CAMBRIDGE STUDIES IN RUSSIAN LITERATURE

Dostoyevsky and the process
of literary creation

CAMBRIDGE STUDIES IN RUSSIAN LITERATURE

General editor MALCOLM JONES

Dostoyevsky and the process of literary creation

JACQUES CATTEAU

PROFESSOR OF RUSSIAN LANGUAGE AND LITERATURE
UNIVERSITY OF PARIS–SORBONNE

Translated by Audrey Littlewood

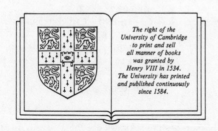

The right of the
University of Cambridge
to print and sell
all manner of books
was granted by
Henry VIII in 1534.
The University has printed
and published continuously
since 1584.

CAMBRIDGE UNIVERSITY PRESS

CAMBRIDGE
NEW YORK   NEW ROCHELLE
MELBOURNE   SYDNEY

d by the Press Syndicate of the University of Cambridge
itt Building, Trumpington Street, Cambridge CB2 1RP
32 East 57th Street, New York, NY 10022, USA
10 Stamford Road, Oakleigh, Melbourne 3166, Australia

Originally published in French as *La Création littéraire chez Dostoïevski*
by Institut d'études slaves, Paris, 1978
and © Institut d'études slaves, Paris, 1978
First published in English by Cambridge University Press 1989 as
Dostoyevsky and the process of literary creation

English translation © Cambridge University Press 1989

Printed in Great Britain at
the University Press, Cambridge

British Library cataloguing in publication data
Catteau, Jacques
Dostoyevsky and the process of literary
creation. – (Cambridge studies in Russian literature).
1. Fiction in Russia. Dostoevskii, F. M.
(Fedor Mikhailovich), 1821–1881
1. Title. 11. La Creation litteraire chez
Dostoievski. English.
891.73′3

Library of Congress cataloguing in publication data
Catteau, Jacques.
[Création littéraire chez Dostoievski. English]
Dostoyevsky and the process of literary creation /
Jacques Catteau: translated by Audrey Littlewood.
p. cm. – (Cambridge studies in Russian literature).
Translation of: La Création littéraire chez Dostoievski.
Bibliography.
Includes index.
ISBN 0 521 32436 X
1. Dostoyevsky, Fyodor. 1821–1881 – Criticism and interpretation.
1. Title. 11. Series.
PG3328.Z6C3313 1988
891.73′–dc19 88-11843 CIP

ISBN 0 521 32436 X

The publishers wish to acknowledge the generous assistance of
the "Direction du livre et de la lecture" of the French
Ministry of Culture, in providing a grant to cover
the translation expenses for this volume.

CE

Contents

Preface to the English edition

'In the last thirty years', as J. L. Backès remarked, 'Dostoyevsky has inspired numerous books and studies, many of them excellent ... The irritating question of technique remains. Dostoyevsky is obviously an artist, but this has never been clearly shown.' If my work has any claim to originality – and here the reader must be the judge – it is in showing the technique of the novel and, more generally, Dostoyevsky the artist at work. I have reversed the procedure adopted by most literary critics, such as Vyacheslav Ivanov, L. P. Grossman and M. Bakhtin, who use the finished novels to infer Dostoyevsky's literary vision. With the advantage of writing after the complete, or almost complete, publication of the manuscripts of Dostoyevsky, I was able to begin with the first hints of creation, the sketches, the rough drafts and their various states, and to track the writer as he worked, in an attempt to grasp his creative logic. The birth of the novel, the writer as artist, is the main subject of this book. Naturally, since no technique exists without its metaphysics, analysis of the creative process led me to the great structures of the finished work, to the poetics of Dostoyevsky.

My book appeared in French at the end of 1978, to be followed almost immediately by further volumes of the great Soviet Academy Edition and by other works of scholarship. Without changing my basic ideas, which depend on the text of the novels, I felt it necessary to modernise, and so have standardised the references and provided a selective bibliography, noting essential works as well as newer contributions which relate to my own research. Besides bringing the book up to date, I have condensed the text to clarify the main ideas, cut such notes and references as were not directly relevant, and corrected the minor factual errors of the first edition which were drawn to my attention by readers and critics and by my eminent colleagues in the field of Dostoyevsky studies, as, for example, G. M. Fridlender of the Academy of Sciences of the USSR and Joseph Frank, Dostoyevsky's great American biographer, to name only two. I should like to express my gratitude to them, to Terence Moore, Katharina Brett, and the staff at Cambridge University Press, to Malcolm V. Jones, who initiated and supervised this translation, to W. J. Leatherbarrow, who revised the bibliography for the English edition, to William M. Todd III of Stanford University, who read the proofs, and finally and especially to Audrey

Littlewood, my translator – indeed, almost co-author – on whom I am aware that I inflicted trials comparable – if I may be excused the analogy – to those which Dostoyevsky inflicted on his heroes in the notebooks.

It is my hope that this book, which springs from a fifteen-year-long passion, may meet with the same reception among the general English-speaking public as it was fortunate enough to find in my own country, not for my own personal satisfaction, but for love of Dostoyevsky.

Abbreviations

The titles of basic works, all in Russian, are abbreviated in the notes. The number which follows them indicates the volume or, when referring to *Diary of a Writer*, the years.

A   *Academy: Complete works of F. M. Dostoyevsky*, in thirty volumes, being published by the Institute of Russian Literature of the Academy of Sciences of the USSR in Leningrad.

Bakhtin   M. Bakhtin, *Problems of Dostoyevsky's Poetics*, second edition, revised and corrected, published in Moscow in 1963 (first edition, entitled *Problems of Dostoyevsky's Art*, published in Leningrad in 1929). Page numbers in brackets refer to the English translation by Caryl Emerson, *Problems of Dostoyevsky's Poetics*, Manchester, 1984.

Biography   The first volume of the first posthumous edition of the *Complete Works* of F. M. Dostoyevsky in fourteen volumes, 1882–3, which includes O. F. Miller's *Materials for a Biography* and N. N. Strakhov's *Memoirs*.

D   *Diary:* The three volumes published by YMCA Press in Paris, containing the *Diary of a Writer* and several articles from the 1860s by F. M. Dostoyevsky. This is a reprint of volumes 10, 11 and 12 of the 'Jubilee' edition, the sixth after the death of the writer, published 1904–6.

Letters   *Letters of F. M. Dostoyevsky*, published in four volumes, 1928–59, under the editorship of A. S. Dolinin.

LH   Volumes of the series *Literary Heritage* published by 'Nauka' referring to F. M. Dostoyevsky, essentially volumes 15, 77, 83 and 86.

Life   L. P. Grossman, *Life and Works of F. M. Dostoyevsky*, Moscow–Leningrad, 1935.

Memoirs   The two volumes of A. S. Dolinin's collection, Moscow, 1964: *F. M. Dostoyevsky in the memoirs of his contemporaries*.

M Anna   The *Memoirs* of the widow of the writer, Anna Grigoryevna Dostoyevskaya, published in Moscow and Leningrad in 1925, under the direction of L. P. Grossman.

T   Tomashevsky: *Complete Works of F. M. Dostoyevsky*, in thirteen volumes, published under the editorship of B. Tomashevsky and K. Khalabayev, 1926–30 in Leningrad.

General editor's note on transliteration and references

Transliteration from Russian follows the system used by the *Slavonic and East European Review*. In the text soft-signs are omitted in proper names and deviant forms of some proper names are preferred where they have become familiar in English-language texts.

Where possible, references to Dostoyevsky's works and letters are to the Academy edition, which had reached volume 29 at the time this book went to press. Following Professor Catteau's own preference in the French edition of his book, references to Dostoyevsky's notebooks are to the versions published in volumes 77, 83 and 86 of *Literary Heritage* (*Literaturnoye nasledstvo*).

General introduction

Dostoyevsky's world is a vast universe, far beyond the grasp of any one reader. This book is not an attempt to make a synthesis of the universe of his works. Vyacheslav Ivanov and Mikhail Bakhtin, who focus on Dostoyevsky's poetic vision, and Leonid Grossman, Konstantin Mochulsky and Pierre Pascal, whose subject is Dostoyevsky's life and works, are the best of many writers who have tried to do so. But no book can include everything; in particular, it may fail to convey the totality which is the essence of Dostoyevsky's work. Most books devoted to the novelist rip the seamless web to pieces.

How can we preserve a sense of plurality in unity without attempting a synthesis? Perhaps we shall find the answer by analysing the reasons which make a perfect synthesis impossible.

There are roughly three main tendencies in Dostoyevsky studies. In the first, the novelist is overshadowed by the philosopher, prophet and seer, who debates abstract and eternal questions throughout his works: good and evil, God and Christ, socialism and revolution, the Golden Age, the future city, the freedom of man. These problems are so finely balanced and debated with such incandescent passion that philosophers of various schools – Rozanov, Merezhkovsky, Shestov, Berdyayev, Camus – have made forays into Dostoyevsky's works to carry off the heroes best suited to their own systems. As Bakhtin says:

If we consider the vast literature devoted to Dostoyevsky, it may seem that we are not discussing a novelist writing novels and stories, but a series of arguments set out by different philosophers, such as Raskolnikov, Myshkin, Stavrogin, Ivan Karamazov, the Grand Inquisitor, and so on. In the eyes of many critics, Dostoyevsky's work has disintegrated into a collection of independent philosophical structures defended by his heroes, among which the author's own viewpoint is secondary. For some critics, Dostoyevsky's voice fuses with the voice of one particular hero: for others it is the synthesis in which all the contradictory voices originate; for others, the heroes simply shout down the author. The reader has discussions with the heroes, and learns from them; their opinions are developed into systems.[1]

The second tendency, which originated while Dostoyevsky was still alive, when numerous accounts and memoirs of him began to appear, abandons the literary work to concentrate on the fascinating paradoxes of his life and character: an epileptic, an invalid, a man condemned to execution, a

I

convict, a gambler, a brilliant journalist, a political turncoat, a passionate orator, an apostle of love and an anti-Semite, a heart torn between sacred and profane love, a devoted father, possibly because he secretly hated his own father, and finally a soul rent between faith and doubt. According to some critics, all this is reflected in his heroes, who are assumed to be concentric mirrors of their creator. We owe a debt of gratitude to the scrupulous biographers who have resisted idolatory and romance, but recently, especially in the West where there is no hesitation about psycho-analysing the dead, Freudian criticism has successfully invaded Dos-toyevsky's personal life. Psychoanalysis has its uses in the study of Dos-toyevsky, but Freudian analysis, based on obscure and unprovable data, has arbitrarily distorted his life and character, and I have felt obliged to try to rectify this.

Finally, a third tendency begins with the text and tries to clarify its deep structures. This kind of criticism appeared at the beginning of the Silver Age, and flourished during the early years of the revolution. The ground was prepared by the immense and admirable effort of Anna Grigoryevna, the writer's widow, who died in 1918, and by the patient labour of some remarkable scholars. Seven posthumous editions of the *Complete Works* appeared from 1882 to 1906, containing *Materials for a Biography* by O. F. Miller and N. N. Strakhov's *Memoirs* which show Dostoyevsky's method of working, V. V. Rozanov's essay in critical biography, numerous letters and several extracts from Dostoyevsky's note-books. From 1911 to 1918 there were two more editions of the *Complete Works* edited by L. P. Grossman, one in twenty-one volumes, the other in twenty-three, including rough drafts published here for the first time, articles attributed sometimes rather too hastily to Dostoyevsky, and the translation of *Eugénie Grandet*, which is not available elsewhere. From 1926 to 1930 thirteen volumes of the *Complete Works* edited by B. Tomashevsky and K. Khalabayev were published, providing the best text available at the time, and containing variants of the printed texts. These editions were accompanied by numerous other studies: collections of materials and articles by L. P. Grossman (1921), by A. S. Dolinin (1922 and 1924), and by N. Brodsky (1924), Works of the Academy of Science in 1923 and later the four compilations of A. L. Bem, published by the Free Russian University of Prague. In parallel, from 1928 to 1934, three volumes of the complete, or almost complete, correspondence from 1831 to 1877 were published. The work on the notebooks went on more slowly, due to disagreement about methods, but by 1935, thanks to I. Glivenko, P. Sakulin, N. F. Belchikov, B. Tomashevsky, N. Ignatova and Ye. Konshina, the scholar had at his disposal all that had survived from the notebooks of *Crime and Punishment*, *The Idiot*, *The Devils* and *The Brothers Karamazov*. There were many other studies and articles, too numerous to list here. The harvest was so abundant that it enabled the critic to take new directions: he could clarify the structure of Dostoyevsky's novels, or he could enter the laboratory of the writer. Precursors of modern criticism, V. V. Vinogradov, Yu. N. Tynyanov, A. G. Tseytlin, M. Bakhtin and V. Shklovsky, formalists or structuralists as they would now be called, published works which are still unequalled. Like the more traditional L. P. Grossman, they were interested in the poetics of Dostoyevsky and based their work on the written novel, using linguistics and stylistics to support their conclusions. G. L. Chulkov (*How Dostoyevsky Worked*, 1939) and A. S. Dolinin (*In the Laboratory of Dostoyevsky the Writer*, 1947, and *The Last Novels of Dostoyevsky*, 1963) turned to the actual creation of the novels, but their studies, valuable as they were, proved unrewarding, and their works were published only just before or even after the Second World War. This resulted in a significant time-lag between these two groups, one studying the written work and the other the process of writing, so that the work of the first groups was necessarily somewhat premature. This is one of the reasons for my book. Since the complete notebooks for *A Raw Youth* were published in 1965 and the other notebooks have been reorganised in the new Academy edition of the complete works, which has been appearing since 1972, the disproportion in materials for studying the text of the novels and studying their creation has been reduced.

But my chief reason for writing this book relates to the more general argument I have just developed in describing the different tendencies in Dostoyevsky criticism. Three main approaches have been distinguished. These critical arguments are used for other writers besides Dostoyevsky, but in his case the difference of approach is exacerbated by the character of the novels, which are swarming with ideologies, by the man and his destiny, which form a novel within the novels, and finally by his art, a challenge to classical ideas. The fragmentation of Dostoyevsky criticism is caused by the originality and richness of Dostoyevsky himself. Forced to choose between subject or form, man or work, criticism is trapped in the traditional dichotomy between idea and expression. Every critic of Dostoyevsky conceals a philosopher, a moralist, or a psychologist, each subconsciously trying to muzzle the others. Bakhtin's attempt to discover the 'profound and constant structures of Dostoyevsky's literary vision' and his insistence that Dostoyevsky was first and foremost an artist, not a philosopher or a journalist, is salutary, but it is an excess replying to an excess. All art refers back to first principles. Bakhtin's stress on carnivals and Menippea, where everything is permitted and nothing decided, dissolves the metaphysics of Dostoyevsky, whose creative thought is a struggle to reconcile four antinomic freedoms, two of which oppose the other two.

It was while Dostoyevsky was planning and researching his novels that the effort of reconciliation and struggle was at its most intense. At this point

Dostoyevsky, developing his plans and grappling with the original chaos which he had to reduce to order, felt split in two. There were two men in him, the poet or creator, and the artist. The plans of the poet often exceeded the means of the artist, or at least so he thought, but the novel was created by the efforts of both, by the fruitful tension between them.

I have given the texts of the notebooks and the novels priority over the abundant literature which accompanies them, and so I hope, like the biologist or the geneticist, to try to find the constants which preside over the procreation, labour, birth and adolescence of each text, and then to grasp the structure of the finished novel. As far as possible, I shall try to follow Dostoyevsky's steps, reversing the usual critical procedure which uses the finished work to understand the idea and analyse its expression. There is a wide gulf between the notebooks and the novels, which makes the task difficult, but at least we shall have the joy of seeing the novel come to life. We shall follow the natural period of gestation, first studying the conditions in which it takes place, the creative environment, then the creative process itself, and lastly the created work in its essential structure.

If we can see how the novel is created, we may perhaps come to understand its first causes and clarify the laws which bind Dostoyevsky's rich and overflowing universe into one great kingdom.

PART I

The creative environment

Introduction

However independent it may appear to the reader, every literary work is created in specific circumstances. The universality, the perennial quality later recognised in it, is rooted in a definite time, a specific environment, in the living flesh of the many who created it. Lansonian criticism, the traditional biographical school, postulates that a work cannot be approached seriously without first studying the surroundings in which the creative act took place, in other words, without studying the author in all his individual, social, biological and spiritual aspects. This provides a safeguard against whimsical interpretations and makes the work of fiction credible as part of the experience of a real man. Even psychoanalytical criticism, dizzy from building its own towers of Babel and its inversion of the usual scholarly procedures, using the works to find out about their creator, is now reforming itself and, renovated under the name of psychocriticism,[1] is checking its discoveries, based on the comparison of texts, against the good old biographical sources.

However, traditional criticism juxtaposes the author and the work, omitting the creative act which binds the two. Certainly there are gangways leading from one to the other; correlations are noted, but the result is still a juxtaposition of two mirrors showing images which are occasionally in agreement but for the most part very different, as the work seems to escape from and surpass its creator.

In this static approach, the creative function, the act that connects the man and the work in a functional relationship, is forgotten, although it is the essential point of this critical method. For this reason, we shall not make a study of the character of Dostoyevsky, a complex and engaging subject, but still a very obscure one. If we consult the best biographers, K. V. Mochulsky, L. P. Grossman, P. Pascal, or the interesting but fundamentally unsound essay of Freud, two or three different Dostoyevskys emerge. Moreover, even a circumspect reading of the evidence and memoirs of contemporaries – school friends, prison inmates, fellow writers, fellow editors, friends and relations, brother, wife, daughter, lover – will compound the confusion, as the man was so protean and the opinions so partial. Only his letters, written hastily and without preparation, innocent of all literary ornament, seem to offer the best means of fathoming the personality of the author, though here too his intentions towards his correspondents must be taken into account.

For the same reason, we shall not analyse autobiographical features in Dostoyevsky's work. There are many of them in the great novels, although they are nearly always unacknowledged and the reader accepts them as part of the life of the characters. They range from the great experiences, such as the scaffold, prison, epilepsy, the passion for gambling, poverty and the need for money, the sufferings of love, literary creation itself, and so on, to the most personal details of everyday life, such as Dostoyevsky's way of thinking while pacing about the room, his mania for soliloquising in the street, his habit of brushing his clothes every day to make them last, and his obsessions and beliefs, such as the sensation of being spiritually crushed in rooms with low ceilings, the premonitory value of dreams, and so on. There are also many characters in the novels which Dostoyevsky took straight from life or, more often, fused from multiple prototypes. These projections of reality in his works have been extensively studied and it is pointless to draw up an additional catalogue.[2]

But if we refer to the creative function, if we ask why the writer chose one experience rather than another for his work, if we begin to suspect that the form and structure inherent in that particular aspect of the personality or in that specific experience determine their use in the novels just as much as their content does, without making any general inference about the life and personality of Dostoyevsky as a whole, then a new path is opened. In simple terms, our intention is to assess the great constants of the environment which the writer created for himself, to evaluate them dynamically as a physicist gauges pressure and weight.

We can best define these invariable factors by comparison of texts, especially of the letters, passionate and revealing even in their reticence. If the specific content of each letter is ignored, the obsessive themes remain: the creative impulse, already revealing embryonic forms of creativity, and the feverish and gluttonous assimilation of culture dominate the early letters, while the problems of money and health and discussions of literary work in progress fill the pages of all the letters and notebooks from adolescence to death. These themes dominate the creative environment, which we are about to analyse.

1

Forms of creativity in embryo

Everything implied by the words *will*, *desire*, *concentration*, *nervous intensity*, *explosion*, is felt and sensed in his works. I do not think I am deluding myself or anyone else by affirming that I see in them the principal characteristics of the phenomenon which we call *genius*.   Charles Baudelaire about Richard Wagner

The indomitable force of Dostoyevsky's literary vocation is always set against a background of agony. 'Exhausting chronic illnesses, a succession of bereavements, fear of bailiffs, material need made worse by a mad passion for gambling, but caused in the first place by his own generosity, incessant humiliations, the need for sordid calculation – and constant confidence in his own genius and the future' – this is Pierre Pascal's description of the terrible conditions in which Dostoyevsky struggled to write *Crime and Punishment*.[1] The conditions in which he wrote, especially when he was fighting with the worst fate could send him, are certainly important, but the nature of his first creative impulses, although just as significant, has been studied very little. Dostoyevsky himself was always questioning the psychology of creation as he wrote his novels; in trying to discover his first creative intentions, the embryonic forms and structures in the making which appeared when he first became aware of his vocation as a novelist, comparing them if need be with the great creative statements of his later years, we are following a path he took before us.

In May 1837 Fyodor Mikhaylovich and his brother Mikhail were travelling to Petersburg with their father, to study at the Kostomarov school in preparation for the Academy of Engineering. The heads of the two boys (Fyodor was just fifteen) were buzzing with everything they had read. As soon as they arrived in Petersburg they planned to rush off to the place where Pushkin, their hero, had been killed in a duel, only two months earlier. 'We had a passionate faith in one thing, and although we both knew everything we needed for the mathematics examination, we dreamt only of poetry and poets. My brother wrote verses, two or three poems every day, even when travelling; as for me, I was continually composing a novel about Venetian life in my mind', Dostoyevsky recalled in 1876.[2] Vague as it is, the admission is instructive. The form is chosen; it will be the novel. The first stage of the creative process is foreshadowed: 'continually' (*bezpreryvno*) and 'in my mind' (*v ume*). While Mikhail was writing in black and white,

9

Fyodor was happily ruminating over his plan, letting it expand and ripen, without going so far as to write it down.

Even in his first novel, Dostoyevsky showed what N. N. Strakhov ambiguously called 'a writer's laziness':

Fyodor Mikhaylovich always put his work off until the very last minute: he never began it until he had barely time to finish it and even that meant working day and night. It was a laziness sometimes carried to extremes, but not at all simple, a special writer's laziness . . . His brain was working incessantly, ideas were springing up and moving about all the time, and he always had difficulty in tearing himself away from this inner work and beginning to write. His thoughts seethed, new ideas flowed into his mind, new plans were being constructed, and the old ones were growing and developing.[3]

Ivan Petrovich, the writer in *The Insulted and Injured*, echoed Strakhov's observation: 'It has always been pleasanter to me to think about my works and dream about how they are going to be written, than actually write them, and really this is not from laziness. Why is it then?'[4]

Strakhov attempted a reply: Dostoyevsky was one of those profound writers who need to let their idea ripen until the moment of release when it is written directly on the paper, without correction. Bakhtin went further: the slow and indispensable ripening of the idea follows from the polyphonic structure of Dostoyevsky's novels, from his wish to prolong the clash of universes and the dialogue of numerous opposing voices. Gabriel Marcel noted that for Dostoyevsky 'the conflicting elements are never reduced, never completely dissolved'.[5] But these are later critical interpretations and young Fyodor was not consciously aware of the process.

His one creative awareness came from a series of intuitions, 'concentric circles of self-analysis and self-perception', in the words of K. K. Istomin.[6] One of these intuitions, very precocious since it occurred in a letter written to his brother Mikhail on 31 October 1838, forms the beginning of an answer to Strakhov's question. Pursuing a philosophical argument inspired by the vogue for Schelling, young Fyodor assumed a mantle of prophecy. The knowledge of nature, of the soul, of God, of love comes 'by the heart and not by the mind', 'the soul or the mind lives by the thought which the heart whispers to it'.[7] Dostoyevsky perceived at the age of seventeen the second dominant characteristic of his creative thought, which may be called the 'awareness of the heart'. Much later, the mature writer formulated this law of his genius in large letters in the notebooks for *A Raw Youth*:

To write a novel, one must first provide oneself with one or several strong impressions, really lived by the author in his heart. This is the business of the poet. From this impression a theme, a plan, a harmonious whole is developed, and this is the business of the artist, although the artist and the poet help each other in both cases.[8]

Another letter to his brother, written about ten months later, 16 August 1839, revealed the great idea which inspired him to become a writer. The vocation was becoming more demanding, and Dostoyevsky, as a pupil in the Academy of Engineering, was finding his studies and the regimented way of life more unbearable. He wanted freedom to fulfil his 'most sacred hopes'. But he mastered his impatience and, accepting his present life, disclosed the basis of his vocation as a novelist:

My soul is inaccessible to the impetuous enthusiasms of earlier times. Everything is calm in it, as in the heart of a man hiding a deep secret; to study 'what man and life mean' – I am fairly successful at this; characters I can study in the writers with whom the best part of my life flows freely and joyfully. I am sure of myself. Man is a mystery. It must be brought to light, and if one puzzles over it all one's life, let it not be said that one is wasting one's time: I am studying this mystery, for I wish to be a man.[9]

The serene gravity of this assertion, remarkable in a youth of eighteen, reveals Dostoyevsky's intentions: the psychological exploration of man, this creature of infinite enigmatic variations. There is also a hint of one of Dostoyevsky's methods of work: constant dialogue with the great masters of literature.

His intention, to reveal the mystery that is man, is clear, though immense, but the forms and methods to be used are still only gleams on the threshold of consciousness: the appeal of the novel, the necessary rumination over the idea and the birth pangs when actual writing begins, the awareness of the heart, and the reference to other writers. Young Fyodor only sensed the laws of his creative process. All this required such an effort that he began by deviating from his plan; he wrote plays and made translations.

Three plays which have not survived were begun, 'childish things'[10] as Dostoyevsky was to say later: 'Boris Godunov', 'Mariya Styuart' and 'The Jew Yankel'. He certainly began to write down the first two. Dr A. E. Riesenkampf, one of the young Dostoyevsky's friends, remembered a farewell party organised in Mikhail's honour, on 16 February 1841, at which the future novelist read fragments of these plays.[11] Fascinated by the actress Lilli Loewe who was enjoying a triumph in the part of Schiller's *Maria Stuart*, then being played in German on the Petersburg stage, Dostoyevsky dreamt of making a free adaptation in Russian, more faithful to history.[12] Andrey, the writer's younger brother, who lived with Dostoyevsky for some time, surreptitiously read a few pages of 'Boris Godunov'.[13] The third attempt, 'The Jew Yankel', which Dostoyevsky mentioned in a letter as being 'completed',[14] remains a mystery.[15] A passion for the theatre and for actresses, the guardian shades of Pushkin, Schiller, perhaps Shakespeare (Shylock in *The Merchant of Venice*) and Eugène Sue (*Le Juif errant*) seem to be the main reasons for this deviation from the novel.

Deeper causes can be sensed in the background: a passion for history and a love for dramatic form. The use of scenic space in the great novels, their division into scenes, their theatrical effects, scenery, lighting and vocabulary, and especially their exploration of man by means of dialogue show that Dostoyevsky's early enthusiasm for the theatre left deep traces. But the infatuation was brief. On 24 March, after two years of 'childish nonsense', Dostoyevsky drew his own conclusion: 'Writing plays! It would need years of work and tranquillity, at least for me! Today, it is good to write. At the moment the drama is turning to melodrama. Shakespeare grows pale in the twilight and, through the mists of our playwrights, he seems a god.'[16] Dostoyevsky was drafting *Poor Folk* when he sent this letter to Mikhail. The allusion to Shakespeare foreshadows his characteristic attitude towards the novel: his dream of creating a universe, which, as we shall see later, emerged clearly in about 1844.

So at the age of twenty, in the thick of examinations and competitions, the student Dostoyevsky was dreaming of the theatre. In 1843 he was promoted to second lieutenant and appointed to the drafting department of the Engineering Command; a wearisome office life began. At the same time he was drawn by a new enthusiasm, the translation of novels, again distracting him from his cherished plans. He was taking a side path which linked up with the main highway of his dreams, but it was an unexpected one. Dostoyevsky, as was fairly common in the nineteenth century, never worried about the art of translation and was completely confident of his powers as a translator, although, unlike Pushkin, Lermontov, Turgenev and Tolstoy, he had not been born into the kind of family where there were armies of tutors for the children, nor did he have the solid training which might have been gained at university. No matter, he could read French easily and Eugène Sue, Balzac and George Sand were his idols.[17] Of his three original projects, *Mathilde* by Eugène Sue, *Eugénie Grandet* by Balzac, and *La Dernière Aldini* by George Sand, only the Balzac translation was to be published.

For Dostoyevsky, translation was not so much a school of writing as a publishing transaction, a way of beginning a career in letters in the most ambitious and lucrative sense of the term. It was the Balzacian dream of becoming his own literary entrepreneur. The letters of 31 December 1843, of January, 14 February, April and summer 1844 are revealing: Dostoyevsky busily formed teams which were immediately broken up, suggested risking a small amount of capital which he hadn't got, made detailed estimates, calculated returns, and lovingly chose the colour of the book's cover ('a pretty salmon-coloured or light green cover'). He hurried to get ahead of competitors, gave up a translation he had begun (*La Dernière Aldini*) on hearing it had been done by someone else (in 1837!), and without apparent regret took advantage of current events and the fame of the moment (Balzac's visit to St Petersburg in July and August) to finish in the greatest secrecy during the Christmas holidays of 1843 a translation judged 'incomparable': *Eugénie Grandet*![18]

Brief enthusiasms, naive dreams, juvenile excitement; perhaps, but in his keenness for concocting schemes the young Dostoyevsky was forging his future weapons. His love for the risk in the publishing game, his instinct for organising teams, his pride, his inflexible will to make his way in the world of letters, his certainty that he could make a living from it, all this indicated the future editor-in-chief, prime mover of reviews and journalist of unfailing pugnacity.

However, Dostoyevsky's *Eugénie Grandet*[19] could only be considered 'a marvel' in the judgement of its young author, who paraphrased, skipped difficult parts, inflated descriptions (unlike his sober landscapes in the novels), used exaggeratedly Russian terms ('steppe' instead of 'country-side'), reversed the logic of the Balzacian sentence by promoting subordinate clauses to main ones, inserted sensational adjectives ('horrible', 'mysterious', and so on), darkened the colours ('pale' and 'cold' are strangely called 'gloomy'), in short, made an extremely free translation in the liberal spirit of the time, sapping Balzac's vigour and energy in the process. This may have been haste or inexperience, but more probably Dostoyevsky was still handicapped by the theatrical style that he affected at the time, dominated by sentimental hyperbole, melodramatic vagueness, conventional attitudes and grandiloquent gestures. Dominique Arban has made a detailed comparison of Balzac's text in the Bechet edition of 1834 and Dostoyevsky's translation, published in June and July 1844 in the *Repertory and Pantheon of all Russian and European Theatres*. She suggests that the gratuitous bombast of the translation is reminiscent of the sentimentalist style much loved by Dostoyevsky's father, with its use, for example, of the word *zhiznenochek* (dear little life).[20] In any case, it was a useful exercise. Dostoyevsky was able to study a kind of composition, which admittedly did not interest him long, and to discover two great types of character which remained imprinted on his mind: the gentle woman who is a willing sacrifice, and the 'predator' (*khishchnyy*) who crushes and tortures. In this cruel dialectic of oppressor and oppressed, *Eugénie Grandet* foreshadows *The Insulted and Injured* rather than *Poor Folk*. It was the first work of Dostoyevsky's to be finished (in three weeks) and printed, and it left traces in the stories and novels he was to write.[21] The treasure of the miserly Prokharchin with his 'rare coins', his 'gold Napoleons', is oddly reminiscent of the treasure in *Eugénie Grandet*. The description of Rogozhin's house in *The Idiot* recalls M. Grandet's; Prince Myshkin uses Balzac's title *La physionomie d'un logis* when he tells his rival 'Your house has the physiognomy of your whole family and your whole Rogozhinian life.'[22] Meanwhile Dostoyevsky 'thought' Balzac; in the letters of 1844 he quoted expressions from 'papa Grandet' and naturally measured his first attempt as

a novelist by the Balzacian yardstick: 'I am finishing a novel of the importance of *Eugénie Grandet*.'[23]

Unfinished dramatic sketches and rapid, potboiling translations were
marginal activities for the young officer, drafts for future work, attempts
limited by the structure of military life. The great royal road to the novel
demands much more; the writer who follows it must be totally free. It is
open only to original creators such as Cervantes, Dickens, Balzac, Tolstoy,
Proust; writers possessed by creative passion who bring into being vast and
crowded new worlds which vie with reality while nevertheless sharing its
texture and its very flesh, worlds which are at once the conscience and the
aesthetic redemption of their age. Dostoyevsky had an obscure intimation
of this; he felt torrents of ideas seething within him; worlds were emerging,
pushing forward to take wing. His 'vision', probably in January 1844, suddenly illuminated this latent creativity.

He gave an account of it in 1861 in an article for the magazine *Time*:
'Petersburg Dreams in Verse and Prose':[24]

I remember once, one winter evening in January, I was hurrying home from the
Vyborg district. I was still very young then. Reaching the Neva, I stopped a moment
and cast a penetrating glance along the river into the smoky, icily hazy distance,
which was suddenly becoming crimson in the last purple of sunset, burning out in the
misty firmament. Night was settling on the city; the dense air trembled at the smallest sound, and, like giants, from all the roofs of both quaysides there rose and were
carried upwards in the cold sky columns of smoke which twined and untwined on
their way, so that, it seemed, new buildings were rising above the old, a new city was
being formed in the air . . . It seemed finally that all this world, with all its inhabitants, weak and strong, with all their houses, shelters for beggars or gilded palaces,
were in this twilight hour like a fantastic vision, like a dream which in its turn would
immediately disappear and turn to smoke in the dark blue of the sky. Some strange
thought suddenly stirred in me. I shivered and my heart at that moment seemed to
be drenched by a sudden surge, suddenly boiling up from the tide of a powerful
feeling never known before. It was as if I had only just understood at that precise
instant, something which until then had been stirring in me without my realising it. It
was as if I had suddenly begun to see clearly something new, an entirely new world
unknown to me and known before only by some kind of dark rumour, some kind of
mysterious sign. I suppose from that precise moment my existence began.[25]

His existence as a writer, that is. It was the beginning of a fantasy of reality
which marked the death of the romantic dreamer and the writer's move to
more human themes in *Poor Folk*. The universe to be created had come to
light.

Another text, written in autumn 1846, makes this intuition clearer. It is a
passage from 'The Landlady', a fantastic novella which was poorly received
by Belinsky, but later admired by the symbolists; Dostoyevsky had poured
his heart into it ('the source of an inspiration which jetted directly from my
heart guides my pen'), and much of himself, although the hero also resem-

bled the romantic companion of his youth, Shidlovsky, especially as hero and friend were both writing a history of the Church. The hero himself matters less than the description of his creative suffering and vertigo, in which Dostoyevsky analyses the psychology of creativity:

Again terror attacked him: the fairytale was being embodied before him in faces and forms. He saw that everything, beginning with his vague childish dreams, all his thoughts and longings, everything that he had experienced in life, everything that he had read in books, everything that he had long ago forgotten, all this was coming to life, taking shape, putting on flesh and rising before him in colossal forms and images, it was walking and swarming around him; he saw magical luxuriant gardens stretching before him, whole towns forming and falling to pieces before his eyes; whole cemeteries sending him their dead, who were beginning to live again; whole tribes came and were born and lived out their time before his eyes; and finally now round his bed of sickness, every thought of his, every fleshless dream was taking on flesh almost at the moment of birth; and finally, he saw that he was thinking not in fleshless ideas but in whole worlds, whole creations, and was being carried along like a speck of dust through this whole endless, strange, inescapable world.[26]

Strakhov observed Dostoyevsky at work and caught a glimpse of this incarnation of ideas that took place in the writer:

The most general and abstract thoughts acted on him with great power ... A simple thought, even a common or ordinary one, suddenly set him on fire and appeared to him in all its significance. He seemed to feel thoughts with uncommon vividness. Then he would set the thought out in different ways, sometimes giving it a picturesque, arresting image without elucidating it in a logical way or developing its content. He was primarily an artist, thinking in images and guided by feelings.[27]

This evidence is valuable, but Dostoyevsky's own writings, quoted earlier, allow us to be bolder: he not only felt but saw the thoughts rising in him, completely formed, in the shape of new worlds imperiously demanding their right to exist. A lava of images poured out from his deepest self, his past experience, his education, to attack and overwhelm him. His ego was carried away, exploded.

The fears repeatedly mentioned by the young author, fears of losing his reason, of giving in to the seductive call of madness, probably originated in this creative vertigo. At least at first. In 1838, as a young Hoffmannesque dreamer, he confided to his brother Mikhail: 'I have a plan: to go mad.'[28] In 1845, intense work on *Poor Folk* gave him another idea: 'As regards literature, I am no longer the person I was two years ago. All that was only childishness and folly. Two years of study have brought and taken away a good deal',[29] and he burst out: 'I have just read an article about German poets who died of hunger, of cold, or in madhouses. About twenty of them, and what names! ... One must be a charlatan.'[30] From then on madness haunted him; not common pathological dementia but the destruction of reason by the intense stress of literary creation, when his overheated imagination was assailed by new worlds rushing upon him. Many of Dostoyevsky's heroes created in this period go mad, like the unfortunate Golyadkin with his dual personality, the miserly Prokharchin with his 'burning head', and the 'weak heart' Vasily Shumkov, or come close to it, like Katerina and Ordynov in 'The Landlady'. Still more interesting is the case of Netochka Nezvanova's stepfather, a violinist who dies mad because he lacks the superhuman stature required for genius. Oddly, the obsession with madness caused by uncontrolled creative power suddenly vanished in the Peter-Paul fortress when Dostoyevsky was imprisoned there in 1849: he wrote a peaceful, smiling, almost Stendhalian work 'A Little Hero'. Ambiguous fate inflicted cruel ordeals on the man, but gave the writer, exhausted by the abundance of his genius, the pause necessary for his great work in the future.

An intuitive sketch of creation, an outline of the forms of creativity in Dostoyevsky, is beginning to appear. The concentric circles beginning to touch the awareness of the writer are: choice of the novel as a form, the slow gestation of the idea and the birth pangs when writing begins, the crucible of the heart, constant reference to the literary heritage, and finally the perilous vision of entire worlds, living incarnations of ideas, clashing against each other, threatening their creator's reason. This assault of structured universes is precisely what determined Dostoyevsky's vocation as a novelist.

This had practical consequences. He could not serve two masters at once, and in August 1844 he asked to be retired. Oddly, the reason given was not a solemn commitment to literature. The first time he mentioned retirement, in a letter of April 1844 to his brother Mikhail, he justified it by: 'service bores me, it bores me as much as potatoes'. In the letter of 30 September 1844, again to his brother, he was not much more explicit:

I have asked to retire because I have asked: I swear I couldn't go on any longer. Life is no fun when you are forced to waste the best part of your time. Really I never meant to serve long; so why should I squander the best years of my life? And lastly, the main thing: I was to be sent to the provinces. What on earth could I do without Petersburg?

And a few lines later, 'I shall soon find myself a slice of bread. I am going to work like a demon. Now I am free.' He had a definite hope: he was finishing a novel.[31] Evidently he did not mention his vocation because it had been discussed so often by the brothers that it was taken for granted. It was certainly obvious to Mikhail, his eternal confidant, who interceded in his brother's favour with the family guardian, P. A. Karepin, even before he received the letter of 30 September. The text of Mikhail's letter has recently been published: 'I learnt with astonishment from your letter that my brother Fyodor had asked for retirement . . . I knew nothing about it . . . I admit I knew of his plan, but I did not know he would carry it out this year.' And later,

He has mentioned a posting to the provinces. If this is the reason for his action, I agree that he had no choice. He cannot leave Petersburg without breaking the links which promise him a great path of glory and wealth in the future. He wants to devote himself to literature; until now he has worked just to make money; that is, translated for journals ... I predict great things for him. He is a man of vigorous personal talents and vast erudition.

And Mikhail concluded in prophetic vein: 'A difficult task awaits him: to cut out a path, to win a name. He has sacrificed everything to his talent, and his talent, I know, I am sure, will not betray him. God grant that he does not surrender, that he may be able to bear the first blows and then ... Who can know what awaits him?'[32] Permission to retire was given in October 1844. From then on, Fyodor Dostoyevsky was free to move on to the stage which follows the call and the vision, that of writing the novel.

2

The heritage

If man is a creator, he is also and above all created by his culture.
Professor Dobzansky at a colloquium at the Sorbonne:
'Biology and the Development of Man', *Le Monde*, 21 September 1974

The creative work of the writer is intimately based on his culture. It is his standard, his model, his reference, his stern school of apprenticeship, his constant critic. Like a parent, it educates, dominates, even oppresses. Yury Tynyanov's study *Dostoyevsky and Gogol, towards a theory of parody* opens with the words: 'In discussions of tradition or literary heritage, one usually imagines a straight line linking the young representative of any literary movement with his predecessors. The thing is really much more complex. There is no direct line of descent, but a deviation, a repulsion from a particular point, a struggle.'[1] This is a literary critic's view of the eternal dialectic process of the creator, who is both a creature of his own culture and a rebel against his heavy and paralysing inheritance, before he becomes the bearer of a 'new word'.

So the search for influences, confluences, rejections should be general and dynamic. Each study of individual influences has its dangers, since Dostoyevsky received different legacies at the same time, and accepted only part of them; sometimes he took a universal theme, sometimes a form, reacting against them at the same time. Besides, Dostoyevsky was not a man for detail. He always elevated the discussion, generalised spontaneously, and threw himself heart and soul into his judgements. He admired and condemned with sweeping generosity. Certainly there were some precise and limited reminiscences, striking confluences, but we are not going to linger over them here. For years students of sources have been exploring the immense subterranean network where the culture of the writer lies buried. Their work is valuable. Great rivers spring from underground torrents, streams and lakes. But only those rivers which emerge into the light are strong enough to reach the creative sea. These are the ones whose course we shall follow.

Dostoyevsky's culture

Some biographers have had doubts about Dostoyevsky's culture: he certainly read a good deal, they think, but was not a cultured man. P. P.

Semyonov-Tyan-Shansky, who knew him from 1846 to 1849, protested against this harsh statement:

In his childhood he received an excellent training from his father, an educated man, an army doctor in Moscow. F. M. Dostoyevsky knew French and German well enough to read texts in detail. His father had even taught him Latin. To sum up, until the age of seventeen, the date of his entry to the Academy of Engineering Dostoyevsky received a regular and systematic education. In this establishment, and just as strictly, he not only followed the general course of studies, but also studied higher mathematics, physics, mechanics and all technical matters of military engineering with complete success. Besides this regular education, he read widely. If one considers that, since childhood, he had read and reread all the Russian poets and novelists, that he knew Karamzin's *History of the Russian State* almost by heart, that he had studied French and German authors with great interest and was especially keen on Schiller, Goethe, Hugo, Lamartine, Béranger and George Sand, that he had studied numerous historical works by French authors, such as Thiers' *History of the French Revolution*, the works of Mignet and Louis Blanc and *The Course of Positive Philosophy* by Auguste Comte, and that he was still reading the socialist works of Saint-Simon and Fourier, it must be admitted that Dostoyevsky was a cultured man. In any case, he was more cultured than a number of Russian writers of the time, such as Nekrasov, Panayev, Grigorovich, Pleshcheyev, and even Gogol.[2]

One of those mentioned, the writer D. V. Grigorovich, agreed readily. He was amazed by Dostoyevsky's vast culture, he said, adding that all the pupils of the Chermak school, where Dostoyevsky had prepared for the Academy of Engineering, were distinguished by exceptional erudition in literature.

The first twenty years of a man's life are of supreme importance in his education, so we have placed these two dated accounts first. But there are other accounts of Dostoyevsky's reading, often richer and also precisely dated: the pages which Andrey, his younger brother, devoted to childhood and family reading; the enthusiastic letters from Fyodor to Mikhail during their adolescent years; evidence from K. A. Trutovsky for the period before Dostoyevsky's arrest; the diary[3] and memoirs of Anna Grigoryevna, his wife; the catalogue of Dostoyevsky's last library,[4] however incomplete for earlier years; and the novelist's own letters, where he asks for books, criticises those he has read, gives advice about what young people should read, and so on. If we were to spread all these out on a table and superpose them like snapshots, noting convergences and similarities, we could trace the cultural heritage and image of Dostoyevsky in its broad general outlines.

The sciences

Dostoyevsky received a scientific and technical education at the Academy of Engineering, in which he differed from all his great contemporaries and is closer to Chekhov. Besides physics, chemistry, geology, analytic and descriptive geometry, integral and differential calculus and theoretic and applied mechanics, he studied military and civil architecture, the art of fortification, architectural drawing, and so on. Is there any reflection of this scientifically based education in Dostoyevsky's works, as, for example, mathematical ideas and the technique of naval architecture are occasionally reflected in the work of Zamyatin?

Natural, exact, economic, social and political sciences do play a part in the novels. Dostoyevsky was not an enemy of science. He did not challenge it scientifically, even epistemologically: scientifically educated, he knew its use. Sometimes he illustrated his hero's complex thought by an image borrowed from Cuvier's theories, from the non-Euclidean geometry of his compatriot Lobachevsky, or from astrophysics, as in *The Brothers Karamazov*. Science is simply an object of philosophical thought, and is used in debate because some thinkers base their theory of knowledge on its authority. So in *Notes from Underground*, a commination service against the historical determinism and biological materialism of the 'new men', the hero does not deny the 'laws of nature', which he calls a 'stone wall'. He rejects them in the name of metaphysical freedom. His allusion to Darwinism is typical: he does not use scientific argument to support his rebellion – this is simply not interesting to him – but chooses his side in the philosophical dispute between defenders of determinism and those of freedom, a wider version of the great contemporary debate between fundamentalists and those in favour of a freer interpretation of the Bible.

Otherwise Dostoyevsky forgot all the science he had learnt, except for architecture, which he had studied as a military engineer. He describes urban architecture with true knowledge; Petersburg architecture in *The Petersburg Chronicle*, an article of 1847,[5] pages of which he was to use again in 'White Nights'; the architecture of the Crystal Palace with its cast-iron roof, which he went to see in London in 1862, and of its hefty twin, the dismal Palace of the Third Universal Exhibition in 1862.[6] Architecture, unlike other sciences, gives concrete images rather than abstractions, volumes inhabited by man and forms which express 'the contemporary idea', as Dostoyevsky says in *The Petersburg Chronicle*.[7] The space of Dostoyevsky's novels with all its measured and numbered surfaces, all its planes of light and shade, with its volumes defined geometrically and in terms of the relationship of their masses, is arranged with an architect's vision.

The plastic arts: church architecture and sculpture

Dostoyevsky was interested in living architecture, the monuments of Petersburg and the modern buildings of his time, but his artistic taste inclined towards the past: Byzantine and Gothic. He was naturally drawn, as a Christian and a nationalistic Russian, to the grandiose and solemn architecture of Byzantium; the enthusiasm he felt for St Mark's in Venice came from a well-developed aesthetic sense as well as the nostalgia of an exile. His love for Gothic art is stranger and may be explained by the mystic ideal – Aglaya, in love with the luminous knight Myshkin, wants to go and see Gothic cathedrals[8] – and also by the influence of Ossianism at the beginning of the century. But beyond the symbolic use of Gothic, there seems to have been a sense of kinship with Gothic form. Dostoyevsky drew Gothic windows in the spaces of his manuscripts and thought that the enormous cathedral of Milan all built in variegated marble with its Italian Gothic, 'pierced with light', was 'fantastic as a dream'.[9] This seems to indicate a basic affinity between Gothic art with its lanceolated pyramids, nets of flame culminating in a paroxystic point, and the composition of Dostoyevsky's novels where the action always converges towards incandescence. In both, complexity is narrowed down to an arrow point.

Dostoyevsky hardly mentions sculpture. He admired the most celebrated classical and Italian masterpieces, especially the *Apollo Belvedere*, which was his ideal of beauty as early as 1861, 'a majestic, infinitely beautiful image', inspiring a 'sensation of divinity' and capable of arousing 'lasting change' in the soul of anyone who admires it.[10] But if his wife Anna had not taken him to museums and made a record of his taste, we should know little. She tells us that in Florence Dostoyevsky never tired of praising the famous bronze gates of the Baptistry of St John. He confided that he would have liked a 'full-size' photograph of Lorenzo Ghiberti's masterpiece and particularly of the 'Gate of Paradise', as Michelangelo called it, in his study, where he could see it all the time.[11] What was the attraction, besides the religious theme, of these ten scenes? Worlds set out in relief, in depth, as Dostoyevsky saw them arise in his own creative imagination, no doubt. But they also have characteristics which reinforce our conclusions about architecture: first, the precious trace of Gothic art, and second, a new treatment of space and movement, a perspective which Ghiberti, architect as well as sculptor, borrowed from the innovations in painting at the end of the trecento. Here again we find creative temperaments akin in composition and vision.

Painting

Painting, on the other hand, plays an important part in Dostoyevsky's work, both as novelist and journalist. It appears in three forms: paintings discussed in critical articles, real paintings mentioned in the novels, and imaginary pictorial compositions. Dostoyevsky's brief writings as an art-critic, though he refused the title and commissioned reviews of the art salons for *The Citizen*, need not detain us long. His choice of painting was dictated by current events: some pictures by the Wanderers were being sent to an exhibition in Vienna. Dostoyevsky singled out *The View of Valaam* by A. I. Kuindzhi, *Lovers of the Nightingale's song* by V. Ye. Makovsky, *Hunters resting* by V. G. Perov, *Volga Bargemen* by I. Ye. Repin, and *The Last Supper* by N. N. Gay, but his praise was very moderate. The title of the article 'About an Exhibition' shows that painting is only an excuse for deploring the European failure to understand the Russian landscape, for discussing the mediocre level of Russian visual art as compared with Russian literature, and especially for expressing Dostoyevsky's hostility towards a preconceived tendency in art, art 'in uniform' as he calls it, and his idea of the synthetic nature of true realism. We learn more about the art of Dickens, Cervantes, Gogol and Dostoyevsky himself than we do about the pictures.

Dostoyevsky was not a great lover of painting, or even a connoisseur. He made no attempt at discovery; he went to see something he had already read or heard about. He had the classic tastes of the Russian nineteenth century, which preferred the quattrocento and especially the cinquecento to any form of Russian art; and, like Tolstoy, he was an average educated Russian of his time with regard to painting. He took no notice of exhibitions of painting during his travels abroad and avoided museums, with the exception of Dresden.[12] He went to galleries only in 1867, dragged there by his young wife, Anna, who noted, first in her diary and then in her memoirs, the objects of their admiration in Dresden, Basle, and Florence.[13] One example is enough to show that Dostoyevsky was influenced by established names. In Dresden, he certainly admired the eternal masterpieces of Raphael, Correggio, Titian, Annibale Caracci, Murillo, Ruysdael, Rembrandt, Van Dyck, Claude, but he did not hesitate to place Pompo Girolamo Battoni, a cold and limited painter of the eighteenth century, once admired at the Russian court, in the same pantheon.

Dostoyevsky's brief infatuation with the *Chocolate Pot* of Jean Liotard and Watteau's *Comédies sentimentales* may be explained by traces of the tender sentimentalism of his youth. However, amid all this eclecticism, the works which Dostoyevsky deeply admired stand out; they form the museum of his imagination. In this case, the picture was no longer an object of pure aesthetic pleasure for Dostoyevsky, but a total emotion, which overcame him and lasted for ever. It was a fascinated adherence of heart and soul, a metamorphosing appropriation. Anna Grigoryevna describes him 'glued to the spot', his face transfigured by enthusiasm or convulsed with horror 'as if an epileptic fit were beginning'. The fascination lasted for minutes on end, even an hour, and Dostoyevsky, without worrying about fines, would pull up a chair to immerse himself in the picture more thoroughly.[14] She noted this enraptured ecstasy before Titian's *Christ and the Moneychanger*,

Raphael's Sistine *Madonna*, Claude's *Acis and Galatea* and Holbein's *Madonna* at Dresden,[15] Raphael's *Saint Cecilia* in Bologna, *The Madonna with the Chair* in Florence, and mystic terror before *The Dead Christ* (*Christ in the Tomb*) of Holbein in Basle.

Dostoyevsky approached the sublime apparition of Raphael's Madonna, soaring on clouds above mortals, or Holbein's livid corpse of the dead Christ, or the enchanting Attic landscape of Claude's *Acis and Galatea*, three pictures which he loved, in the same way. He forgot the particular subject of the painting as the eternal universal figures on which his heroes, good or bad, comment throughout the novels arose before him. Metamorphosing these pictures into allegories, he forged his own pictorial mythology.

The Sistine *Madonna* was no longer one of the many gentle Madonnas painted by Raphael, but 'this fantastic face, this face of a mad mystic submerged in affliction', to take Svidrigaylov's cruel phrase.[16] For Stepan Trofimovich of *The Devils*,[17] for Versilov of *A Raw Youth*,[18] and for Dostoyevsky himself, who from 1879 kept a photographic reproduction of it over his desk,[19] it was the Ideal of perfect Beauty attained by suffering, a grief which art had transformed into longing.

In the same way, *The Dead Christ*, a copy of which hangs in the sombre house of the Rogozhins, was no longer Holbein's masterpiece, but an allegory, as the comments of Myshkin[20] and Ippolit[21] show us, of that 'obscure, impudent and senselessly eternal force', that 'enormous, pitiless, dumb beast', ugly as a tarantula, the nothingness which annihilates life and overcomes faith.

Claude's innocent landscape, his serene picture of the loves of Acis and Galatea, was no longer a pictorial commentary on the thirteenth book of Ovid's *Metamorphoses*, where the Nereid Galatea tells of the death of the beautiful Acis, crushed by a rock hurled by the jealous Cyclops, Polyphemus. For Stavrogin and Versilov it becomes the almost philosophical landscape of the Golden Age, the 'cradle of humanity', 'universal harmony', the dream Utopia, balm of hardened hearts, hope of lost souls; though it is menaced, as Acis is by Polyphemus, by a tempest of fire and blood: the flames of the Paris Commune, the red spider of crime.[22]

Dostoyevsky thus created for himself, late in life, an imaginary gallery, where the exhibits were few, but were integrated in his creation with such authority that he seemed to supplant their original painters. Painting only appears in his work after 1862, the year of his first visit to Europe. *Notes from Underground* contains an allusion to N. N. Gay's picture *The Last Supper* and Raphael's *Madonna* is mentioned in *Crime and Punishment*, but in *The Idiot*, the most pictorial of the novels, many pictures, including Holbein's *Madonna* and *Dead Christ* and *The Beheading of John the Baptist* by Hans Fries, are recalled and even imagined. In *The Devils* there are several other references to Raphael's *Madonna* and Claude's *Acis and Galatea*. *A Raw Youth* and *The Brothers Karamazov* bring nothing new; the same chosen pictures were used again. In other words, the great pictorial inspiration of the novelist essentially corresponded to his four-year stay in Europe from 1867 to 1871. After 1871, Dostoyevsky, like all great artists absorbed by their own creation, showed a pictorial immobility which was not disturbed by the distant sounds of French Impressionism or even, in spite of the chance article quoted, by the sudden fame of the Wanderers. He remained stubbornly loyal to his few chosen pictures, which had become ideal allegories to which he continually related his heroes.

When his museum was not enough, he tried – and this is an original part of his work – to create a pictorial composition in words, endowing his heroes with his own gift of transmutation. When Nastasya Filippovna wishes, without speaking openly, to associate in an allegory of ethereal love the man she considers Christ-like, Myshkin, and the girl she calls 'an angel of purity', Aglaya, she turns to painting. She writes to her rival:

Yesterday, after meeting you, I came back home and imagined a picture. Christ is always painted from the Gospel stories; I would paint him differently. I would show him alone – for his disciples sometimes left him alone. I would leave with him only a little child. The child would have been playing near him, perhaps he was telling Christ something in his child's language. Christ has been listening to him, but now He is thinking. His hand, absently, forgetfully, is resting on the fair head of the child. He is looking into the distance, to the horizon; a thought as great as the whole world is reflected in His eyes; His face is sad. The child has become silent; leaning against Christ's knee, propping up his cheek with his little hand, he has raised his head and is looking at Christ attentively, thoughtfully, as children sometimes do grow thoughtful. The sun is setting . . . That is my picture.[23]

This whole composition of tender longing is in the spirit of Raphael and there is a reminiscence of Claude in the sunset theme,[24] a theme of death and purifying rebirth. In the following lines, Nastasya Filippovna refers to her own death and to Aglaya's innocence.

Another example shows that Dostoyevsky, in the heat of creation, could turn from his own classical preferences to discover true popular art, preceding the brothers Zdanevich, Goncharova and Laryonov, and approaching the folk art of the primitives or of Niko Pirosmanashvili, the Georgian painter whose frescoes tell a detailed story, uniting the naivety of the birch-bark painting with the symbolic supernatural quality of the icon.[25] This picture appears in *A Raw Youth*, in the parable of the merchant Skotoboynikov, who repents after the suicide of a boy of eight, for which he is responsible. Tormented by remorse, the merchant asks Peter Stepanovich, a drunken teacher and amateur painter, to draw the whole story before the child's final act:

Paint me the biggest picture, all over the wall, as big as the wall, and paint in it first of all the river, and the slope and the ferry, and all the people who were there then must be in it. There must be the colonel's wife and her little girl, and that little hedgehog. And draw me the other bank too, all of it, so it looks just as it is, the church, and the square, and the shops and where the carriages are standing; all of it, draw it just as it is. And near the ferry, the little boy, right on the bank of the river, at that place, he must be pressing his two little fists like this to his chest, to his two little nipples . . . that must be there! And then in front of him, on the other side, above the church, open up the sky, and have all the angels in heaven flying to meet him.[26]

There were no angels, but there was a ray of light falling from the sky and a 'river all blue', running the whole length of the wall, and all the real details ordered by the merchant, which are the details of naive primitive art.

In describing these imaginary pictures,[27] we have entered the landscape of Dostoyevsky. We may go on to ask if his taste in pictures had any influence on the form of the novel. His art is closer to expressionism than anything else in painting. Like Munch, Ensor, Nolde, Rouault, Kokoschka and Sutin, Dostoyevsky resolved purely plastic problems as a function of violent emotional expression, in which metaphysical or social sufferings were treated in a tragic or derisive fashion. His use of colours as signs, significant deformations, and deliberate dissonances show that there is no relationship of form between his work and, for example, the serene composition, the wide and graceful, almost heavenly harmony, the delightful geometry of reversed triangles, diagonals and ovals in Raphael's Sistine *Madonna*. At the most there are thematic echoes: the slanting rays of the setting sun in Claude's picture, one of Dostoyevsky's favourite references, is used only as a recurring theme which appeared for the first time in 1847, in 'A Weak Heart'.[28] In the same way, the dead Christ, which Holbein drew with such cold and incisive realism,[29] recalls the corpse described in the chapter 'In the Hospital' from *The House of the Dead*.

However, Dostoyevsky's technique in description, especially in his lighting and the contrast of light and shade, is very similar to that of the great engravers. He particularly admired the etchings of *The Holy Night* by Correggio and of *Saskia* by Rembrandt, with whom he had an amazing affinity.

Dostoyevsky is a master of engraving a scene in ebony, with gleams of water, of what L. P. Grossman calls his 'sombre etchings'. One of the most beautiful is the scene which old Ikhmenev indicates to Ivan Petrovich in *The Insulted and Injured*:

and with a swift, involuntary gesture of the hand, he pointed out to me the misty perspective of the street, lit by lanterns feebly glimmering in the damp fog, the dirty houses, the pavement stones sparkling from the dampness, the gloomy, angry and soaked people walking along, this whole picture, embraced by the dome, black as if drenched in Indian ink, of the Petersburg sky. We were coming out on to the square; before us in the darkness was the statue, lit from below by gas jets, and further on rose the dark, enormous mass of St Isaac's, hardly distinguishable against the gloomy colour of the sky.[30]

The best illustrations for his work have always been black-and-white engravings or woodcuts, such as Dobuzhinsky's for *Crime and Punishment* or Ushin's for *The Idiot*.[31]

The lighting from one source in many scenes of Dostoyevsky's stories and novels is strikingly reminiscent of Rembrandt etchings,[32] such as *The Raising of Lazarus, Angels appearing to the shepherds, Dr Faustus, The Three Crosses* and especially *The Hundred-Guilder Piece, or Christ healing the sick*, where a supernatural light flows from ordinary lamps, lanterns, candles or nocturnal suns to imbue the shadowy night. These Rembrandt-esque lightings appear in the earliest works of Dostoyevsky. A guttering candle end lights up the treasure seekers above the straw mattress where the corpse of Prokharchin is lying. In the convict prison, the wavering light of the lantern passes over the faces of the sleeping convicts one by one. A guttering candle throws fantastic gleams on the mad face of the violinist Yefimov, who is playing for the last time before his death, and brings the immobile lines of his dead wife jutting from the darkness. The most famous example is the scene in *Crime and Punishment*, where the murderer and the prostitute, by the trembling light of a candle end in which mad and tragic shadows are dancing, are reading the eternal book.

Dostoyevsky found the same Rembrandtesque lighting in N. N. Gay's picture *The Last Supper*, as if the light flowed from an invisible source placed between the group of Christ and his disciples and the shadowy Judas. He mentions this picture again briefly in *Notes from Underground*, where the most revealing example of chiaroscuro is to be found. The scene is a brothel, with two characters: Liza, the prostitute, and the underground man. 'The darkness was almost complete. The candle end, which was burning in a corner on a table, was just burning out and cast only feeble beams.'[33] As the light grows feebler and the face of Liza fades away, the underground man takes pleasure in drawing an appalling picture of the degradation which lies in wait for the poor girl. The darkness grows as he tortures her: finally in complete darkness he sadistically tears open the wound. But when Liza becomes hysterical, he hastily lights the candle, to escape his own terror. With the return of light the idyll begins. A. L. Rubanovich has commented on the symbolism of this scene: the struggle between light and shadow reflects the struggle between Good and Evil.[34] But in Rembrandt, 'the shadows are dense, gentle, teeming', breathing an almost luminous warmth, echoing a 'tender and solemn music', creating the mystery of light itself.[35] For the painter, the patches of darkness and gleaming light have the same mystical secret; for the writer, shadows and light illustrate the eternal conflict of Good and Evil. The sumptuous velvety shades of Rembrandt contrast with the tragic and anxious shadows of Dostoyevsky. The plastic form is the same, but the difference in treatment stresses the divergence of their paths.

Music

Three important witnesses give a fairly complete picture of Dostoyevsky's attitude towards music. Riesenkampf, a friend of his student years, noted that, although Dostoyevsky, as an engineering student, worshipped at the fashionable altar of Liszt, who gave concerts in Petersburg in the spring of 1842 and in Lent in 1843, he did not show the same devotion to music as his elder brother, Mikhail.[36] Sofiya Kovalevskaya remembered the year 1865, when Dostoyevsky was in love with her sister, Anna Vasilyevna Korvin-Krukovskaya, and often visited their home, where Sofiya, who was to become a famous mathematician, used to play the piano. Her judgement was even more categorical: 'Fyodor Mikhaylovich was not a musician, he was one of those people for whom the pleasure of music is dependent on strictly subjective reasons. The most beautiful and perfectly played music might simply make them yawn, but a barrel organ yelping in the courtyard below could move them to tears.'[37] Anna Grigoryevna completed the picture: 'Without being particularly keen on music, my husband was very fond of the works of Mozart, Beethoven's *Fidelio*, Mendelssohn-Bartholdy's *Wedding March*, Rossini's *Stabat Mater* . . . Fyodor Mikhaylovich did not like Richard Wagner at all.'[38] We also know, thanks to N. von Vogt's reminiscences of the summer of 1866, that Dostoyevsky, besides his preference for Mozart and Beethoven, liked the works of Glinka and Serov, especially his opera *Rogneda*, more than the 'tubercular' music of Chopin.[39] However, A. A. Gozenpud, a Soviet musicologist, finds these judgements on Dostoyevsky's musical culture too severe.[40]

Like all the educated classes of his time, Dostoyevsky loved Italian opera and bel canto. He was not immune to fashionable enthusiasm; he rushed off to hear the virtuoso Liszt in 1842 and 1843, the Belgian clarinettist Joseph Blaise in 1843, the Norwegian violinist Ole Bulle, the tenor Giovanni Rubini, the Austrian violinist Heinrich Ernst, whom he mentions three times in the 'Petersburg Chronicle' of 1847 and who is supposed to be the original of the 'famous virtuoso S.' in *Netochka Nezvanova*,[41] the Russian pianist Anton Rubinstein whom he probably met at Buteshevich-Petrashevsky's house[42] and later in 1862, and the composer Glinka, whom he is said to have met in 1849, at the houses of Palm and Durov.[43] These were not simply meeting places where politics and socialism were discussed; musical evenings were organised as well, and each visitor paid three roubles a month for the hire of the piano, played by Nikolay Adamovich Kashevsky, with Aleksey Dmitriyevich Shchelkov accompanying him on the violin; there were discussions about the role of music, about Rubini, Viardot and Tamburini. Dostoyevsky therefore had a fair knowledge of music, and it played a large part in his own family circle. He often visited the family of his sister Vera, the Ivanovs, whom he loved and who discussed music with enthusiasm. The father, Aleksandr Pavlovich, was a fanatic about operas and knew them by heart, and his charming daughter, Mariya Aleksandrovna, was learning the piano and was to become a brilliant musician, tutored by Nikolay Rubinstein, Anton's brother.[44]

However, Dostoyevsky, as Sofiya Kovalevskaya noted, was, apart from his undying devotion to Mozart and Beethoven, only responsive to music 'in situation'.[45] His response even to Beethoven could be subjective. In July 1876, Dostoyevsky wrote to his wife from Ems: 'My angel, this morning I heard the overture from Beethoven's *Fidelio*. Nothing higher than this has been created. It is in the light and gracious style, but with passion. Beethoven has passion and love everywhere. He is the poet of love, of the happiness and longing of love.'[46] In the same letter, he had just made a jealous scene to Anna, who innocently told him of her unexpected meeting with a former suitor. These last words of music criticism might well be a tactful way of asking forgiveness, an indirect love-song.

What Dostoyevsky particularly liked were romances, operatic arias adapted to popular taste, in popular songs. They speak the simple language of the heart and soul, they are the supreme example of popular poetry, the dream that floats through the streets. They play an important part in the novels, sometimes echoing the mood of their surroundings, sometimes creating a grotesque, even tragic dissonance.

In the 'Petersburg Chronicle' of 1847, Dostoyevsky described the melancholy which overcame him on hearing street music: 'It is rather like when, for instance, you are coming home, late in the evening, without thinking of anything, looking round on all sides with profound boredom and suddenly you hear music. A ball, yes, it is a ball!'[47] He felt then that life stirred and vague longings appeared within him:

You can see something else, beyond the colourless theme of our daily life; you hear something else sounding, penetrating in its vitality and sadness, like the Ball of the Capulets in Berlioz. Melancholy and doubt pierce your heart, like that profound sadness which appears in the refrain of the plaintive Russian song drawn out to infinity which echoes like an intimate appeal.[48]

The frontier between the classical *Romeo and Juliet* and the popular song has been wiped out. Later, in prison, Dostoyevsky was keenly interested in the convict songs, distinguishing various types, and noting couplets, refrains and even variations.[49] He described in minute detail an orchestra of eight convicts: two violins, three balalaikas, two guitars and a tambourine acting as double bass, to which two accordions were later added. He had come to understand folk music: 'The harmony of the sounds, the play and especially the soul, the quality of understanding and rendering the very heart of the theme were simply astonishing. I understood for the first time all that was infinitely swaggering and unfettered in the swaggering and unfettered songs of the Russian people.'[50]

In the novels, there is no better example than Raskolnikov, who stops in a street near the Haymarket to listen to the singing of a little girl of fifteen dressed up like a street walker and accompanied by a player on a barrel organ who is grinding out a 'very sentimental romance': 'Do you like street songs?' Raskolnikov suddenly said to a man, already middle-aged, who was standing beside him in front of the barrel organ, and who had the appearance of an idler. The man looked at him in a strange way and was surprised. 'I love them', went on Raskolnikov, but as if he were speaking of something completely different: 'I love hearing someone sing to the barrel organ on a damp dark and cold autumn evening, especially damp, when all the people going by have greenish and sickly faces, or, better still, when wet snow is falling straight down, without wind, you know? and through this snow gas jets are shining.'[51] The sentimental song and the landscape of wet snow form a cocoon in which Raskolnikov weaves his morbid dreams. In *A Raw Youth*, Versilov, sometimes struck with deep melancholy, confesses that he too loves, in the same setting, the music repeated by a barrel organ 'broken and out of tune' and 'hiccupping' the aria from *Lucia di Lammermoor*, a favourite of Dostoyevsky's own.[52] Another example, in a totally different setting, is Glinka's 'When you open your lips in the hour of joy', which Velchaninov in 'The Eternal Husband' sings so passionately. Dostoyevsky remembered exactly when he had heard this in 1849,[53] but in the novel it matches the mood of the passage where a tormented Don Juan returns to his former pastime for an instant, burning with desire for the willing young girl who is listening to him. It is a musical kiss.

At another point, the melody heard by the writer in happy times, in the warm atmosphere of the Ivanov family during the summer of 1866 at Lyublino, Georg Stiegele's romance to Heine's verses,[54] appears in a completely different context – that of poverty and madness. In *Crime and Punishment*, Katerina Ivanovna Marmeladova, in the last stages of consumption, goes mad and tries to make her frightened children sing and dance in the streets. The charming romance

> Du hast Diamenten und Perlen
> Du hast die schönsten Augen
> Mädchen, was willst du mehr?

assumes a grotesque and ironic air which heightens the tragedy of the scene.

There is even one romance, *Mein lieber Augustin*, which is used in two different ways. In *The Insulted and Injured* it is a musical colouring given to the Hoffmannesque scenery of the Muller bakery haunted by Smith and his starving dog. In *The Devils* it is an impertinence which mingles its biting counterpoint with the martial sounds of the 'Marseillaise' in the parody by the Jew Lyamshin, 'The Franco-Prussian war', which ends in a frenetic shout.[55]

Is music anything more than an accompaniment to the soul or a counterpoint in Dostoyevsky's novels? Is there any reflection of musical art and technique in his creation? The first part of one of his books, *Netochka Nezvanova*, is devoted to the story of Yefimov, a violinist who dies mad. Any reader looking for musical commentary will be disappointed: technique, counterpoint, a new theory of music are certainly mentioned, but vaguely. There are several reasons for this: first, the theme of the mad musician was a convention of romantic literature at the time, as we see from Hoffmann's *Gluck*, Balzac's *Gambara*, Heine's *Florentinische Nächte* and V. F. Odoyevsky's musical stories; second, Dostoyevsky has transposed some of his own problems of artistic creation in general, after becoming disillusioned with literary people in 1846 and 1847; and lastly, the story is told by a child, who would not be likely to make technical remarks. However, one of the main contributions of music to Dostoyevsky's literary creation appeared in this unfinished work: the recurring theme which is both visual and aural, with a defined symbol uniting the image and the musical theme. In one fantastic scene the orphan, Netochka, hidden behind a curtain, is listening to the concert of the great violinist S., whose true genius sobers Yefimov and drives him into madness. The great hall, 'like an ocean of light', which Netochka sees from behind a red curtain, and the music of the concert immediately make the girl remember her old 'slum in the twilight, the window too high, the deep street with its lights, the windows opposite with their red curtains', she hears once more 'the shouts, the noise, the distant music'.[56] The 'red curtains' associated with music, symbols of an 'eternal Sunday', 'of eternal happiness', are echoed by the red curtain which rises upon a 'paradise' steeped in music. It is a musical landscape where sounds and colours blend in an unchangeable and significant association. Insistent in *Netochka Nezvanova*, it becomes more discreet in *Notes from Underground*, where the memory of the hero's pathetic adventure with Liza recurs to his mind 'like one of those musical themes that won't leave you alone' and is associated with the landscape of damp, yellow and dirty snow.[57] In the great novels, as we shall see, the landscape, even without music, retains its musical essence.

The composition of the great novels, with their sudden conflagrations and tempests of passion, slowly prepared by cunning gradations of tension, their vast orchestration in magnificent crescendos, is reminiscent of Beethoven, for whom Dostoyevsky always had a great passion.[58] Paul Claudel, another master of powerful lyricism, sensed this affinity: 'I consider *The Brothers Karamazov* an immense work. I am speaking purely from the point of view of form. And from this formal point of view, I have learnt much from Dostoyevsky, as I should say that I have learnt much from Beethoven . . .'[59] He gives an example: Dostoyevsky 'knew very well what he wanted and his novels are a model of composition. There is no more beautiful composition, in a tone that I shall call Beethovenian, than the beginning of *The Idiot*: the first two hundred pages of *The Idiot* are a true masterpiece of composition which recalls the crescendos of Beethoven.'[60]

Dostoyevsky himself in *A Raw Youth* proposed a musical mirror for his creation. He made an attempt at opera, or rather oratorio, where the orchestra plays a more important part, in Trishatov's dream:

if I were composing an opera, you know, I would take the subject from *Faust*. I am very fond of that theme. I keep composing a scene in the cathedral, just in my head, I imagine it ... A Gothic cathedral, the interior, choirs, hymns, Gretchen comes in, and you know – medieval choirs, so that you feel the fifteenth century. Gretchen is heartbroken, first a recitative, quiet, but terrible, torturing, while the choirs thunder gloomily, sternly, indifferently:

Dies irae, dies illa!

And suddenly – the voice of the devil, the song of the devil. He is unseen, just the song, at the same time as the hymns, almost coincides with them, but it's quite different – somehow or other it has to be done like this. A long song, unwearying, it is a tenor, it has to be a tenor. It begins quietly, tenderly: 'Do you remember, Gretchen, when you were still innocent, still a child, you used to come with your mother to this cathedral and lisped your prayers from an old book?' But the song becomes stronger, more passionate and impetuous; the notes are higher: there are tears in them, and tireless, inescapable grief and, at last, despair: 'There is no forgiveness, Gretchen, there is no forgiveness for you here!' Gretchen wants to pray, but only shouts tear out of her breast – you know, when you are choked with tears in the breast, and the song of Satan goes on and on, piercing deeper and deeper into her soul, like a blade, higher and higher – and suddenly breaks off with something like a shout: 'Everything is finished, accursed woman!' Gretchen falls on her knees, clasps her hands in front of her – and then we have her prayer, something very short, half recitative, but naive, without any sort of decoration, something as mediaeval as possible, four verses, only four verses – Stradella has some notes like this – and on the last note she faints! Confusion. She is lifted up, carried ... and suddenly there is a thundering chorus. It is like a great blow of voices, an inspired, triumphant, crushing chorus, something like our 'Dori-no-si-ma chin-mi', our hymn to the Cherubim – so that everything totters on its foundations – and it all changes to an ecstatic, joyful general cry of 'Hosanna!', like a shout of the whole universe, and they are still carrying her away, carrying her, and here is when the curtain must fall![61]

Dostoyevsky was stirring all his musical favourites together: Stradella's oratorios, the chant of the Latin liturgy 'Dies irae, Dies illa!' whose themes were used by Berlioz in his *Symphonie fantastique*, and the hymn of the Cherubim in the Orthodox liturgy. His notebooks show us that he also remembered Gounod's *Faust*, and Meyerbeer's opera *Robert the Devil*: 'like Meyerbeer, in whose *Robert* you can really breathe the tenth century'.[62] Perhaps he also recalled the commentary of V. F. Odoyevsky, an acquaintance of his, on the *Faust* of Radziwill, which appeared in *The Russian Invalid* in 1837:

Marguerite is talking to her conscience, personified by Mephistopheles, and listening to the choir singing the first phrases of the Requiem ... After a short introduction, the choir begins to sing 'Requiem aeternam' and at the same time Mephistopheles delivers his first monologue in recitative ... The terrible cry of conscience is drowned in the peaceful decisive chords of religion, and after that, how affecting the solo in the chorus is! At the same time as the menacing staccato phrases of the 'Dies irae' you hear the desperate lament of Marguerite.[63]

Whatever his memories might be, the grandiose musical dream of Dostoyevsky surpasses all those who set this famous scene to music, with the possible exception of Mahler, who uses the rigorous polyphony of Bach and the principle of construction of the symphonies of Beethoven in his remarkable Eighth Symphony.[64] At least, this is the opinion of A. A. Gozenpud:

No composer who has attempted this scene in the cathedral has so much richness in his musical images, so much power in dramatic contrast as Dostoyevsky, from the austere accents of the 'Day of Wrath' to the joy of the 'Hosannah'. All the musical incarnations of this scene are dominated by a sombre and overwhelming atmosphere which culminates in the finale. With Dostoyevsky the musical action, after reaching a tragic summit, moves to another sphere, a sphere of light, and this is followed by a new culmination in a major key.[65]

The formal structures which Dostoyevsky discovered in the plastic arts and in music were often more productive than the subjects. Dostoyevsky had the typical creator's attitude towards art. He fed only on that which was the same substance as himself. He felt kinship and mysterious correspondences rather than influences. He was completely uninterested in anything happening after 1870. With slight changes as regards paintings, he functioned as a creator in an aesthetic world which was completely immobile and conservative.

However, this world was strongly individual. As in literature, Dostoyevsky's mythologising power created throughout his works a system of metaphors based on aesthetic objects (pictures, songs or operas), which he detached from their original creators and invested with a completely personal mythological value, which his different heroes then took over for themselves.

3

The heritage: literature

The stories and novels of Dostoyevsky are swarming with literary references and allusions. All his writings are an immense passionate interpretation of literature, which he took to include philosophy and history. For
Dostoyevsky the book had infinite powers. The hero is described psychologically by the books he reads; man in society and his rebellious mind are
reflected in literary discussions; spontaneously and sometimes inaccurately
quoted, flattered or parodied, exalted or cast down, the book allowed the
author to define himself, to find his place in the literary conflicts of the time,
which seethed with anathematising revolutions. Dostoyevsky's dialogue
with the ghosts of past and present literature went on for the whole of his
working life. Filled with awe for the profession of literature, and eager to
win a place in its ranks, he engaged in a trial of the writing in the magazines
and books of the time,[1] and soon after his first creative work, he began to
cross-examine his own image as a writer, which criticism, with its eagerness
for labels, tended to freeze. In an agony of uncertainty, trying to escape
from the prisons created by his first idols and his first works, he moved
towards his guiding stars through the dense thicket which he continuously
created around himself by his prodigious appetite for reading. But he was
always accompanied by his good geniuses: the writers who were his peers.

Anchorage of youth

Childhood and youthful reading leave such a deep trace on the mind that an
ocean of libraries studied in later years is powerless to wash it away. This
was particularly true for Dostoyevsky. If anyone asked him, at the height of
his fame as a writer in 1880, what books should be given to a child, he would
always recommend, apart from the Russian writers who had appeared since
then, the books he loved in his youth:

You say you have not yet given your daughter anything literary to read, as you are
afraid that her imagination (*fantaziya*) may be developed too vividly. I don't think
this is quite right: imagination is innate in man, and especially in every child, in
whom, from the very earliest age, it is more developed than the other faculties and
needs to be satisfied. If it is opposed, it dies or, on the contrary, it is left – which is
harmful – to wither away by itself. The tension which would certainly result from this
would only drain the spiritual side of the child. It is precisely the impressions of the

sublime which are necessary in childhood. When I was ten, I saw Schiller's *Die Räuber* in Moscow, in the theatre, with Mochalov, and I assure you that the strong impression I received then exercised a very beneficial effect on my mind. At twelve years of age, in the country, I read the whole of Walter Scott, and if I developed my imagination and my impressionability too much, I did on the other hand direct them very well ... Walter Scott has a high educational value. Let her read the whole of Dickens. Let her know the literature of other centuries (Don Quixote and even Gil Blas). It would be best to start with poetry. She ought to read the whole of Pushkin, poetry as well as prose. Gogol too. Turgenev, Goncharov if you like: as for my works, I do not think that they would all be suitable for her. It would be good for her to read all Schlosser's history[2] and Solovyov's Russian one.[3] Do not forget Karamzin.[4] For the moment, don't give her Kostomarov.[5] The conquest of Peru, of Mexico, by Prescott, is indispensable[6] In general, historical works have enormous educational value. Leo Tolstoy should be read in entirety. Shakespeare, Schiller, Goethe.[7]

In a second letter, addressed to an anonymous correspondent, on the same problem of reading matter for a youth from thirteen to sixteen, Dostoyevsky repeated his advice, giving the same names, but adding Zhukovsky, Lermontov, Ostrovsky, the critic Belinsky and repairing a grave omission in his first letter by the recommendation: 'The Gospel and the Acts of the Apostles *sine qua non*.' The main idea is: 'Take and give only what produces sublime impressions and gives rise to great thoughts.'[8]

The historians, except for Karamzin, were not those he read in his youth, but this is not important: his love for history is clear. In these, two of his last, letters, Dostoyevsky was expressing the high moral and spiritual significance of his childhood reading, and the three dominant ideas already implicit in it: the dream, the literature of fiction; the real, historical works; the spiritual, the sacred texts.

The gates of the dream

Fedya, an ardent soul, was introduced to the marvellous world of dream and imagination by the stories he heard as a little boy. After dark, the family nannies, Alyona Frolova and especially Lukerya whispered to their audience of enchanted and frightened children fairy tales about the Firebird, Alyosha Popovich, Bluebeard, and adventure stories like *Yeruslan Lazarevich* or *The Story of the valiant Paladin Bova Korolevich*, widely distributed in popular editions since 1750, illustrated by naive and coloured woodcuts.[9] When the children were older, their parents read to them in the evenings, sharing their taste for sentimentalism, the reverie of the heart, with their elder children. They read poets: Derzhavin of the great odes; Zhukovsky, master of the ballad, of majestic and simple sentiments, whose marvellous translations of the pre-romantic and romantic poets of England and Germany, especially the Greek ballads of Schiller and Byron's *Prisoner of*

Chillon, opened the gates of Western literature to the child. They read prose, the sensitive, charming Karamzin, who is reminiscent of Sterne in his *Letters of a Russian Traveller*, and who melted the hearts of his contemporaries with his tragic story *Poor Liza*; Pushkin, whose poetry did not appeal to Dostoyevsky's parents; and other authors now forgotten but part of the living literature of the time, such as D. N. Begichev, who wrote a poetic moralising chronicle of the noble Kholmsky family also remembered by Tolstoy, and romantic authors, followers of Scott, like M. N. Zagoskin with his much imitated work *Yury Miloslavsky, or the Russians in 1612*, I. I. Lazhechnikov, the more gifted author of *The House of Ice*, K. P. Masalsky with *The Streltsy*, V. I. Dal, who used a pseudonym for *Tales of the Cossack Lugansky*,[10] and many many others published in the *Reading Library*, the magazine of Baron Brambeus, so often derided in Dostoyevsky's early works.

As soon as he could read, the young dreamer naturally turned towards the most exciting and fantastic works. The Gothic horror novels of Ann Radcliffe, which he read as early as eight,[11] with their parade of ruined castles, perilous pathways, duels, desperate flights, elopements, ambushes, terrifying criminals, virtuous and sensitive heroes, foreboding dreams and pale apparitions, gave him a sensation of delicious terror. The writer's friend and collaborator, Apollon Grigoryev, stressed, in *The Epoch*,[12] journal of the Dostoyevsky brothers, the 'magical influence' which Mrs Radcliffe exerted over his heart as a child. Writing of the Rembrandtesque colouring of her descriptions, 'her nervous intuition of the life of shadows, ghosts and phantoms', her 'profound comprehension of sombre and savage passions', the critic was close to the sensibility of Dostoyevsky, who recalled *The Mysteries of Udolpho* in his last novel, *The Brothers Karamazov*,[13] where he returned to the books of his childhood.

Walter Scott, who was influenced by Mrs Radcliffe, was Dostoyevsky's favourite reading as an adolescent. According to his brother Andrey, he read and re-read *Quentin Durward* and *Waverley*, undiscouraged by clumsy translations. In 'Petersburg Dreams in verse and prose' Dostoyevsky recalled the time of his youth, when he imagined he was 'a Knight in a tournament' or 'Edward Glendinning of *The Monastery*', and when he read the story of Clara Mowbray in *St Ronan's Well*.[14] The boy's imagination was inspired by Scott's sentimental mediaevalism, prodigies of magic and demonology, exotic backgrounds. But he was also subconsciously absorbing an aesthetic model, which prepared him to welcome the more vast but related universe of Balzac: the art of Scott with his strong and patient depiction of surroundings, his long expositions, his solidly contrived plots, leisurely and exciting in turn, his vivid and natural dialogue, his power of conception and his talent as a storyteller. According to Turgenev, Scott's work is 'a vast and solid edifice with unshakable foundations set in the natural and popular soil, with ample introductions shaped like porticoes, with waiting-rooms and dark corridors linking everything together'.[15] If we substitute public places, drawing rooms, and so on, where the great crowd scenes of Dostoyevsky take place, for 'waiting-rooms', and uncertain places such as dark staircases and thresholds for 'dark corridors', the link between the complex architecture of Dostoyevsky's novels and the composition of Scott becomes clear.[16]

These two examples show that youthful dreaming can take different forms. Sometimes the imagination is playing a game of adventure, the game of mimicry which every child plays when reading. Sometimes technique and craftsmanship are cunningly introduced into the game, and the imagination is secretly fashioning the artistic means of the future.

With his adventure books, the young Dostoyevsky wandered through time and space. Paradoxically, it was through English writers, Mrs Radcliffe and Shakespeare (*Romeo and Juliet*),[17] and the French George Sand (*L'Uscoque* and the novels of the Venetian cycle) that he formed his idea of Italy. In the same way, by the magic of books, mediaeval Europe, chivalrous in Scott and popular in Hugo's *Notre-Dame de Paris*, came back to life for him. So did the bloodthirsty dynastic struggles of England with Shakespeare and Schiller's *Maria Stuart*, the black Spain of the Inquisition with *Melmoth the Wanderer* by Charles Robert Maturin, then very popular, and Schiller's *Don Carlos*; the North American epic with Fenimore Cooper;[18] the heroic age of the Cossacks with Gogol's *Taras Bulba*; the Time of Troubles with Pushkin's *Boris Godunov* and Zagoskin's *Yury Miloslavsky*. Through Gnedich, translator of the *Iliad*, and Zhukovsky's *Odyssey*, he discovered ancient Greece and Homer, that 'fabulous' man, whom he enthusiastically compared to Christ.[19]

But this kaleidoscope of times and tribes may be deceptive. As Dostoyevsky waded, apparently at random, through a plethora of major and minor writers, he was subsconsciously following his own path. He continued his quest: man and his mystery. As his culture became more organised and disciplined, with his teachers as well as his taste to help him, he began to attach less importance to any particular work than to the great idea represented by a particular writer. This gigantic effort of synthesis, of final judgement, to create his personal hierarchy of literature was subconsciously accompanied by the search, in the vast arsenal open to him, for adequate forms to suit his future creation.

The quest for the synthetic idea

From the age of seventeen, Dostoyevsky showed his own strong individuality. He made a spirited attack on his brother Mikhail:

But tell me, if you please: on the subject of form, what has possessed you to say that neither Racine nor Corneille can please us because their form is bad. What a pitiful person you are! And you set me this really intelligent question! Do you think they have no poetry? Racine has no poetry? Racine the ardent, the passionate, a man in love with the ideal, has no poetry? And someone can suggest this! But have you read *Andromaque*? Have you, brother? Have you read *Iphigénie*?[20]

And he forged ahead to compare *Phèdre* with Shakespeare, as well as making a case for Corneille, admirable in his 'gigantic characters, his spirit of romanticism'. *Cinna* 'would have done honour' to Shakespeare; Karl Moor, Fiesko, Tell, and Don Carlos[21] would grow pale before the divine scenes of Augustus Octavius; the characters in *Horace* would be envied by Homer himself. And what could one say about *Le Cid*? 'What does romanticism want if its highest ideas are not shown in *Le Cid*?'[22]

Dostoyevsky refused to accept the clichés and taste of his time; he was eager to move on to the idea of a synthesis uniting men of genius of all times and all schools. But this total and personal vision of his chosen writers did not crystallise immediately. It changed with time, faded (as in the case of Byron) or became richer (as with Pushkin) when, in his maturity, Dostoyevsky set it in historical perspective. The kernel, however, never changed and he remained faithful to his first choices: Balzac, Dickens, Schiller, Pushkin, and even to those who might have been called old-fashioned, such as Scott, Fenimore Cooper, and George Sand. When his young wife Anna admitted in 1867 that 'to her very great shame' she had never read Balzac and knew practically nothing about French literature, asking her husband to choose books for her in the Geneva libraries 'the best and exactly what was worth reading so as not to waste time on pointless things', Dostoyevsky brought his wife his own favourite authors and read or reread them himself with amazing speed.[23] Later he behaved in the same way with his children Lyubov and Fyodor, who were still too young to appreciate it.[24]

The will to synthesise appeared very early in Dostoyevsky, essentially in his letters to his brother Mikhail, his literary confidant of student years. On 9 August 1838, he says he has read the whole of Hoffmann in Russian, and *Kater Murr*[25] in German since it was not translated, almost all Balzac, Goethe's *Faust*, Victor Hugo except for *Cromwell* and *Hernani*, but the interesting thing in his letter is his attempt to define the genius of Balzac: 'Balzac is great! His characters are products of the intelligence of the universe! Not the spirit of the age but thousands and thousands of years, entire millenia have prepared by their struggle this conclusion in the soul of man.'[26]

On 31 October 1838, he was severe in his judgement of Byron. He had probably just been reading Pushkin's *Yevgeny Onegin*, where Byron is described as 'poet of pride', of 'egoism without hope'. He wrote: 'Byron was an egotist, his dream of glory is derisory, hollow.'[27] But later in *Diary of a Writer* he celebrated the spirit of the great English poet, finally discovering the idea of synthesis:

Byronism is a phenomenon which is perhaps momentary, but great, holy and necessary in the life of the peoples of Europe and even in the life of all humanity. Byronism appeared at a moment of terrible longing, of disenchantment, almost of despair ... At that moment a great and powerful genius appeared, a passionate poet! His songs conveyed the distress of humanity at that time, its sombre disillusionment and its frustrated ideals. It was a new and unheard-of muse, the muse of vengeance and grief, of despair and malediction.[28]

In the same letter, Dostoyevsky begged his brother to tell him 'what is the central thought of Chateaubriand's work *The Genius of Christianity*.[29]

In a letter of 1 January 1840, the same will to synthesise was applied to Homer: 'In the Iliad, Homer gave the ancient world an organisation of life which is both spiritual and earthly in the same sense as Christ gave one to the new world.'[30] Twenty years later, in 1861, Dostoyevsky took up the subject again:

The Iliad is an epic poem of a life so powerful, so full, of such a high moment in the life of a people and, let us note once more, of the life of such a great race that in our time, a time of aspirations, struggles, doubts, faith (for our time is a time of faith), in a word, in our time of a more intense life, this universal harmony incarnated by the Iliad can act on the soul in the most decisive fashion.[31]

It would be pointless to go on giving examples (here embryonic) of Dostoyevsky's ability to find the essential thought or spirit of a writer. The approach is clear. He never wrote as a critic, who is by definition excluded from creation, but as a visionary of the Ideal. He apprehended the literature of others not from a technical and professional point of view, but with the wish to belong to a spiritual band of brothers, to take part in a feast of souls. As in painting, he ranged the immense field of literature to find a personal mythology for himself, a world of chosen beings, reflected towards him by their existing works. The great writers whom he exalted to the skies, Schiller, Shakespeare, Dickens, Cervantes, George Sand, Pushkin, and in secret Gogol, are not simply influences on him. They are living waters which nourish his independent creations. Indeed, as we shall see, his sources of spiritual inspiration are, with a few exceptions, distinct from his masters in form and structure.

The annexation of the inspirers of the Ideal

Except for Pushkin, who to Dostoyevsky was a universal figure dominating and including all the others,[32] Schiller was the first and last great inspirer of the Ideal. At the age of ten, Dostoyevsky was enthusiastic about *Die Räuber*, performed in Moscow with the great actor Mochalov in the part of Karl Moor;[33] in his last novel, *The Brothers Karamazov*, he pays Schiller a vibrant homage, exceptional in a novelist. From the depths of degradation, Dmitriy Karamazov celebrates the ecstasy of love in his 'confession of an ardent heart: he first declaims two lines from 'Die Götter Griechenlands', then some verses from 'Das Eleusische Fest', in Zhukovsky's translation, and finally he thunders out the third and fourth stanzas of 'An die Freude' translated by Tyutchev. Old Karamazov blasphemously says Ivan is 'the very respectable Karl Moor', while he himself is the 'Regierender Graf von Moor in person'. Dostoyevsky's long journey in the company of Schiller ended with the tragedy he had admired so much as a child.

Between these two moments, half a century apart, Dostoyevsky never stopped mentioning or recalling Schiller, in his letters, in his plans (*Maria Stuart* for example), in his stories and novels, from *Poor Folk* (where, among other poems by Schiller, he mentions 'Die Kraniche des Ibykus') and *Crime and Punishment*, to his last novels, in his articles for *Time* and *Epoch*, in his critical articles, and in *Diary of a Writer*.[34] His brother Mikhail, encouraged and instructed by him, translated *Die Räuber* and *Don Carlos*.[35] Dostoyevsky carefully kept these texts in his library, in the famous nine-volume edition by N. V. Gerbel, a collection of all the best Russian translations of Schiller from 1837 to 1861.[36]

Dostoyevsky's allegiance was whole-hearted. From the beginning Schiller was the archetype of the pure desire for the Ideal, to whom Dostoyevsky and his heroes referred throughout his philosophic and creative evolution. Schiller is seen first as delirium incarnated in another person, then as delirium incarnated in the character of the writer himself; soon as a type of independent character; finally, in the last years, as an act of faith in man and universal creation.

Schiller and all his works entered Dostoyevsky's life in the person of I. N. Shidlovsky, friend of his romantic youth,[37] a strange, strong and tormented nature, whose future life, wavering between asceticism and debauchery, faith and doubt, irresistibly recalls the Great Sinner, hero of an immense abortive plan by Dostoyevsky. In a letter of 1840 Dostoyevsky described him transfigured, like a Schillerian hero, by an unfortunate love affair: 'he was not a cold being, a dreamer set on fire by his servitude, but a beautiful, sublime creature, an exact copy of the man presented to us by Shakespeare and Schiller'.[38] His admiration for Shidlovsky was so great that the terms of reference were inverted: reality verified delirium:

I have worked hard at Schiller, I talked Schiller, I raved Schiller, and I believe that destiny has done nothing more timely in my existence than giving me the knowledge of this great poet at this time of my life ... Reading Schiller *with him*, I would verify the noble, ardent Don Carlos, the Marquis Posa and Mortimer *by him*[39] ... As for the name of Schiller, it has become a sacred name for me, magic in some way, summoning so many dreams.[40]

Literature had clothed the real person who, in return, was an inspiration for literature. Schiller then left the body of Shidlovsky to install himself in Dostoyevsky, transforming him into the romantic 'dreamer' whose 'mute, secret, morose tragedy with all its savage horrors, its catastrophes, peripeteia, plots and endings' is described at the end of the 'Petersburg Chronicle' of 1847.[41] When in 1861 Dostoyevsky recalled his time as a Schillerian dreamer with a journalist's acid verve, he removed the mask from this hero enmeshed in inertia and futile daydreams and awoke to the reality of Gogol: 'I saw some singular characters then. They were all strange astonishing figures, completely prosaic, not at all like Don Carlos or the Marquis de Posa, but one and all titular councillors.'[42] Gogol poisoned the kind of Schillerian idealism where love ends in disaster, as in the idyll between the narrator and a whimsical and colourless Nadya, who has been renamed Amelia after Karl Moor's ethereal fiancée: 'If I had married Amelia, I should certainly have been unhappy! What would have become of Schiller now, of my freedom, of roasted barley coffee, and of sweet tears and daydreams and my journey to the moon . . . For after that I went to the moon, gentlemen.'[43] Anyone who reads the sarcastic comments which the underground man loaded on romantic dreamers might think that Dostoyevsky had rooted Schiller the idealist out of his heart after the experience of prison, but in fact the Schillerian inheritance remained under its most seductive form, revolt in the name of the Ideal. There is a startling thematic likeness between, for example, Schiller's *Die Räuber* and *Fiesko* and *Crime and Punishment*. Raskolnikov the rebel is destroyed by pride, as Fiesko the humanitarian idealist is destroyed by ambition. Raskolnikov the criminal is the brother of Karl Moor, the robber who breaks the law, 'which has not yet formed a great man', while freedom – let us substitute 'All is allowed' – lets 'Titans and extraordinary beings' flourish. Svidrigaylov is not deceived by the change of name; twice in the novel he stresses the relationship between the Schillerian hero and Raskolnikov: 'Are you claiming you have any strength? He-he-he! You've surprised me just now, Rodion Rodionovich, although I knew beforehand that was how it would be. You are the one going on about debauchery and aesthetics! You are Schiller, you are an idealist!'[44] and a little later, he replies with lucid sarcasm to Raskolnikov's brusque and disgusted attempt to silence him: 'That's Schiller, our Schiller, Schiller again. Où va-t-elle la vertu se nicher?'[45] All this philosophy of revolt in the name of humanity, doomed in advance to failure and punishment, prison for Raskolnikov and madness for Ivan Karamazov, is foreshadowed in the suicide of Karl Moor. Like Dostoyevsky, Schiller, as he wrote in *Letters on the Aesthetic Education of Man*, did not believe in a freedom which destroyed the moral law and the justice for which it claimed to be fighting. If the inner man did not change, all external reform would be pointless. The Cult of Beauty is the only way of regenerating the social organism. 'Beauty will save the world', as Myshkin says. These are Dostoyevskian themes.

To Dostoyevsky, Schiller, like Shakespeare, was the bard of the passion for the Ideal rather than a herald of the Ideal. The Schillerian hero provided the writer with two abiding characters. The first, suspect because it was tainted with impotence and libertarianism, was the philanthropic dreamer of whom Dostoyevsky had personal experience and which he then created as an independent character, the Schillerian, which obsessed him from the sixties onwards. This is shown by the first lines of the notebooks of *A Raw Youth*, where the name of Schiller appears,[46] and a few pages later a young boy says to Lambert: 'I do not wish to be Schiller ... because it is disgusting.'[47] This Schiller, too political, is the 'friend of humanity' to whom the Convention granted the title of French citizen and whom Dostoyevsky the journalist rejected in *Diary of a Writer*.[48] The second, the Russian transformation of Schiller, has Dostoyevsky's complete devotion. This is the undying source of universal love for 'all peoples and all creatures'.[49] Karl Moor, Fiesko, Ivan Karamazov, who rebel against God and society, who seek freedom in violence, death and coercion, are reflections of the first Schiller; Don Carlos and Dmitry Karamazov, who worship the Ideal through suffering and sacrifice, represent the second.

The case of Schiller is exemplary. First he was worshipped, exercising a profound literary oppression; then, apparently cast out, but really buried in the depths where he loses his identity, he inspired the creator of the great rebellious heroes; finally in the last novel he was no longer a constraint but rose again, sublimated and reconciled in the serene vision of eternal love. A violent love which degenerated into combat, he ended in peaceful communion before the altar of the Passion for the Ideal. The path of Schiller in Dostoyevsky reflects the history of a synthetic thought which finally became independent.

This kind of annexation is even more obvious with George Sand. The notebooks of 1876–7 reveal how important she was to Dostoyevsky: 'A study (learned) on how writers (Schiller, George Sand) influenced Russia and the extent of this influence would be an extraordinary and serious work. But we shall have to wait a long time for this. History of the metamorphosis of ideas.'[50] This last laconic note shows that Dostoyevsky was conscious of the transformation which he forced the heroes of his youth to undergo.

George Sand practically rocked Dostoyevsky's cradle, as he recalled in 1876: 'How many of my admirations and enthusiasms go back to this poet, how much joy and happiness she gave me! I do not hesitate in my choice of words, for this was literally so.'[51] He loved, he goes on, 'in her first works, a certain number of figures of young girls, the ones for example in what were then called her Venetian novels (to which 'L'Uscoque' and Aldini belong), whose most finished type was the later heroine of her novel Jeanne, this time a work of genius'.[52] We do not know exactly which of George Sand's books Dostoyevsky read;[53] on his own admission, he particularly loved 'the first novellas' of the French writer,[54] but he was silent about her great works: *La Mare au Diable, François le Champi, La Petite Fadette and Les Maîtres Sonneurs* which appeared in France from 1846 to 1853, too late for Dostoyevsky, who was arrested in 1849, to have the time to read them as they were published. Possibly he read them later, during his years of exile abroad, from 1867 to 1871, with Anna, whom he was introducing to Western literature, or during his cures at Ems in the 1870s, when he outlined a vast programme of European literature for himself, with George Sand in first place.[55] But it was the early works of George Sand, the novels of the years 1830–40, such as *L'Uscoque, La Dernière Aldini, Teverino*,[56] *Lucrèce Floriani*,[57] although published only in 1846, and especially *Mauprat* and *Spiridion*[58] which left the deepest impression on Dostoyevsky. A relationship has been traced between Carol, hero of *Lucrèce Floriani* and Ordynov of 'The Landlady'. The novels which he read in early youth, *Mauprat* and *Spiridion*, reappear in his last novel, *The Brothers Kara-mazov*, exactly as happened with Schiller.

Mauprat, an atmospheric novel about the redeeming power of love, tells the story of some noble country bandits and shows a family grouped round a crime, with the father, the two brothers, Jean, suggestive of Smerdyakov, Antoine, foreshadowing Ivan, and the nephew Bernard, recalling Dmitriy. In *Spiridion*, the relationship between the aged monk, Alexis, and the young novice, Angel, in the abbey founded by Spiridion is strangely like the one established between Alyosha and Zosima in *The Brothers Karamazov*. In both novels, the mortal remains of Spiridion and Zosima disillusion their disciples in the same way; and Alyosha's entry into the world recalls the destiny of Angel.[59] But the similarity of themes and situations does not lead to an identity between Dostoyevsky's religious ideas and those of George Sand, as Ivan Pouzyna would suggest. Her ideas, indebted to *The Eternal Gospel* by Pierre Leroux, and embodied in *Spiridion* by the heresiarch Joachim de Flore, the thirteenth-century Cistercian who was so appealing to Renan, possibly played some part in the contamination of Zosima's very personal ideas on Christianity, where 'the tender light of the Golden Age is flowing and the shadows of the eternal return appear',[60] but there is no sign of this in the notebooks. They do introduce the atheist theme of the Golden Age, which Dostoyevsky's heroes, Versilov, Stavrogin and the Ridiculous Man, experience in dreams. Apparently Dostoyevsky, in his obsessive syncretism, took over George Sand, wiped away her traces, and kept only what suited him.

A master proof of what one might call the *passionate unconsciousness of a genius avid for synthesis* is given by Dostoyevsky himself in his obituary of George Sand, which appeared in *Diary of a Writer*, 1876.[61] The eulogistic tone of sublimity, the praise of the heroine and the 'universally human', and especially the amazing transmutation of ideas and intentions in these pages foreshadow the famous 'Pushkin speech', which was not so much a critical analysis of Pushkin as a profession of faith by Dostoyevsky. Although he was sincere in his homage to George Sand, her basic themes of socialism and Christianity were an embarrassment to him.

On the first, he could not be duped; he knew all about the different forms of socialism from bitter experience. In 1873, in another article devoted to Belinsky, 'People of Other Days', he placed George Sand with her true peers: Cabet, Pierre Leroux and Proudhon.[62] In his preparatory notes for the obituary of 1876, he recalled the Utopian socialism of the 1840s: 'George Sand. My youth. Faust . . . L'Uscoque. School. Love of humanity! Venice. Socialism. George Sand especially during our exile. Humanity.'[63] Moreover, he let his wish to cross swords with the ideological enemy show through: 'She is a landowner.'[64] In the article he abstained from attack, but emasculated George Sand's socialism, depriving it of its 'social organisation' in favour of its 'moral basis', a thoroughly Dostoyevskian theme: 'She based her socialism, her convictions, her hopes and her ideals on the moral feeling of man, on the spiritual thirst of the human race, on its longing for perfection and purity, and not on the necessity of the ant-heap.'[65] This assertion was incautious from the author of *The Devils*, who defined the relationship between Granovsky–Verkhovensky and Nechayev–Verkhovensky, between Utopian socialism and ant-hill socialism, as that of father and son.

Moreover, to assert that George Sand was 'probably one of the most perfect followers of Christ without knowing it herself',[66] she who extolled the doctrine of the Eternal Gospel, the religion of the Holy Spirit which was to be the successor of the Christian religion and was to cast out all sacraments, is pure and simple extrapolation. However, Dostoyevsky finally qualified his statements; at the end of the article, he noted that in her works there are no 'humiliated persons, no just people who give in, no humble and poor of spirit as there are in almost every novel of the great Christian, Dickens'. On the contrary, she portrays 'proud heroines, true sovereigns'.[67] These 'haughty pagans', whose mystery Dostoyevsky was never able to solve,[68] whom he loved and hated at the same time, are related to Netochka Nezvanova, Nelli, Polina, Dunya, Aglaya, Liza, Katerina Ivanovna, the proud and heroic women who stalk the pages of Dostoyevsky's novels and are one of the clearest signs of George Sand's legacy.

In conclusion, if we are to find grafts[69] from George Sand in Dostoyevsky's work, they appear first in the fascination of the dominating female, and secondly, in the faith in man, 'respect for the individuality of man and for his freedom (beginning with his responsibility)'[70] found in her books, in spite of the Christian viewpoint that Dostoyevsky tried to impose on her.

This second example makes it clear that Dostoyevsky changed the great inspirers of the Ideal to fit his own spiritual quest. He made myths of them, even gods, and woe to anyone who might dispute it![71] But their status owed nothing to the consecration of the external world. A new Pygmalion, Dostoyevsky elevated them to godhead in the mirror of his soul where their forms exactly match the outlines of his secret aspirations. They themselves would have been amazed, or enchanted, by the places they occupy there.

Before the creation of Prince Myshkin,[72] it would have been outrageous to take Don Quixote or Mr Pickwick as archetypal images of 'the absolutely beautiful man', whose supreme model is the Christ of St John's Gospel. Dostoyevsky's suggestion of this comparison is partly due to his conviction that no human creator is capable of matching the sublime image of holiness.

Dostoyevsky had always dreamt of describing the spiritually perfect man: the Idiot was his first attempt; Makar Ivanov (or Ivanych) of *A Raw Youth*, Zosima and Alyosha of *The Brothers Karamazov* were to be his last. And this was why he chose in his heart those great apes of God, Dickens, Cervantes, and Hugo and tried to fathom their approach. This is another indication of the link between imagination and learning the technique of creation; the search for the Ideal is accompanied by the search for an adequate structure to express it. Let us examine the models he chose.

Why does Mr Pickwick, tubby, self-important, pompous and not very bright, in short, ridiculous, change before our eyes into an example of loving charity, an angelic soul? Why does Don Quixote, that beanpole in bizarre costume, shouting the name of Amadis de Gaulle to the nearby windmills, eternally deceived, beaten, tossed in a blanket, in love with the chubby Dulcinea, become a magician whose sad eyes clothe the universe in miracles, a great hero who dies because he is exiled from the Kingdom of the Ideal? Why does Jean Valjean, a branded pariah, a dark force whose misfortunes should have made him a beast ravening with hatred, change into a creature full of light and love?[73] Dostoyevsky replied in his famous letter of 1/13 January 1868:

Every writer, not only ours, but even all European ones, anyone who tried to describe the positively beautiful, has always given up. Because the task is measureless. The beautiful is the ideal; now the ideal, ours or that of civilised Europe, is still far from being worked out! There is one single positively beautiful character in the world, Christ ... But I am going too far. I will simply say that of all the beautiful figures in literature, Don Quixote is the most finished. But Don Quixote is beautiful only because he is ridiculous at the same time. The Pickwick of Dickens (an infinitely more feeble idea than Don Quixote, but all the same immense) is also ridiculous and this is why it attracts you. People feel compassion for a beautiful figure which is laughed at and ignorant of its own value, and there is sympathy in the reader. This arousal of compassion, this is exactly the secret of humour. Jean Valjean is also a powerful attempt, but he arouses sympathy by his terrible misfortune and the injustice of society towards him.[74]

What did Dostoyevsky take from these examples? He realised that if he wished to create a figure which was absolutely beautiful, he had to use counterpoint, the contrast between the beam of light presented by Don Quixote, Pickwick, Valjean or Myshkin, and the dark shadows which the opinions of others project on their candid goodness. The beautiful creature can only be seen against the background of a leprosy which is outside him, through ridicule, idiocy, and the brand of the outcast, all those prisons in which an aggressive society locks the heretic. There is an implicit corollary: the beautiful creature must die. The unsatisfactory development of the Ideal does not matter; failure is present from the beginning, for it is failure which reveals beauty and makes it holy. Don Quixote, dying because he is no longer driven mad by the Ideal, foreshadows the social defeat of Myshkin and Zosima. Christ, the archetype, was crucified by men, and, but for the Resurrection, the failure would have been complete. Dostoyevsky was fascinated by triumphant holiness, but it is through social failure that some of his heroes approach it, as in, for instance, 'The Dream of a Ridiculous Man', where social disgrace ends in spiritual rebirth. This was the lesson Dostoyevsky drew from Cervantes, Dickens and Hugo. His insane idea for a novel – the imitation of Christ, divine excess – grew out of it.

Besides this great central inspiration, Dostoyevsky naturally used other situations, characters, or themes from these three authors, but they are difficult to trace. Certainly *Netochka Nezvanova* recalls *Dombey and Son*, while the first pages of *The Insulted and Injured* (old Smith and Nelly) resemble *The Old Curiosity Shop*, as the Touchard boarding school resembles Mr Creakle's school in *David Copperfield*.[75] *The Last Day of a Condemned Man* by Victor Hugo furnished elements of *Crime and Punishment* (the dream of the repetition of the crime with the malicious old woman) and many arguments to Prince Myshkin, while *Les Misérables* resembles *Crime and Punishment*. But all this is part of the process of creation which is not satisfied with mere literary reminiscences, one isolated vector in a sheaf of many elements fused by the creative will. A great deal of critical ingenuity has been expended on the search for the literary sources of Raskolnikov's famous dream, where the poor nag is martyred by a drunken coachman, although Dostoyevsky himself suggested an autobiographical source, the brutal scene of the 'Feldjäger' in *Diary of a Writer*, January 1876.[76] Might one influence be 'Melancholia' from Hugo's *Contemplations* (1856) or Nekrasov's poem 'Before Twilight' from the cycle *On the subject of time* (1858–9)? Numerous schemas have been analysed: from Hugo *to* Nekrasov *and* Dostoyevsky, from Hugo *and* Nekrasov *to* Dostoyevsky,

from Hugo *to* Nekrasov and then *to* Dostoyevsky. Another possible source
has recently appeared: the episode of the death of the horse in *Les
Misérables*, so that the Hugo of 'Melancholia' might have inspired the
creator of Raskolnikov's dream through Hugo in *Les Misérables* and
Nekrasov in 'Before Twilight'.[77] Dostoyevsky, if interrogated about various
influences, would probably have replied: 'I didn't think of it at the time, but
the critic is probably right.' But he would have added that the important
thing was the central thought of Hugo; 'the fundamental thought of all
nineteenth-century art: ... a Christian and highly moral thought: the
formula is the raising of the fallen human being crushed by the unjust yoke
of circumstances, secular stagnation and social prejudices'. He defined this
thought as 'the rehabilitation of the humiliated and all the outcasts rejected
by society'.[78]

Even when the reminiscence is attested and signed by the hero, it is so
free and personal that it becomes general rather than specific, that is, it is
mythologised. Trishatov, for example, recalls *The Old Curiosity Shop* of
Dickens in *A Raw Youth*:

Do you remember a part at the end, when they – that mad old man and that
charming thirteen-year-old girl, his granddaughter, after their fantastic flight and
their wandering – find a refuge at last somewhere in the depths of England, near
some Gothic mediaeval cathedral, and this little girl got some kind of job there, she
showed the cathedral to visitors ... And once the sun was setting, and this child on
the porch of the cathedral, all bathed in its last rays, stood and looked at the sunset
with quiet thoughtful contemplation in her childish soul, as if she were faced with
some mystery.[79]

Dostoyevsky has dramatised, magnified, transmuted. In Dickens there is no
Gothic mediaeval cathedral, but a modest country church; still less are there
any rays of the setting sun, a theme dear to the Russian novelist, but, in
romantic contrast, the radiant morning sun, and there is no 'thoughtful
contemplation' in the 'childish soul', but a young girl about to die who finds
consolation and serenity in reading the Bible and who dreams of spring and
eternal renewal. However, while unfaithful to the letter, Dostoyevsky was
true to the myth, the spirit of Dickens: for to Dostoyevsky the setting sun
was the double symbol of death and resurrection. And Trishatov adds: 'you
know, there is nothing much, in this little scene of Dickens', absolutely
nothing, but you will never forget it, and it has remained through all Europe
– why? There is beauty! There is innocence!'[80] Later, in 1873, reproaching
painters for 'not giving the idea its head more and being afraid of the ideal',
Dostoyevsky suggested they should follow the example of Dickens, who in
Pickwick, *Oliver Twist* and in 'the grandfather and the little girl of The Old
Curiosity Shop' had created 'something ideal'.[81]

Three books which Dostoyevsky knew and loved illustrate the quest for
the Ideal: *The Posthumous Papers of the Pickwick Club*, a book he read in

difficult times,[82] and on which he meditated as he did on the Gospel, the only book allowed in convict prison;[83] *Les Misérables*, bought volume by volume and read in one week in 1862, in Florence,[84] and reread on 21 to 22 March, while he was imprisoned in the guardhouse at the Haymarket;[85] and finally *Don Quixote* which Dostoyevsky had in his library, in Louis Viardot's fine translation.[86]

Dostoyevsky never tired of praising *Don Quixote*:

Until now it is the supreme and most grandiose expression of human thought, it is the bitterest irony which a man has found to express his thought, and if the end of the world came and someone were to ask men: 'Tell me, have you understood your life on earth, and what have you concluded from it?', someone could hold out Don Quixote in silence: 'Here is my conclusion about life, can you condemn me?' I am not sure that he would be right, but...[87]

The following year, in September 1877, Dostoyevsky went back to his theme: 'Oh, this book is a great book, different from the ones which are being written now; of books like that, only one appears in several centuries.' And further on: 'This book, the saddest of all books, man will not forget to take with him to the Last Judgement. There he will show the most profound and fateful secret of man and humanity revealed.'[88] And the development which followed led to the main idea which made Cervantes, Dickens and Hugo into prophets: *Don Quixote* is the bitter history of the failure of the most sublime, the most pure, the most tender and the most courageous Ideal: 'The sight of so many great and noble forces which are lost in vain is enough to drive more than one friend of humanity to despair, to arouse him not to laughter but to bitter tears, and to embitter for always by doubt a heart until then pure and believing.'[89] These might be the bitter words about an eventual loss of faith pronounced by Myshkin in *The Idiot*, and by Dostoyevsky in reality before another work of art where Nothingness casts out the Ideal, Holbein's *Dead Christ*.

For Dostoyevsky, as for Schiller, George Sand, Cervantes, Hugo and Dickens, the Ideal was a belief necessary to man. The romantic illusion may be doomed to failure, but this is not important: he chose, to parody one of his famous statements, to be with the Ideal rather than with truth. It is an odd company, but it was never arbitrary in Dostoyevsky's mind. In 1876, tempted by the idea of sketching a vast panorama of world literature from antiquity to his own time, he sanctioned his youthful choice by regrouping all these inspirers of the Ideal under the banner of what he called the 'literature of Beauty', which he distinguished from the 'literature of the sacred' (ancient classical tragedy), or the 'literature of action' which is contrasted with the 'literature of despair'.[90] Although he was keenly aware that the Ideal remained inaccessible and that failure was the rule, he braced himself by an act of faith: 'Beauty in the ideal cannot be attained because of the extraordinary power and depth needed. Isolated manifestations.

Remain true. Christ gave the Ideal. Only the literature of Beauty will save.'[91]

The Prometheans

The distinction which Dostoyevsky made between kinds of literature was not absolute. Cervantes and Shakespeare belong to antagonistic categories, as an equivocal note of 1876 shows: 'Classical tragedy is in the service of the gods, but Shakespeare is despair. What is there more despairing than Don Quixote? The beauty of Desdemona is only brought as a sacrifice. The sacrifice of life in Goethe ... A Shakespeare of our time would also have brought despair. But in Shakespeare's time belief was still strong.'[92]

The young Dostoyevsky was not simply a soul thirsting for the Ideal. He knew that even the great inspirers of the Ideal, whom he had annexed, were not as naive as that. They had decked their exemplary heroes in the tawdry rags of the Fool, the tatters of the outcast, the garb of the bandit, the eccentric habits of the figure of fun, all the varied forms of social ostracism. Thanks to them, Dostoyevsky also discovered the other side of man, the shadow cast by the light of the seeker after holiness; the social man, the human being in society.

Then the great masters of the human soul confronted by society, by history, rose before him: Shakespeare, Balzac, Goethe, Gogol, and, to a lesser extent, the despairing, Byron and Lermontov. These great poets do not turn away from holiness, but they erect a pedestal for it, where it may stand remote from the arena of reality where the mystery of man is acted out. For the inspirers of the Ideal, man cannot exist without a paragon, Christ or another; for the great poets, man does not exist without other men. Besides their aspirations towards heaven, whose fire they wish to steal, they have the imperfection, the complexity of the world here below. Like the masters of the Ideal, whom Dostoyevsky called the 'Christian' writers, they are fascinated by the humble, the poor, the victims. But they are also drawn to the other end of the chain: the souls of pride, the strong, the lords, the dominant.

These Arguses – a word Vyacheslav Ivanov applied to Dostoyevsky – these explorers of the human soul enter the labyrinth by different paths: 'poetic rather than historic' truth for Shakespeare,[93] the powerful perception of the human comedy and its most secret springs for Balzac, the duel between Heaven and Hell for Goethe, the sense of 'eternal resonance and universal reconciliation' for Pushkin,[94] the demonic laugh and the parade of masks for Gogol, the terrible lucidity of despair for Byron and Lermontov. In Dostoyevsky's eyes, they are all prophets of the human soul, the bearers of a 'new word'. With them he rediscovered the vocation he felt at eighteen. His phrase 'the mystery of man' had been vague then. He tried to clarify it in the notebooks to *The Devils*, with a reflection on 'eternal' art: 'Day-to-day life is not the whole of reality, for a huge part of it is in the form of a latent word which has not yet been said. Very rarely prophets appear, who divine and pronounce this word in its entirety. Shakespeare is a prophet sent by God to proclaim the mystery of man, of the human soul.'[95] All Dostoyevsky's judgements of literature are affected by this main idea: the mystery of the word hidden under the bushel of daily life, to be revealed by the writer.

This is the source of the wish which he repeated again and again, to accumulate details, to forget nothing, to force the idea or the conflict into its last entrenchments, to create the 'overflowing' universe characteristic of Shakespeare, Balzac, Goethe, Gogol, Pushkin and Dostoyevsky himself. E. M. de Vogüé applied to Dostoyevsky the words Balzac wrote of Beethoven and Scott: 'What is most remarkable is the way the dialogues are woven together as if by the thinnest of electric wires through which a mysterious current flows uninterruptedly. A word which we may have left unnoticed, or the slightest fact, mentioned in one line, has its significance fifty pages further on.'[96] Paul Claudel confirmed this: 'I find many analogies between their [Beethoven and Dostoyevsky] system of composition, systems of abundance. They forget nothing. Perhaps for a Frenchman there is rather too much abundance, but there is also remarkable art and unity of plan.'[97] 'Abundance' has nothing in common with prolixity. It expresses the tireless quest for that unity in complexity which we shall call totality. It comes from a power which is both analytic and synthetic, which does not express everything but which gives prior importance to the hidden idea which gathers everything together. In 1876, Dostoyevsky formulated the image of the prophet who perceives and transmits the hidden sign to the profane watchers: 'In poetry there must be passion, there must be your idea, and it must be demonstrated with passion. Impassiveness and concrete reproduction from the real are worth nothing and above all they have no meaning.'[98]

These passionate and prophetic voices range over the whole of Dostoyevsky's works, sometimes as lords, sometimes as brothers; the imperious voice of Gogol, the serene voices of Pushkin and Shakespeare, the underground voices of Balzac and Goethe. They are always present, but each has his time of power. For Gogol, this was from the beginning of Dostoyevsky's career up to *The Village of Stepanchikovo and its inhabitants* (1859). *Crime and Punishment* marks the culmination of Balzac's influence; Goethe, who is noted, whatever A. L. Bem may have to say about it, as an essential stage of his youth by Dostoyevsky himself,[99] has the full weight of his *Faust* from *The Devils* onwards. As for Shakespeare and Pushkin, they have the immense privilege of being present from the first plans to the final works. This vast literary dialogue took many forms, but in their attitude towards the human soul and its mystery the voices unite. As opposed to the writers of the Ideal, who take Christ as their model and end up with heretics and martyrs, the 'Prometheans' are tempted to make man god. Their hero is no longer the elect sacrifice of Goodness, but a man in whom and around whom Good and Evil are opposed. They were prophets of the protean quality of man, his 'breadth', as Dostoyevsky was to call it. Their brutal clearsightedness schooled Dostoyevsky's imagination: the dream is killed and the glance is sharpened.

First they offered the young novelist heroes whom his generous heart was inclined to welcome; the victims, the insulted and injured. Eugénie Grandet and Marguerite[100] in *Faust* foreshadow the pure young girls, sacrificial victims of love, such as Varenka in *Poor Folk*, Natasha in *The Insulted and Injured*, the lame Mariya in *The Devils*, and the Gentle Woman in the novella of that name. It is a truism that Devushkin of *Poor Folk* and all the poor clerks of the novellas of the forties, of which 'A Weak Heart' is the most striking example and *The Double* the most profound, are descended from Gogol's 'Greatcoat' and 'Diary of a Madman'.[101] Le Père Goriot and Pushkin's Samson Vyrin, pitiful victims of their deep paternal love, foreshadow old Pokrovsky of *Poor Folk*, running desperately behind his son's coffin and letting the books he had bought him fall in the mud.

But they also offered him the demoniacs, the strong proud souls whom Byron and Lermontov celebrate, the seekers after power, as well as the Napoleons obsessed by the doctrine that 'all is permitted' to superior souls, and the Rothschilds, possessed by the same idea of domination but substituting the modern weapon of money for blood and violence. Raskolnikov is the bloodthirsty rival of Rastignac[102] and Pushkin's Hermann;[103] Arkady in *A Raw Youth* recalls Pushkin's 'Covetous Knight',[104] just as Prokharchin echoes Grandet. Stavrogin in *The Devils* is given, as Stepan Trofimovich remarks, the actual debauchery and the potential virtue of Prince Harry, the future Henry V of Shakespeare's play; he is even accompanied by his own Falstaff, Captain Lebyadkin, buffoon, drunkard and poetaster in love with an Amazon.[105] Stavrogin, a hypercerebral power obsessed with experiments on living creatures, is also reminiscent of Faust. Dostoyevsky does not draw an explicit analogy, but there is a clear reminiscence of *Faust* in the fantastic scene where Mariya Timofeyevna, the cripple whom Stavrogin secretly married and abandoned to the knife of the convict Fedya, repeats Marguerite's prison ravings. Like Goethe's heroine, she does not recognise her beloved and confuses him with the executioner, and she also weeps for a child drowned in a pond.[106] Stepan Trofimovich, who loves puns, might have associated Shakespeare's Henry with Goethe's Heinrich; he would have revealed another component of Stavrogin's character.

Beyond these parallels, hidden in the subconscious of the creator or

endorsed by his heroes, there is the great revelation which all the Promethean writers have: the vertigo of the Amoral Absolute, the dizzying
temptation of sensuality. It is from his understanding of this that Dostoyevsky came to defend Pushkin's 'Egyptian Nights' with such enthusiasm,
in his article in *Time* 1861, 'A Reply to the Russian Messenger'.[107] By this
time, Dostoyevsky had had his prison revelation that absolute evil did exist
in concrete form, incarnated, among others, by Aristov, 'that moral
Quasimodo', capable of cold-blooded murder to satisfy 'his unquenchable
thirst for the most perverse and vulgar pleasures'.[108] Dostoyevsky then
introduced in his own works the great criminal souls of which Prince
Valkovsky in *The Insulted and Injured* is the first brutal theorist and
Svidrigaylov and Stavrogin are the refined images.

His prose commentary on Pushkin, although not equalling its subject in
beauty, is much more profound. Two elements are dominant in Dostoyevsky's version of Cleopatra's banquet, where Cleopatra offers a night
of love in exchange for death at dawn. The first, not present in Pushkin, is
the sociological and historical motivation, indispensable in the Promethean
universe: Cleopatra

represents a society whose foundations have long been overturned. Already all
belief has been lost ... thought is darkening and fading: the divine flame has left it;
society has lost its way, and in cold despair senses the pit gaping before it and is ready
to fall into it ... Everyone takes refuge in flesh, everything rushes towards carnal
debauchery, and, to fill the gap of the great spiritual impressions which are lacking,
irritates its nerves, its body with anything capable of arousing sensuality.[109]

The second is the theme of sensual pleasure in 'strong souls':

What unheard-of inexpressible sensuality, what still untried enjoyment, what
demonic happiness to kiss her victim, to love it, to be for several hours the slave of
this victim, to fulfil all its wishes with all the secret caresses that can be imagined,
with all the tenderness of mad passion, and at the same time to be aware every
moment that this victim, this brief conqueror will pay her with his life for this love
and the proud audacity of his momentary power over her.[110]

And Dostoyevsky, leafing through the bestiary of horror, found first the
wild beast, then the serpent, and finally the image which he used to
symbolise evil throughout his works: 'It is the soul of a spider, whose
female, it is said, devours the male at the very moment of coupling with it.'
However he is not so much interested in evil as in the frenzied search for
pleasure, in which the distinction between good and evil is lost, and,
ironically for the idealist, in the triumph of the demonic hero. The
'predatory' type, who occupies so great a place in Dostoyevsky's novels, is
present in embryo in this commentary on Pushkin's 'Egyptian Nights'. At
the beginning of 1866, in his notebooks for *Crime and Punishment*,
Dostoyevsky defined it:

A measureless and insatiable thirst for pleasures. An unquenchable thirst for life. Diversity of pleasures and *satisfactions*. Complete consciousness and analysis of every pleasure, without fear that it will be weakened by this, because it is based on the requirement of nature itself, on the bodily structure. Pleasures artistic to the point of refinement and next to them coarse pleasure, but just because extreme coarseness touches refinement (the severed head). Psychological pleasures. Criminal pleasures in breaking every law. Mystic pleasures (with terror at night). Pleasures in repentance, in a monastery (terrible fasting and prayer). Pleasures of beggary (asking for alms). Pleasure in Raphael's Madonna. Pleasures in theft, (banditry, burglary) pleasures of suicide . . . Pleasures of education . . . Pleasures of good deeds.[111]

This is the Promethean thought, balanced between good and evil, based on the supremacy of man and ignoring the divine mediator. Man comes first, and a part of his mystery is his thirst for freedom and for a life lived in a way which is totally unpredictable. Man burns with a godlike flame, interested only in his own pleasure, or, at the other end of the scale, his own abandon. The absolute quality of the test, the vanity of the ego refusing the paradigm of the Ideal, flinging itself into the maddest extremes, seeing and admiring itself in others, such are the sources of intoxication and horror, to use Dostoyevsky's terms. However much he tried, the prophet of humility and visionary of the Ideal was never able to persuade the novelist to close his Argus eyes and ignore the Promethean hero, lost in pride and imprisoned in egoism.

The Promethean writers are not mythologised, except for Shakespeare and Pushkin who are promoted in Raphael's company to be standard-bearers of Beauty.[112] But thanks to these geniuses who embrace life in its protean entirety, Dostoyevsky made a great discovery in form: the barbaric art of the novel,[113] which assimilates 'civilised' and elaborate genres, adding its modern vigour, and is constantly open to new forms, without worrying about ranks or rules. The breadth of man implies ceaselessly renewed openness to new tones, registers, and styles.

For instance, Gogol is a lyricist who makes use of hyperbole, a master of fantasy, a great comic writer,[114] a penetrating realist who discovers the souls ossified under the living masks of puppets.[115] Balzac, a titanic clockmaker, dismantling the huge machinery of the Human Comedy with furious realism, has a fantastic quality equal to that of Hoffmann and Edgar Allan Poe. Goethe called *Faust* a 'poetic monster', 'a rhapsodic drama' where poetry and naturalistic prose appear in the same scene.[116] Myriad-minded Shakespeare depicted a world where burlesque and tragedy go hand in hand, where power and dreams of happiness turn into derision and madness. Finally, Pushkin, a protean and inventive writer who took all the literary traditions he could find and shook them together, creating a new form for each of his works, explored all the kingdoms of literature and made them his own. The universality which Dostoyevsky recognised in him is a pluralism of forms as well as a reconciliation of ideas. Setting out in search of the mystery of man, Dostoyevsky learnt from the Promethean writers that the way to reach the enigma would not be a single triumphant highway, but a maze of paths, a network of disparate forms, for which he would have to sacrifice the idea of harmony.

Teachers of novelistic form

Dostoyevsky's chosen affinities among the giants of literature did not involve élitism. Realising that the mysterious freedom of the human soul and the great variety of forms used in the novel were closely connected, he began to rifle the immense treasure chest of past and present literature. Dostoyevsky did not scorn instruction from any work, provided it was very popular. The idea and the purpose were the most important things to him, so that he was completely pragmatic when selecting his models for the craft of literature.

In his youth, Dostoyevsky was an enthusiastic reader of picaresque novels, beginning with the illustrious *Lazarillo de Tormés*, which were widely read throughout Europe until the middle of the nineteenth century. He admired Lesage's *Le Diable boiteux*[117] and *L'Histoire de Gil Blas de Santillane*, especially the scene where the archbishop of Grenada asks Gil Blas to be quite frank about his sermons ... and kicks him out for his frankness.[118] He read *The Seminarist*[119] and probably *The Two Ivans, or the passion for trickery*, which Belinsky called the 'first Russian novels', and *A Russian Gil Blas, or the Adventures of Prince Gavrila Simonovich Chistyakov*, all works by Vasiliy Trofimovich Narezhny which also inspired Gogol.[120] He knew *Heart and Thought* by Aleksey Fomich Veltman,[121] as well as *The Pilgrim* and *The New Emilian* which appeared in 1845, and whose charm he praised in his correspondence.[122] It is thought, for reasons that will be shown later, that he also read *Salome* (1846–8), the first novel of the cycle *Adventures drawn from the sea of existence*. These authors who parade their heroes, with their easy-going consciences or their unlucky destinies, through all possible kinds of places and environments, taking the opportunity to depict manners and criticise society suggested concrete themes to Dostoyevsky. *Heart and Thought* turns out to be an ancestor of *The Double*,[123] although the theme is fully developed by Gogol and Hoffmann. There was also probably some influence from *Salome* (where an ex-officer, an adventurer and a gambler, is linked by a complex love–hate relationship with his mistress, the haughty and vindictive Salomeya) on a number of similar relationships in Dostoyevsky, such as that between Versilov and Akhmakova in *A Raw Youth*.[124] But this was not the main point.

It was the narrative skill of these authors, their extraordinary ability to

manage a plot crammed with intrigue and dramatic effects, which fascinated
Dostoyevsky. A passage in his notebook of 1870, while he was sketching the
plan of what was to be his master work 'The Life of a Great Sinner', shows
this clearly:

First pages. (1) the tone (2) condense thoughts artistically and concisely. NB. *Tone*
(narrative in the style of hagiography, that is, it may be by the author, but concisely,
without skimping explanations, but also presenting it in scenes. Harmony is needed
here.) Dryness of narrative, sometimes as much as Gil Blas. In effective and scenic
places – as if there were nothing at all to value here.[125]

Why was this assumed detachment of Lesage and his Russian followers so
appealing to Dostoyevsky? Was it because the narrator was so distinct from
the hero, and thus gave the hero more independence? A hero who is
apparently the plaything of destiny, but always manages to escape by
bootlicking or trickery, is observed by a narrator who is apparently
detached and seems to be surprised by the rush of events. This corresponded to Dostoyevsky's natural dislike for the narrator seen as God and his
preference for chronicle form in the novel. The quotation from the
notebooks also shows Dostoyevsky's surprising freeedom with regard to the
forms which literature offered him; he is using an element of the picaresque
novel for a plan of hagiography.

Dostoyevsky was even more interested in the direct heirs of the picaresque novel; the great French novelists of the nineteenth century, whose
works, published serially in the columns of *Débats* or *Le Constitutionnel*,
kept French readers of all social classes in suspense and were keenly
imitated throughout Europe.[126] They were closely related to the picaresque
novel. Fréderic Soulié, whose *Les Mémoires du Diable* Dostoyevsky read
eagerly,[127] freely imitated *Le Diable boiteux* of Lesage, who had himself
adapted a Spanish novel. Eugène Sue, in *Les Mystères de Paris*, which
Dostoyevsky thought of imitating,[128] and in *Le Juif errant*, adapted the
theme of wanderings and tribulations typical of the picaresque novel. The
surroundings he depicted were certainly new; they were the backstairs of
society, the aristocracy and the grasping bourgeoisie of Louis-Philippe, and
the lower depths of Paris. Perverted and ferocious, even Satanic, beings
such as Baron François de Luizi, or the criminal pair, the Screech-owl and
the Schoolmaster, persecute pure humiliated souls doomed to misfortune,
such as the angelic Fleur-de-Marie. The social satire is acid, the realism
black; a humanitarian moral in the mode of George Sand and the socialist
ideas of Fourier, Saint-Simon and Owen are implicit in the story. Crime
reigns; the whole is a succession of thefts, kidnapping, adultery, incest,
fratricide, parricide, abominations and dirty deeds of all sorts, in spite of
noble souls such as Rodolphe, the worker Morel, and repentant sinners,
like Le Chourineur, a magnanimous assassin. Nor is high society exempt;

another book of Sue's, *Mathilde, ou les mémoires d'une jeune femme*,[129] had little success in high social circles.

The feelings of justice and generosity, which led French serial writers, especially Eugène Sue, to adopt positions of open socialism, were certainly one of the reasons that endeared them to Dostoyevsky in the forties. He composed a whole gallery of characters and types for which, particularly in *The Insulted and Injured*, *Crime and Punishment*, *The Idiot* and *The Devils*, he was partly indebted to Eugène Sue. L. P. Grossman has made a melodramatic catalogue: the stepmother who drives her sixteen-year-old stepdaughter to prostitution; escaped convicts capable of any sacrilege; noble and heroic prostitutes, epileptic marquises, debauched old men, and so on.[130] To the end of his life Dostoyevsky remained a faithful admirer of Eugène Sue. For example, he advised one of his relatives, Yelena Andreyevna Shtackenschneyder, to read Dickens, *Gil Blas*, and also *Martin l'enfant trouvé* (in twelve volumes!) by Sue. She came to the conclusion: 'Dickens, Sue and Dostoyevsky are the bards of the insulted and injured.'[131] But this was probably not the only reason for Dostoyevsky's lasting interest in French popular novelists of the nineteenth century.

From 1845 onwards, his judgements about the quality of these novels were tinged with moderation. He found that French popular novelists were incapable of conveying the idea in its profundity, and they were offhand in their attitude towards art. As opposed to Pushkin, Gogol, Raphael and Vernet, who devoted months and years to their masterpieces, they were only 'scribblers', and 'decorators'. Their main talent was for a 'broad and powerful gesture' in the service of 'a monstrous and unfinished idea'. In other words, he concluded, quoting Béranger, they are 'a bottle of Chambertin in a bucket of water'.[132] Two months later he wrote: 'The Wandering Jew is not bad. However, Sue is fairly limited.'[133]

Dostoyevsky was essentially interested in popular French novelists because they adapted the old form of the picaresque novel which treats the hero's life as a reckless succession of adventures, misadventures, ephemeral triumphs and tribulations, to the new theme of the city, the great modern industrial capital. Hoffmann in Berlin, Dickens in London, Hugo and Balzac in Paris, Gogol and Pushkin in Petersburg had already seized the theme of the city, but Eugène Sue, 'the genius of the crowd', as Belinsky called him, went furthest in developing it, precisely because he was not so great an artist. More than those geniuses whose horizons embraced both town and country, he showed that the great city, the capital, with its fever, its mysteries, its brutal clash of interests, its violent passions, its solitary individuals who rise and sink like mad Cartesian divers in a tiny space, is the true setting for the unexpected adventure. Events take place not at the crossroads, but at the corner of the street, behind a thin partition. The rhythm of natural cycles as it exists in Pushkin and Tolstoy, allowing a slow and profound maturation, is replaced by a convulsive whirlwind. A labyrinth of alleys, corridors, staircases, palaces and slums chokes up the natural space so necessary for human life. There is no more open arena for glorious and heroic deeds, but the mysterious shadows of ambushes, plots, conspiracies, secret murders or solitary agonies. A social hell, instigator of crime, the city horrified writers and poets, whose fear transformed it into myth. Like Pushkin in 'The Bronze Horseman', Gogol in the Peterburg stories, and later Andrey Bely in his novel *Petersburg*,[134] Dostoyevsky denounced the city. He too wrote social novels where realism and fantasy joined to condemn these modern Babels.[135] As a thinker he rejected both Western capitalism of the industrial age and the Utopian socialism which was to create ant-hills for slaves:[136] he dreamt of a 'great Garden' where everyone would have his little piece of earth and sun.[137] But to the novelist the city was the place for modern life, for uprooted and dangerous existence, for new awareness. 'Only the modern town offers the spirit a place where it can be fully aware of itself', wrote Hegel, and Camus, who quotes this, continues:

We live in the time of great cities. The world has been deliberately cut off from all that gives it permanence: nature, sea, mountains, evening meditation. Consciousness exists only in the streets, because history exists only in the streets, so it is decreed. And it follows that our most significant works bear witness to this bias. We seek in vain for landscapes in great European literature since Dostoyevsky.[138]

A lucid artist, Dostoyevsky turned away from harmony, the heroic epic and the noble tragedy: he chose cacophony, chaos, the fever of popular novels, the disordered heartbeats of the urban universe, the focus of modern life. It was not a conscious choice, at least not until *A Raw Youth*, but it is evident throughout his creation. The sentences and the composition of the great novels reflect the breathing and the fever of great cities.

However, Dostoyevsky was aware of the faults of this literary movement. He brusquely rejected melodrama and vaudeville, its theatrical and bourgeois heirs. He made fun of the masters of the popular melodramatic novel: Ducray-Duminil, who inspired Pixérécourt 'the father of melodrama' and is quoted in *Poor Folk*,[139] the amiable Paul de Kock, for whom Belinsky had a weakness and whom Stepan Trofimovich in *The Devils* reads behind closed doors: and especially Alexander Dumas fils, Emile Augier, Victorien Sardou, and Eugène Scribe, whom he executes at the end of his article 'Winter Notes on Summer Impressions' with a parody of Augier's vaudeville, *Le Notaire Guérin*. But his cormorant genius responded to some of the techniques of vaudeville (imbroglios, *coups de théâtre*, reversals, stolen letters passing from hand to hand, parts inside parts, etc.), with which he contrived powerfully grotesque and tragic effects.

D. V. Grigorovich, one of Dostoyevsky's fellow-students at the school of military engineering, indicates two other great teachers of novelistic form in his literary memoirs: 'The first literary works I read, translated into Russian, were suggested to me by Dostoyevsky. They were Hoffmann's *Kater Murr* and Maturin's *Confessions of an English Opium-Eater*, a book of sombre content which Dostoyevsky much admired.'[140] As for the *Opium-Eater*, Grigorovich, though less cultured than Turgenev or Herzen,[141] might have corrected the error of its first editors by the time he came to print his memoirs. They had judged that it would be more profitable to attribute the work to Maturin, the famous author of *Melmoth the Wanderer*, rather than to its real author Thomas de Quincey. The two works and the two authors, Hoffmann and De Quincey, are not associated by chance. They belonged to the literary tendency sometimes called pathological, which accepted the supernatural and was the inspiration of travellers to other worlds like De Quincey, Poe, Hoffmann, Gérard de Nerval, Lautréamont and Lovecraft. For Dostoyevsky, these were experimental writers, explorers of parallel but real universes: as opposed to the Prometheans, they found in themselves something other than themselves and in particular new forms of psychic experience.

As with Eugène Sue, Dostoyevsky was first drawn by the social themes of the *Opium-Eater*, and especially by the story of De Quincey's unhappy youth. He never forgot the great dilapidated house, cold and empty, where Thomas slept on old papers and shared with his companion, a poor lost girl, the crumbs which the landlord, a London businessman, left for them, nor the love of the young man for Ann, the fifteen-year-old prostitute, for whose loss De Quincey was never to be comforted.[142] M. P. Alekseyev notes that Sonya Marmeladova owes more to Ann than to the later figures of Fantine in *Les Misérables* or Fleur-de-Marie in *Les Mystères de Paris*.[143]

But beyond this pity for the disinherited, Dostoyevsky was passionately interested in the strange, fascinating, painful and truthfully recorded experience of the opium-eater. De Quincey was a drug addict as one is an epileptic, that is, without choice; he took the first grains of opium to dull the stomach pains caused by constant famine. He struggled against his addiction, and, gifted with a rare talent of analysis, and a literary genius without which the experience would have been only a shifting of horrible images, he described his sensations, pleasant or painful, with creative honesty and power. They recall the visions of Ordynov in 'The Landlady', where, as we have seen, 'entire worlds' emerge, 'entire creations', universes which are at once given the breath of life. (This may also be linked with epileptic symptoms, which Dostoyevsky quite probably had at the time, although the illness was not yet recognised.) But 'the astonishing and monstrous architecture', the 'dreams of terraces, towers, ramparts reaching unknown heights', resemble the pictures of entire cities which De Quincey builds in his brain. Like the opium-eater, Ordynov sees his childhood reappear; he is 'borne like a grain of dust through this whole infinite strange inescapable universe'.[144] Dostoyevsky, drawn by the creation of worlds parallel to the existing world, discovered new structures of time and space which De Quincey describes as follows:

The sense of space, and, in the end, the sense of time were both powerfully affected. Buildings, landscapes, etc., were exhibited in proportions so vast as the bodily eye is not fitted to receive. Space swelled, and was amplified to an extent of unutterable infinity. This, however, did not disturb me so much as the vast expansion of time; I sometimes seemed to have lived for 70 or 100 years in one night; nay, sometimes had feelings representative of a millennium passed in that time, or, however, of a duration far beyond the limits of any human experience.[145]

These phenomena of dislocation or expansion of space and time are like those described by Ordynov, and Dostoyevsky later attributed them, with or without cause, to the epileptic aura. Through De Quincey, he discovered that the imagination was no longer a pale and extravagant rival of reality, but was capable of building surreal universes to be experienced by body and soul. He realised that these so-called deviations, pathological or not, were also ways of penetrating man's mystery and sources of truth and knowledge.

As for Hoffmann, Dostoyevsky was a devoted disciple. He read the whole of Hoffmann, in Russian, German and French. Grigorovich's memoirs showed that even after reading *Kater Murr* in German, in the summer of 1838, Dostoyevsky had a copy of the same work in Russian from 1844 to 1845. Later he had one of the three French editions (1829–43) of *Fantasiestücke* in his library.[146] In 1861, recalling his bookish youth, Dostoyevsky relived the joy of first reading and the happy memory of Hoffmann[147] in his introduction to three stories by Edgar Allan Poe, 'The Black Cat', 'The Tell-Tale Heart' and 'The Devil in the Belfry' in *Time*. Poe's fantasy, according to Dostoyevsky, was only a *trompe-l'oeil* effect; with all his extraordinary power of imagination and vigorous detail, Poe 'admits only the external possibility of the supernatural event'. He was a 'material' fantasist.[148] 'Fantasy in Hoffmann is quite different. He gives an animated form to natural forces; he introduces witches and spirits into his stories, sometimes he even seeks for his ideal beyond the earth, in a sort of extraordinary world which he considers superior, as if he himself believed in the existence of this mysterious enchanted world.'[149] Dostoyevsky concluded:

Hoffmann is immeasurably superior to Poe as a poet. Hoffmann has an ideal, sometimes not precisely formulated, it is true; but in this ideal there is purity, real true beauty right for man; it is seen best in his realistic stories, as for instance, Master Martin, or that marvellous, enchanting tale of Salvator Rosa, not to mention his best work *Kater Murr*. How much truth, masculine humour, what vigorous reality, what malice, what types and what portraits, and also what a thirst for beauty and the luminous ideal.[150]

In fact, Dostoyevsky, in this article of 1861, had become rather disillusioned: the ideal was 'not precisely formulated' and he left out the subject he was really dealing with, fantasy, to prove Hoffmann's superiority. But he also showed what drew him to Hoffmann; the search for a supernatural world which the fantasist wants to believe in, and which, far from being a refuge, becomes a wish, as with De Quincey, to reach a dimension whose revelation demands total consecration of the whole being. The supernatural is not outside the natural; it is within man. Albert Béguin, in his discussion of *Kater Murr*, confirms Dostoyevsky's feeling. 'Hoffmann', he writes, 'as opposed to the majority of German romantics, always tends to accept reality, to place the exceptional individual within it, rather than escaping to the world of imagination.'[151] Hoffmann's myth, present in all his works – the dilemma of life which is unlivable and of art which is merciless to the artist devoting himself to its service – is a transposition of his actual experience. In *Kater Murr*, the adventures of the musician Johannes Kreisler, alternating with the adventures of the tomcat, are a transposed autobiography. All Hoffmann's themes occur in it, and a number of them inspired Gogol and Dostoyevsky: the dangers of art with Kreisler and the painter Ettlinger who die mad (Gogol's 'Portrait' and Dostoyevsky's *Netochka Nezvanova*); the impossible love affair with Julia, already sketched in 'Berganza' (*Poor Folk*, 'White Nights', *The Insulted and Injured*); the female enemy with councillor Benzon's wife; the magician with old Abraham, who continues the line of the archivist Linhorst in 'Der goldne Topf' and the teacher of 'Die Automate' Dr Coppelius; the motives of guilt, bloodshed and incest which occur in *Die Elixiere des Teufels* ('The Landlady'). While De Quincey drifted on his ships of opium back to his tragic childhood and strange psychodelic universes, Hoffmann took flight on the back of a chimaera, composed of aesthetic intuition, occult science, and 'the equivocal sorceries of the exaltation of love' towards a world torn between 'Mozartian innocence' and reality stained with mysterious original sin. With him, Dostoyevsky discovered for the first time the immense field of secret impulses and complexes embedded in the subconscious.

It is difficult to distinguish Hoffmann's direct influence from the influence passed to Dostoyevsky through Gogol, who was also strongly marked by Hoffmann. All three have left strange stories, which appear romantic, but which in fact introduce, before Freud and Jung, the submerged world of psychic experience, the murky waters teeming with repressed fears, dark longings of the ego and shadows of ancestral myth. 'Die Irrungen' by Hoffmann (1820), 'The Terrible Vengeance' by Gogol (1832) and 'The Landlady' by Dostoyevsky (1847)[152] repeat the same triangle: a young, enchanting beauty, both offering herself and escaping, fantastic and sometimes feeble-minded, oppressed by some mysterious sin which seems to be either incest or parricide: a young man madly in love with her and ready to kill the third person, an old man who holds the beauty captive by hypnosis or enchantment and has powers which are either occult or come from a mysterious father. In Hoffmann this is a learned old Jew of Smyrna, exegetist of the Koran, in Gogol a sorcerer in the tradition of Ukrainian poetry, in Dostoyevsky a mystic sectarian. Although the tones are different – Hoffmann is ironic, Gogol echoes folk legend, and Dostoyevsky's story is realistic fantasy – the trios echo each other: the beautiful Greek, the baron Theodore de S., Schuspelpold in 'Die Irrungen'; Katerina, Danilo, Katerina's father in 'The Terrible Vengeance'; Katerina, Ordynov, Murin in 'The Landlady'. Although he ends his work with a pirouette,[153] Hoffmann, transmitted by Gogol, led the young Dostoyevsky to venture among the hidden depths of the human heart. Forbidden themes are touched; the Electra complex, the obsession with incest, the invitation to the young mediator, both seducing and giving value to the loved one (a deviation perfectly expressed by Dostoyevsky in 'The Eternal Husband'), the pure soul abandoned to the powers of evil (the old myth of the maiden and the dragon), the prison of an endlessly prolific crime (original sin or guilt), the terrified retreat before the rise of suspect and obscure forces which threaten the soul and the ancestral land.[154] All the themes of fantasy based on spiritual and civic crisis which Dostoyevsky was to use in his great novels appeared for the first time in 'The Landlady'. Andrey Bely completed the theme of Hoffmann, Gogol and Dostoyevsky with an identical trio in *The Silver Dove*: Daryalsky–Matryona–Kudeyarov.[155]

Dostoyevsky was partially indebted to Hoffmann for his novella *The Double*, poorly received by critics in 1847, and dug up from its grave by the Russian symbolists. Contemporaries noted that it had been heavily influenced by Gogol ('Notes of a Madman', 'The Nose' and *Dead Souls*) and K. S. Aksakov, using the pseudonym Imyarek, accused Dostoyevsky of imitation and even direct borrowing.[156] Hypnotised by the style, which was indeed dominated by the Gogolian sentence,[157] they ignored everything that Gogol himself owed to Hoffmann.[158] A. A. Grigoryev, though clearly repelled by Dostoyevsky's novella, saw more accurately: '*The Double* is a pathological therapeutic work, not a literary one. It is the story of a madness examined, certainly, to its depths, but still repugnant, like a corpse. Moreover, as we read *The Double* we cannot help reflecting that if the author continues along this path he will be condemned to play the same part in our literature as Hoffmann did in German Literature.'[159] Grigoryev was stressing not only the reminiscences from Hoffmann (*Die Elixiere des Teufels*, *Kater Murr*, 'Die Brautwahl', 'Die Doppeltgänger') but also the relationship of style and composition. The stupefying prolixity, the repetitive exacerbation of the analysis, characteristic of *The Double* in the unanimous opinion of the critics, echoed the luxuriance, the confusion of dreams, letters and events typical of Hoffmann. The numerous corrections which Dostoyevsky made to his novella in 1866 worked as much against Hoffmann's legacy as against Gogol's. He suppressed many secondary episodes, laborious digressions which slowed the action down without contributing any nuance of Sterne-like humour, and the long chapter-headings which were meant to be witty.[160] In 1846, Dostoyevsky had transformed Hoffmann's embarrassed and grimacing irony, intended to mask the revelations of the subconscious, into a mask plastered on from the outside, which altered the tragic reality of the subject, the *dualism*, and made it barren. Dostoyevsky was sometimes witty in his pamphlets, and could use burlesque and grotesque for a dissonant effect to accentuate the tragic and pathetic, but he was incapable of romantic humour when the drama really gripped him. At this point he preferred the flame which burns flesh and the steel which cuts it to pieces. In 1877, returning to the failure of *The Double*, he blamed the form:

I failed with this novella, but the idea was fairly luminous, and I have never done anything in literature more serious than this idea. But the form I gave to this novella was a complete failure ... and if now I were to come back to this idea to develop it again, I should choose a completely different form: but in 1846 I was not able to find that form.[161]

The luminous idea was not simply a common pathological dualism, as in the schizoid process, but the discovery of the irreconcilable duality of the human soul and its breadth. In his notes of 1872–5, Dostoyevsky expressed his pride at having created in Golyadkin, the hero of *The Double*, his 'most important type of underground man'.[162]

De Quincey and Hoffmann opened the gates of psychic infinity to Dostoyevsky. They taught him that the paths of the dream, the pathological state, abnormal symptoms also led to the depths of man and should not be condemned in themselves because they were dangerous or foreign to our everyday experience. Through them the imagination was able to grasp the whole of the universe, true because experienced. No heaven or hell are forbidden to them, but heaven and hell must be tested by the flesh and the spirit. Dostoyevsky learnt that reality does not live in the world, but inside man. He was to formulate this lesson at the end of his life: 'While remaining fully and completely a realist, find man in man ... People call me a psychologist: it is false, I am only a realist in the highest sense, that is to say that I paint all the depths of the human soul.'[163]

We have drawn the literary universe of the young Dostoyevsky only in its main lines, deepening the outlines to reveal the images which crystallised in the years of his distant maturity. A writer forms his relationships with his predecessors only after giving them a completely personal meaning sometimes quite opposed to the literary fashion of the time.[164] They become a part of himself and his own creative aspirations. The potential writer, or the writer at the beginning of his career, is the least innocent of readers. This was a dominant feature in Dostoyevsky, whose attachment to the favourites of his youth was particularly sentimental, and whose power of mythologisation was highly developed. The dialogue which he began with his great Russian contemporaries in the sixties was completely different.

4

The heritage: history and philosophy

Literature, bestowing worlds and forms, offers a free and immense field to the creative imagination, but history, philosophy and religion are received as instruction, objective or revealed truths, less malleable and less capable of being metamorphosed. But although Dostoyevsky's powerful ability to synthesise could not dispose so freely of the reality delivered by history, by didactic systems of philosophy, or the sacred texts of religion, he imprinted his own personal seal on the materials he used in the creation of his novels.

There was a great difference between these materials and the literary heritage, which was settled in its main lines before the period of the great novels, at least with regard to universal literature, for Dostoyevsky followed Russian literary development with close attention all his life, especially the writings of his peers and rivals: Turgenev, Saltykov-Shchedrin and Tolstoy. But though he endlessly read and reread the favourite authors of his youth, bringing them back to life in spite of fashion in his *Diary of a Writer*, from 1863–4 onwards he was relatively indifferent to everything newly published in the West and particularly in French literature, which he loved and read in the original. He practically ignored Stendhal, whose talent Pushkin had recognised as early as 1831,[1] and never mentioned Baudelaire, who is a kindred spirit. Michel Cadot in 'The "Double Postulation" of Baudelaire and its Dostoyevskian version' compares 'Mon coeur mis à nu', Baudelaire's proposed definition of *Tannhäuser*, with some passages in *The Brothers Karamazov*: there are the same words, the same formula: 'the human heart a field of battle between Satan and God', the same double postulation towards heaven and hell.[2] Dostoyevsky died before Baudelaire appeared in Russian translation, but he must have heard, either while he was living abroad or from magazines, echoes of the trial of *Les Fleurs du Mal* and of the poet who introduced De Quincey and Edgar Allan Poe into France. Of Flaubert's works he admired *Madame Bovary*, which Nastasya Filippovna, heroine of *The Idiot*, is reading on the eve of her death, but he is supposed to have read it in summer 1867 only because it had been recommended by Turgenev as the best work 'of all world literature in these last ten years'.[3] However, the creator of *A Raw Youth* gave no indication of having read *L'Education Sentimentale*, and when he quoted 'La Légende de Saint Julien l'hospitalier' in *The Brothers*

Karamazov, he made the mistake of writing 'St John the hospitaller', patriarch of Alexandria.[4]

He forced himself to read Zola, who published his *Lettres de Paris* in the Russian magazine *Messenger of Europe*, introducing the Russian public to naturalism and the theories of the experimental novel, but frankly detested him. In 1876, he wrote to Anna from Ems: 'I have taken a subscription for a reading room (a pathetic library), I took Zola because these last few years I have neglected European literature terribly: I can hardly read it, it's such filth. At home people are shouting about Zola as if he were a celebrity, a great star.'[5] He had the first Rougon-Macquart books on the shelves of his library: *La Fortune des Rougons*, *La Curée*, *Le Ventre de Paris*, *La Conquête de Plassans*, and *La Faute de l'Abbé Mouret*. *L'Assommoir* lay about on his desk for some time, but no one knows if he read it.[6] Except for Flaubert and Zola, who appeared in a Russian magazine to attack the idols of Dostoyevsky's youth, Balzac and George Sand,[7] Western literature left him basically indifferent. His creation was entirely turned towards Russia.

In the field of ideas, this tendency was reversed. Everything was on the move, and there was ceaseless research and passion. It is difficult to retrace the history of Dostoyevsky's intellectual development education, for three reasons. First, it went on throughout his life, with eclipses, desertions and returns; it was more dependent on Dostoyevsky's itinerary than on the movement of ideas in general. Secondly, his fantastic ability to seize an idea and immediately transform it into images, into a world, hides the theoretical sources. A comparison of Hegel's *Phenomenology of the Spirit*, for instance, with *Notes from Underground*,[8] or Kant's *Critique of Pure Reason* with *The Brothers Karamazov*[9] may be interesting, but is never conclusive. Last but not least, Dostoyevsky, who was an attentive reader of the foreign and Russian journals in which these ideas were expressed, often picked up ideas without worrying about their origins or their contradictions. Dostoyevsky the man read historians with passion and was keenly interested in the history of his time, on which he commented in *The Citizen* and *The Diary of a Writer*; he entered the politico-social and philosophic debate when scarcely out of his youth, first as a follower of Utopian socialism, then of Slavophilism – under the mask of the manifesto of the 'national soil' movement – and finally of Panslavism and reaction, without ever being completely devoted to any of them, and without ever losing all his doubts; after the great ordeal, he returned to the fold of the Orthodox Church, not without feeling a great mistrust which was fully reciprocated. Yet Dostoyevsky the novelist, in spite of his touching wish to make his own personal convictions triumph, never stopped listening closely to many varied and contradictory voices in debate, and allowed his heroes, open to life and experience, to draw their own conclusions. For these reasons, Dostoyevsky's culture cannot be defined as a closed ideological system, since it was a continual search for ideological food for his novels.

From history to Utopia

Dostoyevsky's love for history went back to his childhood and appeared at the same time as his love for novels.[10] History inspired his dreams and imagination. In *Diary of a Writer* for 1877, Dostoyevsky recalled a 'grandiose phrase' from the voluminous *History of Russian Imperial Diplomacy* by Kaydanov:[11] 'A profound calm reigned through Europe when Frederick the Great closed his eyes for eternity; but never did such a calm precede so great a tempest.'[12] And he exclaimed: 'Do you know a more sublime sentence?' This was the comment of a novelist attracted by rhetorical art, or the exaltation he felt as a youth when reading Russian historical novels or the novels of Scott.

Karamzin's *History of the Russian State*, according to Andrey, was Dostoyevsky's 'bedside book'.[13] This history of the Russian land until 1612, told with charm and energy, was read at one gulp like a novel and had the faults and virtues of fiction: a vivid and polished style; leading parts played by individual heroes and villains, princes as it happened; the intervention of supernatural elements, which play the part of the dream, comets and other prodigies of nature; and a dramatic skill which did not hesitate to rearrange facts. The feelings which inspired it – adoration of the Russian land, the cult of the State built on suffering, moral condemnation of egotism and tyranny and corresponding praise of virtuous sovereigns – enchanted the child's Manichaean soul. It had an immense success with Russian writers, who readily accepted Karamzin's debatable theory of history, and even with Russian liberals, who objected to his celebration of autocracy. The book inspired in Dostoyevsky that intransigent, even jealous, love for his country, which was a constant of his life and work.

One of Dostoyevsky's first visions of history was literary, or rather epic, as he was fascinated by the Odysseys and Iliads of the modern world. In 1848–9, imprisoned in the Peter–Paul fortress, he devoured the historical works of William Prescott: on 27 August the prisoner wrote to his brother Mikhail: 'There is no article in it [Annals of the Fatherland) which is not read with pleasure. The section on the sciences is brilliant. The Conquest of Peru is an Iliad in itself, and really is fully equal to The Conquest of Mexico of last year.'[14] History, seen from this angle, feeds the imagination as the illusion of the novel does, but, unlike fiction, it marks emotion with the seal of authenticity. This precocious and continuous love for history shows the beginning of that search for the real which marked the whole of Dostoyevsky's literary career. It was the beginning of the introduction of the *document*, and later, as he turned to contemporary life, of the *newspaper cutting*.

Between 1838 and 1848 there was a strange absence of remarks in Dostoyevsky's correspondence about his passion for history. On 9 August 1838, Fyodor told Mikhail that he had just finished *The History of the Russian people* by Nikolay Alekseyevich Polevoy, but said nothing more about it. Polevoy, brought up on Guizot and Thierry, was less than tender to Karamzin, Dostoyevsky's childhood idol, considering his work a portrait gallery lacking in historical perspective. Polevoy thought that a historian should grasp the main stages of Russian history and integrate them with the wider European movements. Dostoyevsky's silence may have been a sign of disaffection. History had never been more relevant; it was leaving the past and turning towards the present to assume economic and social attributes. Everywhere, in Russia as well as in the West, the fashion for historical novels had been replaced by the fashion for physiologies,[15] atomised analytical essays about society and preliminary exercises for social novels. There were the first social novels too, whose way was prepared in Russia by the 'naturalist school' and especially Gogol. Moreover, Belinsky, in his enthusiasm for *Poor Folk* had proclaimed Dostoyevsky the first master of the Russian social novel and this praise drew Dostoyevsky to consider the theory of socialism. In contrast with George Sand, who had encountered Utopian socialism very early and had fully accepted it, Dostoyevsky, like Victor Hugo and Eugène Sue, came to the heart of the social question through his creation. *Poor Folk*, apart from its genius, marked the height of the Russian literary evolution of the time, the conscience of an age which was becoming more sensitive to social themes. An ardent plea for the dignity of poor people who ventured to pronounce a few timid words of rebellion, and an indirect indictment of an unjust society, the novel was received as social propaganda. Its author immediately became part of *avant-garde* thought, energetically driven on by Belinsky's committed analysis, feeling that it was his duty to deepen his own vision by turning towards theory, towards a forward-looking idea of history, which in his own words had become 'a science of the future'.[16] In doing this, he was betraying not his convictions, but his natural behaviour as a creator, which was to transform ideas into images.

In 1847, Dostoyevsky began to frequent the Thursday-evening gatherings of M. V. Butashevich-Petrashevsky, whom he first met in spring 1846. His political reading before this time is unknown. Since November 1846 he had been living in an 'association', a kind of phalanstery, in an apartment on Vasilyevsky Island with the Maykov brothers, Apollon the poet and Valeryan the critic, the poet Pleshcheyev, the Beketov brothers, Andrey the future botanist and Nikolay the future chemist, all young people attracted by socialist and Fourierist ideas. Moreover Belinsky, who had made Dostoyevsky famous, had converted him to atheistic socialism. As Dostoyevsky wrote in 1873: 'As early as 1846 I had been initiated into all the *truth* of this "regenerated world" to come, into all the *holiness* of the future communist society by Belinsky.'[17] Belinsky pushed him into reading more radical works. In 1847 his culture became richer: he was able to dip freely into the vast 'collective' library which Butashevich-Petrashevsky put at the disposal of his guests: there was Saint-Simon, Considérant, Proudhon, Pierre Leroux, Louis Blanc, Fourier, Engels, Marx, and so on. Dostoyevsky borrowed *The Story of Ten Years* by Louis Blanc, one book by Proudhon (perhaps the one which was impounded at his arrest on 23 April 1849), *Introduction to Social Science* by Garnier-Pagès, *True Christianity following Jesus Christ* by Cabet, Strauss' *Life of Jesus*, and a study by Gustave de Beaumont of the American slave-traders, *Mary, or Slavery*. On the morning of 23 April, the police seized two forbidden works: Eugène Sue's *Shepherd of Kravan* and Proudhon's *Celebration of Sunday*.[18] The list is short, but clearly Dostoyevsky was obsessed by the problem of socialism and Christ. The inclusion of Strauss might suggest that Dostoyevsky was moving towards Belinsky's views, which demythicised Christ.[19] Numerous lectures, dealing not only with Fourierism, various Utopias and communism, but also with the problems of serfdom, judicial and military reforms, constitutionalist or revolutionary methods, enabled Dostoyevsky, who was quick to understand systems through partisan exposition, to acquire a fairly complete political education. On 22 April 1849, one of the Petrashevtsy, A. P. Balasoglo, expressed doubts about the education of the literary men who frequented the Petrashevsky circle, the Dostoyevsky brothers and Durov: according to him, they had read 'not one single serious book: neither Fourier, nor Proudhon, nor even Helvétius'.[20] The statement is exaggerated, but not without a grain of truth. Dostoyevsky was not a theoretician by nature: he was a poet of the Idea. Fourierism, he wrote in his 'Deposition' (or 'Explanation') was a 'purely scientific system', but he went on lyrically: 'Fourierism is a peaceful theory: it charms the soul by its elegance, seduces the heart by the love for humanity which animated Fourier while he was developing his theory, and amazes the spirit by its harmony.'[21] This kind of excessively literary reaction probably irritated the realistic Balasoglo. But however rapid or unscientific Dostoyevsky's reading was, it was supplemented by the explanations of competent men such as Timkovsky,[22] or by the conversations he had with his 'Mephistopheles',[23] Nikolay Aleksandrovich Speshnyov, a thoughtful Fourierist and convinced socialist, one of the prototypes of Stavrogin in *The Devils*, and also by the more daring plans of the Durov circle, who were plotting to set up a printing press to disseminate them.

Dostoyevsky's adherence to Utopian socialism ended in failure and in the harsh reality of convict prison, but it had enabled him to discover how profoundly literature was entwined with history, economy, social themes, philosophy and religion. It formed his first ideological experience of a *closed system, in profound contradiction to the thought of the novelist.*

At Christmas 1849, Dostoyevsky set out for Siberia with chains on his feet. What was the state of his philosophical culture at this point? He knew a fair amount about Rousseauism, Comte's positivism, Fourierism, Cabétism and other Utopian socialisms. But, not being a university student like Stankevich, Granovsky, Turgenev, Herzen, Bakunin and others,[24] he had not plunged into the Germanic sea of Kant, Fichte, Schelling and Hegel, the philosophers who bred the Russian circles and generations of the thirties and forties. The way of Belinsky, his friend of 1847, which began with Schillerian romanticism and ended in atheist socialism, had passed through Schelling's aestheticism, Fichte's idealism and the rational real of Hegel, but Dostoyevsky only knew the beginning and the end of it, although he was going to Siberia because he had read Belinsky's famous letter to Gogol before an audience. He knew only the most marginal Hegelians, the ones who had gone astray philosophically, such as Max Stirner and David Strauss. A copy of Marx's *Poverty of Philosophy* existed in the Petrashevsky library, but it is not likely that Dostoyevsky ever read it; moreover the book is a criticism of Proudhon's reformist socialism and leads back to Utopian socialism.[25] There were also Chaadayev and the Slavophils, especially I. Kireyevsky and Khomyakov, who were also indebted to Schelling and Hegel, but their influence, which was to become greater, was then overshadowed by the frankly Westernising choice of the author of *The Petersburg Chronicle*[26] and the prisoner of the Peter-Paul fortress, who, in his *Deposition*, sang the praises of the 'great helmsman', Peter the First.[27]

Reconstruction 'in another fashion'

From Dostoyevsky's imprisonment until 1864-5 a new period of reading began, marking his wish to go back to the sources of his thought and to compare the ideas he had had since his ordeal with those of his past life. This was to be done by studying the texts which had been overlooked or despised because of partisan passion, or which he had not managed to read. After the ideological change of course, which had probably begun when he quarrelled with Belinsky in 1847, the dialectic of texts, a precondition of the polyphonic construction of the novels, began. This reading, whether it took place at the base of the damp ravelin of the Petersburg fortress, or in a remote corner of the prison of Omsk, or in the smoky hut at Semipalatinsk after the day's work as an ordinary soldier, gave a different direction to Dostoyevsky's thoughts, allowing him, as he himself wrote on 18 July 1849, to remodel them, to 'reconstruct them in another fashion'.[28]

First, he returned to his religious sources. His childhood had been pious, as was proper in a noble but fairly modest household of the time; his father before becoming a military doctor had been a seminarist; his mother was from the Moscow merchant classes.[29] The Dostoyevsky children had a typical religious education; they began their Biblical history with the pictures from *One Hundred and Four Histories from the Old and New Testaments*, the Gospel was read to them, and a few episodes of the Bible were explained, including the story of Job, which marked the writer for life; they had to learn the *Rudiments* of the metropolitan Filaret by heart, in preparation for examinations. Their religious practices were intense; personal prayers, pilgrimages to the Saint Sergius Trinity, passionate commentaries on the Holy Scriptures by the deacon, their teacher.[30]

Until 1844 Dostoyevsky followed the main religious observances with a devotion which was remarked on by his fellow-students. But after that neither his letters nor his works touched on the question of religion. Ordynov in *The Landlady* is writing a history of the Church, but Murin, reader of the Holy Scriptures and probably an Old Believer, is disturbing, incestuous and criminal. In this novella of 1847, piety is linked with despotism and the cruelties of the past. Clearly Dostoyevsky was detaching himself from the Church and churches, if not from Christ. At the mock execution, on 22 December 1849, all the condemned except Shaposhnikov refused to take confession, but they all kissed the cross which was offered to them.[31] Even after convict prison, Baron Vrangel tells us, Dostoyevsky hardly ever went to church services and disliked clerics, especially the Siberian parish priests.[32] Much later, recalling his disputes with Belinsky and apparently Nekrasov about Christ and socialism in an article 'People of Other Times', Dostoyevsky tried to prove to the readers of *Diary of a Writer* for 1873 that he had preserved his admiring devotion for Christ in 1847 and this was probably true. The Utopian socialists, whom Dostoyevsky in his plan for an article on 'Socialism and Christianity' in 1864 called 'poets', claimed that Christ was their predecessor. *The Words of a Believer* by Lamennais, translated into Slavonic by A. P. Milyukov, a friend of Dostoyevsky's, was read aloud in 1849, at an evening party at Durov's house.[33] But it is not clear what Dostoyevsky thought of the nature of Christ: was He an incomparable man, the supreme Ideal, the founder of a civilisation based on love, or God become Man? Even the beautiful letter which Dostoyevsky addressed to N. D. Fonvizina on 15 February 1854 was not decisive about Christ's divinity. The credo which he composed for himself: 'To believe that there is nothing more beautiful, more profound, more appealing, more reasonable, more manly and more perfect than Christ, and not only that there is nothing, but – I tell this to myself with a jealous love – that there cannot be anything' is cancelled out to some extent by the preceding assertion: 'I am a child of the century, child of disbelief and doubt until this day, and will be so (I know it) until the grave', and by the assertion that follows: 'More, if someone proved to me that Christ is outside the truth, and that it were a fact that truth were outside Christ, I would rather stay with Christ than with the truth.'[34] By placing these words in the mouth of Stavrogin, at the time when he wanted to believe, and of Shatov, who had reached the gates of belief but was paralysed by the idea of transcendence, Dostoyevsky confirms the negative analysis of this text.[35]

The question remained unanswered, at least until 1864, when Dostoyevsky reversed his priorities. In 1848, socialism was a kind of 'correction and improvement of Christianity, in conformity with the needs of the century and of civilization'.[36] In 1864, socialism was only a transitory 'sickly' means towards the 'dissociation of the masses into personalities' – the author called it 'the socialism of separate twigs'[37] – while Christianity was 'the ultimate development of the personality and of individual freedom', the Ideal attained and so, logically, the 'future life'.[38]

But the problem of Dostoyevsky's faith, which has been traced by Pierre Pascal,[39] is different from the problem which faces us here: the reconstruction of his religious culture. From the beginning this revision took place in parallel with the remodelling of his philosophical, historical and economic culture. He was not trying to reinforce his beliefs but to reconstruct a cultural heritage, to remake a basis even of antinomic ideas.

On 18 July 1849, the prisoner wrote to Mikhail that he had read with interest two accounts of the *Journey to the Holy Land* and the works of the famous eighteenth-century preacher, Dmitry of Rostov.[40] On 27 August, still in prison, he asked for a Bible: 'Both Testaments. I need them. If possible, in French translation; if you can add the Slavonic text, that will be the height of perfection.'[41] This Bible was to be stolen from him,[42] but in Tobolsk the wives of the exiled Decembrists gave him a Gospel which was to be his only – or almost only – reading in his years as a convict. For four years he kept this big book under his pillow; it was an old edition of 1823, but in modern Russian, bound in worn black leather, which he later had rebound in morocco.[43] He read it for himself and the other convicts, he used it to teach Ali, the young Mohammedan, to read, and on the day of his death he opened it once more, at random, to find out God's will.

As soon as he left convict prison, he set out, in a letter to Mikhail on 22 February 1854, a reading programme of astonishing breadth: 'If you can, send me this year's magazines, even if it is only Annals of the Fatherland. But here is what is indispensable to me: I need – an extreme need – historians of antiquity (in French) and modern ones, economists and Church fathers.'[44] And later, 'Send me Carus,[45] Kant's Critique of Pure Reason and, if you can do it by a non-official channel, send me Hegel immediately, and particularly his History of Philosophy. My future depends on it.'[46] On 27 March 1854 he repeated his appeal, making it more complete and definite:

Send me books, brother. No need for magazines, but send me European historians, economists and Church fathers, and if possible all the classical historians: Herodotus, Thucydides, Tacitus, Pliny, Flavius (Josephus), Plutarch and Diodorus (Sicilius), and so on, they are translated into French. Finally Carus and a German dictionary. Of course not all at the same time, but what you can. Send me also Pisarev's physics and a physiology . . . Understand how much I need this food for the mind![47]

Did he receive these works? On 15 April 1855 Dostoyevsky learnt that his brother had indeed sent him, in spring 1854, 'some books, as for example the Church Fathers, the ancient historians', which had not yet arrived![48] However, the list alone was significant; Dostoyevsky wished to reconstruct a solid culture for himself and to build on it. He was faithful to his interests of the forties: Guizot, Thierry, Thiers gave him information about Europe, the eternal problems of representative government, the Third Estate, and the Republic,[49] though in more moderate terms than the Utopian socialists. Augustin Thierry developed an interesting theory on race and dominated and dominating peoples.[50] Leopold von Ranke stressed the importance of the personal factor in history and the unity of historical events, taken as moments in the development of the Absolute Spirit. Giambattista Vico thought that the history of nations moved in cycles.[51] Although we cannot be sure exactly what Dostoyevsky read,[52] these themes are surprisingly close to the themes in the novels: for example, Raskolnikov's cult of the superior man, Shatov's theory of great dominant peoples. Like Vico, the hero of *The Devils* places the gods as the origin of the greatness of peoples. Vico again, with his cyclic concept of history, evokes the myth of the Eternal Rebirth as it appears in Dostoyevsky's works.

Religious thought was also widely covered. Tacitus,[53] Pliny and Flavius Josephus, as Pierre Pascal suggests, provided Dostoyevsky with contemporary evidence of the origins of Christianity;[54] while Ranke's works, *History of the Popes of Rome* and *History of the Reformation*, dealt with its further development. Even if he did not ask for the Koran, Dostoyevsky had discovered it through his Cherkassian friends in prison.[55] The Koran and the Church Fathers encouraged him to rethink the nature of Christ, Man–God or prophet, and to grapple with the problem of divine transcendence from a more universal viewpoint.

The repeated juxtaposition, in the two letters of February and March 1854, of economists and Church Fathers, foreshadowed the great debate of the sixties about socialism and Christ. Nothing indicates that there was a confrontation; on the contrary, Dostoyevsky was proceeding to verify his opinions and his knowledge by comparison and conglomeration. Abstract philosophy was part of this vast plan: Dostoyevsky asked for the indispensable German dictionary to read Kant, Hegel and Carus. But even if after April 1855 he finally received the books he asked for, it is not certain that he read them in depth. Kant is quoted only once in his novels, in 'Uncle's

Dream', and in a context which has nothing metaphysical about it,[56] but there are no other signs of Kantian influence, in spite of Golosovker's ingenious transformation of Ivan Karamazov into a 'dialectical hero of Kantian antinomies', while admitting that the name of Kant never appears in the novel. As for Hegel, who is never mentioned in Dostoyevsky's novels,[57] the evidence of Vrangel, a friend of the Semipalatinsk period, is puzzling. On 2 April 1854 he wrote to his father: 'Destiny has brought me close to a man rare in qualities of both heart and mind. It is our young and unfortunate writer Dostoyevsky. I owe him much. Every day I work with him and we are now going to translate Hegel's *Philosophy* and Carus' *Psyche*.'[58] This note is precious; however, a few pages earlier, Vrangel reported that Dostoyevsky, immersed in Gogol and Hugo, was trying to convert him to literature and to dissuade him from reading 'professorial works'.[59] For Karl Gustav Carus we are reduced to conjecture. To make him out, the apprentice translator would have needed a German dictionary, besides textbooks of physics and physiology, but it would have been worth it. Dostoyevsky, devoted as he was to Hoffmann and De Quincey, would have been fascinated by the preponderance given to instinct and especially to the unconscious in psychic experience by Carus in his work *Psyche, history of the development of the human soul* (1846).[60] But while there is still some doubt about Carus, it seems fairly obvious that Dostoyevsky gave up the struggle to dive into the German sea of Kant and Hegel. A last, brutally frank witness convinces us of this; Strakhov said that Dostoyevsky offered him, 'without having read it', Hegel's *History of Philosophy*, which had finally arrived from Mikhail.[61]

Dostoyevsky's culture became more solid in exile, although he did not forget the controversies of the past. In 1846–7, he had come to blows with Belinsky over the nature of Christ and, as a corollary, over the Ideal and the Beautiful in literature. In 1856 he returned to this subject, undertaking to write a pamphlet about 'The mission of Christianity in art'. This article, 'Letters about art', the result of ten years of meditation, long pondered in the convict prison of Omsk, unfortunately never saw the light of day,[62] but it is proof that he felt confident enough to discuss aesthetics and base them on philosophic and religious meditation.

Garnering in commitment: the journal Time

Besides the works mentioned, Dostoyevsky in exile either procured or was sent Russian and foreign journals, containing numerous articles and reviews of historical, economic and philosophical books. Unfortunately, although he mentioned new literary works in his correspondence, he hardly ever referred to critical or learned articles. Our only guide to his interests is the first journal published by Mikhail and Fyodor Dostoyevsky from January

1861 to 1863, *Time*. According to Strakhov, who was recruited by Dostoyevsky at this point: 'Mikhail Mikhaylovich took on all the material tasks, but the intellectual leadership came from Fyodor Mikhaylovich.'[63] Dostoyevsky confirmed this in 1865 in a letter to Vrangel: '*I* was the one who started *Time*, not my brother, *I* directed it and I edited it.'[64] He took the main part in formulating the programme of the magazine, the vague doctrine of 'the native soil' (*pochvennichestvo*) and in choosing the serious articles, which first appeared in the third section of the magazine ('Scientific Articles, Economic, financial and philosophical questions of contemporary interest'), and which were later scattered under other headings.

We must warn the reader at once that our object is not to analyse the theory of 'the native soil', which was founded on the principle of reconciliation between civilisation and the national spirit, the need to build a bridge over the gap opened by Peter the First between the educated classes and the people, and on the assertion, subconsciously Pan-Slavist, that the Russian idea might form a synthesis of all the ideas developed in the different peoples of Europe. Nor do we intend to study the important and varied works of literature which were published in *Time*. We are only going to examine the culture which Dostoyevsky stored up in the course of the battle. This culture was far in advance of anything he needed; it was liberal and perpetually changing, in spite of the programme, fairly vague, announced at the beginning of the magazine, and it was dialectic, taking care to give both sides of an argument. The important thing is not the commitment but the cultural harvest. All the leading tendencies of political economy and European philosophy were set out, dissected, attacked and defended by writers who did not always share the same viewpoint and were sometimes far from being 'native soil' enthusiasts.[65]

Strakhov, a biologist and right-wing Hegelian, who, with Apollon Grigoryev, was one of the pillars of the magazine, introduced German idealist philosophy in a preface to two extracts from his translation of the first volume of *The History of Modern Philosophy* by Kuno Fischer: 'Principal characteristics of the History of Philosophy' (*Time*, 1861, no. 7),[66] and 'The doctrine of God in Spinoza' (*Time*, 1861, no. 9). First he repeated the thesis that the history of philosophy should be studied as an immanent development of thought, outside all social or historical conditioning, and then he attacked atheism, 'the greatest of absurdities'. Spinoza was cleared of the reproach of atheism, though he accepted neither Christ nor a personal God, nor the dualism of the Jewish religion. An unsigned review of the second volume of Fischer's work *The Century of German Culture* (*Time*, 1863, no. 2) completed the argument by an attack on *The Contemporary*, the utilitarian and materialist magazine.

M. L. Mikhaylov and Chernyshevsky of *The Contemporary* took John Stuart Mill as their master. Strakhov attacked them by giving a translation of Taine's article on modern English philosophy and the logic of J. S. Mill (*Time*, 1861, no. 6), this system which leads 'to the negation of thought, i.e., to absolute scepticism'. He broke a few lances on P. L. Lavrov and his 'practical philosophy', denouncing the underlying egoism of this system and defending his own conception of Hegelianism (*Time*, 1861, no. 2). Accused by Antonovich, a radical critic from *The Contemporary*, of not understanding Hegel properly, he returned the argument in 'Letter to the editors of *Time*. About Turkeys and Hegel' (*Time*, 1861, no. 9).

Strakhov, an experimental scientist as well as a philosopher, one of the best qualified men of his time to reply to biological materialism, analysed Darwin's *Origin of Species by Means of Natural Selection*, which had just been translated into French, in 'Bad Signs' (*Time*, 1862, no. 11). Although Strakhov admitted the immense progress made possible by the natural sciences, he was firmly opposed to the idea that Lamarck's transformism or Darwin's 'struggle for life' could be applied to human beings, a step which the French translator had cheerfully taken: this lady regarded compassion towards the weak as disastrous and had sketched a theory of 'superior and inferior races'. It was an aberration which Dostoyevsky, from *Notes from Underground*[67] to *The Brothers Karamazov*, would not forget.[68] Strakhov crowned his anti-materialist struggle with a copious article: 'Matter (*veshchestvo*) according to materialist doctrine (*Time*, 1863, no. 3). The epigraph from Schelling – 'Matter is the most obscure of things' – indicated the idea; the article was a formal refutation of the works of Ludwig Büchner, *Force and Matter*, translated in 1860, and *Physiological Pictures*, translated in 1862, the bibles of nihilists like Bazarov.

Dostoyevsky followed Strakhov's vigorous assault on materialism with close attention. However, as a counterbalance, he published articles which were totally alien and even opposed to Strakhov. He even praised these articles before his adversaries did; for instance an enthusiastic critical review of George Henry Lewes' *Physiology of Common Life*, translated into Russian in 1861 (*Time*, 1861, no. 11), was published three months before Antonovich's eulogy in *The Contemporary* of 1862. The author of the review in *Time* congratulated Lewes on uniting exact science with very cautious deductions. Lewes had stated that chemistry and physics were not a sufficient explanation for the laws of life: new concepts were needed. These wise words probably explain why this little book passed from the hands of the socialist Lebezyatnikov – viewpoint of *The Contemporary* – into those of the pure Sonya – viewpoint of *Time* – in *Crime and Punishment*.[69]

With a very different philosophy from that of Strakhov, Vladimir Fuks devoted a study to Taine's philosophical methods (*Time*, 1861, 6). Unlike German philosophy, which proceeded by 'geometrical construction', Taine followed the path of experiment, using the method of abstraction, hypothesis and verification to reach the unique essence. Fuks stressed the importance of the initial fact, from which all the others are deduced and which gives rise to all of them, allowing the unity of the universe to be revealed. When, in *Notes from Underground*, the hero launches into a diatribe against supporters of first causes and the chain of causality, his main target is Chernyshevsky, but he is probably also attacking the narrow determinism of Taine.

The articles on general history are relatively alien to the official programme of the magazine, the cause of 'the native soil'. There are signs of an inclination towards the socialism of the forties, and if a few new names, such as Friedrich Engels and Jules Simon, appear beside the old Utopians like Fourier, Owen, and Proudhon, it is because they continued the attack on the miserable conditions of workers in Europe. Dostoyevsky joined his voice to theirs in an article published in *Time*: 'Winter Notes on Summer Impressions' (1863, 2 and 3): he described the hell of London, the poisoned Thames, the air heavy with coal dust, Whitechapel with its 'famished, strange and half-naked' population, where men and women stupefied themselves with alcohol and forced their children into begging or prostitution.[70] However, the policy of the magazine remained cautious. An unsigned analysis of the Russian translation of Bruno Hildebrand's *Political Economy of the Present and Future* (*Time*, 1861, 3) allowed its author to distinguish, unlike the German historian, between communism which forbade private property and a socialist federative system of private economies grouped in associations, and to praise Fourier and Owen, whose systems constitute 'the essence of all European socialism in its positive contribution to economic science'. He opposed Hildebrand's conclusions on England, quoting against him *The Situation of the Working Class in England*, by Friedrich Engels, 'one of the most gifted and erudite German socialists'. The article ended with open praise of the associative system. In the same spirit, Vladimir Fuks sang the praises of the Genevan radical party in *The present state of Swiss Democracy* (*Time*, 1861, 7).

But the most striking thing is the consideration which the editors of *Time* show for Proudhon. One of the most radical critics, at least at that time, Dmitriy Fyodorovich Shcheglov, a friend of Dobrolyubov, used the appearance of Jules Simon's book *The Working Woman* as a pretext for an article about the social vision of Proudhon, 'the greatest thinker of our time' in Shcheglov's opinion (*Time*, 1861, 11: 'The family of the French working class'). In the following edition of *Time*, P. Bibikov analysed Proudhon's *War and Peace* in a study called 'The phenomenology of war'. A long article by R. Fuks (*Time*, 1862, 1 and 3) dealt with Proudhon's *Theory of Tax*. To complete the picture, Eugénie Tur (Yelizaveta Vasilyevna Salias de Turnemir) gave an account of her meeting with Proudhon in Brussels (*Time*, 1862, 4).

This eclecticism in philosophy and political economy might be used to show the gap separating Dostoyevsky from the Slavophiles or to stress the bonds which still connected him with socialism, but it is difficult to deduce his ideological position. Which side was he on? Was he inclined towards Strakhov, for example, or Shcheglov? They had a common adversary in materialism, as embodied by Chernyshevsky and Marx, and the same care for the human personality.[71] It would be risky to draw any conclusion, although the evolution of Dostoyevsky's thought is clearly shown towards the end of 1863 in the open struggle he conducted against Saltykov-Shchedrin.[72] Whether Dostoyevsky adopted the ideas of one writer or another is not the essential part of our subject. The important thing was that he swept them all in together, clasped in each others arms like wrestlers in mortal combat, and stored them all ready for use in the polyphonic and polemical language of the novel. Hegel, Spinoza, Kuno Fischer, Fourier, Owen, Darwin, G. H. Lewes, J. S. Mill, Engels, Proudhon: chaff and wheat mixed, since Dostoyevsky received them through the interpretations and visions of his collaborators: this is the rich harvest which the novelist was preparing to use in *Notes from Underground* and his future works.

As for his historical culture, we must examine first the field of general history and then that of Russian history. Four historians of Europe drew the attention of writers for *Time* and their moral director: the German Georg Gottfried Gervinus, the English Henry Thomas Buckle, the Russian Timofey Nikolayevich Granovsky and the French Jules Michelet.

Gervinus, author of *Introduction to the History of the 19th Century* (from the treaties of Vienna to 1830), much admired by the writers on *The Contemporary* – Antonovich translated it, with a preface by Chernyshevsky – owed his success to his social commitment and his open militancy. N. P. Barsov, who introduced and translated Gervinus' article, 'Theoretical Viewpoint on History' (*Time*, 1861, 11), stressed the guiding idea of Gervinus' research, the pursuit of progress. The case of Buckle was even more explicit. He died on 31 May 1862 and two articles were devoted to his unfinished book *The History of English Civilization*.[73] The first was another study by Barsov about 'The Importance of Buckle' (*Time*, 1862, 6). The second was N. Shulgin's translation of 'Perceptions of the History of the Movement of Ideas among the Spanish people from the 5th century to the middle of the 19th century', an extract from *History of English Civilization* (*Time*, 1863, 2). This illustrated the central theme developed in Barsov's article, that the intellect and its laws guide humanity towards progress, a fundamental idea which Chernyshevsky summarised as: 'History progresses through the development of knowledge.' Two years later, Dostoyevsky, in a violent diatribe against men of systems, 'logistics' and abstract deductions, abandoned the unfortunate Buckle to the deadly rage of his hero, the libertarian of *Notes from Underground*:

For asserting, say, this theory of the renewal of the whole human race by means of a system of its own interests, that, it seems to me, is almost the same ... well, as asserting, for example, like Buckle, that man is mellowed by civilisation, and consequently becomes less bloodthirsty and less capable of war. It's because of logic, is it, that he thinks it turns out like that ... That's why I take this example, as it's such a glaring example. Just take a look around: blood is flowing like a river, and in such a jolly way too, as if it were champagne. That's our nineteenth century for you, which Buckle was living in as well. There's Napoleon for you – the Great one as well as the one still here. Take a look at North America – the eternal union. Take a final look at that ridiculous Schleswig-Holstein ... what is it that civilisation mellows in us there? ... Civilisation simply develops a versatility of sensations in man ... and absolutely nothing more.[74]

'Courses in Mediaeval History' (articles in *Time*, 1862, 4 and 6) by Timofey Nikolayevich Granovsky, the prototype of Stepan Trofimovich in *The Devils*, also use past history as a lesson for contemporary politics. This liberal and Westernising historian compared the mediaeval struggles between feudal lords and people with those between propertied classes and proletariat in the nineteenth century. Finally, in a long article 'The state of historical science and recent historical works in France' (*Time*, 1862, 7) V. Fuks praised Jules Michelet for his forceful criticism of the politicians of the sixteenth and seventeenth centuries in *History of the French Revolution*, where a whole school of semi-fictional writers (Victor Cousin, Mignet) succumbed to the glamour of the French aristocracy, resolutely ignoring the spectacle of the masses sunk in ignorance and in material and moral suffering. All these articles from *Time* have a modern ring. They illustrate the words Dostoyevsky used at his judicial inquiry in 1849: 'History is the science of the future'. It was, at any rate, no longer in an ivory tower.

In the field of Russian history, the journal was influenced by Apollon Grigoryev, creator of 'organic' criticism and principal theoretician of 'the native soil' movement, and also by a small fairly radical group of publicists, a sort of old students' club from Kazan University, Nikolay Aristov, Afanasiy Shchapov, linked through the proof-reader Sungurov with revolutionary students.[75] There were two main themes: the schism of the Russian Church in the seventeenth century, or *raskol*,[76] and, more generally, the reasons for the break between the people and the upper classes, together with an indictment of Peter the First and his century.

The lengthy inquest which *Time* held on the significance of this schism was apparently inspired by Dostoyevsky's article 'Two camps of theoreticians' (*Time*, 1862, 2), where he dismissed orthodox Slavophiles and radical Westernisers in one fell swoop. Here is his declaration of intent:

What does the schism show us? ... It is remarkable that neither slavophiles nor westernisers can properly appreciate a phenomenon which looms so large in our history. This is, naturally, because they are theoreticians. From their theories, it turns out that there is nothing at all good in the schism. The slavophiles, cradling the moscovite idea of ancient Rus in their hearts, cannot show any sympathy for the people when they turn aside from the orthodox faith . . . The Westernisers, judging the historical phenomena of Russian life by German and French books, see in the schism only a sort of vulgar and primitive theory, product of popular ignorance . . . They have not understood in this strange negation a passionate aspiration towards truth, a profound dissatisfaction with reality . . . Now this manifestation of Russian obstinacy and ignorance is, in our opinion, one of the most important facts of our Russian history and the best pledge of hope in a better future for it.[77]

A series of leading articles, documents and reviews formed a record of great richness. Shchapov, a professor who had served a term in prison for making a revolutionary speech at a funeral service in memory of rebellious peasants, was the most important contributor. In his article 'Zemstvo and Raskol. The sect of fugitives' (*Time*, 1862, 10 and 11), he expressed the fundamental idea, present in all the other articles, that the sect of fugitives (*beguny*) and Old Believers in general represented a democratic opposition to Peter's centralism. The whole doctrine indicated a sudden national awareness, an effective and total refusal to accept the institutions and principles of the Empire, of the state system. It contained elements of original socialism, of civil and religious democracy. Lastly, it illustrated that profound Russian tendency to turn to Christs, prophets and teachers, flowing parallel with the other, more violent current, that of Pugachov, Razin and the impostor tsars.[78] Three other articles, one probably by Strakhov (*Time*, 1861, 10), the second by Aristov, a disciple of Shchapov (*Time*, 1862, 1), and the last by M. Rodevich (*Time*, 1861, 12) reviewed seven works, one of which was the remarkable *Life of the Protopope Avvakum, written by himself*, edited by Tikhonravov. Accounts of schismatics, legends of Novgorod and critical works were described and dissected by Strakhov, who was prudent about the social aspects, by Aristov, who was bolder and closer to the slavophiles, and by Rodevich, who was much more interested in the social revolt than in the religious aspect. Discussing a book by Shchapov, *The Beggars of Holy Russia*, Rodevich implicitly distinguished charity from social justice and expressed reserve about almsgiving and charitable societies, which encourage rather than allay poverty. This passage must have made an impression on Dostoyevsky, who refuted it in a discussion between Razumikhin and Raskolnikov which occurs twice in the notebooks to *Crime and Punishment*.[79]

Time devotes just as much space to books and articles about the reign of Peter the First and the first half of the Russian eighteenth century. This was logically connected with the debate about schism, but showed more clearly that the doctrine of the 'native soil' was based on Slavophilism. All the authors, M. Semyovsky, M. Khmyrov, Rodevich, D. Maslov, M. Vladislavlev, denounced the taming of individuality by Peter, the weakening of Russian culture by a systematic invitation to 'culture colonisers' – in reality despots and adventurers – the merry-go-round of favourites before a silent people (Khmyrov's article on the Balt Biron, *Time*, 1861, 12), the part played by foreign diplomats in palace revolutions (Rodevich's review of Pekarsky's book *The Marquis de la Chétardie in Russia* (*Time*, 1863, 4), and the cruelty, depravity and crime which reigned at court. Reputations were challenged; Derzhavin, who allowed himself to sneer at Radishchev, condemned to Siberian exile, is contrasted with Novikov, the preacher of enlightenment (Maslov, *Time*, 1861, 10); Karamzin himself was shown to have been incapable of understanding the part played by the 'great Russian reformer' Speransky, whom Vladislavlev contrasts with Belinsky (*Time*, 1861, 12 and 1862, 8). Dostoyevsky was much more reserved about these severe judgements on Peter the First and Karamzin. He jibbed at an article by Semyovsky about Ustryalov's *The Tsarevich Aleksey Petrovich*,[80] in which Peter the First was treated as a 'personal enemy'. This did not prevent him from publishing more than twenty printed pages written by this same Semyovsky in *Time* in 1861 and 1862! Drawn by Strakhov and Grigoryev towards the slavophiles, Dostoyevsky, as a former westerniser, could not forget his old convictions so easily.

However, he was influenced by Vladislavlev and especially Grigoryev to make a vast revision of his historical ideas. He had always loved Karamzin. Vladislavlev recalled the merits of Polevoy and had a fondness for S. M. Solovyov. Grigoryev suggested N. I. Kostomarov, a historian who was at loggerheads with the authorities and was interested in the communal system of the Russian peasantry. In an article on the work of Kostomarov (*Time*, 1863, 1) Grigoryev, in quest of the 'organic principles' of the national life, distinguished two main tendencies, centralism and federalism, and naturally preferred the latter. According to him, Solovyov represented the centralisers, while Kostomarov, Shchapov, and D. I. Ilovaysky, author of *History of the Principality of Kazan*, represented the federalists. This was the time when Dostoyevsky began to be deeply interested in Kostomarov, even though Kostomarov had had the nerve to question the heroism of Dmitriy Donskoy in an article in 1864 about the battle of Kulikovo. An argument with Pogodin followed. Dostoyevsky undertook to write an article about this dispute[81] for *Epoch*, the magazine which followed *Time*, but never actually wrote it. On 5 March 1864, he confided in his brother; 'My article (to be) on the quarrel between Pogodin and Kostomarov will be in any case a considerable article . . . I do not know history as they do, but I still think I have something to say to both of them.'[82] He was always to show respect for Kostomarov, 'a great name' whom he placed beside Turgenev and Goncharov,[83] though there were some reservations in his praise.[84]

We might continue this demonstration for *Epoch*, the second magazine of the Dostoyevsky brothers, which made a first delayed appearance in March 1864. Fyodor guaranteed its survival until February 1865, in tragic con-

ditions. His wife, Mariya Dmitriyevna, died on 14 April 1864, his brother
Mikhail on 10 July, and his close colleague Apollon Grigoryev on 22 July.
The number of subscribers dropped, debts piled up, and his epileptic fits
became more serious. There were to be only thirteen editions (one double).
Moreover, a battle raged between *The Contemporary* and *The Russian
Word*, magazines of the nihilist camp, and *Epoch*, where Dostoyevsky
openly declared war on materialism and socialism. To find the basis of
economic, historical and philosophic ideas in *Epoch*, we should have to
wade through acres of slag, zoological metaphors ranging from insects to
crocodiles,[85] puns,[86] and personal attacks,[87] removing the crust of hatred
which formed over this virulent battle of the press. Dostoyevsky fed the fire,
but continued his harvesting. Strakhov, attacking more openly since his
editor was now on his side, and Vladislavlev used scientific articles to dis-
mantle materialism, which they now linked closely with socialism. Strakhov
refuted the theses of Heinrich Heine in 'Religion and Philosophy in
Germany from Kant to Hegel' (*Epoch*, 1864, nos. 1–2 and 3). (Kant and
Hegel both seemed conservative to the liberal Heine). He brought Renan
into action, praising his *Life of Jesus*, which appeared in 1863, and his *Essays
in Morality and Criticism*, where Renan asserted that revolution led to a
reign of mediocrities and prevented the rebirth of the individual conscience.
He laid into the 'desperate pessimism' of Feuerbach, whose anthropological
principles and militant materialism had influenced Belinsky, Chernyshevsky, Marx and Engels. With Strakhov we are at the heart of the metaphysical debate.[88] Vladislavlev made a specific attack on people such as
Wilhelm Wundt and Karl Vogt,[89] who based their philosophy of progress on
experimental science. In the religious field there were four articles, partly
historical, partly polemical, about the Papacy and the Jesuits: one is by
N. A. Osokin, 'Jerome Savonarola, an attempt at historical monography'
(*Epoch*, 1864, nos. 1–2), solidly documented, praising Savonarola and
branding Alexander VI. These few examples are enough.

With *Epoch*, Dostoyevsky took the high ground. His field of vision grew
to universal dimensions. The debates in *Time* had been entangled in the
old-fashioned opposition between Westernisers and Slavophiles, and in the
national problems originating in the schism of the Russian Church, concerned with the 'native soil' movement; they were followed by the great
modern disputes of *Epoch*: materialism against idealism, atheism against
spirituality, scientific socialism against the freedom of the true Christ. Dostoyevsky, in these five years of journalism, had restructured his basic
culture.

Crystallisation

In these wide-ranging debates on history, politics, philosophy and religion,
Dostoyevsky had been forced to understand his adversary in order to fight

him. He was now able to use in the great novels those opposing concepts whose 'coupling', in Proust's words, 'is the law of life and the principle of fecundity'.

The first public act of this dialectic of the idea began with *Notes from Underground* (*Epoch*, 1864, 1–2, and 4). It was so important that for the first and last time Dostoyevsky made a formal dichotomy between the ideological briefing, which even contains dialogue, and the novella which illustrates it. The philosophy of the 'underground man' is set out and this is followed by a novella, 'On account of wet snow'. Again for the first time, a vision of the world directly linked with the great economic, historic, metaphysical and even religious[90] problems is about to emerge. A man is soliloquising, but he is talking to his own ego as well as a whole cultural universe. It is a true dialogue, where an 'anti-hero' – the term is unambiguous – endlessly addresses other anti-heroes. The speaker is one but the voices are many. From the negative clash of the dialogue, a third voice emerges which expresses itself in obstinate silence, like Christ before the Grand Inquisitor in *The Brothers Karamazov*. The double negation of determinism and of total unlimited freedom forms the affirmation. Dostoyevsky was inaugurating the structure of the novel which was to be his own, but in a vacuum. By this time his ideological culture had basically been shaped, but his thought was not fossilised and his cultural background was to become much richer.

This is shown by two important texts which Dostoyevsky sketched out in 1864 but did not complete, the prolegomena to his future philosophy.[91] Their form, exceptional in Dostoyevsky, as philosophical discourses, tightly packed, abstract, deductive, devoid of images, is another proof of their ideological and cultural importance. The meditation before the mortal remains of Mariya Dmitriyevna dates from 16 April 1864,[92] and *Socialism and Christianity* from 14 September 1864.[93]

The thinker's maturity is shown boldly, if not always clearly; he sketched out and dominated broad systems and types of thought. Besides an exact exegesis of verses from Revelation and from the Gospels of Matthew, Mark and John about the ultimate development of humanity, foreshadowing Dostoyevsky's interest in the thesis of Nikolay Fyodorovich Fyodorov on the 'duty of resuscitating our ancestors',[94] we find Proudhon and his intuition of the origin of God, a symbolic interpretation of the religious rite (the 'Eternal Memory' of the service for the dead is said to symbolise the perpetuation of generations), an allusion to the Ideal of Christ according to Renan, whose *Life of Jesus* Dostoyevsky had just read, a lapidary definition of materialism as 'universal inertia and mechanism of matter, i.e. death', a mention of the rational study of nature by Descartes and Bacon, a sketch of the theme of peoples who lose their God because of civilisation, foreshadowing Shatov's theories, a vast conception of the three ages of humanity: patriarchal, civilised, and Christian, the definition of true freedom as a renunciation of the will, and an analysis of the socialism of the ant-heap, in short, a display of consolidated thought, by a man capable of original philosophical creation.

While Dostoyevsky's literary culture was settled in its main lines of force before his arrest, his political, economic and philosophic culture only began to crystallise after five years of journalism, towards 1864–5. This explains one of the great surprises for the modern reader of Dostoyevsky; the difference, almost a time lag, between bold, innovatory, contemporary thought, and obviously dated forms linked with Gothic and popular novels, even with the tradition of the serial novel.

From 1864, the evolution of Dostoyevsky's historical, social, philosophical and religious culture followed the natural curves of the literary work, which was inflected in response to a variety of factors: the journalist's inclination towards a spiritual and Pan-Slavist ideology, the reinforcement of the writer's original ideas by related concepts, the interest in systems of reconciliation and finally and above all the search for materials useful for literary creation. At least, this is what emerges from Dostoyevsky's correspondence and the catalogue of his library, re-formed after his European exile and notably different from the library dispersed during his absence, which was, according to Anna Grigoryevna, very rich.[95]

The new direction is clear. The main Slavophile guides, spurned until 1861, but reread during the second journey to Europe in 1863,[96] have come back with a cohort of secondary writers whose works reinforced their theories. These were P. V. Kireyevsky's collection of *Popular Songs*, with P. A. Bessonov's pseudo-scientific commentaries, which were highly irritating to Dostoyevsky,[97] the works of Yu. F. Samarin, 'that firm and deep thinker', and of A. S. Khomyakov, N. V. Gerbel's *Poetry of the Slavonic Peoples* in translations by Russian writers, *Old Slavonic Literature* by Professor P. V. Yestafyev, *The Life and Works of Lomonosov* by N. A. Lyubimov, and the works of the disciples, Grigoryev, Strakhov and Danilevsky, whose book *Russia and Europe* ought to have been, according to Dostoyevsky, 'a reference book' for the whole country.[98]

Religious texts were even more numerous. The Gospel in several copies, the Psalms, the Commentaries of St Ephraim the Syrian, Simeon the New Theologian, Isaac the Abbot of Syria, the Book of Job, which Dostoyevsky reread with tears in his eyes, in Ems in 1875,[99] a choice of the *Lives of the Saints*, according to the *Menologia*, published in monthly journals (1860–1), the works of the metropolitan Bishop Filaret, *The Imitation of Christ* by Thomas à Kempis, the journeys of the monk of Mt Athos, Parfyony, *The Life of the Elder Leonid from the Hermitage of Optino*, a 'Historic Description' of this hermitage, etc, were supplemented by books of prayers, a liturgical calendar, works of piety and also of documentation for the author of *The Devils*, *A Raw Youth* and *The Brothers Karamazov*.

Dostoyevsky's broad vision was not confined to orthodoxy. *Selected Works* of Massillon, the Koran in French translation, *The Moral Ideal of Buddhism and its Relationship with Christianity* by A. Gusev showed his interest in other religions. He had some knowledge of theosophy: *The Gospel according to Swedenborg, The Heavens, the World of Spirits, and Hell, as They have been Perceived and Seen by E. Swedenborg, The Rationalism of Swedenborg* appeared on the shelves of his library, beside works about experiences of spirits, in which Dostoyevsky refused to believe. It is a vast collection completed by the work of Vladimir Solovyov, the young idealist philosopher with whom he travelled to the Optino hermitage. Dostoyevsky's keen interest in Solovyov's writings, which were crucial for the 'Russian renaissance' to come, is shown by the contents of his library, which included Solovyov's book attacking positivism, *The Crisis of Western Philosophy* (Dostoyevsky was a member of the audience when Solovyov defended his thesis on this subject on 6 April 1880,[100] *Critique of Abstract Principles*, and the text of an informal lecture, 'The Three Forces'.

But the library had its black stains: dismal anti-Semitic works such as *The Book of Kahal. Materials for studying Judaism in Russia and its Influence on the Populations among whom it Exists* by the converted Jew, Jacob A. Brafman, and a pamphlet of 1876: 'Pernicious Influence of Jews on economic life in Russia and the Jewish system of exploitation' by Marcellus Ivanovich Grinevich.[101] Dostoyevsky adopted their basic arguments.

Syncretism

In 1865 the cultural background of Dostoyevsky had already crystallised, but he sometimes reinforced his beliefs later when he came across ideas close to his own. The clearest example comes from the work of a penitent Fourierist, Nikolay Ivanovich Danilevsky: *Russia and Europe*, which appeared in 1869[102] and which Dostoyevsky read with enthusiasm. It set out, in a scientific way, a theory about culturo-historical types of people exactly illustrating the confused idea which Dostoyevsky had always had in his heart.

Danilevsky founded his historical naturalism on the zoology of the founder of palaeontology, Cuvier, who, in opposition to Lamarck and evolutionism, thought that types were not degrees of development in the scale of creation as it moved towards perfection, but were distinct planes inside which creatures developed to achieve their own perfection. Danilevsky distinguished a dozen culturo-historic types and defined them according to the dominant feature which each developed and achieved in its own sphere: for example, the religious type among the Hebrews, the cultural type among the Greeks, the political type among the Romans, the socio-economic type among the Germano-Romans, or Europeans. The Slavs were supposed to have the privilege of uniting all these tendencies and so forming the universal type, the summit of the other four. Dostoyevsky welcomed this idea enthusiastically:

The essay by Danilevsky in my view is becoming more and more important and fundamental. It must certainly be the reference book for Russians for a long time! ... It coincides so well with my own conclusions and convictions that I am even amazed, on some pages, at the resemblance of the conclusions; for a very long time, about two years now, I have been noting many of my own ideas with the aim of preparing an article too, with almost the same title, exactly the same thought and the same conclusions. And imagine my joyful amazement when I come across almost the very same thing that I longed to write in the future – already written – and with elegance, harmony, with extraordinary logical power, and with a degree of scientific method that I could never have achieved, however much I tried.[103]

In spite of the perfection of this meeting of minds, Dostoyevsky expressed some fears: 'I am not sure that Danilevsky will show in its full strength the definitive essence of the Russian vocation, which is to reveal the Russian Christ to the world.'[104] His fears were justified; Danilevsky, in his work published in 1869 in *Aurora* and re-edited in 1871, 1888 and 1889, did not entrust the Russian people with any mission: the Messianic spirit was foreign to him and he had no dreams of resurrecting Europe or spreading Orthodox civilisation throughout the world. Dostoyevsky, using Shatov as a mouthpiece, and probably remembering Vico, thought that all great peoples originated with their gods, extrapolating the more modest conclusions of Danilevsky. Here the creator's power of metamorphosis was working on historical and philosophical material. Dostoyevsky's own thought, however, remained perfectly independent and self-controlled; it existed before the works which it uses as additional arguments.

Dostoyevsky once told Strakhov: 'I am weakish in philosophy (but not in my love for it; and in my love for it I am strong).'[105] This was over modest: he had a true talent for finding the thoughts of reconciliation which are in harmony with the syncretism he showed as a novelist. The paradox is that while the committed journalist and editor battled on vigorously and seemed impervious to doubt, except in the finished novellas in *Diary of a Writer*, the novelist created worlds of independent consciences, a polyphony opposed to the need for any conclusion except through tragic experience, and this is often interpreted as the creator's own ideological indecision. The paradox is not as harsh as it might appear; both militant thinker and novelist were attracted by the idea of reconciling the irreconcilable and seduced by syncretic concepts, as the following examples show.

On 7 November (26 October) 1868, from Milan, Dostoyevsky advised his niece, S. A. Ivanova: 'Read "The Congress of British scientists" in the September issue of "The Russian Messenger". Don't miss it'.[106] The article in question was an account of the annual meeting of the British Association for the Advancement of Science. The botanist Joseph Hooker, defender of Darwinism, and the famous physicist John Tyndall, taking the philosopher Herbert Spencer as his reference,[107] agreed that religion and science were not incompatible, and admitted that, even if there is a parallel between the brain structure and the activity of thinking, this is not a cause-and-effect relationship, but the organic expression of a mystery reserved for religion. Dostoyevsky was naturally attracted by this affirmation of the independence of the soul which took the conquests of science into account, as he knew that the strong point of materialists and nihilists was their insistence on the benefits of scientific thought.

In the same way G. Struve's book, *The Independent Principle of Mental Phenomena*, which made a stir at the time, was read 'attentively' by Dostoyevsky in May 1870,[108] and was very appealing to him, at least until Strakhov tempered his enthusiasm. Struve vigorously defended the existence and independence of the soul, trying to make his defence respectable even to materialists by comparing the soul with apparently immaterial phenomena, such as electricity, warmth, weight, and so on. The more lucid Strakhov attacked this sleight of hand in his article in *Aurora* of May 1870: to him, Struve's spiritualism was only materialism in disguise, or at least a dangerous concession to materialist thought.

Dostoyevsky's profound syncretism found its best expression in the passionate interest which he, like Vladimir Solovyov and Tolstoy, felt towards Nikolay Fyodorovich Fyodorov.[109] Fyodorov was a man of one great idea, like Shatov and Kirillov; the general and real, bodily resurrection of ancestors. Rejecting both objectivity which leads to an abstract truth and subjectivity which leads to indifference towards the truth, he founded his philosophy on 'projectivity' (*proyektivnost'*). Scientifically, this aimed at the rational and material domination of nature and even of space by man. In morals and religion, it was supposed to lead to the advent of universal brotherhood. This extended to the living as well as the dead, our ancestors, whose real resurrection it is our duty to bring about. Fyodorov was vague about the means; it might be done by 'mastery of molecules', by collecting the particles dispersed throughout the universe or through some 'divine act' of a transcendent kind. It was a daring project, half way between futurology and metaphysics. It responded in many ways to Dostoyevsky's secret desire to incarnate, to feel the immaterial and to his dream, repeated often in his later works, of a true Golden Age, where Christianity and the pagan myth of the eternal rebirth might be united.[110] Dostoyevsky probably did not read Fyodorov, he simply discussed the philosopher's ideas, which attracted him while he was writing *The Brothers Karamazov*, as his notes on the resurrection of ancestors show.[111]

Completion

Dostoyevsky completed his culture, like most writers, by making technical notes whenever his creative art required it. It would be pointless to dwell on this banal habit, except that in Dostoyevsky it has an originality which completes our picture of his cultural background.

Whatever field he chose, religion, law, medicine, manners, literature, Dostoyevsky knew the value of exactly the right detail and of the weight of amassed information. Among a hundred other examples there are two 'technical files' from the Karamazov notebooks. In its first stage the novel was to introduce a great many children, so the writer, to complete his personal experience as stepfather and father, asked the eminent educationalist V. V. Mikhaylov, head of a kind of modern technical college (*realnoye uchilishche*), about the world of the child: 'Incidents, habits, replies, speech and words, features, life in the family, faith, naughtiness and innocence; nature, the schoolmaster, Latin, etc. In a word, everything you know yourself, you will be doing me a great service.'[112] At a more advanced stage of his work, he needed the ritual of monastic burial for his chapter 'The odour of putrefaction'. He turned to his friend, K. P. Pobedonostsev, future procurator of the Holy Synod, who replied in this note: 'My dear Fyodor Mikhaylovich, I have just been visited by the Archimandrite Father Simeon who has brought me details he found in various texts, to be sent on to you, about monastic burial; he had completely forgotten to explain them to you when he last saw you.'[113]

However Dostoyevsky, unlike Zola, was never overwhelmed by his material. He resorted to documentation only when he was writing and when it was strictly necessary. When he left prison, he had a unique file of information about convict society: proverbs, adages, short and burlesque elegies, new words, popular assonance, which formed what has been called *The Siberian Notebook*. But it was not his intention to write a physiology of prison camps. He used his treasure trove hesitantly, with circumspection and in the right place. While a number of his expressions naturally occurred in *The House of the Dead*, others appeared in the novellas and novels, from *The Village of Stepanchikovo* to *The Idiot*, including *The Insulted and Injured* and *Crime and Punishment*.[114] Dostoyevsky never used his 'technical files' mechanically. He explained this clearly in the *Diary of a Writer* when he was attacking the 'lie' of some documentary writers, such as N. S. Leskov. He said that the author who carries a pencil and notebook around with him to note down typical expressions will end up by collecting hundreds of them.

When he begins a new novel, as soon as a merchant or a man of the church starts to speak, he gives him a way of speaking which is directly taken from his notebook. The readers laugh and appreciate this so-called fidelity; absolutely according to nature.

But it soon appears that it is worse than a lie, precisely because the merchant or the soldier of the novel have their speech reduced to its essence, that is, they speak as no soldier or merchant really does speak. In reality, the merchant or the soldier says ten sentences and it is only in the eleventh that he will use the expression taken down in the notebooks.[115]

For Dostoyevsky reality transcribed from documents or linguistic facts was not intended to make something seem realistic or to guarantee a naturalism which counted on the reader's admiring approval: it was the framework supporting the fiction of the novel. He never deviated from this rule in his own practice. The antithesis both of Zola and of the Goncourts, he had no vanity as a stylist or as a realist; he went directly to his aim, which is not to say that the aim was simple. Surprising as the comparison may be, Dostoyevsky belonged to the great line of direct writers, such as Tolstoy or Hemingway, who do not recreate reality but tell it as it is.

Dostoyevsky used printed and oral sources together. With his religious characters, elders or wanderers, such as Zosima in *The Brothers Karamazov*, it is difficult to distinguish the part played by Dostoyevsky's religious readings from his memories of meeting the elder Ambrose in the Optino monastery, at the end of June 1878.[116] Similarly, while Dostoyevsky's library, at the time of writing *The Brothers Karamazov*, contained a few law books, some general ones about church law, political, international and civil law, criminal procedure, statistics, the history of Russian law, and others describing scenes witnessed in magistrates' courts or commenting on judgements,[117] he also used the technical advice of the public prosecutor Anatoliy Fyodorovich Koni, who had been his friend since 1873 and also of the brilliant jurist Adrian Andreyevich Shtackenschneyder, brother of Yelena Andreyevna, whom he frequently visited, especially from 1879 to 1880.[118] V. S. Nechayeva suggests another source, both printed and oral: in 1865, N. M. Sokolovsky was one of Dostoyevsky's colleagues on *Epoch*, which published extracts from Sokolovsky's *Memoirs of an Examining Magistrate* in the May and November issues. This appeared in book form in 1866 and is a mine of valuable information about criminal psychology. *Crime and Punishment* is heavily indebted to it and so is Book IX of *The Brothers Karamazov*: 'Preliminary Examination'.[119]

Dostoyevsky's documentation, like his general culture, was collected dialectically. When he confided his plan for a huge novel, 'Atheism', to Maykov on 23 (11) December 1868, he added that he would first have to read 'almost a whole library of atheists, catholics and orthodox believers'.[120] He was setting the terms of a double debate, in which both the godless and the Caesaropapists are opposed to the 'true' Russian believers. Another letter tells us that in the winter of 1868–9 he had indeed read 'for his pleasure and profit' Diderot, Voltaire and the Slavophiles, especially Khomyakov, the most religious of them all.[121] We shall give only this one example, since to give others would be to move on to Dostoyevsky's creative process, where collation of written documents is only one part of the whole.

The heritage: general conclusion

Although we have followed a time scheme for Dostoyevsky's philosophic and historical culture, our sketch of his cultural background has been synchronous. Dostoyevsky was not only a writer who first felt and then mastered successive influences; he was primarily a creator who transmuted a vast world of culture and built from it a personal world.

In literature, he took over his inheritance in a fairly disorderly manner, but relatively fast. In *Poor Folk*, indebted in subject to Gogol, the Russian naturalist school and the French sociological novel, and indebted in form to the epistolary tradition and the sentimentalist style, Dostoyevsky had fused, in an original and sometimes irritating way, Gogol's form of the oral tale (*skaz*) with sentimental effusion in the style of Karamzin to express the tragedy of the poor clerk and of poor folk in general. In *The Double* and 'The Landlady' he was even more influenced by Gogol, especially in style, but also by Veltman, Hoffmann and De Quincey in matters concerning dualism and the supernatural. In *The Village of Stepanchikovo* he used parody and stylisation to free himself from the haunting obsession with Gogol. *The Insulted and Injured* has some pages which suggest Hoffmann, Dickens and the incredible plots of Eugène Sue. In this novel, he killed, symbolically as it were, his *alter ego*, the writer Ivan Petrovich. This novella of 1859 and this novel of 1861 are the last fires of a creation which took place while Dostoyevsky was appropriating his literary heritage, and which is highly indebted to this heritage. In these two works he began to free himself from his literary heritage; complete freedom began with *The House of the Dead*, the first book born entirely from experience, from reality, detached from any literary influence.

The strengthening of the historical and philosophic legacy, preceded by a vast revision which went on from 1848 to 1860, took place during the period of journalism from 1861 to 1865. For the first time, in 1864, Dostoyevsky wrote a predominantly ideological work: *Notes from Underground*. From then on, the politico-economic, historical, philosophical and religious basis of his culture was fixed in its main lines. After 1866, and especially from 1867 to 1871, Dostoyevsky's journeys abroad gradually brought to life a purely aesthetic culture, especially in the field of the plastic arts.

On the whole, on the eve of writing the great novels, Dostoyevsky's cultural basis was settled. He was forty-five! The cultural heritage was no longer the immobile and over-significant landscape, one of the dead cities cluttered with the paralysing past in which remnants from Schiller or

Pushkin or Gogol were clearly visible. It was a fertile and transformed world, where the good geniuses and teachers of form lived and worked behind the scenes. They had all lost their identity: Shakespeare, Schiller, George Sand, Cervantes, Balzac, Gogol, Pushkin, Raphael, Claude, Holbein, Fourier, Proudhon and a hundred others, each one metamorphosed by the formidable assimilating and syncretic power of Dostoyevsky. The thinker had ideas and the journalist publicised them, but the novelist had forged a dialectic basis of impressions, of ideas, of images, of systems in perpetual conflict to serve his creation. To use a formula of Dostoyevsky's own, he 'grafted on to his organism, his flesh and his blood'[122] a culture which was always questioning itself through its various representatives.

5

Illness

> Immediately a place
> Before his eyes appeard, sad, noysom, dark,
> A Lazar-house it seemd, wherein were laid
> Numbers of all diseas'd, all maladies
> Of gastly Spasm, or racking, torture, qualmes
> of heart-sick Agonie, all feavorous kinds,
> Convulsions, Epilepsies, fierce Catarrhs,
> Intestin Stone and Ulcer, Colic pangs,
> Dropsies, and Asthma's, and Joint-racking Rheums.
> Dire was the tossing, deep the groans, despair
> Tended the sick ...   John Milton, *Paradise Lost* (IX, 477–87)

For most readers, illness is the key word in Dostoyevsky's creation: the man is sick and the whole of his work – characters, writing, plots, massacres, lighting – is permeated with sickness. This idea is deeply rooted because it implies that the overpowering effect of Dostoyevsky's genius, his disturbing and uncomfortable analysis may be discounted as the results of his illness, an illness with mysterious and terrifying names: the falling sickness, the comitial sickness, sacred sickness, St John's evil, epilepsy. In recent times, some of the legends attached to epilepsy have been cleared away; but psychoanalysis has filled the gap by attaching to Dostoyevsky the all-powerful Oedipus complex, in its most interesting form, the obsession with parricide. However every legend is based on some fact and illness certainly played a part in Dostoyevsky's life and work. Our main task here is to examine the relationship of Dostoyevsky's illness with his creative genius.

The legend: the lazar-house of the novels

Dostoyevsky's works have a morbid side, and Dostoyevsky himself was mainly responsible for the disturbance they caused and the accusations brought against them while he was still alive. If we were to take the part of devil's advocate, we might use the quotation from *Paradise Lost* as an introduction to his works.

Humanity in his novels is ill, with rare exceptions, and seriously ill. People spit blood, wither away: consumption carries them off in a flash. A sudden pallor, a fall: an epileptic fit strikes the hero down. Someone dreams too much, or becomes delirious: it ends in fatal madness. Sex becomes a little too urgent, so an innocent little girl or haughty virgin has to be raped.

If violence breaks out, the axe and the knife appear at once . . . And if death appears, it must be haunting like Kirillov's suicide, or poignant like the agonies of Nelli in *The Insulted and Injured*, Liza in 'The Eternal Husband', or Ilyusha in *The Brothers Karamazov*, child-like souls matured by suffering, cut down as they were just beginning to blossom. And when a character does not die, when he or she is neither consumptive, nor epileptic, nor hysterical, nor paranoid, nor schizophrenic, nor alcoholic, nor a sick prostitute, nor a sexual pervert, there is still evidence of morbid behaviour: sudden pallor, vivid blushes, burning eyes, trembling and fits, swoons. Behaviour in an untenable situation is almost stereotyped: the heroine who is at the end of her tether has a hysterical fit, while the hero takes refuge in a bout of fever, like Liza and Stavrogin in *The Devils*.

This is the usual caricature of Dostoyevsky's characters. A. Grigoryev and Belinsky attacked the pathological aspect of the heroes of *The Double* and 'The Landlady' as early as the forties. But after the publication of *The Devils*, the violence of the critics, especially of the radicals cut to the quick by the anti-revolutionary tone of the novel, was unrestrained. N. K. Mikhaylovsky declared that the favourite heroes of the novelist were 'on the frontier between madness and normal intelligence'.[1] V. Burenin spoke of a 'gang of idiots'.[2] P. N. Tkachov, in a violent article 'About sick men', extended the accusation; Dostoyevsky had limited himself, in all his works, to 'the analysis of psychiatric anomalies of the character of man and to the depiction of the inner world of mental patients': all his heroes appeared at the moment when they were crossing the frontier from sanity to abnormality, and this had been going on since *Poor Folk*.[3] Dostoyevsky sketched a postscript: 'Who is sane and who is mad. Reply to Critics.'[4] He gave this reply later in the *Diary of a Writer* for 1877 discussing the trial of Kornilova. Kornilova, while pregnant, had flung her little step-daughter out of the window and her acquittal was partly due to the struggle in her defence which Dostoyevsky conducted in his *Diary*. A critic sneered at the writer's imagination, which was powerful enough to have 'a clear notion of the irresistible nature of the morbid impulses of pregnancy' and accused him of a 'weakness for the pathological symptoms of the will' which was, he added poisonously, 'quite excusable on the part of the author of *The Devils* and *The Idiot*. Dostoyevsky replied:

As for my 'weakness for the pathological symptoms of the will', I will simply say that I have indeed sometimes succeeded, it appears, in my novels and stories, in unmasking some people who thought themselves sane and showing them that they were ill. Do you know that there are very many people who are ill simply because of their health, that is because of their excessive certainty that they were normal people.[5]

This could hardly be a satisfactory answer to rational atheists and materialists.

The legend: from the characters in the novels to the creator

It used to be thought that work reflects its maker. The morbid and violent
humanity of Dostoyevsky's characters was projected on to the writer; his
heroes were lined up, inspected, and compared with everything that was
known about him, including sensational gossip and innuendo. His reputation is still suffering from the conclusions which were drawn. Even among
liberal critics, he is one of the few writers, possibly including Nietzsche, who
is judged by his biology.

Which were the most frequent illnesses in his works? Statistically, and
especially in the early works, consumption takes first place. It might have
been deduced that the author was tuberculous, if Dostoyevsky, unlike the
unfortunate Belinsky, had not taken too long to die. Critics then turned,
quite reasonably, to the history of the writer's life. From his childhood, in
the Pauper Hospital where his father practised, and among the poor
patients of Dr Riesenkampf, whose apartment he shared in his youth,
Dostoyevsky had met, observed, and even cared for a great number of
people suffering from consumption. It was known that his own mother
probably died from it, that he saw tuberculosis slowly killing his first wife,
Mariya Dmitriyevna, and that some details of great clinical precision, such
as the persistence of hope and dreams of the future up to the final moments
of death, which are noted in Katerina Marmeladova in *Crime and Punishment*, came from his own painful experience. Besides, the frequent use of
this scourge in literature, especially to get rid of heroines, was not far from
the reality which everyone at the time could see around them, in London,
Paris or Petersburg. In short, consumptives were allowed. Nevertheless,
Dostoyevsky's death at the age of sixty was probably due to haemoptysis.

However the heroes who sprang from his feverish pen from 1845 to 1848
came to a different end: Golyadkin of *The Double*, published in February
1846, Prokharchin in 'Mr Prokharchin' of October 1846, the dreamer
portrayed in 'The Petersburg Chronicle' of June 1847, Ordynov of 'The
Landlady' of autumn 1847, Vasya Shumkov of 'A Weak Heart' of February
1848 and the musician Yefimov of *Netochka Nezvanova* of the first months
of 1849. With them madness showed its grinning mask and anxious eyes.
Four of them go mad: Golyadkin, Prokharchin, Shumkov and Yefimov, of
which two, Prokharchin and Yefimov, die, while the others are taken to the
asylum. The 'dreamer' (*mechtatel'*) and his brothers, the hero of 'White
Nights' and the writer Ivan Petrovich of *The Insulted and Injured*, Ordynov,
hero of 'The Landlady', with the disturbed Katerina and the frightening old
epileptic Murin, see the gates of delirium and unreason open before them.
Dostoyevsky personally was not believed to be mad, although he later
showed an annoying predilection in his works for dangerous dreamers,
monomaniacs like Shatov and Kirillov, and the feeble-minded, such as the

simpleton and Mariya Timofeyevna, the cripple of *The Devils*. But the theme of madness was common enough in contemporary literature: it occurred in Balzac, Hoffmann and Gogol. Some critics, however, made disturbing comparisons which refer particularly to 1846–8. They recalled the sensational entrance which the 'new star', the 'new Gogol', made into the world and the literary salons with *Poor Folk*. The pale young man with a sickly complexion, timorous, reserved, gauche, fainting before a society beauty,[6] had soon changed into a 'Knight of the Doleful Countenance', eyeing his less fortunate rivals with contempt, ready to quarrel with anyone and tortured by self-conceit, so enraged by an epigram which Nekrasov and a few friends made up about his vanity that he was ready to challenge Nekrasov to a duel. It was said, and the rumour was tenacious, since Dostoyevsky had to deny it once more in 1880,[7] that the young author of *Poor Folk* had insisted on a special border for the text of his masterpiece in the magazine where it was due to be published. In the epigram Belinsky is supposed to say:

> I will put you in vogue,
> I will act like a rogue
> I will let you have a border
> And place you last in order.[8]

A young novelist who was touchy or hypersensitive might have been accepted; as he was quick-tempered, he was persecuted.[9] He was seen as a sick soul, a genius whose natural speech was delirium.

Soon after Dostoyevsky returned from prison, his epilepsy became common knowledge. The news spread widely beyond the circle of his acquaintances; his enemies even sneered at his doctor in the virulent battle between the magazines of the Dostoyevsky brothers and *The Contemporary*. As if to offer his critics a better target, Dostoyevsky was hardy enough to introduce a real epileptic in *The Idiot*, to analyse his pathological symptoms at length and even to glorify the benefits of the morbid ecstasy. With blameworthy stubbornness, he repeated the offence in *The Devils* with Kirillov and Stavrogin, and again in *The Brothers Karamazov* with Smerdyakov. It was a clear case: the tortured genius of Dostoyevsky owed a great deal to his illness and this illness was not at all imaginary.

After the writer's death, a new and serious accusation was added to the legend. Behind Prince Valkovsky of *The Insulted and Injured*, Svidrigaylov in *Crime and Punishment*, Stavrogin of *The Devils*, behind the salacious and lewd old men who occur throughout Dostoyevsky's works, such as Yuliyan Mastakovich in 'A Christmas Tree and a Wedding' (1848), Totsky in *The Idiot* (1868–9), Trusotsky in 'The Eternal Husband' (1870),[10] and the father Karamazov, who all have a sweet tooth for young flesh and innocence, lurked the shadow of de Sade. Readers were surprised at the frequent occurrence of little girls humiliated and threatened with rape. While Nelli in

The Insulted and Injured just manages to escape her fate, poverty forces the youthful Sonya of *Crime and Punishment* into prostitution. Moreover, Dostoyevsky seemed to enjoy depicting the sexual anxieties of children, such as Netochka Nezvanova and the boy in 'A Little Hero', and Nelli, and later on describing Arkadiy's erotic dream in *A Raw Youth* where the haughty Akhmakova yields to his desire because of blackmail. In 1913, a letter which Strakhov, Dostoyevsky's first biographer, had sent to Tolstoy on 26 November 1883 appeared in *The Contemporary World*. Strakhov began:

You have probably received my *Biography* of Dostoyevsky by now . . . I must make you a confession about this. While I was writing I never stopped struggling, I fought against the disgust rising in me, I tried to repress this bad feeling. Help me to free myself of it.

I cannot see in Dostoyevsky either a good man or a happy man (which basically go together). He was bad, envious, perverted, and he passed his whole life in upheavals which made him pitiful and would have made him ridiculous if he had not been so malicious and intelligent. He himself, like Rousseau, judged himself the best of men and the happiest.[11]

He went on, before spitting out his poison:

Often I did not reply to his outbursts, which were unexpected and very indirect and roundabout, just like a woman's; sometimes, two or three times, I allowed myself to say very irritating things back. But of course in the matter of insults he generally had the upper hand of normal people, and the worst is that he enjoyed this and never really repented his wickedness. Wickedness attracted him and he boasted about it. Viskovatov told me that he had boasted of raping a little girl whom her governess had brought to him in the public baths. Note also that with his animal sensuality he had no taste, no feeling for the beauty and charm of woman. This is obvious from his novels. The characters who resemble him most are the hero of *Notes from Underground*, Svidrigaylov in *Crime and Punishment* and Stavrogin in *The Devils*. There is one scene with Stavrogin (the rape, etc.) which Katkov refused to print, but D[ostoyevsky] read it to many people.[12]

The scene referred to, the chapter 'With Tikhon', usually called 'Stavrogin's Confession', was only published as a whole in 1922, but part of it appeared in the Jubilee edition of 1904–6, in time to confirm the terrible accusation – crimes of that sort could not be invented. It is pointless to carp at Strakhov's methods: the identification of the writer with his most sensual and satanic heroes and the affirmation that he must have committed the crime to describe it so perfectly. If we accepted this logic, the prisons would be full of writers. As for the obsession with rape, it looms no larger in Dostoyevsky's work than obsessions with murder and suicide and also with pure love, with aspirations towards holiness and perfection. As Pierre Pascal noted,

Dostoyevsky was intensely sensitive to the unhappiness of children and to him rape was the most tragic and long-lasting symbol of this unhappiness; besides rape is, for the rapist, the most repellent symbol of sin. The image which obsessed Dostoyevsky was vicious power faced by helpless innocence. As for trying to find aspects of his own character in the characters he created, this requires a great deal of caution: why should we choose to find them in Stavrogin rather than prince Myshkin, or the underground man rather than Ivan Karamazov?[13]

Tolstoy's reply is a discreet recall to prudence and a refusal to condemn.[14] He was clearly embarrassed by Strakhov's volte-face and shaken in his admiration for the author of *House of the Dead*. He hinted that it was because Strakhov had exalted Dostoyevsky to the skies that he now felt the need to decry him and show his dark side:

Your letter has made me very sad and disillusioned. But I undersand you perfectly; and, unfortunately, I almost believe you. I have the impression that you have been the victim of the false and lying attitude which you, not you personally but everybody, have had towards Dostoyevsky, you have exaggerated his importance and exaggerated in the usual way, raising to the rank of prophet and saint a man who died at the burning point of his inner struggle between good and evil. The writer touches and interests us, but it is impossible to place a man entirely composed of struggle on a pedestal to edify posterity.[15]

After this came Freud and Jung and psychoanalytical literary criticism, subtle but less formidable from the scientific point of view. For Freud, Dostoyevsky was a neurotic.

One of the first and frankest analysts, the German Jolanka Neufeld, whose conclusions were mainly approved and taken up by Freud in his famous essay 'Dostoyevsky and Parricide' (*Dostojewski und die Vatertötung*) concluded her *Sketch for a Psychoanalysis* of the novelist with these words:

We have examined the life and creation of Dostoevsky in the light of psychoanalysis and we have found the desires which determined his life and work. The picture which rose before our eyes was of a little boy, somewhat neglected by his mother and submitting to the severe discipline of his father. Solitary at home and at school, full of strong repressive tendencies, desires and thought of riches, domination and power which could not be realised, he escapes from reality into the world of imagination and dream, where all his unsatisfied desires can be fulfilled. From these dreams his works are born. Their basis is the erotic tendency, their object is the unconscious desire for incest. The life and work of Dostoevsky, his acts and feelings, his destiny, all come from the Oedipus complex'.[16]

On the basis of the eternal Oedipus, whom Dostoyevsky apparently never managed to escape, the system was erected with amazing skill, always falling on its feet by adroit use of the two ideas of ambivalence and sublimation. Let us summarise Neufeld's analysis.

Hatred of the father, who is the fortunate rival for his mother, is shown by his fear of the 'wolf' at Chermashnya, the property bought by Dr Mikhail Dostoyevsky,[17] in the feeling of guilt towards the tsar, the 'Father' (*batyushka*) and the passive acceptance of a disproportionate prison sentence, in the ambivalent feelings of Arkadiy towards Versilov in *A Raw Youth* and, naturally, in the clear obsession with parricide in *The Brothers Karamazov*. The celebration of the Ideal of Christ is a form of assimilation with the suffering son, abandoned by his father. Dostoyevsky's religious feeling is a sublimation of father hatred, but he also idealised his father: this explains the first marriage (but not the second) with a widow, already a mother, Dostoyevsky's generous treatment of his dead brother's children, and his attempts to bring up his own children as he was brought up. The fear of dying which the young writer experienced in the forties, the continence which he is supposed to have observed until he was forty years old,[18] and the Manichaean concept of earthly and celestial love in his novels show a propensity to incest. The heroes of his novels love two women at the same time, and, as an additional proof, see marriage as depravity in a mother or future mother: Natasha of *The Insulted and Injured* and the mother of Arkadiy in *A Raw Youth* have gone astray, Sonya is a prostitute, Nastasya Filippovna is a fallen woman, etc. Dostoyevsky sublimated his incestuous tendency towards the Mother-Earth into ardent patriotism. The analyst surpassed herself in a study of the erotico-anal component of Dostoyevsky's libido, of which the ambivalence is constriction–liberation and the equivalence is excrement as experienced by the child and money conceived as a gift. Dostoyevsky suffered from constipation,[19] showed an inclination for disgusting smells (the smell of the Elder Zosima's corpse), kept his work at the planning stage as long as possible and seemed to regret finishing a book. However, unlike his father, who was sordidly avaricious, he was astonishingly generous, gambled and even squandered money. To Neufeld, gambling was not a substitute for onanism[20] as it was to Freud, but a way of receiving the gifts of heaven – a perfectly sensible analysis. Some aspects of the work and the novels are studied from this point of view; for instance, there are no descriptions of nature, which is always assimilated to the mother's body, and this shows that the tendency to exhibitionism has been repressed. *The Idiot* is an abortive attempt to escape the Oedipus complex. *The Devils* is an illustration of algolagnia – masochism and sadism mixed – a final expression of self hatred. Lastly, *The Brothers Karamazov* is the supreme expression of the obsession with parricide, which had never been conquered.

This is a very rapid summary which the reader may complete by reading the more learned but basically similar essay by Freud. It does give an idea of the use of psychoanalysis for clarifying some characters in the novels, but it can hardly be deduced that these characters represent the writer. Moreover there are some grounds for complaint from the Freudian viewpoint, but we shall concentrate solely on its analysis of literary creation.[21]

First, it is risky to psychoanalyse a dead author. In Dostoyevsky's case, the analyst was forced to rely on biographers, so that she fell into bad habits, sometimes explaining the man by his hero, sometimes the characters by the man. This would be excusable if she had not ignored everything that did not fit in with her thesis and made too much of doubtful and unauthenticated material. Orest Miller, in his 1883 biography, analysed all the evidence about Dostoyevsky's epilepsy: he particularly examined all the hypotheses relating to the date of the first fit, and, anxious to include everything, added a note at the end of page 141:

There is another very strange piece of evidence about the illness of F[yodor] M[ikhaylovich], placing it in his early youth and linking it with a tragic event in his family life. But although someone personally very close to Dostoyevsky reported this to me directly, I have never found any confirmation of this rumour, and this is why I have decided not to go into detail about it.[22]

What could this tragic event be? Questioned by Leonid Grossman, Dostoyevsky's widow confirmed that the fact existed, but kept silent about its nature. The author of the most detailed chronology of the novelist, relying on the evidence of Lyubov, Dostoyevsky's daughter, and of A. S. Suvorin, placed the event in June 1839. According to family tradition, Fyodor had his first epileptic fit when he learnt, towards the end of the month, of the brutal death of his father, murdered by his serfs on 8 June.[23] We shall return to this statement, which Freud used as a basis for his theory of the neurotic nature of Dostoyevsky's epilepsy, in which fits are supposed to be 'self-punishment for the wish for the death of the hated father'.[24] Dominique Arban went further, arbitrarily placing the event in 1828: Fedya was seven, he heard groans in his mother's bedroom and saw an unforgettable sight. Arban is discreet but suggestive about the nature of the sight; it was probably the primitive scene enhanced by a few brutalities. The dramatic page which she devoted to this sybilline phrase must be read to gauge the full imagination of the psychoanalyst, who had no qualms about basing the whole of her Oedipean edifice on feet of clay: a note at the foot of a page, freely interpreted and promoted to the rank of a crucial event.[25] Freud himself, although he admitted that the anamnestic data on Dostoyevsky's epilepsy were defective and untrustworthy, was unhappy that the facts did not quite corroborate his theory: 'It would suit our purposes very well if it could be established that they [epileptic fits] completely stopped while he was a prisoner in Siberia, but other data contradict this hypothesis.'[26] However he craftily used a note – when will the subversive power of notes be realised? – as justification: 'Most of the data, including Dostoyevsky's own, show on the contrary that the illness only assumed its final epileptic character during the Siberian exile. Unfortunately, there is reason to distrust the auto-biographical information of neurotics. Experience shows that their memory introduces falsifications which are designed to break an unpleasant causal connection.'[27] With all due respect to Freud, there was other evidence and the medical certificate given to Dostoyevsky by the major of the seventh Siberian battalion of the line, Dr Yermakov, did not spring from a neurotic imagination.[28]

Secondly, psychoanalysis stresses the contrast between the banality of the complex and the originality of the creation. A network of convergences is constructed, a complex scaffolding is built, a marvellous reticulated structure is erected simply to end up with the universal Oedipus complex. As Charles Mauron remarked: 'We all have more or less the same complexes, as we all have a liver and a spleen.'[29] What can we do but pace round for ever inside the cage built by the virtuosos of the Oedipus complex? When the progenitor, the tsar, God-the-Father are the powerful Father, object of hate and identification, when woman, nature, the Earth and the Motherland are the Mother, to whom incestuous desires converge, no one can take a step without falling over them. In Freudian terms, it is not ambivalence which is interesting, but sublimation,[30] which is the natural element of genius.

Third, medical analysis destroys the innate quality of the work of art. What happens to the emotion, the beauty and, especially for Dostoyevsky, the pugnacity of the ideas debated? Behind the dilemmas of Christianity, atheism, socialism and individuality, there is only the derisive mask of a complex. This is perfectly well known to psychoanalysts, who claim, falsely, that they do not meddle with the sacred question of aesthetics and thought: in Freud's words, 'before the problem of the creative artist analysis must, alas, lay down its arms'.

Fourth, Dostoyevsky is well aware of the unconscious and the subconscious. As Jolanka Neufeld remarked, the chapter of the 'Eternal Husband' where Velchaninov examines the deep and unconscious motivations (the impulses, in Freudian terms) which have driven Pavel Pavlovich to try to kill him after curing him, is called 'Analysis'. Dostoyevsky, long before Freud, brought some of his heroes to the state which the psychoanalyst calls self awareness, for instance, Ivan Karamazov in his terrifying formula: 'Which man does not want the death of his father?' But this is not the cold statement of an analyst, it is a jagged flash of lightning which reveals the rebellious mind, a cry of suffering. Dostoyevsky's analysis of dreams and characters could often be called Freudian. The beginning of 'Dream of a Ridiculous Man', for instance, contains this sentence: 'Dreams, it appears, are directed not by reason, but by desire, not by the head but by the heart, and yet what tricks of infinite cunning has reason sometimes played on me whilst I dreamt.'[31] In their exploration of the mystery of man, psychoanalysts, psychiatrists and Dostoyevsky have a good deal in common, but one basic difference: Dostoyevsky does not reduce man to his libido and is primarily interested in his freedom of choice, in his power to rise above his complexes. There is one branch of psychoanalytical theory, the analysis of destiny (*Schicksalanalyse*), of Dr Leopold Szondi, which is less narrow than that of Freud, since the set of impulses which it proposes introduces, among other factors, the intervention of the impulse to be or to participate. The Oedipus complex is joined by the antinomic complexes of Cain and Moses,[32] and ethics is not left out. Why is Szondi so moderate? Simply because he created analysis of destiny from his reading of Dostoyevsky and Freud and from the idea that all destiny is choice (*Schicksal ist Wahl*).

Finally, Freud is not beyond reproach scientifically. Thérèse Neyrant-Sutterman has shown that his essay is just as informative about his own psychology as it is about Dostoyevsky's.[33] Moreover, Freud was lucid enough afterwards to disown his analysis, which had been inspired by Neufeld and which he had written in parts over several years.

The most serious charge against the general attitude of psychoanalysts towards Dostoyevsky is that they confused neurosis with epilepsy. For Freud, epilepsy originated in a traumatic neurosis:[34] for some of his disciples, epilepsy was a response to environment; it existed in the people around the subject, rather than in the subject himself. Neurologists admit that epilepsy may sometimes be linked to a schizoid process – this might have been the case with Van Gogh – but they define it as a chronic disorder, a continual tendency to fits resulting from an excessive discharge of cerebral neurones, whatever clinical or paraclinical symptoms happen to be associated with it. Neurosis is not the origin of epilepsy.[35]

Before we turn to the real evidence about Dostoyevsky's health, we have to deal with another obstacle posed by the legend, this time created by men of letters. In fact, a heap of accusations charging Dostoyevsky with the ills, perversions, deviations and crimes of some of his heroes without a word about the rest of his work, lead to the totalitarian view expressed in the theses of Lombroso and the pathographic German school, based on the study of poets, writers, painters and philosophers who clearly suffered from psychosis or from organic cerebral affection (Hölderlin, Nerval, Maupassant, Strindberg, Van Gogh, Nietzsche). For this school, genius was only an 'epileptoid variety of madness'[36] and the giants of thought paid for their intellectual superiority by degeneracy and psychoses. Erroneous as this theory may have been, it reinforced the image which many people had of Dostoyevsky. While a number of these, such as Merezhkovsky,[37] Gide,[38] and Mauriac,[39] gave an important and fair place to illness in literary creation, they took care not to make it the basis of genius. Others failed to avoid the trap. Thomas Mann, fascinated by the two great sick geniuses, Nietzsche and, according to him, Dostoyevsky, adopted a theatrical attitude in the face of the monster: 'My terror, a mystic terror which leads me to silence, begins before the religious grandeur of the accursed, the genius-illness and the illness-genius, before the type of the damned, the possessed, in whom the saint and the criminal are fused into one.'[40] After stating that a feeling of guilt and an obsession with crime are the consequences of 'the sacred illness, the sickness which is mystic in the highest degree' he joined the psychoanalysts: 'I do not know what neurologists think of "the sacred illness" but in my opinion it is undoubtedly rooted in sexual life, whose dynamism shows itself in this savage and explosive form. It is a deviate and transfigured sexual act, a mystical debauch of the brain, an action of psychological depravity.'[41] And further on:

It is certain that his genius is closely linked with his illness, and receives its characteristic hue from the illness, which is indissolubly connected with his psychological penetration, his familiarity with crime, what Revelation calls the 'satanic depths' and particularly his aptitude for suggesting the mystery of transgression, and in causing it to emerge in the background of the existence of his sometimes terrible creatures.[42]

Finally came the confession: 'Life is not finicky, and we may well say, illness impregnates, illness dispenses genius.'[43]

So, at the end of this road bordered with grimaces and the glittering eyes of madmen, the black signal of illness shines in a mystic half-light. Its sickly flame dissipates all obscurities; Dostoyevsky's heroes are only ill because he has all the defects of neurosis based on the Oedipus complex, epilepsy linked with this neurosis, and sexual depravity. His genius had no other source but the great sacred illness with which he had been blessed, and of which his work was only a by-product. We must get this myth out of the way before we examine the part played by illness in Dostoyevsky's creation.

Reality: medical file from 1821 to 1857

First, Dostoyevsky had common illnesses which were not at all mysterious. When he was nearly sixteen, in 1837, he had a sore throat which was finally treated with homeopathic methods. After they failed and were abandoned, the illness disappeared of its own accord, but left the writer with that hoarse chesty voice which was so striking to audiences at his public lectures.[44] In 1848, he had haemorrhoids and was treated by Dr Stepan Dmitriyevich Yanovsky.[45] In 1849 he was in prison: haemorrhoids appeared again, very painfully; from then on he suffered badly from them, especially after 1864, as he confided to a friend of the Siberian period, Baron Vrangel, in a letter of February 1866:

And now I've been suffering from piles for a month. You probably haven't the least idea of this illness and its attacks. It's been going on for three years on end, two months every year, February and March. What a nuisance it is. *For fifteen days* I had to stay lying on the sofa and for fifteen days I couldn't hold my pen. And now I have just fifteen days left to write five printed pages! I was in perfect health, but I had to stay lying down since in fact I couldn't stand or sit from convulsions every time I left my couch ... Besser looked after me.[46]

Finally, at the beginning of 1874, Dostoyevsky caught a chill from going to and fro, in all weathers, between the overheated room where he corrected the proofs of *The Citizen*, and his home. His coughing increased, he felt stifled. Professor Koshlyakov prescribed compressed air treatment and Dostoyevsky, three times a week, spent two hours under a dome in Dr Simonov's clinic. Anna Grigoryevna recognised that the treatment was beneficial, but she also remarked on the immense waste of time for Dostoyevsky, who, after his usual late night, had to get up early, rush out to be in time for the dome, and wait patiently for latecomers, his companions under the dome; his mood was spoilt for the rest of the day.[47] Emphysema, which Dostoyevsky described as his other great illness after epilepsy,[48] began at this time. The treatment, which Dostoyevsky followed grudgingly, lasted five to six weeks, between June and September, in 1874, 1875, 1876 and 1879, in Ems. In a letter of August 1876 he described the constrictive routine of this cure, grumbling that he could only spend two hours in creation and one and a half hours in correspondence.[49] From year to year the illness became worse and Dostoyevsky had no illusions about its serious nature. He mentioned it in his letters, as on 15 September 1880: 'The catarrh of the respiratory tracts that I have has changed into emphysema: an uncurable business ... and my days are numbered.'[50] This was a premonition: the curtain call was due. On 26 January 1881 he had a haemorrhage; on 28 January, he died. Although they did not say as much to Anna, the doctors who were called to Dostoyevsky's bedside[51] immediately saw that the case was fatal: the pulmonary artery was broken. According to Von Bretzel, the family doctor, dissection of the pulmonary cavity indicated that consumption had probably developed with the emphysema.[52]

All these illnesses, which temporarily ruined the energy and the mood of Dostoyevsky, which robbed him of hours and days of work, were purely and simply an obstacle to his creation, which does not reflect them in any way. Before we deal with epilepsy, whose symptoms were badly defined at the time, we must examine the childhood and youth of the writer, noting only conclusive evidence.

In *Diary of a Writer* for February 1876, Dostoyevsky recalled an auditory hallucination, which took place in broad daylight. This was the episode of the 'Peasant Marey' which happened in August 1831, at Darovoye. The boy of ten was playing in a thicket. Suddenly in the profound silence he *distinctly*, *clearly*, heard a cry: 'Wolf!' he shouted and fled in terror into a clearing. There a solitary labourer, the peasant Marey, caressed his cheek and reassured him with a sign from 'his large thumb with a black nail, speckled with earth', with a 'slow maternal smile' and with simple words. Dostoyevsky concluded:

I realised at last that there was no wolf and that I had only believed that I heard the cry of 'Wolf'. Besides, the call had been so distinct and clear, but two or three times before I had believed I heard the same cries (not always about wolves) and I knew it. (Later, when I grew up, these hallucinations disappeared.)[53]

Is this a phenomenon relating to psycho-motor epilepsy, as some specialists think? Opinions differ about the diagnosis: organic epilepsy of the left temporal lobe (Théophile Alajouanine) or essential, idiopathic or genuine epilepsy (Henri Gastaut).[54]

In any case, the child, fiery Fedya, as his parents called him, had a nervous and sensitive temperament. When Dr Yanovsky treated him in 1846 and suspected 'some nervous illness', Dostoyevsky confided that he had had nervous symptoms several times in his childhood,[55] but the term he uses (*nervnyye yavleniya*) is too vague to allow us to draw any conclusion.

In June 1839, the tragedy exploded: Dostoyevsky's father was struck down in a field by an apoplectic fit. Hearing of this brutal and possibly suspicious death, Fyodor is supposed to have had his first epileptic fit. At least, this was what Aleksey Sergeyevich Suvorin asserted in 1881: 'Something terrible, unforgettable, torturing happened in his childhood, and the result of it was the falling sickness.'[56] Orest Miller's note echoed this statement, which was later endorsed by Lyubov, the novelist's daughter, and by Leonid Grossman, who based his conclusions on family tradition. The arguments in favour are slender: the peremptory statement of Suvorin, a family tradition reported by the whimsical Lyubov, but no tangible facts. V. Shklovsky noted that if Dostoyevsky had been a declared epileptic at this time, he would never have been kept at the Central Engineering School, where at least it would have been noticed.[57] None of the fellow-pupils or superiors of the 'clerk' Dostoyevsky, when they collected their memories of the writer, mentioned even the hint of a fit.[58]

When Dostoyevsky, with his brother Mikhail, became an orphan and had to show responsibility, he changed from a quicksilver child into a precociously mature adolescent, solitary, with a few chosen friends. Intent on his dreams of literature, the 'monk Photius', as his school-fellows called him,[59] passed the long hours of night in reading and writing, with a blanket over his shoulders, in the draughts of the window overlooking the Fontanka canal. He worked too hard, took no relaxation and ruined his health. In 1843, one of his friends, Dr Riesenkampf, who shared an apartment with Dostoyevsky, gave a detailed medical portrait of his companion. Dostoyevsky, he wrote, was always in an unhealthy state: 'First of all, he was of scrofulous complexion and his voice was hoarse, to which was added a frequent swelling of the sub-maxillary ganglions and the neck, while his earthy colour showed bad blood (caxechia) [*sic*] and a chronic illness of the respiratory passages. Later there were inflammations of the ganglions and in other places abscesses.'[60] After recalling other complaints which were first picked up in Siberia, Riesenkampf returned to 1843:

But he bore his sufferings with stoicism and had recourse to medicine only in extreme cases. What chiefly worried him were his nervous disorders. More than once, he complained that during the night he seemed to have the impression that someone was snoring beside him, which caused him insomnia and a sort of distress, so that he could not stay still. Then he would get up and often spent the night reading and most of the time sketching stories. In the morning nothing went well, he got annoyed about the smallest thing, quarrelled with his orderly, set off in a bad temper in the direction of Planning, cursed his service, complained about senior officers who had a grudge against him, and thought of nothing but retirement.[61]

Beside this morbid irritability, Riesenkampf noted that he was afraid of being caught unawares by lethargic sleep.[62] Andrey Dostoyevsky recalled this strange phobia in 1881: 'At this period (I cannot remember the year it began) he showed some irritability and seemed to be suffering from some nervous illness. I often chanced to see notes, which he left during the night, approximately as follows: Today I am going to fall into a lethargic sleep, so do not bury me for so many days.'[63] Konstantin Aleksandrovich Trutovsky, a school-fellow of Dostoyevsky's, noted that in 1849, the writer, who was his guest for a few days, regularly asked before going to bed 'that he should not be buried for three days if he fell into a lethargic sleep'.[64] Besides this morbid nervousness, there were fits which are difficult to diagnose. Of the year 1845, Grigorovich noted:

Several times during our rare walks he had fits. One day, as we were going along Trinity Street, we met a funeral procession. Dostoyevsky turned away and wanted to go back, but we had only taken a few steps when a fit occurred, and so violent that I had to carry him into a nearby shop with the help of passers-by: there was great difficulty in bringing him round. After this kind of fit there was usually a state of exhaustion which lasted two or three days.[65]

For 1847, Dr Yanovsky, a doctor who had become such a friend in 1846 that he met Dostoyevsky every day, said that once, struck by a presentiment which made a deep impression on Dostoyevsky, he went towards Senate Square to find his friend there 'without hat, with coat and waistcoat unbuttoned, his tie in disorder, supported by a quartermaster sergeant and shouting at the top of his voice: 'Here he is, here is the one who will save me . . .'[66] Yanovsky treated Dostoyevsky for three years, from 1846 to 1849. He noted that at this time the author of *Poor Folk* was anxious about his health to the point of being ridiculous – he worried about tea being too strong and only drank a warm herbal brew – that he had violent headaches which he called *kondrashka*, a lay word for apoplexy. Yanovsky examined him: 'The lungs are intact but the heart beats are irregular, the pulse unsteady and very rapid as it is with women and particularly nervous people.'[67]

How did Dostoyevsky react to these difficulties? Before 1845 he rarely spoke of his health. Although he twice mentioned suicide in his letters, in 1838, where in a youthful romantic flight he invoked the shade of Hamlet,[68] and again in 1845, when he threatened to fling himself 'perhaps' into the Neva if he did not succeed in 'placing' his novel, *Poor Folk*,[69] these rare attacks of pessimism were insignificant compared with his usual enthusiasm and creative hyperactivity. But after 1845 there were certainly changes of mood and undeniable cyclothymic symptoms. Periods of exaltation, aggression, open vitality alternated with hours of depression,[70] in which he was haunted by fears of madness[71] and obsessions with fever[72] and nervous strain. After *Poor Folk*, the sudden fame and the intoxicating social celebrity, came the first criticism, the first sneers and with them the first wounds: the young writer fell 'ill of grief'.[73] In April 1846 there was a first warning: I have been close to death, in the full meaning of the word. I was extremely ill with an irritation of the whole nervous system, and the illness went to my heart, producing a rush of blood and an inflammation in the heart, which was only just controlled by leeches and two bleedings. Now I am out of danger.'[74] In spite of the advice of the doctor: to keep to a diet, to exercise, to lead a calm regulated life, Dostoyevsky went on with his intense work, thinking it was enough to swallow a great number of concoctions and mixtures. Boredom, apathy and hypochondria were strange neighbours for his tense and febrile expectation of 'something better'.[75] There was an improvement towards the end of 1846, but his nerves were still strained by the ordeal of uninterrupted creation. Every failure, he wrote to his editor, brings back his illness which finished, he added without mincing his words, in an 'inflammation in the brain'.[76] At the Peter-Paul Fortress, where he was incarcerated in 1849, he felt his nervous disturbance was rapidly getting worse. His throat felt stifled, his appetite fell, insomnia increased and when he did manage to fall asleep he was assailed by morbid dreams;[77] moreover he had felt for some time that the floor was swaying under him, as if he were in a ship's cabin.[78] If we compare the cyclothymic states, obsession with madness and cerebral crisis, compression of the throat, insomnia, hypochondria, morbid nightmares, and coenaesthesic anxieties described in the letter with the evidence we already have: an obsession with lethargic sleep and death, violent headaches, faints, irritability, a sensation that someone else was present, a feeling of being persecuted by his colleagues, over-confidence, we might conclude that this was not epilepsy but some severe psychosis, such as that defined by psychiatrists as 'acute organic psychiatric syndrome'.[79] This would mean ignoring the immense effort of creation, the incessant affirmation that he had inexhaustible stores of vitality (*zhiznennost'*), the lucid, possibly liberating use of his own anxieties in his works, and especially the constant vigilance of the writer who never gave in to illness but analysed himself with clinical precision. However, it is possible that Dostoyevsky, from 1846 to 1849, may have entered the schizoid process, that he may have been on the edge of mental illness, and that he caught a glimpse of its terrifying depths, as this letter to Mikhail in 1847 shows:

you see, the more spirit and inner substance there is in us, the more beautiful our place and life is. Of course it is a terrible dissonance, a terrible disequilibrium which society presents to us. The *external* must be balanced by the *inner* life. Otherwise, with the absence of external occurrences, the inner world will take the upper hand too dangerously. The nerves and imagination would take a very great place in one's being. Every external occurrence, because one hasn't got used to it, appears colossal and in some way terrifying. You begin to be afraid of life.[80]

The door half opened on psychosis had not opened in vain: through it Dostoyevsky caught a glimpse of that extraordinary faculty of the dissociation of the ego, the dualism, which he had possessed all his life, as he later realised in a letter of 11 April 1880, and which is both 'a great torment' and 'great pleasure'. But in 1880 he analysed it not as a pathological condition, but as the strong awareness needed for critical understanding of one's moral duty to oneself and others.[81]

The psychotic element was not removed but dominated; although it is true that some of the syndromes might be characteristic not of epilepsy but of the disorders which follow it, particularly after the fits. According to Professor Thieffry, an epilepsy may very well begin in a degraded form, causing psychic symptoms reminiscent of psychosis or neurosis.

After the death of Dostoyevsky, a battle royal broke out in the correspondence columns of the newspapers over the date of his first epileptic fit. Suvorin, who placed the first fit in the writer's early youth, was opposed by Andrey Dostoyevsky and especially by Dr Riesenkampf, who chanced to visit Omsk in 1851, where he had a conversation with the army doctor Ivan Ivanovich Troitsky, who is supposed to have said: 'I am very sorry for Dostoyevsky. They've gone so far that he has contracted epilepsy here.'[82] Two witnesses related this to the year 1851: Riesenkampf, who was repeating the statements of Troitsky, a doctor at the military hospital, and Pyotr Kuzmich Martyanov, a writer who described Durov and Dostoyevsky in prison, from oral sources. Here is the Troitsky version: one day, Dostoyevsky, ill, was lying on his bunk instead of working like the other convicts and the terrible major of the fortress, Krivtsov, the wild beast in human form depicted in *House of the Dead*, burst into the cell and threatened him with flogging. This flogging is supposed to have taken place and caused the first fit of epilepsy.[83] In Martyanov's version, Dostoyevsky, according to a marine guard who was discreetly looking after him, had stayed in his bunk because he had previously been the victim of an epileptic fit, and for this reason the flogging had been prevented by General De Grave, commander of the fortress of Omsk, and Krivtsov had been reproved: sick people were not flogged.[84] This episode of corporal punishment is doubtful: Dostoyevsky, in his first non-official and very detailed letter to Mikhail after leaving prison, said nothing about it and simply reported that the 'scoundrel' Krivtsov had threatened him with corporal punishment for any misdemeanour, but that God had delivered him from Krivtsov, who was court-martialled two years later.[85] The only official document, unfortunately dated 16 December 1857, was based on information given by Dostoyevsky himself: the report of Major Yermakov, doctor of the 7th Siberian battalion of the line, on the ensign Dostoyevsky:

Aged about 35,[86] of average constitution, in 1850 for the first time was struck by a fit of the falling sickness (epilepsy) with the following symptoms: a sudden shout, loss of consciousness, convulsions of the extremities and the face, foam at the lips, stertorous gasping, rapid short pulse. The fit lasted about fifteen minutes. It was followed by general weakness and a return to consciousness. In 1853 the fits were repeated and from then on appeared at the end of every month.

At present, Mr Dostoyevsky feels a general weakening of his strength, a complete exhaustion of the organism and suffers from facial neuralgia following an organic ailment[87] of the brain.

Although Mr Dostoyevsky has followed a continuous course of treatment for four years, there has been no improvement and this is why he cannot continue in the service of his Majesty.[88]

In a petition to Alexander II, Dostoyevsky repeated, in 1859, that epilepsy appeared 'in the first year of his forced labour', which was 1850.[89] Another tiny piece of evidence is in favour of this date: the description of the political criminals in the Omsk prison records of 19 June 1850 indicates that Dostoyevsky had a small scar above his left eyebrow.[90] Earlier descriptions make no mention of it,[91] and we know that Dostoyevsky injured himself several times by falling down during his fits,[92] so that this scar may have been caused in the same way. To summarise, the first generalised epileptic fit, medically recorded by Dr Troitsky, took place in 1850 or 1851.[93]

A medical statement and the presence of the illness are two different things. Dr Yanovsky, who was best placed to describe the years 1846–9, now entered the battle and modified the diagnosis. Recalling all the symptoms already described, and then a first fit which Dostoyevsky is supposed to have had in 1847 and a second, which possibly followed the news of Belinsky's death, at the end of May 1848, he declared:

The late Fyodor Mikhaylovich Dostoyevsky was already suffering from epilepsy in St Petersburg and, moreover, three years and possibly more before he was arrested for the Petrashevsky affair, and so before he was sent to Siberia. It must be said that this overwhelming illness known as epilepsia only showed itself in a slight form in 1846, 1847 and 1848. Moreover, although others did not notice it, the sick man was aware of it, although confusedly, and called it a stroke with an aura or breeze [*kondrashka s veterkom*].[94]

Had Yanovsky concealed his diagnosis from the nervous Dostoyevsky, or was he influenced by later events when he made his diagnosis? In any case, Dostoyevsky himself had no idea about it until 1850, so that it could have had little effect on his creation. The important thing for the literary critic is what Dostoyevsky himself experienced.

How the illness was experienced

Dostoyevsky knew about the falling sickness before 1849; he described an epileptic, Murin, in 'The Landlady'. Anxious about his own ailments, he often consulted works about mental illness, lent to him by Yanovsky.[95] If Yanovsky, inadvertently or even conjecturally, had made a diagnosis of epilepsy, Dostoyevsky would certainly have made full use of his infirmity before the Commission of Inquiry in 1849 – he was always to use it in this way later. However in this case, he gave another interpretation: 'Half my time is taken up by work, which gives me my living, the other half is constantly taken up with illness, crises of hypochondria from which I have been suffering for almost three years.'[96] Later, recalling the past in a letter of 1856 to E. I. Totleben, he repeated that before the political drama he had been ill for two years with a 'strange moral illness': 'I had fallen into hypochondria, there was even a time when I lost my reason; I was too irritable, with a morbidly developed sensitivity and an ability to distort the most ordinary facts and give them a totally different appearance and a totally different dimension.'[97] But Dostoyevsky was never to confuse his nervous illness before 1848 with epilepsy, whatever links there might have been between the two in reality. As early as 1857, he said in a letter to Vrangel: 'I was a hypochondriac to the highest degree, but the brutal upheaval [arrest, trial, condemnation and convict prison] which suddenly occurred in my destiny completely cured me.'[98] A letter of 1872, to Yanovsky in fact, clears away any confusion. Here are two sentences from it, twenty lines apart: 'My health (that is, epilepsy) has quietened down compared with what it was, but it is not radically cured' (sic), and 'You loved me and you were concerned about me when I was affected by mental illness (I realise this now) before my departure for Siberia, where I was cured.'[99]

These statements prove that, while Yanovsky was probably right, Dostoyevsky himself thought that his epileptic symptoms were an indeterminate nervous illness (a beginning of the schizoid process). It is rather odd that he should declare he was cured of the latter at the very time when he had no more doubt about the former. Possibly the revelation of a precise medical statement appeased the troubled spirit of the writer, who was desperately aware of increasing anxiety and emotional changes. Yanovsky's interpretation is confirmed retrospectively by Dostoyevsky, who, at Semipalatinsk in

1854–6, is said to have confided in Baron Vrangel that the first signs of epilepsy, which had become open in prison, went back to his time in Petersburg.[100] We may assume then – and this is the essential point for his creation – that he did not experience the real pathological symptoms of the years 1846–9 as epilepsy, nor did he interpret them later as epileptic symptoms. It is precisely because of the uncertainty about the nature of this strange nervous illness, and so because of its imaginative possibilities, that it was so fruitful for the creation of psychotic heroes. These heroes are the fruit of a creative spirit determined to perceive and dominate its anguish, and not the by-products of an epilepsy of which the writer was still unaware.

When epilepsy was medically declared in 1850 or 1851, all doubts about the indeterminate nervous illness of previous years vanished. At first, Dostoyevsky did not seem completely convinced. In letters to Mikhail (22 February and 30 July 1854 and 14 May 1855) he recognised that he had epilepsy, but minimised its seriousness: fits are 'rare' and, though 'very disagreeable', only come at 'long intervals',[101] they are like epileptic fits, he was still saying, but they are nothing of the kind.[102] In 1856 he was frankly worried. On 9 November he wrote to Vrangel: 'If I wanted to return to Russia, it is only to embrace my family and see competent doctors and find out what kind of illness (epilepsy) I have, what these fits are which are being repeated all the time and deaden my memory and my faculties a little more every time and are making me afraid of going mad.'[103] Apparently it was only when he was immobilised by a terrible fit in Barnaul, in February 1857, a month after marrying Mariya Dmitriyevna Isayeva, that he took medical advice and realised the full extent of his illness.

My fit shattered me, in body and mind; the doctor told me I have real epilepsy and predicted that if I don't take steps immediately, that is, follow the correct treatment, which is only possible in complete freedom, my fits could take the worst character, and in one of them I would be stifled by the throat spasm which always happens to me during the fit.[104]

In June and July 1857, he had leave from his commander to go to the outpost Ozernyy to treat his epilepsy,[105] and soon after this he pleaded illness as an excuse for retirement, which took place on 18 March 1859, Dostoyevsky having the rank of sub-lieutenant. From then on, his epilepsy was clear to him and everyone else. He was now able to describe it and use it in his works.

Epilepsy declared

The majority of fits took place at night or during morning sleep. Their frequency depended, according to Dostoyevsky himself, on three factors; climate, work, conditions of life. Emotion caused by outside events did not seem to affect them. Although specialists in epilepsy do not admit the influence of climate, Dostoyevsky noted that the dampness, cold and sudden changes of climate typical of Petersburg or Geneva were harmful to him; he had weekly fits, rather than the usual monthly ones. On 21 October 1867, he wrote:

All the same, what an obscenity Geneva is. I was really wrong about it; I have fits here almost every week, and also bad palpitations. It's a horror, not a town. It's Devil's Island. Winds and blizzards for days on end and on ordinary days very sudden changes of weather, three or four in a day. And this is for someone with haemorrhoids and epilepsy.[106]

But his stay in Florence in March 1869 was beneficial, the fits were, he wrote, 'literally twice as rare as in Petersburg, at least since we came to Italy'.[107] In Dresden, a few months later, in December 1869, he observed that 'in spite of the unsettling work', he has not had a fit for three months.[108] Strakhov also mentions this rhythm of Dostoyevsky's fits, adding a psychological argument which was probably decisive: 'His fits came about once a month, this was their normal rhythm. But sometimes, though rarely, they came more often, as many as two a week. Abroad, where he was more peaceful and also because of the better climate, he sometimes went for four months without a fit.'[109]

Intense work also caused repeated fits. The specialists whom Dostoyevsky consulted did not mince their words: to be cured he must stop writing.[110] The idea of following this advice, which would deprive his life of all meaning, was not a serious option for Dostoyevsky. He simply took it that his illness was incurable[111] and went on with his immense task,[112] particularly heavy when he was working on magazines, only stopping when his illness struck him down. So in April 1861, the editorship of *Time* apologised to its readers for publishing only two chapters of *The Insulted and Injured* 'because of the author's illness'. This illness, Strakhov tells us, was a terrible epileptic fit which struck Dostoyevsky almost entirely unconscious for three days.[113] Serial fits took place just at the same time as the most violent creative effort. This was not when the novel was being written down, which was comparatively easy, but during the tormented search for the right form, structure and composition.

In November 1865, for instance, an important change took place in the genesis of *Crime and Punishment*: Dostoyevsky abandoned the form of *Icherzählung* (or first person narrative), the hero's confession, and changed instead to a narrative by the author. The notebooks are clear on this point and Dostoyevsky mentioned it in his letter to Vrangel of 18 February 1866: 'At the end of November a lot was written and ready. I burnt it all, now I can admit it. I didn't like it myself. A new form, a new plan drew me away and I began it all again from the beginning.'[114] It was precisely at this point of dissatisfaction, creative doubt and gestation that Dostoyevsky endured a series of fits, closely following each other. He wrote to Vrangel on 8 November, alluding to his return from Copenhagen at the end of October: 'As soon as I arrived I immediately had a fit on the first night and a very strong one. I got better, and about five days later had another fit, even stronger. Finally, three days later, another, though weaker, but these three fits in a row have disturbed me horribly.'[115]

The parallel between the painful birth of the novel in its essential structure and the increase in the number of fits is equally clear in the genesis of *The Idiot*. On 31 December 1867 (Julian calendar) Dostoyevsky wrote to A. N. Maykov:

For the whole summer and autumn I have been putting together various ideas (some of them were very ingenious) but my experience made me sense the falseness or the difficulty and immaturity of one or the other. At last I stopped at one of them and started work. I had written a lot when on the 4 December (to follow the local calendar), I flung it all out . . . Then (as my whole future was hanging on it) I began to torture myself with thinking of a *new novel*. I didn't want to go on with the old one for anything. I couldn't. I thought about this from the 4th to the 18th of December, new style, inclusive. On average, I think, it came out at about six plans (no fewer) a day. My head turned into a windmill. Why I didn't go mad – I don't understand. At last, on the 18th of December, I sat down to write a new novel.[116]

Now in this period, which we know today from the second part of Anna Grigoryevna's diary, which has recently been deciphered,[117] fits followed each other at an unusual pace: 6 September (aborted), 10 September at ten past five (very strong), 14 September (aborted), 24 September at four thirty-five (normal), 8 October at ten past two (strong), 15 October (aborted), 16 October (aborted), 18 October at three (normal), 9 December at twenty past four (normal), 15 December at ten past seven (normal). On 22 December, Anna Grigoryevna wrote: 'He began to dictate to me his new novel, the old one being given up.'[118] Even if the fit of 8 October, following the overexcitement of gambling and losses at roulette, is left out, it seems clear that the gestation of *The Idiot* alone cost Dostoyevsky five epileptic fits. He was aware of the connection; in his letter to Maykov of 2 March 1868, he wrote: 'Last night, the whole plan of the third and fourth parts [of *The Idiot*] was radically recast, and this is for the *third* time (and so I need three more days, at least, to rethink the new arrangement); increasing disturbance of my nerves and the number and strength of my fits – in a word, that's my situation.'[119]

The conditions of Dostoyevsky's life also played a part. First there was the work at night until four or five in the morning. All specialists in epilepsy stress the importance of regular sleep. If sleep time is reduced, fits become more frequent. Then there were the misfortunes of Dostoyevsky's life, mourning, indebtedness, passion for gambling and other evils. When Dostoyevsky was working hardest to overcome the most difficult con-

ditions, the rhythm of fits accelerated. A comparison of the years 1861–2
with the years 1864–5 makes this clear. The first were the triumphant years
of the return to Russia and the success of *Notes from the House of the Dead*
and *The Insulted and Injured*, the friendly welcome for *Time* from the public
and the other journals. The fits were spaced out, every three months: '1
April (strong), 1 August (weak), 7 November (medium), 7 January
(strong), 2 March (weak).' In May 1863 *Time* was banned. In March 1864
the new journal of the Dostoyevsky brothers, *Epoch*, appeared with its trail
of catastrophe: relative lack of success, open hostility of the other reviews,
successive mourning (brother, wife, friend), multiplied debts, collapse of
the journal in February 1865, Dostoyevsky being obliged to make a binding
and unequal contract with a literary entrepreneur. Fits followed in rapid
succession: '5 July [1864] (average), 21 August (strong), 18 September
(average), 29 September (average), 15 November (average), 12 December
(great), 22 February [1865] (important), 2 May (important), 9 May (average).'[120]

If we leave out 1867, spring 1868 and the year 1870 (fourteen fits between
January and October), the years between Dostoyevsky's second marriage
and his death were marked, if not by a radical diminution in the number and
intensity of the fits, at least, as Anna Grigoryevna noted, by a stabilisation
equal to that of the best years: 'The diminution and weakening of the fits
was a great blessing to us. They freed Fyodor Mikhaylovich from that truly
terrifying and gloomy mood which sometimes lasted a whole week and
inevitably followed each fit.'[121] All praise for this was due to the young and
energetic wife who gradually took in hand Dostoyevsky's financial and
editorial affairs and set them in order. She gave him the valuable help of her
stenographic skill, as well as the comfort and peace of her steadfast naive
love and of an ideal married life.

Dostoyevsky's own observations on his fits are very valuable as they
contain his records for 1873–6 and 1879–80, with descriptive and interpreta-
tive commentaries. There are comments which might make specialists
smile, such as those on climatic and lunar influence, but there are also
precise descriptions of the experience of the fit, important not only for
diagnosis (which is the business of doctors), but also in showing the part
played by illness in literary creation. It is a tragic chronicle, especially in its
description of the confused state after the fit. Here are a few extracts:

> [1874] 16 APRIL (strong, headache, legs sore)
> N.B. Saturday 20 April. My head and mind have just begun to clear, was very
> gloomy, obviously I have been seriously affected. Three days until the 19th
> were the most painful. On the 20th April, at ten in the evening, although it was
> still painful, seems to have begun to go away.
>
> 13 MAY (fairly strong).
>
> 27 JUNE (fairly strong)

9 JULY (Saturday 29 June) Head and mind heavy, legs still sore.

15/27 JULY (fairly weak). Full moon. Weather very changeable, for about five days: sun, wind, rain, calm, all on the same day.

8 OCTOBER (at night, strong, at five o'clock in the morning). Days dry and clear.

18 OCTOBER, fit at five o'clock in the morning, fairly strong, but weaker than the preceding one. Days clear. 28th December, in the morning, at 8 o'clock, in bed, one of my strongest fits. My head suffered worst of all. The blood was squeezed on my forehead in an extraordinary way and the pain was echoed in the temple. Confusion, sadness, remorse and fantasy. I was very irritated. Clear day: frost went down to 1.5°.
In all, in 1874, from the 28 January, 8 fits in the year.

[1875] Afterwards, two more fits, one on the 4 January and the other on the 11 January.[122]

8 APRIL. Fit at 12.30 a.m. I had a clear presentiment of it during the evening, even the day before. I had only just made some cigarettes and settled down to try and write at least two pages of my novel, when, I remember, I flew into the middle of the room. I lay there for forty minutes. I recovered consciousness in a sitting position, with my cigarettes, but I wasn't making them. I don't remember how my penholder got between my fingers: I had ripped my cigarette case with it. I might very well have plunged it into my body. All week the weather has been damp, it is full moon and there seems to be a slight frost. 8 April full moon.
N.B. An hour after the fit, I was thirsty. I drank three glasses of water at a gulp. It is not that I have much headache. It's an hour since the fit took place. I am writing and I am still mixing up words. The fear of death is beginning to pass already, but it is still extraordinary, so that I dare not go to bed. My sides and legs hurt. Forty minutes later I went to wake Ania [Anna] and I was amazed when Lukerya told me that the mistress had gone away. I questioned Lukerya in detail about when and why she had gone away. Half an hour before the fit I took *opii banzoedi*: forty drops in water.
    All the time of complete unconsciousness, i.e. after getting up, I remained sitting and filling my cigarettes with tobacco, four if one added them up, but rather messily, and for the last two, I felt a violent headache but it took me a long time to understand what had happened to me.[123]

[1876] 15 NOVEMBER, at ten o'clock in the morning, while asleep. Clear day and frost. Very tired condition. Fantasy. Vagueness, false impressions, arms and legs aching. Fairly strong [fit].

19 FEBRUARY, fairly significant fit.

17 MARCH, one of the biggest. Clear change of weather. Moon begins to wane.[124]

[1880] 7 SEPTEMBER 80. Fairly strong [fit] at a quarter to nine. Dislocation of ideas, return to earlier years, revery, thoughtfulness, guilt, I have dislocated a bone in my back or injured a muscle.

6 NOVEMBER 80. At seven o'clock in the morning, in first sleep, but the sickly state was very hard to bear and lasted almost a week. The more this goes on, the more the organism is weakened for bearing fits and so the fits are harder to bear and their effect is stronger.[125]

Did Dostoyevsky know when his fits were coming? He said he did several times, but sometimes his fears were not justified, and mainly the fits came on him without warning. In *The Brothers Karamazov* Ivan tells Smerdyakov: 'I know an epileptic fit can't be forecast in advance. I've checked it out, so no use telling lies. The hour and the day can't be forecast.' To which Smerdyakov replies very truly: 'It's certain you can't tell the day and the hour in advance for a fit, but you always have a feeling about it beforehand.'[126] However, Dostoyevsky made every effort to find personal warning signals: irritability, profound sadness, hypochrondria, obsession with madness,[127] palpitations or a feeling that the heart had stopped, stifling[128] or somnolence, a heavy head, an itch in his hands at the base of his nails.[129]

The generalised fit, for the outside observer, was always the same: a hoarse shout, convulsions of face and limbs, loss of urine. Anna Grigoryevna also noted a rocking of the head, the blood leaving the face so that the nose was frozen, grinding of the teeth (she was afraid that Dostoyevsky, who had false teeth, might swallow them and choke), squinting, and so on.

It is she who gives us the most complete description of a double fit which occurred during Lent 1867. After their marriage on 15 February, the wedded couple made the traditional visits. Dostoyevsky, who was a great smoker, but did not drink, allowed himself a glass of champagne. He was particularly lively and talkative.

Suddenly he did not finish the word he was pronouncing, paled, tried to get up from the sofa and leaned towards me. I watched the changes in his face with amazement. But suddenly there was a terrifying shout, or rather a howl and he began to bend forwards . . . I seized him by the shoulders and forcibly put him back on the sofa. But what was my horror when I saw the inert body of my husband sliding off the sofa and when I was unable to hold it . . . Gradually the fits stopped and he began to recover his senses; but at the beginning he had lost consciousness of where he was and was even incapable of expressing himself; he wanted to say something but he kept saying the wrong word and it was impossible to understand him . . . Another fit followed an hour later and this time so violent that Fyodor Mikhaylovich, two hours after regaining consciousness, was still uttering cries of pain . . . It was then that I saw for the first time what a terrible illness Fyodor Mikhaylovich was suffering from. Hearing him shout and groan for hours, seeing his face deformed by pain, so different from usual, his eyes madly fixed, and being incapable of catching his rambling words, I almost had the conviction that my dear husband was about to go mad.[130]

Strakhov describes a much less dramatic fit, adding a valuable commentary on the singularity of the aura, the symptom and signal immediately before the fit. The text will be given in parallel with Sofiya Kovalevskaya's account, written later and oddly reminiscent of Strakhov's. One might even wonder if Kovalevskaya had been influenced by Strakhov's 1883 text, which she had read before beginning her *Childhood Memories* in 1887.[131] Or possibly Dostoyevsky, whose memory was bad, had spoken of the same fit on an Easter night (which would explain the very clear religious colouration of the second account) while placing the event in Siberia around 1854–7 and substituting a convinced atheist for the Orthodox believer Strakhov.

STRAKHOV

It was, I believe, in 1863, exactly on *Easter Eve*. It was late, after ten o'clock when Dostoyevsky called in to see me. We had *an animated conversation*. Without remembering the exact subject, I can say that it was *very important and abstract*. Fyodor Mikhaylovich, in an exalted mood, paced about the room; I was sitting at my desk. What he was saying was full of *nobility and joy*. When I made a remark in agreement, he turned towards me *an inspired face* which proved that *his exaltation had reached its height*. He stopped a moment as if to find the exact words, with his mouth already open. I looked at him with increased attention, expecting some extraordinary word, some revelation. Suddenly a strange, long drawn out, absurd sound came from his open mouth and *he fell unconscious* in the middle of the room.

This time the fit was not too violent. Seized with convulsions, his body stiffened and foam appeared on his lips. Half an hour later he regained consciousness and I took him home, which was not far.

Fyodor Mikhaylovich told me several times about the *moments of exaltation which preceded the fit*: For a few brief instants, he used to say, I feel *a happiness unthinkable in the normal state and unimaginable for anyone who hasn't experienced it* ... I am then *in perfect harmony with myself and the entire universe*; the sensation is so strong and so pleasant that *one would give ten years*

S. KOVALEVSKAYA

... in Siberia. He was then terribly bored with being alone and whole months would go by without his meeting a soul with whom to exchange deep thoughts. Then he was visited quite unexpectedly by an old friend (I have forgotten the name mentioned by Dostoyevsky). *It was exactly on Easter eve*. But the joy of reunion made them forget even the festival and they passed the whole night in the house, chatting without noticing the hours passing by or feeling tired, *intoxicated with their own words*.

They were talking about *the things closest to their hearts; literature, art and philosophy*. They finally came to religion.

Dostoyevsky's friend was an atheist, Dostoyevsky a believer, and each ardently believed that he was right.

'God exists, he exists!' cried Dostoyevsky, *at the height of exaltation*. At that very moment, the bells of the nearby church rang out for the Easter morning service. The air began to shake and dance.

'And I had the feeling,' he continued, 'that the sky had come down to earth and swallowed me up. I apprehended God in reality and I was absorbed by him. I cried out once more: Yes, God exists! *I remember nothing more*.

You, you healthy people, you cannot even guess *what such happiness is, the happiness that we epileptics feel a second before the fit*. Mahomet says, in the Koran, that he saw *Paradise*. All the intelligent imbeciles are convinced that *of life, perhaps even one's whole life* in exchange for a few seconds of such *felicity.'*[132]

he is only a liar and a charlatan. But no, he is not lying! He really was in Paradise when he had an epileptic fit, because he was affected in the same way as I am. I could not say whether this *felicity* lasts a few seconds, hours or months, *but believe me, I would not exchange it for all the joys in this world.'*[133]

This violent ecstasy, so well described in *The Idiot*, the summit of Dostoyevsky's epileptic experience, should not let us forget the terrible consequences of each fit. Every one was a shipwreck of the whole being: physical, sensory, intellectual, emotional and moral. The following day was always a painful reconstruction of the body, of awareness, mind and soul: Dostoyevsky had to relearn perception, speech, writing and memory, and to drive away the black mood and mystical terror, 'fantasy' as he called it in his notes. He had to master his irritability and free himself from the terrible feeling of guilt, the impression that he had deliberately lost and buried the dearest creature in the world.[134] In the fits cited above, Dostoyevsky noted with precision the disturbing symptoms characteristic of the obsessive cloudy state after the fit. The notes of 1870 are still more revealing:

13 JANUARY; Strong fit after an imprudence about 6 o'clock in the morning[135] ... It is the *fifth day* after the fit and my head is still not clear.

19 JANUARY. Fit at six o'clock in the morning ... Headache, whole body aching. N.B. In general, the consequences of the fit, i.e. *nervousness, faulty memory, a state of the haziest and somehow contemplative*, go on longer than in earlier years ... In the evening, especially *by candle light, pointless hypochondriacal sadness, pointless and as it were a red bleeding (not a colour) halo over everything! Impossible to work on these days* (I am noting this observation *on the sixth day* after the fit).

10 FEBRUARY. At three o'clock in the morning a fit of extreme violence, in the lobby, while awake. Fall and wound on the forehead. Without remembering anything and without being aware of it, I carried the lighted candle in a perfect state into the bedroom, closed the window and only guessed later that I had had a fit ... I was beginning to calm down when I suddenly had another fit ... When I regained consciousness I had a horrible headache and was unable to speak properly for a long time. Anya spent the night with me (*Extreme mystic terror*) ... *Impossible to think of work; profound hypochondria during the night* ...

23 FEBRUARY. Fit during sleep, I had just gone to bed at ten past five in the morning ... weak ... although the consequences of the fits (that is, *heaviness and even pain in the head, nervous disturbance, nervous laugh and mystic terror*) last longer than before ...
Sleep with *dreams not always agreeable.*

1870, MAY. Fit in a waking state, after twenty-four hours of travelling in

Homburg ... At the hotel, in my bedroom, I felt the attack and fell. Without harm, I simply bruised the nape of my neck, the swelling remained for a good week. When I became conscious, *I didn't fully recover my senses for a long time* and I remember I paced all around the hotel and talked about my fit to everyone I met, among others the hotel-owner ... Strong fit *mystic sadness and nervous laugh.*

1870, 13 JULY. Fit while sleeping, morning ... *Anguish* ...

25 JULY. A fit in the morning when I had just gone to sleep. Before, terrible shudderings. The evening before, imprudence.

28 JULY. A fit while sleeping, in the morning, at a few minutes past eight ... Very strong afflux of blood to the head, the face had gone blue. It is *the 3rd of August already* and my head is still not clear. *State of mind very sad.* On the 1st of August I *did something stupid* in the study. I definitely attribute it to my state after the fit.[136]

After reading the tragic chronicle of these fits, it is hardly possible to feel that Dostoyevsky owed even a part of his genius to the sacred illness. It was a curse which decimated his intellectual faculties, at least during and after the fits,[137] exhausted him, and sapped his memory to the point where he admitted, in 1876, that he had 'literally and without exaggeration forgotten all the subjects and characters of his previous novels, even of *Crime and Punishment*';[138] it changed his work into 'torture',[139] often forcing him to write in a state of irritability, sadness, anguish and even mystic terror. Dostoyevsky, like Flaubert and Van Gogh, who suffered from the same illness, was a genius despite and in spite of epilepsy.

Creative energy

If psychosis, epilepsy or other illnesses were a frequent obstacle to creation, this was only temporary. As soon as he could, Dostoyevsky began to fight back. His reaction to storm and shipwreck – illness, obsessive gambling, debts, mourning, overwork – was a burst of energy, a leap towards life. His whole existence was a perpetual resurrection, and his sun and water of spiritual rejoicing were literature and his faith in his vocation as a poet. The tragic chronicle is echoed by the creative life.

He was just recovering from his first literary disappointments when he wrote on 26 November 1846 to Mikhail: 'Brother, I am reborn not only morally, but physically too. Never have I had so much abundance and farsightedness, so much evenness of character and physical health.'[140] Imprisoned in the Peter-Paul fortress, on 14 September he wrote: 'I expected much worse, but now I see there is so much vitality stored inside me that it can never be exhausted.'[141] About two months later there was the mock execution, the departure as a convict for Siberia, the beginning of madness for others; but Dostoyevsky met it with a hymn to life. He wrote to Mikhail on 22 December 1849:

Brother, I have not lost courage. Life is life everywhere, life is in us, and not in the world outside. There will be people near me, and to be a human being among other human beings and always remain human, in whatever misfortunes there may be, not to despair and not to fall, this is what life is, this is its aim. I have realised this. This idea has entered my flesh and blood. Yes, it is the truth![142]

The paragraph ends with a sentence taken from Hugo's *Le Dernier Jour d'un condamné*: '*On voit le soleil!*' The only worry which crossed the mind of the man who had been spared from execution at the last minute is that he might not be able to create:

Is it possible that I shall never more take a pen in my hands? I think after four years it will be possible. My God! How many images, lived, created by me anew, will perish, die out in my head, or turn to poison in my blood! Yes, if I cannot write, I shall perish. Rather fifteen years of prison, and a pen in my hand.[143]

And a cry of hope: 'Life is a gift, life is happiness; each moment could be a century of happiness. *Si jeunesse savait!* Now, changing my life, I am being reborn in a new form.'[144]

To the fear expressed in the same letter: 'Will my body stand it?' fate replied by the change from latent epilepsy to great generalised fits. Dostoyevsky survived this, went back to Russia, and won back his place as a writer, at the price of superhuman labour and thanks to his talent. The terrible year 1864, with its trail of catastrophes and unsurmountable tasks, should have struck him down, but he regained his forces and summed up on 31 March 1865, writing to Vrangel: 'From all the reserves of my strength and energy there remains in my soul something troubled and vaguely anxious, close to despair ... However, it still seems to me that I am just beginning to live. It's funny, isn't it? As many lives as a cat.'[145] In 1873, asked by 'Madame Olga Koslow' to write in her album, which contained notes by many famous names, he tried[146] to formulate his credo:

In spite of all losses, I love life ardently, I love life for life's sake, and seriously, I am still getting ready to *begin* my life. I will soon be fifty and I still cannot really make out if I am finishing my life or only just beginning it. This is the principal trait of my character, perhaps of my activity as well.[147]

This, which he repeated in 1876 to his brother Andrey,[148] was not a simple profession of faith, it was also confidence in his work. Rash as it might be, this serene projection into the future showed the will and assurance of a creator who moved in time as if he had eternity at his disposal. So on 24 December 1877, about two years before he died, Dostoyevsky sketched an ambitious programme:

Memento for my whole life.
1 Write a Russian Candide.
2 Write a work on Jesus Christ.

3 Write my memoirs.
4 Write a long poem *The Fortieth Day* [Prayer for the Dead]
(The whole without counting the last novel and the publication already envisaged of the Diary, so a minimum of ten years of work, now I am 56).[149]

And on 8 November 1880, sending off the last pages of *The Brothers Karamazov*, he wrote to his correspondent: 'Allow me not to say good-bye to you. I intend to live and write for twenty more years.'[150]

Given Dostoyevsky's spiritual energy and creative health in the face of the epilepsy which was an undoubted handicap to his creativity, it is manifestly wrong to postulate a causal connection between his illness and his genius.

Epilepsy and creation

Illness in its many aspects played a part in Dostoyevsky's creation. But it did not form or determine genius: his genius, like Midas, exerted its amazing power of changing everything it touched.

The effects of epilepsy on Dostoyevsky's creation may be dealt with in three chronological periods. The first, which ended with the appearance, in convict prison, of generalised epileptic fits, was that of creative interrogation faced with the fact of illness. It was an anxious time, marked by exploration in various directions in the field of literature. In the second phase, culminating in *The Idiot*, epilepsy was accepted and used in the novels. In the last, announced in *Notes from Underground* but especially clear after *The Devils*, the pathological as such was eradicated, dissolved in a psychology which goes beyond the distinction between healthy and unhealthy.

With *Poor Folk* and *The Double*, which are in the same social vein although the choices of form are different, Dostoyevsky revolutionised his approach to the mystery of man and made a daring synthesis between the 'Inspirers of the Ideal' and the 'Promethean' writers. Beginning with the precarious balance between inner and outer worlds, mentioned by Dostoyevsky in his letter to Mikhail, the hero himself discovers what may be called the *dialectic of desire* and its tragic or grotesque dimensions. Torn between the desire to change, socially, emotionally, or even aesthetically, and the compulsion (inner as well as outer) to renounce his desire, the creature suffers, struggles, mutilates and sometimes destroys himself. There is no doubt that this tragedy has a social basis, an unjust society defined historically, as Belinsky, Dobrolyubov and Soviet critics think. It is probable that there were other psychological compulsions, reflections of the heavy taboos of Dostoyevsky himself. But from the beginning Dostoyevsky set the problem in more philosophic and universal terms: man is defined by the tragic dialectic of desire. This is the unforeseen, the unknowable and indeterminable factor which preserves life in the fixed and castrating social group. It forms the unity of Dostoyevsky's thought from Devushkin and Golyadkin to Versilov and Karamazov. In 1875, in a plan for a preface to *A Raw Youth*, Dostoyevsky revealed his pride in this:

I am the only one who has known how to clarify the tragedy of the underground man, which consists of suffering, self-punishment, the awareness of the best and the impossibility of reaching it and especially the clear conviction of these unfortunate men that the whole world is like this and so it is not worth the trouble of correcting oneself.[151]

The heroes of the years 1846–9 do not say that they are giving up, as the Underground man does, but they are brought to renunciation and, after anxious struggles, to madness or death. Like the 'Heautontimôrouménos' of Baudelaire, they are 'the wound and the knife', 'the slap and the cheek'.[152]

At this time, as we have seen, Dostoyevsky believed he was ill. Whether this was a schizoidal mental illness or early epileptic syndrome is not important; the writer believed his illness was a strange moral ailment, of nervous origin. His troubles worried, even tormented him, but at the same time he was observing them: hypochondria, irritability, nervous disorders, a sensation of dualism, a feeling that outside events and inner life were dissociated and, in consequence, that he was trapped in dreams or reverie. These morbid symptoms were perfect images of the tragic dialectic of desire, perfect paths for the exploration of human psychology. As Dostoyevsky had experienced them, they directed his imagination and kept it within bounds. Strange and violent, they grip the reader and hold his interest (*zanimatel'nost'*). Illness was not the master but the servant of the creative plan. It was valuable as an enlarging mirror, suggesting strongly marked and distinctive material. On the basis of what he experienced without being able to name it, Dostoyevsky suggested various hypotheses in the novels, constructed subjects, developed literary lines of pathological logic. At the beginning there is the observation of a morbid symptom, at the end, there is a tragic dénouement, sometimes equally morbid. Premises and conclusion draw an almost psychiatric landscape, but the centre of the novel remains the exploration, to exhaustion point, of the dialectic of desire in its most tragic form, the failure of the dream.

The Double is the best example. A psychiatrist would have a ready diagnosis for Golyadkin: schizophrenia, complicated by paranoia with erotomaniac delirium. The hero who suddenly discovers a plot and sees 'enemies', 'masks' and 'burning eyes' everywhere is a perfect example, with his twin, of the paranoic schema of persecutor and persecuted. His love for a person of high rank, normally inaccessible to him, Klara Olsufyevna, and the different stages of this love are undoubtedly erotomania; first he has a revelation of the love of the Object, the Object encourages him by a sign known only to him (the letter suggesting an elopement), then doubt appears and finally hatred for the Object, who has entered the general conspiracy against him. The ending confirms this analysis: Golyadkin is put in an asylum. Yet, beyond the psychiatric landscape, the intended fiction of the double made real, there is the 'normal' idea of the tragic dialectic of desire, of a double Golyadkin rather than the double of Golyadkin,[153] of the small Gogolian clerk, humiliated and crushed, who breaks every social barrier, and incarnates in his impertinent twin his own strategems, his own wish to rebel against a caste which is keeping him out. The renunciation is at the heart of the desire, and the hero, instead of destroying the universe, dissociates from himself and destroys himself. He frequently decides on an action and then 'suddenly', 'sharply' changes his mind, acting in a totally different way; this translates sometimes too schematically the non-transgression within transgression. The overwhelming dream cracks its fragile dwelling-place in the man and then leaves it, withered, with freedom aborted at birth. All Dostoyevsky's literary work until 1848 is imprisoned in this swamp of desire, both imperious and fatally powerless: every dream is shipwrecked, ripped open on the reef of the dreamer himself, who cracks under the shock. Illness is nothing more than a literary image of failure.

Prokharchin is another personification of failed desire: he dreams of riches and dies on the treasure hidden in his mattress, in complete destitution, that is, at the heart of renunciation of riches. With the type of the 'dreamer', whom Dostoyevsky sketches in 'The Petersburg Chronicle' of 1847, this is an analysis of the schizoid process, that is, the loss of vital contact with reality which leads to madness if it is not stopped. In 'The Landlady' the construction is more consciously artistic: there is a clash between two dreams: Ordynov painfully frees himself from his own dream, enters the morbid universe of the beautiful Katerina, who is trapped in a prison of guilt and self-punishment, and is then tossed out from it gasping on the edges of real life. 'A Weak Heart' (1848) is the culmination of this theme; the dream, even when realised against all expectations, kills. Vasya Shumkov goes mad because the will to renounce the desire was stronger than the desire. In 'White Nights' the desire is clothed in enchanting poetry, but the dream is once more abortive. Finally, a tragic failure in *Netochka Nezvanova*: Yefimov dies in a fit of delirium tremens because he desired genius without accepting the necessary servitude: patience in poverty, courage and work. This last case is apparently a lesson which the worried Dostoyevsky was giving to himself: illness and madness are the fate only of those who give up. The analysis of Yefimov's tragedy, made by his friend, B. – attacks of despair, excessive pride, irritated self-love, loneliness wounded by the jealousy and indifference of others[154] – traces the difficulties which Dostoyevsky himself experienced. It is also evidence of his certainty that he is not doomed to the same fate as Yefimov.

With this brief survey of the literature of 1845–9, we see what the creator has made of illness. Accepting its dark face, he has drawn strange and varied figures which go beyond the neurotic or psychotic to illuminate the depths of the human mystery common to both pathological and normal experience: the tragic dialectic of desire. Facing his nameless illness, he has also tamed it and made it an integral part of his creation.

Moreover, and this is perhaps the only point where creation adapted itself to illness, Dostoyevsky asserted that he wrote better in the state of tension caused by his nervousness. In a letter of 27 August where he told Mikhail of his discomfort, his impressionability, his morbid dreams and a sensation of pitching on his bed, he added: 'From all this I conclude that my nerves are upset. When this sort of nervous time came on me before, I used it to write: in this state you can always write better and more.'[155] He confirmed this admission in *The Insulted and Injured*, where Ivan Petrovich replies to Natasha, who asks if he has hurried too much and spoilt the novel: 'What can I do about it? Besides, it doesn't matter. With concentrated work like this, a sort of particular irritation of the nerves comes over me; I think more clearly, I feel more vividly and more deeply and even the style obeys me completely, so in this very concentrated work it comes out better.'[156] In fact creation is a protection against illness: specialists in epilepsy agree that intellectual stimulus prevents the appearance of epileptic fits.[157] The mention of style is another argument against Dostoyevsky's schizophrenia. F. Minkowska, studying Rorschach tests and children's drawings, has shown that the personality of schizophrenics is 'vague, without relief and contrast' while that of epileptics is 'strongly defined, with strong relief and strong colours'.[158]

However, from this time on, the neurologist may find conduct and behaviour in some of Dostoyevsky's heroes which some specialists in epilepsy, though not all, connect with epilepsy and especially with the states after the fits: illusions of *déjà vu*[159] ('faces, events long forgotten'), of having heard something before ('themes from stupid songs pursued him') in Golyadkin;[160] the mechanical walks of Ordynov, who wanders distracted and unconscious through the streets,[161] his mechanical tidying activity repeated 'for the hundredth time', accompanied by a 'sort of painful and sickly oblivion',[162] the dreamy states. But these take place in the context of behaviour which is experienced by the hero and conceived by the writer as psychotic rather than epileptic.

There remains the troubling case of Murin, who, before Ordynov's eyes, is struck down by a generalised case of epilepsy; first the 'harsh, almost inhuman shout', then the tonoclonic symptoms: 'Murin lay on the floor; he was jarred by convulsions, his face was distorted with pain, and foam appeared on his twisted lips. Ordynov guessed that the unhappy man was in the grip of a violent epileptic fit.'[163] 'The Landlady', written in 1847, does not prove that Dostoyevsky already knew he was epileptic. The description is classic and occurred in several other novels of the time, for example, those of Eugène Sue, who was not an epileptic. More probably Dostoyevsky had already had, as Yanovsky asserts, an experience of epilepsy which he did not recognise as such and which he compared with what he read in medical textbooks lent by his friend. Unconsciously, he repressed it, relegating it in his creation to the black arsenal of mysticism and sorcery surrounding Murin. Here Dostoyevsky is at one with common sense and tradition, which are repelled and horrified by the Sacred Illness. This is the one exception, revealing deliberate blindness, a repressed admission.

Once epilepsy was diagnosed, his attitude changed. From 1860 onwards, with increasing serenity, he made it part of his creative material, an involuntary experience which he was to use in its essence, its dramatic effects and revelations. *The Insulted and Injured* shows this transition. As before prison, Dostoyevsky borrowed one of the symptoms from the post-critical state of epilepsy, fully aware of it but without naming it. The autobiographical confession is clear, even if it is attributed to Ivan Petrovich:

Whether it was from the disturbance of my nerves, from new impressions in a new flat, from my recent melancholy perhaps, but little by little and gradually, from the very beginning of dusk, I began to fall into the state of mind which so often comes to me now, in my illness, at nights, and which I call *mystic horror*. This is the heaviest, most painful fear of something, which I myself cannot define ... This fear usually grows stronger and stronger, in spite of any arguments of reason, so that finally the intelligence, although it acquires, in these minutes, perhaps, even more clearness, nevertheless is deprived of any capacity to stand out against these sensations. It is not heeded, it becomes useless, and this doubling makes the terrifying anguish of waiting even stronger.[164]

But Dostoyevsky also created for the first time an epileptic heroine, Nelli. Three fits are described, rapidly, in two or three lines.[165] In the second, Dostoyevsky paid particular attention to the stage after a fit: inability to speak, intolerable distress and anguish. But the main point was the dramatic effect: the epileptic fit was the culmination of an artistic orchestration which is not morbid. Nelli's final epileptic fit, for example, was combined with the other elements, with the storm, the growing darkness, the poignant intensity of her last confession, which all marked the rise of emotion.

In *The Idiot* epilepsy is described with striking clinical realism which often repeats, word for word, the observations of the author and the evidence of Anna and Strakhov. The awareness of the hero dictates the method of description. Prodromata and sequels are described from inside by the sufferer, Myshkin: the tonoclonic fit is observed from outside by another person.

The familiar prodromata – extreme distraction, impossibility of concentrating and disappearance of the idea, confusion in seeing (objects and faces), anguish, oppression and suffocation (dramatised by the coming storm), disorganised walking around, impatience – are described at length in the pages preceding Rogozhin's attempt at murder and the explosion of the fit.[166]

Next the fit is described:

Then suddenly something seemed to gape open before him: an unusual *inner* light dawned on his soul. This moment lasted, perhaps, half a second; but he, however, clearly and consciously remembered the beginning, the very first sound of his terrible howl, which tore out of his breast of its own accord and which he could not have stopped by any force. Then his consciousness went out instantly and complete darkness fell.

He had had an epileptic fit . . . It is well known that attacks of epilepsy, in fact the true *falling sickness*, come in an instant. In this instant the face, especially the look, are suddenly extraordinarily distorted. Convulsions and shudders master the whole body and all the features of the face. A terrible, unimaginable wail, unlike anything else, tears out of the breast; in this wail everything human suddenly seems to disappear, and it is impossible, at least very difficult, for the spectator to imagine and admit that the man himself is shouting. It even looks as if some one else were shouting from inside this man.[167]

The sequels, as Myshkin sums them up, are a state of stupefaction, loss of memory, difficulty in thinking (logical course of mental activity interrupted, inability 'to link more than two or three ideas together in sequence'), intolerable sadness.[168] All this is commonplace and has been described many times.

But the writer had become more daring: epilepsy was made part of a bolder orchestration and given a significance which had nothing in common with the pathological. Myshkin's walking is not as disordered as it seems; it is because he is unconsciously drawn between two impulses that he seems to wander, hesitate, return and set out again, first, to go to see Nastasya Filippovna, about whom he feels guilty, and second to escape the immediate danger, whose obscure face is symbolised by the two eyes spying on him and the object with the deer-horn handle which fascinates him in the window of a cutlery shop. The morbid anguish is experienced as the premonition of a crime – Rogozhin is there, lurking in the shadows, with his knife. The pathological becomes a dramatic means of slowing down the final realisation and the theatrical effect. The tension is increased by the sudden explosion of the storm (an effect already used) and the redoubled darkness of the clouds, the hotel corridor and the niche where Rogozhin is hiding. The epileptic collapse, linked to the murder attempt, is vividly dramatic: the body of the prince, agitated by 'convulsions, pulsations and spasms', falls down the fifteen steps of the staircase, and a pool of blood forms round his head.

The whole orchestration, the significance given to the episode reveal the metamorphosing power of Dostoyevsky's genius and set epilepsy in a framework of normality. They may also lead us to think that Myshkin's analysis of the strange aura which he has the privilege of experiencing, one second before the fit, is a construction after the event by Myshkin himself, whose spirit is seeking 'a high synthesis of life', the Ideal of the Imitation of Christ. The hero's words reveal Dostoyevsky's conception of illness.

First, what does the aura consist of? The prince, with a prudence which is more restrained than the evidence given by Strakhov and Kovalevskaya, tries to work it out by waves of Proustian elucidation, creating a feeling of the inexpressible, the indescribable:

Amid the grief, the spiritual gloom, the pressure, at moments his soul seemed to catch fire and in an extraordinary surge of feeling all his vital forces were strained to the limit. The sensation of life, of self-knowledge became almost ten times greater in those moments, which were as long as lightning. Mind and heart glowed with an extraordinary light; all emotions, all his doubts, all anxieties seemed to calm down at once, to be resolved in a kind of higher peace, full of clear, harmonious joy and hope, full of reason and the final cause.

. . . flashes and gleams of a higher self-awareness and self-knowledge, and so of 'the highest state of being'.

. . . it is harmony and beauty in the highest degree, it gives a feeling, unheard of and unguessed until that point, of completeness, measure, tranquillity and ecstatic fusion in prayer with the highest synthesis of life . . .

. . . extraordinary increase in self-knowledge . . . and at the same time of self-awareness which is immediate to the highest degree.[169]

Myshkin realises that this happiness, this ecstasy which 'might be worth the whole of life'[170] – an echo of Dostoyevsky's own assertion – is probably only an 'illness', a 'disturbance' or one of those visions related to visions caused by 'hashish, opium or wine, degrading the reason and distorting the soul, abnormal and unreal'.[171] But since the aura is felt to be real, it does not matter if it is caused by illness. Myshkin's choice is clear: experience sanctions reality, which is primarily existential and makes no distinction between the pathological and the normal. The prince even admits that his conclusion and his judgement may be wrong: but the 'reality of sensation' makes him trust his visions.

This conviction, born from the piercing reality of the vision and tested in the crucible of the heart, is formed in the same way as Dostoyevsky formed his own convictions. If it is one of his fertile wagers such as 'Rather Christ than the truth if the truth is outside Christ', an examination of the link between illness and the transforming power of genius may not be the right approach. The epileptic aura may be a true gift of Heaven, a true revelatory ecstasy like the mystic illumination reached through asceticism[172] or it may be no more than a sensation of vertigo rationalised after the event, like an elevation or assumption.[173] Possibly it was Dostoyevsky's secret inclination towards themes of universal harmony, eternity, God, which gave the aura its feeling of happiness and joy. In short, Dostoyevsky may have mytholo-gised the aura so as to experience a transcendence which he could not reach by other means.

We may remember, since Dostoyevsky invoked the ghost of De Quincey by mentioning opium, the witticism in *The Opium-Eater*: 'If a man "whose talk is of oxen" should become an opium eater, the probability is, that (if he be not too dull to dream at all) he will dream about oxen.'[174] Dostoyevsky was always talking of universal harmony, the Age of Gold, paradise on earth, Christ and God in his works. In this case, the epileptic aura would be only one of numerous paths leading to a universe of love and harmony, although one of a rare quality. Moreover, only Myshkin among Dos-toyevsky's epileptics was granted the experience of this singular aura; the others only know the dark face of epilepsy: Murin in 'The Landlady', Nelli in *The Insulted and Injured*, Smerdyakov in *The Brothers Karamazov*, who even illustrates one of the blackest symptoms of the illness: suicide during a fit.

But paradoxically, the non-epileptic characters who by one means or another have the same revelation as Myshkin's, either in a pure halluci-nation (the dream of the Golden Age), like Stavrogin in *The Devils*, Versilov in *A Raw Youth*, the hero of 'The Dream of a Ridiculous Man', or by an existential feeling of eternity like Kirillov in *The Devils*, all have a sickly constitution, or even, in the case of Stavrogin and Kirillov, a tendency to epilepsy.

We would tend to agree with Myshkin. Whatever the scientific truth may be about the reality of the epileptic aura, Dostoyevsky was convinced that he experienced it as a form of intuitive and privileged awareness of divine or universal harmony. If there has been mythologisation, the metamorphosis has been repressed and faith has taken its place.

The revelation given by the epileptic aura made Dostoyevsky clearly aware of something he had been using subconsciously in his earlier works: this was not so much the idea, already formulated by De Quincey and Hoffmann, that illness was useful for exploring the human mind, but an awareness of the way in which sickness and health are entwined in real life. In the name of realism, as opposed to tradition, he refused to accept the reassuring fictional convention that sickness should be relegated or dis-counted. His systematic paradoxes can even be annoying; why must the sombre Svidrigaylov, Stavrogin, Lambert and Versilov be handsome and strong, with arrogant health and a colour which is 'too' vivid, while the more virtuous Raskolnikov, Myshkin, Stepan Trofimovich, Mariya Timofe-yevna, Tikhon, Makar Dolgoruky, and Zosima are condemned to ruined health or even terrible illnesses. Dostoyevsky's rage against the arrogant appearance of health (in fact Svidrigaylov has hallucinations, and so does Stavrogin, besides attacks of fever) was iconoclastic; health is sometimes simply a mask. The Underground man knows this perfectly well; he chooses illness to increase his self-awareness. Dostoyevsky's daring, at least in his time, was to assert that pathological symptoms, if they are truly experienced, reveal the tragic dialectic of desire, which is the basic structure of the normal man, more reliably than the healthy state does. Let us recall Svidrigaylov, a man of insolent health. However, simply from hearing the rustle of Dunya's dress,[175] he fears he may become epileptic and sees once more, fully awake, his late wife, whom he has undoubtedly killed, coming to talk nonsense to him. He is at the opposite extreme to Myshkin, and yet he reasons as Myshkin does: 'I agree that visions appear only to sick people; but surely this only proves that visions can appear in no way except to sick people, and not that they do not exist in themselves.'[176] And a few lines later, he makes an analysis:

Visions – they are, so to speak, rags and tatters of other worlds, their beginning. A healthy man has obviously no reason to see them, because a healthy man is the most earthly of men, and so must live only an earthly life, for the sake of completion and orderliness. But as soon as he falls ill, as soon as the normal earthly order in the organism is disturbed, the possibility of another world appears, and the iller he is, the more contact there is with the other world.[177]

Illness is, 'like everything which goes beyond the bounds' (to use another of Svidrigaylov's expressions) a passage beyond everyday life to reach another reality, another side of the human mystery. The contrast between normal and abnormal disappears, to be replaced by the complementarity of normal and supernormal,[178] not because Dostoyevsky celebrated illness, but because he accepted it.

In contrast with the opium dreams of De Quincey, the voluntary asceticism of St John of the Cross, the pure psychic automatism of André Breton, the mescalin of Henri Michaux, Dostoyevsky did not choose to be epileptic. It was a fact with which he had to come to terms. If the aura is the lightning flash which reveals another world, this does not lessen the violence and darkness of the storm. But the supreme virtue of the creator was that he took some features from the violent storm and from epilepsy in general for use in his work. From *The Devils* onwards, he moved to what we have called 'eradication of the pathological'. This is shown by the description of the behaviour of the heroes: basically epileptic according to some analysts, but given a different psychological, dramatic and philosophical significance by the novelist. The shift began with *The Idiot*, where epilepsy is only one voice in the dramatic orchestration, but a voice which is always recognisable. After this novel, epilepsy was always invited to take part in the action, but asked to remain anonymous: it became the masked servant of the true creative plan.

The strange behaviour of Stavrogin is a perfect illustration of this. We recall his first impertinence before going abroad. Without any warning 'in an almost dreamy way', 'as if he were going mad', he gripped the nose of the respectable Pyotr Pavlovich Gaganov, a habitué of the club, who had an innocent habit of saying excitedly that he wouldn't be led about 'by the nose' and pulled him along for two or three steps in this uncomfortable position.[179] When Mrs Liputina had her birthday, he kissed the pretty creature 'on the lips, three times in a row, long and voluptuously', without reason, unexpectedly and in the presence of her husband.[180] Finally, on the pretext of whispering in the ear of his kinsman, the governor Ivan Osipovich, the reasons which had made him attack Gaganov, he suddenly gripped the upper lobe of the unfortunate man's ear between his teeth and savagely bit it.[181] This incongruous behaviour might be seen as a symptom of epileptic fury (or *raptus*). The hypothesis becomes more plausible since, after this scandal, Stavrogin has an attack of fever. But there is never any question of epilepsy. The victims suspect that Stavrogin is perfectly well aware of what he was doing. The chronicler maintains the mood of burlesque and ambiguity, stressing only two points: the savagery of the act, the 'rapacious' sensual side of the character – 'And suddenly the wild beast showed his claws', he repeats – and the taste for scandal, the slap in the face of society. Dostoyevsky's aim was to create a halo of mystery around Stavrogin from the very first. His notebooks tell us 'The prince does not reveal himself to anyone and everywhere mysteriously',[182] or 'The prince reveals himself gradually in action and without any explanation.'[183] The more unusual, unexpected, even ridiculous his conduct is, the more disturbing it is to the imagination. This was the creative line, the 'tone', as Dostoyevsky says, which a masked epilepsy helped to create. There is another moment, in *The Devils*, of a pathological nature. Stavrogin's mother Varvara Petrovna surprises him sitting and asleep:

It seemed to amaze her, as it were, that he had fallen asleep so quickly and that he could sleep like that, sitting so straight and so motionless: even his breathing was almost unnoticeable. His face was pale and stern, but seemed to be completely frozen, motionless; his brows were slightly bent and frowning; decidedly, he looked like a soulless wax figure. She stood over him for about three minutes, hardly breathing, and suddenly fear seized her . . . He slept for a long time, more than an hour, and still with the same rigidity; not a single muscle of his face moved, nor did the slightest movement appear in the whole of his body; his brows were still just as sternly bent. If Varvara Petrovna had remained for three more minutes, then probably she could not have borne the stifling sensation of this lethargic immobility and would have woken him. But he suddenly opened his eyes himself, and, motionless as before, sat on for about ten minutes, seeming to be gazing obstinately and curiously at some object which had caught his attention in the corner of the room, although there was nothing there either new or particular.[184]

A neurologist might see this as the *dreamy state* described by Jackson, but again Dostoyevsky abstained from all reference to the pathological. His aim was to arouse fear and horror by a fantastic scene, deliberately unexplained, and to suggest – which is not at all the case in the epileptic dreamy state – the immense cerebral gestation of Stavrogin, a monster of intelligence; he too is wrestling with the tragic dialectic of desire, but he carries out his struggle through other people.

Basically, Dostoyevsky had rediscovered his method of using illness in the earlier works. But between *The Double* and the last novels he passed from ignorance to awareness, from the mask imposed by lack of knowledge to the mask deliberately chosen.

The contribution of epilepsy to the structure of the novels is more difficult to grasp: creation took place outside and in spite of fits. When the fit passed, another, normal life began again; the intellectual faculties were reborn intact, except possibly for memory. However the precise description of the generalised fits makes one wonder. After his usual night of work, from ten or eleven at night to five o'clock in the morning, Dostoyevsky sometimes had a fit at about five or eight in the morning. After the storm had passed, he struggled against exhaustion, the confusion and the flight of ideas, taking from three to eight painful days to toil up the slope once more. The hours preceding the fit of which he was still unaware, the hours of anxiety, sometimes of terror, always of feverish nervousness, during which he was working, those other hours between the crushing stage after the fit and the gradual recovery of complete creative freedom, during which he was still working, must have had some effect on the writing of the novels. Although the part played by epilepsy is never decisive, there is still the matter of convergence, of appropriateness, or orchestration, and epilepsy must have had an effect on some forms such as colouring, time-scheme, composition and even style.

Red on a black background is the dominant colouring of *The Devils*, with rare notes of yellow, pale green, white and gold. As always with Dostoyevsky, the connotations are varied and numerous. A number of scenes are nocturnal, and Russia sinks into the nihilist shadows. Blood flows and the red of the revolutionary Apocalypse invades the picture. It is the red tie of Stepan Trofimovich – 'What a red idea!' cries Varvara Petrovna – the name of Karmazinov, formed from the root 'crimson', the red spider of Stavrogin's dream, the reddening blaze of the fire against the black night, the pool of blood in which the Lebyadkins lie, the large red box of matches belonging to Kirillov, the wardrobe splashed with his blood, etc. The night bursting into stains of blood is the hell of crime, Revolution and Satan; this was undoubtedly the original symbolism. But the effect was experienced by Dostoyevsky himself when he observed, in the notebooks for *The Devils*, on the sixth day after the fit of 19 January 1870, that in the evening, especially by candle light, he was overcome by hypochondriac melancholy and that he saw 'a kind of red halo, bleeding (not a tint) over everything'. But this may be only a subconscious convergence between his experience of illness and the use of colour in the novel, since these colours have a political and spiritual significance also found in Gogol and Andrey Bely.[185]

There is a clear connection with the odd structure of time suggested by the epileptic aura. Dostoyevsky himself talked of the indescribable happiness which he felt during the aura, which was accompanied by a half-mystical experience of time: accession to eternity, physically experienced. In *The Idiot*, when Prince Myshkin is talking to Rogozhin, he comments on this feeling of eternity, using the Koran and Revelation to make his point: 'At that moment I have the impression that I understand the strange sentence, that "there should be time no longer."'[186] 'Probably', he added smiling, 'it was the very second in which the overturned water jug of the epileptic Mahomet[187] did not spill a single drop, though in that second Mahomet visited all the dwelling places of Allah.'[188] Eternity is experienced as past, present and future united in a single moment, and as the annunciation of a resurrection of the whole being, a renewal, and an eternal return to the innocence of morning. Strangely, the feeling given by the aura was more convincing than the idea itself. When, in 1864, Dostoyevsky was meditating by the body of Mariya Dmitriyevna about the life to come, he used the same expression from Revelation: 'There should be time no longer', but he could only persuade himself that Eternity existed by taking Christ as a mediator.[189] The great virtue of the aura was that it replaced discursive adherence by spontaneous faith. In 1847, when epilepsy, though present, was not experienced as such, Dostoyevsky gave Ordynov, the hero of 'The Landlady', this feeling of eternity which regenerates existence. The young man is delirious:

Sometimes moments of unbearable, annihilating happiness flashed by, a moment when the vital force convulsively increases in the whole human frame, when the past becomes clear, the present moment of light rings with triumph and gaiety, and the unknown future is like a waking dream: when inexpressible hope falls like a reviving spring on the soul; when you want to shout with ecstasy; when you feel that flesh is powerless against this weight of impressions, that the whole thread of existence is being torn apart, and when at the same time you are celebrating the renewal and resurrection of your whole life.[190]

We are in the presence of a true psychic aura which dare not say its name and which as yet has no religious content.[191] In *The Devils*, Dostoyevsky strengthened this link between the feeling of eternity and the idea of renewal, even of physical change in man, in a speech by Kirillov, the atheist who dreams of imitating Christ. The epileptic aura is invoked, but its temporal structure is detached from the symptoms of illness:

There are some seconds, just five or six of them come at a time, and you suddenly feel the presence of eternal harmony, perfectly attained. It is not an earthly feeling; I am not saying it is heavenly, but just that a person in earthly form cannot bear it. You have to change physically or die. It is a clear and indisputable feeling ... It's not as if you love, oh – this is higher than love! The most terrifying thing is that it's so horribly clear and such joy. If it were more than five seconds, the soul couldn't stand it and would have to disappear. In these five seconds I live through a lifetime and for them I would give my whole life, because it is worth it. To stand ten seconds, you would have to change physically.[192]

Kirillov uses a free quotation from the Gospel to make his point about harmony attained: 'in the resurrection they will not give birth, but will live like the angels of God.'[193] Shatov, the Christian, counters with the materialist suggestion that this feeling is caused by epilepsy, taking up the image of the Koran:

An epileptic once described to me in detail this feeling before the fit, exactly like you; he specified five seconds as well and said that it was impossible to bear any more. Do you remember Mahomet's jug, which did not have time to spill while he flew on his horse through the whole of paradise? The jug is those five seconds: it is too like your harmony, and Mahomet was an epileptic.[194]

Kirillov tells Shatov jokingly he will have no time to get epilepsy, that is, that he is not epileptic. This reversal of connotations previously established in *The Idiot*, this deliberate paradox, is almost a confession of the principle of creation; yes, the feeling of eternity (though not the idea) comes from the psychic aura, and for me it assumes a religious colouring, but in this case I am making it an independent phenomenon, felt by an atheist who is not ill. The origins are obscured; only the reality of revelation counts.

It is always rash to track down the biological side of an author, to delve into his personal mythology and it is still rasher to gauge the part played by pathological experiences in the formation of style and composition. But since these are, to plagiarise Roland Barthes, 'an equation between literary intention and the bodily structure of the author', it may be allowable in this case, especially as Dostoyevsky admitted that he often wrote in a state of nervous tension.

Without giving a detailed analysis, we may note that composition and style in Dostoyevsky are marked by a violent and convulsive impetus, which appears miraculously theatrical to some people while to others it is simply excessive. The style is immediately striking: Dostoyevsky overwhelms the reader by his analytic clarity and psychological frenzy. Euphemisms and diminutives (especially before 1849), repetitive adjectives meaning almost the same thing, superlatives, intriguing approximations, disturbing adverbs (suddenly, sharply, too much), triple repetition of words formed from the same root, particularly characteristic of *Notes from Underground*, all these elements show a kind of rage in the writer, an obsession with the idea, which is turned in all directions and explored to the point of exhaustion, a wish to compel, almost to bully the reader into adherence.

On a higher scale, the composition reflects the same fever. In the great novels the action rises in a serrated curve. There are long dead times of shadow, the stages in which the event is prepared, conflicts are established and the voice of the hero is swallowed up in the secret mysterious voices of the crowd. These are followed by violent convulsions which suddenly burst into dramatic storms and culminate in echoing sonorous explosions. Certainly the feverish incandescence of the verb, the brutal discharge of the action in scenes of high tension is not merely a mimicry of the epileptic storm in writing, but their violent and convulsive tenor indicates that the writer had a secret inclination for the *noble* form of excess: aesthetic excess which is a metaphor for 'what goes beyond bounds' and so weighs heavier and penetrates more deeply. It is the *explosion* which reveals the truth.[195] It is interesting that another creator, also epileptic, should mention Dostoyevsky when stressing the close connection between excess and profundity. This is what Van Gogh writes to his dear Theo, on 10 September 1888: 'The idea of the "Sower" continues to haunt me all the time. Exaggerated studies like the "Sower", and like this "Night Café" usually seem to me atrociously ugly and bad, but when I am moved by something, as now by this little article on Dostoyevsky, then these are the only ones which appear to have any deep meaning.'[196] This is one of the rare cases which might be thought to show the 'colouring' given to the work by illness. But this is again only a secondary matter: the creative choice is the important thing.

To conclude; from epilepsy, a sinister black column rising across his creative path, Dostoyevsky retained and used only the parts which were consubstantial with his genius, except perhaps for the strange revelation of the psychic aura. And in this case, like Perseus seizing the single eye of the Graiae, he took from his blind aggressor the power of experiencing eternity.

Diagnosis of neurologists: renewed polemics

According to Professor Alajouanine, a neurologist, Dostoyevsky's descriptions of epilepsy are exceptional: 'Few doctors would be capable, without personal experience, of describing these fits in a way which combines the precision of certain details and the vagueness of their succession with that blurred image of the background which is characteristic of the memory which some epileptics have of their fits.'[197] On the basis of all these descriptions by Dostoyevsky and by his epileptic heroes, the professor concluded: 'There is no doubt that Dostoyevsky suffered from an organic illness: an epilepsy with rich and varied symptoms giving evidence of a cerebral process whose most notable symptomatology may be placed in the context of temporal epilepsy.'[198] He even said that Dostoyevsky, due to his introspective genius, was the first to describe temporal lobe epilepsy, even before neurologists were aware that this illness existed.[199] He has analysed the evidence of the man and his friends and relations together with the use of epilepsy in the novels, and summed up his diagnosis as follows: temporal epilepsy

contains, given the structural and functional importance of the temporal lobes, varied elements (sensorial and psycho-sensorial disturbances; auditive, visual or olfacto-gustative disturbances, language disturbances for the left lobe, unconscious or hallucinatory psycho-motor activities, affective perturbations, among others); the expression of these more or less dissociated and variable disturbances gives this type of epilepsy a very variable appearance. We find several characteristic elements in Dostoyevsky's fits or those of his characters: sometimes in the form of an aura which precedes the great convulsive fit, sometimes as a phenomenon after the fit, sometimes isolated in an epileptic equivalent not ending in convulsions. So we find notes and descriptions of psycho-motor activity and the activity of subconscious searching, walking around with an obsessive idea, impressions of *déjà vu*, hallucinations which develop like films, hallucinatory activities and dreamy states in the fog of half-consciousness, all of which feature in various works.'[200]

After an attack on the error of Freud, who denied the organic nature of Dostoyevsky's epilepsy, since he thought that the psycho-affective disturbances characteristic of temporal fits were hysterical symptoms, Professor Alajouanine stressed the importance of one of these disturbances: 'The ecstatic aura is the most remarkable: it is also the most exceptional in its purity and the least well known, even to doctors.'[201]

In spite of this reservation, this diagnosis was commonly accepted by neurologists at the time when I was writing this chapter, but, due indirectly to this book, the scope of the arguments has increased. In fact, aware of my medical ignorance, I made a point of consulting specialists who were all passionately interested in Dostoyevsky, such as Professor Henri Gastaut, a specialist of international standing. At this time he shared the general opinion that Dostoyevsky suffered from psycho-motor or left temporal lobe epilepsy (complex partial seizure), a thesis he had defended for the past twenty-five years. The description I have given and the method I chose (a double distinction between the document and the experience, between the experience and the literary use of it) has made him change his diagnosis. This would have little importance in our consideration of the literature if Professor Gastaut had not questioned the scientific reality of the epileptic aura.

Gastaut's hypothesis does not modify my conclusions; it even confirms my position on the negative, rather than inspiring, role of epilepsy in literary creation; it changes nothing in my analysis of the experience of the illness and especially of the relationship between epilepsy and the novels. However it does stress the mythologising power of Dostoyevsky. It goes a step further than I would go; Dostoyevsky is thought to have invented the ecstatic aura and so led neurologists into error. This conclusion is outside my range of competence. If there has been mythologisation, it is completely unconscious: Dostoyevsky believed in his feeling and clung to it with all his being. His good faith may have deceived the good faith of neurologists and his persuasive genius may have played a trick on science.

Let us broadly summarise the thesis of Professor Gastaut:[202] Dostoyevsky did not suffer from organic epilepsy, secondary to a lesion of the temporal lobe, but from functional epilepsy, independent of any cerebral lesion: a primary generalised epilepsy, formerly called essential, idiopathic or genuine.

The arguments are as follows: the psycho-motor phenomena which occur in temporal lobe epilepsy before and during the fits always occurred in Dostoyevsky after the fits. Psycho-sensorial phenomena (illusion or hallucination) have never, or seldom, been noted in connection with his fits. The ecstatic aura, as distinct from confidences about it, is never mentioned in the notebooks, where, on the contrary, Dostoyevsky insisted on the brutally sudden appearance of his fits. None of the epileptic heroes of Dostoyevsky's novels show symptoms characteristic of 'temporal epilepsy': a number of symptoms which have been wrongly connected with it may be observed in psychopaths, neuropaths and even normal people (the sensation of *déjá vu*, for example).

However, there are many arguments in favour of a diagnosis of primary generalised epilepsy: a family predisposition to fits (unexpected death of one of Dostoyevsky's two sons from epilepsy, at three years old): the absence of any neurological sign of organic cerebral disease; the time of the fits (night, during first sleep) and especially the fact that some fits are preceded by trembling (massive bilateral myoclonia) and shaking. Gastaut concludes: 'I have no hesitation in saying that an epileptic who has had more than four hundred generalized convulsive fits in about forty years, without a single initial symptom which could be related to a focal electrical discharge, must be considered as suffering from generalised rather than partial epilepsy.'

The ecstatic aura which Dostoyevsky describes could be the specific but relatively ordinary psychic state he felt at the beginning of the few fits which occurred when he was awake, transformed and idealised by the metamorphosing power of his genius. The description given by Anna and Strakhov of his absentmindedness before the fits is evidence of this.

Developing his argument, Gastaut, after studying the medical literature devoted to the evolution of the aura through the ages, undertakes to show that there is no reference to a joyful aura, let alone an ecstatic one, from antiquity until the end of the nineteenth century (on the contrary, the aura is always based on fear and anguish);[203] secondly, doctors discovered Dostoyevsky's ecstatic aura at the beginning of the twentieth century, and considered it an exemplary and unique phenomenon impossible to generalise;[204] and finally the notion of a joyful and even ecstatic aura was erroneously added to the arsenal of medical semiology, influenced by the twentieth-century discovery of temporal lobe epilepsy (and Gastaut frankly confesses his own mistake).

6

Money

Superfluous money is much more important to me than necessary money.

Trishatov in *A Raw Youth*.[1]

Next to epilepsy, money is the ruling power in Dostoyevsky's creative environment. No writer has spent more time asking for money and no writer has hated money so much. The attitude of Dostoyevsky and his characters towards it is a perfect illustration of the tragic dialectic of desire: between creator and created there is only a difference of dramatisation. Money and Dostoyevsky, money in Dostoyevsky's works are themes which have been exhaustively researched,[2] so we shall give only a rapid summary. Two points deserve closer analysis: the part played in the act of creation by the need for money, so far nimbly eluded by critics, who see it only as a motivation, and the part money plays in the novels to reveal the human mystery.

Thirst for money

From his youth to the eve of his death, 26 January 1881, when he begged his editor to send him 400 roubles,[3] Dostoyevsky, as his letters show, never stopped asking for money. He had a complete repertory of approaches: from a timid request[4] to his father while he was a student, for money to buy boots, a chest and his own tea, to an insolent and violent attempt to obtain 1,000 silver roubles from his guardian, P. A. Karepin, in return for giving up part of his inheritance.[5] He turned with natural confidence to his brothers Andrey and Mikhail when he had no wood to keep himself warm and only a few kopecks to live on, and to his friends, Pleshcheyev, Vrangel and Maykov: he was humble to his fellow-writers, Turgenev, Herzen and Ogaryov, when he had ruined himself gambling abroad. He paid them back honestly when he was in funds, although sometimes a little late – on 24 December 1880 Pleshcheyev received the incomplete residue of a sum borrowed in 1859[6] – but as his account-books were badly kept, quarrels resulted. Turgenev, for instance, claimed that he had not been repaid fifty thalers lent in 1863. When it was a question of extracting 10,000 roubles from a rich aunt,[7] Dostoyevsky turned to strategy, a curious mixture of coarse frankness and psychological cunning. He used a lying and pardonable assurance – the work was never so far forward as he claimed – when he needed an advance from an editor. When, after one of his escapades in some 'Roulettenburg', he repented of having lost everything at the gambling tables and begged his young wife to pawn the family clothes and jewels, his approach was conscience-stricken and full of agony. He knew some desperate moments: for example, in Wiesbaden in 1865, after squandering all he had at roulette, he found himself confined in his hotel, penniless; he could not even buy a stamp, was deprived of candles, kept himself alive on tea and pretended, under the contemptuous gaze of German lackeys, to go and dine elsewhere between three and six, while for the rest of the time he forced himself to sit and read, so as not to whet his appetite.[8] These were brief moments, among thousands of others, in the eternal search for money reflected in his letters.

Solvency: the wager of the novel

However, Dostoyevsky was not at all like the former officer in several of his novels, correctly dressed and expressing himself with studied elegance, who collects money at street corners. He did not beg, and he denounced the sordid motives of the rich in giving charity. He borrowed with the assurance of someone perfectly creditworthy. As opposed to some of his heroes, who fall into the clutches of moneylenders only to postpone their inevitable doom, he offered a priceless guarantee: his literary production, his work. The whole difficulty was to transform this into coin of the realm. So if, by mischance, his friends Maykov, Milyukov and Strakhov, whom he trusted to cash in his works with the editors, failed, he did not worry too much.[9] It was simply one of the inconveniences of his job.

The precarious life of the proletarian writer who lives by his pen and risks his independence in order to exist is fairly familiar to readers: but the boldness of Dostoyevsky, who gambled on his future work by trying to sell an idea for a novel in advance, is less well known. He must have had great faith in his creative genius to risk so large a stake, at a time when there was no literary patronage, in a country where the writer was at the mercy of arbitrary censors and greedy editors, who might be incompetent like Krayevsky or sharks like Stellovsky, and where the public, at least initially, was limited and fluctuating, dependent on the fate of the magazines in which the novels and novellas appeared. But to this vital and exacting game Dostoyevsky brought stakes in which he had complete confidence and which made the martingales he thought necessary for roulette seem small by comparison: his name, doubly famous since *Poor Folk* and his transportation to Siberia, the unique quality of his subjects, the guarantee of his experience, his passion for the modern and newsworthy, and finally his extraordinary power to work.

He gambled on the black squares of the convict prison (*The House of the*

Dead), alcoholism and poverty (the first plan of 'The Drunkards', which became the Marmeladov plot in *Crime and Punishment*, the drama of Nelli in *The Insulted and Injured*), madness, disease and epilepsy (the works before his trial, *The Idiot*). He gambled on the red squares of crime (Raskolnikov, Rogozhin, *The Brothers Karamazov*), of bloody nihilist revolution (*The Devils*). He bet on the odd numbers of the mediation of the rival ('The Eternal Husband') or double paternity (*A Raw Youth*), of money and gambling (*A Raw Youth*, *The Gambler*). Finally he placed large bets on the even numbers of his ideal heroes, Myshkin, Tikhon, Makar the wanderer, Alyosha and Zosima.

Dostoyevsky played to win in literature. The letter of 9 October 1859 where he set out his plan to Mikhail is a perfect illustration:

These Notes from the House of the Dead have taken on a complete and definite plan in my head. It will be a little book of six or seven printed sheets. My personality will disappear. These are the notes of an unknown person; but, for interest, I can guarantee it. The interest will be enormous. There will be serious and gloomy parts, humour and folk language with the special convict colouring (I have read you some expressions, from those I noted *on the spot*), and the portrayal of individuals still *unheard-of* in literature, and touching parts, and finally, the main thing, my name . . . I am sure the public will read it greedily . . . Of the interest, I am as certain as I am of my own existence. Two thousand copies will be sold out in a year (even, I am convinced, in six months); let's suppose 1 rouble 25 – there's 2,000 roubles in a year. For the first time, money, and absolutely certain money![10]

When the work had appeared, and the success of *Time* was assured, he proudly told Strakhov: 'My name is worth a million!'[11] In 1863, planning to write *The Gambler*, he insisted in exactly the same way that he had a fascinating subject based on his own experience:

If The House of the Dead drew the attention of the public, as a portrayal of convicts, whom no one had described realistically until The House of the Dead, this story will be bound to draw attention as a realistic and most detailed description of the roulette game . . . It won't be bad at all. The House of the Dead was certainly curious. Now this will be the portrayal of a kind of hell, something like the 'bath-house' scene at the prison.[12]

Elsewhere Dostoyevsky stressed the newsworthiness of his subject. The letter of September 1865, where he set out to Katkov the Raskolnikov theme in *Crime and Punishment*, is full of significant phrases: 'The action is contemporary, this year, in fact', 'A young man . . . under the influence of some of these strange half-digested ideas which float around in the air', 'I have seen this even among backward people', 'A man of the new generation', 'Several cases occurring lately have convinced me that my subject is not at all eccentric', 'Last year I was told the story of a student', 'In a word, I am convinced that my subject is partly justified by the time we live in.'[13] He took up the same arguments when, from Dresden in February 1870, he announced to Maykov his plan for *The Devils*, a novel about revolutionary plots in Russia: 'I have set to work on a rich idea, it's not the treatment I am talking about, but the idea. One of those ideas which have a definite effect on the public. Something like Crime and Punishment, but still closer to everyday reality, directly touching the most serious question of the time'.[14] And he hoped to earn as much money with this novel as he did with *Crime and Punishment*, perhaps even 14,000 roubles if the second edition was counted.[15]

But sometimes Dostoyevsky felt the vertigo of the gambler at the roulette table. This was true for *The Idiot*, a dangerous enterprise. The winning cards were not strong: illness is not very attractive, money, which is the newsworthy subject in the novel, is only a secondary theme, and the stake is not pure gold: the idea of the ideal man is immature and can only end in failure. Dostoyevsky anxiously staked everything: the vivid expressions repeated in his letters to Maykov in October 1867 and January 1868 prove that the metaphor 'game of money and chance – wager of the novel' is not gratuitous:

What is going to happen to us? – I can't think! Meanwhile, the novel is the only salvation. The worst thing is that it must be a very good novel. It can't be anything else: this is the *sine qua non*. But how can it be good with my faculties completely beaten down by illness! I have imagination, and even a rather good one ... Nerve too. But no memory. In a word I am charging on the novel, (*na ura*), headlong, everything all at once on one card, come what may![16]

And again from Geneva, three months later: 'Only my desperate position has forced me to take this premature idea. I have taken a risk, as with roulette, thinking it would develop as I wrote! Unforgivable.'[17]

And it is precisely in connection with roulette and the passion for gambling that the aspect of risk in literary creation is shown most clearly, as if the situation inspired the subject, or as if the subject, which had been at Dostoyevsky's disposal since 1863 but was used only in 1866, imposed the method of creation. The subject of *The Gambler* is a bet: Aleksey Ivanovich, to save Polina who is in debt, rushes, full of hope and certainty, to the casino, where he wins 200,000 gold francs. *The Gambler* was also a bet for its writer: to escape the trap set by Stellovsky, he had to write a novel in less than a month. To show the full extent of the risk he was taking, we shall go back to the year 1865.

Dostoyevsky's wife and brother had just died and he found himself in sole charge of six people: his stepson, Pasha Isayev, and the wife, Emiliya Fyodorovna, and four children of his brother Mikhail, with 10,000 roubles in debts, mostly as bills of exchange which he endorsed with a total lack of common sense, his credulity matched only by his natural generosity.[18] He was the administrative, financial and moral director of a magazine, *Epoch*, which, in the throes of an economic crisis, had seen the number of its subscribers fall to 1,300, where 4,000 had been hoped for. He was no longer writing, he was hacking his way through a financial jungle, giving, with or without his sister-in-law's signature, fresh bills of exchange, 435 roubles here, 500 there. He paid back outstanding debts: 300 roubles to Turgenev for his novella *Apparitions*, 45 roubles to Arthur Benni, who was himself in prison for debt; 1,000 roubles lately borrowed from the Literary Funds.[19] He was seething with plans. In April 1865, having a pressing need for 3,000 roubles at once, and for 2,000 more roubles to buy back the right, which he had mortgaged, to reprint his works, he began to dream of the 15,000 roubles which he would make with a novel 'in instalments, as they do in England', with a new illustrated edition *de luxe* of *The House of the Dead*, and lastly with a collection of his works.[20] On 14 April he confessed to Vrangel:

Oh, my friend, I would willingly go back to prison for the same number of years only to pay my debts and feel free again. Now I am going to write a novel again under threat of the stick, that is to say, by necessity, hastily. It will cause a sensation, but is that what I need? This forced labour has crushed and consumed me. And all the same to start off I need at least three thousand. I am turning to all sides to get them, – otherwise I am lost. I feel that only chance can save me.[21]

June was even more hectic; on the 5th an attorney Lyzhin (the future Luzhin of *Crime and Punishment*) threatened him with foreclosure for two debts of 249 and 450 roubles and he was saved only at the last moment by a loan granted on the 6th by the Literary Fund. On the 8th he asked Krayevsky, editor of *Annals of the Fatherland* for 3,000 roubles as an advance for a novel to be delivered in October, 'The Drunkards'. He proposed a payment of 150 roubles per signature, rather than 250. Krayevsky refused on the 11th. Dostoyevsky, with his back to the wall, now sold himself, in a contract registered on 2 July, to a literary entrepreneur, Stellovsky: in exchange for the fateful 3,000 roubles (the figure was to be a symbol in his works)[22] he gave up to Stellovsky the right to publish all his work which had appeared until then, besides a new novel of at least ten signatures (seven according to Strakhov), to be supplied by 1 November 1866.[23] If this last clause were not fulfilled, for the next nine years Stellovsky would be able to publish all the works of Dostoyevsky freely and for nothing. Dostoyevsky signed, with the fatalism of someone expecting a catastrophe but hoping he would be spared.[24] He paid off a few creditors, kept 175 roubles and went abroad . . . to lose at roulette and to beg Herzen, Vrangel and his mistress Suslova to get him out of trouble. With the help of Vrangel and Yanyshev, the Russian priest at Wiesbaden, Dostoyevsky went back to St Petersburg. There he learnt that Katkov, editor of *The Russian Messenger* had accepted his plan for the future *Crime and Punishment* and sent him an advance of 300 roubles. During the winter, Dostoyevsky worked like a slave; he was encouraged by the success of the first chapters of the novel in January 1866. He received further advances, but lived like a hermit, on a few kopecks. 1,500 roubles have vanished without trace, he told Vrangel.[25] In fact, his life went on as before: rent for the flat, English tailor, keeping his brother's family, repayment of loans and creditors (the more they are paid, the more insolent they become). He was writing his novel obsessed by the debtors' prison, but in hope ... Time passed, and Stellovsky began to haunt his dreams. Dostoyevsky had tried hard to buy the contract back, to obtain a delay. It was useless. Stellovsky refused, not even trying to hide his schemes: as Dostoyevsky had not yet written half of *Crime and Punishment* he would not be able to deliver twelve signatures by 1 November 1866, and so would be in his editor's power.[26] There was the danger: serfdom for nine years.

The gambler reacted boldly, even aggressively:

I intend to do an unusual and eccentric thing: write thirty signatures in two different novels within four months. I shall write one in the morning, the other in the evening, and finish in time. Do you know, my dear Anna Vasilyevna [Korvin-Krukovskaya], I rather like these eccentric and extraordinary things. I don't fit in among the sober-living folk. Excuse me, that's boasting! But there's nothing left to do, except boast ... I am sure none of our writers, living or dead ever wrote in the same conditions as I *constantly* write. Turgenev would die just to think of it! But if you knew how painful it is to spoil the thought which is born in you, which has filled you with enthusiasm, which you know to be good, and be forced to spoil it deliberately![27]

The wager did not come off exactly as planned: Dostoyevsky dictated *The Gambler* from 4 to 31 October 1866, ten signatures in twenty-eight days.

This real feat of strength, made materially possible by stenography, probably succeeded only because the plan of the novel, one and a half signatures, which is quite substantial, had been written in advance, as early as autumn 1863. This is shown by the letter of 30 September 1863, where Dostoyevsky was already setting out to Strakhov a precise plan for a 'narrative', of which the two polarities were Russians abroad and a passion for roulette: '*Now*, I have nothing ready. But I have a fairly good plan (if I am any judge) for a narrative. Most of it is jotted on bits of paper. I was even on the point of writing it, but it's impossible here. It is hot and secondly, I've come to a place like Rome *for a week*: can anyone write if he's only got a week *in Rome?*'[28] This reservation is important for the rest of our analysis. However this might be, Dostoyevsky had recovered his freedom; *The Gambler* had won the game for him.

Gambling and creation

The parallel between gambling and creation, with money as the common stake, might convey the image of a genius sure of himself, waiting for the last moment to carry out his mission, and might blot out the more credible image of the writer tormented by need of money and knocking at every door to ask for help. The reality was quite different. If there was a game, it was vital, even tragic. The stake was literary life or death.

The game is a road without return. Bets are laid; there is complete commitment. At roulette, when 'les jeux sont faits' and 'rien ne va plus', the gambler must wait for the verdict of the roulette ball. In the same way, when Dostoyevsky had committed himself to an editor and received advance pay, he could not go back; although only the idea and the plan were ready, he had to write without a break, supplying signatures of an agreed number for an agreed time.

Roulette and creation had the same superficial motive, the dream of being rich or the need for money, as well as the same deep motive: the serious passion for risk, for leaning over the abyss. They had the same initial success: Dostoyevsky's first novella, *Poor Folk*, was a triumph: his first stake at roulette, at Wiesbaden in 1863, brought him 10,400 francs. As a gambler and as a writer, Dostoyevsky abandoned himself to the logic of the game and the novel. But gambling and creation differ in one fundamental point: roulette, in spite of its runs, is the despotic kingdom of chance, while literature is ruled by genius and the active will. We shall sketch the development of Dostoyevsky's gambling to show the strange connections between the two passions.

Before 1863 Dostoyevsky was never really attracted by gaming. He played cards like all children and even, according to his younger brother Andrey, cheated. Like his officer companions, at their parties in 1842–3, he tried whist, preference, and even a few games of chance: *la banque* and *stoss*, a sort of faro,[29] but he did not game in prison or the army.[30] He could have 'tried his luck' as he liked to say, during his first journey abroad in 1862, but he did not.[31] It was only in 1863 that he caught his violent passion for gambling. Unfortunately he began by winning, which convinced him that his system was reliable: the secret 'is terribly stupid and simple and it consists of self-control at every moment of the game, of never getting excited'.[32] But he found it difficult not to be carried away, even with 'an iron character', and the next day he lost 5,000 francs. From then on, Dostoyevsky played incessantly, still convinced of the virtue of his method, and still losing, for he was incapable of stopping after a win, still dreaming of reversing the course of fate, saving his family and safeguarding his independence as a writer. As he wrote to Mikhail in September 1863:

At Wiesbaden, I created a gaming system for myself, made use of it and immediately won 10,000 francs. The next morning, I changed the system, got excited, and immediately lost. In the evening, I went back to the first system, observing it strictly, and I had soon won back 3,000 francs. Tell me: after this how can I stop being carried away, how can I fail to believe – if I follow my system, happiness is mine for the taking. I must have money for myself, for you, for my wife, for writing novels. Tens of thousands are won here, easily. And I went there to save you all and to shield myself from trouble.[33]

At Baden-Baden, there was the same failure: '*In a quarter of an hour* I won six hundred francs. That made me excited. Suddenly I started losing, I couldn't stop any more and I lost completely.'[34] He gambled four more napoleons, won thirty-five in half an hour, risked it all and lost again . . .

The passion for gambling became an addiction, particularly violent in 1865 and 1867. In 1865, at Wiesbaden, after heavy losses, he had to live locked up in his hotel. In 1867, at Homburg, he became enthralled, played for ten hours at a stretch, lost more than 1,000 francs, sold his watch and chain, won a few gulden, lost again, staked his watch (repurchased), won, lost, wagered the money sent to help him and lost: this took up most of May. From June to August at Baden-Baden, he rushed to the gaming table almost every day, and lost large sums, to the despair of his young wife, who pawned rings, dresses, mantilla, and other family possessions to allow him to go back to the game. In September and October, at Saxon-les-Bains, he won 1,300 francs which he lost the next day. And the eternal litany began again: remorseful letters, supplications, pawnbrokers. After this the passion seemed to wane, with one flare-up in April 1868 at Saxon-les-Bains, and a final fling in April 1871 at Wiesbaden: Dostoyevsky had lost thirty thalers, and thirty more thalers which Anna had sent him to come home; he repented bitterly and asked her to send thirty more, but this time for his journey back to her. Above all he now declared himself cured, definitely cured!

A great thing has happened: the vile fantasy torturing me almost ten years has vanished. For ten years (or rather since the death of my brother, when I was suddenly crushed with debts)[35] all the time I dreamt of winning. I dreamt seriously, passionately. And now this is all finished! That was the last time, absolutely! Can you believe, Anya, I now have my hands free; I was bound by gambling, and now I am going to think of work and not dream of gambling all night, as I used to.[36]

The date of 28 April 1871 was memorable: Dostoyevsky kept his word. At Bad-Ems, in 1874, 1875, 1876, 1879, he was no longer tempted. It is true that all the gambling houses in Germany had been closed at the time, but as Anna Grigoryevna noted, there was still Saxon-les-Bains or Monaco and the distance would not have discouraged a really passionate gambler.[37]

The sudden appearance of this infatuation with roulette, and its sudden disappearance have not been really discussed. Why, moreover, during that unhappy period from 1863 to 1871, did Dostoyevsky resist his passion in 1864, 1866, 1869 and 1870? His life and creation give the answer.

From 1863 to 1866 Dostoyevsky was confused by his sexual liberation and emotional solitude. His first love had faded; Mariya Dmitriyevna, ill and erratic, made pointless scenes: he looked after her diligently, but became more and more detached. He fell in love with Apollinariya Prokofiyevna Suslova, whom he had known since 1861 or 1862, and who became his mistress. In 1863, they agreed to meet abroad, in Paris. On his way, at Wiesbaden, Dostoyevsky played roulette. He arrived in Paris 'too late', as Apollinariya said: she had already found consolation in the arms of a Spanish student, Salvador. However, more or less reconciled, she and Dostoyevsky set out for Baden-Baden, where his passion for roulette became an obsession.[38] It is easy to imagine his contradictory emotions: remorse at betraying his sick wife, who had been sent off to Vladimir or Moscow, shame for a disturbed and impure love, a sensation of sexual liberation, happiness in loving a woman twenty years younger than himself, who was independent, proud, liberal and ardent, torture at being supplanted by a handsome young man whom, moreover, she did not love, bitter-sweet reconciliation, redoubled and undeserved humiliations, which the 'colossal egoism and self-love'[39] of the imperious Salome-Apollinariya inflicted upon him, and roulette. This was all part of his infatuation with adventure, the gamble on passion, the magnetism of the abyss and the voluptuous surrender to vertigo, the rush towards the future to forget or resolve his obsession with money and creation.

1864 with its tragic succession of events plunged Dostoyevsky into despair:

And now I suddenly found myself alone and I was simply afraid. My life had suddenly broken in two. In one half, which had already gone, there was everything I had lived for, and in the other, still unknown half, everything was strange and new to me, and not one heart which could replace the two I had lost![40] . . . Everything around me had become cold and deserted.[41]

Besides sinking under the burden of editing, old and new debts, and the worsening of his epileptic fits, Dostoyevsky now felt so alone that in 1865 and 1866 he behaved like a drowning man, trying to cling to any straw.

He first had a mysterious liaison, apparently short and sensual, with an adventuress, Martha Brown, née Panina.[42] In March–April 1865 he proposed marriage to Anna Korvin-Krukovskaya, the elder sister of Sofiya, and waited patiently for her reply. The girl refused because of their difference in opinions: she later married the future communard Jaclart. In 1865 he found Apollinariya once more, cool and whimsical, with the inevitable accompaniment of roulette wheels and croupiers. However, in November he proposed to her and was again refused. In desperation, in March 1866, on Easter night, he proposed to a lively and fearless young girl, Mariya Sergeyevna Ivanchina-Pisareva, whom he met at his sister's house and whom he pictured as Mariya Nikitichna in *The Eternal Husband*.[43] She refused, but sweetened her refusal with poetry and laughter. In summer 1866, his sister had a plan: her sister-in-law, Yelena Pavlovna Ivanova, whose husband was on the point of death, would be an excellent future wife for her brother, who, she sensed, was worried and bewildered.[44] But Dostoyevsky was too impatient to wait. On 4 October he engaged a young stenographer, Anna Grigoryevna Snitkina, to take down *The Gambler*. On 8 November 1866 he asked her to marry him. At last he was accepted, and with true love.

In this attraction towards women of twenty – nearly always the case – there was a violent hurry, an obstinacy which is a mixture of emotional distress and sexual greed, of dizziness and appetite for love. It is not surprising that there was a parallel at the time between Dostoyevsky's intimate life and his passion for roulette, which is also a desperate whirlwind and mad craving. It may be argued that Dostoyevsky played feverishly in 1867, the first year of his marriage. But the first months after the marriage in February were emotionally difficult. Anna received a cool welcome from his stepson Pasha and the widow of Mikhail, and at first Dostoyevsky was not aware of her great virtues. One might even think, from what he wrote to his former mistress Suslova, that he married from lassitude:

My stenographer, Anna Grigoryevna Snitkina, was a young girl of twenty, quite appealing, of good family, excellent secondary education, endowed with an extremely good and pure character ... At the end of the novel, I noticed that my stenographer truly loved me, although she had never said a word about it, and I found her more and more attractive. As, since the death of my brother, I find life dreadfully boring and wearisome, I asked her to marry me. She accepted, so we are now married.[45]

It is true that Dostoyevsky was writing to a former lover, but these are hardly the words of a man madly in love. With the passing years, he was to see that his dear Anya was the ideal companion, his 'guardian angel', as he said, the saviour who always forgave and put things right. He was to love her completely, body and soul,[46] and as he grew more assured in his love for her, he struggled harder against his passion for gambling. If he was still playing in 1871, it was on Anna's shrewd advice: she had noticed that he came back from 'Roulettenburg' calm and determined to work.[47] When his love was settled and his spirit was at peace, his passion for gaming disappeared like the shadow of a dream. Anna's observation about the 'beneficial effects' of roulette on her husband's work is a clue to the essential link between gambling and creation.

Dostoyevsky said that the dream of gambling stifled him, and distracted him from writing; moreover, the mirage of sudden wealth, falling from the skies, gave him a deceptive hope of writing his novels without haste, of being able to polish them, because then he would be in the envied and comfortable situation of Goncharov, Turgenev and Tolstoy, his aristocratic and pampered fellow-writers. In other words, he thought that his obsession with gambling was an obstacle which he had been struggling to overcome for eight years. But the act of gambling was quite different. Leaving the boredom of Dresden or Geneva, a monotonous existence of intense work, and the intellectual solitude of exile, for Baden-Baden, Homburg, Wiesbaden or Saxon-les-Bains was psychologically liberating. He needed to live his dream, to feel true risk, escape from the monotonous ritual of everyday life and enter the game which recreates equality. He needed to touch bottom, to fall in defeat penniless after trying his luck. The act of gambling, even when doomed to failure, became a storm which cleared the creative sky.[48] It was the explosion, a catharsis of all moral, emotional and psychological tensions. As opposed to the obsession, the act of gambling set his genius free.

When he had lost everything and drunk the cup of shame, Dostoyevsky was reborn to creation, his only source of life in all senses of the word: it raised him from the depths and gave him his daily bread. Chronologically, each failure at roulette inspired a reaction of new literary plans. Moreover, Dostoyevsky, under pressure of want, needing the advances which were to save him, was forced to explain in his letters to friends and editors the exact plans which his writer's 'laziness' would have preferred to keep simmering in the fertile limbo of indecision. Gambling losses caused the deepening of the subject, because it had to be set out, accelerated the creative process by a fresh burst of energy and even sometimes brought about a change of line in the novel, so that Dostoyevsky actually began to write.

In Baden-Baden in 1863 the idea of *The Gambler* was developed in detail and the plan written out. Wiesbaden in 1865 accelerated the fusion of a first plan, 'The Drunkards', with a second 'the psychological account of a crime', which Dostoyevsky, in desperate straits, described minutely to Katkov.[49] Homburg in May 1867 released a burst of creative energy of extraordinary vigour: it was an act of faith founded on material uncertainty:

God will save me somehow. I have never in my life calculated six months ahead, just like everyone who lives by his labour, practically paid by the day. I am really counting on this work now. Understand, Anya: it must be magnificent, even better than Crime and Punishment. Then the whole of reading Russia will be mine and all the booksellers will be mine.[50]

He was alluding to his novel *The Idiot*, over which he had been toiling all summer and all autumn, trying out and rejecting numerous possibilities. The terrible passion for roulette that carried him off in a squall in June and July 1867, at Baden-Baden, prevented him from going on. The obstacle of the game defeated him. But Saxon-les-Bains in November 1867 was decisive. Dostoyevsky was aware of this and on 18 November he wrote to his dear Anya:

I have lost everything! everything! Oh, my angel, do not be sad and do not worry! Be certain that now the time is finally coming when I shall be worthy of you, and won't steal from you like a horrible disgusting thief. Now my novel, only my novel will save us, and if you knew how I am relying on this! . . . It was just like this in 1865. Difficult to be closer to ruin than I was then, but work got me out of it. With love and hope I am going to start work and you will see what will come of it in two years.[51]

And the following month, Dostoyevsky set out his plan to Maykov. Still more revealing was the letter to his wife of 4 April 1868. After the loss he had just suffered at Saxon-les-Bains, he suddenly felt reinvigorated, filled with immense creative energy. He had just had an idea of genius, to ask Katkov for more subsidies in exchange for a promise that he would go to live at Vevey in complete calm, to finish his novel! All his expressions underline the relationship between a gambling loss and a burst of creative energy: 'If this vile disgusting thing hadn't happened, this pointless loss of 220 francs, perhaps I should never have had this sudden astonishing magnificent idea, which suddenly came to me and will be *salvation for both of us*,'[52] He went on: 'This thought crossed my mind and I should never have carried it out if it had not been for this shock, this abominable loss of our last crumbs.'[53] And finally a lucid and generalised statement: 'The idea came to me at about 9 o'clock when I had lost everything and I had gone wandering through the streets (it is exactly like Wiesbaden, when I lost and then thought of Crime and Punishment and decided to get in touch with Katkov).'[54]

Money and the creative process: speech for the prosecution

Gambling is only a mad dream of unexpected fortune, a gift from Heaven: it is a hand stretched out to the blind goddess in a moment of despair. The other mad hope in the lottery of existence – the bequest, which, with the figure of the Babulinka, appears in *The Gambler* – is linked to it, but this celestial manna, which falls freely on Versilov who gets through three inheritances in *A Raw Youth*, is tainted by its association with death. But the game of chance or the game of life are both the extreme form of the need for money.

There remained the eternal and daily need for money, which began in 1844 and was to last to the end of the writer's life, or nearly so. It was only in 1880 that the wise and diligent Anna Grigoryevna finally liquidated her husband's debts, which, in 1871, had come to 25,000 roubles[55] (some 22,000 roubles due in 1867 with interest added). 'We had to pay for thirteen years. One year only before the death of my husband, we freed ourselves from debt and could breathe freely, without being afraid that someone would come and torment us with calls, explanations, threats of seizure, sale of our goods and other such unpleasant things,' she wrote in her *Memoirs*.[56] And with a touch of regret for the peaceful happiness she might have

known, she recalled her husband's superhuman toil, the privations he and
his family endured, and the disastrous consequences of his permanent
indebtedness on his creation.[57]

The first consequence was financial.

While pampered writers (Turgenev, Tolstoy, Goncharov) knew that the magazines
would quarrel over their novels and got 500 roubles per signature, Dostoyevsky,
who was financially embarrassed, had to tout for work himself, and, as a person who
asks always loses, he received much less from the same magazines. For Crime and
Punishment, The Idiot, and The Devils he received 150 roubles per signature, for
A Raw Youth 250 roubles, and only for his last novel The Brothers Karamazov did
he get 300 roubles.[58]

Dostoyevsky always resented the injustice of this disparity in pay,[59] which
he saw as a flagrant illustration of a society founded on 'the cult of moneybags'.

The second consequence is directly concerned with the aesthetic value of
his work: hurried writing, rushed out because of financial need, is supposed
to be the origin of 'the faults', the artistic failures and the muddled complexity of Dostoyevsky's novels. This is, at any rate, an opinion commonly
accepted by critics and also by Anna Grigoryevna, who used it as a defence
plea.[60] Dostoyevsky's own correspondence from 1846 to 1881 is full of complaints about this 'great artistic affliction', to use his wife's expression.

His whole existence as a writer, except for the years 1844–5, devoted to
Poor Folk – a work meditated at length, remodelled and written with care –
was full of recriminations about the slavery of money, curses on the tyranny
of need, dreams for recovering his lost independence. As early as 1846,
Dostoyevsky was accusing his editor: 'The system of permanent debt which
Krayevsky propagates is the system of my slavery and of my literary
dependence.'[61] In 1849, he told him frankly: 'To keep my word and deliver
the work in time, I have done violence to myself, written such bad things
and such a bad thing as The Landlady and so I became doubtful and lost
confidence.'[62] At Semipalatinsk, in January 1858, he recognised that nine
years ago he had printed 'bad things', profaned his best ideas and his best
plans by working 'in haste, for a set date'. He tried to start again, pleading
with his editor Katkov a cause which was lost from the start: 'To me, work
for money and work for art are two incompatible things.'[63] In December
1858 he wrote the truth to Mikhail: 'I don't want to write to order. But what
can I do? . . . For money, I must make up stories. It's horrible! The disgusting trade of the poor man of letters!'[64] In 1859 he was still explaining to his
brother that he needed a year and a half to write his novel and for this period
his existence would have to be materially assured, but now he had nothing:

You never stop telling me that Goncharov, for example, got 7,000 roubles for his
novel . . . and that Katkov himself (from whom I am asking 100 roubles per signature)
gave 400 roubles to Turgenev for his Nest of Gentlefolk, that is 400 roubles a

signature. My friend, I know very well that I write worse then Turgenev, but really, not so much worse, and I hope eventually to write no worse than he. Why then do I, with all my needs, take only 100 roubles, while Turgenev, who owns 2,000 souls, takes 400. Because of poverty, I am *forced* to rush and write for money and so *inevitably spoil* things.[65]

The same year, just before going back to Petersburg, he confided in a former school-friend that he hoped to re-publish his works himself and, for the first time, to be able to 'write not to order, not for money, not for a deadline but conscientiously, honestly, taking time to think, without selling my pen for a piece of daily bread'.[66] But by 1863 he had realised the vanity of this hope and analysed the situation lucidly to Strakhov:

Let Boborykin know, as The Contemporary and Annals of the Fatherland know, that, (except for Poor Folk) I have never in my life sold my works without receiving advances. I am a proletarian writer, and if anyone wants my work, he must pay my expenses in advance. It is a system that I myself detest. But it's established like this and apparently won't change.[67]

This was to be a constant complaint; 'I must work with all my strength, work without reading over, rush off to catch the post.'[68] 'All my life I have worked for money and all my life I have never been free of need.'[69] 'Believe me, I am certain that if I had two or three years ensured to write this novel, like Turgenev, Goncharov or Tolstoy, I should write one of those things people would be talking of a hundred years later!'[70] And finally: 'No, this is not how works of literature are written, to order and under threat of the stick: but with time and freedom.'[71] Sometimes it was a real cry of despair, like the long letter to Maykov in October 1869, when Dostoyevsky, who had been waiting for money from his editor for twelve days, let his rancour explode: people are 'spitting' on his hunger, insulting his wife who has just had a baby, every day he runs to the bank for news, he is tearing his hair, can't sleep, thinks all the time of this accursed sum, just cannot work. He ended: 'And after all this, I'm supposed to write artistically, with the purity of a poet, without tension, without heat, and people point at Turgenev and Goncharov! They should just see the conditions I'm working in.'[72]

Anna Grigoryevna, wishing to frustrate possible attacks, but shackled by her own traditional taste in literature, summed up:

Dostoyevsky's works are often compared with those of other talented authors and he is reproached with the outrageous complexity, confusion and overcrowding of his novels, while the creations of others are polished at leisure and with Turgenev, for example, cut like a jewel. But people rarely take the trouble to recall and consider the conditions in which other writers lived and worked and those which my husband experienced ... Fyodor Mikhaylovich was suffering from two serious illnesses and burdened by a large family and debts; he was preoccupied by the painful thought of the morrow and his daily bread. Could he polish his works in such conditions? How many times it happened, in his last fourteen years, that two or three chapters had already appeared in a magazine, the fourth was at the printer's, the fifth might be in the post on its way to The Russian Messenger and the rest were not yet written but only imagined. And more than once, Fyodor Mikhaylovich, on reading a chapter already printed, caught sight of a mistake, and was in despair, well aware that he had spoilt his plan: If one could go back, he would sometimes say, if one could revise. Now I see where the mistake was, I see why the novel does not succeed. Perhaps I have definitely killed my *idea* by this mistake.[73]

According to this theory, money, in the form of need, played a double and necessarily contradictory part in creation: first it incited creation and secondly it degraded it and lessened its artistic value. It was a poisoned goad, an equivocal *agent provocateur*. It drove Dostoyevsky to ceaseless production, to kill himself with work, like Balzac, with the difference that, whereas Balzac dreamt of luxury and riches, Dostoyevsky only wanted to live, sometimes just to survive. The need for money forced him to steal precious time from his creation, to exhaust himself in unworthy struggles, to spur himself on and so spoil his best ideas, to neglect the final polish, in fact to do jobbing work, if not exactly piece work. Is this an exact image of reality?

Money and the creative process: speech for the defence

Dostoyevsky lived through hours of real destitution and days of poverty, he was haunted by the debtors' prison, but he was not a poor man. He knew the sufferings of poverty, its distress and tragedy, dramas, revolts, and psychological springs, which he described in *Poor Folk* and *Crime and Punishment*, but he never learnt its lessons. A really poor man can distinguish need from luxury, but Dostoyevsky was always perfectly incapable of this: he was sometimes forced to live on milk or do without food, but as soon as money appeared he went out for a feast with his friends and colleagues. Every evening, with a technique of which he was very proud, he carefully brushed his overcoat to make it last, but he had an expensive English tailor and bought linen for two years at a time. He was always late with the rent, but he changed apartments more often than necessary and wanted them light and spacious. He was sometimes up to his eyes in debt and pawned necessities, like his wife's dresses, but he gambled and lost huge sums at roulette. No, Dostoyevsky was not a poor man, but he was always short of money. He had a vocation for being short of money, or to put it bluntly, was a spendthrift.

For this 'poor man' earned a good deal. Not much, it is true, at the beginning of his career, when *Poor Folk* brought him only 250 roubles, *The Double* 600 roubles, 'The Novel in Nine Letters' 125 roubles,[74] 'A Little Hero' and 'Uncle's Dream' 2,000 roubles. But after his return to literature in 1860 his earnings were much larger: the journals *Time* and *Epoch* brought him on average 7,000 to 8,000 roubles a year, for *Crime and Punishment* he received 14,000 roubles, for *The Idiot* 6,000 roubles and later the editorship of the *Citizen* brought him a yearly salary of 3,000 roubles and political articles and *Diary of a Writer* added about 2,000 roubles.[75] ... But, as he never stopped repeating in his letters, money burnt a hole in his pocket: 'Money is running off in all directions, like crayfish',[76] and 'As for money, alas! there isn't any. The devil knows where it has vanished. But I haven't many debts',[77] or again, 'All winter I have lived like a hermit, worked, wrecked my health, lived on a few kopecks and spent 1,500 roubles! Where has it gone? Money seems to burn a hole in my pocket!'[78]

Biographers have had a field day with this extravagant life. We shall simply sum up the motives, mainly psychological: Dostoyevsky's childish lack of common sense, his credulity (he was robbed by his servant, cheated by his collaborators and swindled by his creditors), prodigality (he gave huge banquets or doubled his shopping bills when he was in funds), his passion for gambling, his unlimited generosity (he fed the patients of his friend, Dr Riesenkampf: he supported the lazy Pasha, his stepson, nearly all his life, and kept the widow and children of Mikhail for about ten years), and finally, more deeply, an unconscious reaction against the severe principles of economy, almost amounting to avarice, of his father, Dr Dostoyevsky. Dostoyevsky's attitude to money is like that of the convicts, whom he describes as slaving for long months 'sweating blood' to heap up a few kopecks, which was a 'treasure' in the convict prison, and then spending them 'thoughtlessly, with such childish absurdity'.[79] He often compared his literary slavery to a convict prison, worse than the real one. If we transpose word for word what the author of *The House of the Dead* says about the part played by money in prison, his feelings are more easily understood:

For money the prisoner is greedy to the point of convulsions, to the point where his reason is overcast and if indeed he scatters it to the four winds when he is celebrating, he scatters it in exchange for something he thinks is even higher than money. What is higher than money for a prisoner? Freedom or at least some kind of dream of freedom.[80]

Here there is clearly a last motive, this time linked with the creative life: the dance of money, the squandering of money was a celebration of life, a fountain of joy which interrupted the harsh effort of writing. It signified the use of power, freedom regained for a day, a month, even a year, by possession and dissipation of the thing which caused the slavery. Dostoyevsky's deepest nature always impelled him to return to the fertile instability of desire. Although he sang the praises of wise men who had given up earthly longings, he was never able to kill the desire for money in himself. He needed the moderation and experience which his young wife slowly but surely acquired. The search for money resulted from Dostoyevsky's nature and not from the system of literary production he adopted.

In other conditions he might not even have produced his extraordinary work. The arguments developed by Anna Grigoryevna and by Dostoyevsky himself, who never hesitated to give his eternal need for money and his haste as an excuse to foil eventual criticism and to account to editors for the failure of his first works, are not really valid.

They suggest that, plagued by necessity, he had no time to reread his works. This is a quibble, for Dostoyevsky was a man who wrote in the heat of inspiration. When his inspiration was in full flight, he could not go back to revise what he had written, except for minor points of style. On 19 July 1866, replying to Katkov about the proofs of some chapters of *Crime and Punishment*, he wrote: 'Personally I have a strange characteristic; when I have written something I completely lose the ability to consider it critically, at least for some time.'[81] He knew what he had written and stuck to it. He had harsh battles about the editor's censorship. For example, he struggled to keep a stronger version of the scene in *Crime and Punishment* where the murderer and the sinner are reading the Gospel.[82] It was only after long resistance and even endangering publication of *The Devils* that he finally agreed to the suppression of the shocking chapter 'Stavrogin's Confession'. He later managed to save the part about the Golden Age and put it in *A Raw Youth*. We only have to look at the correspondence between the author of *The Brothers Karamazov* and N. A. Lyubimov, who was in charge of proof-reading and printing the novel at *The Russian Messenger*, to be convinced that Dostoyevsky read over his work, weighed every word and every detail, and cherished each one like the apple of his eye. He was very anxious that the *tone* of words should not be changed, energetically defending the strong or coarse word, the poetic verb or the concrete phrase.[83] He was a copious genius because, desperate to reach the depths of the idea or the emotion, he was unable to cut anything he thought necessary. This was the true origin of the prolixity (*mnogoslovnost'*) he recognised as his 'literary vice',[84] which had nothing to do with money. It was present in *Poor Folk* and tended to disappear just when there were great financial difficulties, in *The House of the Dead*, *Crime and Punishment* and 'The Eternal Husband', and to reappear in the more peaceful times of the great novels of the sixties. Dostoyevsky was not at all like a journalist who pads his work for financial reasons, at least not in his novels. Repetitions of whole passages are rare, if we distinguish them from his recurrent themes.[85] When we consider, for example, the work most admired by Gide, no doubt because it is the most harmoniously constructed, the most concise, the most 'French' from the point of view of form, 'The Eternal Husband', we find that Dostoyevsky had reread it 'with his pen in his hand', and yet it swelled from two and a half signatures to ten, for creative and not financial reasons: 'My novella is ready but it has grown to a terrifying size: exactly ten signatures of The Russian Messenger. Not because it unravelled as I was writing, but because the subject changed as I wrote and new episodes came in.'[86]

Moreover, misled by the taste of novel readers of the time, which was essentially formed, with the immense exception of Gogol, on the French school, a taste embodied in the novels of Turgenev with their clear and harmonious architecture, where poetic natural descriptions balance a limpid and linear action, Anna Grigoryevna and Dostoyevsky himself, who was extremely sensitive to criticism, could not imagine that a different aesthetic standard was possible. But this was exactly what Dostoyevsky was creating without daring to defend it openly, though he made a timid attempt at the end of *A Raw Youth*. Why should simplicity be preferable to complexity, if genius is more inclined to express the increasing complexity of modern life? How can we blame an author for introducing too many characters, if the future is with the crowd and the city? Why is the interweaving of ten or twenty subjects a fault if the writer is trying to penetrate the texture of motives which are naturally entwined? Why celebrate the artistic perfection of the monophonic novel when Dostoyevsky, an innovative and original genius, was constructing the polyphonic novel with its infinite possibilities? These novels demanded, in Dostoyevsky's words, a modern 'enthralled and passionate' form of writing, whose essential characteristic was the contrasted succession of two phases: a slow patient exploratory elaboration and free improvised feverish writing. The part played by the need for money must be analysed at these two levels.

When he was ruminating over the Idea, when the plan was coming to birth, Dostoyevsky *did not hurry*, whatever his money problems. Even if he wanted to, he could not. Strakhov has explained this time for ripening as 'writer's laziness': but it appears to be a profound necessity arising from the polyphonic nature of Dostoyevsky's novels, prolonging the non-resolution of the conflict to infinity. The motive of need for money came into play only when the writer made an effort to move from the state of *poet* to that of *artist* and when he sought with amazing energy – we may recall the plans which swarmed in his head during the gestation of *The Idiot* in December 1868 – the turning point from planning to writing. Money, or at any rate his imperious need for it, impelled him to break away from the creative dream and begin writing. Dostoyevsky, in his letter to Strakhov of 10 March 1870, gave a clear explanation:

I will tell you directly that I have never invented a subject for money because I had contracted to deliver a text at a particular date. I have only signed contracts and sold in advance when I already had the theme which I really wanted to write and which I judged necessary to write. It is a theme of this sort that I have now . . . Seldom has anything appeared to me newer, fuller and more original. I can say this without being accused of vanity, for I am only speaking of the theme, the thought which has become flesh in my mind, and not of its execution.[87]

On 5 April he returned to the subject:

All my life I have always worked for the money I was given and given in advance. It's always been like this and was never different. It is bad for me from the economic point of view, but what can you do! But when I took money in advance, I was always selling something which already existed, in other words, I sold only when the poetic idea had been born and, as much as possible, had ripened. I didn't take money *for an empty space*, that is, with the hope of *inventing* and *composing* the novel by a given date.[88]

This distinction between the stage of imagination and the stage of composition as far as money is concerned is very valuable. Creation, as one might expect, had other sources than the need for money, although money assured its continuity and gave it impetus. Nor was money responsible for Dostoyevsky's prolixity or for what a classical mind might see as artistic imperfection. It intervened at a crucial moment for the creative process, at the transition from idea to writing. It then precipitated the appearance of a precise and definitive plan and a choice of narrative viewpoint: it released the writing and so accelerated the birth, brusquely ending the prolonged gestation. Like a brutal midwife using instruments to tear the child away from its maternal dream, money is the hateful mediator, in creation as in life.

From this trauma in his life as man and creator, Dostoyevsky took the dialectic vision of money in his work. Money is the object of simultaneous desire and hatred. The great merit of Dostoyevsky was not in using this dualistic relationship in his novels, but in embracing modern history by assuming the necessary mediation of money and dramatising this mediation until it became an aesthetic principle.

Money, before being the object of passionate reactions, is first of all a fact. To escape it one must flee society, shutting oneself in a monastery like Tikhon or Zosima, or wandering through the roads of Russia like Makar Ivanovich, or escaping from reality in the dreamlike Utopia of the Golden Age or the 'Great Garden' described in *Diary of a Writer*. As Tolstoy wrote in his *Diary* on 31 October 1853: 'A strange thing, we all hide the fact that one of the mainsprings of our life is money, as if we were ashamed of it', adding: 'But it is the most constant interest of our existence, and it is through money that a man's character is expressed.'[89] This reproach could not be applied to Dostoyevsky: the whole of his work tells us that money is *a category of the knowledge of our social and even spiritual being*, like space.

But first we need to define the different faces of money in Dostoyevsky's work, stressing the imbalance between the statements of the artist and novelist and the diatribes of the thinker, who was a product of the artist. The thinker dreamt of banning money from society, and so from man, but the artist could not imagine man without the mediation of money.

Irreducible alienation

For the young writer, preoccupied with social questions and still strongly influenced by Gogol, money was the source of inequalities, injustice and alienation. The first works of Dostoyevsky: *Poor Folk, The Double*, 'Mr Prokharchin', 'A Weak Heart', and later the Marmeladov theme in *Crime and Punishment* dealt with a theme dear to Russian literature in the thirties and forties, the poor civil servant, whose line of descent has been traced by A. G. Tseytlin.[90] Dostoyevsky went beyond the traditional scheme of the naturalist school to deal with the riven consciousness, the wounded dignity, the tragic dialectic of a desire unable to rise above its alienation. He showed the ridiculous and bewildered humanity of Devushkin, Golyadkin, Prokharchin, Shumkov, Marmeladov, with their absurd names.[91] In the earlier novellas, Dostoyevsky was concerned with individuals, although there are several families in *Poor Folk*. In *Crime and Punishment* the theme was extended to society: poverty was dramatised by alcoholism, prostitution, and crime, and the petty clerk or the deprived student dragged their families into their tragedies. The peasant or the industrial worker, however, whose situations were far worse, did not enter Dostoyevsky's field of vision. Besides the many historical, political, personal reasons: non-existence of a Russian proletariat in the Western sense, the servile condition of workers before the end of serfdom, the essentially city vision of the writer, the danger of treating these subjects directly, there is one which is decisive: poverty is most painful when inaccessible riches are in sight. The prisoners of destitution struggle more furiously if they can see the gilded carriages of their excellencies, the marble walls of their pompous drawing rooms, the treasured and disturbing beauty of their daughters, from their basement windows. The tragedy of the petty clerk is that he is looking at something else, near, everyday and inaccessible. If he were to climb up one grade in the table of ranks, if His Excellency were to notice him or the young daughter of His Excellency suddenly fall in love with him, the brilliant world of the capital would fling open its doors. This is the dream he pursues, sometimes to the point of madness. It is by contact with insolent wealth that the need for dignity and justice is born. The seeds of revolt begin to sprout, and, stamped down, they poison the bed in which they were coming to life. The prison built by money is more unbearable because one of the ways of escape, work, turns out to be impossible. It has often been noted that the majority of Dostoyevsky's heroes do not work.[92] Heaven or relatives support them. The petty clerks in the early works are paid so wretchedly that they cannot even buy necessities.[93] No one in Dostoyevsky can make money by honest toil.[94]

If we except gifts from heaven (unexpected win at gambling, fabulous inheritance), the slaves of money have three choices: revolt, revolution or retreat. Sometimes the hero revolts by committing theft, crime, fraud or breaking the law, like Raskolnikov and several characters in *A Raw Youth*. Sometimes he wishes to destroy a society built on injustice: these are the socialist and nihilist themes of *The Devils* and the Vasin episode in *A Raw Youth*. Sometimes he leaves the world to its adoration of the Golden Calf and follows another Ideal, that of Christ. Dostoyevsky has created a universe where all these solutions are tried out.

After the poor clerks, Dostoyevsky continued his passionate indictment with examples of the most helpless and innocent victims, children and women. The little boy, the governess's son whom Yulian Mastakovich unjustly accuses and drives out in 'A Christmas Tree and a Wedding', Netochka Nezvanova, Nelli in *The Insulted and Injured*, Sonya Marmeladova, a prostitute at fifteen in *Crime and Punishment*, the unfortunate Matryosha, raped by Stavrogin, who hangs herself in *The Devils*, the little girl driven away in 'Dream of a Ridiculous Man', the boy who commits suicide in the episode of the merchant Skotoboynikov in *A Raw Youth*, the child who dies of cold in 'The Little Boy and the Christmas Tree', which is practically an Andersen fairytale, the little serf devoured by his angry master's mastiffs in *The Brothers Karamazov*, and lastly Ilyusha Snegiryov, so sensitive about his father's honour, who dies at the end of the novel: the list of accusing shades in the sordid trial of money is endless. For women the nets are still finer. Confined in a gynaeceum of laws and customs, they depend on men, who hold the money and who buy and sell them. As adults, they feel their slavery more passionately; women in heart and body, they are forced to sacrifice everything that makes them unique and sensitive beings. They may be driven by real poverty into prostitution, like Sonya, or doomed to an unequal marriage, like Varenka in *Poor Folk* or the 'gentle one' in the eponymous novella. There are numerous young girls who are picked out at market by men like Julian Mastakovich, Svidrigaylov, Totsky, Trusotsky or Fyodor Karamazov. Some have been abused since their childhood like Nastasya Filippovna or have sacrificed themselves for others. But all of them know they have only one form of coin valid for pampered males: surrender and grateful submission of body and soul. The fact that their love is inextricably linked with money is flung in their faces. Natasha in *The Insulted and Injured* sacrifices her family for love, but immediately loses Alyosha, for whom his father, the ignoble Valkovksy, has arranged a golden marriage: a dowry of three million! In compensation, 10,000 roubles ... and Count N. are offered as a tip. The proud Polina, in *The Gambler*, sees the market price of her love fluctuate as the accounts change: when the inheritance has gone, Des Grieux thinks only of getting himself out of a tight spot; as soon as the Gambler wins a fortune for her, he feels his love, which is now spoilt, decline and he runs off with Mlle Blanche. Every time a woman appears to ask for something, Akhmakova to recover the document which would compromise her future and her fortune, Katerina Ivanovna to obtain the 4,500 roubles which would save her father, the men who have the money, Arkadiy Dolgoruky in dreams, Dmitriy Karamazov in thought, feel the 'thought of centipedes'[95] or 'their spider soul'[96] stirring inside them. These impulses are more terrible because they appear in ardent creatures such as Dmitriy the Schillerian and Arkadiy the raw youth. In Dostoyevsky, love between man and woman is always affected by money, if not caused, destroyed or defiled by it.

No one escapes the alienation of money, not even those who organise and could moderate it. The majority yield to its fascination and are tormented by their surrender, like Ganya Ivolgin, or hide their wounds by a grotesque mask, like those clowns of the drawing room, Polzunkov, Yezhevikin and Lebedev. There is a long list of criminals, gamblers, cheats, blackmailers, legal and shady businessmen, moneylenders, officers and civil servants who have misappropriated state funds, princes and generals compromised by some financial scandal, all worshipping the golden idol. Except for a few really evil beings like Valkovsky and Lambert, they are all guilty but suffering creatures, wounded and wounding, humiliated and humiliating. They carry the 'threadworm' of the vast historic scourge which swept down on Russia after contaminating Europe, which Dostoyevsky denounced in *Diary of a Writer* with the passion of a prophet. In January 1876, for example: 'Everywhere in the air there is a sort of opium, a kind of decaying smell. Recently there has appeared among the people an incredible perversion of ideas, with an inclination to materialism on all sides. I here call materialism the fact that people bow down before money, before the power of moneybags.'[97] In October 1876 he saw the 'monster of materialism advancing on the people in the form of moneybags',[98] while the true élite was supplanted by great millionaire merchants, speculators in the European fashion, and gamblers at the Stock Exchange. The conventional hierarchy was overturned to the profit of banks, stock companies, railway companies, whose rise was so brutal that Lebedev, in *The Idiot*, compares the railway network to the deadly star Wormwood in Revelation.[99] In 1877, Dostoyevsky the thinker denounced the illusion of money, from which he had long suffered as a man:

Irregularity of wishes only leads you to be your own slave. This is why the world of today, almost all of it, sets freedom in financial security and the laws which guarantee it? – 'I have money, so I can do what I please. I have money, so I am not lost and I will not go and ask for help and not to ask anything from anyone is supreme freedom'. While this is basically not freedom, but a new slavery, the slavery of money.[100]

Dostoyevsky did not deny that the cult of money had always existed. But now the contagion had spread to the people, who until then had been the guardians of true values and an example for the élite,[101] but were now bowing down before material things; the soul of Russia was threatened by money's soul-destroying power. Dostoyevsky painted an apocalyptic picture of humanity entirely submissive to Mammon. His hatred of money explained why, in 1863, in his article 'Winter Notes on Summer Impressions', he placed capitalism and socialism under the same materialist banner. They are, as Berdyayev said later, 'of the same flesh and blood', both aspiring to be substitutes for Christianity[102] and to replace Christian Messianism by the dream of the earthly kingdom of Utopia. Capitalism and socialism have the same God – matter; the same motive – interest, which is that of the carnivore, 'predator' or 'herd'; the same result – the alienation of the freedom of the majority and the reign of the Rothschilds or the Grand Inquisitor; and the same method – metaphysics and the transcendental are relegated to the attic, and efficient scientific tools like utilitarianism, mathematical organisation and economic realism take their place. This was the position of the journalist and thinker. That of the novelist was not very different, except for some indulgence towards socialist youth in *A Raw Youth*.

Dostoyevsky went even further in the novels, for he showed that the structures of money lay at the heart of socialist thought, although it claimed to dominate them. First there is the character of Luzhin in *Crime and Punishment*, who, in the name of realism, decides to exploit for his own sordid interests the pure but naive formulae which Chernyshevsky and his followers preached in the sixties. Nikolay Mikhaylovsky, the populist leader, noted that there were thousands of Luzhins ready to 'hook the rags of their base moneygrubbing' to radical or socialist slogans and to reason as follows:

We spit on all idealism and we hold to the strict prescriptions of science and realist philosophy. We are realists and as, from this point of view, all that is natural is moral and we base our ideas on the natural struggle for existence, we say that it is natural to crush feeble creatures who are formed differently. We are realists and as, from this point of view, the victim counts for nothing, we live only to fill our own stomachs.[103]

Mikhaylovsky considered this an adulteration of true socialism, but for the author of *The Idiot* and *The Devils* it was socialism's essence. All the socialists he describes, from these novels to *The Brothers Karamazov*, Liputin, Pyotr Verkhovensky, and Rakitin, fit in perfectly with Stepan Trofimovich's diagnosis: 'All these desperate socialists and communists are such boundless misers and collectors and proprietors, so much so that the more socialist a person is, the further he's gone, the more acquisitive he is.'[104] Even in *A Raw Youth*, where Dostoyevsky showed disinterested young socialists such as Dergachev's group and particularly Vasin, it is stressed that socialism and capitalism are alike. There is a note in the notebooks, not used in the novel, where he fuses Chernyshevsky's ideo-

logy, parodying its syllogisms, with the capitalist structures of joint stock
companies:

The idea of Vasin. One can only live happily when men are good to you. But men are
only good when they feel good. And this is why everyone must make every effort to
make things good for everyone. Therefore a joint stock company must be created.
The shareholder will be a philanthropist willy nilly, for otherwise men will be bad to
him and he will be unhappy.[105]

Vasin was indifferent to riches and even to comfort,[106] but even he could
not imagine society outside the structures of capital. Moreover, nihilism,
the radical form of socialism, gave rise to an idealism dedicated to money,
as if to restore the balance. The money cycle is inescapable: this is the lesson
contained in that paradoxical heir of nihilism, the *Rothschild idea, the idea
of capitalisation* which germinates in the brain of the raw youth.[107]

The ring closes. Money, source of injustice, suffering, humiliation, and
death for the innocent, slavery for all, destroyer of souls, is reborn of the
very theories which propose it should be abolished. As a basis of capitalist
as well as socialist thought, money is a category of life in the world of the
novels which cannot be suppressed. Only the rare Utopian dream forms,
the 'Great Garden' of 'The Earth and the Children',[108] and the Golden Age
of Stavrogin, Versilov and the Ridiculous man, expel money from society.
Everywhere else, man, even while he aspires to another ideal, is irreducibly
alienated by money. The true modern realism of Dostoyevsky is that he
placed the weight of the social being at the centre of his analysis of the
human mystery, and introduced the mediation of money between the two
terms of the tragic dialectic of desire.

The dream of capital

The novel is illusion. Dostoyevsky, like Balzac who built up fabulous
fortunes in his works, was dreaming of the impossible. A million, in his
eyes, could only be a gift from Heaven. His heroes imagined it would be the
fruit of their tenacity, their privations and their knowledge. Time and
money would bring capital: the million would be heaped up patiently, and
alienation would be overcome by a reversal of relationships, in which the
slave of money would become the master of his master and its power would
be his. The dream of capital is Promethean.

The theme of capitalisation appeared very early in Dostoyevsky. He had
translated *Eugénie Grandet*, read *Gobseck* and admired Molière's *L'Avare*.
He knew Pushkin's *Covetous Knight* by heart, and loved to recite it like the
hero of *A Raw Youth*, and he knew Gogol's unforgettable Plyushkin in
Dead Souls. Moreover, his early need for money had resulted in a fair
acquaintance with moneylenders.

In his first attempts to deal with this hackneyed theme, Dostoyevsky did not distinguish very clearly between two entwined motives: first, avarice which makes one the slave of money and destroys everything around it, and second, patient accumulation which soon goes beyond the sterile cult of money to reach the vengeful kingdom of gold, the enjoyment of absolute power, as Pushkin's Baron expresses it:

> What is not subject to me? Like a demon,
> Henceforth I have the power to rule the world.
> I need but wish, and palaces will rise,
> And joyful nymphs come flocking to my gardens.
> The offerings of the muses will be mine,
> Free genius be my slave, and sleepless toil
> And virtue humbly wait for my reward.
> I need but whistle: bloodstained crime will creep
> Gently and timidly into my presence
> And lick my hands and look into my eyes
> To read the signs of my all-powerful will.
> All is within my power, and I am free.
> I am above all wishes: I am calm.
> I know my strength: this knowledge is enough.[109]

The primary form of avarice appeared as early as 1846 in the novella 'Mr Prokharchin', with its echoes of Gogol (madness) and Balzac (the inventory of the savings hidden under the mattress, and an allusion, noted by Shklovsky,[110] to the theme of power: the episode where a neighbour reproaches Prokharchin for thinking he is Napoleon.[111] In 1861, in 'Petersburg Dreams in Verse and Prose', a potboiler for *Time*, Dostoyevsky returned to the subject with an account of Solovyov, who had been found 'dead in the most horrible poverty on heaps of gold'.[112] He suggested that Solovyov might have been a perfectly normal young man who suddenly 'caught a glimpse of something and was afraid'. From that instant, he began to heap up money: his lust for gold might have originated in a fear of life.[113] The article came to nothing, but Dostoyevsky had found two ideas in his journalism which he was not to forget as a novelist: the type is 'colossal' and the deep motive for avarice is probably a fear of perishing in the social jungle. This is the origin of the dream of capitalising a million – a reflex of self-preservation, a withdrawal into one's shell. Later, in 1877, when he was writing an obituary of Nekrasov, whom critics unanimously recognise as a relative of Arkadiy in *A Raw Youth*, Dostoyevsky expressed this idea very clearly:

The million, that is the demon of Nekrasov! Is he supposed to have loved gold, luxury, pleasures so much that to obtain them he flung himself into 'business deals'? No, it was a question of a very different demon, the most shadowy and degrading of tempters. It was the demon of pride, the thirst for security, the need to cut himself off from men behind a solid wall and to consider their wickedness and their threats with detachment. I believe this demon was already clinging like a leech to the child's heart, when he was fifteen years old and suddenly found himself on the streets of Petersburg, after somehow running away from his father ... It was a sombre, morose thirst for security, which deliberately cut itself off so as not to depend on anyone any more.[114]

The evolution takes place in depth in the novels. Arkadiy in *A Raw Youth* changes these motives of fear and pride into a theory of inner freedom. Dostoyevsky stressed this when he drafted a plan of reply to critics in 1876: 'Some have taken it that I wanted to represent the influence of money on a young soul, but I had a broader aim.'[115] He set out the double 'poetic' aspect of the Rothschild idea: first, the aspect sketched by Pushkin in *The Covetous Knight*: money is not an end in itself, but a way of acquiring Napoleonic power: second, the part which Pushkin had only envisaged: a refusal to use money as a weapon. Arkadiy wishes to possess power, but to be loved without having to use it. The fascination of piling up treasure originates in a wish for freedom without any change in society (power is simply transferred) and in the Promethean dream, voluntarily repressed. It is not simply the tragic dialectic of the unreal desire, but the voluptuous retention[116] of a desire which may be realised at any moment, power over others and over oneself.

How did this movement from 'Mr Prokharchin' to *A Raw Youth* take place? In *Winter Notes on Summer Impressions* Dostoyevsky had noted that freedom without money was only an illusion:

What is freedom? An equal right for everyone to do everything he likes within the limits of the law. When can you do what you like? When you have a million ... What is a man without a million? A man without a million is not a person who does everything he likes, but a man to whom other people do what they like.[117]

The stakes are raised in *The Gambler*: 'Money is everything' changes to: 'With money I will become a different person.'[118] Raskolnikov, who is not a hoarder[119] but a man *impatient for capital* endows money with symbolic, even superstitious, value: a little nest-egg would allow him to begin a new life in a halo of humanitarian ideals. He then commits murder for a few gold objects and a purse, which he immediately hides under a big stone, so that its contents are only revealed at the trial: 317 silver roubles and three twenty-kopeck pieces.

Ganya Ivolgin in *The Idiot* does not break the laws of society, but his impatience is akin to Raskolnikov's. He despises the mediocre but efficient Ptitsyn, a small capitalist of the American type. 'At seventeen Ptitsyn slept on the street, traded in penknives and started with a kopeck; now he has sixty thousand, but only after a lot of gymnastics. Now I am going to jump over all that gymnastics and start straight from capital: in fifteen years they'll be saying: "There is Ivolgin, the King of the Jews".'[120] Skipping a few stages, he dives 'into the shades' of degradation and agrees to marry Nastasya Filippovna for 75,000 roubles. When Prince Myshkin taxes him with weakness of character and absence of any particular talent, not even honouring him with a place among the 'great scoundrels', Ganya retorts: 'When I have made money – I will be a man of the greatest originality. The most vile and hateful thing about money is that it even gives talent.'[121] In *A Raw Youth*, Arkadiy develops the same theme with even more passion: 'Money is the only way which takes even a nobody to *first place* ... but if I were as rich as Rothschild – who would worry about my face? I would only have to whistle and thousands of women would rush at me with their charms. I am even sure that they would, quite sincerely, start thinking that I was really handsome.'[122] Money makes one wittier than Talleyrand, goes on the youth, concluding: 'Money is, of course, a despotic power, but at the same time it is the highest equality, and in this is its main force. Money makes all inequalities equal.'[123] This is the first point; the second is access to freedom:

I don't need money, or, rather, it's not money that I need; it is not even power: I just need what is acquired by power, and what can't be got without it, the calm and solitary knowledge of strength. This is the most complete definition of freedom, which everyone is struggling over. Freedom! At last I have written this great word ... Yes, the solitary knowledge of one's strength is fascinating and beautiful. I have strength and I am calm.'[124]

The third term of reasoning is repressed desire. 'If I only had power, I reasoned, I should not need it at all; certainly of my own free will I should always take the last place ... I can eat a piece of bread and ham and my knowledge would be enough to fill me.'[125] Arkadiy can accept accusations of mediocrity and lack of talent, but not of lack of power:

I was horribly pleased with the idea of being a creature who was just talentless and mediocre, standing before the world and telling it with a smile: You may be Galileo and Copernicus, Charlemagne and Napoleon, you may be Pushkin and Shakespeare, you may be army marshals and courtiers, but look at me – ungifted and illegitimate, and all the same I am higher than you, because you are money's servants.[126]

The idea of *A Raw Youth* is poetic in Dostoyevsky's sense:[127] it creates a new being. The conqueror of money, instead of using it to serve his ambition, vengeance or profit, will spurn it and return to his solitary life. The superiority of the hero is not in the reversal of roles, but in his power to free himself from money, which society is unable to do. Arkadiy will have conquered everything, others, money, and finally himself. This is the holy madness of his idea. There is a profound similarity between his dream and the choices made by Makar the wanderer and the elders Tikhon and Zosima; the choice of leaving the world and entering the desert.[128] The young miser even dreams of redistributing the money he intends to make and going off into the void. He would recreate the original state of society, wipe out all traces of his passage and would even become a beggar – like Solovyov – to enjoy his solitary state to the full. 'Just the knowledge that I had had millions in my hands and I threw them into the mud would feed me in my desert, like the raven.'[129] This reveals the whole hateful and infamous power of money: to gain inner freedom, one must first contemplate and kiss the hateful face of gold. One must bargain with it to control it. The infamous mediation of money has never been clearer.

The means Arkadiy uses are original. They form 'a summary of the perfect little capitalist', which is very like a collection of monastic rules. Besides 100 roubles, the starting capital, one needs, As Arkadiy sums it up, 'courage, obstinacy, constancy, perfect isolation and secrecy'.[130] The idea has nothing in common with the narrow miserliness of the modern Harpagon and Plyushkin, with the wealthy beggars in the newspapers, or with the laborious capitalism of the German *Vater*, cruelly satirised in *The Gambler*. The former accumulate, but do not multiply: the latter add, but also subtract, endlessly sacrificing to appearances and the family. The secret plan of the Youth for the imitation of 'saint' James de Rothschild is first to refuse family and society, and secondly to work his apprenticeship not in capitalisation, but in the mechanics of capitalism. He distinguishes two phases; the first is the period of commission and petty resale: i.e., the resale of cheap objects, like the album bought at auction for two roubles and five kopecks, and resold for ten roubles, and the assimiliation of 'street knowledge'; the second is the application of the techniques of 'the Stock Exchange, shares, banks and the rest',[131] tempered by great prudence; he will try to make as much money as the railway magnates, Kokorev, Polyakov, and Gubonin,[132] but he will know how to sell shares in time and profit cautiously from the movement of affairs, like the hunchback in Law's time, who cashed in on people using his hump as a desk. In fact Arkadiy knows very little about modern economics. His whole experience is only a few trials at the preliminary stages; he can save small sums, deprive himself of food and comfort, save on boots and clothes, sell a cheap object, but as for 'the rest', as he calls it, he remains evasive and only proposes his 'will'.

The reason was that Dostoyevsky himself found it difficult to understand the complex mechanism of high finance. He had a detailed knowledge of the moneylending system, of borrowing and bills of exchange, but he knew nothing about the manipulations of capital, banking credit and the movement of monetary variations. Of course, economic life in Russia was simpler than it was in Western Europe; there were no attorneys or notaries, who play such a large part in Balzac. The Frenchman loved analysing the history of a crash or a fortune: the Russian stated the existence of one or the other and judged as a moralist. This economic innocence is clear not only in

Dostoyevsky's neglect of the relationship of money to work, but also in his absolute conviction that large sums could only be *gifts from Heaven* (inheritances, wins at gambling), *dishonest gains*, *thefts* or what he calls *conjuring tricks (fokusy)*. In the notebooks of *The Devils*, the 'Prince' is talking about the rouble and about European and Russian capitalism:

Just look at Russian capitalists and their capital: it's as if everything had been won at roulette. The father gets a million together and not by hoarding, not by work, but by[133] some sort of trick. Most of our capital is won by tricks. And more often than not, and it's no surprise to hear it, the heirs have turned into noblemen, have given up business and gone off to join the hussars or frittered it all away. That means, all this is a trick, so much so that there isn't even an idea here how capital is formed.[134]

Dostoyevsky never dealt with the basic question of what Marx called surplus-value, which gives rise to capital and large fortunes. He reacted to any speculation on a large scale by shouts of 'Theft!' Proudhonian in soul, he could think of high finance only as shady and scandalous:[135] in this sense, he remained faithful to the socialist doctrines of the forties.

It is a sordid spectacle which greets Arkadiy when he 'enters his career'.[136] All around him is decay (*razlozheniye*), especially in society,[137] and one of the chief agents of decay is naturally an unquenchable thirst for money. In the first stage of his plan, Arkadiy expressed his contempt for borrowing on wages and moneylending, the province 'of the Jews and those Russians who have neither intelligence nor character'.[138] Then he finds it happening all the time, on a much larger scale, from top to bottom of society. Everyone he meets is deep in the sewers: Lambert and his gang of master-blackmailers, Stebelkov, who forges railway shares[139] with Prince Sergey Sokolsky, Darzan, the aristocrat who falsifies bills of exchange, all those nobles who conceal gambling dens behind their aristocratic façades and visit Stebelkov's pawnshop, Anna Versilova, who sells herself to the senescent Prince Sokolsky to acquire title and fortune, the beautiful Akhmakova, who weaves a great web of intrigue to recover an imprudent letter, written to safeguard her inheritance ... Faced with all this corruption, Arkadiy feels that his *idea* is swelling with mud. Is he going to be carried away by the dance of money? He gambles, gets into debt, is accused of theft and involved in blackmail. But fortunately, he has broken the rule of isolation he imposed on himself: his heart wins, and he adopts a baby; in spite of all his sufferings as a bastard and his rejected love, he renews his ties with his sister, mother and two fathers, Versilov the aristocrat and Makar Ivanov, the man of the people, and he falls in love with the haughty Akhmakova. His idea is a failure, but he discovers himself. From this point of view, *A Raw Youth* is more than 'The story of the searches, hopes, corruption and rebirth'[140] of a young soul. It is also a novel about the beneficial failure of an *idea* based on money, about a mind and thought which is reformed while keeping the powerful fecundity of the feeling experienced. It is a spiritual education through the hateful mediation of money.

The mediating function of money: the ordeal of the world of the novels

Whether we consider the slavery it causes or the powerful lever it represents, money in Dostoyevsky's work forms a *mediation* in the Hegelian sense of the term, i.e., an intermediate action which produces a second stage, different from the first.

In the novels, money, besides being hateful, is mobile and indestructible. Dostoyevsky's world is like a huge system of circulation, where a diseased and mad blood, money, runs through the individual cells, starving some and stuffing others, and goes on its disorderly wanderings without ever being destroyed.

Money never stays in the same place, it is not *sensible* and only settles down with landowners, rare in Dostoyevsky's works, old-style merchants such as Rogozhin's father, and usurers, but at the price of 'gymnastics' as Ganya Ivolgin says. Arkadiy's dream of sensible money is a chimaera and a foreign and non-Russian one at that – it is only practical for the Napoleonic bourgeois, the German *Vater*, the Pole, the Jew. Ptitsyn is the exception that proves the rule. For the great heroes of Dostoyevsky, money is mad,[141] especially when they reach a crisis. This unleashes a movement of money, not a waltz or a merry-go-round but a sort of deadly blind man's buff. Small or large sums get lost, reappear, disappear again; they are seldom used for the hero's daily needs, but usually end up with someone else. For instance, what becomes of the 35 roubles given to Raskolnikov by his mother, who has taken it from her tiny monthly pension of 120 roubles? Apart from the 9 roubles 55 kopecks which Razumikhin spends on second-hand clothes, 15 kopecks are given to a prostitute on the Haymarket, 30 left in a cabaret 'The Crystal Palace', with a 20-kopeck tip, a coin is given to the people who help to move Marmeladov after his accident, and finally 20 roubles are left with Marmeladov's family . . . In *The Gambler*, tidy sums come and go, like a roulette ball, from Polina to the Gambler, from the Gambler to Polina (700 florins), then again from the Gambler to Polina (the hoard of 200,000 francs, whose deadly fires gleam in the night of love), from Polina to the Gambler, and then from the Gambler to Mlle Blanche, who changes them into smoke, though, like a careful Frenchwoman, she puts a good part of them into sensible money first. The last great novel, *The Brothers Karamazov*, is constructed on the deadly confusion of two sums of 3,000 roubles, the fatal 3,000 roubles, a gilded and tragic web in which Dmitriy struggles like a captive fly. This extraordinary muddle in which truth vanishes has been described in detail,[142] so we shall simply pick out the main parts.

The first 3,000 roubles have been entrusted to Dmitriy by Katerina to give to someone else. In fact, she is using them to test the man she believes she loves, since he has saved her from dishonour. Dmitriy had just replaced 4,500 roubles, which Katya's father, an officer, had stolen from the Treasury. The 3,000 roubles originating with Katya, instead of returning by this complicated circuit to their starting point, are going to be lost, partly for another woman with whom Dmitriy is in love: Grushenka. Dmitriy, who fully intends to repay them, is tempted by another 3,000 roubles which his debauched father has hidden and is saving for his 'angel', Grushenka. Old Karamazov is killed, as we learn later, by Smerdyakov, who takes the 3,000 roubles intended for Grushenka. So in both cases, the two fatal sums associated with the two women loved by Dmitriy have been diverted: the first has been, on two occasions, almost entirely dissipated at a riotous party; the second is in the hands of Smerdyakov. The demonic power of money allows these 3,000 roubles, which are really no longer in circulation, to continue an imaginary existence for other people: for the innkeeper, Trifon Borisych, who gives evidence that he has seen Dmitriy spend 3,000 roubles at his first orgy, for the Poles, to whom Dmitriy has offered 3,000 roubles if they would give up Grushenka. Ironically, the imaginary 3,000 roubles decide the fate of Dmitriy. And when they become real again, in the form of another 3,000 roubles given to the lawyer to save him, they are useless. This uncontrollable threesome reel of the 3,000 roubles: 3,000 roubles–Katya, 3,000 roubles–Grushenka, 3,000 imaginary roubles causes the judicial error.

In Bulgakov's novel *The Master and Margarita*, after the Master has burnt his novel, the Devil returns it to him, with the words 'Manuscripts do not burn.' This is true of money in Dostoyevsky: notes, which appear to be perishable, are always miraculously preserved from destruction. Foma Opiskin, for example, in *The Village of Stepanchikovo*, is given 15,000 roubles to get out of the colonel's house and acts out a scene of disdain and disinterestedness: 'Give me these millions that I may stamp my feet on them, give them that I may tear them in pieces, spit on them, scatter them to the wind, dirty them, dishonour them.' And after this virtuous tirade 'Foma scattered the whole bundle around the room. It was remarkable that he did not tear or spit on a single note, as he had boasted he would; he only crumpled them a bit, and that fairly carefully.'[143] Again, in *The Brothers Karamazov*, Alyosha brings Captain Snegiryov 200 roubles from Katya; the unhappy man speaks of the good he is going to do to his family, but suddenly he crumples the notes in fury, clenches them in his fist, flings them to the ground and stamps on them with all his might before running off. When Alyosha picks them up, they are 'quite whole, and even crackled, like new notes, when Alyosha unfolded them and smoothed them out'.[144] As Shklovsky says: 'The heroes of Dostoyevsky despise money, timidly and unprofitably.'[145] Money only appears indestructible because men cannot or dare not destroy it; the slave creates the master.[146] But the recurrence of the theme, originating in a psychological judgement, finally creates a much stronger impression: money seems to be indestructible in itself. This change from psychological realism to symbol is particularly clear in the famous scene where Nastasya Filippovna throws the 100,000 roubles brought by Rogozhin into the fire and challenges Ganya to pull them out. At first the bundle nearly puts the fire out.

But one little blue flame was still clinging underneath on the corner of a log. At last a long thin tongue of fire licked the bundle, the fire caught on it and began to run upwards along the corners of the paper, and suddenly the whole bundle caught fire in the hearth, and a brilliant flame leapt up. Everyone cried out.[147]

The ordeal lasted for another moment, Ganya fainted, Nastasya Filippovna pulled the 100,000 roubles out of the fire with tongs; 'Almost all the outer paper was scorched and smouldering, but you could see at once that the inside was untouched. The bundle was wrapped in three layers of newspaper, and the money was intact. Everyone sighed with relief.'[148] Bank notes do not burn, jeers Dostoyevsky's devil. They even have a life beyond the grave: in 'Bobok', the decomposing corpses in the cemetery do nothing but talk of money, which has held them prisoner all their lives: false coins (15,000 roubles), dowries (90,000 roubles), embezzlement (400,000 roubles). Money is imperishable.

As for the mediating function of money and its terms, there is no better expression of it than the one which Nastasya Filippovna proposes when she flings her challenge at Ganya and the 100,000 roubles into the fire. 'I want to look at your soul for the last time.'[149] The ordeal by money is one of the most recurrent ways of exploring man in the world of the novels. It is not artificial, since it is suggested by a realistic vision of society. With Tolstoy, for example, in *Three Deaths*, *War and Peace*, and *The Death of Ivan Ilych*, the passage from life to death is the test which illuminates and reveals the soul of man: with Dostoyevsky, it is the test of money. The test by money is the trial by ordeal in the world of the novel, with all the barbarous madness and tragic chance that this implies. The natural elements used in mediaeval times, fire and water, have been replaced by the eminently modern and artificial element of money.

Even the heroes who have conquered the demon of gold, the just and the holy, make their terms with it and know its power in the world. They oppose it with the law of love and voluntary poverty for themselves and try to direct and control its action. Myshkin is indifferent to poverty and riches, but when he inherits a vast fortune, his acts lose their purity of intention. The wanderer Makar Ivanych takes Versilov to court, so that his wife, mother of the raw youth, can be sure of the 3,000 roubles (a fatal sum) still owing from Versilov. Tikhon and Zosima have renounced all worldly goods, but they

receive donations for others. Alyosha himself, who has a marvellous talent
for living without money, is well aware of its value for the poor and for their
self-respect. All these men of God suffer from the wound of charity and
take infinite precautions to bestow charity without humiliation. The other
group indifferent to money, the spoilt aristocrats, are equally aware of its
power for good and evil. Stavrogin assents to the murder of the Lebyadkins,
and so of his own lawful wife, by throwing notes to Fedka the convict.
Versilov causes the suicide of Olya, a young unemployed governess, by
misplaced charity.[150] Katerina Ivanovna cruelly tempts Dmitry by entrusting him with 3,000 roubles, which sets the tragedy in motion.

As for the heroes who are struggling with the 'demigod' of money, in the
phrase of Makar the wanderer, they suffer a double mediation. First money
is a dazzling surface, a screen which hides real awareness, real motives, but
also a mirror reflecting the image of the soul. Raskolnikov, Nastasya
Filippovna, Dmitriy Karamazov have to kiss the infected face of their idol, so
that they can see it clearly. Raskolnikov has to murder the old money lender
and the gentle Lizaveta for the miserly sum of 317 roubles and a few gold
objects, thus sealing the alliance of money and blood,[151] so that the true
motives of his crime can gradually appear to him: poverty, his morbid state,
no doubt, but above all Promethean pride, the intimate conviction that he is
a Napoleon, the bewilderment caused by new ideas, the impatience for
justice, grief at the social tragedy of the Marmeladovs, of Sonya, of his own
family, and lastly the imperious need to break the paralysing dialectic of
desire, to move on to the act, to submit himself to the ordeal. Nastasya
Filippovna has to put herself up to public auction, reject the 75,000 roubles
of Totsky, choose Rogozhin, who offers her 100,000 roubles which are at
once proudly abandoned to Ganya, disdain the 1,500,000 roubles inherited
by Myshkin whom she loves, bargain with her flesh and her passion, so that
Myshkin can see, beyond the capricious courtesan, a pure and proud
woman who suffers, who deliberately submits to the knife of the murderer
to expiate a crime which she has not committed but which has stained her
for ever. Again, Dmitriy Karamazov has to be the pawn in the confused
game of the real, imaginary, imagined or sought 3,000 roubles, gold and
blood have to form a monstrous union, before this ardent heart, torn
between the Ideal of the Madonna and the abyss of Sodom, can discover
true love and his vocation of suffering and sacrifice. It is not by money but
by means of it, that the tragic hero is lost, finds himself, is reconciled with
himself or redeems himself in the eyes of the Other.

Velchaninov in 'The Eternal Husband' is perhaps the best illustration of
the mediation of money. The originality of this novella is in its symmetry, its
closed cyclic movement. It ends at its starting point, as the word 'eternal'
implies: at the end the two heroes, the cuckolded husband and the aging
Don Juan, take up their former parts and places. What has happened to

Velchaninov? At the beginning he is happy, healthy, perfectly 'balanced'. Suddenly everything falls apart: his health and especially his financial affairs. He comes to the capital for a law suit, which is going wrong. The man with a mourning band on his hat, Trusotsky, a husband he once deceived, intervenes. The fascination, a curious mixture of love and hate, which Trusotsky exerts on him, his secret need to drain the abscess, the monstrous tragedy of the innocent Liza, who pays for the faults of adults with her own life, all this causes a profound crisis for Velchaninov. He analyses himself and sees himself as he really is. He is on the point of reforming himself. Then he unexpectedly wins his law case, obtains 60,000 roubles and finds himself back on 'solid ground'. He forgets his secret shame, his retreat from the world; he changes morally and even physically: 'He looked cheerful, open, self-assured. Even the malignant worrying unhealthy wrinkles, which had begun to gather round his eyes and on his forehead, had almost entirely gone; even the colour of his face had changed, – it had become whiter, rosier.'[152] Money hid from Velchaninov his deepest self; the threat of losing money partly contributed to the beginning of his self-interrogation, his crisis and cathartic analysis. The return of money screened his conscience again; 60,000 roubles was all that was needed for Velchaninov to recover his comfortable blindness and to fall back into the rut of mediocrity.

But there is no such escape for Dostoyevsky and his great heroes. However much they might hate money, it was a necessary mediation for all of them. It clarified and accelerated the painful birth and the actual writing of the novels; it acted as a modern trial by ordeal in the world of the novels, bringing to birth the tragic and secret being whom all Dostoyevsky's heroes discover at the crisis point of the drama.

PART II
The process of creation

Introduction

Before we break into the study of the writer, or cross the threshold of his laboratory, or rummage among the artist's rough sketches, we must ask ourselves if this intrusion is right or profitable.

Any creative artist, especially a novelist, is by nature a public person and Dostoyevsky, who wrote for 'all the Russian reading public', was well aware of this. A literary vocation may be described as a will to gain power over people's minds, just as politics is a struggle for power in the city. Although literature was not a publicity stunt for Dostoyevsky, who uses the word 'I' very little in his works, he knew that he was placing himself, like a prophet, in full view of the crowd and of posterity.

But apart from the confidences which he authorised about his way of working, would he have allowed anyone to enter the inviolable and mysterious realm of the gestation of the novel, an opaque kingdom as fruitful and incalculable as life itself? Apart from his vanity as an artist, he would have doubted whether this was a valid approach to his work. He knew too well how the work changed as it developed, how creatures, forms, chains came to birth, faded, aborted, were fused and divided, how plan succeeded plan without apparent profit, how long hours of research, of experiment, of trial were followed by minutes of illumination and joy, how periods of discouragement succeeded instants of fallacious lucidity. And who could find his way amidst the jungle of the notebooks, this maze of notes, unfinished sentences, ellipses, sections of edited text, signs, without the reference system to which he alone had the key, and which only made sense to the writer who was using them as a working plan? And most of all, what is the value of drafts, sketches, projects, abandoned experiments compared with the finished work? Have we the right to favour the unformed, the uncreated, mere traces of a rich and complex path, when only the final novel is sanctioned by the creator?

However, the work is born of chaos: it is the genesis of a universe. As we are unable to experience the act of writing, to rediscover the bridge between the creation which has reached independent life and the world from which it came, we can only try to note the essential stages of the passage. Spying on the creative action of the artist, we can, at least if there are sufficient traces, infer the movement of creation. The creator's attitudes and his way of working are similar for each novel, and defined psychological types facing

171

identical situations recur insistently and obsessively in the notebooks, so that we can generalise to some extent. This area of criticism remains limited: it removes the unique quality of each novel and it is not a substitute for specific analysis of the genesis of any particular work. It disengages general structures, that is all.

The laboratory of the novelist is no longer a realm which is totally obscure. Large areas of it have been illuminated, if only incidentally. The embryonic forms of Dostoyevsky's creation of the novel have been sketched, the fertile transposition of his cultural resources has been shown, the dominant features of epilepsy and money have been measured. From these two chapters, dramatic, even tragic images remain. But no ordeal – and there were ordeals infinitely more cruel than financial distress or repeated attacks of epilepsy, such as confinement in the fortress, the mock execution, the four years of convict prison – no ordeal could turn Dostoyevsky aside from his literary vocation. He has been seen as a born writer, sure of making his mark in the arena of literature, cherishing his secret ambition of equalling the best, devoured with an ardent passion for writing, in a word, steadfast in his greatness. It is time to show him at work, in his daily existence.

7

The writer at work

I go to matins and there is always a light in his study. He is at work.

The merchant Alonkin

The night writer

The venerable merchant Alonkin owned the apartment in Petersburg at the corner of Carpenter Street and Little Meshchanskaya, which Dostoyevsky rented in 1866.[1] Since the penniless writer was a diligent worker (*velikiy trudolyubets*) before the Lord, Alonkin forgave him his slowness in paying the rent.

If Dostoyevsky needed night, with its mystery, its living silence, its shadows dancing in the candle-light, it was not to summon the powers of darkness, or to enjoy the romantic shadows which sometimes influence his descriptions, but to be free of daily hindrances and material worries, and to continue his concentrated and lonely struggle with the plans he had been forming all day. Night was the time for experiment, for testing the fruits of the laborious idleness of the day by writing. Night was the chosen time not for the Dostoyevskian universe, where the solar sun and night coexist, but for the creation of the novels and the creative process.

His preference for working at night was a habit he formed at the Engineering School. In the midnight hours, when everyone else was asleep, the officer on duty, Savelyev, used to find the clerk Dostoyevsky at his desk, with a blanket over his shoulders.[2] It is also a symbol of the creation of the novels, an immense and laborious effort to drive the shadows away from an idea which was originally obscure, since it was heavy with dense thought, drawn in thousands of different directions, a monsoon cloud, saturated, nourished by reality, by experience, by news items read the day before, by plans cherished for months, jostled by contemporary events, restrained by what had already been created, drawn into the whirlpool of the uncreated, enslaved by the appearance of 'entire worlds', 'colossal images', anxious to conduct a dialogue with the great shades of the past, the great contemporaries, impassioned about philosophy and worried about the effect needed. It was the painful night of labour, the passage between two certainties: the realms of light from which the first inspiration came and the final creation. This creation is not uncontrolled excess, as Strakhov thought,[3] but a complex whole, accepted in its complexity. The Dostoyevskian world looms up like a mountain range when each novel is begun. How could inspiration fall as the gentle dew from heaven, as it came to Mozart, Veronese, Pushkin and Stendhal? Dostoyevsky's creation, like the man and his thought, is, in Tolstoy's words, 'all struggle'.[4] Hesitant, feeling its way, experimenting, it directs a chaos of many different lives which cannot be described in its entirety but which must be expressed so that the novel reflects the whole of the first vision. The immensity of this task required not only genius, but also a method and rhythm of hard work.

Always pen in hand

Dostoyevsky was a born writer. He wrote all through his life, from his early years at the Engineering School, where, according to Savelyev, he had already begun *Poor Folk*, to his last breath: on the eve of his death, he was still correcting the proofs of *Diary of a Writer* for January 1881. He wrote a great deal, divided between his activity as a journalist and editor and his work as a novelist, using his journalistic work in his novels and his novels in his journalistic work.[5] He complained that he was working too hard and building himself a literary prison, a metaphor which was no idle ornament. About three months before his death, on 15 October 1880, he repeated this once more to an impatient correspondent:

Why haven't I replied to you? You will not believe me: if there is a man labouring like a convict, then I am that man. I spent four years in a hard labour camp in Siberia, but life and work were more bearable there than they are today. From 15 June to 1 October I have written up to twenty printed pages for my novel and I have published three signatures of Diary of a Writer.[6]

But this complaint is an expression of overwork, not renunciation. Dostoyevsky always had a keen awareness of his mission as a writer. He went on in the same letter: 'And yet I cannot write straight from the shoulder, I must write artistically. I owe it to God, to poetry, to the success of what I have written and literally to the whole Russian reading public who are waiting for the end of my work. And this is why, for literally days and nights, I have been sitting and writing.'[7] This determined, uninterrupted creation was accompanied by an equally large amount of correspondence, which, first limited to his exchanges with family, friends, dealings with editors and affectionate relationships, grew, especially after 1873 and *Diary of a Writer*, to be an animated and copious dialogue with the Russian reading public. Dostoyevsky did not shirk this task, but he reserved his writing talent for the creation of the novels by giving up the art of letter writing. He could have written brilliant and polished letters, as his first novel, *Poor Folk*, proves, but he had neither the time nor the taste for it. He poured out all his problems, his feelings, his worries and his anguish in a passionate muddle without worrying about repetition or obscurity. When he took up his pen, Dostoyevsky did not imagine posterity leaning over his correspondent's shoulder; he wrote like a man in a hurry exchanging a brief confidence with his next-door neighbour. The indifference to style in the letters, rare in a writer, was the result of complete concentration on his great works.

At the beginning of his literary activity, this concentration took place at all hours and everywhere, with a preference for night. There are plenty of witnesses. A. I. Savelyev remembered the nocturnal hours which Dostoyevsky wrested from the full and regulated existence of the Central Engineering School. Riesenkampf described the sleepless nights of Dostoyevsky, who sought refuge in reading and writing, and Grigorovich recalled the enthusiastic secret period of *Poor Folk*:

Dostoyevsky spent whole days and a part of his nights at his desk. He never said a word about what he was writing, he answered my questions unwillingly and laconically. Knowing his extreme reserve, I stopped interrogating him. However, I could see a mass of sheets covered with the handwriting so characteristic of him: the letters appeared naturally under his pen, close and clear like pearls.[8]

Later Dostoyevsky, through Ivan Petrovich, the hero of *The Insulted and Injured*, remembered those hours of intense creation when he was carried along by a morbid feverishness.[9] He wrote in the most difficult circumstances and the most unlikely places: in the humid ravelin of the Peter-Paul fortress, in the convict prison itself. There, thanks to Troitsky, the chief doctor, who prolonged his stays in the hospital and brought him paper and pencil, he composed the Siberian notebook, a garland of proverbs, dialect forms, assonances, folk treasure, fragments of playlets, and oddments from *chastushky* about the life of the convicts, which was a goldmine for future works. Baron Vrangel described Dostoyevsky as an ordinary soldier, exhausted by the harsh military day, the reviews, the marches and countermarches, suffering from eye trouble because he spent whole nights writing in a smoky hut in Semipalatinsk.[10] Other images appear, more anecdotal: Dostoyevsky in October 1865 scribbling a few notes for *Crime and Punishment* on *The Viceroy*, the boat taking him from Copenhagen to Petersburg: Dostoyevsky, cleaned out but ever hopeful, feverishly working at a new idea in a German hotel, after his disillusionment with gambling: Dostoyevsky trying to win a few hours for creation or his correspondence from the draconian timetable imposed by the doctors for his cure at Ems. Like many writers, he had pocket books, on which he scribbled lightning ideas as they flashed by; the irregular writing, so different from that of the notebooks, shows that the writer was moving about as he made these notes.[11]

However, Dostoyevsky did not habitually write in noisy restaurants or railway stations. He imposed discipline on himself, he made a rhythm of work which he forced himself to keep, even if it became boring. While he was finishing *The Idiot*, he described his daily existence in Geneva to his niece S. A. Ivanova in January 1868:

Anna Grigoryevna and I live like hermits. This is my life: I get up late, I make a fire in the fireplace (the cold is terrible), we drink our coffee, and then it is work. Then, about four o'clock, I go to the restaurant, where I have lunch for two francs, wine included. Anna Grigoryevna prefers to have her meals at home. Then I go to a café, and while I drink my coffee I read the Moscow News and The Voice, from beginning to end, not leaving a single letter out. Then I walk about the streets for half an hour to get some exercise; after this I go back home to start work. I make the fire in the fireplace again, we drink tea and I begin to work again. Anna Grigoryevna says she is terribly happy.[12]

This was the rhythm which Dostoyevsky, according to Anna Grigoryevna, observed until the end of his life, at any rate while he was writing novels.

The study

Let us go back to the last years, when the Dostoyevsky family occupied the six large rooms on the second floor of 5, Smith Street, St Petersburg.[13] It is night: eleven o'clock strikes. Fyodor Mikhaylovich is standing in the doorway of the drawing room, and Anna Grigoryevna knows it is time for her to go to bed.[14] They say goodnight. The writer looks round his study. It is opulent and severe, and furnished in the classical Russian style, with rectilinear and massive forms, cornices, friezes, columns, pilasters and arches, but the general effect is of sobriety. To the left is the cupboard, behind the desk is the leather divan with its straight back, and above it a full-sized reproduction of the Sistine *Madonna*, but without the people at her feet.[15] With a glance, Dostoyevsky makes certain that everything is as pedantically tidy as he could desire. On the desk, everything is in place (Anna herself has seen to this): newspapers, correspondence, books needed for reference, boxes of Russian cigarettes, as her husband is a heavy smoker, notebooks.[16] The pens are shaped and sharpened as he likes them: he hardly ever uses pencil. The paper is thick and of the right format with the lines barely visible.[17] Everything is in order. The two candlesticks cast their living light.[18] Work begins.

If Dostoyevsky was writing, a pile of sheets appeared, covered with beautiful writing. If he was at the research stage, he jotted down in the notebooks the ideas which occurred to him with a nervous, sometimes pensive pen, distracted by the odd Latin word or some name written with loving calligraphy, but elsewhere firm and decisive, with frequent additions of 'very important', 'capital', 'Nota bene' or NB, 'A new idea', 'a splendid idea', 'an idea in flight' and 'or perhaps'. At other times, his pen doodled disturbing or jeering faces between the columns of notes starring the pages, or inscribed the flames of Gothic ogives in the empty margins. From time to time he rose to meditate, strode around the room, turning sharply, or, to recover his spirits, he drank another glass of lukewarm or cold tea, or used the candle to light a cigarette which he had filled with tobacco. The writer has entered the night of creation. The pen scratches, the wax sputters, the shadows come to life in the smoke: these are the only visible outward signs of the mystery of creation. At last, towards four or five o'clock, in the pale dawn of the white nights or the deep silence of early winter mornings, Dostoyevsky went to bed.[19] He was sometimes so exhausted that an attack of epilepsy followed his first sleep. He got up at eleven o'clock at the earliest, at two at the latest.

Activity by day and improvised writing

A good way through the day, Dostoyevsky's ordinary life began again. There were meals to be eaten, his wife and children coming to tell what they had been doing and to be read to, the necessary walks, friends calling to see him, letters to write, and sometimes the crushing tasks of the editor. Dostoyevsky prepared for his day with a few gymnastic exercises and a careful toilette: he had a passion for cleanliness and was not casual and relaxed at home. His daughter had never seen him in slippers and dressing-gown. He always appeared wearing shoes and a tie, linen of dazzling whiteness and starched collars. He had a holy horror of stains, which distracted him and made him incapable of concentrating.[20] One might suppose that this strictness in dress, refusal to be the Bohemian artist, like his manic passion for order and cleanliness, were a legacy from the difficult years of poverty and dirt in prison and the army, but they may also show an organising will, which is exerting itself in a field more easily mastered than that of creation. In his daytime activity there were two main times devoted to creation: that of expression, writing, and of ingestion, reading.

Before *The Gambler* and his second marriage, Dostoyevsky wrote like most of the writers of his time. From more or less detailed notes, he composed, corrected, went over his works several times, especially *Poor Folk*, and ended with the definitive manuscript, of which he himself made a fair copy, as he had no money to pay a copyist. When stenography, in the youthful form of Anna Grigoryevna, entered his life, he inaugurated a method whose originality has not been sufficiently stressed: dictation on the basis of a manuscript.

Anna Grigoryevna has preserved the memory of his first improvisations:

While I was getting ready, Fyodor Mikhaylovich had begun to pace to and fro fairly quickly, crossing the room diagonally, from the door to the stove which he invariably struck with two small blows. Meanwhile he was smoking, taking fresh cigarettes all the time, which he just started to smoke and then threw into the ashtray at the end of the desk.[21]

But soon the novel, *The Gambler*, had grown and Dostoyevsky was no longer improvising directly, but dictating from the manuscript he had written during the night. The habit was formed and Dostoyevsky, often between two or three o'clock in the afternoon, before the main meal at four, dictated the results of his nightly work to his wife.[22] When he was doubtful, he would check his 'effects' by reading the whole chapter aloud, for he had noticed that his dear Anna's reactions coincided with those of his readers. She was wise enough to make no judgement on essentials, according to the memoirs of their daughter Lyubov, and proposed only minor changes: a blue dress turns to pink, a wardrobe slides furtively from right to left, the hero's hat alters shape or perhaps the hero sheds his beard.[23] After dictation Anna copied out her stenography and Dostoyevsky corrected this text, expanding it where necessary. Anna then only had to make a fair copy and the manuscript was ready to be sent off. It was a rapid and economical way of working: no more wearisome copying for the writer, and no more temptations to perfectionism; but it raises an observation and question.

While Dostoyevsky was dictating, he never stopped pacing around the room and even, at difficult moments, pulled his hair, which he then wore long, as we are told by Anna Grigoryevna.[24] The style with its triple repetitions, its sentences punctuated as in speech, its accumulation of nouns and adjectives with similar meanings, its constant reticence, reflects this uninterrupted pacing within a confined space. From this time on, the rhythm of the Dostoyevskian sentence may be defined as a walking movement, where the breath of the spoken word is marked in the written style.

But the essential point remains a mystery. How far was the manuscript finished when Dostoyevsky began to dictate? What was the part played by improvisation? The manuscripts, even the most complete, like those of *A Raw Youth*, give only the planning or drafting stage, or at the most the beginning of writing. They are essentially the three notebooks for the years 1861–5 and the seventeen work books for the years 1856–81 preserved in the Lenin Library in Moscow and the Central Archives of the USSR, supplemented by the Anna Grigoryevna Dostoyevskaya bequest at Pushkin House in Leningrad. Certainly these manuscripts include written texts of various sizes which are found without much change in the finished work: for example, several pages of Raskolnikov's diary, although in the finished novel the third person is used instead of the first. But there is no linked text to be handed in to the printer as it stands. L. M. Rozenblyum may be right in supposing first that there were probably some separate sheets,[25] now lost, from the stage between the notebooks and the finished text, and second, that improvisation played a 'considerable' part during the dictation.[26] The phenomenon of improvisation is still mysterious, even to Pushkin, who introduces an Italian improvisor in *Egyptian Nights*. However, for Dostoyevsky, it did not go beyond the limits of a text spoken freely on the basis of a rapid, incomplete but substantial written text. The framework of the novel was firm, the strong expressions noted, the links defined. It now had to be joined together and brought to life, and the details had to be connected. But this improvisation, however relative it may have been, gave the writing the conviction of the voice, a modulation full of shades and slight differences, the twists and turns and emotion of a spoken thought. Improvisation gives the written speech the mobility of the unfinished, the vibration of *non-finito* so dear to Michelangelo. Dictation from notes keeps all the options open, preserves a freedom, a play between the definite state of the written text and the notes of the stenographer. This original method of work reinforces the profound tendency of the thought of Dostoyevsky, who keeps to the wavy and irresolute line of life. V. V. Rozanov compares Tolstoy as 'painter of life in all its finished forms'[27] with Dostoyevsky, 'analyst of the changing movements in the life and mind of man'.[28] It would be absurd to claim that Dostoyevsky's method of writing was determined by the nature of his creative genius, but it matches the movement of the writer's thought perfectly.

The second important time of the daily creative activity was reading, mechanically and gluttonously devouring the written text. This, different as it may seem, was one of the fundamental building blocks of creation, just as the experience and the dream were. But, in contrast with experience and dream, which are directly linked with the creator, reading comes from the Other, and appears as such. A written text is the transcribed word of the Other, often of a collective Other: in modern terms, it is one of the media. As soon as the text appears, the world disappears into the universe of the novel; with the writing of the Other, the dialogue begins. Usually writers who have a sense of being an élite do not converse with anyone who happens to come along. If they refer to previous literature – 'great' literature, if possible – to define their own thought and their own aesthetic theory, they do it with discrimination. An aristocratic line of descent is established and the writer becomes its guardian. Dostoyevsky had none of this literary snobbishness. He hunted all sorts of game: the Sacred Word, the classical work of art, contemporary writing with its depths of its passing charms, the popular adventure novel, the article where voluble prose clothes a stinging epigram, serious scientific works or works of popular appeal, reviews with their ideological battles, newspapers with their chronicles of current events, their echoes, their ephemera and their sensational news items. For Dostoyevsky as creator no source was noble in itself; there were only voices in a dialogue: the Bible, voice of God; the great classics, voices of inspiring genius; the Press, the anonymous voice of underground history, of the time to come.

8

The great dialogue: the news item

Every newspaper is nothing but a tissue of horrors from first line to last. War, crimes, thefts, lewdness, tortures, crimes of princes, crimes of nations, crimes of individuals, intoxication with universal atrocity. And every civilised man drinks this disgusting brew with his morning meal. Everything in this world reeks of crime: the newspaper, the wall, the face of man.

I cannot understand how a pure hand can touch a newspaper without a shudder of disgust.　　　　　　　　　　　　　　　　Charles Baudelaire, *Mon coeur mis à nu*

News items in creative research

Unlike Baudelaire, who was writing in the 1860s, Dostoyevsky considered the Press an indispensable tool with nothing sordid about it. In this field he was the initiator of the great American and European literatures of the twentieth century, where the newspaper, even in its raw form, is an integral part of the novel.

Dostoyevsky could not live without the Press, especially abroad, where he needed to keep in touch with his native country. In Geneva, in 1867 and 1868, he found true 'happiness' in reading the Russian Press from cover to cover: *The Voice, The Moscow Bulletin, The St Petersburg Bulletin*, and the foreign papers.[1] He is always mentioning his newspaper reading in his letters.[2] And the two hours, from five to seven, which he spent on this daily activity in some café, were so enthralling to him that, while he was walking in the evening with his young wife, he loved to tell her what he had been reading about, so that she could keep up with 'everything that was happening in Russia'.[3]

Once he was so indignant about a story that Anna Grigoryevna noted the event in her *Diary* of 14 October 1867 (2 October of the Russian calendar). 'In the evening we went for a walk and Fedya told me a long story of what he had been reading in the papers, that is the story of Olga Umetskaya, poor girl; how sorry I felt, what strength of character.'[4] The story filled the Russian legal chronicle and Dostoyevsky followed the trial attentively in the Russian newspapers he found in Geneva:[5] in *Moscow* 23 and 24 September 1867 (nos. 136 and 137), and *The Voice* 26, 27 and 28 September (nos. 266–8), which for Europe is the 5, 6, 8, 9 and 10 October. Dostoyevsky's strong reaction is understandable: he might have created Olga Umetskaya himself. At fifteen, she was still a child but already a woman, and desperation had driven her to rebel.

The Umetskys, well-off provincial landowners but always squabbling about money, were what would now be called inadequate parents. Carefree progenitors, they would leave their children in a village in the heart of the steppes until they were seven or eight. Then they took them into the family, but it was a martyrdom for the survivors (five out of twenty), who were regularly beaten and sent to sleep in the stable, so that the two little brothers of Olga 'did not know how to speak' at seven years old. Olga had twice tried to throw herself out of the window, and even to hang herself, but each time she had been stopped. Finally, in desperation, she tried to burn the family house down four times: just before the last attempt she had been beaten black and blue for giving some honey to a workman. Brought to court, this humiliated and injured soul was proud enough to take complete responsibility for her action and to deny nothing.

The future creator of Nastasya Filippovna understood her perfectly, and was much struck by the picture of this family of Russian provincial nobility, rent by money quarrels and gnawed by the leprosy of dirt and disorder. He had been working on a similar theme for about a month: life was strewing manna in his path.

The first sketch of the novel *The Idiot*, on 14 September 1867, begins with the words: 'A family of ruined landowners.'[6] Certainly the situation is different; the characters have a 'name' and live in Petersburg. The father is a general who was ruined abroad and is trying 'to get money by stupid calculations'. The mother is 'worthy of respect, noble but extravagant'. There is not much resemblance to the Umetskys: the son, 'the handsome young man' is proud and ambitious 'with some claim to originality' (the future Ganya): the daughter is 'stupid, cruel and bourgeois', the second son, nicknamed 'the Idiot' because he is epileptic and his mother hates him, is a soul who has 'a burning need for love and immeasurable pride' (a very distant predecessor of Myshkin). But there is also an adopted child, an orphan (daughter of the mother's sister-in-law): 'a resentful Mignon and Cleopatra'.[7] The poor orphan is terribly ill-treated and 'less than a servant in the house'. 'Naive, proud, envious' she hates the family and longs for revenge; she is also 'terribly intelligent and notices everything'. She tells her dreams to the Idiot, with whom she forms an alliance, since they are both humiliated.[8] Like the future Nastasya Filippovna, she has been physically humiliated; the general tries to rape her; the 'handsome young man', 'the Idiot' and in later plans a certain Vladimir manage to do so.

She is 'the resentful Mignon and Cleopatra' at the same time. Dostoyevsky was creating his heroine with reference to his cultural heritage, thus beginning his dialogue with 'great literature'. Mignon is the heroine of *Wilhelm Meisters Lehrjahre*, by Goethe, a strange child uprooted from her family, who accompanies a *troupe* of wandering actors, singing nostalgic airs from the country 'where the lemon trees bloom' and finally dies of love for Wilhelm. Dostoyevsky transforms this image to represent the bitter poetry of loneliness and the deadly power of dreams of love. Cleopatra, as we have seen, is a disturbing and powerful beauty with the soul of a praying mantis, a legacy from Pushkin's *Egyptian Nights*. She is more than an image of debauchery; Dostoyevsky was fascinated by her 'ferocious irony', her desire to 'enjoy the contempt' which she feels towards the suitors for the deadly night of love, or in other words, her pleasure in vengeance. Like Cleopatra, his heroine dreams of revenge on those who possess or rape her. And like the queen, who, for one night, wishes to become a low courtesan, a slave, she proposes, in an extreme challenge, to become 'a bad woman'.[9]

This was the first sketch. And suddenly reality, in the form of a news item, had given a seal of authenticity to the literary figure which he was drawing with the help of images from Goethe and Pushkin. Dostoyevsky took up his notebook at page 27 and opposite 'resentful Mignon' he wrote in the margin 'Olga Umetskaya'. On page 29 he added directly: 'The story of Mignon is just the same as the story of Olga Umetskaya.' Reality, enhanced by the sanction of public opinion since it was a fact chosen by the press as an example of a social tendency, fertilised the research which had begun with the cultural background and personal inspiration of the writer.[10] It was still a long way to the complex living figure of Nastasya Filippovna, the result of trial and error, hesitation and changes, as well as many experiments with successive heroines: Mignon, Hero, the very real Olga Umetskaya, the newcomers Ustinya and Nastya. But Dostoyevsky now knew that he was going forward on a path cleared by reality, and that the tragic figure, extravagant as it might seem, was not an arbitrary construction, but a creature living in this world. Reality freed the artist from the poet's doubts. In fact, this operation remained hidden; the contemporary reader of Dostoyevsky, unlike the critic who has access to the notebooks, was aware only of the fascinating Nastasya Filippovna, though he sensed some truth behind the image. Dostoyevsky, with the science of the true realist, had used the vague and dark background of buried but still palpable memories of things read before. This was not a simple procedure, but a characteristic of the way in which Dostoyevsky constructed the novel: he did not describe reality or give it a concrete image, but allowed its presence to be felt, and admitted its first existence. Reality was thus no longer the projection, the transcribed perception of the author, but emerged from the heroes, as it was an essential part of them when they were first created.

The news item inserted in the novel

In this way the news item was detached from the writer who had discovered it in the Press and became the quotation, the object of the heroes themselves, who use it to express their own fantasy, their own convictions, forebodings or misery. *The Idiot* gives us four revealing examples, from comic to tragic.

Let us listen to General Ivolgin as he tells a story. He is in a railway carriage, smoking a cigar. Two ladies sit opposite him with a charming little lapdog, Princess Belokonsky and her companion, Mistress Smith. The Englishwoman, dressed in blue, suddenly springs up, seizes the cigar and flings it out of the window. The general delicately seizes the dog and sends it after the cigar. The lady slaps him, he hits her: great commotion! Everyone laughs at this story, but Nastasya Filippovna, with deliberate cruelty towards Ganya, who is suffering because his father is talking such rubbish, reveals the lie: 'I read the same story in *The Independence* – it is my newspaper – five or six days ago: it happened on one of the lines by the banks of the Rhine, between a Frenchman and an Englishwoman: the same cigar snatched away, the same lapdog thrown out of the window, the same ending as in your story, even the same light blue dress!'[11] And she mercilessly promises to send him the newspaper so that he can check it. The use of the news item here has no mystery; it is psychological or dramatic.

The next one is more characterisitic. At one point, Lebedev, with his usual clownishness, is trying to annoy his insolent nephew, a 'rebel' and a 'conspirator' who has come to 'touch' him after a gambling loss. Lebedev turns to Myshkin:

> 'Have you been following the murder of the Zhemarin family in the news-
>   papers?'
> 'Yes', said the prince, rather surprised.
> 'Well, here he is in person, the murderer of the Zhemarin family. This is the
>   very man!'
> 'What do you mean?' said the prince.
> 'You understand, I am speaking allegorically. I mean it is the future second
>   murderer of the future second Zhemarin family.'[12]

Dostoyevsky, writing for the Russian reader of 1868, says no more. He knew that the reader could easily fill in the hint, since the average reader, like Dostoyevsky himself, had seen the account of this amazing crime in *The Voice* of 10 March 1868 (no. 70), where it was generally supposed to show the influence of nihilism on educated youth. The murderer, Vitold Gorsky, of noble family, a schoolboy of eighteen, was giving lessons to the son of a merchant from Tambov, Zhemarin. He had prepared his weapons with great care, and when the right day came, he had cold-bloodedly murdered six people: Zhemarin's wife, mother, and eleven-year-old son, a relative and two servants. The news item which Dostoyevsky noted in his notebook no. 5, page 132, should originally have been an episode experienced by the prince, who released Gorsky, the murderer of the Zhemarins.[13] In the final novel, Dostoyevsky uses it as an obsessional theme, which passes from mouth to mouth. The crime haunts people's minds. The scene just before before Rogozhin's attempt to murder the prince and the epileptic fit is typical. Myshkin foresees these two events; he wanders through the streets, vainly trying to order the chaos of his ideas, to stop the terrible devil's dance of images which are assailing him. And suddenly, like a 'musical theme, obsessive and wearisome', he sees the images of Lebedev's nephew, of the murderer of the Zhemarins, of the waiter with whom he discussed this news item, which he had recently seen in the newspapers, and especially of Rogozhin, an imminent murderer who will kill but 'not in such a disorganised way'.[14] Yevgeniy Pavlovich mentions the affair too. He makes fun of Gorsky's lawyer, who is supposed to have said: 'It is natural that poverty should have put it into my client's mind to kill these six persons. Who would not have had the same idea in his place?'[15] Finally, Mme Yepanchin, enraged by this method of reasoning, foresees the end of the world, the coming of the 'last times'.[16] Dostoyevsky was competing with the Press and describing the process of the formation of public opinion. It is his tribute to the Press's power over the mind.

The third news item, which also concerns murder, is not explicitly mentioned. We remember that before exchanging crosses, Myshkin and Rogozhin have a long discussion about faith. The Idiot, as if he knew in advance about the knife which 'his brother in Christ' is to raise against him, recalls a personal experience:

In the evening, I stopped in a provincial hotel for the night, and a murder had just been done in it, the night before . . . Two peasants, who were getting on in years, and not drunk, and who had known each other a long time, friends, had been drinking tea and decided to go off to bed in a room they had rented together. But one of them had noticed the other wearing, in the last two days, a watch, silver, on a beaded yellow chain, which, apparently, he hadn't seen him with before. This man wasn't a thief – he was even an honest man, and, by peasant standards, he was not at all poor. But the watch appealed to him so much and it tempted him so much that he finally couldn't stand it: he took a knife and when his friend turned his back, he came up to him cautiously from behind, found his target, raised his eyes to heaven, crossed himself and saying a bitter prayer to himself: 'Lord, pardon me for the love of Christ!' he cut his friend's throat with one blow, as if he were a ram, and took the watch from him.[17]

This is linked with a news item which Dostoyevsky had noted on page 87 of notebook 4: 'NB. Cf. The Moscow Bulletin of 5 November 1867. The affair of the murder of the bourgeois Suslov by the peasant of the province of Yaroslavl, Myshkin district,[18] Balabanov (cut Suslov's throat to take his watch while Suslov was blowing on the coals of the samovar, saying 'Lord, pardon me for the love of Christ')'.[19] In fact, the item appeared in *The Voice* of 30 October 1867 (no. 300) and Dostoyevsky had freely transposed reality: Balabanov was a poor man who came to Petersburg to survive: he killed to pawn the watch for eight roubles.[20] Dostoyevsky was especially struck by the prayer said at the moment of the crime, which illustrates the words of Myshkin: 'The essence of religious feeling is beyond any reasoning, or any faults or crimes, or any forms of atheism.'[21]

The last example of a news item, equally bloody, is the boldest and the most revealing. There is a double use of it. On one hand, the news item is dissolved in the creative process to arouse an existential reality, as in the Balabanov case which we have just discussed, and on the other hand, like the Gorsky case, it keeps its character as a piece of news with the value of an example, even a warning. The news item has its twin inside the novel: two murders, real and fictional, the murder of Kalmykov by Mazurin and that of Nastasya Filippovna by Rogozhin, endlessly echo and clarify each other.

Even before going abroad in March 1867, Dostoyevsky had learnt from the papers that a Moscow merchant, V. F. Mazurin, had managed to hide for eight months in his own house the corpse of the jeweller I. I. Kalmykov, whose throat he had cut. The trial was held on 26 November 1867 and *The Moscow Bulletin* (no. 259) and *The Voice* of 29 November (no. 330) gave accounts of it. Mazurin, like Rogozhin, had inherited two million from his father and was living with his mother in a house which was exactly like Rogozhin's. On the 14 July 1866, using a razor with a blade firmly bound on to it, he cut Kalmykov's throat. And that evening he covered the corpse with an 'American oil cloth' and placed two bowls of 'Zhdanov water' on the window sill, to get rid of unpleasant smells. Mazurin, like Rogozhin, was condemned to fifteen years hard labour.

In one of Nastasya Filippovna's three letters to the prince, there is a surprising parallel between Mazurin and Rogozhin:

I read my fate every day in those terrible eyes, which are always looking at me . . . These eyes are silent now (they are always silent), but I know their secret. His house is gloomy, boring, and there is a mystery in it. I am sure that he has a drawer in which a razor is hidden tied up in silk, like that murderer in Moscow: he lived with his mother too and he bound his razor in silk to cut someone's throat. All the time when I was in their house, I kept on thinking that somewhere under the floorboards a corpse had been hidden, perhaps by his father, and covered with oilcloth, like the Moscow one, and surrounded with bowls of Zhdanov water.[22]

This premonition had such an effect on Myshkin that even during the terrible final scene, on the verge of madness, he remembered the Mazurin affair. Rogozhin explained his sinister precautions after the murder:

'I covered her with an oilcloth, a good, American oilcloth, and over the oilcloth with a sheet, and I put four bottles of Zhdanov water uncorked, they're still there now'. 'It's like there . . . in Moscow?'[23] stammered the prince.

This is obvious mimicry on Rogozhin's part, reinforced by Nastasya Filippovna's obsession with the news item. One might say that she imposed the means of her own death on the murderer. The extraordinary thing in the novel, and the contemporary reader was aware of it, is that the action begins on Wednesday, 27 November 1867, so that Nastasya Filippovna had read of Mazurin's crime in the newspapers on the day before or on the very morning of the day when Rogozhin and Myshkin enter her life. As Dorovatovskaya-

Lyubimova writes: 'From this day on, the crime of Mazurin was engraved on her memory and pursued her like a musical theme for the whole of the novel.' And later: 'Nastasya Filippovna is described so that two visions always appear at her side: that of the murderer Rogozhin and that of his prototype the murderer Mazurin.'[24] By this subtle intrication of novel time and real time, Dostoyevsky shows the reader how the creative process began with this sensational news item, and also how important the news item was to him.

A social, spiritual and moral Socratic dialogue

Dostoyevsky explained the significance of the news item in *The Idiot*:

I know a real case of murder committed for a watch. It has been in the newspapers. If a writer had imagined this crime, those who know about the life of the people and critics would have said at once that it was impossible. But if you read it in the newspapers as a fact, you feel that this is exactly the sort of fact that is most instructive about Russian reality.[25]

The words are Myshkin's, but the idea is Dostoyevsky's own, as it also appears in the long letter he wrote to Strakhov, 10 March 1869, from Florence. *The Idiot* had then been completed and Dostoyevsky, as if to disarm the critics, defined his idea of reality hidden in the unique, exceptional, 'fantastic' event – fantastic in the Dostoyevskian sense, that is, improbable but not unreal since it is factual – and marked himself off from his fellow-writers by a hymn of praise to the news item.

I have a personal vision of reality (in art) and what most people call fantastic and exceptional is sometimes for me the very essence of reality. Daily occurrences and the commonplace view of things are not realism in my opinion, but just the opposite. In every newspaper you come across stories of the most real and complicated facts. To our writers they are fantastic, so they take no notice of them, or they are reality because they are facts. Who will be capable of noticing them, explaining them, noting them down? They happen every instant of every day, but they are not at all exceptional . . . We let the whole of reality escape from under our nose. Who will be capable of discerning facts and going deeply into them? . . . My fantastic Idiot, is it not reality, and the most everyday reality at that?'[26]

For Dostoyevsky, the news item, whether it was a crime of passion, a vast confidence trick or financial catastrophe, a scandalous verdict, a personal or collective attempt at arson, a suicide caused by despair or ideology, a train crash, children plotting against their father, or the numerous cases of ill-treated children, had its roots deep in changeable reality and its appalling or amazing oddity revealed the subterranean upheavals of society. It illuminated the hidden depths of the collective soul, just as illness or hallucination cast a sudden unexpected light on the soul of the individual.

The news item had a quality of universal prophetic experience, a power of persuasion that no other material in the novel possessed. Its great strength was that it belonged to the collective heritage of the writer, his heroes and his readers. It is the voice of the crowd returned to the crowd. The novelist was giving back to the reader something the reader had already assimilated more or less absentmindedly, but he added an interpretation, a new sense. As material of the novel, the news item becomes the vehicle of a Socratic dialogue, social, spiritual and moral. As Jean-Paul Sartre says: 'The most everyday facts may be interpreted in depth. Analysis of a news item, for instance, may reveal more about the nature of a society than a commentary on a change of government.'[27] Dostoyevsky says the same thing in his advice to his niece, S. A. Ivanova: 'Get several newspapers, and for heaven's sake read them, this is really necessary nowadays, not for fashion's sake, but so as to get a strong and clear impression of the visible bond between all affairs, public and private.'[28]

A list of the news items used in the other great novels, all found in the most immediate, 'most fantastic', 'most unexpected' and 'most unlikely' reality, as Dostoyevsky said in his *Diary of a Writer* 1876[29] would never be finished. The most important, with their correspondences in the novel in brackets, are: in *The Devils* the political murder of the student Ivanov (Shatov) by the five headed by the nihilist Nechayev (Pyotr Stepanovich Verkhovensky): in *A Raw Youth* the activities of the secret society of the Dolgushintsy (Dergachev, Vasin, Kraft), the suicide of the student Kramer (Kraft),[30] the issue of false railway shares for the Tambov–Kozlov line (Brest–Grayev in the novel) by the criminal Kolosov (Stebelkov) and the aristocrat Nikitin (the young prince Sokolsky):[31] and finally in *The Brothers Karamazov*, the attempt to murder the Austrian carpenter Anton Fleisner made by his own children, aged from eight to ten[32] (the guilt of all the Karamazov brothers in parricide) and especially the tragic story of Lieutenant Ilinsky (Dmitriy Karamazov), condemned on evidence for parricide and recognised as innocent after spending ten years in the 'House of the Dead', where Dostoyevsky met him.[33] However the novelist did not make a servile copy of reality. The factual background and the idea which he saw in it were only the first inspiration. His characters, especially the main ones, have only a behavioural resemblance to their originals in the newspapers. Reality is only a launching pad for the imagination, but it is the indispensable basis and guarantee, as Dostoyevsky is always saying. On 10 May 1879, he wrote to the editor of *The Brothers Karamazov*:

Everything which my hero, Ivan Karamazov, says in the text I have sent you is based on reality. All the stories about children really took place, they have appeared in the newspapers and I can show you where: I have invented nothing. The general who hunted a child with his dogs and this whole fact are a real event, it was published in The Archives, I think, this winter and reprinted in many papers.[34]

However, in making this statement, Dostoyevsky was silent about his true achievement, which is the supercomposition of reality.

Supercomposition of the news item

In *Diary of a Writer*, October 1876, Dostoyevsky made an admission which applied to the news item:

Observe a certain fact of real life, even something which is not particularly striking at first sight, and, if you are at all capable of it and you have the right vision, you will find a depth in it which does not exist in Shakespeare. But this is the whole question: whose vision and who has the ability? For not only to create and write literary works, but also simply to notice a fact, an artist of some kind is needed.[35]

An artist is needed to imagine the life behind the formal document and to resurrect the news item. *The Diary of a Writer* is often called a laboratory for the creation of the novels: one might add that it is often a laboratory open to the sky, where the chemist freely shows the secret of his operations. In 1873 Dostoyevsky demonstrates his method of supercomposition of the news item. It comes to life before us, develops, and puts on flesh in a scene like that of a novel where ends and beginnings are revealed. It is the history of a poor peasant girl who, beaten black and blue a whole year long, tormented and maimed by her husband, driven to despair by everyone's lack of understanding, her suit dismissed by the village court, finally committed suicide.[36]

First he gives the plain facts:

The story of this woman is well known: it is quite recent. It has been read in all the papers and possibly not forgotten. The thing is very simple: she hanged herself to escape from her husband's blows: the husband was tried and judged worthy of clemency. But this story has haunted me for a long time, and still haunts me.[37]

He began by noting the appearance of the husband as it is given in the official document: 'It is said that he was tall, solidly built, strong and fair.' But the artist could resist it no longer: 'I would have added, sparse hair, white skin, a full body, slow grave movements, a concentrated look, speaking little and seldom, letting his words drop like precious pearls which he enjoys before others do'.[38] Then he imagines the dead woman: 'She was probably a tiny thin little woman, thin as a rake.' And, putting in a plea from experience, he goes on: 'It is not rare for a big robust man with a full white body to marry a tiny little woman (they are even inclined to this choice, I have noticed).'[39] He even felt that something was 'missing' in the picture: it would have been better if the woman had been pregnant. Then his imagination carries him off into a long description of the peasant torturing the unhappy woman, his increasing sadism following his cruel indolence, their frightened little daughter watching the violence. Continually referring to the document, he justifies his development of the story by repetitions of 'probably' (*dolzhno byt'*), and by reference to his own experience: 'Have you seen a peasant beat his wife? I have.' The process is clear: by a dialogue with the imagined voices of the crowd, always going back to his own experience and that of the anonymous reader, Dostoyevsky supercomposes the news item. The aim of the exercise was to prove that 'the philosophy of the environment', summarised as 'His social environment is to blame', is an excuse for everything, justifies any plea for clemency, and so should be rejected or at least amended. In the chosen passage, the story from the newspapers comes only after the reasoning: it is an illustration of the theme. The journalist makes a plea; the artist convinces. The supercomposed news item, the result of a Socratic dialogue whose essential purpose is to convince the inner conscience of the reader, is not a fact which forces Dostoyevsky into a particular philosophical view point, but is bound to his philosophy as body is to soul. He uses this force of persuasion, springing from the tacit dialogue between writer and reader, with sovereign skill in his great novels.

Conclusive proof

A vast catalogue could be made of all the news items collected by Dostoyevsky, with their exact sources, their 'technical files' in the note-books, their use in the novels. This would give a clearer image of Dostoyevsky's fantastic realism, a true vision of the future, whose boldness escapes the modern reader, since he is deprived of the innumerable echoes which Dostoyevsky's works aroused in a contemporary.

At the time the effect was so strong that reality sometimes came back like a boomerang to confirm the supercomposition of the news item which Dostoyevsky had chosen. *Crime and Punishment* is the most striking example. G. F. Kogan discovered in *The Voice* 7–13 September 1865 (nos. 247–53) a news item which the novelist had probably read: a passage from the 'Diary of Raskolnikov', a first version of the novel, gives us reason to think so.[40] A young man of twenty-seven, son of a merchant, a *raskolnik* (old believer), Gerasim Chistov, had murdered two old women in January 1865 during a robbery of their mistress. As in the novel, the crime took place between seven and nine in the evening and had been committed with an axe; as in the novel, the two victims lay in a pool of blood and one of them had been unlucky enough to come in unexpectedly; as in the novel, the murderer had left several objects behind and hidden the gold and silver, not under a stone, but in the snow.[41] The coincidences are so numerous that it is reasonable to think that the Chistov case inspired Dostoyevsky before his first plans for *Crime and Punishment*.

The first chapters were published in the edition of *The Russian Messenger* for January 1866. In mid January, while the novel was still at the printers, the newspapers carried an account of a crime very similar to that of Raskolnikov. Danilov, a well-educated and intelligent student, with a firm and serious character, and as handsome as Dostoyevsky's hero – he had large expressive dark eyes and a mane of hair – had murdered and robbed a retired Captain Popov, a moneylender, and his housekeeper Nordman. The coincidence struck everyone: there was still talk of it three years later.[42] The dates give no room for doubt: reality had confirmed Dostoyevsky's interpretation of intellectual crime. There was another surprise in November 1867: it was learnt that a man held on suspicion, Glazkov, had freely confessed, like the painter Mikolka, to the crime committed by Danilov.[43] It was the final proof that Dostoyevsky had written a scenario for reality, and he was very pleased about it. In a letter of 23 December 1868, written from Florence to his friend Maykov, he recalled this success:

The idea I have of reality and realism is quite different from that of our realists and critics. My idealism is more real than their realism. Lord! If we give an intelligent account of what we Russians have experienced in the last ten years of our spiritual development, are our realists not going to shout out that this is pure fantasy? But this is precisely what realism is, but deeper: theirs floats on the surface ... With their realism, you couldn't explain a hundredth part of the things which have really happened: whilst we, with our idealism, have even foretold some things which actually took place. That has happened. My dear fellow, do not laugh at my conceit. I am like St Paul: if I am not praised, I will praise myself.[44]

The book of contemporary Russian life

Dostoyevsky was not a mere casual reader, but a deep student of newspapers and went beyond the modest idea of a catalogue. He dreamt of making a true book of contemporary Russian life, a vast collection of all striking news items, not only for his own use as a novelist, but for the public. As soon as he finished *The Idiot*, which is full of news items, he wrote from Florence on the 6 February 1869 to his niece S. A. Ivanova:

I have another idea, a work consisting almost entirely of compilation and quite mechanical: it is a work which will appear every year in January, an immense and useful book, indispensable, a reference book for everyone. It will have about sixty pages of fine print and will be published in a large edition which will certainly be sold out. I will not tell my idea to anyone, it is too good and too valuable: the profit is obvious. My own work will be simply as editor. This editing, though, will have to be done with an idea, with a serious knowledge of the business.[45]

A. S. Dolinin thinks that Dostoyevsky was alluding to the future *Diary of a Writer*, a plan which appeared in autumn 1867 in a letter to the same correspondent: 'Moreover, on my return (to Russia), I am absolutely determined to publish something like a newspaper (*gazeta*) (I remember I mentioned it to you before, but now the form and the intention are completely clear). But for this, I must be at home and see, perceive with my own eyes.'[46] In 1867, Dostoyevsky wrote 'newspaper'; in 1869 he wrote 'immense book of sixty printed pages'. It seems to us, given the size of the work, the plan to have his niece as a helper, as well as others, and the words 'compilation' and 'mechanical work', that Dostoyevsky was referring to a vast collection of press cuttings, significant news items, which was another of his favourite plans.[47] He was later to develop it in the words of Liza in *The Devils*.[48] Liza's literary enterprise is as follows:

Many national and provincial papers and other newspapers are published in Russia and every day many things are reported in them. The year passes, the newspapers are put away in cupboards or thrown out, torn, used for wrappers and parcels. Many published facts produce an impression and remain in public memory, but as the years pass they are forgotten. A lot of people would like to check things later, but it is an immense task to find anything in this sea of paper, often knowing neither the day, nor the place, nor even the month of the event. However, if all these facts for a whole year were collected in one book, with a set plan and a set idea, and with chapter headings and indices, set out by the month and date, a collection like this might show the essential characteristics of Russian life for the whole year.[49]

Shatov, whom Liza has chosen as helper and co-editor, shows some scepticism. She then enthusiastically goes into detail about the nature of the events to be collected, but above all she stresses the point of this kind of book:

Of course, not everything could be collected and reprinted. Government acts and decrees, local administration and laws, all the really important facts could be omitted in a publication of this sort. A lot could be omitted and choice could be limited to actions which express moral personal life to a greater or lesser degree, the personality of the Russian people at a given moment. Of course this could be anything: curiosities, fires, sacrifices, all kinds of good and bad deeds, all kinds of words and speeches, perhaps even news about floods, perhaps even a few Government decrees, but from everything only the things which describe the time must be chosen: the entries must be chosen with a definite point of view, with an indication, an intention, a thought which illuminates the whole, the entirety . . . It would be, as it were, a picture of the spiritual, moral, inner life of Russia for the whole year.[50]

And, repeating the exact words of the letter of 6 February 1869, she finishes: 'Everyone would have to buy it, it would have to be a reference book.'[51] Liza's plan has the recurrent theme of universality which is so characteristic of Dostoyevsky's creation.

Another of Dostoyevsky's heroes takes up the torch and uses the idea for personal profit. This is a creator much more like Dostoyevsky himself: Ivan Karamazov, author of *The Legend of the Grand Inquisitor*. He confides in his brother Alyosha: 'You see, I am a keen collector of certain little facts, and believe me, it is in newspapers and by word of mouth that I find them, and I note their origin, little stories as it were: I have a fine collection already.'[52]

The dream of the great book of contemporary Russian life, a vast organised Press review, was never to become reality, at least in the mechanical and business-like form that Dostoyevsky envisaged. Certainly, *The Diary of a Writer*, which is full of direct news items, at least in its polemical parts, is a descendant of this plan. But Dostoyevsky, a born novelist, was incapable of 'mechanical work', of the simple task of 'compilation'. As soon as he touched a news item he made a supercomposition reality. As the title indicates, it is the diary of a writer. The best example is that of 'A Gentle Spirit', a novella originating in an old plan of 1869,[53] but suddenly brought back to life by a disturbing news item of 1876: the suicide of a young dressmaker called Borisova. She had flung herself from the roof, clasping an icon of the Virgin.[54] Dostoyevsky had remarked on this news item in October 1876, in the chapter of *Diary of a Writer* called 'Two Suicides'.[55] In November, he supercomposed: the news item became a novella. The movement of the narrative is something like a Socratic dialogue: a man, the husband of the gentle woman, is questioning himself and gradually replying. He soon reveals the dead silence of his soul, his frozen solitude of being. The news item, significant as it is, is only the launching pad from which the imaginary fiction of the writer soars in search of the ends and the beginnings, which, as Dostoyevsky himself says, appear fantastic.[56]

9

The great dialogue: migrant images

You want to force humanity not to talk in images ... From the very earliest times, man has always talked in images. Every language is full of images and metaphors. You are attacking the expression of thought in images, you are conspirators against progress, you poor unhappy morons.

Dostoyevsky to the 'destroyers of aesthetics'[1]

There is another fruitful and stimulating dialogue in the novels of Dostoyevsky: a dialogue with great living and contemporary literature. The profound realism sustained by assiduous reading of newspapers acquired a new dimension as Dostoyevsky orchestrated a confrontation between the anonymous and factual voice of the crowd and the great voices of literature.

The novel: chosen place of literature

The great ghosts of the past, transformed by Dostoyevsky, continually interrupted and challenged him. As soon as a plan took possession of him, they rose and freely offered their images, characters, even their aesthetic forms. In the very first sketches for *The Idiot*, Goethe brought forward Mignon, Pushkin Cleopatra from *Egyptian Nights*, Shakespeare the young, unjustly accused beauty from *Much Ado about Nothing*, Hero.[2] As soon as Dostoyevsky decided to create a 'positively good' hero, Cervantes suggested Don Quixote, Dickens Pickwick, and Victor Hugo Jean Valjean. The Christ of the Gospels, a figure which Renan, mentioned several times in the preparatory notes, was trying to show in more human dimensions, appeared as the great model. During the research, Pushkin contributed 'The Poor Knight' and Shakespeare *Othello*,[3] though traces of this appeared only in an unused variant. The novelist N. I. Grech, a suspect ghost from the beginning of the century, inspired the theme for the final scenes of *The Idiot*: the tragic vision of the *Woman in Black*.[4]

Dostoyevsky's novels are supremely literary. They are a field where literature is also an object of the novel's action, like Courbet's famous picture, *The Painter's Workshop*, which shows the model and the work, the setting and the action, the artist and his chosen friends, forming a picture within the picture. The literature of others is present everywhere: in the initial plan, the process of work, the novel itself, the houses and conversations of the heroes. The characters are defined by the books they read in the same way as they are defined by their favourite pictures and music. As Leonid Grossman noted:

If Trusotsky is interested in Apollon Grigoryev's article on predatory or gentle types, or Alyosha Valkovsky enjoys Childhood and Boyhood by Tolstoy, or Liputin reads and rereads Considérant, or Stavrogin shows an interest in Balzac, or Nastasya Filippovna is reading Madame Bovary on the eve of her death, or the older Verkhovensky rereads Hugo and Chernyshevsky, if Rogozhin reads Solovyov's History, or Old Smith has a geography book and the New Testament on his table, or there is a general interest in Schiller in the Karamazov family, this is never merely the result of chance. Even in the image of Sonya Marmeladova the bibliographical aspects are not forgotten. We learn that she has studied ancient history up to Cyrus, king of Persia, has read several books of "romantic content" and was very interested in Lewes' Physiology. We also learn that the Gospel is her constant companion.[5]

The dialogue with literature within the novel allowed Dostoyevsky to define his characters, as well as defining himself in relation to others.

The first dialogue with literature: Poor Folk

Viktor Shklovsky has noted that the novel in letters was useful for 'inserting elements of literary criticism, without apparent malice'.[6] But in *Poor Folk*, where the heroes talk freely about literature in their letters, the struggle of the young novelist cannot be understood until the polyphonic obstacle is overcome. Dostoyevsky does not reveal his own literary choices: it is his heroes who speak. This is stressed by Dostoyevsky himself in a direct attack on the public: 'They don't understand that one can write in this kind of style. They are accustomed to see the author's mug all over the place in everything: but I haven't shown mine. It doesn't even come into their heads that it is Devushkin who is speaking and not me, and that Devushkin cannot speak in any other way.'[7] Devushkin, a petty clerk without much education, indiscriminately admires the pastiches of Ratazyayev, his neighbour, the works of Paul de Kock, Ducray-Duminil, Zhukovsky and Pushkin: but he loathes Gogol. However, the reader is not deceived. By placing the literary hero in the life of his own hero, and by the passionate reaction of his own characters to this literary hero, Dostoyevsky forces the public to consider the image which he, as a writer, has of the masters of literature. The author opposes himself and breaks free of his opponent by stylisation and parody.

Ratazyayev, the neighbour of Devushkin, involuntarily takes charge of the parody and stylisation. He is a poor literary hack, who, as his name indicates,[8] swallows all the mannerisms of the flowery, romantic literature which was then very fashionable. His *Italian Passions* where Vladimir declares his raging passion to Zinaida, who then betrays the count, her worthy husband,[9] is a parody of the Gothic society novel of the followers of Bestuzhev-Marlinsky and of 'rhetorico-horror' literature, as V. V. Vinogradov calls it, child of the French frenetic school. *Yermak and Zuleyka,* where the famous conqueror of Siberia bursts into imprecations over the corpse of his beloved, murdered at night by her own father, the blind Kuchum,[10] is a tasty pastiche, complete with wild scenery and shamanic magic, of the pseudo-historical novels of exotic adventure by Bulgarin and Kukolnik, possibly even of Polevoy. The facetious extract which begins 'Do you know Ivan Prokofyevich Yellowbelly? Yes, the very same one who bit Prokofiy Ivanovich',[11] with its jingle of names and patronymics and the comical oddity of its surnames, recalls the clumsy imitations of Gogol which were then fashionable.[12] Here a doubt appears; could Dostoyevsky, a devoted admirer of *The Greatcoat*, actually be making fun of Gogol himself? Is this the point where he sets light to the charge which, moving underground, finally explodes in *The Village of Stepanchikovo and its Inhabitants*? Could Gogol be placed – by means of Ratazyayev – on the same footing as the 'decadent literature' (*literatura tli*), in Panayev's phase, of Marlinsky and Polevoy? It seems more likely that Dostoyevsky, in thrall to Gogol's enchanting style, distinguished two authors in him: the cruel demon who transformed his heroes into soulless puppets, and the author of *The Greatcoat* and 'Diary of a Madman', who was trying to reconcile the naturalist school with the forms of sentimentalism which it had destroyed.[13]

It is the right to sentiment which makes Devushkin love Pushkin and protest vehemently against Gogol. The primacy of sentiment is the theme of *Poor Folk*, but sentiment is not the same as sentimentalism, as the attitude of the hero shows us. Devushkin passionately longs for heart. But, a gaping and timid listener to Ratazyayev's 'literary lectures', he stands respectfully at the gates of literature, which he regards from afar as a strange, enchanting world. On the other hand, he clings to the language of Pushkin and Gogol, where everything is so 'natural', so 'exact', so 'real' and he enters candidly, by means of dialogue, into the world of Samson Vyrin and Akakiy Akayiyevich, into the trap of true mirrors. Literature, with all its connotations of artifice and spectacle, enchants him like an inaccessible country: but the absence of literature in the stories of Pushkin and Gogol sets free the living dialogue. Devushkin reaches true literature by repudiating the literary. The hero serves the purpose of the novelist.

In his letter of 1 July, Makar Devushkin overflows with praise of Pushkin: 'I have read "The Station Master" in your book;[14] and I must tell you, my dear, it might turn out, you could be going on with your life and you wouldn't know that there is a book like this right under your elbow, where your whole life is set out as clear as the palm of your hand.'[15] And a few lines further on: 'It's just as if I wrote it myself; as if, for instance, my own heart, such as it is, as if somebody had taken it, turned it inside out to show to people and then gone and described it all in detail.'[16] The universality of Pushkin's hero is so striking that Devushkin identifies himself with Vyrin: 'I feel exactly the same thing, just the same as in the book, and I've sometimes found myself in just the same situations, as, for instance, this Samson Vyrin, poor soul. And how many Samson Vyrins there are among us, poor unlucky loving souls!'[17] He even lets his verbal mask slip: 'All this goes on nearby . . . take for instance our poor official, – he may very well be another Samson Vyrin, only he has another name, Gorshkov.'[18] The homage to Pushkin in *Poor Folk* is almost idolatrous. Eleven volumes 'prettily bound' of the *Complete Works* of Pushkin are offered to the student Pokrovsky by Varenka and his father: this is symbolic, a first indication of the famous speech of apotheosis in 1880.

The case is quite different with Gogol. Makar Devushkin hastily sends back his 'malevolent' *Greatcoat*. In Pushkin, everything was clear, harmonious, shining with love, and Devushkin, completely confident, gradually identified himself with Samson Vyrin, without pain or any feeling of indignity. With Gogol, he wakes to his suffering, he feels the knife turn in the wound. The hero does not sense a gradual identity; his own being is brutally revealed. In his letter of 8 July, Devushkin does not admit that he is Akakiy Akakiyevich Bashmachkin; he does not discuss the evidence, he simply becomes the accused: he is Bashmachkin to such a degree that the hero of *The Greatcoat* loses his name.[19] The unhappy Devushkin, feeling himself accused, immediately begins a long defence against his prosecutor, Gogol. With naive and comic anger, he admits that Gogol has drawn him from life. He reproaches the author of *The Greatcoat* for failing to respect the law of modesty, for exposing, with a kind of malicious enjoyment, something which Devushkin, in his dignity as a poor man, tried to hide from others:

You hide sometimes, you hide, you cover yourself up with anything you can find, you're even at times afraid to show your nose – anywhere at all, because you're terrified of gossip, because out of anything, anything at all, out of anything somebody will make up a clever lampoon for you, and all your public and private life goes around in literature, all printed, read, laughed at, gossiped over! And then you wouldn't be able to show yourself on the street; everything's set out so clearly there that a man like me would be recognised just by the way he walks.[20]

This is a magnificent act of homage from Dostoyevsky to Gogol's power of observation and creation in spying out – spying on, according to Devushkin – the poor clerk of the fifties; it is indirect praise of Gogol's merciless art. Dostoyevsky created his hymn of praise to Gogol's art in the negative, in the impression made on Devushkin, who has misinterpreted *The Greatcoat*, at least if we take it as a humanitarian story. Devushkin is funny, but his virtuous indignation and his plea for justice is moving: the little people, 'the microscopic individualities' have a right to sentiment and especially to the Ideal. With this complex treatment, Dostoyevsky indicated the direction of his literature; he wished to bring back sentiment and even sentimentalism, seeking it not in drawing-rooms or the conventional surroundings of

previous novels, but in 'garrets and attics', in Belinsky's words. His choice
of the letter form, where ideas are debated as in *La Nouvelle Héloïse*, *Die
Leiden des jungen Werther*, and George Sand's *Jacques*, and his refusal to
follow the rosecoloured literature of Nicolas-Germain Léonard and his
Russian rivals, who propagated novels such as *Thérèse and Faldoni*,[21]
make his central position clear; Dostoyevsky wished to renovate sentimentalism, and to reconcile the right of the heart to express itself and
especially to live according to the Ideal with the pitiless realism of the
naturalist school, which, with *The Greatcoat*, had ended in a move towards
the sociological novel. V. V. Vinogradov observed that in *Poor Folk* Dostoyevsky was asserting himself as the original creator of the 'school of
sentimental naturalism', where the 'little man' raises a social protest never
before heard in Russia.[22] This is true, but it needs an adjective stressing
the importance of the Ideal to complete the statement.

This is the first kind of literary dialogue. By using literary types familiar
to the contemporary reader, by setting familiar images in his heroes' lives,
Dostoyevsky defined himself and marked his place in the history of
literature.

The migrant image

After prison, Dostoyevsky gave up sentimental naturalism, which was still
present in *The Insulted and Injured*. Without completely deserting socio-
logy and sentiment, his great novels, rooted in reality, moved towards a
literature which is mainly psychological and philosophical. The emotional
idea, that is to say the idea indissociable from the person who holds it,
takes over his work. Its clash in reality with the other emotional ideas
determines its victory or defeat. The great novels go beyond the tragic dialectic of desire; the hero is committed by his action. But the tragedy
remains; for many of Dostoyevsky's characters, the idea is 'like a rock
which half crushes them'.[23] They struggle under their heavy burden,
unable to escape. For others, the idea 'shines like a great sun',[24] so brilliant that no one can live up to it. For others, Stavrogin, Versilov, Dmitriy
Karamazov, it is many-sided and irreducibly complex, light and darkness,
the Ideal of Sodom and the Ideal of the Madonna, the seduction of the
depths and the call of the heights, a magnetic field with tragic oscillations.

The novels of Dostoyevsky do not read like a thesis; for the reader they
are the dramatisation of the conflicts of the mind in its varied explorations.
The novelist's privilege, as Belinsky remarked to Dostoyevsky, is to show
meaning through images:

We publicists and critics only reason, we try to explain in words, and you, the
artist, with a single line, make us see the very heart of the matter in an image. It is
so real that it can be touched, so that even the reader who is least capable of

reasoning must understand it at once! This is the secret of creation, the truth of art![25]

The immense originality of Dostoyevsky is that he made more use than all his great contemporaries of the image with conceptual value, the image clothed in metaphysics. He was not afraid to borrow ideas from his ideological friends and enemies, either simply to express something or turn it to his own profit, or to create other symbols and images which aroused an echo in the reader's mind by their reference to the original. This is one of the most original and skilled aspects of the dialogue with literature, or, more broadly, with all the ideological movements of the time. The symbolic image had the same persuasive force as the news item for the public of that time. Just as the writer used a news item to stir the anonymous strata of events left by time in the memory of newspaper readers, he used the symbolic image to appeal to the collective store of ideas in everyone's mind and exploited the echoes between the reality of ideological debates and the fiction of the novel.

The images which Dostoyevsky transferred from the common heritage to his work might be a literary type, an object, or a subject. As they wander through the novels, they sometimes suffer a sea change. The important thing was that, through all their changes, the reader should be able to recognise them. They were useful not because they were original, but because they were commonplace public and popular images. They sometimes really do become commonplace, but Dostoyevsky was indifferent to this.

The literary hero and the historical hero

As opposed to several of his peers, such as Turgenev with *Hamlet of the Shchigry region*, *King Lear of the Steppes*, Leskov with *Lady Macbeth of Mtsensk*, or later Bulgakov with *The Master and Margarita*, Dostoyevsky made very little use of the direct symbol connecting the hero to a famous literary line. At least on the work's surface, for, as we know from the notebooks, Dostoyevsky was continually interrogating Shakespeare, Cervantes, Goethe, Dickens, Balzac, and especially the Russians, Pushkin, Lermontov, Gogol, Turgenev, Saltykov-Shchedrin, and Tolstoy while planning the novels. Direct references and allusions were plentiful in the notes and correspondence; but for the reader of the novels there are few images of literary heroes.

In the first works, they are used to deride and debunk: in *Poor Folk*, Thérèse and Faldoni, N. G. Léonard's two lovers from Lyons, give their elaborate names to the disgraced servants of Devushkin's landlady. In *The Gambler*, Des Grieux, Manon Lescaut's naive lover, lends his name to a French émigré, the predatory cheat who is after Polina's fortune. In both cases, the name is a grotesque mask, transparent to the reader.

Very soon the onomastic mask gave way to comparison between Dostoyevsky's hero and a famous literary figure. In *The Idiot*, for example, Myshkin is openly and publicly compared to Don Quixote and Pushkin's *Poor Knight*; in *The Devils* Stavrogin is compared to Prince Harry from Shakespeare's *Henry IV*. This again was an original approach to literary comparison; the comparison was not presented directly by the novelist, as if to give the reader a clue, but was a myth created by the other characters in the novel.

Aglaya begins the game, suggesting with grave irony that Myshkin is both the Poor Knight of Pushkin's poem, with Nastasya Filippovna as the beautiful lady, and a Don Quixote 'who would not be funny'.[26] But it is Kolya Ivolgin who sets the theme going and Prince S. recalls that they are all responsible for the idea. They have in fact suggested that Adelaida, Aglaya's sister, should paint a picture of the Poor Knight, and seeking a model among their acquaintance, they have chosen Myshkin.[27] The comparison between Myshkin and the heroes of Cervantes and Pushkin is the result of a plot, which Aglaya reveals with cruel enthusiasm.

The case is even clearer in *The Devils*. At the beginning of the novel, Stepan Trofimovich, to calm Varvara Petrovna's fears about her son's pranks, compares Stavrogin with Prince Harry, who spent his youth in debauchery with Falstaff, Poins and Mistress Quickly, before he took himself in hand and became the grave and severe Henry V.[28] But Stavrogin himself, as Pyotr Stepanovich Verkhovensky reports, gives the name of Falstaff to his clownish drinking companion, Captain Lebyadkin.[29] Here again the myth of Stavrogin–Prince Harry, the young rake who is destined to a glorious future, is sanctioned by the public voice. The subjective dialogue between the writer and his predecessors becomes objective; it emerges, in the finished novel, from the literary awareness of the characters. It is even more objective when the novelist gives up his pen to the hero. In *A Raw Youth*, Arkadiy tells his own story and considers his recent past. The literary mythology with which he surrounds himself is naturally affected by his own preoccupation with money. An inferno of vile or powerful creatures devoted to money, including Harpagon, Plyushkin of *Dead Souls*, Pushkin's *Covetous Knight*, Hermann from *The Queen of Spades*, a fantastic story in which Pushkin created a 'colossal figure of the Petersburg period', parade through the pages of the novel.

However, Dostoyevsky's heroes are never pedantic. If they sometimes recite Pushkin, as Aglaya does in *The Idiot*, or Schiller, like Dmitriy Karamazov, or show a serious knowledge of Heine, like Versilov, or Pushkin, like Arkadiy, they do so with such passion and understanding of the idea behind the text that art never becomes a sophisticated pastime reserved for the élite. The literary heroes recalled are those who have entered the cultural mythology of the novel's readers.

More generally, Dostoyevsky and his characters refer to real people who have become, or are becoming, historical symbols or myths. Like the Greeks, who evoked a science, art or activity by the name of a muse or a god, they draw on the collective and mythical source of the history of their own time: the faces of ideas. Besides their literary museum, the novels offer a portable gallery of famous character symbols, without originality but perfectly efficient, which the heroes of Dostoyevsky carry from novel to novel, giving them a few sly kicks on the way. When Arkadiy, the hero of *A Raw Youth*, imagines his triumph over the world, he gives a magnificent example of historical mythology: 'You are Galileo and Copernicus, Charlemagne and Napoleon, Pushkin and Shakespeare, marshalls of camp and court, while here am I, without talent or birth, but still above you.'[30] The symbols are direct; the geniuses of science, politics, arts and arms, the summit of human history. They form recurrent themes in Dostoyevsky's work.

Besides Galileo and Copernicus, whose eyes will be put out by Peter Stepanovich in *The Devils*, there is 'Bernard' (Claude Bernard), who, for Dmitriy Karamazov champion of the Ideal, is a symbol of all positivist scientists, men who, like the seminarist Rakitin, only believe in chemistry, the scalpel, and materialist determinism.[31] Galileo and Copernicus are positive symbols, the unfortunate Claude Bernard is a negative one. The choice of Bernard as symbol reveals Dostoyevsky's attitude: he might have substituted Bazarov, the nihilist of *Fathers and Sons*, who represents scientific ideology in Russian literature. The meaning would have been the same, but he preferred to make use of current events. Bernard, a great physiologist, had just died in 1878 and his works, particularly those on the nervous system which Dmitriy vaguely remembers, had been widely discussed in the Russian Press.[32] Dostoyevsky preferred an illustration from life to one from literature.

In the political field, Dostoyevsky's heroes are mainly interested in great men, such as Caesar or Mahomet, who seize the right to break the laws accepted by nine-tenths of humanity, the men to whom 'all is permitted', the Napoleons. This theme was sketched by Napoleon's contemporary Pushkin in *Yevgeniy Onegin*:

> We think everyone else is zero;
> we are the only integers.
> We all dream of becoming Napoleon:
> millions of two-legged creatures
> are simply tools to us.[33]

The idea is taken up by Dostoyevsky's first heroes, briefly by Prokharchin, ironically by the Underground man, seriously by Raskolnikov. Raskolnikov distances himself from the Napoleonic legend propagated by Balzac, Stendhal and even Victor Hugo, who saw Napoleon as the people's avenger. Raskolnikov, like Bezukhov in *War and Peace*, does not forget the blood, but he is mainly fascinated by the inhumanity and contempt that Napoleon was capable of, which he knows is beyond his power. He praises the tyrant ironically;

> No, these men are made differently; a conqueror to whom everything is permitted, who crushes Toulon, causes a massacre in Paris, *forgets* an army in Egypt, *wastes* half a million men in the Russian campaign and gets out of it with a pun at Vilna: and this man, after his death, is idolised: that means *everything* is permitted to him. No, these men obviously are not flesh, but bronze![34]

Crime and Punishment is the novel of the failure of the Napoleonic dream, since Raskolnikov also kills for money. The bronze statue of the violent, haughty and impatient conqueror casts another shadow on the peeling walls of Raskolnikov's attic, that of James Rothschild, a more modern image of power, a subterranean and patient conqueror. Arkadiy in *A Raw Youth* made Rothschild his Napoleon. Rothschild and Napoleon are the two images of the wish for power, the Nietzschean pride devoid of any romantic idealism. The underground man had begun their dethronement, sneering at Rothschild's philanthropic dreams: 'I receive uncounted millions and I sacrifice them all to the human race,'[35] and at the cultural mission of Napoleon: 'Barefoot and starving, I set out to praise new ideas and crush the unenlightened at Austerlitz.'[36] As we go further on in the works, the heroes tempted by the Napoleonic or Rothschildean idea of power renounce it more clearly: Raskolnikov discovers that he is an insect, 'a louse' by nature, and ends by confessing his crime, Ganya Ivolgin shows that he is incapable of carrying out his cynical plan, and the Raw Youth, who develops his idea of power through money further than the others, finds another idea. In every case, from Prokharchin to Arkadiy, the idea of domination symbolised by Napoleon and Rothschild, and springing partly from social alienation,[37] ends in failure. Ivan Karamazov takes up the torch with the Grand Inquisitor, but this time the symbol was Dostoyevsky's own, while those of Napoleon and Rothschild were derived from the collective awareness of contemporary readers. Even if there was a shift in the movement of creation, such as the overshadowing of one symbol, Napoleon, by another, Rothschild, more rooted in the money-dominated society of the second half of the nineteenth century, the core of the idea remained perfectly clear to the reader. Between him and the novelist a code had been established, with signals from the bank of common reading and common knowledge.

Migrant images of the arts

Every time the reader of Dostoyevsky finds a reference to Raphael, Pushkin or Shakespeare, he knows that this signifies 'sublime ideal of beauty', 'perfect art', 'spiritual perfection'. But he is also aware of the distant sources of the novelist's myths and especially their passage through the reference system of the time. Raphael, Pushkin and Shakespeare, aesthetic units of reference, are perfect illustrations of the migrant images so typical of Dostoyevsky's work.

They appear most clearly in *The Devils*, where Stepan Verkhovensky is the novelist's spokesman. This is obvious because Dostoyevsky makes him a Don Quixote spluttering about beauty, a ridiculous man who is hopelessly out of date. Bitter derision, the fate of most of Dostoyevsky's profound heroes, such as the Underground man, the Idiot, Stepan Trofimovich, the hero of 'The Dream of a Ridiculous Man', even the elders Tikhon and Zosima, is the seal of truth. No one has understood better than Dostoyevsky the great lesson of the Passion: spitting, the crown of thorns, flagellation, mockery, even more than death by crucifixion, mark out the person who speaks the truth.

At the beginning of *The Devils* the chronicler tells us of the fiasco at one of Stepan Trofimovich's last public lectures in Petersburg. He had aroused a storm of whistles by declaring that 'boots are inferior to Pushkin and a good deal inferior'.[38] Later the unfortunate 'knight of beauty' listens helplessly as Varvara Petrovna, won over by nihilist ideas, makes an attack on the Sistine *Madonna*: 'These days absolutely nobody raves about the Madonna or wastes time on that sort of thing, except backward old men.'[39] And later:

It is perfectly useless. This jug is useful, because water can be poured into it; this pencil is useful, because everything can be written down with it, but in the picture there's only a woman's face worse than any other face you could find in nature. Try to draw an apple and put a real apple next to it, which would you take? You wouldn't make a mistake, I'm sure.[40]

Towards the end of the novel, Stepan Trofimovich enters the heart of the question during the scandal he causes at the famous party organised in Karmazinov's honour: 'The question is essentially which is the more beautiful: Shakespeare or boots, Raphael or petrol?'[41] He answers his own question in a piercing voice:

Shakespeare and Raphael are higher than the liberation of the peasants, higher than nationalism, higher than socialism, higher than the younger generation, higher than chemistry, higher than almost the whole of humanity, since they are the fruit, the real fruit of the whole of humanity and perhaps the highest fruit that could possibly be! The form of beauty has already been attained, and without this attainment I, perhaps, could not consent even to go on living.[42]

He continues, before bursting into hysterical tears:

Humanity could very well live without the Englishman, or without Germany, it could get along only too well without the Russian, it could live without science, without bread, but beauty is the only thing it could not live without, because there would be nothing to do on earth! The whole secret is there, the whole of history is there! Science itself could not survive one minute without beauty – do you know anything about this, you who are laughing, – it would turn into cloddishness, you couldn't invent even a nail![43]

The intention of Stepan Trofimovich's exalted speech is clear to the modern reader, just as the sense of Varvara Pavlovna's diatribe against the Sistine *Madonna* is clear, but the chosen images, boots and Pushkin, Raphael's Madonna and a jug, a pencil, a drawing of an apple and petrol, science and bread opposed to beauty may seem strange and unexpected. Dostoyevsky's contemporary reader would immediately recognise the symbols as part of an ideological contest in which the arms (the images) and the battleground (Russia in 1870) were quite familiar. He knew the names of the combatants whose faces were hidden behind the words.

This war, heavily documented, was the dispute about aesthetics begun by the utilitarians of *The Contemporary*, Chernyshevsky and Dobrolyubov, which led to the wholesale destruction of aesthetics by the nihilists of *The Russian Word*, Pisarev and Zaytsev. Without considering the problem as a whole, we shall simply try to find the origin of these migrant images, heavy with accumulated meaning, these ideological strata twisted and broken by polemical earthquakes.

In 1855, Chernyshevsky first opened fire with his thesis 'Aesthetic relations of art and reality', in which he refuted Hegel's aesthetic theory of the sublime and the beautiful, and made an apologia for reality at the expense of art, summarised in paragraph nine of his thesis: 'Reality is not only more living but also more perfect than imagination. The images created by the latter are only the pale and almost always mediocre reflection of reality.'[44] Reviewing the arts to prove this, Chernyshevsky reached still life – roses, apples and oranges: 'It is true that inanimate nature does not think of making its fruits good to eat. But one must admit that until now our art has not been able to create anything like an apple or an orange, let alone the sumptuous fruits of tropical lands.'[45] Dostoyevsky gathered these two sentences into a formula so striking that historians of philosophy later attributed it to Chernyshevsky:[46] 'A natural apple is worth more than a painted apple, especially as a natural apple can be eaten, while a painted apple cannot',[47] a remarkable formula which expresses the utilitarian basis of Chernyshevsky's aesthetics by means of a satirical image suggested by the description 'good to eat'. The denigration of art enraged Dostoyevsky so much that he returned to it several times in his notebooks of 1860–5: 'Nobody eats fruit in a picture.[48] The painted apple and the real apple.'[49] There is even the beginning of a refutation which Dostoyevsky the journalist intended to use in one of his attacks on *The Contemporary*. This fragment ends with the words: 'Exactly if they had set about this real problem of "the apple". Firstly, he should not have expressed himself positively. But they have done it and we shall certainly reply. The problem is too serious.'[50]

In 1861, in an important article in *Time*, 'Mr Dobrolyubov and the question of art', Dostoyevsky counter-attacked and began the great dispute, which is still raging, about the function of art. Far from supporting art for art's sake, he agreed with Chernyshevsky and Dobrolyubov that 'the artist should speak in concrete terms, should serve the general interest, should be faithful to contemporary reality, its needs, its ideals'.[51] But inspiration and creation should be free and the artist should not be dragooned; beauty exists in its own right, unconditional and absolute. More, beauty is a necessity for men. However, Dostoyevsky gave only a brief mention to Raphael, Pushkin and Shakespeare; the central illustration of his theme is the *Iliad* and a classical poem by A. A. Fet, *Diana*. He did not reject commitment in art – his entire work would have contradicted this – but he opposed the narrow reversal of priorities: 'the more man is capable of echoing the historical and the universally human, the wider his nature, the richer his life, the more he is capable of progress and development'.[52]

The supporters of social utilitarianism in art, Chernyshevsky and Dobrolyubov, had set out a dangerous path, along which the nihilist monks of *The Russian Word*, Dmitriy Ivanovich Pisarev, whose intelligence and noble sincerity are praised by Shatov, at least in the notebooks of *The Devils*,[53] and Varfolomey Aleksandrovich Zaytsev, a less famous but incredibly virulent critic, were rushing forward, hatchets in hand. Their reasoning followed that of Turgenev's Bazarov: man is hungry, he is still sunk in poverty, and art is only a secondary need, reserved for a tiny minority of pampered people. Art must be exterminated. Pisarev wrote 'The Destruction of Aesthetics',[54] in which he describes aesthetics as the basic element of 'intellectual stagnation' and 'the surest enemy of scientific progress'. Pushkin, Shakespeare and Raphael were favourite targets, especially Pushkin, whom Pisarev called a mere stylist, a virtuoso who deadened healthy intelligence and bred a generation of sybarites and parasites.[55] It was Pisarev, in 1864, who made an indirect reference to boots: 'If Germany had dozens of archaeologists like Jakob Grimm, it would be no richer or happier because of them . . . This is why I say with complete sincerity that I would rather be a shoemaker or a baker than a Raphael or a Russian Grimm.'[56] Zaytsev, who was particularly acid about Pushkin, made similar statements: 'It is time to understand that any positive number, no matter how small, is larger than zero.'[57] And, gaining in effrontery: 'There is no one washing floors or emptying cesspits who is not more useful than Shakespeare.'[58] The Sistine *Madonna*, already roughed up by Pisarev, did not escape his iconoclastic zeal: 'Contemporary worshippers transform art into a mummy and mummify themselves when they preach art for art's sake, making it an end instead of a means. They have been adoring the Venus de

Milo for two thousand years[59] and the Madonnas of Raphael for three hundred years, without noticing that these raptures are a condemnation of art.'[60] The images all had a hidden meaning: boots and shoes symbolised the Russian people: the cesspit cleaner[61] was the revolutionary who would clean out Tsarist society, and so on. In a vitriolic article, 'Mr Shchedrin, or Schism among the Nihilists',[62] Dostoyevsky regrouped these images, crystallising them into expressions for use in his novels. His target was the quarrel between *The Contemporary*, 'the organ of moderate nihilists', and *The Russian Word*, 'the organ of immoderate nihilists'. The article was supposed to be the manuscript of a novel, entitled *Shchedrodarov*, a transparent allusion to Dostoyevsky's adversary on *The Contemporary*, Saltykov-Shchedrin.[63] The editorial board of *The Opportunist*, i.e. *The Contemporary*, is alarmed by attacks from *The Foreign Word*, i.e. *The Russian Word*, where Skribov and Krolichkov, verbal masks for Pisarev and Zaytsev,[64] are on the rampage. It engages Shchedrodarov, nicknamed 'young pen', and dictates its conditions to him as follows:

Paragraph Four: Young pen, you must henceforth take it as a rule that a pair of boots is always more valuable than Pushkin, as one can very well do without Pushkin, but not without boots, so it follows that Pushkin is a mere luxury and waste of time. Understood?

But Shchedrodarov was silent again. He did not ask what Pushkin might be, for example, to someone who already had boots.[65]

The editorial board continues:

Shakespeare himself is a luxury and a waste of time, because there are witches in Shakespeare, which is very backward indeed: they are particularly harmful for Russian youth, as its peasant nurses have already filled up its head with witches. But attention, young pen! Shakespeare may still be tolerated for the sole reason that Büchner in *Kraft und Stoff*[66] (and the devil knows why) took it into his head to praise him; given that we ought to keep up with all progressive people and especially with Büchner, we may spare Shakespeare, for the time being, of course. But this is such a minor item – added the speaker – that I don't make a special point of it and simply place it under paragraph four, the one about the pair of boots and Pushkin.[67]

Clearly Pushkin and Shakespeare were equivalent symbols to Dostoyevsky. In a plan for an article of 14 September 1864, 'Socialism and Christianity', not much later than the text quoted above, there is another mention of the nihilists: 'They admit it with pride: boots are better than Shakespeare.'[68] Stepan Trofimovich keeps this equivalence and compares Pushkin or Shakespeare indifferently to the wretched pair of boots. On the same model he creates the comparison of Raphael with petrol, clearly alluding to the incendiaries (*pétroleuses*) of the Commune[69] and so to revolutionary nihilists. The end of Stepan Trofimovich's peroration on the impossibility of science existing without beauty was inspired by one of the writers on the second journal of the Dostoyevsky brothers, *The Epoch*. N. I. Solovyov, a military doctor whose naive enthusiasm, freshness of conviction, and total insensibility to literary fashion was much appreciated by Dostoyevsky, wrote six articles for the journal, beginning in July 1864, soon after Dostoyevsky's own article, all directed against Pisarev, who replied in *The Russian Word* by a series of articles regrouped under the title 'Realists'. In his first article Solovyov attacked Pisarev's 'theory of ugliness' and accused him of knowing nothing about real scientists and poetry's contribution to science. Popularised science became trivial and degenerate if it were deprived of aesthetic feeling.[70]

Nor had Dostoyevsky forgotten the comparison of cesspit cleaner with poet, formulated by Zaytsev. He did not use it for Stepan Trofimovich in *The Devils*, because it had already appeared in *Crime and Punishment*, where Lebezyatnikov naively explains nihilist ideas about art:

And besides, tell me please, what is it you find so shameful and contemptible even in cesspools! I am the first, I am ready to clean any cesspools you like! This isn't even self-sacrificing! It's simply work, a noble activity useful to society, just as good as any other and infinitely superior, for example, to the activity of any kind of Raphael or Pushkin, because it is more useful![71]

With this problem of aesthetics and art, Dostoyevsky collected images from articles by his opponents as well as his supporters, and constructed symbols of the same sort, elaborating a code of metaphors which the contemporary reader could easily decipher. This language of images differs from the Aesopian language used by the opponents of the regime to avoid censorship, because it gives both the position disputed and the personal position of the hero (and sometimes of the author). It does not express a thesis, but a living clash of opposing choices, often stressed by elliptical syntax and odd comparisons.

Migrant images of Utopia and materialistic socialism

In my study *From the Crystal Palace to the Golden Age, or the Heirs of Utopia*, I traced the complex path of the symbolic images of Utopia in Dostoyevsky's works from their beginning to their dispersal.[72] The image of the Crystal Palace had several sources and its embryo passed through several stages: the 'palace of marble and gold' quoted by Dostoyevsky himself in an unpublished chapter of *The House of the Dead*; the real Crystal Palace of 1851 and the 'military prison' of the Universal Exhibition of 1862, as described in *The Review of Two Worlds* or *Annals of the Fatherland*, publications read by Dostoyevsky; the fourth dream of Vera Pavlovna in Chernyshevsky's socialist novel *What is to be Done?*; and finally the 'crystal palace' of the Underground man, which disintegrates and forms opposing successors. On one side is the Golden Age described by Plato, transformed by Saint-Simon, disinfected by Dostoyevsky and symbolised in Claude's *Acis and Galatea*, finally experienced by the hero of 'The Dream of a Ridiculous Man' on the planet of the children of the sun, a reminiscence of Considérant's *Social Destiny*. On the other hand, there is the blind and brutal Utopia, announcing happy and docile flocks of sheep, illustrated in turn by the appearance of the bird-Kagan bringing happiness to people in *Notes from Underground*, the Shchigalyovism of *The Devils*, which begins where Chernyshevsky's Utopia, with its columns of aluminium, ends, and finally the kingdom of the Grand Inquisitor in *The Brothers Karamazov*. The journey ends in the syncretic image of an eternal rebirth of the elect and the real resurrection of ancestors on earth. Legions of political philosophers, from Plato to Fyodorov, including Rousseau, Fourier, Owen, Considérant and Chernyshevsky, dozens of articles, accounts of exhibitions, records of political proceedings, political tracts (*The Catechism of a Revolutionary*), and historical works suggested these images used by Dostoyevsky, who resurrects them in the mind of the reader. This transmigration of images, a sort of metempsychosis where the souls are ideas and their descendants are the metaphors, forms the orchestral background typical of the Dostoyevsky novel.

The symbolic images evolve with the movement of the writer's thought, but even more with the passage of time, since the intellectual ferment was so intense that authors grew old within ten years. The images also grew old and died, and others, with the same symbolic meaning, took their place and bore the same message. An example is the changing image used to express material, and materialistic, well-being, to which Dostoyevsky opposes immortality and Christ. In 1860, in the chapter of *The House of the Dead* prepared for the censors, it is the image, commonplace for someone returning from Siberia, of the 'palace of marble and gold' overflowing with all kinds of good things: in 1864, in *Notes from Underground*, it is the 'crystal palace', debased to the level of henhouse or block of flats bearing the signboard of the dentist Wagenheim as a symbol of suffering abolished: in 1868 in *The Idiot* for Lebedev it is 'railways' and 'wagons bringing bread for starving humanity':[73] in 1874–5 in *A Raw Youth*[74] and *The Brothers Karamazov* it is 'stones transformed into bread'. The sources of these symbols were the people with whom Dostoyevsky was conducting a dialogue in his works, because they were at the heart of the ideological debates of the time.

The 'crystal palace', as is well known, was suggested by Chernyshevsky, who in *What is to be done?*, which appeared from March to May 1863 in *The Contemporary*, had alluded to it as an illustration of his Utopia, his phalanstery. In the following year Dostoyevsky fused the comparison and the object of the comparison into one image. The 'railways' and the 'wagons bringing bread to starving humanity' were images from A. I. Herzen, whose historical memoirs *Past and Thoughts*[75] Dostoyevsky was attentively reading in 1867 in Dresden and Geneva, at the time when he first had the idea for *The Idiot*. He probably already knew the pages where these images originated, the chapter 'Pater V. Pecherin', published in 1861 in *The Polar Star*,[76] but they became symbols for him only in 1868. To understand the death of the 'crystal palace' image and the birth of the images which take its place, we must look at the passage describing a correspondence Herzen had in 1853 with Father Pecherin, a Russian emigrant who was converted to Catholicism and became a Jesuit.[77] Herzen, going beyond the Utopian socialism of Chernyshevsky, wrote:

Do not think I have called the phalanstery a barracks[78] by a mere slip of the pen, no, all the socialist doctrines and schools which have appeared up till now, from Saint-Simon to Proudhon, who is nothing but negation, are very poor, this is just the first stutterings, the first stumblings, they are the Therapeuts and the Essenes of the ancient east.[79]

The attack on the 'crystal palace', the primary form of Utopia, was no longer important to Dostoyevsky. The debate was more serious. Pecherin reproached Herzen for relying on literature and philosophy, whose flowering announces the decadence of civilisations, and not on religion; he reproached him for praising the tyranny of a new materialistic world, based on science. Herzen replied:

I do not confuse science with literary and philosophical development. If Science does not regenerate the state, it does not collapse with it either. It is the means, the memory of the human race, it is victory over nature and liberation. Ignorance, only ignorance, is the cause of pauperism and slavery. The masses have been left by their own teachers in an animal state. Science alone can remedy this and give them a piece of bread and a roof over their heads. It is not by propaganda, but by chemistry, mechanics, technology, railways that it can correct their brain, physically and morally repressed for centuries.[80]

This idea horrified Pecherin. Herzen challenged him: 'What are you afraid of? Could it be the sound of wheels bringing their daily bread to a starving and half-naked crowd? Is not the threshing of wheat forbidden with us so that the lyrical delights of idleness are not disturbed?'[81] Herzen was almost certainly thinking of engine wheels in this passage, but his last sentence is a fine evocation of the tyranny of Russian country squires, who forbade wheat to be threshed while they were resting, and it inevitably led Dostoyevsky back to peasant Russia. From it he constructed the formula of 'wagons bringing bread to starving humanity.' He had an amazing ability to seize the significant concrete image, such as the railway, or to fuse similar images into a whole, recognisable without being immediately identifiable.

In *The Brothers Karamazov*, his novel-testament, Dostoyevsky abandoned reference to the great minds of his time, his adversaries, to turn to the powerful and negative Spirit, the devil who tempted Jesus in the wilderness by offering him the temporal kingdom which the Grand Inquisitor finally accepts: 'If thou be the Son of God, command that these stones be made bread.'[82] This symbolic image first appeared in the notebooks for *A Raw Youth* as a rival to Herzen's image of 'wagons bringing bread to starving humanity', which it displaced in the finished novel, but, as it did not belong to the arsenal of the ideological contests of the time, it brought a question from a reader of *Diary of a Writer*, 1876, where Dostoyevsky had used it again; Dostoyevsky then defined its sense: 'Stones and bread mean the social question of the moment, the environment.'[83] It was only after receiving public consecration that it became part of the imagery of *The Brothers Karamazov* as a symbol both universal and contemporary.

In this way Dostoyevsky, during the whole of his work – there are numerous examples – was conducting a dialogue with the living thought of his time, borrowing from the bank of his reading, also used by his readers, the images which cover the various philosophical ideas expressed at the time and which illustrate the conflicting thoughts of his heroes. In doing this, he affirms his belief as a novelist: humanity talks in images and thought is expressed in images. Lebedev in *The Idiot* is saying the same thing when he explains that the 'railways' and 'iron roads' against which he thunders are only 'the image and plastic figuration' illustrating a tendency of civilisation.[84]

The essential structure of the novel of Dostoyevsky, even of his journalistic work, is dialogue. By stressing the supercomposition of the news item and the transmigration of symbolic images, we have tried to show that from the very beginning Dostoyevsky's creation is a dialogue with the Other. Some biographers have stressed the touchy and antisocial character, the solitude of Dostoyevsky. On the contrary, he is the creator in his time who is the least withdrawn, the most desirous of establishing contact with the other person, and so the most certain of establishing his empire over the reader.

10

The play of dialogue

Humility is not the chief virtue of novelists. They do not hesitate to claim the title of creators. Creators! rivals of God!
In truth, they are his apes.
The characters they invent are not created, if creation means making something from nothing. Our so-called creatures are formed from elements taken from reality; we combine, more or less skilfully, the results of our observation of other men and the knowledge which we have of ourselves. The heroes of novels are born of the marriage which the novelist makes with reality.

François Mauriac, *Le Romancier et ses personnages*[1]

Sometimes novelists amuse themselves not by aping God – which is their basic task – but by aping themselves, telling us how one of their marriages with reality has ended in divorce. Once Dostoyevsky, usually secretive about his creative effort, chose himself as subject, the creating subject, though without admitting it openly. It is to the journalist of 'Petersburg dreams in verse and prose', published in *Time* in 1861, that we owe the amused self-portrait of the novelist watching himself in a mirror as he talks to his past, his dreams, his previous works, news items, migrant images. The self-portrait, like some self-portraits of Rembrandt, is spritely, but the eyes of the novelist shine with all their inspiration and wisdom. Before we begin our analysis of the subterranean logic of Dostoyevsky's creation, we shall give a brief illustration of his creative process and the game of dialogue in action.

The author of The Greatcoat *and the author of* Poor Folk *in rivalry*

The journalist began by a survey of his beginnings as a novelist: his romantic youth, haunted by the chivalrous shades of Walter Scott and the dreamers of Schiller, and his tribulations in the lunary world of imagination. Then he remembered his return to earth, where he was sobered by the sarcasms of a merciless demon, Gogol:

And I began to look around me and suddenly I saw some strange figures. They were all strange wonderful characters, quite prosaic, not at all like Don Carlos or the Marquis Posa, but simply titular counsellors. Someone was making faces in front of me, hidden behind this imaginary crowd, and twitching unknown strings and springs and all these puppets moved, while he roared with laughter, and kept on roaring with laughter.[2]

The term 'puppets' betrays an implicit criticism: Gogol's art is a cheerful anatomy lesson, a cruel lampoon. Dostoyevsky then remembered how he came to renew his life and his heart: 'And then I had the fugitive vision of another story, the story, in some dark corners, of a certain "titular" heart, honest and pure, moral and devoted to its superiors, and with it the heart of a very young girl, hurt and sad, and their story tore my heart.'[3] This is a clear allusion to *Poor Folk*, to Devushkin and Varenka. From the creative point of view, it is a valuable indication. Every plan caused a return to the past, and especially to earlier creation. Characters did not die, but came to besiege the novelist in his new creation: 'I have the same visions still, but with other faces, though my old acquaintances sometimes come to knock at my door as well.'[4]

Then the novella begins: 'This is what appeared to me recently. There was once a clerk, in a certain department, of course.'[5] Dostoyevsky was using the beginning of Gogol's *Greatcoat*. The following part, in the cruel and burlesque style of Gogol, is a vivid summary of the portrait of Akakiy Akakiyevich:

He never had a protest, not even a voice; he was a completely sinless character. He had practically no underwear either; his uniform had ceased to fulfil its function. He would go around, odd little soul, hunched up, with his eyes on the ground, and when he was coming home from the office, from the other side of the Neva, and he happened to go along Nevsky Prospect, he was certainly the most humble and submissive creature that the Nevsky Prospect had ever seen, so that even the coachman, who once lashed him with a whip, as a kind of greeting, while he was running across our magnificent avenue, was stunned to see that he did not even turn his head, let alone curse like a trooper.[6]

The first inspiration was certainly Gogol.

But the story changes: the poor clerk has a cantankerous wife and six children. The author of *Poor Folk*, creator of the Gorshkov family, has entered the scene. From then on, the writer became a sort of centaur, half Gogol, half Dostoyevsky: the hero goes mad like the character in Gogol's *Diary of a Madman*, he imagines he is Garibaldi, just as Poprishchin, with whom he is compared in the text, thought he was the king of Spain. Then, going beyond Gogol's legacy, Dostoyevsky tried to find the reason for this madness: 'And so he had gradually become convinced that he was indeed a Garibaldi, a buccaneer, a disturber of the natural order of things.' And further on: 'He saw only one thing everywhere: his crime, his shame and his disgrace.' Here the specifically Dostoyevskian theme of the tragic dialectic of the wish to rebel, expressed in earlier works by Golyadkin and Prokharchin, makes its appearance. The rebellion – Garibaldi is a revolutionary – fails because the character disintegrates. The creative process is clear: Dostoyevsky, tempted by the old Gogolian demons, went back to what he had already created, without interrupting his dialogue with Gogol, whom he surpassed and deepened by stressing the wish for power and rebellion originating in social alienation. The story seems to stop at this point when . . .

The reality of the news item

'The dream suddenly came true. How do you like this, gentlemen? I have found another mystery in the newspapers recently.'[7] And Dostoyevsky went on to say how he had found a 'new Harpagon', a 'new Plyushkin' (again the literary reference) who died in appalling poverty on a pile of gold, or to be exact on '169,022 silver roubles in banknotes and ready money'. This was a retired titular counsellor called Solovyov, who had stopped paying rent, dressed in rags and lived without 'fresh food, even in the last days of his life'. At first this looks like a completely different theme, but it can be traced back to the previous theme in two ways: first, thematically, since the poor clerk who thinks he is Garibaldi and the miser Solovyov both wish for power and are both destroyed by their own dream (Napoleon and Rothschild are not far away); second, creatively, since the reference to the miser Prokharchin in the first part of the article, slight as it is, leads naturally to the subject of hoarding wealth. The original idea, fed by migrant images, has just been fertilised by the news item, supported by literary parallels.

The incarnation of reality

Mediation begins. Dostoyevsky, who also walked the Petersburg streets – always this walking rhythm – suddenly saw his idea take on flesh, blood and bone:

In front of me, in the crush, passed a silhouette, not real but imaginary . . . The silhouette which slipped by me had a padded coat, old and worn, which its owner must have used as a blanket at night . . . When he came up to me, he glanced at me, he blinked his eye at me, his dead eye, without light or strength, as if a corpse's eyelids had been lifted in front of me, and I immediately guessed that this was that very Harpagon who had died with half a million in his rags.[8]

This is the third stage: the intervention of real experience, only described as 'imaginary'[9] because it resurrected the hero of the news item. The individual Solovyov, already a public character, was promoted to the rank of literary and universal type. Dostoyevsky first summoned the ghosts of Gogol and his own creatures, 'his old acquaintances', who had come knocking at his door, and from them he brought into existence a sort of 'blending', in Gide's expression, unified only by the idea that inspired it. Then the news item showed him the deep reason for his hesitations and so made the theme that obsessed him clear. The experience of reality cut the knot so that he was able to go on to original creation.

The true beginning

Now the Rothschild theme, still unnamed, like a kitten with closed eyes, made its appearance: 'Suddenly an image very like that of Pushkin's Covetous Knight appeared before me. My Solovyov suddenly seemed a colossal character. He had left the world and all its temptations, to shutter himself up in his own home. What did all this vainglory, all this luxury which is ours matter to him!'[10] Expressions, later to become familiar with the hero of *A Raw Youth*, who took them over unchanged, reappeared: 'No, he needed nothing, since he had everything there, under his pillow . . . He had only to whistle and everything he wanted would crawl obediently towards him. He had only to wish and crowds of faces would gladden his heart with an attentive smile. He is above all wishes.'[11] There is nothing surprising about these echoes, as Dostoyevsky was playing a game with the reader and indicating his sources. Like Arkadiy in *A Raw Youth*, he was shamelessly stealing from Pushkin. This part of 'Petersburg Dreams' of 1861 must be considered the beginning of the Rothschild theme in *A Raw Youth*, which was written thirteen years later. And as if he were remembering these pages, Arkadiy, after setting out his 'idea', was to recall not only the inspiration they have in common, Pushkin and his covetous knight, but also a kind of double of Solovyov: a beggar found dead on a ship on the Volga, with a treasure of 3,000 roubles – always the fateful sum – sewn into his rags.[12] The two texts, the two newspaper items, illuminate each other.

In this article, Dostoyevsky was still influenced by his guardian angel Pushkin, who had driven out the shade of Gogol. He was aware of this: 'While I was letting my imagination roam in this way, it seemed to me that I was cheating, stealing from Pushkin, and the whole thing happened very differently.'[13] The end of this sentence announced something which was habitual with Dostoyevsky, which we shall call 'variability of situations'. The creator seemed to reason as follows: This literary character is obsessing me, but I forbid myself to copy my predecessors, so let us change conditions, ages and characters and try out the same idea. For example, Little Nell of *The Old Curiosity Shop* fascinates me. In Dickens she is humble and sweet, so let us choose a proud rebellious child and see what happens: the result is Nelli in *The Insulted and Injured*. This was experimental research which went beyond the narrow framework of heroes imitated or borrowed from predecessors, and numerous traces of it can be found in the notebooks. Mauriac describes it as follows:

Life gives the novelist a starting point which allows him to venture along a different path from the one which life has taken. He turns vague possibilities into realities. Sometimes he simply takes the opposite direction to life: he reverses roles; in a particular drama he has known, he looks for the victim in the executioner and the executioner in the victim. Accepting life's information, he takes the opposite course to the one which life has taken.[14]

Dostoyevsky as a novelist extended this method of 'variability of situations'
to characters suggested not only by life but by literature, by news items, and
by himself in previous earlier works. The 'Petersburg Dreams' provide a
perfect example of this 'opposite course'. The journalist suddenly brushed
against the possibility among possibilities which might have led him not only
to the Rothschild idea but also to the hero of *A Raw Youth*. He rejuvenated
Solovyov: 'Some sixty years ago Solovyov surely had a job, he was young,
lively, twenty years old. Perhaps he also had his pleasures, liked going out in
a carriage, knew some Louise or other, or went to the theatre to see *The
Life of a Gambler*.[15] Arkadiy was also to be fascinated by gambling. Two
plans had appeared on the creative horizon: *The Gambler*, to be written in
1866, and *A Raw Youth*, in 1874.

Failure

Unfortunately the author of 'Petersburg Dreams', probably because this
was only a game to him, let the original image slip: he did not place the birth
of the Rothschild idea in the youth of his hero, but made it the result of a
psychic trauma, a kind of break in the personality, so that miserliness was
caused by fear and not by principle. Dostoyevsky was distracted from his
intuition by Vasya Shumkov of *A Weak Heart*; his previous creation
entrapped him: 'But suddenly something must have happened which
seemed to nudge him in the side, one of those events which change a man so
completely in the wink of an eye that he is not really fully aware of it
himself. Perhaps there was a moment when his eyes were suddenly opened
on something and he became timid'.[16] Gogol, still unexorcised, took the
upper hand, and even reclaimed his own property: 'And so Akakiy
Akakiyevich starts putting aside farthing after farthing for a coat lined with
marten, and takes it out of his salary, and saves up, saves up for a rainy day,
he doesn't know exactly why, but certainly not for a coat any longer. He
sometimes trembles and is afraid.'[17] The idea of power through money had
vanished. The hero became an Akakiy Akakiyevich without his dream, a
mixture of Plyushkin and Prokharchin. Dostoyevsky had been wasting his
time by fusing the Gogolian type with the character of the miserly Solovyov,
by producing a brilliant supercomposition of a news item; the true subject,
briefly touched on, failed to appear. In fact, the writer was still imprisoned
by the theme of the tragic dialectic of desire, which always ends in spiritual
and mental disaster for the character who is not yet a hero.

The main point in this reading of the text is the game of dialogue in the
double sense of the term – both amusement and complex exercise. The
short-story writer could hardly be expected to accomplish something for
which the novelist needed months and years. However, the stages of
creation – confrontation with the writer's earlier creation and the literary

heroes of the past; the stimulus of the news item; fertilisation by reality; the experimental variability of situations – were all present, though their order was arbitrary. It is an invitation to a deeper analysis of the creative process in the novel.

11

The unity of thought in the novel

Trying to understand the structure of *The Divine Comedy*, I came to the conclusion that the whole poem is a single united and unbreakable strophe. Or, more exactly, it is not a verse strophe, but a crystallographic figure, a solid.

Osip Mandelstam, *Conversation about Dante*[1]

A genius, in Dostoyevsky's eyes, is someone who brings a 'new word' (*novoe slovo*). The new word is a message, though it may be in the shape of a question, as well as a new vision of the world and the creation of a universe. The best illustration appears in the famous lecture on Pushkin, 8 June 1880. Dostoyevsky took the poet's work as a whole in all its protean shapes, a whole whose meaning seemed so clear to him that he condensed it into four basic points in the 'word of explanation' which acted as preface for the publication of the lecture in the only issue of *Diary of a Writer* for 1880.[2] We are concerned only with his approach, which was the same as that he adopted towards Cervantes, George Sand and Nekrasov. For Dostoyevsky, every great writer gave birth to a total work, whose vector, perfectly drawn at the moment of death, was constantly present at each stage of his evolution. Dostoyevsky always analysed with a view to synthesis. We may go on to consider his attitude towards his own work. Was he creating a unity? Was he, like Dante in *The Divine Comedy*, Balzac in *The Human Comedy* and Proust in *Recollections of Time Past*, pursuing a great continuous design throughout his work? Would he have wished to do so, even if it had been possible?

At first there seem to be too many factors working against the idea that the work was planned and constructed as a whole. First, there were the external factors. These are decisive. Arrest, prison, ten years in Siberia, the years Dostoyevsky devoted to journalism, in spite of their formative and informative value, were gaps in the continuity of creation, which was also interrupted by a succession of bereavements, by epilepsy, gambling and the eternal pursuit of money.

Still more decisive are the inner features of Dostoyevsky's creation: his deep interest in current events, his taste for violent climaxes, his preference for tragic heroes, his conviction that he was living at a time of crisis, upheaval, fever and disintegration, which reinforced his tendency to eschatology. To carry out a task of this sort, he would have needed a more peaceful existence and a world which changed less swiftly.

However, other factors might favour a unified view of Dostoyevsky's work. First, there was his ability to see the universe of his novels appearing as a complex, superabundant world, a swarming whole which was to be set in order and deciphered at the moment when it was first coming into existence. Each new plan was the appearance of a protean universe, part of a new chaos, where earlier creations, the uncreated and the thing to be created seethed in confusion. Finally, numerous major and minor themes recurred, identical situations and actions reappeared, images passed from one novel to another, and obvious genetic chains linked the heroes of different novels.

The brief Balzacian temptation

In some minor early works, the novellas from 1846 to 1848, there was a Balzacian inclination to move characters from one novel to the next. Yulian Mastakovich, Yemilyan Ilich and Astafiy Ivanovich are examples of this.

Yulian Mastakovich (from *mastak*, an expert) appears in a story of 1847, 'The Petersburg Chronicle'. He is an important gentleman, a fifty-year-old dignitary, straightforward and plump, lustful and self-seeking: he has designs on a 'girl of seventeen springs, innocent, well brought up, who left school a month before',[3] and who certainly has a large dowry. While arranging this marriage, he is dreaming of future encounters with his present mistress, a pretty widow. In the shadow of his study, we catch a brief glimpse of an unfortunate copyist 'sitting down to 100 tons of urgent work'.[4] This turns out to be Vasya Shumkov who, in 'A Weak Heart' of February 1848, cannot manage this heavy task in the time fixed and is obsessed by the stern figure of his chief and protector, Yulian Mastakovich. In this story, Yulian Mastakovich, compassionate and moved, gives the lie to the terrifying image which the young copyist has made of him. However, in 'A Christmas Tree and a Wedding', of 1848, he becomes a scoundrel with a formal mask of virtue. Dostoyevsky goes back to an earlier episode in the life of his character, when it is Christmas and the children are gathered round the tree; a charming little girl of eleven who already has a dowry of 300,000 roubles is playing with a redheaded boy, son of a governess. Yulian Mastakovich is swaggering about amongst the guests, and making rapid calculations: 300,000 roubles with five years interest ... He immediately carries out his plan: the little boy is driven away and slandered. Yulian Mastakovich pays court to his future mother-in-law and five years later, the chronicler recognises the poor child on Yulian Mastakovich's arm in a wedding procession.[5]

Yemilyan Ilich is an episodic character from *Poor Folk*: a sacked petty clerk who drags his bad luck around with him and drowns it in alcohol.[6] He reappears in the novella 'An Honest Thief (notes of an unknown man)', where he is one of the two protagonists: the drunkard who steals his benefactor's breeches to buy a drink and who dies confessing his theft.[7]

This novella comes from a cycle of short stories which Dostoyevsky, probably inspired by Turgenev's success with *A Sportsman's Sketches*, had planned in 1848. The hero of them all was to be the worthy man who had taken in the drunk Yemelyan Ilich, a retired warrant officer called Astafiy Ivanovich.[8] *The Notes of an Old Campaigner*, as it was called, was meant to consist of three stories: 'The Veteran', where Astafiy recalls the campaign of 1812; 'The Spirit of the Place' (*Domovoy*) where Astafiy, having retired to Petersburg, is working in a factory;[9] and finally 'The Honest Thief', where Astafiy, out of work, meets the drunkard Yemilyan and takes him in. The first and last appeared in *Annals of the Fatherland* in April 1848, but were rewritten in 1860 and regrouped under the title 'An Honest Thief'.

On the whole, the result is small if not zero. These wandering characters might as well change in every story: the reader would not even notice. Astafiy Ivanovich fades away into the long procession of vaguely characterised Dostoyevskian chroniclers, Yemilyan Ilich is more interesting as a type than as a name – this petty clerk, sacked and desperate, drowning his remorse in alcohol, is a forerunner of Marmeladov in *Crime and Punishment*, who originated in an earlier plan 'The Drunkards'. Only Yulian Mastakovich, well named and well constructed, has some consistency. He takes his place in the fruitful line of important, highly placed men who hide their evil calculations under virtuous or generous masks: Bykov in *Poor Folk*, Pyotr Aleksandrovich in *Netochka Nezvanova*, the husband of Mme M. in 'A Little Hero', Luzhin in *Crime and Punishment*, Totsky in *The Idiot*.

To sum up, Dostoyevsky seems to have quickly lost interest in rivalling the Balzacian novel, if indeed he was ever tempted by it.

The logic of creative thought: the novel of a life

In reality, Dostoyevsky was already pursuing his great design. It is usual to mark a break in his work by his time in prison. A break in his literary production is obvious, and there is also some discontinuity in his ideological development, although Dostoyevsky had begun to change his ideas earlier, when he squabbled with Belinsky in 1847. But there was no break in the search for his great plan. The works before 1849 and those from 1859 to 1863 are all part of a logical preparation for the great novels of his maturity.

This logic is clear from the chronology. In *Poor Folk* Dostoyevsky goes beyond Gogol and the naturalist school haunted by the figure of the poor clerk, by making a detailed analysis of the mental suffering of the characters. Makar Devushkin and Varvara Dobroselova emerge from their class and type and reach human awareness; they proclaim, in spite of social injustice and alienation, their thirst for life and self-respect. Unfortunately, their minds, made self-aware by suffering, are imprisoned by a desire that cannot be fulfilled. Belinsky noted that *Poor Folk* was the first Russian social novel: the failure of the characters incites the reader to break through the barriers, to deliver the prisoners of society. This moral does not actually exist in the text: it resulted from a political reading, though a fully justified one.[10] The heroes of *Poor Folk* feel that the least attempt at rebellion is impossible and unthinkable – this is its tragedy. If *Poor Folk* is the first Russian social novel for the committed reader, for the hero it is a confession that he has totally renounced the idea of revolutionary action. Belinsky admired it because he anticipated the conclusion, but he was disillusioned by the novellas on the same theme which came later, *The Double* (February 1846) and 'Mr Prokharchin' (October 1846). The reasons he gave for his disillusionment were essentially aesthetic, but the apostle of socialism may also have noted the theme of powerlessness and the acceptance of this powerlessness by the artist. The petty clerks who are described: Devushkin, Golyadkin, Prokharchin and Vasya Shumkov of 'A Weak Heart' (February 1848), are so profoundly alienated that they are destroyed by the mere impulse to rebel. They feel guilty and horrified even at the thought of being different. They are paralysed by everything: their bosses, the powerful, a shadow of happiness, a promise of love, other people, the crowd, and most of all by themselves. In 'A Weak Heart', with its significant title, there is a passage which illustrates this perfectly: 'The fact was that Vasya had not fulfilled his obligations, that Vasya felt that he was guilty *towards himself*, felt that he was ungrateful to fate, that Vasya was crushed, shattered by happiness and considered himself unworthy of it, and finally that he was only looking for a pretext to let himself slide down that slope.'[11] These characters are clay vessels resistant to the furnace and the glazes of society, but breakable if touched by a warm breath of happiness, a gentle breeze of love. They are the eternal insulted and injured, crawling creatures frightened by their own movements, the 'beaten down' (*zabityye lyudi*) as Dobrolyubov was to describe them,[12] the outcasts of a merciless society. This was the pessimistic statement of the artist Dostoyevsky. The hostile landscape of ice and fire, the Neva which Vasya's friend contemplates at the end of 'A Weak Heart', and whose evil spirit pursues the journalist of 'Petersburg Dreams' and even Raskolnikov in *Crime and Punishment*, symbolises the castrating power of society.[13]

Obviously Dostoyevsky here thought that the feeling of guilt towards oneself was caused by society. But with 'The Landlady', that fantastic novella of October and December 1847, guilt escaped from its social context (whence Belinsky's wrath) and assumed spiritual and Freudian dimensions. It is not society but an Old Believer, a magician from the mists of Russian folklore, the diabolical Murin, who casts the net of guilt – probably incest –

over the beautiful Katerina. And the saviour who appears is Ordynov, an impenitent dreamer, who does not know if his adventure is dream or reality. This is the dreamer (*mechtatel'*) whose 'mute, desolate and secret tragedy' Dostoyevsky describes in two masterly pages of 'The Petersburg Chronicle' of June 1847[14] and introduces in 'White Nights' of September 1847. These dreamers whose roaming imagination is always ready to catch fire for love of the flame are imprisoned by their solitude and paralysed by their inertia.

Wherever the reader looks he sees only heroes flinging themselves at brick walls because they have caught sight of a dream, heroes deliberately loading themselves with chains of guilt, heroes huddled and motionless in the chrysalis of their dreams. This is the logic of the exploration which the writer doggedly pursues; the tragic dialectic of desire, a feeling of guilt which becomes more and more remote from its social origin, and the sterile idealism of the Schillerian dreamer are its three main elements. The impotence of the hero is the constant.

There is no contradiction between the pessimistic but realistic position of the artist and the commitment of the man to Fourierist socialism. His socialism was only an act of generous charity like that of the Decembrists in 1825, an action born of the realisation that others were in a hopeless position.

However, Dostoyevsky as artist continued his exploration of man. He was looking for reasons and processes, and so in *Netochka Nezvanova* and 'A Little Hero', works unfinished in plan and interrupted by fate, the first by Dostoyevsky's arrest on 23 April 1849, the second by his exile to Siberia at the end of December 1849, he turned towards childhood, which is the beginning of everything, of the process of alienation and the growth of rebellion. The first novella began as a novel which was to have at least six parts.[15] The text published in issues 1, 2 and 5 of *Annals of the Fatherland* 1849 had the significant subtitle 'Story of a Woman', and the three parts were entitled 'Childhood', 'A New Life', 'The Secret'. In the fortress, Dostoyevsky began another story, 'A Little Hero'. Written during the summer and autumn of 1849, it was not published until 1857. The novella, which had expanded by this time, is a sort of echo, or masculine pendant, to the second part of *Netochka Nezvanova*.[16] It was also, originally, a plan for a novel.[17]

Clearly Dostoyevsky was beginning a new kind of novel: the novel of a life, in several parts, of which the first was naturally devoted to childhood. He wished to deal with the mystery of man from his beginnings and as a whole, to escape from the gloomy cycle of the dreamer and his powerlessness. It is significant that one of the characters who was most important in *Netochka Nezvanova* at the beginning, the dreamer Ovrov, should be almost forgotten in the final version, and that the two children selected as heroes should be fighters who are choosing their side. Apparently Dostoyevsky wanted to tell the story of a character as it developed, or more exactly to take the character, for example, of a precocious, proud and sickly child, such as Netochka Nezvanova, the little hero, Nelli in *The Insulted and Injured*, Liza in 'The Eternal Husband', and follow it as it is tested by life, not dreams.[18] To make this test, powerlessness – a frozen form of failure and the end of one part of life – must be banished. The human being must be taken at the time of its spiritual birth, in childhood when everything is possible, when everything shines with faith and love, and body and soul are not yet withered by society. Criticism of the 'philosophy of the environment', so clear in *Crime and Punishment*, has begun. Some months before he reached convict prison, Dostoyevsky went beyond social man. He did not deny him, but he went more deeply. He adopted Rousseau's approach, but without proclaiming the purity and innocence of childhood or celebrating the man of nature and truth. He returned to the hero's childhood to illuminate the mystery of man by beginning with the virgin page where the first letters are to be written, that is, where the possibilities are infinite. He envisaged the history of a life so that he could admit all kinds of different experiences and see the spiritual choices as they were made and prepared.

From different characters with varied experiences to different experiences within the same person

This inner logic, together with the plans for 'the novel of a life', was destroyed by the political drama. But the experience of prison, the submersion among the people, convicts as it happened, showed Dostoyevsky what he was looking for. This was not types of men, but man in all his spaciousness and breadth of character, not 'gold in a poor casing', but gold and casing mingled, that is, the duality, the duplicity and the doubling which are natural to the human being.

Notes from Underground is the gargoyle which forms the keystone of the Dostoyevskian edifice. The hero immediately asserts that he is an anti-hero, like someone suffering from too much awareness, the awareness of being double and multiple, torn by the contradictory impulses which inhabit him and paralysed by their succession in stages (*polosy*): 'I felt that they were swarming inside me, these opposing elements. I knew that they had been swarming inside me for my whole life and were begging to be let out, but I didn't let them, I didn't let them, I deliberately didn't let them out. They tortured me to the point of shame; they drove me to convulsions.'[19] 'Either hero, or mud',[20] he knows no middle point and confesses his inability to choose between them: 'I have not been able to be anything: neither bad, nor good, nor a scoundrel, nor honourable, nor a hero, nor an insect.'[21] He is an anti-hero first on the ideological and metaphysical plane; he rejects the idealism and the romantic lie of the Schillerian dreamer and he refutes the positivist, materialist and utilitarian philosophy of Chernyshevsky and the 'new men'. He affirms his fundamental egoism, as opposed to rational egoism, and so refuses Christian ethics in spite of its implicit recognition of freedom in the theological sense of the word. In short, the Underground man proclaims the infinitude of freedom, but simultaneously he is denying it by his inability to live and experience it. The alienation is no longer social, but comes from the inner depths of being, from the ecstatic stupor of a man contemplating the infinite field of the possible, where the opposing magnetic forces hold him powerless. This is why the Underground man is also a literary anti-hero: he is the negation of the literary type and of its limitations. He is the man without a name,[22] a person in search of identity, for whom, in Rimbaud's words, 'the I is another person'.[23] He tries to find this ungraspable I in the other person, in anyone, in Liza the prostitute, in an unknown officer, in his old school-fellows. With all of them, the Underground man embarks on a search full of distrust, approaches, dreams of desertion, confessions immediately retracted, desired contacts immediately repudiated, impulses of love immediately cancelled by hate, trying to capture the reflection of his own soul. The impression is so strong that Nathalie Sarraute, forgetting the historical links of Dostoyevsky's heroes and the solid texture of echoes from real life, generalised: 'His characters already have a tendency to become what characters in novels will be more and more, not so much human "types" in flesh and blood, like those we think we see around us and whose infinite enumeration seemed to be the aim of the novelist, but simple supports, bearers of states still unexplored which we find within ourselves.'[24] This definition, sensitive but too absolute, was intended to make Dostoyevsky one of the fathers of the modern novel. In fact, Dostoyevsky's heroes give the impression that they are repeating states of mind because they are all seeking their own deeper self, and beyond this the mystery of the human soul.

Dostoyevsky's great asymptotic plan was not intended to destroy the portrayal of character in a novel, but to reduce the multiplicity of individuals to the plurality of experience in one individual. His dream was to write the novel of a life where the hero, of defined identity, passes through all the stages and contradictions of the human spirit. He was tempted by the idea of enclosing the whole of humanity in one man, and exposing this man to an orgy of universal experience.

The first to cross the threshold of fascinated expectancy in which the anti-hero of *Notes from Underground* lives and to venture into the battlefield of infinite liberty to discover his inner self by his experience was Raskolnikov. The great novels begin with him. Certainly, he is defeated: his chosen way excluded others. Enclosed in solitude at the beginning of the action, the hero of *Crime and Punishment* begins his expiation even before he commits the murder. His deadly sin was to have broken his links with others. Salvation comes when he recognises the existence of others, when he gains knowledge of himself by seeing others and their seeing him: the first mirrors are Svidrigaylov and Sonya. We know the epilogue of the novel: 'But here a new history begins, the history of a man's gradual renewal, his gradual rebirth, his gradual passage from one world to another, his discovery of a new reality, until then completely unknown. This could form the theme of a new story, – but our present story is finished.'[25] So *Crime and Punishment* was only the history of a crisis, although the childhood of the hero was recalled, although the future was envisaged. Dostoyevsky still had to write the story of a life, the culmination of the logic of his creative thought, the work which, from the alpha of childhood to the omega of the hero's death, was intended to deal exhaustively with the immense mystery of man in a succession of experiences and new births and to contain the world of the great basic conflicts of mankind. The story of creation must deal with the creative dream, even if it never became reality. The great novels of Dostoyevsky were nourished by the idea and the remains of this great plan which was never fulfilled.

The two creative lines

Two creative lines existed in Dostoyevsky. One, open and above ground, appeared in the finished work, destined for the public. In reality this line was broken into segments to form the novels and these segments were arranged slantingly, like branches bending towards a moving light, subject to the phototropism of contingency. They were variously affected by the writer's experiences, such as material obstacles or encouragement, his reading at the time, contemporary ideological debates, the fascination of news items, and the pressure of political history. The second, underground, line was more continuous: it passed through numerous imaginary, scrapped or abandoned plans, through plans to which Dostoyevsky was always returning because they were essential to him and because they were a goldmine to be explored and used, through censored chapters ('Stavrogin's Confession' is a good example), through confidences in letters to friends and relations. It was less dynamic than the first line, but just as important. It nourished the first, it was, to continue the plant metaphor, the tree bearing the branches, knotted and tormented by the storms of the novelist's personal life and of history, which are images of the novels that the reader sees. Although the sap rises from the roots to the branches, the growth of the tree is also dependent on air and light, or, in other words, the novels in their turn modified the great design which inspired them.

12

The summit of creative interrogation: 'The Life of a Great Sinner'

> The technique of a novel always sends us back to the metaphysics of the novelist.
>
> Jean-Paul Sartre, *Situations I*[1]

There was a typical interaction of these two creative lines in the period from the end of 1868 to December 1870. On the surface, Dostoyevsky was finishing *The Idiot*, of which the last five chapters appeared, late, in the February 1869 issue of *The Russian Messenger*; from September to December 1869 he was writing 'The Eternal Husband', a novella promised to *Aurora* where it was published in January and February 1870; he was then beginning *The Devils*, whose first chapters he sent to *The Russian Messenger* in October 1870. On the underground line, which is clearer in his correspondence than his notes, he seemed to be mainly occupied with two successive plans, thematically linked but profoundly different, 'Atheism' and 'The Life of a Great Sinner' which formed the great project of his entire life.

The reality is much more complex. The working notebooks of Dostoyevsky for this period, and even as early as 1867, contain, besides notes directly relating to *The Idiot*, 'The Eternal Husband' and *The Devils*, numerous other minor plans. They show that Dostoyevsky, even while he was composing, writing and dictating, was constantly tempted by different developments of themes and characters.[2] This is not because he was incapable of maintaining the logic and unity of the narrative, or because he was distracted by the subjects which sprung up like weeds as he wrote, it was rather a matter of the creative dialectic between the novel which had to be finished and the same novel which remained essentially unfinished in its polyphonic mode. It was the elaboration of the main novel which brought these minor plans to birth and then killed them, casting off unrelated happenings like a moulting skin, to keep only the psychological gains. Dostoyevsky, using his method of variability of situations, tried and followed up experiments which reinforced the one he was conducting in the setting finally chosen for the novel, but were carried out in different surroundings. One example will be enough to show this.

'The Emperor' or the laboratory experiment

From October to December 1867 Dostoyevsky was searching for the soul of the hero whom he called 'the idiot' in his first drafts. He made no fewer than

eight plans before he abandoned the proud, despotic and secretly passionate figure first envisaged and ended with the gentle, lucid, and naive,
almost saintly being, who stands upright amid the whirlwind of passions
which carries off the imaginary heroines and families: the future prince
Myshkin. At precisely the same time Dostoyevsky was setting out a plan in
his notebooks which appeared to be completely different.

A THOUGHT (POEM)

A THEME ENTITLED '*THE EMPEROR*'

A cellar, darkness, a youth, does not know how to speak, Ivan Antonovich, almost
twenty. Description of *the nature* of this man. *His* development. *He* develops by
himself, fantastic pictures and images, dreams, a maiden (in a dream) – *He* has
imagined, seen through the window. Conceptions of all objects. Horrible fantasy,
mice, cat, dog.

A young officer, the adjutant of the Commandant, has planned a coup, to
proclaim *Him* emperor.

He gets to know *Him*, bribes the old invalid who is serving the prisoner, gets in to
see *Him*.

Meeting of two human beings. *His* astonishment. Both joy and terror, friendship.

He develops the captive, teaches *Him*, explains to *Him*, shows *Him* the maiden.
(The Commandant's daughter, through whom all this is happening.) The Commandant's daughter is tempted to become empress.

Finally tells *Him* that *He* is emperor, that all is possible to *him*. Pictures of power
('this is why I am so respectful towards *You*; I am not *Your* equal').

(The captive has grown so fond of him that once *He* says: 'If you are not equal to
me, I do not want to be emperor' – i.e. feeling, afraid of losing his friendship.)

He shows *Him* the world, from the garret (the Neva and so on).

Finally the rebellion. The Commandant pierces the Emperor with a sword. *He*
dies majestically and sadly.

He shows the universe. 'It is all yours, if you only want it. Let us go!'

It is impossible; in case of failure, death, what is death? . . . He kills the cat to show
Him: blood.

A terrible impression on *Him*. 'I do not wish to live.'

'If so, if anyone dies for me, if you die, she will die . . .'

Mirovich enthusiastically shows *Him* the other side of the coin and explains how
much good *He* can do when *He* becomes emperor. *He* catches fire . . .

Mirovich is an enthusiast. He gives *Him* the idea of God, of Christ.

NB. (He shows *Him* his betrothed, the Commandant's daughter, making an
agreement with her . . . His betrothed agrees: she comes out to show herself,
splendidly, dressed for a ball, with flowers. Enthusiasm of the Emperor. The
betrothed is amazed by the impression which she has produced. She has dreams: to
become empress. Mirovich notices this, is jealous. The Emperor notices his hatred
and jealousy, his looks of hatred, does not understand, but feels what the matter
is.)[3]

Who are these heroes? History tells us that the imprisoned emperor is the
unfortunate Ivan (Ioann) VI Antonovich, who was proclaimed emperor on
the death of the Empress Anna Ivanovna in 1740, the year of his birth, but
never reigned, since in 1741 Yelizaveta Petrovna seized the throne of
Russia. He was imprisoned and transferred to the Fortress of Schlusselburg.

In the reign of Catherine II, Lieutenant Mirovich, in a plot to restore him to power, attempted an armed rising. The plot failed and the prince was killed by his guards, on the night of 4–5 July 1764.

Dostoyevsky may have been returning to the historical projects of his youth, such as 'Mariya Styuart' and 'Boris Godunov', but he was more probably inspired by his recent reading: by an article, 'Ioan VI Antonovich. An episode from Russian history', in which V. I. Semevsky, the historian, used previously unpublished documents from the archives[4] and especially, as A. V. Alpatov has shown, by the publication in 1863 of a plan for a novel, which remained unfinished, by the Ukrainian writer G. F. Kvitka-Osnovyanenko, whose double subject would have been the life of Mirovich and the fate of Ioann VI.[5] In his plan, conceived around 1840,[6] Kvitka was particularly taken by his heroine, who is very like the ambitious Marina in 'Boris Godunov'. Daughter of one of the two officers in charge of Ivan Antonovich, dissimulating, enterprising, energetic, daring, of limitless pride, she is ready to do anything to gain her ends. She seduces the prisoner, extorts a promise of marriage from him and dreams of freeing him. She meets Mirovich, whose hatred of his superiors makes him her willing tool. She pretends to love him in return for his love and tempts him with dreams of becoming a general in chief.

Kvitka's notes inspired Dostoyevsky to develop the theme of ambitious rivalry between Ivan Antonovich and Mirovich, the origin of the love of prince Myshkin and Rogozhin for Nastasya Filippovna. Other themes characteristic of Dostoyevsky appear. The two men take their place among the young dreamers of his novels. Intoxication with the dream of power, of 'all is possible', which is characteristic of Raskolnikov and Arkadiy, is balanced here by the refusal to accept the suffering of any living creature expressed by Ivan Karamazov in the chapter 'Rebellion'. Love for universal life, celebrated by Makar in *A Raw Youth* and Zosima in *The Brothers Karamazov*, is linked to Dostoyevsky's constant theme of the experience of suffering, without which there is no true awareness. In this plan, as in many of Dostoyevsky's plans, there is a thematic density which is based on earlier works and is a preparation for later ones.

But in our opinion the essential point is elsewhere. In this sketch, Dostoyevsky was approaching the important subject of the history of the formation of a soul. Ivan Antonovich is an empty page: prison has cut him off from the world and preserved him from society. His power to dream is unlimited, his soul is untarnished and – a Rousseauist miracle – all is possible. He is a soul to be modelled and this is done by another dreamer, Mirovich. Gradually the young man, mentally retarded until then, incapable of speaking, wakes to a spiritual life. He discovers, without passing through the experience of sin, that the will to power and Evil are essentially one, and that love, in the widest sense, demands renunciation of the dream of power. Dostoyevsky was struck by the situation which history offered him: a laboratory experiment enclosed in the laboratory, a soul which is born in a 'twin birth', as Claudel would say, 'of itself and the world'. This Gaspard Hauser situation was used for Prince Myshkin, who is also brought up in solitude, plunged in the prison depths of his idiocy, isolated in his Swiss sanatorium, and only awakes to spiritual life during his adolescence, among children and from his meeting with Marie. Preserved by their early suffering and solitude from the wicked society which humiliates, alienates and degrades man, Ivan Antonovich and Myshkin come with only the gift of their 'calm eyes', like Verlaine's Gaspard Hauser, into the coarse atmosphere of life which destroys them. The social failure of Myshkin, like the political ruin of Ivan Antonovich, who dies 'majestically and sadly', is implicit in this rapid leap from childhood to sainthood, without going through the profound and necessary experience of *pro et contra* in life. Socially immature, they reach their deepest self immediately and their brief span of life is ended by their calvary. In the plan of *The Emperor* Dostoyevsky eliminated childhood and adolescence so as to obtain characters who were as new as children: he simply delayed experience. However, the secret wish of the novelist to go back to the childhood of the hero, as he did in *Netochka Nezvanova*, is clear in the first paragraph of the 'Emperor' plan, and in Myshkin's accounts of his childhood to Rogozhin and the Yepanchin family. Until 1869 Dostoyevsky had never been able to carry out his wish. In his novels and stories, his heroes enter their time of crisis as grown men and women, or, on the contrary, their story or sometimes their life (Nelli in *The Insulted and Injured*) is interrupted at the threshold of adolescence. But adolescence is just the time when 'all is possible', the time of immaturity, of falling and rising, of learning to balance. It is a time for experiments in life, the chosen time of the Dostoyevsky novel. The dream of the novelist was to reconcile essence and subject, thought and theme. He wanted to insert real adolescence, lived in the world and not in the hermit's cell of the Emperor or the Idiot, into the story of a life. Even before he tried to do this in 'Atheism' and 'The Life of a Great Sinner', he had chosen adolescence not as a theme, but as a novelistic technique.

The technique of mimic adolescence

When Dostoyevsky tried to define the psychology of his hero, he began a series of experiments which leave little trace in the finished novel, where the dominant feature of the character is more evident. This is the limbo stage of creation which we shall call 'mimic adolescence'. At this laboratory stage all Dostoyevsky's heroes are brothers. They acquire their personality, their identity only when they leave the melting-pot of creation.

There are curious relationships between Raskolnikov, the Idiot (the future Myshkin), the Prince (the future Stavrogin) and Versilov. They are brothers who have experienced a different literary adolescence. Stavrogin and Versilov were created after the character of the Great Sinner, so we shall consider only the initial relationship of Raskolnikov and the Idiot, as it appears in the first sketches.

They are both dualistic creatures, torn between their pride, their feeling of superiority and their need for love. Here is Raskolnikov in the notebooks of *Crime and Punishment*: 'He says: to be able to reign over them! All the baseness around only infuriates him. Profound contempt for people. Pride.'[7] Numerous notes in the same vein follow: 'hatred for humanity',[8] 'satanic pride',[9] 'immeasurable pride, arrogance and contempt for this society', 'despotism',[10] 'pride and haughtiness and confidence in his own innocence continually crescendo',[11] and so on. The same expressions define the original Idiot: 'NB. *Main character of the Idiot*. Self control from pride (and not from morality) and furious freedom: allows himself anything.'[12] If the Idiot, in the first drafts, burns with an 'ardent desire for love', he is still swaying between two extremes: 'Either to have tyrannical power or to die for everyone on the cross'[13] and 'to end with a great crime or a heroic deed'.[14] We know that he will turn towards Christ. Raskolnikov has chosen crime, but after his crime he does not lose hope – in the notebooks, since this possibility is rejected in the novel at the end of the epilogue – of 'redeeming the petty and ridiculous crime of youth by a mountain of goodness and usefulness',[15] or in other words, of becoming a second Haas, a doctor in the Moscovite prisons whom the Siberian convicts remembered with great emotion:[16] 'Is it really impossible that I should become a Haas? Could I really not be like Haas?', or again, 'Why should I not become like Haas? Why is everything lost? A child? Who will forbid me to love that child? Can I not become good?'[17]

There is another relationship between the Idiot and Raskolnikov, going beyond them to unite all the great heroes from the Underground man to the Karamazovs. On 18 October 1867, Dostoyevsky believed he had already reached 'the definitive plan of his novel', *The Idiot*. He had only reached the stage of the stormy love affairs of the heroine Hero-Olga Umetskaya, one of the eight plans of a first version which was to be abandoned. He then underlined a formula: 'Theory of happiness on earth',[18] which he did not develop here because the theory was already clearly set out on the page of the notebooks for *Crime and Punishment* headed 'The Idea of the novel', probably written in December 1865 and January 1866:

There is no happiness in comfort, happiness is bought by suffering. Such is the law of our planet, but this direct awareness, felt in the process of life, is such an immense joy that it is possible to pay for it by years of suffering.
Man is not born for happiness. Man earns his happiness, and always through suffering.

There is no injustice here, for knowledge and awareness of life (that is, what can be directly felt by body and soul, by the whole process of life) is obtained by experience *pro et contra*, which must be slowly and painfully acquired.[19]

The important point for our discussion is not so much the Orthodox idea of the relationship between happiness and suffering as the statement that an experience *pro et contra* is necessary and the insistence that body and mind are a unity. These two ideas define the technique as well as the thought of the novelist. There are no ideas which are not lived, no images which are not felt, no convictions which are not tested in body and soul. Man is an eternal adolescent in the sense that he wavers before committing himself and hesitates even when he is already committed. And the hero lives the main part of his adolescence in Dostoyevsky's laboratory, the working notebooks. Here the character gradually detaches himself from the previous life which he shared with his fellows, so that this literary, mimic adolescence is substituted for real adolescence. The experiments sometimes leave traces, when we find in the finished novel an unexpected recurrence from a previous life under other skies. Myshkin has some dark impulses,[20] inherited from his original character, while Raskolnikov, Stavrogin and Versilov have dreams of the Golden Age and universal harmony, which come from the mythical past of humanity in general, but also from their own past existence in the limbo of the novel, the notebooks.

'Atheism', again the novel of crisis

Dostoyevsky was fascinated by his previous creation. In *The Idiot*, Myshkin, during the party at the Yepanchin house, pronounces anathema on Roman Caesaropapism and its black cohort, the Jesuits: 'Roman Catholicism is even worse than atheism, that is my opinion! Yes, that is my opinion! Atheism only preaches nothingness, but Catholicism goes further; it preaches a distorted Christ, that it has lied about and blasphemed, the opposite of Christ. It preaches the Anti-Christ, I swear to you.'[21] He goes on:

The pope has seized a country, a temporal throne and has taken up the sword; since then everything has been going on just the same, only they have added lying, intrigue, deceit, fanaticism, superstition and crime to the sword, they have played with the most sacred, purest, most innocent and passionate feelings of the people; they have exchanged everything, everything for vile temporal power.[22]

He goes on to lump Catholicism, atheism and socialism together, and then, wounded by a remark that his benefactor Pavlishchev had become a Jesuit, he sketches a portrait of the Russian in the grip of doubt:

You are surprised at Pavlishchev, you attribute it all to his madness or his goodness, but why? Our Russian passion in these cases surprises not only us, but the whole of Europe; with us, if anyone goes over to Catholicism, he is bound to become a Jesuit, and one of the most devious ones; if he becomes an atheist, he is bound to start demanding the eradication of belief in God by force, that is, by the sword![23]

He explains the origin of this 'sudden fanaticism':

It is not just because of vanity, it is not just because of disgusting vain feelings that there are Russian atheists or Jesuits; it is because of spiritual pain, a spiritual thirst, a longing for a higher cause, for a firm shore, for the country they have stopped believing in, because they have never even known it! It's so easy for a Russian to be an atheist, easier than for anyone else in the world! And ours don't simply become atheists, but they always come to believe in atheism as if it were a new faith, without noticing that they have come to believe in nothing. This is the sort of thirst we have![24]

Remember, he adds, that there have been 'in Russia, highly educated men who even entered the flagellant sects ... And how, by the way, are flagellants any worse than nihilists, Jesuits, atheists? Perhaps they are even more profound! But this is what anguish of soul can lead us to!'[25]

This exaggerated expression in Russians of the dialectic relationship between faith and doubt was to be the central theme of 'Atheism', a plan which Dostoyevsky set out to his friend, the poet Apollon Maykov, in his letter from Florence of 23 December 1868.[26] Myshkin's formulation of the idea remained general, not part of the novel, but it occurred before the new project, since Dostoyevsky had just finished chapter 7, part 4, from which these quotations are taken, and was preparing, as he says in this letter, to write the last five chapters.[27] Within a few days, the Idea was embodied in a hero:

At the moment I have an enormous novel in my head, its title is 'Atheism' (this is between us, for heaven's sake) but before I start, I must read almost a whole library of atheists, Catholics and Orthodox believers. Even if I can free myself from all material worries, it will hardly be ready for two years. I have the character ready: it is a Russian of our background, of a ripe age, not very cultured but with some culture, fairly advanced on the promotion ladder, who suddenly, when he is fairly old, loses faith in God. All his life he has only worked, without coming out of his rut and has not been distinguished in anything at all until he reached 45. (Psychological solution: deep feeling, the man and the Russian man). The loss of faith acts on him in a colossal way. (On the whole, the action of the novel and the background are very wide). He haunts the new generations, the atheists, the Slavs and the Europeans, the fanatics and Russian hermits, the priests; among others he is collared by a Jesuit, a Polish missionary; he escapes him to fall into the abyss of the flagellant sect and finally he finds Christ and the Russian land, the Russian Christ and the Russian God. In the name of Heaven, don't tell anyone, but you see for me, if I write this last novel, even if I were to die then, I should have expressed myself in full.[28]

When *The Idiot* was finished, Dostoyevsky returned to the plan which was 'torturing' him, in a letter of 6 February 1869 to his niece S. A. Ivanova:

At the moment I have in my head the idea of a great novel, which in any case, even if I *fail*, will be certain to have an effect, even if only because of the theme: 'Atheism'. (It is not an attack on the convictions of our age. It is something else, a true poem) ... Two or three characters have taken shape in my mind, among others, an enthusiastic Catholic priest (of the type of St Francis Xavier).[29]

Unfortunately Dostoyevsky was torn between two opposing certainties which paralysed him and which he expressed in his correspondence from December 1868 to May 1869. On one hand he was sure that 'Atheism' would be his great work, his testament, the summit of his writing career. 'My aim', he wrote on 20 March 1869, 'is not to acquire glory and money but to carry out a synthesis of my artistic and poetic idea, in brief, to express myself as completely as possible in something before I die.'[30] On 27 May 1869, he called his literary idea: 'Parabola of atheism' and declared that all his past career was only a pale 'introduction' to this work to which he wanted to devote his entire life.[31] On the other hand, he was equally convinced that it was impossible to write it in his present circumstances, in exile, far from the Russia which nourished his thoughts as a novelist: 'I cannot write it here; for that I absolutely must be in Russia, see, hear, take a direct part in Russian life. Two years will be necessary. This is impossible here and this is why I want to write something else.'[32] Returning to Russia would have solved the problem, but he could not do this without settling debts of at least 4,000 roubles and having an income, for the first year, of about 3,000 roubles, 7,000 roubles in all.[33]

The plan appeared only in Dostoyevsky's letters. There is no clear mention of the subject in the notebooks of this period. What happened? Dostoyevsky was engulfed by the tribulations of 1869: leaving Florence in August for Prague, forced return to Dresden, birth of his daughter Lyubov in September, writing 'The Eternal Husband', the novella promised to *Aurora* for autumn. On 10 September 1869, in a letter to S. A. Ivanova, he returned to the plan without naming it and drew up a long list of complaints: 'I have an idea to which I am completely devoted; but I cannot, I must not begin work on it, because I am not ready for it yet. I haven't thought it over properly and I need materials. As a result, I am forced to invent new stories: it is repulsive. What will become of me and how I am going to settle my affairs, I haven't the faintest idea!'[34] It is obvious that Dostoyevsky had begun nothing in August 1869.

From the novel of crisis to the novel of a life

'Atheism', a plan which appeared only in letters, seemed to have been postponed indefinitely; but it was reborn in a different form, changed by Dostoyevsky's underground wish to go back to childhood, to the blank page where everything is still to be written, even the problem of faith and doubt.

The hero of 'Atheism' loses his faith at a ripe age, so why not expand the drama and especially why give it a date? Does not the problem of God go beyond time and society? Would it not be preferable to place it at the beginning of life? Two notes scribbled in 1869 indicated a return to childhood and youth; the second is a development of the first:

1 31 July. Florence
Childhood.
Fathers and sons, intrigue, children's conspiracy, beginning of boarding school, etc.[35]
2 Underground idea for The Russian Messenger 14/2 November.
I (?), family, from childhood, Moscow, everything owing to him. Growth. Chermak, the first is the last, accused of everything. Silent and gloomy, keeps family. All depend on him. Silent. All find this oppressive. The woman he loved (she once spoke to him heart to heart) married his brother. Brother suddenly became ill. Everyone looks at him trembling. He is silent and does charitable deeds. For example, he received a slap. He didn't challenge. In the family they daren't laugh. End in tragedy.[36]

These sketches are the link between the previous plan of 'Atheism' and the new one which appeared in December 1869 and which Dostoyevsky entitled 'The Life of a Great Sinner'. It was not a thematic but a structural turning point: the composition was disrupted. On 26 December 1869, Dostoyevsky, who, delayed by 'The Eternal Husband' promised to *Aurora*, had written nothing for *The Russian Messenger*, confided in his niece, S. A. Ivanova:

I think they will be angry with me at the Russian Messenger and they will have some cause. But what could I do? I didn't know things would turn out like this and I couldn't send The Russian Messenger the story I had written for Aurora. I am planning something much more important for them. It is a novel and only the first book will be published by The Russian Messenger. It will take five years to complete and will be divided into three distinct narratives. This novel is the whole expectation, the whole hope of my life, and I am not referring to money. It is my main idea, it occurred to me only in the last few years. But the writing must not be rushed. I don't want to spoil it. This idea is everything I have lived for. Besides, to write this novel, I must be in Russia. For example, the second part of my first narrative takes place in a monastery. I need not only to see (I have seen a lot), but to live in a monastery.[37]

It was an important turning point. The plan left his letters to enter the notebooks. On 20 December 1869 Dostoyevsky began to collect the first notes for 'The Life of a Great Sinner' in a handwriting firm enough to show the clarity of his inspiration. The dates – 20 December 1869, 1, 2, 24, 27 January up to 15 May 1870 – determine the logical order of the pages, which, as usual in Dostoyevsky, are not placed in sequence.[38] Dostoyevsky was sure that everything would go quickly and on page 14 he calculated the stages of his work: '27 January, 10 February, 15, 22 February, 22 begin the envoys.'[39] At the end of February, he was so sure of his plan that he thought he could send the first chapters of the first book to *The Russian Messenger*. The new plan was ambitious: Dostoyevsky envisaged at least 140 printed signatures, divided as follows:

20 Childhood.
20 The monastery.
40 Before exile.
20 Exile and Satan.
40 The heroic deed (spiritual progress).

The thematic link between 'Atheism' and 'The Life of a Great Sinner' is clear. There is even a word-for-word parallel between the expression in the letter of 27 May 1869 'the Parabola of atheism' and the new plan entitled 'Life [*Zhitiye*, hagiography, saint's life] of a Great sinner'. But the composition and structure are completely different: the Jesuit, the Polish missionary, the priest who is as zealous as Francis Xavier, have disappeared; all the action takes place in Russia and the hero is no longer a mature man who suddenly loses faith. The tragic time of crisis is abandoned for the hagiographic time of experience, of the tribulations of a soul. Dostoyevsky, partly relying on personal memories,[40] as the notes linking the two plans tell us, is going back to the childhood of his hero.

'The Life of a Great Sinner': matching theme and technique

As usual when plans followed each other, Dostoyevsky moved in a spiral, tirelessly returning to his first notes, sometimes concentrating his whole effort on the psychological description of the hero, sometimes rapidly listing all the properties, sometimes noting the canvas, sometimes wondering about tone and form. He kept on surrendering to the experience of writing and these notebooks are more like intimate creative diaries than the linear plans of Tolstoy and Turgenev. His heroes are born in the repetition of the many experiments to which they are subjected, even if these experiments disappear in the finished novel. We have called this technique the mimic adolescence of the hero. With 'The Life of a Great Sinner', the principle is applied to childhood, an amazing childhood which contains the history of a soul. The tendency is so definite that Dostoyevsky, after having developed this crucial period at length in his plan, passed over 'the monastery' in one page, practically omitted 'the exile', which became a 'journey through Russia', and concluded with two laconic lines about 'the exploit'. The plan is fantastic in the Dostoyevskian sense of the word, for this childhood is crammed with extraordinary experiences. The child is certainly unusual; he is one of the strong heroes who forge their power during the humiliations and injuries of early childhood, who are partly the dreamers of the stories before prison, partly proud, rebellious and wounded young souls like Netochka Nezvanova, Nelli of *The Insulted and Injured*, Liza of 'The Eternal Husband' and Nastasya Filippovna of *The Idiot*, and partly Promethean heroes like Raskolnikov, the original character of the Idiot and the future Stavrogin, Versilov and Ivan Karamazov.

'The Life of a Great Sinner' is the summit of the creative search. It is an end and a reversal. Until this point all the works were leading to the final discovery, after many tribulations, of the 'breadth' (*shirokost'*) of man. The embryo of this is the tragic dialectic of desire, where man dies as he is being born. The breadth of the human soul is sometimes so great that it dissolves into a schematic arrangement of opposing types: victims on one side, executioners on the other. This happened in *The Insulted and Injured*, where only Nelli represents rebellion. *The House of the Dead* is the ethnological document which brings irrefutable proof of the breadth of man: even convicts banished from society prove that it is a permanent part of man's nature. *Notes from Underground* is a passionate manifesto of the theory: the breadth is vigorously proclaimed in opposition to monistic, materialistic and romantic ideas, but in total vacancy: the anti-hero obstinately refused to leave the corpses that surround him. *Crime and Punishment* is the first illustration of this breadth: its main lines are the interaction of Raskolnikov's good and bad motives for murder and the ordeal which foretells his redemption, although this is put off to a future beyond the novel. In *The Idiot* Dostoyevsky has been too hasty: the breadth of character shown in the earlier plans is quickly left behind and Myshkin, who has been guarded, like the Emperor in Dostoyevsky's plan, from the necessary experience of adolescence, conquers without fighting and fails as a saint fails. 'The Life of a Great Sinner' is original because the phases of the novel are inverted: the breadth is no longer the conclusion and the result of the ordeal, but is acquired and formed at the beginning of life. It directs the ordeals, it is the dynamic energy of human freedom. The simple scheme of fall and redemption is replaced by the complex succession 'of falls and redemptions' (*padaniye i vosstavaniye*),[41] a sign of the freedom of the hero, who suddenly becomes unpredictable. The complexity of the novels, for which Dostoyevsky was blamed and which he himself deplored, his method of trying out actions, gestures, situations and relationships, of subjecting his characters to varied and numerous experiments and questioning himself about the results did not happen because the novels were difficult to write; the technique was inherent in the idea of breadth, of repeated experiences of *pro et contra*. 'It is exactly this state of *oscillation* which forms the novel', Dostoyevsky noted in his plan.[42]

As a result, the plot as such is devalued. It is not badly structured and finished off, for Dostoyevsky was a master of technique, but it does not matter if the plot is mad or even improbable, as in *A Raw Youth*. There is hardly any plot in the plan of 'Life of a Great Sinner', although events occur in a rudimentary chronological order. At this stage the time scheme, always compressed as much as possible in the final version of the novels, matters less than hagiographical time, in which the oscillations of the soul must come as thick and fast as possible.

'The Life of a Great Sinner': Jacob's night

Mochulsky has reconstituted the four acts of the childhood of the Great Sinner in great detail.[43] In contrast, we prefer to keep the creative disorder, to indicate the recurring elements which link the created with previous creations, to stress the breadth of the hero and above all bring together the multitude of experiences.

The young boy of 'The Life of a Great Sinner' is fiery and passionate, proud and willful, a fighter and a Promethean hero. From the beginning Dostoyevsky collects significant notes:

Birth of violent passions.
Reinforcement of will and inner force.
Excessive pride and struggle with vanity.
Prose of life and passionate faith which always triumphs over it.
Let everyone bow down and I will pardon them.
Fear nothing. Sacrifice his life.[44]
Either slavery or domination.[45]
. . .
Arrogant contempt towards his persecutors and prompt judgements. The extraordinary promptness of his judgements shows a violent, passionate exclusiveness.[46]
. . .
He pardons nothing which is lying or false.[47]
. . .
Tendency to unlimited domination and confidence immovable in its own authority. To move mountains. And he is glad to test his power.
Struggle is second nature to him, but calm, not stormy.[48]

The 'instinctive awareness of superiority'[49] is increased by the sight of the dirt and depravity which surround him, first with 'the little old people' in the country where he has been sent, then in his family, the Alfonskys in Moscow, and at the Suchard boarding school which Dostoyevsky had known as a youth. His contempt and disgust for adults only increases. He quickly realises that they are 'much more stupid and insignificant than they seem'.[50] All of them – the 'little old people', their guests, the teachers and even a respectable scholar, his parents – they are all living for the moment, exchanging cynical or frivolous remarks, copulating, ill-treating their serfs. Alfonsky, his father, goes so far – a memory of the rumours about Dr Dostoyevsky's death is obvious – that the peasants murder him. His step-mother, for he has discovered that he is a bastard, has an affair in which he is involved.

The child is beaten, unjustly whipped, accused of theft. He shuts himself up, meditates about his hatred, wants to 'dirty the whole world', dirty himself, even in the eyes of a woman who falls in love with him, the doctor's wife. To blows and insults he replies by insolent attacks. Humiliation and suffering are the first, involuntary, great experience of his life. He uses his injuries to feed his contempt and his will to dominate. Determined to form his character, he encourages people to inflict ordeals on him and tries other experiments which the hero of *Notes from Underground* had attempted in vain. 'He is treated as a monster and he behaves like a monster.'[51] He questions himself: 'Would it be a good idea to become a flatterer?' and he discovers that it needs 'a spiritual force to become a flatterer'.[52] Or again, 'At the examination he does well unexpectedly, he wanted to appear an idiot. He despises himself deeply because he couldn't resist doing well.'[53]

He feels that the seeds of 'the strongest carnal passions'[54] are coming to life in him and this is followed by a long series of sexual experiments, direct or indirect. He sees the sexual act, he devours an erotic novel *Thérèse-Philosophe*;[55] with Umnov, a class-mate who 'spies on naked women and tries to rape the little cripple',[56] he learns 'to f . . .'[57] With Albert, the future Lambert of *A Raw Youth*, he plunges into debauchery: 'Lambert and he, complete picture of depravity.'[58]

At the same time he trains his body to endure pain: he is silent when unjustly whipped, he fights with 'bigger boys', he struggles against cowardice: 'I will never be afraid any more. I will learn not to be afraid.'[59] Like the Idiot in the first drafts, he inflicts burns on himself; like Arkadiy in *A Raw Youth* he gashes his body 'to test himself'.[60]

'He is amazed himself at what he does, he tests himself and loves going down into the depths.'[61] This fascination with the depths has been a recurrent theme since *The House of the Dead*, where Dostoyevsky described 'resolute men' like his fellow-prisoner Luke:

He was like a man who was getting drunk, or in a raging fever. As if, once having leapt over a forbidden line, he was beginning to enjoy the idea that there was nothing left sacred for him; as if he felt an irresistible longing to leap at once over all law and authority and revel in the most unbridled and unlimited freedom, to revel in the moment when the heart freezes from that horror, which he could not have helped feeling towards himself.[62]

All this, Dostoyevsky goes on, is like 'that feeling when a person on a high tower is drawn towards the depths under his feet, so that finally he would be glad to fling himself down headlong'.[63]

Proud and tyrannical by nature, the hero crosses the forbidden line. He commits sacrilege by taking a star from the crown of an icon, an episode used later in *The Devils*, and by declaring himself an atheist in court. He becomes aware of his taste for blood, first by killing a goose,[64] and then by murdering a deserter from the army with the help of Kulikov,[65] a convict of base origins, who fascinates and indoctrinates him and is an earlier version of Fedka, the convict in *The Devils*. His mad descent into the abyss also allows him the drunkenness of confession: 'Hellish orgy with Albert (Lambert), crime and sacrilege, admission of murder with Kulikov: *straight into the abyss*.'[66]

In parallel he explores all the means of achieving power: 'Intelligence, cleverness and education, he wishes to acquire all this as future means of becoming unusual.'[67] He becomes hungry for knowledge, probably as Dostoyevsky did in his youth, with the same likes and dislikes. He studies French, German, universal history, geography (which is drudgery), tries the sciences which he finds difficult, devours classic and popular novels with passion. He beats Katya, the little cripple, because she is less enthusiastic about Karamzin than he is. Walter Scott inspires his dreams. Shakespeare and Lermontov show him strong and rebellious characters in *Hamlet* and *A Hero of our Time*. He knows Gogol and Pushkin by heart, and reads the Bible 'all through', commenting on it to Katya with amazing maturity.

Seeking a 'fulcrum', a more efficient lever than education and intelligence to conquer power, he ends by 'settling on money'.[68] The first stage of the plan is 'to pile up riches', the dominant experience among the many experiences of the child, whose 'upbringing takes place amid torments and hoarding'.[69] A moneylender, 'a terrifying man, antithesis of Tikhon',[70] infects him with the fever for gold, but this Mephistopheles appears later, after the hero has been in a monastery. The boy does not wait for his encouragement; '*Main nota bene*: he set out to gather money with a confused idea, but this idea became stronger and was proved to him by the course of events which followed.'[71] As with Ganya in *The Idiot*, money seemed to be a guarantee against the risk of error about his own person and his own value: 'Sometimes he thought again that if he didn't become extraordinary and were completely ordinary, money would give him everything, that is power and the right to despise.'[72] Like Arkadiy in *A Raw Youth*, himself inspired by Pushkin's *Covetous Knight*, he knows its power as a weapon: 'Whether they like it or not, they will come to me and bow down.'[73] Momentarily tempted to steal a wallet (a reappearance of the Lebedev episode in *A Raw Youth*), he refuses and chooses the straight and narrow path: 'He decided to get money by honest means.'[74] Here again, money represents trial by ordeal.

However, the child is not a monster. Savage, hard towards others and himself, madly proud, he is very like Kolya Krasotkin in *The Brothers Karamazov*, who hides a heart of gold under coarse and brutal manners. His only way of showing his interest in Katya, the little cripple, is to hit her – like him, for he is beaten. In reality, he feels a true tenderness for the little girl, with whom he shares his dreams, his reading: one day, carrying her in his arms, he finally shows his real affection.[75] He even sees 'the green paradise of childhood loves' which he confesses so innocently: 'When I am big, it's not you I shall marry [*ya zhenius' ne na tebe*].'[76] In spite of his sufferings, he knows 'the poetry of childhood years' and 'the first ideals'.[77] 'He repents and is tormented for having desired so basely to be extraordinary.'[78] And it is because many things 'touch him *to the depths of his heart*' that 'in a terrible fit of malice and rage' he flings himself into debauchery.[79]

Unlike the predator dazzled with sensuality, he never completely surrenders to Evil. When he is on the point of sliding vertiginously into the abyss, he immediately recovers himself, not to repent his crime, but with a wish to do something completely different. In Albert's company he profanes an icon, but thrashes his companion, who has committed blasphemy. He beats the little cripple because she hasn't saved money, but forbids himself to hit her when she crosses his will by refusing to declare herself an atheist. He joins Kulikov in the murder of Orlov the deserter,[80] but ends by giving himself up. He flings himself into a mad orgy in the company of Lambert, who 'drinks it in and can find nothing higher', but he 'enters debauchery, with irresistible desire, with horror too'. 'The emptiness, dirt and absurdity of debauchery amaze him. He leaves it all and, after horrible crimes, bitterly gives himself up.'[81] The constant and fruitful oscillation characteristic of the plan appears most clearly in the relationship of the young hero to money: '*THE MAIN THING*. Sense of the first part. Oscillation, insatiability of design, he is only preparing himself but he is strangely convinced that everything will come of its own accord: money solves *all* problems.'[82] Dostoyevsky then caught a glimpse of the principle on which the novel was composed: 'Although money settles him on the famous firm *point* and solves *all* problems, sometimes the *point* oscillates (poetry and many other things) and he can find no way out. It is precisely this state of oscillation which forms the novel.'[83]

However, the fundamental oscillation, which gathers in all the others, takes place around the question of God. At the beginning, the child has faith. Then 'strangely', he loses it. More exactly, he goes through 'stages (*polosy*) of not believing in God'. Paradoxically, disbelief influenced by August Comte's positivism[84] and by companions like Albert, who do not believe, only becomes definite when the young criminal is placed in a monastery.[85] Atheism was to be experienced in a place of prayer and contemplation: this is the theme of the second book.

But in the first book, as far as one can judge by notes as elliptic as 'Last communion. First confession. Disgust: does God exist? Bible and reading',[86] childhood is not the time when God is denied, but when he is interrogated and confronted. The young hero acts like an atheist, profanes an icon, shows off before the court, but is shocked by blasphemy. He reads the Bible so much that he 'fuses' with it (*slivaet s bibliey*).[87] The Gospel, in spite of his periods of doubt, converts him: '*NB*. Do not fail to speak of the way in which the Bible affected him. In agreement with the Gospel.'[88] The question 'Does God exist' is repeated but 'the main thing for the moment is his own self and his own interests'.[89] God is not denied. He is always present as a rival, an admired and envied adversary. The immeasurably proud soul of the Great Sinner is tempted not by the imitation of Christ, but by the sin of Lucifer.

The child may have been fascinated by the complex Biblical character of Jacob[90] because Jacob tricked his father, his brother and his father-in-law; but probably also because he was a man elect of God who fought against the angel. Why is the hero so enthusiastic, with Osip (Kulikov) – 'they practically slept together' – for the flagellant sect? Is it because the flagellants proclaimed that they were gods?[91] The aspiration to perfection and deification with its consequences of absolute power over the other flagellants, members of the 'nave' (the assembly or lodge of the sect) tempted the domineering child. 'In the wanderings of his imagination, limitless dreams, as far as overthrowing God and taking His place (Kulikov had a strong influence).'[92] The terrible game does the rest; he tells the little cripple, whom he is always testing in mind and body: 'I am God.' And to use his jealous power, like Jehovah, he flings at her: 'I will love you when you have done everything.'[93] The childhood of the Great Sinner contains a dispute with God not about His existence, but about His power, a duel of pride. The 'night of Jacob' will be long. It is only towards the end of the Sinner's life, when he 'sets up a home for children' and becomes a Haas,[94] the holy man who appears in Raskolnikov's thoughts, that the Angel of God touches him and defeats his pride. The Angel takes the form of the monastery elder, Tikhon, who tries to teach him 'the power of humility' and of 'free will' and 'to bless him for fall and redemption',[95] but in vain, for the struggle to come is long and uncertain. The issue of the combat is noted 3/15 May 1870:

MAIN IDEA

After the monastery and Tikhon, the Great Sinner goes out again into the world to be *the greatest of men*. He is sure he will be the greatest of men. He behaves as if he were: he is proudest of the proud and treats people with the greatest arrogance. With this, vagueness about the form of his future greatness, which is in complete accord with youth. But he (and this is the main thing) *thanks to Tikhon* has mastered the thought (conviction): that to conquer the world you need conquer only yourself. Conquer yourself and you will conquer the world. Career has not been chosen, but there is no time: he begins to observe himself deeply. But besides this, contradictions: (1) gold (hoarding) (a family on his hands), the moneylender, a terrible man, the antithesis of Tikhon, inspired him to hoard; (2) education (Comte, atheism, comrades). Education torments him, and ideas, and philosophy, but he masters the essential part. Suddenly adolescence and debauchery. Heroic deeds and terrible crimes. Self-sacrifice. Mad pride. Through pride, he goes off to be a monk and a wanderer. Journey through Russia (affair, love, thirst for humility) etc., etc. . . .

NB. (rich canvas)

An unusual man. But what has he done and accomplished. *Features*. From pride and unlimited arrogance towards people he becomes gentle and humble towards everyone – precisely because he is already infinitely superior to everyone.[96]

The sudden change – humility resulting from pride and not from love – may have been one of the reasons for the abandonment of the plan. However, at another time, on the page for 1 January 1870, Dostoyevsky went back to the statements of Myshkin at the beginning of the first plan, 'Atheism', and brought in Christ and the Russian Land. On the way he resumed his dialogue with literature, bringing an action against Tolstoy:

A completely opposite type to the offspring of the noble aristocratic house described by T[olstoy] in *Childhood* and *Boyhood*, which has degenerated into swinishness. This is simply the type of the native (*Korennik*), who is unconsciously troubled by his own typical strength, which is completely direct, and does not know what to base itself on. Native types like this are often like Stenka Razin or Danila Filippovich, or finish up as flagellants or self-castraters. This is an unusual, a direct strength which is heavy even for them, needing and seeking something to settle on and something to take as guide, desperately needing peace from storms, but meanwhile unable to stop itself from storming until the time when it is quieted. He finally settles on Christ, but the whole of life is storm and disorder ... A limitless direct force, seeking peace, which frets itself to the point of suffering and which joyfully flings itself – during searches and wanderings – into monstrous aberrations and experiments, until it fixes on an idea strong enough to be fully proportional to their direct animal strength – an idea which is so strong that it can finally organise this strength and calm it as though it had been touched by holy oil.[97]

Storm and disorder, searches and wanderings, monstrous aberrations and experiments: these are the expressions we must remember so as to form a picture of the structure and eventual composition of 'The Life of a Great Sinner', which Dostoyevsky, if only by the title, links with hagiography, or the Life of a Saint.

The structure of 'The Life of a Great Sinner': the four freedoms

At first, the choice of hagiography is surprising. There are essentially three kinds of saint particularly venerated and loved by the Russian people;[98] first, the martyr, not a glorious martyr who dies for the faith, but a spiritual imitator of the Passion of Christ, someone who yields to the exhortations of the Gospel in the terror of his flesh and gives up his life, endangered often for reasons outside religion; second, the simpleton (*yurodivyy*), a holy fool who chooses folly, derision, physical and social humiliation, and inverts worldly values to recall the truth of Christ to men; or, third, like Tikhon, he is a *starets* (literally, an elder), a holy monk whose original part in the Eastern Church is perfectly defined in *The Brothers Karamazov* with reference to Zosima:

What is an elder? An elder takes your soul and your will into his soul and his will. Once your elder has been chosen, you abdicate your will and give it over to him in complete obedience, in complete renunciation. He who vows himself to this trial, this terrible apprenticeship, accepts it voluntarily in the hope of finally reaching, by the obedience of his whole life, perfect freedom, that is, freedom with regard to himself, and thus avoiding the fate of those who have lived without finding themselves.[99]

The essentially passive virtues of these saints are summarised by Pierre Pascal: humility, refusal to judge, respect for others, pity.[100]

Now, unlike Myshkin, who is close to the first two kinds of saint, the Great Sinner of the project is gnawed with pride; he despises, judges and condemns others whom he dreams of enslaving. Far from imitating Christ, he confronts God. Unlike the majority of saints who begin their adolescent years with renunciation of self, he practises renunciation only on his deathbed. Dostoyevsky has inverted the situation and deliberately chosen the most distant starting point. He is more interested in the journey than the arrival. He sacrifices the lying simplicity of the usual saint's life and so strengthens its value as an example. Only Tikhon, the elder who later appears in *The Devils*, brings the feeling of Easter joy characteristic of the lives of saints into the plan, and his treatment is purely static.

The Great Sinner, on the other hand, is treated dynamically. Dostoyevsky succeeds in this by using two essential elements of the Russian idea of sanctity: the heroic exploit and the almost Jansenist idea of the election of the sinner rather than the Just Man. 'There is a heroic exploit [*podvig*] whenever you choose the most difficult way, when you have a victory over yourself, to whatever degree or in what order this may be. *Podvig* is Christian heroism, which begins by the attentive practice of the simplest duties, goes on through asceticism, and ends in complete sacrifice.'[101] The Great Sinner commits himself to the steep path of suffering. His obstinacy grows with his sins and his crimes. Here the second element intervenes. The saint is not necessarily a Just Man with respect to the moral law, he is a repentant sinner, mysteriously chosen by grace, who has been pardoned. This theme acquired almost heretical proportions among the Russians, Orthodox believers as well as sectaries. They wanted to believe in final forgiveness, even for the wicked. The idea, close to Dostoyevsky's heart, is illustrated most strikingly in a famous apocryphal book of the twelfth century, Greek in origin: *The Pilgrimage of the Mother of God among the Torments*.[102] In this 'little monastic poem', 'whose scenes and boldness are not inferior to those of Dante', quoted by Ivan Karamazov at the beginning of his legend of the Grand Inquisitor,[103] the Virgin visits Hell and begs mercy for all the damned: she finally obtains a pause in their sufferings from Good Friday to Whitsun each year.[104]

This intertwining of statism and dynamism leads to the double structure of 'The Life of a Great Sinner', which is a problem on the creative plane. On one side there is the partly traditional hagiographic line of Tikhon, clearly conveyed in some notes for the plan which relate to the elder: everything is serene, fluid, profoundly innocent, harmoniously beautiful. On the other side, there is the modern hagiographic line of the Great Sinner, half way between *Les Tentations de saint Antoine* and the oratorio of *Faust*, as Trishatov pictures it in *A Raw Youth*, which should end in the salvation of the sinner: everything here is disturbed, wavering between violent impulses, hesitations, falls and recoveries before the final chord of harmony.

Dostoyevsky realised this formal difficulty. He understood that the field of creation must lie between the time of eternal glory suitable for hagiography, which is relatively poor in historical, political, and sociological details, and the time of uncertainty and power suitable for the novel of a life. He tried to reconcile the teleological nature of hagiography, which is careless of biographical or epic time, and the polyphonic nature of the novel founded on a space–time structure but favouring space over time. To solve this difficult problem, he interrogated himself about the form he should give to the narrative:

FIRST PAGES: (1) tone, (2) squeeze thoughts in artistically and concisely. NB. *Tone* (narrative – *Saint's Life* – i.e. although from the author, but concisely, without stinting on explanations, but also presenting it in scenes. Here there must be harmony). Dryness of the narrative sometimes goes as far as Gil Blas. In spectacular and dramatic places, as if they weren't particularly important.

However the dominant idea of the Life must be visible, i.e. although the dominant idea is not explained in words and is always left to be guessed at, the reader must always see that this idea is pious, that the Life is a thing so serious that it was worth the trouble of beginning it as early as childhood. Also by the choice of what the story is about, of all the facts, something must constantly be made clear and the future man must constantly be shown and raised on a pedestal.

So that at every line it should be felt: I know what I am writing and I am not writing in vain.[105]

The novelist's problem is to make sure that the reader is aware of the muted triumph of the ending as well as being involved in the hazards of a life which, due to the freedom of the hero, is made up of a succession of experiments and crises. G. B. Ponomaryova, in her study of the structure and genre of 'The Life of a Great Sinner', concluded: 'The composition of the Life is apparently defined not by biographical periods or by epic or biographical time, but by a structure based on the crises of the hero's consciousness.'[106] It is also a structure where a tenuous thread of final victory may be traced between the lines.

The freedom of the creator and the freedom of the created must be maintained without distorting one at the expense of the other. This is the summit of Dostoyevsky's creative interrogation, since here for the first time the Idea and the writing of the novel are both faced with the same mystery: how to reconcile two freedoms.

The metaphysical problem at the heart of 'The Life of a Great Sinner' is the difficulty of reconciling the freedom of God with the freedom of man. This is to be the central theme of Dostoyevsky's work. His great chosen heroes are the fighters, those who fall and rise again, who resist and aspire, who move through opposing experiences, who struggle with themselves and with God, who wander to the gates of the City, like Raskolnikov, Stavrogin, Shatov, Kirillov, Versilov, Dmitriy and Ivan Karamazov, or who join battle without knowing whether they will win, like Raskolnikov in the epilogue to *Crime and Punishment*, Arkadiy in *A Raw Youth*, Dmitriy Karamazov at the end of the novel, and even the gentle holy Alyosha. It is true that a number of Dostoyevsky's heroes are Christians bathed in light: Sonya Marmeladova, Prince Myshkin, Mariya Timofeyevna in *The Devils*, Makar Dolgoruky in *A Raw Youth*, the elders Tikhon and Zosima, but the novelist has pictured them already transfigured and set apart, like figures in a jewelled icon, by the faith they have accepted and by which they live. Imitating Christ, they have already made their sacrifice of self. Their grace is a mystery not for the Christian but for the hero who is struggling in the storm. The hero's passion for God and the difficulty he finds in living are the signs of this unending struggle between the freedom of the Creator and the freedom of His creature.

In parallel, as if in blasphemous mimicry – for the writer is the ape of God – Dostoyevsky sets the problem of reconciling the freedom of the hero with the freedom of his creator, the novelist. Bakhtin decided that this reconciliation had taken place and that Dostoyevsky was the creator of the polyphonic novel, a completely new kind of novel, outside the usual literary forms. For him, 'the multiplicity of independent and clear voices and consciences, the authentic polyphony of fully equal voices, is the essence of Dostoyevsky's novels'. The main heroes 'are not only objects of the author's word, but also subjects of their own directly significant word'.[107] This intuition is particularly valuable for the study of dialogue and style, but it seems to me that Bakhtin has made a victory of something which in Dostoyevsky is only a struggle, and has made the intention of the writer in his novels the principle for explaining his universe. In reality, Dostoyevsky never stopped questioning himself about this uneasy reconciliation and hesitating, from *Crime and Punishment* to *The Brothers Karamazov*, about the complex relations between the independent voice of the main hero and the word of the author. Each great novel gives an original and appropriate answer, often with a degradation of the initial choice as the work goes on, as is shown in *The Devils*, for example, by the fluctuating appearances and disappearances of the chronicler.

In 'The Life of a Great Sinner', Dostoyevsky approached this problem from the strange angle of the relationship of hagiography with the novel. Clearly he wished, by the technique of literary adolescence here associated with real adolescence, to preserve the freedom of his hero, who builds it for himself by the number and variety of his experiences inside the novel: concise 'scenes', 'dryness of narrative'. But Dostoyevsky refused to give up his own voice: 'I know what I am writing and that I am not writing in vain.' However discreet and prudent it is, the voice of the hagiographer imprints a secret jubilation (the tone) on the text. In the orchestral outburst of passion of the tempest of life, where the choirs of the sombre and severe *Dies Ira, dies illa!* confront the insidious and ever more powerful voice of Satan, there should be heard the innocent and serious semi-recitative of the hagiographer leading up to the thunderous Hosannah in the finale. Leaving this metaphor, borrowed from Trishatov's description of *Faust* in *A Raw Youth*, the finished work (the author's design) must be visible in the unfinished events of the novel (the hero's experiences *pro et contra*), and certainty (redemption) must appear within uncertainty (oscillation), the end in the progress and the changeable in the light of eternity. The conflict within the hero's own mind and the conflict between the independent and co-existent worlds formed by other minds must be maintained as long as possible, but also life must resolve these conflicts, or in other words the novel must have an ending. The writer must put in the last full stop, which may be as brutal as the suicide of the hero, a solution often considered in the notebooks, or indefinitely suspended like an organ fermata, prolonging the sublime note of reconciliation into the future.[108]

In brief, and speaking absolutely, since the plan was never completed, 'The Life of a Great Sinner' is the place where the crucial experiment takes place, the crossroads of four freedoms, two of them antagonistic but not antinomic to the other two, the freedom of God and the freedom of Man, the freedom of the writer and the freedom of his character. From the formal point of view, it is difficult to harmonise oscillating movement, in which the time of the free action cannot be foreseen, with eternity, where time is dominated. It requires an original structure of space and time which is characteristic of Dostoyevsky. It is possible to see it emerging in his correspondence, which we shall now consider.

'The Life of a Great Sinner': the dream in letters

The plan had been delayed until a return to Russia. Meanwhile Dostoyevsky had to make a living and so, without abandoning his great plan, he plunged, from February 1870, into a 'rich idea', *The Devils*.[109] He had changed his plans: *The Devils* was to go to *The Russian Messenger*, the magazine in which he had promised to publish 'The Life of a Great Sinner', which he now wished to give to *Aurora*. He intended to work quickly, finish his satirical novel by autumn and then plunge 'with delight' into the writing of the 'first book' of his life's great work.[110] The writing of *The Devils* did not stop him developing the plan of his future book. Two important letters, of 5 and 6 April, the first, more reserved, to Strakhov, the second, freer and more expansive, to the faithful Maykov, take up the initial plan of 'The Life of a Great Sinner'. In the second letter a basic difference in form between the plan of the notebooks and the new plan of the letters emerges:

This thing for Aurora has been ripening in my head for two years. It's the same idea I told you before. It will be my last novel. In the dimensions of War and Peace[111] ... This novel will contain five great narratives (each of about fifteen printed pages, the whole plan has been worked out in two years). The narratives are quite independent, so that they could be sold separately.[112] The first I am reserving for Kashpirev [*Aurora*], the action takes place in the forties. The overall title of the novel is The Life of a Great Sinner, but each novel will have a separate title. The principal question which is treated in all the parts, the one which has consciously and unconsciously tormented my whole life, is the existence of God. The hero in the course of his life is sometimes an atheist, sometimes a believer, sometimes a fanatic and sectarian, and then an atheist again. The second narrative will be entirely set in a monastery. I have set all my hopes on it. Perhaps people will finally stop saying that I have only been writing nonsense. (I will admit to you alone, Apollon Nikolayevich, I want to have Tikhon of Zadonsk as my principal character in this second book, by another name, of course, but he will also be a bishop retired to a monastery). A boy of thirteen, who has been the accomplice of a criminal, very forward and depraved (I know this type, he is from our educated classes), the future hero of the novel, has been shut in the monastery by his parents to be brought up there. This wolf-cub, this nihilist of a child becomes attached to Tikhon (you know the character and appearance of Tikhon very well).[113]

Up to this point there is nothing we do not already know. However the rest of the letter indicates a new direction, partly effaced in the plan of the 'Life' found in the notebooks of May 1870:

In the monastery I shall also put Chaadayev (by another name of course). Why shouldn't Chaadayev spend a year in a monastery? Suppose that Chaadayev, after that first article, which caused him to be certified insane by the doctors every week, had not been able to resist printing, abroad for instance, a leaflet in French: it might very well have happened that he was sent, to punish him, to repent his crime for one year in a monastery. Other people would have come to see him: Belinsky for instance, Granovsky, even Pushkin (for in my novel Chaadayev would be only a type.) In the monastery there is also Paul of Prussia, and Golubov and the monk Parfyony (I am an expert on this matter and I have known the Russian monastery since childhood). But especially Tikhon and the boy. For the love of Heaven, do not tell anyone the contents of the second book ... Don't say anything about Tikhon. I have mentioned the monastery to Strakhov, but I have said nothing about Tikhon. Oh, if only I could create a majestic, *positive*, holy figure! Quite different from that sugary Kostanzhoglo[114] and that German (I have forgotten the name) in Oblomov.[115] And how should we know: perhaps it is really Tikhon who is our positive Russian type, the one our literature is looking for, not Lavrovsky,[116] Chichikov,

Rakhmetov, Lopukhov,[117] etc. In fact, I shall not be creating anything, I shall simply show the real Tikhon, who has long had a place in my heart . . . The first narrative is the childhood of the hero, naturally it is not children who appear: there is a love affair.[118]

Several figures, with the exception of Tikhon and Chaadayev, are missing in the plan appearing in the notebooks of May 1870, which contains no mention of Belinsky, Granovsky, Pushkin,[119] Golubov, Paul of Prussia or Parfyony. There must have been an intermediate stage, in the letters, between the notes of December 1869 and February 1870 and those of May 1870, an idea of 'The Life' which was imagined but which Dostoyevsky did not even begin to write down. It is interesting because it seems to have been an original attempt to create a spatio-temporal structure which could reconcile hagiographic time with the time of the novel.

To approach it, we shall make a biographical and historical detour to describe the great figures, apart from Pushkin, mentioned in Dostoyevsky's letter to Maykov.

Tikhon, whose worldly name was Timofey Savvich Kirillov (1724–83) was the bishop who had just been canonised in 1861. Prelate of Elets and Voronezh, he had given up his place as a bishop because of bad health, and retired in 1769 to the monastery of Zadonsk, where he became a famous elder. In 1861 and 1862 a *Life of Tikhon* was published for the edification of the faithful. His thought was based on pietism rather than scholasticism and influenced by folk poetry, and his teaching about universal love, humility, the complementarity of Good and Evil, suffering as a means to happiness, and hope of redemption even for the most desperate criminals, together with his visions of the future which sometimes brought him to a degree of enthusiasm which he later repented, and his way of experiencing the sufferings of sinners within his own body: all this is reproduced in the censored chapter of *The Devils* and in Book 7 of *The Brothers Karamazov*.

Parfyony (Parthenos) was a monk, a hermit of Mount Athos, who died in 1868. His book, *Stories from pilgrimages and journeys in Russia, Moldavia, Turkey and the Holy Land*, was very popular and Dostoyevsky thought so highly of it that he took it abroad in 1867.[120] Parfyony had also published many books attacking the schismatics.

Paul of Prussia (1821–95) and Konstantin Yefimovich Golubov, his disciple, were Old Believers (*raskol'niki*) who had returned to the Orthodox faith in 1868. Golubov thought that false morality and dissension among men were the cause of universal evil and opposed inner freedom to outer, material, freedom. On 7 March 1870, Dostoyevsky summed up: 'Golubov's ideas are humility and self-mastery and that God and the kingdom of heaven are with us, in self-mastery, and freedom is there too.'[121] 'Golubov says: Paradise on earth, it exists now, and the world has been created perfectly . . . God has created the world and the *law*, and He has performed yet one more miracle – He has demonstrated the law to us through Christ, in example, in life and in formula. It follows that misfortunes come only from abnormality, from failure to observe the law.'[122] This idea of paradise on earth through self-mastery became a theme in Dostoyevsky, appearing in Zosima's teaching, in 'A Pocket Age of Gold' (*Diary of a Writer*, January 1876) and 'The Dream of a Ridiculous Man' (*Diary of a Writer*, April 1877).

Pyotr Yakovlevich Chaadayev (1795–1856) was the former Guards officer, an aristocrat, 'extremely intelligent, quick, remarkably cultured extremely handsome, and spoilt and independent to the highest degree', who, after the Napoleonic campaign of 1812 and the occupation of Paris, after his resignation in 1821, his wanderings throughout Europe and a great spiritual crisis, had published in *The Telescope* of 1836 the first of his *Philosophical Letters addressed to a Lady*, written in French.[123] This caused such a storm of indignation throughout the Russian Empire that, by order of the Emperor, the author was declared insane: every week a doctor would come to certify him mad. He had declared that Russia's form of religion was a mistake, since instead of turning to Catholicism, in which the social and the spiritual were joined together, she had 'sought the moral code for her education in wretched Byzantium, which the West regarded with deep contempt', and so had dedicated herself to sterility.

The experience of the ages is nothing to us. It might be thought that for us alone the general law of humanity had been revoked. We alone in the world have given nothing to the world, and have taken nothing from it; we have contributed not one single idea to the mass of human ideas; we have made no contribution to the progress of the human spirit, and such of this progress as has come to us, we have disfigured.[124]

Dostoyevsky was fascinated by the ideas and character of Chaadayev, whose complex thought he discovered gradually, mainly from 1862 onwards. Versilov, partly inspired by Chaadayev, casts light on the way in which Dostoyevsky would have probably liked to represent Chaadayev in 'The Life'.

Everything converges, the ideas and the biography. Without detailed examination of the numerous ideological likenesses between Versilov, this 'prophet of housewives' and Chaadayev who ironically called himself 'the women's philosopher', it is enough to quote some extracts from the notebooks of *A Raw Youth* to be convinced of their reality:

He [Versilov] considers squarely that the independence of the Russians as a people and of Russians as individuals is impossible and that this has been proved.[125]

We Russians have no memories which do us honour, and those which there were, we have lovingly dishonoured and cast out.

I do not accept or admit that there are people in Russia who think and act freely: they are all lackeys, you hear, lackeys and not slaves. And if there are any signs of

Russian boldness, it is only the impudence of a lackey, with his constant cowardice about himself: how he ought to act, what is to be done.[126]

The lives of Versilov and Chaadayev are strangely alike. Both are handsome and spoilt by admiring, protective women. Both are both proud, egoistic and careless of others. Both are remarkably intelligent and witty, profound and ironic. They have the same spoilt aristocratic manners and refined dandyish elegance. They served in the same Guards regiment, both loftily refused to fight a duel, wandered for a long time throughout Europe, and were attracted by Catholicism. Both loved a whimsical and sickly young girl (Lidiya Akhmakova for Versilov, Avdotya Norova for Chaadayev) before falling in love with a woman who is longing for a world more noble and less empty than theirs (Katerina Akhmakova for Versilov, Katerina Panova for Chaadayev). However, Versilov is a complex figure with many connotations and the character in 'The Life of a Great Sinner' whom Dostoyevsky calls Chaadayev was only supposed to be the historic type of the author of *The Philosophical Letters*.

The same may be said of the pure Westernisers introduced into the monastery: the atheist and revolutionary critic, Vissarion Grigoryevich Belinsky (1810–48) and the 'pure and ideal Westerniser in all his beauty', Timofey Nikolayevich Granovsky (1813–55).

Belinsky was a literary parent to Dostoyevsky, first worshipped and then hated. Turgenev considered Belinsky the 'central figure' of the forties in Russia, a Westerniser who was basically patriotic. According to him, Belinsky

was deeply convinced that Russia needed to gather in everything developed by the West so as to develop her own strength, her own significance. If we accept the results of Western life, and apply them to our own, allowing for the particular features of Russia – history, climate – then, he thought, we might finally reach our own original genius, which he valued much more than is supposed.[127]

Granovsky, a professor of history at Moscow University, a friend of Herzen, who was to write his obituary in *Life and Thoughts*, was one of the prototypes of Stepan Trofimovich in *The Devils*. The notebooks for *The Devils* for 3 February 1870 contain a page, entitled 'T. N. Granovsky' and beginning 'Portrait of a pure and ideal Westerniser in all his beauty'. In constructing Stepan Trofimovich, Dostoyevsky also recalled the spirit of the famous lines in Nekrasov's *Bear Hunt*:

> So you stood before the fatherland
> Pure of heart, righteous in mind,
> Like a reproach incarnate,
> You, the liberal idealist.

This brief historical and biographical information shows us the vast panorama which is beginning to appear. The gathering of historical figures mentioned in Dostoyevsky's two letters of 5 and 6 April 1870 reveals an ambitious plan which would have transformed 'The Life of a Great Sinner' into a magnificent fresco.

What did we have in the plan of the notebooks? The eternal non-historic theme of the perpetual adolescence of the human soul, set in real childhood and youth, and a long trial of saintliness, which is always deferred until the last page. This theme would have been treated as a series of opposing experiences, existentially describing the metaphysical spaciousness of man as well as shaping the novel. The freedom of the human being and the free will of God, the independence of the character and the free will of the writer were to be the four convergent slopes of this pyramid.

However, in the letters, the history of almost all Russian thought, from the eighteenth century to 1870, the history of the great movements of literary, philosophical, political and religious thought, gathering all the great basic questions – man, organisation of society, God, Russia's future – into one vast and unique debate, suddenly makes an appearance. At the beginning of this fresco, if we follow a chronology which Dostoyevsky expressly denies, Tikhon the elder of the eighteenth century, incarnates hope and the model of goodness. Then comes the other model, Pushkin, who, according to Dostoyevsky, created true national Russian literature at the beginning of the nineteenth century. With Chaadayev, in the thirties, the crisis, the great spiritual and civic schism, emerged, and Russia and the Russian Church were abruptly challenged by Catholicism and the West. With Belinsky and Granovsky in the forties, there was the dangerous explosion of Westernism, liberalism and atheism, openly attacking Slavophilism, whose torch was taken up, in the fifties and sixties, by those whom Dostoyevsky calls the 'new Russians', true Orthodox believers like the monk Parfyony, whose adoration of God has passed though the crucible of schism and doubt, and those former Old Believers who have become reconciled with the official Church and therefore with Russia, Paul of Prussia and Golubov, who were never afraid to cross swords with revolutionary emigrants like Herzen. However, their real enemies are missing – the atheist nihilists and destroyers, the Nechayev who rages like a plague fever in *The Devils*. It is obvious that the historical fresco has been amputated at the top: this is because it is being used for *The Devils*, which was begun in February 1870. Like this plan, *The Devils* gives living shape to the debates and events of Russian history from the forties to the sixties, with the Westernisers T. N. Granovsky, I. S. Turgenev (the writer Karmazinov), the nihilists, Nechayev (Peter Verkhovensky) and all his real accomplices of the group of five called 'The People's Vengeance'; the structure of the novel has inspired the new idea for 'The Life of a Great Sinner' expressed in the letters of 5 and 6 April 1870. The open creative line of the novel has revived the underground line.

'The Life' is now an immense fresco, representing about a hundred and fifty years of the history of ideas and movements in Russia. Great historical figures (by other names) are confronted with people whose names are unknown to history, but who are solidly anchored in the childhood and youth of the writer. It is a true concilium, an ecumenical assembly which is striking in the boldness of its aesthetic design. It is reminiscent of Dante's *Divine Comedy* and the second part of Goethe's *Faust*.[128]

The plan of the letters is clear – it preserves hagiographical time, where the critical instant comes into contact with eternity and denies historical time its determining role. In scientific terms, it substitutes synchrony for diachrony. It does not suppress human time, the time of the free action, and it gives back freedom to historical time by spatialising it in a privileged place; the monastery is an enclosed space where a whole set of ideas, historically formed over centuries, are to be debated at the same moment. This pictorial concept of time is more familiar in paintings than in novels. The plan for 'The Life', as it appears in the letters in March 1870, is reminiscent of Raphael's *School of Athens* and even more of Courbet's *Atelier*. Less ambitious than Raphael's composition and less allegorical and less centred on the personality of the creator than the *Atelier* of Courbet, Dostoyevsky's plan for 'The Life of a Great Sinner' reveals the ideal image of the space and time structure of the novels, where mutilating time is dissolved into liberating space. In the great novels to come, this is to be the pure form towards which Dostoyevsky strives without ever reaching it, except perhaps in *The Brothers Karamazov*.

The fertile death of the plan

For the whole of 1870, Dostoyevsky was struggling with this plan which was to be 'the last word of his literary career'[129] and which was so dear to his heart. But the same obstacles kept appearing between him and his dream; he had to be in Russia, he had to have a few years of freedom, untroubled by the need for money. He wanted to write his future novel, which had been ripening for three years, not for a fixed date, but 'as Tolstoy, Turgenev and Goncharov work'.[130] Moreover, he had to finish the novel he was writing, *The Devils*, which had been promised to *The Russian Messenger*, 'with whom it's impossible to break'.[131] These arguments followed each other in his letters from 19 May to 14 July 1870 to S. A. Ivanova, of 14 December to Strakhov, and of 27 December to Maykov, the last letter in which 'The Life of a Great Sinner' made an appearance.

These were the material reasons which Dostoyevsky gave, but there were others connected with the creative process. Work on *The Devils* modified the initial structure of 'The Life of a Great Sinner', but it also caused a haemorrhage which left the original project bloodless. First, there was the escape of historical types, such as Granovsky and Tikhon, whose encounter with Stavrogin, a successor of the Great Sinner without the dimension of adolescence, pillages a number of basic themes, such as the need for humility and the struggle against pride, which would have merited more extended treatment. The life-blood of the plan is transfused into the trio formed by Stavrogin, Shatov and Kirillov. Stavrogin represents the continual oscillation between fall and recovery, the variety of experiments and the search for heroic achievement. Shatov is a hesitant approach (whence his name, formed from *shatat'*, to waver) to the strong personalities of Paul of Prussia and Golubov, with the idea of the contribution of different peoples to history, developed by Danilevsky in *Russia and Europe*, in the background. Kirillov is the atheist who admires Christ and is a rival of God, like the Great Sinner in his childhood, who wants to commit suicide to prove his freedom to himself and the world. Many of the eternal questions raised in 'The Life' are resurrected within the historical plan of *The Devils*. Moreover, there is a betrayal of the opposing experiences of the Sinner, and Stavrogin is partly substituted for the novelist. He indoctrinates Shatov, Kirillov, and Pyotr Stepanovich at the same time and launches them in various directions: he is vivisecting others to test his own broad nature. This is his essential imposture, his spiritual dishonesty, his ontological impotence. The Great Sinner had at least the merit of exposing himself to experience and living through his own experiments instead of exposing and observing others, crouching like a monstrous spider – it is Liza's image – as they struggle in the web he has created. Lastly, the space–time structure sketched in the 'Life', the presentation in a concilium, becomes more complex. Extending his old obsession with doubles, Dostoyevsky breaks his hero up into pieces: Shatov, Kirillov, Pyotr Stepanovich are all hypostases of Stavrogin's being. Literary space replaces pictorial space, without attaining the vastness which it was to have in *The Brothers Karamazov*.

A. L. Bem has suggested another reason, founded not on the design which appears in the letters of 5 and 6 April, but on a careful analysis of the plan in the notebooks. We are left, he says, with an impression of ambiguity: 'the criminal side of the hero is clearly depicted and psychologically convincing, but the luminous side remains confused and one has to take the final victory on trust.'[132] Bem recalls Dostoyevsky's own question: 'An extraordinary man. But what has he done and accomplished?', and senses a false note in Dostoyevsky's creative conception[133] in the last sentence of the plan: 'He ends by setting up a school for children and becomes a Haas.' We also have noted the rather abrupt departure from humility caused by pride and not by love, but faith may well be a sudden illumination and a sharp reversal of values. Love and hatred are as close to each other in Dostoyevsky's psychology as they are in Racine's.[134] Finally it must be remembered that this is a plan, of which only the first part, childhood, is developed at length.

However Bem is right in stressing that the second book of the novel would have given Tikhon a place equal to that of the main hero, and that Dostoyevsky would have been forced to insert a hagiography of Tikhon within the hagiography-life (*Zhitiye-zhizn'*) of the Great Sinner.[135] This is the real dilemma with regard to form: there is a confusion between the two Lives of Saints. One is serene, narrated by the hagiographer who is already aware of the final triumph, and the other is restless, letting the author's jubiliation appear, but also preserving the freedom of the hero in his tragic search. Apparently Dostoyevsky had not yet solved the problem set by this complex game of hagiographical mirrors. In the first case, there is no difficulty about the writer becoming a hagiographer, but in the second the hero, an independent, free mind, would have to celebrate, discreetly of course, his own final sanctity, although he would not yet know where his opposing experiences are leading him. A solution is found in *A Raw Youth*, where Arkadiy himself is the chronicler of the edifying stories of the wanderer Makar, and especially in *The Brothers Karamazov*, where it is the postulant for holiness, Alyosha, who narrates 'The Episodes from the Life of the Elder Zosima, hiero-monk of strict observance, departed in God, written from his own words'. The note of triumph and jubilation is given to another character, the young hero whose own freedom remains absolute and complete. The hagiography is set in the novel of a life, without losing any of its effect, since it is psychologically motivated by the desire, still unconscious in Arkadiy but clearly expressed in Alyosha, to adhere to the ideal of holiness, to imitate the model.

This is the story of why and how 'The Life of a Great Sinner' was abandoned, a powerful subterranean source, bred of earlier works of which it is the logical and ideal conclusion and whose living waters are to fertilise the three last great novels. At the end of the analysis, it is clear that in the letters of 1870 the plans 'Atheism' and 'The Life' are bolder and more far ranging than the drafts given in the notebooks. In passing from creative intent to concrete elaboration, Dostoyevsky seems less free, more subdued by the complex game of experimentation, the mimic adolescence of the hero and the appearance of new structures. As we know, he often distinguished two selves: the poet and the artist. The poet had the power to dream and the privilege of feeling the dream 'in his heart'. The artist's task was to develop the theme, construct the plan, and create a 'harmonious whole'. In fact the first proposes and the second disposes, as this failure, at least at the level of execution, shows.

Dostoyevsky might have used the same words for the great design of 'The Life' that he often used about his finished works, especially *The Devils*: 'Being more a poet than an artist, I have always taken themes beyond my strength',[136] or again 'I always take themes beyond my strength. The poet in me is always racing in front of the artist and this is bad.'[137] Strakhov, referring to *The Devils*, knocked in the final nail:

For content, abundance and diversity of ideas, you are the first and even Tolstoy is monotonous compared with you ... But it is also clear that you write mostly for an élite, and you overload your works and complicate them too much. If the web of your narratives were simpler, they would have a greater effect ... This fault is naturally linked with your merits. A clever Frenchman or German, with a tenth of your subject matter, would have become famous over two hemispheres and would enter literary history as a star of the first magnitude. And his whole secret would consist, it seems to me, in weakening his creation, diminishing the subtlety of analysis, and instead of using twenty characters and a hundred scenes, he would stop at one character and ten scenes.[138]

Strakhov's judgement is valuable, in our opinion, for its implicit recognition of Dostoyevsky's supreme genius as a poet. Dostoyevsky accepted the reproach with modesty, and also took the compliment by comparing himself with Hugo and Pushkin:

Yes, I do suffer from this fault and always have. I have never yet learnt to control my means. A crowd of separate novels and stories slides together into a whole, so that there is no measure of harmony in it ... The worst is that, without even considering means, I am carried away by poetic fury, I rush in to express an artistic idea which is beyond my powers (NB. This is why the power of poetic inspiration, in Victor Hugo, for example, is always stronger than the means of carrying it out. There are traces of this duality even in Pushkin.)[139]

'The Life' is an attempt to reduce this duality. To construct a harmonious work, without mutilating his art by false simplification, but keeping the hundred scenes and the twenty characters, to construct a novel which would preserve the whole vision, the plurality, the intertwining, and arrange it like a new world in an eternal and orchestrated space: this was the dream of an artist raised to the height of poet.

The fact that it was a failure does not detract from its value as an interrogation, necessary for future creation. The poetic impetus was broken because it reached an idea of the space–time structure which was too pure, too pictorial, where time was removed in favour of space. However, the destruction of the plan gave rise to new imperatives: the need to invent a space, the natural structure of freedom, which was not concrete, and the need for a time which did not deform this freedom. Literary space and the time of power are already visible. This is why we see 'The Life of a Great Sinner' as the pure ideal, where metaphysics and the technique of the novel are in complete harmony. Would it be a paradox to say that all the works of Dostoyevsky could be referred to a single novel that was never written?

13
A Raw Youth: reasons for choice

The novels of Dostoyevsky are seething whirlpools, gyrating sandstorms, water-spouts which hiss and boil and suck us in. They are composed purely and wholly of the stuff of the soul.　　　　　Virginia Woolf, *The Common Reader*[1]

There is something paradoxical in approaching the creative process through abortive plans, however important or typical. We must leave the Ideal, and turn to its asymptote, the reality of the finished novel. Our choice of *A Raw Youth* needs to be justified.

Arguments

A Raw Youth is a tributary of the previous novels, *Notes from Underground*, *Crime and Punishment*, *The Idiot* and *The Devils*, and springs from the resurgence of the great underground river, 'The Life of a Great Sinner'. It announces and prepares *The Brothers Karamazov*, a novel where theme and structure are perfectly controlled and balanced. This gives it a key position in the works of Dostoyevsky as a whole, chronologically and ideologically; it is a place where all the great novels meet. Embryologists say that all the potential of a species, even in its evolutionary form, is present, though not differentiated, in the potential of any individual. *A Raw Youth* contains all the actual or possible characteristics of the Dostoyevskian novel, planned or achieved.

Moreover it is an extraordinarily complex work, the most 'mad' and so the most neglected book in the canon. It is a concentration of all those elements of the Dostoyevskian novel which are most irritating to the Euclidean mind. There is an enormous number of themes, abandoned for page after page in a more or less carefree way, a swarm of ideological echoes and wandering images to unsettle the reader, a subtle confusion ordered with such skill as to appear casual and, in parallel, a practically non-existent plot composed of psychology, a juicy muddle of the resolutions, contradictory decisions, impulses and aversions of the young hero, an exuberant dramatisation of events – in the notebooks Dostoyevsky drew up a list of all the pyrotechnical metaphors he could think of: 'crowning piece', 'firework display', 'Bengal light' and even the prosaic 'burning' – an accumulation of uncertainty and approximation, rumours and mysteries. It is enough to drive Strakhov, that giver of good advice, to the depths of despair, it is enough to make a correct summary of the novel impossible, and it is more than enough to vindicate critics of the time such as Avseyenko and Skabichevsky, who denounced the author's morbid taste for the 'stifling shades of the underground' and 'the devouring strength of the idea' and accused him of having misunderstood and even mutilated living reality.[2] But the liveliness and chaos of this novel are fully justified. Psychologically, the hero is passing through the confused, rich and uncertain time of adolescence. Aesthetically, the central idea is universal disorder and disintegration. To go more deeply, this is all typical of Dostoyevsky's creation, since it was his vocation to embrace the whole vision in one single glance, to express the emergence of entire universes by means of the broad character of his hero, to display within a literary space the thousand possibilities of action. From this viewpoint, *A Raw Youth* may not be the culminating point of Dostoyevsky's work – *Crime and Punishment*, *The Devils* and *The Brothers Karamazov* have a better claim to this – but it is the most revealing challenge and the most modern in form.

Lastly, there are about six hundred pages of preparatory notes for it. None of the great novels, according to V. S. Nechayeva, who has catalogued Dostoyevsky's archives,[3] gives us such a rich, complete and continuous whole. Only the notebooks for *A Raw Youth* allow us to follow the creative process from the pre-history of the novel to its final stage.[4] It must be stressed, however, that there is still a gap between Dostoyevsky's last rough drafts, though some of them are considerably elaborated and occasionally contained passages which appear unchanged in the book, and the copies made by Anna Grigoryevna for the printer. This gap is the result of Dostoyevsky's amazing improvisation while dictating the novel.

In the thicket of the manuscript

Dostoyevsky's manuscripts have often been described,[5] but the facsimiles,[6] published from time to time, are much more appealing to the imagination. The first impression is of an enormous lumber room, a disorganised builder's yard, a laboratory littered with junk and humming with activity. Three worlds mingle: everyday existence, reverie and creation. Sums of author's fees, calculations of receipts and expenditure, addresses, and notes about epileptic fits show the intrusion of daily life.[7] Reverie, a mock sleep of the creative imagination, is expressed by doodles and semi-automatic drawings in the main body of the text or the margins: lanceolated arches with unorthodox rose windows, decorated with circles and lozenges, profiles and faces of men, sullen or cheerful, and often bearded,[8] elegant flourishes, lovingly formed words, short pen tests, a dream set out in calligraphy.[9]

The main columns of the notation, horizontal, vertical or slanting, often isolated by a vigorous line or enclosed in a balloon, are written in a sloping hand, clear and firm. The ornamental borders of the NBs (*nota bene*), uncial capitals, single, double and even triple underlining, headings in the middle of the page, thick transverse lines linking spheres and other signs like this mark out the pages.[10]

The graphic arrangement of the page sometimes betrays a lightning flash of thought or emotion, the fever of inspiration or research. L. M. Rozenblyum, in his introduction to the notebooks for *A Raw Youth*, quotes some passages close to poetry. Sometimes it is the word-play of contrasting pronouns, stressed in Russian because pronouns are morphologically identical with possessive adjectives (*ego* and *ego*), which gives dramatic intensity to the hero's soliloquy:

> He is the purest of men, and he must not know,
> But I will prove to HIM what she is like.
> . . .
> She placed herself across His path
> She ruined His life,
> It cost her nothing, but it was torture for Him,
> And *she* triumphs, while He is lost.
> I want to save Him.
> I want to break His idol
> Give him back to me, I want Him to become what he was three days ago.[11]

Sometimes the lyrical repetition of the same phrase gives the style a rhythm reminiscent of Claudel:

> *He* is senseless to him, although dear, and he argues ceaselessly.
> And senseless is the submission of the family,
> And senseless his growing love for the princess
> And senseless and wavering his idea, which has sent him whirling,
> And senseless is Vasin,
> And horrible is Liza's affair,
> And what good is the truth?[12]

As Bakhtin says, the sense of the words is 'pedalled' (as the pedals of the piano muffle or increase the sound) by their arrangement on the page. This pedalling was not intended for the novel, though the wordplay with pronouns does appear in it, but to help the writer examine his creation. It is a sign of aesthetic reflection.

This is the arrangement of the page in these manuscripts: the thickets are tangled, the 'growth is thick' but not inextricable. Is there any overall arrangement, chronological order, or even a system of reference? Only the first exercise book, in its first half, pays any attention to the calendar and gives us the valuable pre-history of the novel. The great majority of notes, rarely marked with dates or signs, which in any case are indecipherable, is committed, as Louis Martinez writes,

to the hazard of nocturnal inspiration without regard to page numbers. Pages are skipped, the writing begins at the end of the exercise book, progresses indifferently from left to right and right to left, stops (rarely, it is true) in balloons on the margins, overlays other lines obliquely or vertically, jumps into one corner and then across into another, and even appears upside down on a page already written.[13]

There is a strong temptation to preserve the complex whole of the notebooks, as was done in the first publications of the notes for *Crime and Punishment* and *The Devils*, and to show the genesis of *A Raw Youth* in all its 'nebular beauty and confusion, all its coils and distortions'.[14] This would put us in the same position as the novelist when he read over his notes. In fact, Dostoyevsky read the accumulated material fairly systematically so as to distribute his 'main columns' or 'nests' concerning some idea or person evenly over the different parts of the book, or over the chapters of one particular part, or over a particular climax. This is clear from numerous annotations in the margin or in the body of the text, such as this one relating to the second part:

27 February [1875]
Detailed arrangement (*komponovka*) of the 2nd part. (Big problem).
(At the beginning, a general but detailed idea of the 2nd part, and after that by chapters. Then composition of already separate chapters and especially of the *first*. Particular and detailed reading of the *material*, clearly ticking the places chosen.)[15]

Or again:

1/2 March. Compose the first chapter in detail, the others, given the materials already existing, *will come of themselves*.
The point, the axis with which to begin, the starting point, the essence of the plot!
!   Reading of materials!
2 March: reading of materials,
3 March: composition of the axis,
and 4 March: begin![16]

Dostoyevsky read over his notes but was not trapped by them. He kept his freedom of choice and simply tried to immerse himself in the certain and definitive elements, such as fragments of dialogue, 'verbal' portraits which suddenly emerged as a whole (old prince Sokolsky with his curious French phrases, odds and ends of an aristocratic memory in decay, or Makar Ivanov the wanderer with rhythms, assonances and images from poetry and popular religion) and also the development of important emotional ideas (Kraft, Vasin, and Versilov). Dostoyevsky is like a speaker who would consider it undignified to write out his text, but carefully consults innumerable notes relating to several possible speeches, ticks those he judges adequate for the speech he is about to deliver, organises them and begins to speak or dictate, ready to modify his choice at any moment.

Moreover this rereading did not cover the whole of the notebooks, but only the part which was to appear in the finished novel. So, before we define our method of analysing the materials, we must describe Dostoyevsky's profoundly original way of doing research and writing at the same time.

Writing in instalments

Dostoyevsky worked on *A Raw Youth* from February 1874 to November 1875. The novel appeared in Nekrasov's periodical, *Annals of the Father-land*,[17] in January, February, April, May, September, November and December 1875.

There was therefore a long period of full-time research, about eleven months, followed by publication irregularly spaced out over a year, with a gap from May to September. In fact, the planning of the last parts went on throughout 1875. Serial publication in magazines, invented in France and England, had the great advantage of sustaining the writer by giving him a guaranteed number of readers, the subscribers. It had its dangers: while allowing expansive writers like Tolstoy and Dostoyevsky to spread their abundantly solid books over a period of time, it could give rise to a rather irritating fluency. It also had its constraints, which must be noted if we are to understand Dostoyevsky's creative process.

The system entailed, first of all, a science of interest or suspense (*zanimatel'nost'*), which was just as important for the novelist writing in instalments as artistic quality (*khudozhestvennost'*). Of course the art of keeping the reader on tenterhooks is characteristic of the novel published in book form, but for instalments the author has to make more effort: he must finish each part and especially each episode with a cliff-hanger.

For example, Nekrasov, in his enthusiasm for the 'freshness' of the first part of *A Raw Youth*, advised Dostoyevsky not to spoil such a good beginning by hurrying.[18] Dostoyevsky then suggested leaving out March, to which Nekrasov agreed, and handing in the second part for April and May;[19] in return Nekrasov proposed spreading the publication of this part over three months, April, May and June. Dostoyevsky refused: he would have had to stop at the end of the third chapter, which had too many mysterious allusions and was falling flat. For the sake of effect,[20] the firework, he preferred to force the pace and deliver the fourth chapter in April. This ends in a climax: the meeting between the beautiful Akhmakova and the Youth, where he naively admits his love for the person he thinks he hates by composing a dazzled eulogy of her body and other graces. This example was typical.

The whole system was also constraining. Copy had to be handed in on a set date, Dostoyevsky had to catch the post, forge ahead in spite of sadness and isolation (the summer cure of 1875 in Ems), in spite of being disturbed or threatened by epileptic fits.[21] There was the eternal fear of being short of money, his obsession that he might be forced to take a tiresome break from everything, his fear of spoiling his work. On 13 July, in Ems, Dostoyevsky lamented: 'No, this is not how a work of art should be written, to order and under threat of the stick, it needs time and freedom.'[22] All this is familiar to us and partly explains the gap in publication between May and September 1875: but only partly, for Dostoyevsky was capable of writing in the worst conditions and even of forcing the pace. The main reason for the interruption was creative, as Dostoyevsky admitted to his wife on 7 June: 'I am not yet ready to harness myself to work, I haven't yet cut my plan up into parts.'[23] And some lines further on: 'On the 22nd or 23rd I must begin to make a fair copy and make the plan.'[24] 10 June he complained that he had not 'tidied up' his plan and that he was having terrible difficulties.[25] In short, from the end of May, when he arrived in Ems, to the beginning of July, when he left, Dostoyevsky was continually 'tormented' by his novel. He recovered only in August. What did this long interval mean? Quite simply, that Dostoyevsky was not only writing in instalments, but he was also developing the plans relating to different parts of the novel in instalments. The plan was never firm or finished: it was constructed as the novel progressed. There was certainly an organisation of the whole, roughly defined by the fateful gestures, but it was versatile and supple, open to many possibilities. The plans of the different parts came from the truth of the many experiments and experiences attempted with and by the hero.

The writing and research on the parts of the novel were thus parallel but not simultaneous. Even the accumulation of material went on after the writing of the first chapters and went far beyond what was needed. A note, for example, which was meant for the first part and left out, could very well turn up in the second or third. On the other hand, another note which Dostoyevsky had originally saved for the third or fourth part (he began by envisaging four parts) might suddenly be inserted in the last chapters of the first. Remarks of a psychological nature or fragments of dialogue were interchangeable in Dostoyevsky's creative method. The creative logic always followed the research; it arose from the experimentation and the mimed adolescence of the hero.

The methodological dilemma

There are two possible attitudes towards the manuscripts of the notebooks: we can either wander joyfully among the galactic nebulae of the notes and so preserve the potential richness of the novel, which in this case would be only the final preferred version of the notes; or else, since time and the mobility of plans play such a large part, we can try to reconstruct a chronological order, in spite of insufficient or non-existent dating.

The first course simply hides the critic's helplessness. In fact the disorder and discontinuity of the notebooks exists only in our eyes. Dostoyevsky himself, who sowed these thickets of annotation, certainly did not get lost, but moved about them with ease. To understand the labyrinth, the genesis of the novel, we must find its maker, Daedalus, and forget Theseus, for whom the labyrinth is only an obstacle.

A. S. Dolinin chose the second method. He tried to overcome the disorder and reduce the chaos by putting the immense mass of notes in chronological order. His principle is clear: the first part of *A Raw Youth* was published in January and February 1875, and the first dated sketches go back to February 1874, which allows us to divide the manuscripts into two parts: (1) the rough drafts before publication began, and (2) the rough drafts during publication. The definitive text of the novel is used to determine the form of the notebooks. On this solid principle, Dolinin divided the notes into six periods.

The first three show the passage from the pre-history of the novel to its historical age. From February to July 1874 there was primaeval chaos, the sudden appearance of the whole complex universe. From August to September the subject emerged; from 8 September to November it took shape.

After this came the notes referring to different parts of the novel, which are dated by the times when the final copy was handed in. For the notes referring to the first five chapters this time is December 1874. The notes concerning the last chapters of the first part must have been written before January 1875, and so on. This method gives a coherent view of the novel's gestation, but there may be some danger in it. We may feel that we are not justified in explaining the unfinished work by the final version, the work in process by the work done, or that we do not have the right to exclude all the possibilities of the original plans in favour of those few retained for the final version.

Both attitudes have advantages and disadvantages. The first, keeping the raw material in its original state, preserves the complex whole of the first vision, but leaves the critic helpless. The second, which replaces synchrony by diachrony, is more productive, but sins by being too teleological. The first gives us the romance of the mysterious labyrinth, the second is sterile and doubtful history. A compromise is necessary, so that time and totality may be reconciled – an attempt to analyse the fundamental creative structures without ignoring chronology, or, in words which are possibly too scientific, to use genetic structuralism. This compromise is close to Dostoyevsky's own creative method, which is characterised, very roughly, by research in a spiral within an emerging whole, by gradual and systematic clearance of the exuberant growth which invades the pages, by deepening the ideological themes which recur again and again, by perpetual interrogation about form, by multiplying the different possibilities and experiences offered to the hero, by long and slow saturation in the memory, and by meticulous planning of the times of crisis, with a view to improvisation while the novel is dictated.

The artificial part of all this, and we admit that it is inconvenient, is that we have to study in chronological order structures which, in the notebooks, were sometimes formed simultaneously.

14

A Raw Youth: the appearance of
the vision

The poet is truly the thief of fire. He is burdened with humanity, even with *animals*; he will have to make his inventions feel, sense, and hear; if what he brings from *out there* has a form, he gives it a form; if it is formless, he gives the formless.

Arthur Rimbaud, Letter to Paul Demeny, 15 May 1871

For Dostoyevsky, the urge towards a new novel always began with vast and laborious rumination. Themes and characters from earlier works which he had failed to exorcise returned, accompanied by even more demanding themes and characters from the underground creative stream, of which 'The Life of a Great Sinner' is the boldest vision, all impetuously clamouring for life.

The new novel began by exploding other novels and gathering them together in one gigantic puzzle, into which unpublished pieces, prophetic of later works, tended to glide surreptitiously. This was not a mechanical process; it was the appearance of a whole universe. Like the poet Rimbaud, Dostoyevsky brings the formless back from his rumination. The unity of the work and the continuity of the creative interrogation are inscribed at the beginning of the notebooks, where identifiable relics from earlier works and the meteorites of future ones are crushed together. The novels of Dostoyevsky have an epilogue only for the reader, never for the writer, who is constantly deepening and resurrecting people he has killed or doomed to oblivion.

The fantastic novel-poem

The Devils, the satirical novel which caused Dostoyevsky to postpone his grandiose design of 'The Life of a Great Sinner' indefinitely and left it bloodless, reappeared in the very first lines of the notebooks of *A Raw Youth*. The theme of a nihilist revolution, purely levelling and destructive, of Utopia betrayed, of atheist mankind in the future, as expressed by Peter Verkhovensky-Nechayev in *The Devils*, becomes more general, leaving the narrow frame of the Russian province and embracing the whole of humanity.

Socialists and nationalists in Jerusalem.[1]

A fantastic *novel-poem*: future society, the commune, the insurrection in Paris,

262

victory, 200 million heads, *terrible wounds*, debauchery, destruction of arts, libraries, the child tortured. Combats, anarchy. Death.[2]

This apocalyptic fresco foreshadows the passages in the finished novel where Versilov imagines the destiny of humanity. At the beginning of the novel, a gigantic financial collapse and the seizure of power by the proletariat is evoked. And in the 'confession', immediately after the dream of the Golden Age, there is the reddening picture of Europe in agony, the burning of the Tuileries, the bell tolling for the old world, crowned by the derisive vision of future humanity curled up in a fragile fraternity which is to replace the idea of immortality. It also announces the theme of the revolutionary plot, which was to be confirmed by real events at the end of 1874.

The theme is in fact very old. Carried to incandescence in *The Devils*, it goes back to the epilogue of *Crime and Punishment*, where Raskolnikov has a morbid dream of 'terrible wounds', symbolised by threadworms attacking humanity, and of the beginning of total fratricidal war. But in the notebooks for *A Raw Youth*, it is enriched by the theme of suffering familiar to the writer, the suffering of the child. And in this context, it is no longer simply a cry from the heart, but support for the argument set out by Ivan Karamazov: can one accept universal harmony, whether created by God or by men, if even one child has to be tortured to get it? In these few lines, the whole of Dostoyevsky's creation is present: the novels written, the novel being planned by the writer, and the novel to follow.

The empire or republic of children

As always, Dostoyevsky was on the alert for a news item to illustrate the theme of undeserved suffering, and he noted the atrocious 'Report from Bakhmut', which appeared in *Moscow News* on 26 February 1874: an account of the calvary of a peasant woman from the village of Andreyevka. Weary of being beaten by her husband, the unhappy woman had taken refuge with a woman friend. The chief elder of the commune refused her permission to stay and she was dragged back by her husband. To punish her, he harnessed her to his cart, set the horse off at a gallop, and flogged her every time she fell.[3] It is the great theme of the suffering of the innocents, which was to be treated broadly in *The Brothers Karamazov*, where all the victims of human and divine cruelty are gathered in one immense synthesis: the little children tortured (the 'Rebellion' of Ivan), the 'withered black mother' with her starving child, against a background of burnt charred beams and denuded steppe (Mitya's dream at the end of the third part), and tormented animals (Ilyusha's dog).

But as soon as Dostoyevsky began to sketch this fantastic novel of a nihilist apocalypse, with this movement towards martyred childhood, his

mind, always oscillating between opposing points, returned to the old
dream begun in *Netochka Nezvanova* which had crystallised in the sketch
for the first book of 'The Life of a Great Sinner', the novel of childhood:

NOVEL ABOUT CHILDREN, EXCLUSIVELY ABOUT CHILDREN, AND WITH A
CHILD-HERO'.[4]

Conspiracy of children to form their *empire of children*. Arguments of the children
about republic and monarchy. Children form relationships with criminal children
locked up in a fortress. Children-arsonists and [spoil] saboteurs of railways.
Children try to convert the devil. Children debauched and atheist. Lambert.
Andrieux. Children murderers of their father (*Moscow News*, no. 89, 12 April).[5]

Dostoyevsky linked the two ends of the chain: the end of time and the
entry into life. These two plans, the fantastic novel of the nihilist apocalypse
coming directly from the last novel he had written, and the novel of the
children's empire, issuing from the subterranean line, supported each
other. The gloomy perversion of a society of children appeared to Dostoyevsky as the violent image of civic and spiritual apocalypse. He used the
extreme motive of parricide – whether the father is the real father, the earth
of the Fatherland, the tsar, or God – to reach the central idea of his plan. On
4 May, 1874, he formulated it: 'The revolution of reforms has fragmented
the basis of society. Sea has risen. Definitions and frontiers of good and bad
have disappeared and *been wiped out*'.[6] And more clearly some pages and
probably some weeks later:

The main thing. The idea of decomposition is everywhere, for everything *is
dislocated* and there are no bonds left not only in the Russian family but even just
among people. Even among children, dislocation.
Decomposition is the great idea to be seen in the novel ... Society is chemically
decomposing.[7]

In *A Raw Youth*, neither of these two plans for the novel appeared. The
first came to life only in Versilov's conjectures, the second nourished *The
Brothers Karamazov*, although there the theme of parricide and that of
childhood (Kolya Krasotkin and Ilyusha) are radically opposed.[8] But the
search for the central Idea of the novel has been carried out through them.
The idea of decomposition, which in Dostoyevsky's words is one of the
'great ideas' of the final novel, appeared gradually. The fantasy novel of the
nihilist apocalypse and the novel about the republic of children were the
preliminary scaffolding which could be discarded when the great idea
emerged, although at first it was abstract and general. These two sketches
for novels are the placenta of the Idea, which, although it was not first cause
of the novel, was present at the very beginning of creative activity,
embedded in a nourishing matrix. The novelist proceeds like the poet,
through images, through a vision of the world. It is a world which is now
becoming clear: the two novels, complementary opposites, express a whole

which is defined by the thing that unites them, that 'family look' which the novelist is struggling to decipher: the Idea.

The two plans for novels, extensive and daring as they are, did not express the whole vision. They were inscribed in an approach which is essentially historical and social, therefore political, embracing the licensed time of degradation (the apocalypse of the old world, placed at the end of history) and, in a bold foreshortening, the shocking time of disintegration (the perversion of childhood). Both the bud and the fruit are decayed.

The novel of the 'predator'

Childhood is also a return to 'The Life of a Great Sinner'. As we know, this great plan tended not to suppress history but to present it in pictorial space and integrate it in a metaphysical and psychic dimension. Dostoyevsky called this dimension the 'breadth of man'. Dmitriy Karamazov describes this vastness, as Montaigne might say, in spatial images: 'There the banks join, contraries exist together'; or again 'There the devil struggles with God and the battlefield is the heart of man.'[9] It is a space which opens out on two infinities – the Ideal of the Madonna and the Ideal of Sodom whose magnetism creates the tragic hero.

All Dostoyevsky's creation is a desperate struggle against historical time. He was too attentive to reality, to the events he scrutinised, to reveal the future, but he wished to repudiate the blind external force of history and incorporate it in a larger debate which he placed in the heart of man, a creature of total freedom. There are traces of this struggle in *The Devils*, the novel which preceded *A Raw Youth*. The original theme, the Nechayev affair, and beyond this the menace of nihilist revolution, is historical and political. But while the novel was being written, Dostoyevsky was carried away by the underground theme of the 'broad' man, Stavrogin. He drew Stavrogin from the line of broad natures, which existed in an unformed state in the notebooks, but which until then had always been splintered before finding their way into the novels: Raskolnikov–Svidrigaylov, Myshkin–Ganya–Rogozhin, and later Dmitry–Ivan–Alyosha in *The Brothers Karamazov*. However, influenced by his original theme, which was to paint the hatred swooping down on Russia, he distorted Stavrogin. He made him a broad nature who had aborted, a Prince Harry incapable of becoming the austere King Henry, a 'knight of the spider' – a sort of inverted Don Quixote – empty of all desire, an impostor, a Narcissus who, as Tikhon says, has only one fear left, that the mirror may return a derisive image. Hanging is not a punishment for Stavrogin at the end of the novel; Dostoyevsky was admitting failure and salvaging the remains of his hero's greatness.

In the notebooks of *A Raw Youth*, he was obsessed by the image of a truly broad nature which would never admit defeat and it was naturally through the prism of Stavrogin that he took up, in the first pages of the notebooks, his unwearied design of grasping the vastness of man. This was more natural because *The Devils* had been castrated by the loss of a chapter, 'At Tikhon's house', which Dostoyevsky, in spite of all his efforts, had not been able to force on Katkov and of which the contemporary Russian reader was entirely ignorant. In this chapter the mystery of Stavrogin thickens, as his broad nature is shown moving towards the two extremities of the chain: Evil, the ideal of Sodom with the rape followed by little Matryosha's delicious attempt at suicide, and Good, the ideal not of the Christian Madonna, but of the pagan Acis and Galatea, with the indescribable dream of the Golden Age. The Stavrogin of the 'Confession' came back to life in the character of the 'predatory type', the still unnamed and universal HE of the lines written in spring, 1874.

The first note was inspired, as so often, by the work of other, even minor, authors. Reacting against an article by Vasily Grigoryevich Avseyenko about a bad historical novel by Yevgeniy Andreyevich Salias, *The Companions of Pugachev*, which appeared in *The Russian Messenger* for April 1874 (this date is valuable for the notebooks), Dostoyevsky called Prince Danila, the 'predatory type' of the novel, 'a fool'. Danila, dithering between his passion for Milusha, the savage maiden, and the career awaiting him at the imperial court, chooses Milusha while snivelling over his lost ambitions. Dostoyevsky objected to Salias' illogicality: 'The true predator would have married Milusha and returned (to the court). It would have been immoral, the really predatory type would even have felt some remorse about it, but he would have gone on with all his sins and passions.'[10] And he resolved to create a true 'predatory type' for his novel of 1875:

Predatory type (1875)
Passion and immense *breadth*. The most abject vulgarity united with the most refined greatness of soul. However the strength of this character is that it bears this infinite breadth extremely well, so that it ends by seeking a burden and does not find it. Both fascinating and repellent (the red insect, Stavrogin).[11]

Keeping the word 'predatory' (*khishchny*), Dostoyevsky gradually moved away from the old definition in the notebooks of *Crime and Punishment* for 1866, which was more centred on pleasure; still in the shadow of the overwhelming ghost of Stavrogin, he moved towards a definition which placed more stress on the duality of the broad nature, the existential duplicity of the hero, who comes closer to the character of the Great Sinner than the impostor in *The Devils* had managed to do:

Think of *predatory type*. As much awareness as possible in evil. I know it is evil, and I repent, but I do this to the accompaniment of noble impulses. Can do it this way: *two ways of acting* at one and the same time; in one (with certain people) form of action he is a most righteous man, with all his heart, he is noble in soul and joys in his actions, in infinite tenderness. In the other form of action he is a terrifying criminal, liar and debauchee (with different people). When alone with himself he looks at both one and the other with haughtiness and despondency, puts decisions off, waving them away. He is drawn by passion. *Here* there is a passion with which he cannot and does not wish to struggle. *There* is the ideal which purifies him and his saintly deed of compassion and of compassionate action. Both sides and the people who are concerned in them meet towards the end of the novel.[12]

In spite of this tendency to foreshadow Versilov, the possible genetic programme of this character oscillated between past and future creation: his frenzied egoism comes from the Underground man, his atheist convictions and the corollary 'all is permitted' from Raskolnikov and Ivan Karamazov, and his obsession with suicide and hallucination from Svidrigaylov, Stavrogin and Ivan Karamazov:

The suicide and a demon in the Faust style.[13]

This predatory type is a great sceptic.[14]

He has a conviction (though not a theory): there is no other life, I am on the earth for one instant, why stand on ceremony. But since the conditions of living together have been established by society in a kind of contract, then cheat in secret, break the contract in secret and if harmony is broken by this and it ends in dissonance for future society, then – 'What business is it of mine, even if they were to perish not just in the future, but at this very minute, and I with them, *après moi le déluge.*'[15]

He is an atheist not only by conviction, but completely.[16]

Note. This is the picture of an ATHEIST. This is the main thought of the drama (that is, the main essence of His character).[17]

Dostoyevsky has already begun the profound game of experiment, the literary adolescence of the character. *He* has been slapped, he has secretly avenged himself by dishonouring someone: or he will receive a slap from a child, one of his step-sons. Like Stavrogin, like the future Versilov, he is loved by women. There are tragic loves: he has a wife, 'a saint', who has sacrificed everything to him and whom he subjects to infernal tortures so as to enjoy her sufferings, of which she finally dies; the daughter of this woman, his step-daughter, a lively mischievous child – reminiscent of Netochka Nezvanova, who is half in love with her father, Liza in 'The Eternal Husband' and Matryosha of *The Devils* by her action – falls in love with him; gnawed by feelings of remorse towards her mother, whom jealousy and maternal love tormented to death, she hangs herself ('Put the insect there', noted Dostoyevsky). There are glowing loves: He loves a young girl or the wife of someone else.[18] The love relationships of the future novel emerge from the mist: a double family, with the children of the first marriage (these are to be Versilov's in fact), three women loved: the gentle Sofiya Andreyevna, mother of Arkadiy, Lidiya Akhmakova, the sickly and whimsical adolescent who tries to poison herself with sulphur matches, the haughty Katerina Nikolayevna Akhmakova.

Thinking of the Great Sinner, Dostoyevsky complicated the metaphysical problem: *He* is an atheist but, a few pages later, *He* preaches Christianity.[19] The main gestural image symbolising the essential dichotomy of the character, the spiritual and civic flaw, then appears:[20] this is the breaking of the icon (in the novel the icon of Old Believers bequeathed by Makar Ivanov, the wanderer). Dostoyevsky was also thinking of Stavrogin, who, in the unpublished chapter of the *Confession*, mechanically broke the elder Tikhon's ivory crucifix. In *The Devils* this was only a sign to the reader: neither Tikhon nor Stavrogin, who saw it only as an object costing twenty-five roubles, made much of it. In *A Raw Youth*, the scene, prepared at length, commented on by Versilov himself, who describes how the desire to make a scene grows in him irresistibly (the mad wish to stamp on the flowers he offers to Sonya, to whistle or to burst out laughing at Makar's funeral, to break the icon on the corner of the earthenware stove), assumes a highly symbolic, even allegorical value: it is a farewell, since Versilov is leaving Sonya to fling himself into the abyss of his passion for Akhmakova. The gesture appeared at the beginning of the notebooks, but its timing was not yet settled: '*He* is a preacher of Christianity and this is why the princess has left her own world and everyone and married him. And then he breaks the icon (before or after her death, before is preferable). I am depraved, an atheist.'[21]

The character designated *He* is like *The Captives*, the unfinished statues by Michelangelo, which Dostoyevsky had possibly seen in Florence. Some forms or features had emerged from the material, but they were not yet living. *He* was still a plan, handled in the third person. However, here and there the *I* was already appearing and became more frequent in May and June 1874. The voice of the hero was being shaped, gradually becoming freer, in soliloquy or dialogue. The polyphonic structure was absent at this stage. Paradoxically, *He* came to life only when, on 11 July, Dostoyevsky threw him out for another hero, 'the boy'.[22] He ceased to be the property of the creator, as he became the admired, desired, sometimes hated Other Person for the Raw Youth.

The three novels

In these first months of 1874, three still unformed worlds have emerged in parallel, if not simultaneously: 'the fantastic novel-poem' of a nihilist apocalypse expressing Dostoyevsky's fascinated horror at the rise of revolution: the novel about the republic or empire of children, which came directly from the underground source, 'The Life of a Great Sinner', but has been transformed by the sociological vision of a group; finally, the novel about the predatory type, prepared by earlier monsters, particularly by Stavrogin in *The Confession*, but already inclining towards the more ambitious theme of the broad nature, the metaphysical axis of 'The Life of a Great Sinner' and later of *The Brothers Karamazov*. The three worlds have faces scarred by the same sickness, the basic idea, whose name is decomposition, or disintegration, or perversion, or dislocation, flaw, fissure. They are three sections of the same whole on different planes: historic and social (crisis of civilisation), sociological and psychological (the generation of childhood), psychic and metaphysical (the essential dualism of the self).

Dostoyevsky the poet, possessed by these visions unfurling before him, ceaselessly interrogated Dostoyevsky the artist: how can these three stages, these three spheres be reconciled? More exactly he tried, as the subjects flowed towards him, to note the intersections, the entwinement, stressing this or that vision, but never rejecting any of them. At the beginning of February 1874 he wrote:

A man who shot himself and a devil like 'Faust'. Can be joined to the *novel-poem*, and so on.[23]

In May, after trying the predatory type, he saw a connection with the theme of the children:

/?/ Problem. To unite the novel: *children* are more natural with Him.[24]

A little later he expressed some doubt:

PROBLEM: SHOULD CHILDREN BE BROUGHT IN?[25]

These instructions and questions addressed to himself are like the stairways of Piranesi's imaginary prisons; groups of people remain isolated beneath the vaults, and communication seems impossible. Some of them must move and establish contact. Dostoyevsky tackled the thorny problem of the unity of the novel by using characters as bridges of flesh between the different worlds: in their migration from one sphere to another, they carry elements which unite the two and they take from the broad nature some of the potential which this nature cannot express in the novel.

The messenger: Fyodor Fyodorovich

This is how Fyodor Fyodorovich is born, a unique and original character in Dostoyevsky's work. He is the messenger who expresses a secret inclination of Dostoyevsky's own,[26] the Christian in spite of himself. He is also the messenger who vanishes once he has played his part as a link-man; coming straight from *The Idiot*, he appears as the antithesis of the Great Sinner and the *Him* of the notebooks of *A Raw Youth*, and soon dissolves into other people as different from each other as Vasin, the impassive revolutionary who inherits his coolness and the strength of his socialist convictions, and

Arkadiy and Alyosha Karamazov, to whom he bequeaths his love of children.

Fyodor Fyodorovich is a kind of atheist Myshkin: like him, he is considered an 'idiot'[27] and 'a great child': 'NB. He himself is a grown up child, only full of the strongest living and painful feeling of love for children';[28] like him, he is perfectly at ease in the empire or republic (still undecided) of the band of children whose guide and counsellor he becomes, whom he inspires by talking about Schiller and communism, and whom he treats as equals, addressing them as 'Gentlemen';[29] like Myshkin he has a gift of innocent shrewdness and can see into womens' hearts: 'SHE (and many people) consider Fyodor F[yodorovi]ch a child, understanding nothing about life and people, and suddenly Fyod[or] Fyodorovich, when the time has come (but quite unexpectedly and not thinking of preparing the scene) told her the whole psychology of her soul, to a depth which terrified her, but calmly and almost coldly.'[30] This atheist who shares Belinsky's ideas about Christ (a sublime man who would have joined the ranks of the revolutionaries),[31] the fanatical socialist who is not terrified by the logic of the revolution, the inevitable bloodshed, the fires which will break out and devour works of art (the *Venus de Milo* and the Sistine *Madonna* will be saved from the flames, however)[32] is the opposite of the predatory type, although his younger brother in the plan for the novel. 'Fyod[or] Fyod[orovi]ch is all faith, while *He* is all despair.'[33]

This faith, which is faith in communism, is suddenly affected by love for a foundling child,[34] which paradoxically changes Fyodor Fyodorovich into a Christian. This would be heresy in the doctrine of the Orthodox Church, in which the faith is more important than the nature of its object. However this bold syncretism which favours the ardent man of zeal was not new in Dostoyevsky's work. It appeared in the passage from Revelation: 'Unto the Angel of the Church of the Laodiceans write', which Tikhon recites to Stavrogin:

Those things saith Amen, the faithful and true witness, the beginning of the creatures of God.

I know thy works, that thou art neither cold nor hot: I would thou werest cold or not.

Therefore because thou art lukewarm and neither cold nor hot, it will come to pass that I shall spew thee out of my mouth.[35]

Dostoyevsky, in a bold construction which would have been considered blasphemous, entrusts to an atheist, *He*, whose misfortune is that 'HE does not believe in the Resurrection',[36] the defence of freedom in Christ, and grants another atheist, Fyodor Fyodorovich, a fanatical socialist, the privilege of Christian grace:

The elder brother (HE), in the presence of his wife and younger brother, proves to Fyod[or] Fyod[orovi]ch that Christ based society on freedom and that there is no other freedom than his ... and that he, the communist Fyod. Fyod-ch, bases it on slavery and idiocy. Fyod. Fyod-ch is defeated in the argument, but not defeated in feeling. 'Well then, we can accept the system of Christ as well', he says. 'Only we must correct some of it'.[37] 'But then nothing will remain of Christ', says his brother. 'I admit, I'm not going to argue', says Fyod, Fyod-ch, for 'this is only words' and does not go with what is really happening. And he goes away from the argument calm.

But suddenly he is struck by something: a deserted baby. And *directly* he becomes a lover of children and a Christian. They tell him that in the new society the children will be without fathers, for there will be no family (for the family is like private property). He says that probably, if this is natural, things will not be like that. 'For is it possible not to love children. You see, father and mother have deserted them; there will always be people like me. O! they will be a thousand times better than us, for everything will be love and harmony! They will all be fathers and mothers ...

'You are not far from the kingdom of God', someone says to him. 'You have mixed Christianity up with communism. Many people make this impossible compromise, it is true, nowadays.'[38]

Fyodor Fyodorovich has visibly been invented as the opposite of the Great Sinner and the broad nature; he knows no doubt, goes directly on his way and is completely true to his beliefs, whether communist or Christian. He is certainty as opposed to dualism, unity opposed to division.

For Dostoyevsky, he was mainly the flesh-and-blood character who gathered the whole together and established a network of living relationships between the three plans for the novel which appeared in the first months of 1874: the fantastic poem-novel about the destructive and bloody revolution, the novel about the empire of children, and finally the novel, sketched at greater length, about the predatory type which is in fact, in spite of the screen of Stavrogin, the broad nature.[39] However, Fyodor Fyodorovich was to disappear. Perhaps Dostoyevsky realised that the character was a psychological contradiction, too cold with adults and too passionate towards children: perhaps he recoiled from the temptation to make an open alliance between communism and Christianity or from the difficulty of creating a hero who accepts, even with a grief-stricken heart,[40] the necessity of revolution by fire and sword, while loving children with a passionate love. Only Dostoyevsky's later work allows us to suggest a reply. *The Brothers Karamazov* refuses this composite. Alyosha is first a Christian before becoming, perhaps, a 'Russian socialist' and Ivan rejects the divine universe or any kind of universal harmony constructed by the hand of man in the name of the suffering of one child.

However, at the first stage of research on the novel, Fyodor Fyodorovich was the common denominator of the three lines which have been sketched, the messenger who cemented the three parts of a whole vision which now had to be organised to form the novel.

15

A Raw Youth: the human architecture

The formal relations in a work and between works constitute an order, a metaphor of the universe.   Henri Focillon, *Vie des formes*

The architectural space which we are considering is simply the way in which the chaotic whole which has just appeared is organised, or, in material terms, the complex construction of relationships between the various characters. This is originally a random movement of particles, which is gradually organised by experiment into a formal arrangement directed by the Idea.

Gravitational disposition

The human architecture in Dostoyevsky's great novels is ordered, directly or indirectly, by the underground but fundamental dream of the broad nature, which is shown at its most brilliant in 'The Life of a Great Sinner', where Dostoyevsky was trying to rearrange the abundant growth of the universe by developing it geometrically within the immense soul of the hero with his impulses and his contradictory actions. At the extreme point, and we have caught a glimpse of this in the plan mentioned only in the letters, Dostoyevsky would have tried to include a large slice of the history of Russia, all the great eternal questions of God and humanity, and many burning contemporary problems, or in other words a history of thought, within the sum of this monstrous creature's experiences.[1] His first impulse was to concentrate the world, the totality which had just appeared, in the one living cell of the broad nature. This enthusiastic plan was immediately doomed to failure, or at least so it seemed.

First, the novel about the broad nature could not take place in a desert peopled with abstract phantoms. The need for experiences and trials required the creation of many other characters, men, women and children loved, hated, dominated, despised, sacrificed, tortured, objects which might become subjects in the course of the novel. Since the broad nature is attractive, the first architecture to be sketched showed a gravitational movement. At the beginning of the notebooks, all the characters are willingly or forcibly introduced into the orbit of the predatory type. Dostoyevsky was repeating the structure of *Crime and Punishment*, *The Idiot*, and especially *The Devils*, where all the characters gravitate round the main heroes, Raskolnikov, Myshkin and Stavrogin. In the first two novels, Dostoyevsky had constructed his system of gravity by using natural ties, such as family and friends, but he also used chance meetings. In *The Devils*, he made almost no use of chance, or almost none, if we exclude the chance presence of an escaped convict. All those who are apparently magnetised by the mysterious black sun of Stavrogin are in fact attached to him by real connections which gradually become clear; the three women love him, while Kirillov, Shatov and even Pyotr Stepanovich are all his spiritual sons, to whom he has bequeathed his obsession with the imitation of Christ.[2]

At the beginning of the notebooks of *A Raw Youth*, Dostoyevsky tried to re-create an identical network of dependence, from which artifice would be banished, as if he wanted to preserve the unity of the broad nature at all costs. The world would no longer be confined within one saturated atom, ready to explode under the pressure of its conflicting tensions, but would be extended to a group of characters revolving round the central planet, the predatory type. Three women, as in *The Devils*, revolve in the hero's orbit: the wife, 'a believer, his infernal victim', who is to die; her daughter, who is her rival, in love with her own step-father, and hangs herself after her mother's death; and lastly a young girl or the wife of someone else, perhaps a vaguely seen princess. The empire or republic of children is drawn into the orbital movement; more exactly, subject to a double attraction, it splits into two groups: the first group, including the little boy, the hanged girl's brother, who slaps his stepfather, remains faithful to Fyodor Fyodorovich; the second group turns into worshippers of Him, especially one 'heroic boy', the leader of the group, a fascinated renegade.

In the second place, the predatory type, too close a copy of Stavrogin, does not exhaust the potential of the true broad nature, of which it is only the dark side. It is pointless for this type to feel 'all the vilenesses of the fall and all the sensations of the highest thought';[3] he remains embedded in his impotence and his irremediable weakness makes him almost pathetic. Dostoyevsky was dimly aware of this:

NB. Even out and concentrate (realise) this character more strongly. Make him more attractive. (A depraved man. Depravity).

NB!!! In HIM there is tiredness and indifference and suddenly (often) a quick impulse to some kind of action (and mostly depraved and horrible), often to a noble action (but without fail HE will make it nasty and finally end with something depraved, secret and horrible).[4]

Just as rapidly, Dostoyevsky placed two other characters beside the predatory type, which, united with him, overlap to form the broad nature again. The first is our old friend Fyodor Fyodorovich, the inverted twin of the mysterious He, whose weakness as a character probably results from his systematically antithetical construction. The second, inspired by the Great

Sinner, is an attempt to escape the gloomy cycle of oscillation between fall and recovery by a movement spiralling upwards towards holiness, in fact an image of the redemption which Dostoyevsky involuntarily refused to grant the predator:

A young man (NB the great sinner) after a series of progressive falls suddenly reaches the highest of heights in spirit, will, light and consciousness. (Do not explain to the reader, just suddenly. The whole point is that the rudiments of the moral change lay in his character, which had indeed submitted itself to evil not naively, but because of [conscious] evil thought etc.)[5]

Two forces confront each other. The first, centripetal, is trying to move the crowd of characters who have arisen in Dostoyevsky's mind into the orbit of the 'broad', though not broad enough, hero, and to keep them there. The second, centrifugal, tends to weaken this central hero, by leaving out many of his possibilities. On one side there is a gravitational arrangement: on the other a twinning which is simply the incarnation of the inner struggle experienced by the broad nature.

The horizontal structure: brothers

The broad nature absorbed and took over the antagonisms which formed totality, but it was now on the point of splitting and endangering the unity of the novel. Dostoyevsky tried a solution; the twins who come from the broad nature will be brothers in the same family and blood will ensure unity. By this choice Dostoyevsky was avoiding the impasse of Stavrogin's impotence by allowing the broad nature, horizontally distributed among brothers, to have experiences separately, but he was still able to show that there was only one nature in all these characters. First there were to be two brothers:

HE is *forty*, but Fyodor Fyodorovich, HIS younger brother (or better still *half-brother*), is *twenty-seven*.[6]

The structure is admirable: unity (they are brothers) and antinomy (they are only half-brothers) are shown materially. But it is not enough, since it deprives the novel of its glorious ending: hope, the final redemption of the Great Sinner. Dostoyevsky then suggested another architecture, that of three brothers:

So, one brother is an atheist. Despair.
The other is a complete fanatic.
The third is the future generation, the living force, the new people.[7]

The predatory type, Fyodor Fyodorovich, and the young man (the Great Sinner who conquers himself) or possibly – his age is indefinite – the boy who 'pursues the path of righteousness'[8] form the brotherhood which constitutes the broad nature. It is the Karamazovian structure, the perfect human architecture of the Dostoyevsky novel. Each of the Karamazov brothers represents 'the Karamazov nature',[9] as it is called by themselves and others. Dmitriy describes it at length in Schillerean terms in his 'Confession of an ardent heart'. Rakitin the cynical seminarist puts all the Karamazovs in one basket, even Alyosha, who is supposed to be a 'voluptuary like his father' and 'a holy fool like his mother'.[10] He repeats this during the trial and the prosecutor follows his lead, commenting ironically about Dmitriy's 'sincere' dualism:

> Why is this? It is because we are broad, Karamazovian natures – this is the point I was leading to – natures capable of containing all possible contradictions and of contemplating two infinite spaces at the same time, the heights above us, the infinite height of the highest ideals, and the abyss below us, the abyss of the lowest and most fetid degradation. Call to mind the brilliant thought expressed recently by a young observer who has considered the whole Karamazov family profoundly and closely, Mr Rakitin: 'The sensation of the depths of degradation is just as necessary to these unbridled, impetuous natures as the sensation of the highest nobility'[11] – and this is the truth. They need this unnatural mixture permanently and continuously ... We are broad, broad as our dear mother Russia, we will contain everything and we will reconcile everything![12]

Within this horizontal structure, which stopped before July 1874, Dostoyevsky began to experiment by subjecting his characters to gestures which tested and committed them. HE finds that He has a savage enemy, his young brother:

> The young boy, the brother (who is with Lambert and all that) gives a slap on the face to his elder brother. Runs after this from the family. Then he draws closer to the elder brother, *discreetly* but *irrepressibly*. He does not want to show respect – and listens to him with terrible curiosity. HE listens to him, seeing in him some interest. At the end – HE dies from the beetle,[13] while the younger brother is resurrected in a heroic deed. Mix them both in the same intrigue (with the Princess) the y[oung] man paralyses HIS evil deeds.[14]

In this paragraph the complex relations between Versilov and the Raw Youth, even the intrigue which unites them, already exist. The Raw Youth suddenly acquires a dimension which brings him close to the Great Sinner and distances him from Stavrogin. The Copernican revolution of the novelist has begun and the way is clear. The characters no longer gravitate around Him, the predatory type, but move into the orbit of the new hero. On 23/11 July 1874, Dostoyevsky decided:

> The HERO – not HE, but the BOY.

And further on:

> HE is only an ACCESSORY, but what an accessory!!

Across the page there appears, like a title:

A portrait of the youth follows, with some of his surviving features: his touchy naivety, his youthful egoism, the Rothschild idea, the mixture of hostility and fascination he feels for Him, the despotic Him.[16]

The promotion of the new hero does not immediately modify the relationship between the characters. It even complicates them, since the characters already organised round the predator resist the change. The novelist hesitates and questions himself. Is Liza necessary?[17] He forgets her for a moment before returning to his first idea, which was to make her the victim of the predator,[18] and, before she hangs herself, a 'fairy queen' who enslaves the youth.[19] He also considers the wife of the predator, analyses the complex process of the victim who turns into a 'female Don Juan' and suddenly comes to believe that she too is 'cruel and predatory', before realising, on the eve of her death, that she is only a betrayed soul troubled by the depravity of her husband, only an 'eternal poor little victim', full of compassion, who had spent all her life trying to submit.[20] Dostoyevsky invents a lover for her, a young prince, from whom he means to create a type: the future Sergey Sokolsky.

Dostoyevsky then sketches the husband of the princess whom the predatory type desires: the old prince (Sokolsky in the novel). There is no hesitation; the character appears armed from top to toe, as he does in the final novel, from the imagination of the novelist. He springs to life before us. First outwardly: he is an 'old gossip', a general, a former Guards officer who has become a shrewd capitalist, even a shareholder, a little stingy. He is being duped and people are trying to guess his will. A strange mixture of good nature and selfishness, he enjoys the effect of his witticisms, likes to pretend to be a gay dog who is ruled with a rod of iron, rushes off to see light women (French, of course) like Mlle Andrieux, and finally plays the part of a rational atheist. Dostoyevsky passes gradually from the indirect style with its use of 'they say' (*deskat'*) to a dialogue where the interlocutor is only indicated by the apostrophe, here 'my dear' (he is probably speaking to his young wife) or by questions and answers.[21] As we have noted, these are the 'atoms' of dialogue in which a character first begins to appear.

Two rival systems of gravity

At this stage, nothing is stable. Dostoyevsky multiplies his characters, but seems to have forgotten the structure of brothers. He even gets lost: HE and the old prince are supposed to marry sisters,[22] promising a family muddle. But Dostoyevsky immediately recovers: 'EVERYTHING CAN BE CORRECTED IF HE and the old prince are NOT married to sisters.'[23] And he weaves another complex web of relationships between Him, the old prince and the young prince. On 24/12 July, probably disappointed by the turn the novel was taking, he admonished himself:

TRY CHILDREN TOMORROW, *JUST CHILDREN*.[24]

In a supreme effort, he tries to gather into one plan the Raw Youth and his Rothschild idea, the predatory type and his spirit of negation, and also the children who want to kill and rob their father: either the Youth comes to know them before the parricide, or he sees them immediately after the murder.[25] In fact the three great plans envisaged at the beginning of research, without being detached from the original axis of the predator, are moving insensibly toward the orbit of the Raw Youth and losing their strength in the novel. They are no longer subjects of the novel, but subjects of a dialogue between Him and the Youth, as in the final work. More exactly the plans are taken over by the heroes, in whose minds they become themes for debate. This note about the predator is the first indication of the beginning of polyphony:

All this THEORY (i.e. *influence on wife*). HE himself explains it all at the time of action and *gives a commentary* to the reader on the whole thought of the novel, how the thought particularly affects HIM. And take this rule for the whole novel, that the actors themselves should explain and THAT IT SHOULD BE MORE UNDERSTAND-ABLE.[26]

Two examples show how the original plans for the novel are absorbed by the mind of the new hero, so that the problem of the novel's unity is solved.

The 'fantastic novel-poem' about the doom of civilisation is absorbed in a passionate discussion:

Conversations with the boy . . . In Europe they want (bourgeoisie) to stop this fourth estate by force. HE foretells the destruction of the world and civilisation in fiery words. 'We've already seen the prelude. *You* (i.e. youth) must prepare, for you will be participants, the time is near, just at the door, and just when it seems so secure (armies of millions, explosive bombs). All this force, destined for the defence of civilisation, will turn against it and swallow it up.' The youth listens to these conversations with a sinking heart.[27]

The original novel about atheism, the tragedy of the predatory type was illustrated by two images: first, an ardent sermon about the freedom brought by Christ,[28] and second, the breaking of the icon,[29] which Dostoyevsky placed at the beginning and end of the final version of the novel. The tragedy is now reflected in the independent mind of the Youth, who weighs, judges and gives evidence:

'Now I understand his sufferings', says the youth. 'HE was not pretending when he preached about Christ so *forcefully*, on the contrary, he preached with the greatest of sincerity. He kept assuring himself that he *believed*. He was trying to prove to himself that *belief* existed, he was fighting with the monster of his doubts, he crushed it, but it finally gobbled him up (the monster).[30]

The youth gains an independence which threatens the predator and takes over the theme of the novel. Better still, the novelist commits his young hero to follow the predator's tracks. This is worth a whole series of notes on the goad of the flesh with Lambert, the inevitably cynical and salacious Frenchman who played such a large part in the childhood of the Great Sinner. This sadist, who would really enjoy 'feeding dogs with bread and meat, while the children of the poor are dying of hunger',[31] becomes the damned soul of the two heroes. He tells the Youth how he '*had* Viktoriya by threatening to tell her mother about her',[32] he takes the youth to brothels ('scene with various young ladies'),[33] and he suggests to the predator that he can use the same method to get the princess's *strawberry* as the one used with Viktoriya.[34] This test shows us how the paths of the Youth and predator divide. After his experiences the Youth feels only remorse, and the simple animal satisfaction of his desires does not affect his capacity for love.[35] The predator, on the other hand, loses all his ability to love freely; for him, to possess a woman is only an act of vanity or a slap in society's face:

HE says to his wife: 'I never loved her (i.e. the princess). It was only vanity, only envy, perhaps.
– But why did you seduce Liza?
– Liza was an enemy from the start, I needed her submission. It flattered me.[36]

Like the predator, the Youth wants to experience evil, which is incarnate in Lambert, the black angel who seals the alliance of sex and money. He refuses to be a Schiller, learns nihilism.[37] In short, it seems that the Youth wants to follow the dangerous paths already trodden by his brother. There is a parallel in their experiences, if not in their way of overcoming them, and this leads naturally to a parental relationship.

The vertical relationship of parenthood

The structure which makes these two characters brothers no longer seems suitable if they are to repeat each other's experiences. In fact the brothers become both complementary and antinomic pairs for the broad nature at the same time. Solving this problem means abandoning the horizontal structure which makes them brothers and adopting the vertical structure of linear descent. On 1 August Dostoyevsky caught sight of this solution, though he put it in question form:

IDEA

Is HE not a contemporary father, and the youth HIS son? (*Think about it.*)[38]

This simple question freed the novelist. He then took up his old notes, remodelled them to fit the new structure, gave the character of the predator some new psychological features, and went on, as usual, in a spiral. We still come across the ruins of the old human architecture – the name of Fyodor Fyodorovich, the little child whose mouth is torn by the predator – but the outline of the final novel is now becoming clear, unwinding telegraphically to show its final structure:

> Step-son and stepfather.
> Artistic nature.
> Charming character (he refused inheritance).
> Exhibitionism.
> Captives (literally).
> Terrible mean actions with the princess and almost a conspiracy (think of one).
> The young man turns away and abandons HIM (secret depravity).
> He cuts up the icons (it turns out that everything in HIM is serious.)
> For the wife.
> The little beetle (wife). The ideas of Geneva have destroyed him.
> The youth becomes honourable.
> Meanwhile the comrades of the youth are disappearing. Episode with aunt. (NB. This is a poem of first youth). He talks with his stepfather, asking him how much education he needs, how to behave. He is angry that he has said all this to his father ... The youth himself with the letter which has been found imagines raping the Princess in a dream, and sets out the idea to Lambert who has just arrived. He is frightened by Lambert's acceptance of the idea. How he happened to go to [Mlle] Andrieux. About Liza. And continually about HIS charm for him. In a word, never leave the youth for a moment, the aroma of first youth, the poem. Better if FATHER is natural father.[39]

This is a surprising passage. It is clear that Dostoyevsky, hastily collecting all the gains of previous research, was not aware of the slight but important change – it is in the middle of the text that he changes step-father to father – until he reached the end of his summary. He accepted it at once: HE is to be the natural father of the youth.

From now on, the human architecture of the novel was clear and stable. All the characters are to enter the double orbit whose two planets were to be father and son. On 7/8 August, Dostoyevsky gave himself a pat on the back: a large 'GOOD!' in the middle of the page,[40] and some time later, still in capitals:

IDEA

'FATHERS and CHILDREN' – CHILDREN and fathers.[41]

The novel was to be an original and argumentative treatment of the work of Dostoyevsky's great rival, Turgenev, with whom Dostoyevsky, by a rather acrobatic form of reasoning, tried to link his hero: 'For the son who intends to be a Rothschild, is in essence an *idealist*, i.e. a new phenomenon as an unexpected consequence of nihilism.'[42] In fact, Dostoyevsky was to invert the terms; the disorder is on the father's side, and the desire to overcome disintegration is felt by the son, whose happy ending is to be achieved by abandoning the Rothschild idea.[43]

The rivalry between the two heroes as pivotal characters is resolved by its incarnation as the ambiguous relationship, attraction–repulsion, imitation–opposition, of son towards father. Nevertheless it sets a serious compositional problem: 'Who is the hero? The youth or HE?'[44] Dostoyevsky was still struggling with this dilemma in 1874, in spite of his growing preference for the Raw Youth.

The majority of characters, those grouped in the family and those close to it, could be ranged naturally round the two heroes, but the role of other characters now becomes doubtful, because they were important mainly for the development of the original heroes, the predator and his antinomic twin Fyodor Fyodorovich, and for showing disturbing obsessions. These characters are essentially Liza and the little boy of eight, whose mouth is torn by the predator.

In almost all Dostoyevsky's notes, the little boy, a sick child, ends by drowning himself. The writer promises to depict his character, but does not, as he is more interested in the crime, the revealing action of the predator,[45] than in the psychology of the victim. The martyred child, injured to the depths of his young soul and on the point of suicide, can no longer be used as a hero in the novel; he is a universal symbol, an illustration to be used in Ivan Karamazov's collection of tragic stories about tortured children. This is the reason why this theme, so powerful in the notebooks,[46] appears in another form, half epic and half hagiographic, in the final novel. The wanderer Makar Ivanov tells the moving and edifying history of the sin and redemption of the merchant Skotoboynikov.[47] This change of route is very instructive: forced to mutilate the original whole and so expel one of his characters, Dostoyevsky returns to this character in the course of the novel, using the form of the traditional folktale (*skaz*) to give it the power of universal truth.

Liza, originally the little girl seduced by the predator who hangs herself, plays the same part as the little boy with the torn mouth. She is a victim, so she ought to have disappeared, especially as she is a repetition of Matryosha in Stavrogin's confession. In fact she loses her right to existence, especially after the appearance of the character of the Youth: 'No need for Liza', notes Dostoyevsky towards the end of July.[48] Then, suddenly gripped by his obsession with the demonic hero, he brings an adult Liza back to life, not from the novel but from the notebooks of *The Devils*: 'A Lermontov in a skirt'[49] fighting with the 'Pechorinian' Stavrogin as an equal. Let us follow her metamorphoses. At the stage where the heroes are brothers, she is emancipated: she is the sister, 'purest of young girls', who may suddenly become a 'prostitute'.[50] At the father–son stage, she lets herself go: mistress of her stepfather, whom she hates, she tries to poison her own mother.[51] She is to be the predator, a female predator, and not HE, notes the novelist.[52] She will even be 'a giantess', 'a Satan'; she will crush the Youth and her end must be 'solemn and terrible, like the sound of a funeral bell'.[53] She is an intriguer who will hatch the plot against the princess, extorting the letters from the Youth by her charm,[54] and then a passionate lover who will surrender to the young prince and tragically drown herself.[55] She then frees herself from this melodramatic part and becomes 'a simple Russian maiden of inexpressible sublimity.'[56] Liza's season in hell is so horrifying that Dostoyevsky casts her out of the Youth's family, and invents a more discreet sister, Olya, who in the final version is the unhappy teacher helped by Versilov. The tragic Liza at last returns to her difficult and shadowy role as discarded lover. Her silence and mystery are profoundly ambiguous, a badly healed scar of her eventful life in the notebooks during the creation of the novel. Anna Andreyevna Versilova, the Youth's half-sister, goes some way to embody the novelist's dream of creating a female predator. A cold strategist and adventuress of the drawing rooms, she will stop at nothing to marry the old and immensely rich Prince Sokolsky; when he is dead, she refuses the 60,000 roubles he leaves her and declares that she wishes to enter a convent. Basically three young girls in the final novel, all three linked with Him and the Youth (Liza, daughter and sister, Anna Andreyevna, daughter and half-sister, Olya, helped by Versilov and meeting the youth at Vasin's house), inherit their natures or their destinies from the original Liza. The breadth of character of the female predator, which might have overturned the chosen architecture of the novel, has finally exploded into several characters depending on the two main heroes.

Dostoyevsky may have wished to keep the whole of his original inspiration (theme of the martyred child: the little boy who drowns himself, the little girl who hangs herself), or he may have been trying to include characters sketched in previous notebooks who had deviated from their original nature (the female predator), but the canvas of the novel, in spite of all these internal pressures, remained solidly based on the parental structure of father and son, from August 1874 onwards.

The perfect human architecture: the fissure at the heart of unity

The horizontal Karamazov structure of half-brothers expresses both the relationship and the fissure, the antinomy at the heart of unity, and it does this in material terms. But whereas the vertical father–son structure translates unity and parenthood by repetition, it does not express fissure. The conflict of generations will certainly explode or will be absorbed, but it is not signified in the chosen human architecture. The fissure is not yet illustrated within the relationship itself.

However, from the very first drafts, Dostoyevsky gave the predator a family where the break was clearly inscribed. The children, in particular the boy of eight and Liza, were not his. The disintegration took place within the step-family and it was the predator who caused it. The problem abruptly becomes more complicated when the Youth becomes a step-son and then a son, rather than a brother. The fissure has to be recreated, to be clearly shown within the relationship.

In fact, in July 1874, when the Youth became the chosen hero, Dostoyevsky had inscribed the break in the facts, even if he had just reached the brother stage. The boy who was brought to Petersburg to replace the elder brother who had married was only the half-brother of the predator: 'Besides they are half-brothers, and the relatives who are aunts of the boy are nothing to HIM.'[57]

When Dostoyevsky chose the father–son structure in August 1874, he instinctively repeated the same distortion, substituting half-fatherhood, as it were, for half-brotherhood. As with the Verkhovenskys in *The Devils* and later with the Karamazov family, Dostoyevsky used the theme of the irresponsible parent, distributing the various children, the accidental results of his marriages, among various good souls, poor and distant relatives or devoted servants. The child, tossed from family to family – this is the case with Dmitriy Karamazov – placed in a boarding-school where he endures insult after insult, dreams of revenge in his emotional solitude. The child, painfully aware of his father's indifference, feels that he is a bastard. It is not surprising that Pyotr Stepanovich or Dmitriy Karamazov drag their fathers through the mud. In the plan of *A Raw Youth*, the relationship of father and son is more complex. It is dialectic: the Youth is fascinated, enchanted and attracted by his unknown father (he embraces Versilov's hand in the darkness with tears of joy, the first tears since he left school);[58] but he rebels against the family despotism of the predator and especially the indifference shown by Him: 'And during the whole of the novel, the Youth is tormented by HIS reserved character, pride, mystery, inhumanity, inability to love people and him, especially him.'[59] If the repulsion matching this attraction or the fissure at the heart of the union is to be clear, the obstacle must come not only from the father, but from some deeper reality: briefly, that bastardy is not only a feeling but a truth inscribed in the human architecture.

After days devoted to digging up the Idea and to research about how the story should be told, Dostoyevsky suddenly discovered a solution. On 8 September 1874, a character whom the novelist must have had in his mind for a long time suddenly appeared fully grown, already modelled verbally, stylistically, psychologically, and spiritually: the wanderer Makar Ivanov. This was a miraculous and inspired birth, without a shade of hesitation, quite different from the literary adolescence so typical of the other characters, immediately sealed by the serene and metaphorical speech of folk and religious language, with its rich imagery, its assonance, its poetic metaphors, its precepts and wise proverbs, its trace of Slavonic.[60] But at the same time, Makar is born into a situation: he reveals a whole universe of light to the Youth, to whom he never stops talking:[61] he stigmatises modern man, who has given up his freedom in exchange for the golden calf; he also converses with the amazing fool in Christ, Lizaveta Smerdyashchaya, and quotes her words of hope for those who are suffering, words directly inspired by the apocryphal *Pilgrimage of the Mother of God among the Torments*.[62] A clear column soaring amid the stormy movement, Makar Ivanov stresses the break and particularly gives it a name: he will be the Youth's father, his legal father. it is a 'new story':

Death of Makar Ivanov. He has lived honourably. After 19 February [1861][63] he collected money to build churches of God. He returned to Petersburg to die and died among his family. The family is composed of his wife aged 37 (NB. She had always been a beauty, but eight years ago, when her youngest child, the sickly little boy, was born, she suddenly became all bent), of the youth, of Olya who is 17, of the sickly little boy of eight. They are all HIS children and Makar has only been the husband who gave them his name.[64]

And, by an irony embittering the Youth, sharpening his pain and his secret wish for revenge, the name Makar has given them is Dolgoruky, the illustrious name of a Russian princely house. Bastardy is experienced tragically in suffering and mutilation. A fissure publicly inscribed, illegitimate birth is a material symbol of the idea of disintegration within the human architecture.

Bastardy also introduces a double polarisation of the novel. On one hand, the son throws himself into a clumsy and passionate re-conquest of his real father: 'In general, the whole novel is a poem of the love of the youth for HIM.'[65] On the other hand, even while he is making this attempt, he discovers in Makar Ivanov a spiritual (and legal) father who bequeaths a different ideal to him. From this point of view, *A Raw Youth* illustrates the universality of fathers dreamt of by Fyodor Fyodorovich.[66]

The arrangement of the characters, if not their destinies, may now be summed up:

HE is the old type of nobleman. Precious features of scepticism, nobility, disbelief, lazy atheism, laziness, liberalism, despotism. Above all passion, predatory type. But passion, refuge in Christianity ... Secret atheism and despotism in the family. Almost the same as in the previous novel. This is how the youth finds him.

Olya is an angelic type. The frightened ones. She is frightened because the y[oung] prince has come courting. But it was terribly flattering to her, she was happy. She refused, drowned herself.

Mother. Russian type (huge character), they are trodden down, submissive and firm, like saints.

Makar Ivanov (Russian type). He is amazed.
The youth as he was.
Dolgushin and p[eople] near Vasin – very briefly.[67]

A last summary clearly shows Dostoyevsky's jubilation at having reconstituted the original whole, which had splintered in the course of the research, and at having expressed it in a human architecture which is now clear:

In the novel all the elements. Civilised and desperate, idle and sceptical, of the higher intelligentsia: HE.
Old Holy Russia – the Makarovs.
The holy and good in new Russia – the aunts.
Degenerate nobility – y[oung] prince (sceptic, etc.)
High society – a ridiculous and abstractedly ideal type.
Young generation – the youth, with only his instinct, knowing nothing.
Vasin – ideal without a way out.
Lambert – meat (flesh), matter, horror – and so on.[68]

The novel can begin. As we look back, the complex path is clear. At the beginning Dostoyevsky wanted to preserve the whole of the universal vision which had appeared to him: at this stage, all the last great novels are strangely alike. He tried to reduce the chaos by flinging bridges of flesh and blood, characters, between the various plans for the novel and he inevitably drifted towards the broad nature which could contain all these plans and was vast enough to contain the universe. The necessary experience which the broad nature must pursue in its tragic search inspired a group of characters fascinated by the hero and organised around him in an unstable gravitational system. At the same time a process of parthenogenesis began: the broad nature, torn by opposing impulses, split up into several broad natures which were arranged in the horizontal structure of brotherhood or the vertical one of father and son, and in which the splitting of the initial being, the fissure within the single character, is necessarily inscribed within the unity (half-brotherhood or half-fatherhood). It was only when this tottering structure had been erected that the other heroes and heroines took their places and this marked a return to the original universal vision. The ones who disappeared (Liza and the little boy) returned to the novel indirectly, in stories which are not part of the main plot (the story of Olya, the parable of the merchant Skotoboynikov), diamonds torn from the primaeval chaos.

The human architecture of *A Raw Youth*, like that of *The Brothers Karamazov* and to a lesser extent that of *The Devils*, springs from Dostoyevsky's perpetual oscillation between his great underground dream of expressing the entire universe in a single broad character, and his need to have other characters in the novel with various experiences and different destinies. It is his metaphysical world expressed in flesh and blood.

16

A Raw Youth: the Idea of the novel

Decomposition is the main visible thought of the novel.

Dostoyevsky in the notebooks of *A Raw Youth*

Confusion of critical ideas

Dostoyevsky's work glows with ideas, as some people glow with health. It arouses more passion and intolerance, inside and outside Russia,[1] than the work of any other writer, furnishing ideologists of all sorts – Christians and atheists, friends and enemies of socialism, egoists and universalists, not counting psychoanalysts, existentialists personalists, and so on – with endless ammunition for their battles. Dostoyevsky, who loved philosophy, would not have questioned anyone's right to make use of any of the ideas in his novels, or at least to take up the theories embodied by his heroes.[2]

This is not the same as saying that Dostoyevsky was a master of the philosophical novel. Engelgardt's idea that his work reveals 'the distinct links of a complex philosophic construction expressing the history of the gradual formation of the human spirit'[3] contradicts the novelist's basic inclination, which was, as we saw in 'The Life of a Great Sinner', to reject historical time in order to preserve human freedom by extending it in space. Dostoyevsky was not a Hegelian, but a novelist who interrogated man in the idea made act. As an artist, writes V. Ya. Kirpotin, 'he never limited himself to the antinomy or even the dialectic of the idea in itself, but tested it in practice'.[4] Bakhtin in particular stressed that Dostoyevsky's novels are not primarily ideological, for they do not show the Idea in a Platonic sense, but particular ideas which always belong to particular minds:

The idea, as the subject of representation, does indeed occupy an enormous place in Dostoyevsky's work, but it is nevertheless not the hero of his novels. His hero was a man, and in the final analysis he represented not the idea in man, but (to use his own words) the 'man in man.' The idea for him was either a touchstone for testing the man in man, or a form for revealing it, or – and this is the last and most important – a 'medium', an environment in which human consciousness could be revealed in its deepest essence.[5]

This dispute results from a double confusion. On one side, the ideas of the hero are mechanically and selectively attributed to the creator, as, for example, in the constructions, the betrayals of Strakhov, Berdyayev, Freud and Shestov, brilliant as some of them are. On the other side, the emotional idea of the hero is confused with the great Idea of the novel. The hero's idea, his emotional idea as Dostoyevsky called it, is the means by which the hero's deepest self is revealed, which shows us whether the hero is Raskolnikov, Shatov, Kirillov, Pyotr Verkhovensky, Tikhon, Zosima or Ivan Karamazov.[6] This is the idea of which Bakhtin is speaking. But the Idea or thought (*mysl'*) of the novel is the real subject or theme which defines the unity of the novel and naturally takes a central place in the research.[7] Guarding the whole vision seen at the beginning of creation, the Idea of the novel embraces and unites the ideas of the heroes, although it does not determine the plot, the *fabula*, which Dostoyevsky constructs in parallel with the subject and which he treats with the casual assurance of an old hand. We propose to analyse the formation and evolution of the Idea of the novel in the notebooks of *A Raw Youth*, and to clarify its organic relationship with the ideas of the heroes.

The formulation of the Idea within the hero's mind

In the first pages of the notebooks of *A Raw Youth* Dostoyevsky formulates the rule of the conscious heart: 'To write a novel, one must first provide oneself with one or several strong impressions, really lived by the author in his heart. This is the business of the poet. From this impression a theme, a plan, a harmonious whole is developed, and this is the business of the artist.'[8]

Let us translate: the strong impressions are the immediate plans for the novel, and the theme is the Idea of the novel, which we have seen as it became detached from its placenta: in the notebooks of *A Raw Youth* this is the idea of universal decomposition, of decay.

In parallel, Dostoyevsky has set himself another rule: the Idea of the novel must be expressed by the characters themselves, or, in other words, become conscious in the hero's mind.[9] From the very beginning the Idea finds its home in living speech. Formulation of the Idea for the novelist's own use is immediately followed by its use in dialogue, as for example, in this passage where the predator is talking to his brother, Fyodor Fyodorovich:

Decomposition is the main visible thought of the novel.
'the tower of Babel', HE says. Well, here we are, a Russian family [He says]. We talk in different languages and don't understand each other at all. Society is decomposing chemically.
–Well, not the people.
–The people too.[10]

This process is essential. It confirms Bakhtin's great intuition of Dostoyevsky's polyphony, which Bakhtin analysed mainly in the finished works but which is here shown in the notebooks. Dostoyevsky transferred to his heroes his gifts as a poet, his method as a novelist: the law of the conscious heart passes to the hero, who ceases to become the object of legislation and himself becomes the legislator. In fact, the process is complex and not at all absolute. Dostoyevsky does not give up his own freedom; he never stops controlling, experimenting, directing the will of the heroes, and he cuts the thread of their destiny with terrible decimations, waves of suicides or deaths.[11] The freedom of the characters is adulterated by the need to go on with the novel.

The passion for the Idea

This polyphony, which is imperfect at the creative stage, is shown in what we shall call the passion for the Idea. Dostoyevsky found the Idea appearing everywhere in the notebooks. Sometimes it was a simple note by the writer for his own personal use, sometimes it was already part of the hero's mind and an object for discussion, sometimes the hero saw it as an object in someone else, and in this case it began the interrelation of minds which is so characteristic of Dostoyevsky's world.

The predator is naturally the person chosen to express and feel the idea of fissure, of decomposition, which he carries within himself.[12] We have seen him, in a dialogue with Fyodor Fyodorovich, expressing his theory of national disorder. On 7 and 8 August, Dostoyevsky defined the theme of the Idea which was to be transformed into the personal theory of the predator: 'Nota bene. GOOD! 7/8 August. (NB. Of the lack of ideology in society, the disintegration of the family, HIS theories and so on).'[13] Formerly Dostoyevsky had shown the inner disorder of the predator by means of the old prince (look of the other):

Important Nota bene. The novel finds HIM already retired and ditching His business career. HE gave up business when he received an inheritance.

'But if He had wanted, He would have been a business man', even the old prince criticises HIM. – 'And, in general', says the old prince, 'I see in HIM a sort of poet. Up to now he has restrained himself but now nature has had her say and He has revealed himself.'

That is how it was, as the old prince says. From the very point at which the novel starts, all HIS inner chaos and the disharmony (lack of faith, etc.) within him has ripened. The demands of conscience have become more insistent etc. And this inner chaos is expressed by an outer disharmony, i.e., he has retired, he is chatty, restless, behaves eccentrically towards his wife; in a word, *disorder*, and just as if he wanted to dissuade himself – an intense preaching of Christianity (relics).[14]

Dostoyevsky collects it all together and makes the point himself: '*Tone of the whole.* HE is always occupied with his own highest idea (decomposition) and His *loss of purpose* and His *chemical* decomposition.'[15]

All the candidates for the predatory nature who are later to be discarded,

such as the step-mother and Liza, are living incarnations of disorder. The
step-mother exclaims 'How horrible all this is suddenly! What disorder
suddenly. No, I am not a predator, I am an eternal poor little victim',[16] just
before her death which is due to 'moral disorder and exhaustion'. Liza is
seen by the predator (the look of the Other and not self-awareness) as a
disorder: '*He* looks on Liza also *as a disorder*, i.e. someone who has lost her
purpose and, with the strongest passions, is tossed around as it were in the
general chaos.'[17] From this observation the novelist passes to the self-
awareness of the character: 'Liza says? If I had lived in the sixteenth
century, I should have been a poisoner. I love disorder (Liza suddenly
says).'[18]

The 'inner disorder' of the hero becomes the general theme of the
novel.[19] Everyone is affected by it: first He, then the step-mother, Liza, and
the young prince, whose revealing actions are noted by Dostoyevsky in
December 1874, and then in January 1875: 'The prince gave a slap in public
(disorder)'[20] and 'The young prince (disorder) has made Lidya pregnant.'[21]

Everyone discovers it in other people. The illness, which is first within the
characters, spreads to become a social and historical phenomenon. Two
examples, situated chronologically at either end of the research, the first in
August 1874, the second in June 1875, illustrate this. Three characters, He,
Vasin and the Youth are discussing the motives of suicides like the
unfortunate Kraft:[22] they conclude that it is the result of general disorder.
Later, in the dialogue between Akhmakova and Versilov, Dostoyevsky
clearly indicates the shift from 'inner confusion' to social decomposition.
Akhmakova first analyses Versilov: 'You are as ready to commit a crime as
to do heroic deeds, there is no control. I repeat, there is disorder in you.'
And a few lines later, she condemns the high society to which she and
Versilov belong: 'There is lying, falseness, deceit and supreme disorder in
everything. Not one of these people could stand up to a test: there is
complete immorality, complete cynicism in every one of them. They are
robbers and cheats every one, do you think I can't see this?'[23]

Even the Youth does not escape the passion for the Idea. In August 1874
Dostoyevsky groups together all his methods of approaching the Idea of the
novel. It is a significant passage: besides the simple note, a summary for
personal use and a suggestion for titles, there is a dialogue by the central
character, the predator, showing his own self-awareness and his observation
of the Other, and also the linking of the hero's idea, in this case the
Rothschild idea, with the Idea of the novel:

The title of the novel: 'Disorder'.

The whole idea of the novel is to show that now disorder is general, disorder is
everywhere and in everything, in society, in its business affairs, in its ruling ideas
(which do not exist for that very reason), in its convictions (which for the same
reason also do not exist), in the decomposition of the principle of the family. If

passionate convictions exist, then they are only destructive (socialism). There are no moral ideas, suddenly there is not a single one left, and the main thing is that HE talks as if they had never existed at all.
–But surely you must be religious.
–That's about the last thing I have left.
–You, for instance, says HE to the youth, have chosen the Rothschild idea. You can use this idea as more evidence of moral disorder. You want to go off into *your own* lair away from everyone and you are making your own means of doing this.

Liza is complete moral disorder, she won't agree to live without happiness. The Dolgushins are moral disorder.[24]

Naturally, when the Youth is suddenly promoted to main hero, the Idea of the novel is seen through his eyes and experienced in his mind. He takes the Idea away from the predator and even from the writer, since the Youth now becomes the narrator. But this does not affect the freedom of the predator, whose words are quoted to express his own independent mind. Two brief notes, where the Youth is speaking, perfectly express what Bakhtin called 'the interrelation of minds in the sphere of ideas':

And at the end: disorder of the soul is caused by lack of faith (by atheism). Strange words! I should not have understood them or should have thought them empty, if I had not seen a living example in Him.[25]

I have called all this: Disorder. That is His word . . . *He* used that word most of all.[26]

The idea is endlessly rediscovered in and through the characters, even if some of them are destined to change or disappear.

The dialectic Idea

The Idea becomes more profound and is examined in detail. Finally it is dialectically reversed, a point already inscribed in the fissure, the structure which both unites and tears apart the human architecture which is a metaphor of the Idea. If decomposition is the main Idea of the novel, it must have its opposite, harmony or at least the desire for harmony. The appearance in September 1874 of Makar Ivanov illustrates the oscillating movement of Dostoyevsky's thought, a thought which always clothes itself in images and characters. The predator and the wanderer are complete opposites, but what interests Dostoyevsky is the correlation of these opposites and the path of one towards the other, the correlation of the two poles and their equal attraction. He must therefore have a hero who is neither a saint nor a broad nature stifled by the disorder of his soul and society, but a strong and vulnerable character who experiences disorder, becomes sharply aware of it and tries to root it out of himself. The Idea of the novel is no longer limited to expressing disorder: it becomes a man's uncertain struggle against 'the forces of disorder', to use Dostoyevsky's expression.[27] The Idea of the novel becomes an act, an experience, the subject of the novel.

Dostoyevsky carried on this search for the dialectic idea, acted upon and tested by life, by various means. The first was the search for titles. In August 1874, when the Youth became the central hero, Dostoyevsky tried various titles:

'Confession of a great sinner, for himself'.[28]

Complete title of the novel:

A RAW YOUTH. CONFESSION OF A GREAT SINNER, WRITTEN FOR HIMSELF.[29]

On 26 August, Dostoyevsky was still hesitant but reunited the two ends of the dialectic idea:

NB! SHOULD IT NOT BE ENTITLED: (BEGINNING OF A CAREER) the novel etc.
Another title: DISORDER (26 August).
Another title: A detailed history.
Or: A CERTAIN DETAILED HISTORY.[30]

In parallel, he tries to fix the idea, the true subject, in its dynamics:

MAIN IDEA.

Although the youth arrives with a ready-made idea (*ideya*) the whole thought (*mysl'*) of the novel is that he is searching for a guiding thread of behaviour, of good and evil, which does not exist in our society, this is what he is thirsting for, and trying to track down. The aim of the novel consists of this.[31]

From then on Dostoyevsky held the key to his work. The *fabula*, the external subject, was still in the throes of experiment when he defined the Idea of the novel in dense formulae:

The concluding thought is formulated by the youth at the end of the novel in this way. The only person who will save himself is the one who from his youth onwards has developed for himself that strong moral sensation (feeling), which is called conviction. The formula of the conviction may change in the course of life, but the moral sensation of this feeling is unchangeable throughout life.[32]

Crystallisation was so rapid that towards the end of August 1874, Dostoyevsky noted down a final synthesis:

In general the whole novel shown through the character of the Youth, seeking a living truth (Gil Blas and Don Quixote), can be very appealing.
Do not forget the last lines of the novel: 'Now I know: I have found what I was looking for, what is good and what is evil, and I will never deviate from it.'
Final. In general this is a poem about how *the Youth* enters the world. This is the story of his searches, his hopes, his disillusionments, his defects, his rebirth, learning – the history of the nicest and most attractive creature. Life itself teaches him, but teaches him, the Youth, because another would not have learnt from life.[33]

Relationship of Idea and plot

The last sentence in this quotation, which mentions the exceptional nature who can learn from life and the necessity of learning by experience, leads us to ask about the links between the Idea of the novel, its profound subject and the story of the novel, its dramatic subject, which Dostoyevsky calls the *fabula* or fable (*basnya*).

There is a surprising difference in the elaboration of the two. While the Idea of the novel immediately crystallised in its dialectical dynamics, the *fabula* remains moving, uncertain, constantly referred to and constantly deferred.

However, Dostoyevsky is always spurring himself on. 'A fable, a fable is needed! An eventful interesting plan. Vengeance on the princess', he notes in July 1874.[34] A little later, he writes: 'The affair is going on by itself, the fabula of the novel is developing. The youth himself with the letter which has been found imagines in a dream that he will rape the princess and sets out his idea to Lambert.'[35] Dostoyevsky relies on his immense power of improvisation. He does not forget the need for a subject. He slogs on: 'NB. think of the fable (Lambert, Andrieux, the princess and so on) BETTER, more deeply, MORE WIDELY AND MORE SERIOUSLY.'[36] He calls himself to order: 'THE FABLE! THE FABLE!'[37] At another point, distracted by the subplot of Kraft's suicide, he reminds himself again: 'But then *the fabula*, *the fabula*!, which is to be developed terribly concisely, consistently and unexpectedly.'[38] Roughly, and Dostoyevsky underlines this several times,[39] the spring of the action is the famous letter which compromises the princess and which has fallen into the Youth's hands. But this is only the argument. The true subject is still to be constructed and Dostoyevsky himself gets lost in the tangles of the 'net' (*teneta*) which the Youth has rashly flung out and in which the predator (Versilov) and Lambert meddle whenever they feel like it. Gradually, in the series of detailed plans which could all be called 'plot against the princess',[40] the complicated intrigue of the final novel is constructed. However, there is no connected progression or exact chronological background. The plans drawn up by the writer, except for those concerning the past of the characters (the childhood of the youth, the 'legend' of Versilov), appear as summaries, lists of facts and gestures whose order or attribution can change at any time. The plot cobbled up by the novelist, a daring and sordid affair of blackmail originating in the mind of a humiliated youth in love, can be constructed only if the freedom of the heroes is preserved. The vast experimental stirring up of minds must not be paralysed by a determining plot fixed in advance. On the other hand, the suspense (*zanimatel'nost'*), which Dostoyevsky never forgets, must not be weakened in any way.

Technique of final gestures

This double and contradictory requirement gave rise to the technique, so original in Dostoyevsky, of final gestures. These have two principal characteristics: they are interchangeable at the research stage of the novel, and they are violent, both in the research and in the finished novel, though in the final text they may appear slightly modified, as an impulse rather than a crime. They have a double function: to interest the reader and to test the soul of the hero. This aspect has been vigorously stressed by Kirpotin, though he has confused the Idea of the novel with the idea which is felt by the hero, besides confusing the idea with the gesture which reveals it:

In Dostoyevsky's poetics, the idea only acquires strength enough for the novel when it reaches extreme tension, becomes a mania or even a monomania; in the same way the act to which a man is driven by the idea must have a character of extremity, the intensity and tempo of catastrophe. The acts are always murder, suicide, rape, arson, pillage, blackmail, violent scenes, marriages suddenly made and suddenly broken.[41]

He goes on:

It is only by means of the test [proba], by checking in practice, by real catastrophe that the false idea of Raskolnikov, his plan of reconstructing universal order, founders. Without murder the ideas of Rogozhin, of Peter Verkhovensky, of the Karamazov brothers could not be made clear, as the idea of the Youth could not be made clear without blackmail.[42]

At first sight the final gestures which occur throughout the notebooks of *A Raw Youth* would chill even an addict of horror stories. Death, sex and money are triumphant.[43] There is rape, copulation – here Dostoyevsky uses the vernacular – a child's mouth is mutilated, an adulterous woman is burnt by being placed on a stove;[44] suicide, hanging, drowning; theft or accusations of theft; money or shares are counterfeited, people tear each other apart for inheritances, denounce each other, are arrested, commit arson, slap, provoke others to duels, break icons, die mad or stupefied. Dostoyevsky refuses to say definitely who committed any of these actions. The slap, for example, is sometimes given by the young prince, sometimes by the little boy, sometimes even by the princess. The suicides, to take another example, are innumerable: they come in waves, sweeping Liza, Kraft, Him, the little boy, the young prince and others off the stage.

This is only a first impression. Dostoyevsky is not so much interested in the person who performs the action as in the one who suffers it. The final gesture is less significant of the violence used than of the suffering endured and the revelation given. The slap may be given by different characters, but it is always He (Versilov) who receives and endures it.[45] It is always the little boy whose mouth is torn. Most of the time it is the victims who commit suicide: Liza, Olya, the little boy. It is the Youth who is accused of theft, who is suspected of embezzlement, who dreams of rape and is impelled towards it, who wants to set fire to something; all these actions revive the sufferings of humiliation and the thirst for vengeance.[46] Death, so active in the notebooks and epilogues, is not experienced within the character as it is in Tolstoy: it is only an action which is observed by another person. The suicide of Kraft, obsessed by the secondary role played by Russians in the concert of nations, is important mainly because it reveals disorder to Arkadiy. The final gestures, violent as they are, matter little in themselves. This is proved by the carefree way in which Dostoyevsky moves them from novel to novel and cheerfully forgets them in the epilogue.[47] The only important thing is their significance, their burden of suffering and of awareness, and so, on the plane of the novel, the revelation of the idea that they illustrate. They represent the storm, the tragic experience, a test which is necessary before man can reach the depths of his soul.[48]

The order of psychology

The shocking event, or the final gesture, is only a symbol, the sign by which the idea is recognised. The novelist sees this so clearly that he organises the succession of gestures around one great violent scene of revelation. He does this once and for all at the beginning of his plans and it is not changed. The duel always comes after the slap, the impulse to commit arson after the humiliation, the suicide by hanging after the rape. In *A Raw Youth*, the breaking of the icon by Versilov is always inserted between the movement of Versilov towards his wife and his desertion of her for another, the princess. More subtly, the youth's attempts to make money – economies, bargaining – precede his impulses to use the letter as blackmail. Both originate in his thirst for revenge and power: the Rothschild idea, an emotional idea, may be discarded when he discovers a more powerful weapon. With money, the Youth would have had women at his feet; with the letter he dreams of possessing Akhmakova. The link between sex and money has never been clearer and the fusion of the emotional idea and the plot has never been so subtly designed. The Rothschild idea and its development in the novel create the unity of the plot.

But the unity of the novel is fixed by what Dostoyevsky, in the summer of 1875 when he was questioning himself about the plan of the third part, called in his notebooks 'the order of psychology'. This is the balance sheet which the Youth draws up of all his experiences, all the final gestures which he has seen and analysed. The Idea of the novel, no longer the emotional idea, appears in all its clarity: to be aware of the universal disorder, the hero places himself outside disorder. In this respect, the notebooks in their schematism are more explicit than the novel, where Dostoyevsky has realistically prevented the youth from being too wise and too perspicacious.[49] The order of psychology illuminates the organic link between the gestures and the Idea of the novel and especially, within the human architecture, the division of the characters into creatures of disorder and creatures who yearn for order. Two long pages are devoted to this: we shall give only a few extracts:

Spiritual beauty in Makar (*blagoobraziye*), disorder in Versilov. The youth wishes to go away from disorder. *Order of psychology.* At first the youth under the influence of a bad feeling (vengeance) grows friendly with Lambert and even lets him understand his scheme. But after his meeting with her (alms), after her scene with Versilov, after the death of Makar and, finally, the breaking of the icons and the flight of the old prince – THE UGLINESS (*bezobraziye*)[50] OF THIS ENVIRONMENT SUDDENLY STRIKES THE YOUTH . . . Now it is time to confess: why did I write these notes? *Disorder* amazed me. Oh, I was irritated at school, but until Petersburg I knew nothing. I imagined even worse, I imagined wicked people, but I thought that everyone, good and bad, had something in common that they respected, considered sacred, about which they did not argue . . . *The moral disorder* of Versilov, the absence of principles. Only Makar in order, but can it be possible? Only my mother is a saint, but how does she live? I believed in her [Akhmakova] but how does she live and what is she striving for? . . . Bioring is severe order for her, and 'the world is disorderly and depraved' (she herself says) . . . 'I long for order', she says (to Versilov): 'So do I'. It turns out that the youth has caught the word disorder from her . . .

The youth to Anna Andreyevna his sister (when the old prince ran away): I do not know, Anna Andreyevna, but the disorder of our society continually amazes me. While everything is in its decreed official frame, there is some sort of appearance still in the Russian and the Russian family. But if anything were shaken, immediately everything would come to light, the whole lack of moral basis, and disorder would begin . . . He says this to Versilov, and CONTINUOUSLY, after Makar.[51]

This part of the notebooks is exactly like a laboratory. At the beginning Dostoyevsky is acting as a biologist. From several visions he selects a working hypothesis, an Idea of the novel which he sees: here, universal disorder. This soon reveals its dialectical nature through the broad character of the hero, who is split into two characters, genetically and spiritually related.[52] In a kind of experimental passion, the Idea of the novel is injected, still at the stage of research and reflection, into numerous characters gravitating round the main heroes. Its form is antinomic: disorder for some, yearning for order in others. The crucial, often deadly experiences of the final gestures are then unfolded. At this stage the analogy with the biologist ceases, or rather life and the novelist take its place.

The guinea-pigs, the subjects of experiment, have now become aware of the Idea of the novel themselves, and especially the main hero; he is even capable of summing it up. When this Idea has appeared in the dialogue and has been observed in the characters of others, the final writing of the novel can begin. Some final gestures are taken up to become part of the plot which is only a convention to get them in the right order, so that they may be assembled round the character who is most deeply aware of the Idea, in other words, the Raw Youth.

17

The composition of the novel in Dostoyevsky's work: choice of chronicle form

Reflect, reflect before writing. Everything depends on the conception. This axiom of the great Goethe is the simplest and most marvellous summary and precept for all possible works of art.

Gustave Flaubert, *Letter to Louise Colet*, 13 September 1852

The musical comparison

For Dostoyevsky, to compose was to set the original chaos in order, forging the unity of the novel without betraying the dialectic totality. It was a formidable task. All the elements of the composition had to harmonise in a set of meanings which were perpetually overtaking each other. The novel of Dostoyevsky is essentially teleological, as we have seen from the difficult construction of the human architecture: the antagonistic spheres of the people gravitating around Versilov and the Youth finally dissolved into a vertical structure which signified both parenthood and break. The Idea of the novel, first separated from its placenta and then passionately tested by experience, is another example of the teleological nature of *A Raw Youth*: the monolithic theme of social, family, national and spiritual disorder was succeeded by the fertile dialectic of disorder and the desire for order; the pessimistic and static statement was replaced by the optimistic dynamics of struggle.

Before approaching *A Raw Youth*, we shall consider the problem of composition in Dostoyevsky's work as a whole. Like E. M. de Vogüé[1] and Vyacheslav Ivanov,[2] Leonid Grossman, followed on this point by Mikhail Bakhtin,[3] who sees in this form of composition an eloquent confirmation of his thesis on polyphony, stressed the musical character of Dostoyevsky's works. In his discussion of the creation of *Notes from Underground* at the point where Dostoyevsky was still planning to write three parts instead of the final two, Grossman wrote:

Dostoyevsky himself indicated his approach to composition by drawing an analogy between his system of construction and the musical theory of transitions or oppositions. At the time he was writing a novella in three chapters, different in content, but internally united. The first chapter was a polemical and philosophical monologue, the second a dramatic episode which prepared for the catastrophic ending of the third chapter. Dostoyevsky asked himself if these chapters could be published separately. They echo each other, their themes are different but closely linked, introducing an organic change of tonality but not a mechanical break. This enables us to decipher Dostoyevsky's brief but important indication in a letter to his brother about the publication of Notes from Underground in the journal Time:[4] 'The novella is divided into three chapters . . . In the first chapter there may be about one and a half signatures . . . Must it be published separately? People will laugh at it, especially since it loses all its flavour without the other two (the more important ones). You understand what a transition in music is? This is exactly the same. In the first chapter apparently it is just idle chatter, but suddenly this idle chatter is clarified in the last two chapters by an unexpected catastrophe.'[5]

Here Dostoyevsky with great subtlety transposes the law of musical transition from one tonality to another on to the plane of literary composition. The novella is constructed on the basis of literary counterpoint . . . This is what point against point (*punctum contra punctum*) means. It is different voices singing on the same theme. This is the 'multivocalism' which reveals the multiplicity of the forms of life and the complexity of human feelings. 'Everything in life is counterpoint, that is, opposition,' as M. I. Glinka, one of Dostoyevsky's favourite composers, says in his memoirs.[6]

Komarovich, one of the most subtle analysts of Dostoyevsky, even proposed a precise musical genre; this suggestion, made in 1924, possibly influenced Bakhtin's criticism: 'Teleological co-subordination of elements (subjects) which is pragmatically distinct is the principle of artistic unity in the novel of Dostoyevsky. And in this sense it may be compared to the unity created in polyphonic music: the five successive voices of the fugue developed in contrapuntal harmonies recall the vocalic organisation of the novel of Dostoyevsky.'[7] J.-J. Rousseau in his article about fugue for *The Encyclopedia* says that 'confusion is the chief danger and is very difficult to avoid'. This explains why early readers of Dostoyevsky were confused by his new principle of composition: the first French readers, such as Jean Fleury, reproached him with a complete lack of composition,[8] but later readers, like Paul Claudel, saw his novels as a model of composition in the style of Beethoven.

Although the comparison with music may be indicative for the finished works, Dostoyevsky rarely used musicological metaphors. In the notebooks and in the process of creation he referred mainly to literary models. This is an aspect of the great literary dialogue which has seldom been considered with reference to composition.

Visible dialogue: ideological polemics and aesthetic competition

Dostoyevsky was always keenly aware of what was happening in contemporary Russian literature, just as he was always aware of history and the newspapers. All his works, except for *The House of the Dead*,[9] are thematic echoes, ideological polemics, aesthetic rivalry, or all three at the same time. Before discussing the problem of composition, we shall say a few words about this visible dialogue.

While Pushkin, who died in 1837, accompanied Dostoyevsky from beginning to end of his career as a writer, the other peers of Dostoyevsky succeeded each other. Dostoyevsky always tried to set his pace by writers who were celebrated at the time. There were times which overlapped or went into reverse. So Gogol, who tyrannised over the first works and was finally overcome and supplanted as literary model in *The Village of Stepanchikovo*, reappeared whenever Dostoyevsky caricatured a provincial town with its grotesque society where rumours become monstrously swollen, where ladies revile their cowardly husbands as in *The Devils* or *The Brothers Karamazov*, or even every time the devil appeared in the novels. From the beginning of the sixties until *Crime and Punishment* which ends the cycle, Dostoyevsky, both as novelist and as journalist in *Time* and *Epoch*, was waging ideological war against Chernyshevsky and the 'new men'. The key work of this period is *Notes from Underground*. From *The Idiot* to *A Raw Youth*, a long struggle, which has been partly shown in the analysis of migrant images, began against a more subtle adversary, Herzen. Between these two landmarks there was a phase, from 'The Eternal Husband' to *The Devils*, in which Dostoyevsky mounted an attack on Turgenev, with whom he had quarrelled in 1867.[10] Dostoyevsky seemed to be matching the moves of this rival, who was his complete opposite. Turgenev's charming light comedy *The Provincial Lady* (1851) received a partial reply in 'The Eternal Husband', a tragedy in prose; the famous essay *Hamlet and Don Quixote* (1860), in which Turgenev admitted the impotence of the Russian intellectual, was answered by *The Idiot* and Myshkin, a new Don Quixote with a profoundly Russian soul; Turgenev's famous novel *Fathers and Sons* and his social novels, such as *Rudin* and *Smoke*, were countered by *The Devils*, in which Dostoyevsky transformed Turgenev's simplistic opposition between liberal fathers, disciples of Granovsky and Belinsky, and their nihilist sons into a seditious father-and-son relationship. Stepan Trofimovich Verkhovensky, whose historical prototype is Granovsky, is the real father of the nihilist terrorist inspired by Nechayev, the spiritual father of that sinister Hamlet, Stavrogin, and the person directly responsible for the criminal destiny of Fedka the convict. Dostoyevsky has changed the Westernised and erratically weak-willed intellectuals into dangerous monomaniacs of the Idea. Finally, he parodied Turgenev and all his works in the effeminate pink person of the writer Karmazinov. *The Devils* also contained a challenge to another giant of Russian letters, Saltykov-Shchedrin, whom he admired as a writer but opposed politically.[11] The town which Dostoyevsky ferociously depicted, probably from his memories of Tver (where he lived from August to

December 1859)[12] and from his reading about events in Kharkov,[13] is also reminiscent of Stupidborough (*Glupov*) in *The History of a Town*.

In *A Raw Youth* Dostoyevsky revealed an older ambition: a dialogue with the great Russian writer, 'an artist to the highest degree',[14] whose writings he followed anxiously, Leo Tolstoy. There were several reasons for this: first, Tolstoy had begun to write part of the old Dostoyevskian dream, the novel of a life. His trilogy, *Childhood, Boyhood, Youth* offered Dostoyevsky perhaps not a model, since the work was basically autobiographical in spite of the 'bizarre mixture of events' in the childhood of the friends of the young Tolstoy and his own childhood, but at least some elements of psychology and even of composition.[15] Secondly, *War and Peace* and *A Raw Youth* are both about the Russian noble family. *War and Peace* shows its glory and its epic greatness: *A Raw Youth* shows its disintegration and its wreck as it becomes a 'family of chance'. On this point the last pages of *A Raw Youth* and a variant where Versilov talks of his favourite novelist, Tolstoy,[16] are particularly revealing: on one side there is the age that has gone, beauty and order; on the other, a formless future, a new beauty to be discovered, 'chaos and general disorder'.[17] In *Diary of a Writer*, July–August 1877, Dostoyevsky summed up his ideas in a few lines:

Never has our Russian family been more shaken, more decomposed, more separated, or more amorphous than it is today. Where could you now find a 'Childhood' and a 'Boyhood' which could be recreated in a story as harmonious and truthful as that, for example, in which Count Leo Tolstoy told us of his times and his family, or as War and Peace by the same author. These poems today are only historical pictures from the distant past. Oh, I do not mean to say that they are such enchanting pictures, I certainly don't want to go back there from our time, that isn't my idea at all. I am only speaking of their character, of their finished, clear and definite qualities, which enable a description of the time to be as clear and luminous as it is in the two poems of Count Tolstoy. There is nothing like this today, nothing defined, nothing clear. The modern Russian family is becoming more and more a family of chance. Yes, a family of chance, that is the definition of the Russian family of our day.[18]

In *A Raw Youth* Dostoyevsky issued a double challenge to Tolstoy. Basically, 'not wishing to write only in the historical way and obsessed with passion for the present day',[19] he was challenging the 'historian of the Russian nobility, the psychologist of the noble soul',[20] treacherously praised by Versilov in the unpublished variant. Formally, he was replying to the ideal of clear and harmonious beauty in the Tolstoy epic by affirming the possibility of a new aesthetics which could express modern chaos and complexity.[21] This was, roughly speaking, the visible literary dialogue which Dostoyevsky pursued with his most famous contemporary Russian rivals, although he was also constantly referring to minor writers and masters of the past.

But while he was struggling to deliver the novel, Dostoyevsky was conducting another invisible dialogue with two great masters of the Russian novel, both poets, Pushkin and Lermontov. Their novels, *Tales of the late Ivan Petrovich Belkin* (1831) and *A Hero of our Time* (1840), dominate the search for composition in the novels of Dostoyevsky.

The architectonics of Lermontov

The composition of every novel focuses on two main problems: the structure of the narrative and the choice of narrator. These two closely linked aspects set a limit to Dostoyevsky's polyphony, since they form the voice of the author, which has been so unjustly devalued, and his judgement of the hero.

Leonid Grossman was the first to mention Dostoyevsky's fascination with the 'architectonics' of Lermontov's famous novel.[22] *A Hero of Our Time* is composed of five parts, which, due to a double chronological movement in time, seem to fly and pursue each other like the parts of a fugue.[23] As B. M. Eykhenbaum says:

A Hero of our Time is a cycle of novellas grouped round a hero, a very important point which distinguishes this work from all the collections and cycles of stories common in the literature of the thirties. To achieve this psychological cyclisation and make it aesthetically convincing, the old ways of linking the stories had to be abandoned and a new method had to be found to make the whole composition of the cycle perfectly natural and motivated. This is what Lermontov did: he detached the author from the hero and distributed his stories according to a logic motivated not only by the succession of narrators (as it is in Bestuzhev), but also by a progressive growth of awareness about the life and personality of the hero: from the first description, which the reader receives second-hand (it is the author of 'Bela' who retells Maxim Maximych's narrative), the reader passes to a description which is direct, although made by the author from his oblique observations ... after this 'plastic' preparation, the reader is given the possibility of judging the hero by the memoirs he leaves behind him.[24]

Belinsky remarked on the originality of this novel: he mentioned the distribution of parts 'according to internal necessity'. If the reader did not follow the order fixed by the author, the novel would disintegrate into a collection of short stories. Apollon Grigoryev's article in *Time* said that the various elements of the novel were 'fused by the powerful and imperious hand of Lermontov'.[25] The double composition creates the impression of length of time and complexity which is indispensable for the novel, and also introduces the reader progressively into the universe of the hero, moving from the most external impression to the most inner, even introspective, look at the 'history of a human soul', as Lermontov himself expressed it.

Dostoyevsky must have been impressed by this structure of separate narratives grouped round a hero who could be approached either through the author retelling the narrative of a witness, or through the direct witness and narrator, or through the character himself in his direct written confession. Wishing to discover the 'mystery of man', Dostoyevsky would find here both the means of penetrating this mystery and the form in which it could be incarnated.

From the beginning to the end of his literary career, Dostoyevsky had dreamt of a novel composed in several parts, usually in five, publishable separately but grouped around a central hero. *Netochka Nezvanova* was to have been a novel in six parts and in the journal where it was published in 1849 it was called 'History of a Woman' in three parts: 'Childhood', 'A New Life', 'The Secret'. The political drama, prison and the army cut this attempt short. But in June 1857 Dostoyevsky returned to his dream. In a letter to Ye. I. Yakushkin, he says he is writing a work of 'the size of the novels of Dickens':[26] 'It is a long novel, the adventures of a character, united by an unbroken link but consisting of episodes which are finished in themselves and distinct from each other. Each episode forms one part. So that I can very well publish each episode separately.'[27] Dostoyevsky claimed to have written only the first of the three books which were to make up this novel: the two others were to be given later 'although they were the continuation of the adventures of the said character, but in another form and mode, and a few years later [in his life]'.[28] A. S. Dolinin suggested that this referred to *The Village of Stepanchikovo*, but the existence of two heroes, Foma Opiskin and Colonel Rostanev, in this novel invalidates the hypothesis. In fact, this Lermontovian project had nothing to do with *The Village of Stepanchikovo*, Dostoyevsky's last passage of arms with Gogol. It was one of the connections, between the period before and after prison, of the great underground creative line, or in other words the missing link between *Netochka Nezvanova* and 'The Life of a Great Sinner', the works in which Dostoyevsky's dream of the novel of a life had been partly realised. On 18 January 1856, Dostoyevsky had already confided to A. N. Maykov that he had long cherished in prison, beside the future *House of the Dead*, a great novel, his final work, that he had already composed it 'in his head', but, feeling that he was ill-prepared for it, did not wish to rush into the work without consideration, as it 'required several years of development' and, finally distracted from his task by his love-affair, he had become resigned to never writing it.[29]

His letter to Yakushkin in June 1857 is simply the resurrection of this plan. Had Dostoyevsky begun to write even the first part of the enormous novel? His correspondence leaves this in doubt. Probably he had only reached the stage of the 'heart's awareness'. He had a true passion for the project; he lied to himself as he lied to others, plagued as he was by an urgent need for money. Asking Katkov of the *Russian Messenger* for an advance, he declared on 11 January 1858:

I conceived my novel at leisure while I was in Omsk. When I left Omsk three years ago, I was able to get pen and paper and immediately set to work. But I did not rush, I liked thinking it all out to the last detail, composing and balancing the parts, noting whole scenes in their entirety and especially gathering the materials.[30]

Up to this point Dostoyevsky was telling the truth, repeating what he had already told his brother Mikhail in a previous letter.[31] But the rest about the actual writing of the novel is less assured. Reserves and reticences abound. He has not grown cold towards the work, but on the contrary become more passionate, though he had only just set to work last May. Almost all the first book and a part of the second have already been written in rough, but in spite of that he still could not finish the first book, though, however, work was going on without interruption. Once more he stressed the originality of the composition: 'My novel is divided into three books, but each book (although it could be divided in parts, I indicate only the chapters) . . . is in itself completely distinct from the others.'[32] It was all obviously untrue. Dostoyevsky had announced two months earlier, on 3 November 1857, in a letter to his brother Mikhail, who was asking for the first 'already written' part of the novel, that he had been overcome by doubts and was abandoning it. He softened the bad news with embarrassed justifications about the need not to hurry, not to publish anything unfinished, not to treat art lightly, and concluded: 'This is why the whole novel, with all its materials, is packed in a drawer.'[33] On 18 January 1858, a week after his letter to Katkov, he confirmed that he had definitely abandoned the novel, in a letter to Mikhail:

I am leaving my novel (the big one) for a time. I cannot finish in time! It would simply wear me out. Even so it has worn me out. I am leaving it until the time when my life is calm and settled. This novel is so dear to me, so much part of myself, that I will not give it up for anything. On the contrary, I intend to make it my chef-d'oeuvre. The idea is too good and it has cost me too much for me to give it up altogether.[34]

Nevertheless the novel was not simply a delusion. It was very much alive in the creative imagination of its author, who described it to his brother when they met in Tver at the end of August 1859. On 21 September 1859, Mikhail wrote a valuable letter to Fyodor, which allows us to guess what this novel of a life, with its Lermontovian structure, might have been like:

Here you are, hesitating between two novels, and I am afraid that a lot of time will be wasted in hesitation. Why did you tell me the subject? Maykov once told me, long ago, that if you once told the story of a subject, you would never write it down. My dear, perhaps I am wrong, but your two great novels will be something like the Lehrjahre und Wanderungen of Wilhelm Meister. So if they are written as Wilhelm Meister was, in sections, gradually, over the years, they will be as good as the two novels of Goethe.[35]

Understanding his brother's motives, Mikhail was to become almost an accomplice of his incautious boasting. On 26 October 1859, Mikhail said that he had had an interview with the editor Krayevsky and had praised this long novel, saying that Fyodor had read him extracts from it. He slipped in a conniving postscript: 'It seems you haven't begun anything.'[36] In fact, on 9 October Dostoyevsky told him that he had 'destroyed' his novel,[37] but in the same letter he developed another project which is prophetic of *Notes from Underground* in its aesthetic conception, and which appears, as the allusion to the passionate element proves, to be one of the parts of the 'great novel' transformed, diverging in the same way as *The Devils* later diverges compared with 'The Life of a Great Sinner':

In December I shall begin a novel ... Do you remember I spoke to you about a 'confession' ... It has become joined to the novel (the passionate element) I told you about. First, it will make an effect, and secondly, I have put all my heart's blood into it. I thought of it in prison, lying on my bunk, in hours of sadness and despair. It is naturally divided into about three novels (the different times of life), each novel of about a dozen printed pages. In March–April I shall publish the first in some journal. The effect will be stronger than that of Poor Folk (by a long way!) and Netochka Nezvanova ... A Confession will finally make my fame certain.[38]

The Lermontovian project was temporarily abandoned. It was to be reborn later in the project of 'The Life of a Great Sinner', planned in five parts, and then to be embodied in *The Brothers Karamazov*, of which, if we can believe Suvorin, we possess only the first part.[39]

This composition inspired by Lermontov, so obsessive in the underground line of creation, also affected the work actually done. The notebooks of *The Devils* are full of allusions to Pechorin with reference to Stavrogin or even Liza,[40] and the spirit of Lermontov's structure is present, although the formal architectonics of *A Hero of Our Time* is not. As with Lermontov's hero, the approach of the mysterious Stavrogin is gradual and announced by many voices. At the beginning he is described by the narrator–chronicler, who makes wide use of gossip and the Shakespearean metaphors of Stepan Trofimovich; then Varvara Petrovna conducts her own inquiry, Captain Lebyadkin lets out a few ambiguous words; and at this point Pyotr Stepanovich tells his own version. Finally the hero himself appears and is described only in scenes and action. His mystery is gradually unveiled by the observation of other people, the three women who love him, and the three men who, each in his own way, have taken up his ideas. Finally Stavrogin reveals himself in his writings: the confessional document which he makes Tikhon read, and, since this confession was not accepted by the editor, its substitute, the letter to Dasha. There is the same double chronological structure in *The Devils* as in *A Hero of Our Time*: first, an action which takes place during a precise length of time, and second, the 'history of a human soul', a kind of hero of his time, into which the reader is introduced gradually and progressively first by the incomplete and complementary biographies given by the chronicler and by Pyotr Stepanovich, which form flashbacks, then by the successive explanations of Stavrogin's old theories, now resurrected by Kirillov, Shatov, and Pyotr Stepanovich, and finally by Stavrogin's own writings, which are a substitute for Pechorin's diary.

The chronicler in Pushkin

The contribution of Lermontov to the composition of Dostoyevsky's novels has been little noticed, but numerous critics have analysed the relationship between Dostoyevsky and Pushkin. Every one of Dostoyevsky's works, and examples have been given here, lives and breathes Pushkin. D. D. Blagoy, in a recent article 'Dostoyevsky and Pushkin', has made a rich synthesis, adding his own discoveries and correcting some errors, of about seventy studies on this theme.[41]

However, he devoted only a few words to the fundamental question of composition, and this with regard to *The Devils*: 'In the narrator, the character who relates the strange happenings which form the contents of the novel, we can see the features of Pushkin's hero, Ivan Petrovich Belkin (which, by the way, could be seen earlier, to some extent, in the narrator of *The Insulted and Injured* who is in fact called Ivan Petrovich).'[42] Here Blagoy skimmed over a major problem of composition which, as the notebooks from 'The Life of a Great Sinner' to *The Brothers Karamazov* show, Dostoyevsky always set himself with reference to Pushkin and in particular to the *Tales of the late Ivan Petrovich Belkin*, to which must be added *History of the town of Goryukhino*, containing Belkin's auto-biography.

In the cycle of tales, the late Ivan Petrovich Belkin is a mask for Pushkin: stylistically the prose is that of the author. Belkin appears only in a letter to the author from one of his friends. In the chronicle of the town of Goryukhino, his style and his life assume a definite character. He is an officer who has retired to his estates and leads a calm and modest existence, without much education (his favourite book is a popular *Manual of Literature*) and without much imagination, although he has a mania for writing, without much ability to manage his estates and with an indulgence towards his serfs, who swindle him, which his neighbours consider blame-worthy; in short, he is a simple man devoid of intellectual qualities, but good at heart. This worthy soul is a merciless recorder of facts; he writes down everything, tragic, burlesque, comic, historical, trivial, everyday events, weather reports and social drama: here and there he inserts naive opinions which are a joy to the readers, besides making them think about the condition of the serfs. He is the ingenuous archivist and the compassion-ate poet of this little world, which he knows inside out.

Dostoyevsky admired Belkin's simplicity of soul, and his irresponsibility.

The chronicler clumsily stumbles into the heart of the reader, exposing scandalous dramas and country festivities with the same fearless pen; he is determined to understand everything, surprised at nothing, he follows events in detail and involuntarily makes one think. For Belkin, who has the modesty of someone who knows how little he knows, abstains from judgement. He collects facts, but there is a great deal he does not know. He is the direct observer and assents to his background. In this sense, he is the opposite of the serene Pimen in *Boris Godunov*.

Belkin's roots in the land, his perfect knowledge of his environment, which is 'transparent as a glass roof',[43] and his inability to distance himself from it, in short, his meticulous shortsightedness, was naturally appealing to Dostoyevsky, who, even as early as *Poor Folk*, prided himself on not showing, as he jokingly said, 'his mug as an author'[44] and who had always, on aesthetic principles, refused to play God as the writer. A chronicler like Belkin allows the writer to tell the story without saying everything outright, to multiply reticences, reservations, surreptitious hints, dissimulations, deliberate concealment by an author trying to keep an atmosphere of uncertainty. As N. N. Chirkov said:

Dostoyevsky never fails to show us that there is a good deal unexplained in the action of the hero, while he gives us various explanations for this action. One of his procedures is to leave something unsaid [*nedogovorennost'*] when he represents the movements of the hero's soul. From this point of view, narrative in the first person is a very convenient form. The narrator, as opposed to the omniscient author, cannot know everything.[45]

There was another characteristic in Belkin which attracted Dostoyevsky: his vagueness and inconsistency which allowed the author – and Pushkin could rarely resist this – to slide into his place without the reader being able to guess whether it was the chronicler or the author who was speaking. This resulted in what D. S. Likhachov called 'stereoscopic vision' (*stereoskopichnost'*),[46] the simultaneous presence of two observers; the shortsighted one, the chronicler, always trailing behind and bustling about on behalf of someone or other, but always finally surprised, lost and overtaken by events; and the author, who has taken the high ground and is judging from his own point of view. The author and narrator are no longer distinct, just as there is no distinct hero.[47]

The Dostoyevskian chronicler in The Devils

The chronicler is the vaguest and most elusive character in this novel. The rare pieces of information about him are scattered so subtly throughout the book that they are easily forgotten. He is called Anton Lavrentyevich G-v, and is an official, but no one tells us where. Liputin is more forthcoming about him: 'He is a young man with a classical education and relatives in high society.'[48] One thing is certain: he is the irritated confidant ('out of boredom') of Stepan Trofimovich, the former great man who likes to think he has been banished and 'rises as a reproach incarnate towards his fatherland'. All these elements, his part as a confidant and therefore as an intimate member of the small gossiping and liberal circle around Stepan Trofimovich, his profession, his links with high society, show his omnipresence and his knowledge of everything and everybody. As a provincial chronicler he is also at the receiving end of all the gossip and rumour flying through the town, which he compares with what he sees. He is an ever-open sympathetic ear and he is the shortsighted eye of the informer.

We know enough about his ideas to guess which side he is on. He is a man whose 'eyes have been unsealed' and who has denied his past errors, or his adherence to Western liberalism. Nothing is known about his feelings, except that he was once in love with Liza. His passion is supposed to have died out, but the old jealousy is still smouldering as he watches Liza and the other women fascinated by Stavrogin, the 'subtle serpent'.

Although a spiritualist might describe him as ectoplasm, the chronicler remains 'one discourse among many discourses', to quote Bakhtin.[49] However, Bakhtin has not stressed the essential ambiguity of this voice. The chronicler has his opinions and judgements, but he is strictly obedient to the novelist, or rather to the directives defined by the novelist in the notebooks. His voice is subject to the creative design. When Dostoyevsky, for example, makes it a rule not to explain Stavrogin but to reveal him gradually in action, whereas Stepan Trofimovich is explained all the time,[50] the chronicler is his devoted servant, although from time to time, like an old family retainer, he voices his own opinion. The variations which fall from his lips sometimes express the personal opinions of the insignificant, conformist and servile character of the chronicler in the novel, and sometimes the judgement of the novelist. The frontiers between them are often vague and shifting: this is the fertile ambiguity of the stereoscopic vision. We can illustrate this best by a brief review of the tones used by the chronicler when he refers to the other characters. Anton Lavrentyevich is hypocritically obsequious towards Stepan Trofimovich, whom he overwhelms with treacherous praise, but gradually Dostoyevsky, who 'loves his Stepan Trofimovich',[51] detaches him from the perfidious observation of the chronicler by sending him off on the great journey, away from the diabolical whirlwind of the town, into the redeeming intensity of the Russian Land. And by his own admission the chronicler is amazed when he hears about it; he remains at the level of his own mediocrity. While he carries out a blunt and brutal execution of Liputin, one of Pyotr Verkhovensky's accomplices in the murder of Shatov, his severity towards Virginsky, the Fourierist, has a tinge of understanding. Dostoyevsky, himself a former Fourierist, has prompted him to leniency. Towards the theoretician Shigalyov, to whom

Dostoyevsky is relatively merciful, sparing him direct connection with the murder, Anton Lavrentyevich is pitiless; he is Flaubert's bourgeois, so terrified by Utopia that he becomes cruel. On the other hand, the chronicler's hatred for the Jew Lyamshin, whom he charges with all crimes and all cowardice, reflects Dostoyevsky's deep-rooted anti-Semitism.[52] Similarly, the chronicler's bitter compassion for Erkel, the young fanatic who has strayed into the conspiracy and is faithful to Pyotr Verkhovensky to the end, is explained by Dostoyevsky's tendency to absolve the young who have wandered into nihilism out of generosity of mind. The chronicler shows more intuition than the author about Pyotr Verkhovensky-Nechayev. At the beginning Dostoyevsky had imagined a comic character such as Khlestakov. The provincial Anton Lavrentyevich immediately realised that young Verkhovensky's clowning was only a smoke-screen. He takes him seriously and passionately denounces his plots. Another good example of stereoscopic vision is the case of the writer Karmazinov, whom Dostoyevsky caricatures savagely. The account of the meeting is given by the chronicler, who, like Belkin, is making fun of himself and taking revenge for his own naivety by an attack on the celebrity's appearance. But the introductory remarks about 'second-class writers' certainly belong to Dostoyevsky, who is openly settling his score with Turgenev.[53] Here the chronicler is the menial henchman who inherits Dostoyevsky's own sympathies and antipathies.

But it is quite different when the chronicler is faced with the great heroes of the idea: Stavrogin, Shatov and Kirillov. He is lost and becomes more and more shortsighted, a pure reporter of facts. Shatov is seen from outside; he exists independently of the chronicler, who sets down his awkward and ridiculous features but never manages to scale the wall of silence with which Shatov confronts him. Kirillov remains an enigma; as V. A. Tunimanov has said: 'The true Kirillov shows himself in his meetings with Stavrogin, Pyotr Verkhovensky and Shatov. The chronicler is absent from all these scenes in dialogue.'[54] Finally, while the chronicler is passionately interested in Stavrogin, he is completely incapable of understanding him. His eyes blur because he is staring so hard. It does no good to note external signs such as pallor, look, smile, and gestures so carefully, to measure chronicle time to the nearest minute and second, to collect different opinions from other observers, to say he knows a good deal about Stavrogin; he stays well to the rear of events and even gets totally lost when the second part of the novel begins. The essence of Stavrogin, in conformity with the rules Dostoyevsky has set himself, is shown in his actions and attitudes when faced with danger (Shatov's blow, the duel), love (the cripple, Liza, Dasha) and the great ideas that rule men's actions (Shatov, Kirillov, Pyotr Stepanovich).

The fact that Dostoyevsky has chosen a chronicler with a venomous tongue, completely different from Pushkin's good-natured Belkin, does not change the principle of composition. The narrator with his limited viewpoint and sympathetic ever-open ear preserves the suspiciousness, the reticence, the approximation and also the hypocritical freedom of the novelist, who intervenes without admitting his intervention as an author, and judges without signing his judgement. This is hypocrisy in the basic sense of the word, that is, acting a part, a paradox of the creator, who sometimes appears by the chronicler's side or behind him as he bustles about at the front of the stage. The form which was embryonic in Pushkin became such an elaborate procedure in Dostoyevsky that the novelist thought of the numerous confessions in his works not as real confessions but as chronicles in which the hero as chronicler is always standing a pace behind the person confessing.

The hot-press chronicle

The story of Dostoyevsky's creation of the novel illustrates his tendency to place the chronicle close in time to the events chronicled – the annalist is either a witness or the main hero – and to compose it in the form of memoirs (*zapiski*). These memoirs are not intimate diaries, soliloquies by lone and introspective spirits such as Henri-Frédéric Amiel, or confessions like those of Jean-Jacques Rousseau or Michel Leiris, moving from self-examination to exhibitionism, or 'stripping' (*zagalivaniye*)[55] as Dostoyevsky called it in the notebooks for *A Raw Youth*, or memoirs like those of Chateaubriand or Malraux, who are writing ostensibly as philosophers, historians and politicians. They are notes defined as non-literary, amateur memoirs by writers who, though they do not despise established literature and the art of writing,[56] are always asking the reader to excuse their clumsiness, ignorance and chaotic composition. Dostoyevsky went further than Pushkin in this direction. Belkin, inspired by a love for literature, only writes the chronicle of the town of Goryukhino after he has honestly and humbly examined his own ability and measured the abyss which divides him from professional writers. The Dostoyevskian chronicler, often more cultured, says he is avoiding 'literary beauties' and 'all that literature rubbish' (*literaturshchina*). He thinks of himself as a cut-price writer, who takes up his pen on occasion to relate an event he happened to witness or a critical stage in his own life.

There is one exception: Ivan Petrovich in *The Insulted and Injured*, a professional writer whose first long novel, the twin brother of Dostoyevsky's own *A Raw Youth*, was very successful.[57] But when he is writing his journal (the novel *The Insulted and Injured*) a year after the events – a chronicle close in time – he is an invalid trying to cheat death and boredom in a hospital bed by noting down the story of Natasha and Nelli. In despair, expecting no more from this life, he is indifferent about his readers, and will leave his papers to the orderly, who 'can at least stick them round the windows when the winter shutters are put up'.[58]

Dostoyevsky might be accused of depreciating the man of letters so as to avoid reproaches of prolixity or overloaded composition, which he received even from his friends, but this would be unjust, for in Dostoyevsky's mind the chronicle form was always associated with the idea of rapidity, concision, and strong simplicity 'in the manner of Pushkin'. The refusal to write 'literature' stresses the inexperience of the chronicler and his foreshortened view of events, and, where he is the hero of his own narrative, his misunderstanding of himself. This is how *A Raw Youth* begins:

Unable to stand it any longer, I am starting to write this history of my first steps on the path of life, though I could well have done without it. One thing I know for certain: I shall never start writing my autobiography again, even if I live to be a hundred. You have to be too disgustingly in love with yourself to write about yourself without shame. I can only make the excuse that I am not writing for the same reason as every one else, that is, not for praise from the reader. If I suddenly took it into my head to note down word for word everything that has happened to me since last year, I thought of it because of inner necessity: I was so staggered by all that happened. I am only noting down events, doing my best to avoid everything irrelevant, and especially literary beauties; a man of letters writes for thirty years and at the end of it he doesn't know why he's been writing for so long. I am not a man of letters, I don't want to be a man of letters and I should consider it indecent and vulgar to hawk the inside of my soul and a beautiful description of my feelings around their literary market. It annoys me, though, to feel that some description of feelings and some observations (perhaps even vulgar ones) will probably be unavoidable.[59]

The Youth suggests to the reader that he is not writing a narcissistic confession or a literary work, but an honest chronicle by himself and for himself. The imperious need to write is explained without a real explanation, as the Youth simply recalls the strong impression and the effect produced. Interest is guaranteed. This brief preface assures the reader that he will not be served with a carefully prepared piece of literature, but with a slice of life, a page of truth with its mystery preserved. This is Dostoyevsky's great strength as a novelist: the reader is invited not to be the passive spectator of a play put on by the omniscient novelist, but to be the chronicler's companion, sharing his search amid doubt and sometimes mystery for a truth which is by nature imperfect.

There is a double movement: 'the man of letters' is depreciated and the reader becomes the equal of the chronicler. But since Dostoyevsky is controlling his chronicler, sometimes slipping into his place, unceremoniously turning him out on many occasions such as dialogue scenes, where the chronicler is absent or simply an automatic recorder, and adding ironic chapter headings in *The Devils* or *The Brothers Karamazov*, the reader is on privileged terms, as he receives more information than the narrator.

Dostoyevsky, while keeping his own creative freedom, gives the reader freedom to make his own judgement.

Composition in chronicle form from Poor Folk to The Brothers Karamazov

Composition giving preference to chronicle time was a constant in Dostoyevsky's work, and especially in his creative research. Even the first novel *Poor Folk* (1846), in spite of Dostoyevsky's concession to the letter form of sentimentalism, is in fact an intersecting chronicle, very close to events, where the two heroes set down the events which overwhelmed their souls, unable to master time as it rushes towards catastrophe: at one point they write to each other as much as twice a day. The imaginary author of 'Mr Prokharchin' describes himself as a 'biographer'.

The sub-titles of the following works need no commentary: 'An Honest Thief, fragment of anonymous memoirs' (1848); 'A Christmas Tree and a Wedding, fragment from anonymous memoirs' (1848); 'White Nights, a sentimental novel, extracts from the memories of a dreamer' (1848); *Netochka Nezvanova, history of a woman* (1849);[60] 'A Little Hero, fragment from the chronicle of Mordasov' (1859);[61] *The Village of Stepanchikovo, fragment from anonymous memoirs* (1859).

In the sixties, it was no longer the sub-titles which were revealing but the titles, with the exception of *The Gambler, a novel, fragment of the memoirs of a young man* (1866). The chronicle became a rule. Two words are used for it: *zapiski*, which is variously translated as memoirs, stories, memories, writings, but which means 'notes taken', a clumsy formula which stresses its authenticity, its lack of planning, and its margin of error; and *zametki* (remarks) often translated as reflections, which stresses the rambling form and the effort to understand reality. In 1861–2, there are *Notes [zapiski] from the House of the Dead*, in 1863 *Winter Notes [zametki] on Summer Impressions*, an article in *Time*, and in 1864 *Notes [zapiski] from Underground*. Every time, particularly in the first and last of these works, Dostoyevsky set a radical distance between the chronicler and the actual author, besides stressing the incomplete and fortuitous nature of the chronicle.

In *The House of the Dead* there are two intermediaries between author and reader.[62] A young official meets a life exile, Alexander Petrovich Goryanchikov, a mysterious creature, sensitive and touchy. He is an educated noble who has been condemned to prison for the murder of his wife. The narrator is absent for a time, and on his return he learns that Goryanchikov, who intrigued him so much and confided nothing to him, is dead. The ex-convict has left a bundle of papers. The narrator buys them, although two notebooks are missing:

I carried off his papers and spent a whole day sorting them out. Three-quarters of these papers were empty, meaningless scraps or writing exercises for his pupils. But there was also a fairly voluminous exercise book, in small handwriting and unfinished, perhaps thrown out and forgotten by its author. It was a description, though incoherent, of the ten years which Aleksandr Petrovich had endured as a convict. In places this description was interrupted by some other story, some strange horrible memories, sketched unevenly, convulsively, as if by some kind of compulsion. I read over these extracts several times and was almost convinced that they had been written in madness. But the notes [*zapiski*] from convict prison – Scenes from the House of the Dead, – as he himself calls them somewhere in his manuscript, seemed to me not entirely devoid of interest.[63]

In *Notes from Underground*, the composition is more subtle. The order is reversed. The book begins as a confession by the author and it is only at the end of the first part that the reader realises that the narrator is not the writer. The passage on confession to oneself tallies with the preliminary declaration of the hero of *A Raw Youth*:

Is it possible even with oneself to be completely sincere and not fear the whole truth? I note by the way: Heine asserts that faithful autobiographies are almost impossible, and a man will most likely lie about himself. In his opinion, Rousseau, for instance, certainly lied about himself in his confession, and even lied deliberately, out of vanity. I am certain that Heine is right; I remember very well that sometimes simply from vanity you can nail real crimes on yourself, and I can even understand perfectly what kind of vanity this may be. But Heine was judging the man who makes his confession in public.[64] I am writing just for myself and I here state once and for all that if I am writing as if I were addressing readers, it is only for show, because it is easier for me to write like this. This is a form, simply an empty form,[65] there will never be any readers for me. I have already made this clear . . .

I do not wish to be tied in any way as I set down my notes. I shall not introduce any order and system. I shall simply write down what comes to mind.[66]

Notes from Underground ends unambiguously; it was an interrupted chronicle: 'But that's enough; I don't want to write any more "from Underground"' . . . 'However the "notes" of this paradoxalist do not end here. He could not bear it and went on. But we also think that this is the place to stop.'[67] The *I* of the anti-hero of *Notes from Underground* is opposed by the *We* of the author, who cannot be identified with his character.

This form of chronicle, the confession to oneself, quite different from the public and literary confession,[68] does not appear in the final version of *Crime and Punishment*, but there is no doubt of Dostoyevsky's original intention. In the first notebook, the second by Anna Grigoryevna's numeration,[69] dated August–October 1865, four printed sheets give an almost definitive, though shortened text, which is usually called 'Raskolnikov's Diary', although at this stage the hero only has a Christian name: Vasiliy (Vasya, Vasyuk). It is an incomplete form of 'the novella' which Dostoyevsky had offered to Katkov, editor of *The Russian Messenger*, in September 1865.[70] In this first short version, Dostoyevsky had clearly chosen to give a chronicle of the crime by the criminal himself:

16 June. Two nights ago I began to describe and sat for four hours at a stretch. It will be a document . . .[71]

These sheets will never be found in my room. My window ledge lifts up slightly, and nobody knows this. It has been lifting up for a long time and I have known for a long time. In case of need it can be lifted and put back so that if someone else moves it, it won't lift up again. Besides, it won't occur to anyone. I've hidden everything there under the windowsill.[72]

This is not a confession but a document for strictly personal use, an account given shortly after the event, with a mixture of exactness and confusion. The first page illustrates this perfectly. The murderer has come home after the crime:

Remembering now in detail everything which happened *there*, I see that I have almost forgotten not only how I came through the streets, but also which streets I came through. I only remember that I came home from a completely different direction. I still remember that moment when I got as far as A[scension] Avenue, but further on I can't remember very well. As if in a dream, I remember . . .[73]

In fact Dostoyevsky was hesitating: he envisaged a story as well as a diary[74] covering six chapters, in which the hero had to 'write, speak and appear to the reader partly as if he had lost his mind'.[75] Wavering between chronicle and confession,[76] he solved the problem in the second notebook (no. 1) of October–December 1865. Here there was a more complete version entitled 'In court' and very close to the final version although still written in the first person.[77] There is a greater length of time between the crime and its description. The chronicle fades away to be replaced by complete confession: 'I am being accused and I will tell everything. I will write everything. I am writing for myself but others can read it and all my judges, if they want to. This is a confession. I will hide nothing.'[78] The contradiction between a confession written for oneself which others were free to read, a confession which would hide nothing but which had to convey all the motives, even unconscious ones, for the crime, embarrassed Dostoyevsky. He tried to find a different angle: 'NB. Second part. Confession, story of the murder: "I did not expect that myself", and all the time of the story, there follows as it were amazement at himself, as if it were amazement from someone else.'[79] This detachment from the hero's observation of himself and the need to 'get rid of vagueness'[80] led Dostoyevsky to set the crime further back in time. A new plan appeared:

The story of the criminal
8 years ago
(So as to place him completely outside)
It happened exactly eight years ago and I want to tell it all in order.[81]

Dostoyevsky carried his logic to its limits and resolved the problem in his final version. He first increased the time lapse between crime and narrative, which was originally supposed to be written five days after the murder, then at the time of accusation, then eight years after; and then substituted a distancing in observation by making the narrator the author, rather than the criminal: 'Story from the author, as if unseen, but all knowing, not leaving him for a moment, even with the words: "and all this happened so unexpectedly"'[82] And Dostoyevsky explained to himself the reasons for abandoning the chronicle-confession:

Go over all the questions in this novel. This is what the subject is like. *Story from my own point of view and not from his.* If it is a confession, then it is too much *to the last extremity*, must explain everything. Each moment of the story must be clear.
NB. *For consideration.* Using confession at some points would not be modest and it would be difficult to imagine why it was written.
But from *the author.* Too much naivety and frankness is needed.
Must first suppose the author *omniscient* and *infallible*, setting out in the sight of all one of the members of the new generation.[83]

The author's observation was needed to tell the detailed story of the fatal entwinement of connections and meetings, to gather the many motives together, especially the subconscious ones, and most of all to show the beginning of the punishment before the crime was committed. In fact, the time of chronicle, of uncertainty has left many traces in *Crime and Punishment*, for instance, in the frequent soliloquies of Raskolnikov and the alternation of moments of awareness with long hours of unconsciousness, lit by dreams.[84]

Dostoyevsky also renounced *Icherzählung* in *The Idiot*, where he unhesitatingly adopted the form of narrative by the author. However, the absence of a chronicler does not imply that chronicle time does not exist in the novel. The novelist in his own name is filling the apparent gaps imposed by chronicle form, which are in reality the ways in which truth is sought. First, he gives a favoured place to the rumours at the beginning of the second part, when Myshkin is away for six months. Then, in his notebooks, he gives himself a direct order: 'Write more briefly; just facts; without comments and without descriptions of sensations'[85] and he tries to write as instructed: 'We admit that we are going to describe strange adventures. As it is difficult to explain them, we shall confine ourselves to fact.'[86] Imitating the clumsiness typical of an amateur chronicler, he even accepts the charge of incompetence: 'However, agreed, people might say to us: All this is true, you are right, but you haven't been able to set out the affair, justify the facts, you're a bad artist ... But obviously we can't help that.'[87]

Dostoyevsky had already noted that the creative power of the chronicle was due not to the character of the chronicler but to his literary function. So in his last three great novels he deliberately chose the chronicle, clearly and strongly in *The Devils*, in the form of self-confession for *A Raw Youth*, discreetly and subtly in *The Brothers Karamazov*.

In this last novel, Dostoyevsky seems to be free from the problem of the simultaneous existence of chronicler and author. He introduces himself openly as the 'biographer' of his hero.[88] For the first time, author and chronicler are in alliance, even fused, though the stereoscopic vision does not lose its effectiveness. The chronicler is defined by the only element necessary for his foreshortened vision; he is an inhabitant of the small town where the action of *The Brothers Karamazov* takes place. His life has been reduced to its function. The symbiosis reigning between author and chronicler is expressed linguistically by the double pair: I/my hero (introduction to the novel) and I/our hero (the novel). The biographer novelist is more hagiographical and also more ironic, the chronicler biographer is more innocent and surprised. Both intervene with discretion. When the biographer needs to suggest the constant doubt, the whirlwind which overtakes him and the reticence of chronicle time, he appears as a provincial chronicler. The twelfth book of the novel begins as follows:

On the next day after the events I have described, at ten o'clock in the morning, the session of our local court opened and the trial of Dmitriy Karamazov began.

I shall say in advance and I shall say it insistently: I realise I am quite incapable of giving an account of everything that happened in court, not only as fully as is required, but even in the right order. I think if I had to remember and explain everything properly, it would need a whole book, and even a very large one. So please don't complain if I only give what struck me personally and what I specially remembered. I may have taken secondary events for the most important ones, and even left out the most striking necessary features.[89]

And later during the trial, when Katerina Ivanovna has a fit of hysterics and gives the court the famous letter which is to destroy Mitya, the chronicler plays his part of bewildered purveyor of facts, overtaken by events, to perfection: 'I repeat, it was difficult to follow all the details. Even now all this appears to me in such confusion.'[90]

Dostoyevsky's approach to this kind of composition is unknown, for the notebooks of *The Brothers Karamazov*, very fragmentary in what is left, are mute on this point. However there is an impression of ease, even of grace in this mastery of chronicle time, though this may be a false impression given by the absence of documents. Where they exist, as we have seen in *Crime and Punishment*, the choice of this precise form of narrative and its use is accompanied by interrogation, hesitation and second thoughts. The notebooks of *A Raw Youth* describe this long struggle in detail. They have another merit: they illuminate Dostoyevsky's debt to Pushkin in the field of composition.

18

Composition of the novel in
A Raw Youth: chronicle and stories

The tone and manner of telling the story are said to occur to the artist naturally. This is true, but sometimes you lose your way and have to look for them.

F. M. Dostoyevsky, *Letter to N. Strakhov, 9/21 October 1870*[1]

Research ends and writing begins

The novelist's research ended when he had defined the narrative form and chosen the narrator, in short, with the selection of a definite form of composition. The natural antinomy between thought and writing had been resolved: it was an end and a beginning.

It was an end, because this choice was made only after the appearance of totality, only after the idea of the novel had crystallised and been passionately tested by experiment, only after the ideal structure of the Dostoyevskian novel, with its explosion, dispersal and spatial development, reflecting the 'broad nature', and its rending of the human architecture, had been set in place, only after the main hero had been selected. The decision about composition did not mean that everything had been decided; on the contrary, the testing of the Idea of the novel by its final gestures and the precise distribution of secondary characters went on after the writing had begun. In the notebooks of *A Raw Youth*, Prince Sergey Sokolsky is a typical case; the first chapters had already been written, but Dostoyevsky still did not know the nature of his love affairs with the beautiful Akhmakova, the gentle Liza or the intriguer Anna Andreyevna, how he was going to die (suicide? madness?) or whether he was going to be a political spy. The destiny of the heroes, the plot, the *fabula* keep a margin of vagueness and of possibility, which is gradually defined as the writing goes on.

It was also a beginning, for the choice determined the final writing. The writing, or dictation of the novel only began when the composition was settled, although Dostoyevsky never gave up wondering about his choice. While he was working on the final novel he was still questioning the insufficiencies and difficulties implicit in his choice, and he invented processes of complementary composition to solve these problems.

Birth of the chronicle

The first pages of the notebooks of *A Raw Youth*, from February to July 1874, are entirely devoted to preliminary research, which has already been analysed. Dostoyevsky was not yet wondering about composition.

However, in the process of forming the characters and testing out the ideas, he spontaneously turned to polyphonic form: dialogue and immediate use of the voice of the hero. As soon as an idea or a psychological trait was noted down, the spoken word came to clothe them. It was a natural reflex in Dostoyevsky, who acted less like a classical dramatist than a modern director: he wrote his text and parts with the actors' help, and, after some guidance about the idea to be expressed, he forced them to make an improvised response.[2] These fragments of dialogue, marked out by 'he said', 'she said', 'conversation', or, more dramatically, 'he exclaims', 'he whispers', or, as in a play, by the simple indication of the actor's name, or by the usual inverted commas, form the key points where the characters themselves become aware of the idea. The hero is born of the word. His independent existence is formed through his speech. But the dialogue which frees the creature from his creator and forces him to explain himself implies that the narrative which surrounds him, the tissue of the novel into which he inserts himself, is written in the third person, in the author's name. Dostoyevsky was aware of this from the first draft: 'At the very beginning of the novel *tell the reader* about this and explain that this man of order and measure, the man of affairs has begun *to go astray* to general amazement.'[3]

On 11/23 July 1874 there was a major reversal: the main hero was not to be the predator, but the Youth, who was also to become his son. Only after this revolution did Dostoyevsky begin to ask himself questions about composition. First he questioned the viewpoint of the author and what he called the tone. He naturally referred to his long-term obsession, 'The Life of a Great Sinner', and to his first undoubted success, *Crime and Punishment*. The discreetly dithyrambic tone of the hagiographer is taken from the underground project; Versilov still has a visibly large part:

But the MAIN THING is to keep for the whole of the narrative the tone of HIS undoubted superiority to the youth and *everyone*, in spite of any comic features in HIM and HIS weaknesses, everywhere the reader must be made to feel in advance that a great idea is torturing HIM at the end of the novel and so justify the reality of HIS suffering.[4]

In the notebooks of *Crime and Punishment*, after trying chronicle in diary form, Dostoyevsky tried to keep the objective time of narrative by the author, who 'never leaves his hero for a moment'.[5] In August 1874, he proposed the same kind of composition for his future novel: 'In a word, do not leave for a minute the youth, the aroma of first youth, the poem.'[6]

But in mid August, he took the opposite track:

(12 August) *IMPORTANT SOLUTION OF THE PROBLEM* ... Write *in the first person.*
Begin with the word: *I.*
   'The confession of a great sinner, for himself'.
   I am nineteen and I am already a great sinner. After the disaster which struck me,
I want to note it down. For myself, after, many years later (and I shall live long), I
shall make better sense of all these facts, but this manuscript will be useful to me
then for self-knowledge and so on.
   Begin directly and *concisely.*[7]

A few lines further on, Dostoyevsky sketches out the beginning of *A Raw
Youth*:

'I am writing without style', or: 'I am writing, of course, without style, but only for
myself' or something like that. This is in the middle [of the novel]. Confession
extremely concise (learn from Pushkin). A great number of things left unsaid
[*nedoskazannosti*].[8]

In a few words Dostoyevsky has defined the mode he is going to use: the
chronicle structure, whose essential features are defined in a series of
valuable notes, stretching from August to October 1874.
   The first characteristic of this chronicle is its slight but necessary distancing of the time of action from the time of narrative. The hero wishes to be
simply a reporter, noting down the adventures he has just had almost as
soon as they happen, a naive annalist still overwhelmed by the tumult of the
passing storm. So Dostoyevsky tried to fix the precise lapse of time which
separates the relatively clearsighted narrative from the relatively uncom-
prehended action. As in *Crime and Punishment* the pendulum swings
between two extremes. About 26 August, Dostoyevsky chose a very short
lapse of time for his chronicle: the Youth is supposed to have written his
confession after his second term in prison.[9] On 2 September, he reacted and
increased the time lapse: 'The youth is writing four years after the event,
which explains why he is able to understand HIM, HIS idea etc.'[10] On 10
September, the pendulum swung back: 'If it is in the first person, if it is close
(three months), then the manuscript must bear the traces of a certain lack of
understanding [*neosmyslennost'*]. – If the youth has already lived through
this period, then if there is understanding the naivety is lost.'[11] The problem
was to combine the freshness of passion with the tranquillity of observation,
the fever of the event with analytical reflection on it, the perplexity of the
actor with the relative clarity of the writer's vision, all within a deliberately
equivocal time scheme. Dostoyevsky finally came to a decision and scribbled
the final solution in the margin: 'In the first person – signed and sealed.
Whatever happens. But the person writing is now writing a year after
events. Keep this in mind on every line.'[12] Before this final decision,
Dostoyevsky had thought of another approach which already involved a
time lapse of one year, to solve the problem of Versilov, who was tending to
overshadow the Youth in his plan:

The youth might have HIS posthumous memoirs and copy from them directly.

HIS memories. Now, when (a year later) everything is finished, I have HIS writing book. This, it seems, had been written *after everything* (i.e. in the Finale). It is not anything complete, but scenes, for instance, with Liza, HIS cursory remarks, and everything is unconnected.[13]

Dostoyevsky in this unused hypothesis was going back spontaneously to the use of memoirs or intimate diary, such as Pushkin has used in *Tales of Belkin* or Lermontov in 'Pechorin's Diary', and was introducing the same shortened time lapse between the moment of action and that of writing into Versilov's memoirs. It would have been a chronicle inside a chronicle.

The second characteristic of the chronicle in Dostoyevsky is to allow the 'hypocritical' freedom of the novelist full play, by means of stereoscopic vision. Dostoyevsky was careful not to speak in his own name, but he intended that the reader should share his own estimate of the hero. He imposed the tone, he inflected the voice of the youth as chronicler. He applied the rule he made in 'The Life of a Great Sinner'. At every moment, and on every line, the reader should be aware of the dominant idea, feel that the events place 'the future man' which the Youth, here an apprentice, is to become, 'on a pedestal'. The final triumph must be sensed in the midst of struggle and defeats. In short, the reader must hear, in among the thunderous and tragic chords of Versilov's dark tragedy, the lively clear pipe of the youthful chronicler, as orchestrated by the novelist. On 12 August 1874 Dostoyevsky turned to Pushkin, who had shown him the way in *Tales of Belkin*: 'So that the type of the youth *stands out* of its own accord (in *the clumsiness of the narrative*, and in "how good life is", and in the unusual seriousness of character. Artistry must help. But as in the tales of *Belkin*, Belkin himself is the most important thing, so here the youth is the main thing depicted).'[14] And, towards the end of August, he summed up his intention: 'In general in the character of the youth express all the warmth and humanity of the novel, all the warm passages (Iv. P. Belkin), make the reader grow to love him.'[15] For the whole of September 1874 and even until February 1875, Dostoyevsky kept on admonishing himself and calling himself to order:

Form, form! (simple narrative story; *à la* Pushkin).[16]

The tone is as follows. Story, for instance, of His relations with the princess . . . They parted enemies, and this is the position in which the youth came across the affair, etc. i.e. *à la* Pouchkine[17]

Write in order, more briefly, *à la* Pushkin[18]

Write more briefly (imitate Pushkin).[19]

and

NB. IN A PERFECT SWIFT STORY NARRATIVE IN THE PUSHKIN MANNER.'[20]

This reference to Pushkin's brevity may seem comic, but in fact Dostoyevsky was thinking less of Pushkin's laconic style than of his way of narrating the facts. He wanted to imitate the brusque and ingenuous simplicity of the reporter who tells us what has happened without worrying about artistic transitions. It must, he writes again, 'be more compressed, as compressed as possible'[21] and the plot must be developed 'in a terribly compressed, consistent, and unexpected way.'[22]

The sovereignty of the writer in the chronicle

To clarify our analysis, we have, like Dostoyevsky's chronicler, anticipated. In fact from mid August to mid September 1874 Dostoyevsky was considering the virtues and disadvantages of chronicle structure and only adopted it after long debate. The notes are also the technical diary of a writer questioning himself about his creation. While becoming more and more firmly attached to the *Icherzählung*, Dostoyevsky developed its counterpoint, direct narrative by the author, and it is from this dialectic confrontation of the two structures that he forged the original composition of the chronicle.

As soon as he came to adopt first person narrative, on 12 and 20 August, he was tempted to give it up. He envisaged a composition like that of *Crime and Punishment* and *The Idiot*:

If it is not the youth who is writing (*I*), then do it so as to cling to the youth as the hero and not leave him for the whole beginning of the novel, so that, for example, both the princess, and HE, and the environment of the aunts, and Dolgushin, and everything are described only to the extent (at first of course) *that they gradually affect the youth. It could come out beautifully*.[23]

On 26 August, in another swing of the pendulum, Dostoyevsky returned to his initial plan and tried to summarise the advantages of the hero's confession:

Think over first person narrative. Many advantages; much freshness, the part of the youth comes over more typically. More lovable. I shall manage better with the part, the personality, the essence of the personality . . .

His passion for stirring things up can be described more easily and typically, i.e., the passion for starting a blaze (comparison of the conspiracy against the princess with arson) . . .

Finally, description may be quicker and more condensed. Naive actions. Make the reader grow fond of the youth. If they like him, the novel will be read. If the youth does not succeed as a character, the novel will not succeed either.'[24]

On 27 August Dostoyevsky found another advantage: the unity of the novel. But the problem of tone came up again, in other words, the question of the effective exercise of the freedom of the novelist, of his trademark:

Think about this forcefully. // Colouring. Shall I bring out the character? If in first person, then there will certainly be more unity and less of *that* with which Strakhov reproached me, i.e. multitude of characters and subjects. But the style and tone of the youth? This style and tone may suggest the ending to the reader.[25]

On 31 August, Dostoyevsky stressed the undeniable advantages of factual and concise narrative which keeps the uncertainty of chronicle time:

Remark of 31 August . . .
The youth writes that in the explanation of facts he is bound to make mistakes, and therefore, as much as possible, wishes to confine himself to facts only.
   NB. 31 August. The factual account of the youth in the first person will certainly shorten the prolixity of the novel, *if I am able*.[26]

But at the same time he was still preoccupied with the almost hagiographic tone in which the voice of the novelist can be heard: 'PROBLEM. Towards the end of the first part the reader should sense in advance the importance of the ending (of the idea) and the further development of the thought of the novel.'[27] To suggest the cheerful tone of the chronicle, Dostoyevsky used a surprising simile: 'The youth must write everything (all the novel) as unexpectedly and originally as he does about frou-frou.'[28] On the next day, 1 September, he analysed the dissonances of this tone, which is organically linked with the character of the youth, and also with his own estimate of the hero: 'The tone of the notes is gloomy and naive. Sometimes naively ironical, but sincerely.'[29]

   2 September, the day after, Dostoyevsky was again doubtful, noting the disadvantages of his choice:

Two questions. If it is by the author, will it be interesting? By the youth (by I) it is naturally interesting. And more original. And the character is set out more clearly.
   By I or the author? . . .
   In the first person it is more original and there is more love, and more artistry is needed, and it is terribly daring, and shorter, and the arrangement is easier, mood is lighter, and the character of the youth as main hero is clearer and the sense of the idea as the reason for which the novel was begun is more obvious. But will this originality not annoy the reader? Will the reader be able to stand this I for thirty-five pages? And the main thing, the basic thoughts of the novel – can they be naturally and fully expressed by a twenty-year-old writer?[30]

In spite of his evident preference for the *Icherzählung*, whose different virtues he summed up as if to convince himself, Dostoyevsky had stumbled upon the disadvantage of the confession, in which the author's own evaluation disappears. So, by a new swing of the pendulum, he returns briefly to the possibility of narrative by the author: 'If the story is from the author, then draw it from above, as if I hid my sympathy, controlling myself, and as originally as possible in the tone and distribution of the order of the scenes and objects described.'[31] But he immediately rejected this: 'If it is by the author, then there's been too much of it, and then these techniques of narratives are conventional in literature, and to make the Youth original, i.e. explain why I chose him, is more difficult.'[32] And on 6 September he made his final decision: 'Finally: I.'[33]

After this date Dostoyevsky still had doubts about various difficulties, but he kept to his choice of first person narrative, which was necessary if the Youth was to be the main hero. Three brief notes of regret reveal the main obstacle for the writer. On 7 September Dostoyevsky asked:

NB. There is the question of form: How will the youth describe *in the first person* these psychological explanations with Liza and the antecedents of the link with the princess, even if it is from HIS words?

But if the author is the narrator, then will not the youth be a secondary figure, while HE is the main one? . . .

If the author is the narrator, the part of the youth disappears completely.[34]

On 10 September he solved this particular problem:

In the first person, it is more naive, incomparably more original and even more charming in its departures from regularity and the system of narrative.

The y[oung] prince in the judgements of the youth and all the scenes with Liza will come out more originally in the youth's writing from the youth's pen. By I, by I, by I!

If it is by the author, then it will be unusually difficult to set out for the reader the reason: why is the youth the hero? and justify it.[35]

The obstacle comes from what one might call the transfer of power from the novelist to the hero-chronicler, the transfer of the omniscience of the writer to his character, the nature of the polyphonic principle itself. How could the hero who tells the story know everything – in particular, the previous and secret intimacy of Akhmakova and Versilov, the young prince and Liza – when his function is to discover, to experience his own adventure, to try to understand and to understand himself? Having endowed his hero with an independent mind and voice, Dostoyevsky cannot, for this very reason, grant him godlike privileges. The confession, which assumes full lighting and absolute control of time, is clearly impossible.[36] Dostoyevsky must therefore use the confession to oneself, the diary form where the time lapse between action and narrative is very small, and where the universe is ordered by the subjective view of the hero and ruled by the jagged time of uncertainty.

Dostoyevsky was well aware of this duality. The chronicler-hero is able to abstract himself from clock or calendar time, which the novelist must observe whether he likes it or not. From the ambiguity resulting from the overlapping, the interweaving of the still pulsing time of action and the time of a narrative which is still lacking in clearsightedness, the novelist has drawn a freedom which classic narrative in the third person would not allow. On 2 September he noted: 'NB. Arrangement of the narrative of the youth more original. Tossing from one detail to another. In this arrangement is his own character, but according to chapters.'[37] And a few lines on, he commented: 'First person narrative makes it more original, because the youth can very naively leap from one anecdote or details, to the extent of his development and immaturity, which would be impossible to an author conducting his story correctly.'[38] This deliberate break with objective time is linked with the egocentric view point of the chronicler-hero, which Dostoyevsky defined in a note at the beginning of March 1875, when he was struggling with the second part of the novel: 'The principal character of the second part is that everywhere the youth puts *himself at the front of the stage*. It is not so much the adventures of other people he describes, but *just his own, only his own*, and those of others only as far as they relate to his own adventures.'[39]

With the chronicler-hero, Dostoyevsky gives the first and most direct of the two images of stereoscopic vision. But at the same time he makes his own voice heard, energetically inflects the tones and introduces a superior viewpoint which forms the second image. And to counterbalance the narrative system of the chronicle, he takes his interpreter in hand and exercises strict control over the part he plays. This clear return of the sovereignty of the writer appears in the notebooks just when the first two parts of the novel are being written in their final version. Dostoyevsky manipulates the tone with authority. Sometimes it is tragic: 'NB. To raise the level of the tone, the worries and suffering of the youth, who is observing HIM with emotion, tormenting himself about HIS character, it is necessary *to raise more tragically* the tone of the happenings and accusations which are being heaped on HIM by society as well.'[40] Sometimes it is ironic: '*Feature*. Never show HIM in any other way but with words of deep irony.'[41] Sometimes it is sympathetic: 'Do not leave the youth for a moment. The youth is *the hero*. Make his character come out more sympathetically.'[42] The inflections of the novelist mingle with those of the chronicler, without letting the separating line appear too clearly. This blurring is shown in the chronology as well. The youth is a diligent reporter, but a prisoner of rumour; garrotted by his ignorance, tossed about by the storm of events, he rushes ceaselessly between the recent past and the present, imprudently explaining a gesture which he had known after the event, or being submerged by hypothetical explanations. If the reader is interrogated point blank, he is unable to set the events in order. This impression is deceptive: the chronicle is precise, consistent and meticulously dated, day by day, hour by hour, minute by minute, even second by second. This strict chronological construction, characteristic of all Dostoyevsky's great novels, whether written in the first or third person, is the novelist's doing. In *A Raw Youth* the chronicler-hero respects this construction without noticing it or rather without giving it much importance. He is the novelist's transcriber, at least with regard to objective time.

The novella-parables

The evidence of tone, the construction of the discreet scaffolding of objective time are part of the second image of stereoscopic vision. But it is another procedure of pure composition which creates the superior point of view, both eternal and universal, typical of the Dostoyevskian chronicle: this is the technique of inserted stories, parables embedded in the subjective narrative of the chronicler.

On 14 October 1874, Dostoyevsky remembered Strakhov's reproaches about excessive swarms of characters and subjects in his novels. To avoid the usual trap, he set two rules for himself:

First rule. Avoid the fault in The Idiot and The Devils, that secondary events (many) were expressed in an incomplete, allusive, novelistic form, stretched over a long space, in action and scenes, but without the slightest explanations, in guesses and hints, instead of directly explaining the truth. As secondary episodes, they were not worth this great attention from the reader, and even, on the contrary, the chief aim was obscured by this . . .
To try to avoid and give an unimportant place to secondary events, very shortly, and combine the action just around the hero.
Second rule is that the hero is the youth. And all the rest is secondary, even HE is secondary.[43]

Dostoyevsky was revealing his creative antagonisms. On one hand, to preserve the unity of action he was trying to fight against the complexity which results from the initial appearance of totality. But he refused to renounce this original richness altogether. He reproached himself only for giving a novelistic form to the secondary events which then competed with the essential novel. One must, he said, 'explain the truth directly'.

In *A Raw Youth* Dostoyevsky solved these problems in an unusual way; the first by choosing the chronicle written shortly after the event, centred round the hero and narrated by the hero, and the second by the subtle insertion of stories which are not connected, or only remotely connected, with the main plot, without betraying the unity of the novel.

From the beginning of his research, Dostoyevsky felt strongly that it was improbable that the youth could take the whole variety of human experience on his own shoulders. So he had been tempted by a hybrid solution: 'In the course of the novel (and more and more often towards the end) leave the youth and in separate chapters turn to the other characters in a narrative by the author. This is how the episode of the suicide of the little boy with the bird will be revealed.'[44] The choice of first person narrative prevented Dostoyevsky from applying this principle. He avoided the obstacle by entrusting the narrative of these stories to characters gravitating around the chronicler–hero, who merely sets them down without taking responsibility for them. There are many novellas inserted in the chronicle of *A Raw Youth*: the tragic story of Olya, who, tormented and proud, ends by hanging herself, told by her mother;[45] the clumsy and naively patriotic anecdote of the large stone which only the cleverness of a Russian peasant could move, told by the counsellor Pyotr Ippolitovich, the youth's landlord;[46] the half-philosophical conversation between Makar Ivanych the wanderer and Pyotr Valerianovich, the lay recluse in the hermitage of St Gennadius, who shows him a living cell under the microscope and is assailed by doubt;[47] the parable of the ex-soldier, who, admitting a robbery, pardoned or more exactly declared not guilty, cannot bear his sin and hangs himself;[48] and especially the marvellous and cruel history of 'the little boy with the bird' and the merchant Skotoboynikov who finds redemption in love and giving up the world.[49] These last three stories are told by Makar Ivanych, the legal father of the youth. The dream of the Golden Age, told by Versilov to the youth, is also in this category, although the tone is quite different.

This technique was used again in *The Brothers Karamazov*, where the elder Zosima and Ivan Karamazov are the two great tellers of Lives and Legends, each in his different way. The chapters 'The mysterious visitor' and 'The Grand Inquisitor' are the two diamonds of Dostoyevsky's last novel.

These novellas are easy to recognise: they have a striking similarity, as they come from the immense realm of universal and eternal experience, the anonymous common fund of human wisdom and tragedy, from 'the oral tradition of the people', as the Youth notes on the subject of the half-legendary stories of Makar Ivanych,[50] or from the mythical dreams of the human spirit. They are distinguished from the written text, the literary speech, by their character as oral tales. Particles, especially incidental clauses which express the speech of someone else, the popular words and phrases so lovingly collected in the notebooks, the nervous alert syntax, crammed with verbs, characterise the speech of Olya's mother, Pyotr Ippolitovich and Makar Ivanych. Naturally Versilov's account of his dream of the Golden Age is quite different. But where does this caustic aristocrat find the poetic prose full of musical harmony and smooth alliteration,[51] if not from the exalted word, the speech inspired by collective myth. Whatever tone they may be in, the novellas do not belong to the Youth who copies them down, but to the community of souls. They are rocks of eternity which the novelist places in the mobile and subjective texture of the chronicle.

They are so singular that they form finished wholes and may be subtracted from the chronicle without seeming to harm its structure. Before beginning the story of the merchant Skotoboynikov and the child with the bird, the Youth declares directly: 'You are free to skip the story, especially as I am telling it in its own style.'[52] Apart from their stylistic personality, these novellas are very like the stories used as illustrations in *Diary of a Writer*. Legends, edifying stories, moving visions, coarse anecdotes, philosophic dialogues, they are authentic parables, showing the thought and superior viewpoint of the novelist. The chief chronicler, the Youth, does not always share the moral drawn from the story. He hastily concludes that the recluse with the microscope, Pyotr Valerianych, is an atheist, which the narrator, Makar Ivanych, disputes; he hesitates to decide on Versilov's responsibility for Olya's suicide, and it is Vasin who judges. In general, Dostoyevsky allows another person, such as Vasin, or Versilov for the cock-and-bull story about the stone, or Makar Ivanych for his numerous stories, to draw the right moral or psychological lesson.

However, in spite of their essential strangeness these episodes which are independent of the subjective vision of the chronicler and are placed in the margin of the true plot are not remote from the subject. They play the same part in the life of the chronicler-hero as the concilium of famous people grouped in the monastery in The Life of a Great Sinner. The only difference is that each time – and this is to be the ruling principle in *The Brothers Karamazov* – illustration is preferred to debate or to exposition of ideas. These novellas inserted in the chronicle are the reflections of a higher truth marked by eternity and universality, conferring their absolute value on the subjective experiences of the Youth. 'They directly explain the truth.'

The Dostoyevskian composition of the chronicle written shortly after the event keeps both the freedom of the hero and the freedom of the novelist, who, by the manipulation of tone, the use of objective time, the insertion of parables and novellas, shows his higher viewpoint. The initial antinomy between the narrative of the author, which distorts the independent consciousness of the hero, and confession, which drowns the eternal and the universal in subjectivity, has been overcome.

PART III

Time and space in the world of the novels

Introduction

In the notebooks for *A Raw Youth* Dostoyevsky approaches the space–time structure he had planned in 'The Life of a Great Sinner', especially in the brief period when this unwritten work appeared as a plan in his letters. The link between the two subjects is obvious. During the research the original character of the Great Sinner, of whom Stavrogin was the larva incapable of metamorphosis, has somehow suffered a double change: it has spread out over space and has contracted in time. It has split into the three characters of Versilov, the impenitent sinner, Makar Ivanych, the man of God, and Arkadiy, the raw youth, who is the son of both of them and who occupies a central position, as the human architecture showed us, forging a path to order through the disorder that surrounds him.[1] Time is contracted because the whole life of the hero is no longer the subject of the novel; all the experiences which the Great Sinner would have had from childhood to death have been concentrated in one great crisis during the hero's adolescence. The Raw Youth only has a few of these experiences; the others appear as impulses within the youth or as actions which he witnesses, since besides being subject to experiences, the Raw Youth chronicles and spies on the experiences of others.

The space–time structure of *A Raw Youth* is less ambitious than the structure formerly envisaged for 'The Life of a Great Sinner', but its intention is the same; to reconcile the antinomic freedoms of the novelist and his hero in the writing, and the opposing freedom of God and man in the sphere of thought. The hot-press chronicle, written by the hero, gives both the time of crisis and, within the stereoscopic vision which also conveys the author's viewpoint, hagiographic time, reinforced by the insertion of novella-parables with universal and eternal value.

We shall now leave the writer's laboratory and study this space–time structure in the novels. The gap between notebooks and finished work is immense. Writing, especially when it includes a margin of improvisation as it does with Dostoyevsky, always warps the original plan, which sometimes fades away or sometimes unexpectedly appears more vivid and clearcut. It is only by examining the great novels of Dostoyevsky as a whole that these original forms will appear and that we may attempt to sketch a synthesis of the aesthetics of the novels subordinate to their metaphysics.[2]

19

The master of men and hours

Dear friend, all theory is grey
And the golden tree of Life is green.

Goethe, Faust

The sovereignty of the writer in the notebooks

Between the notebooks and the novels there is more than the usual distance between the draft and the finished work, the plan and the novel. There is the breath of life which animates the clay bird, the free flight which liberates creature from creator. Bakhtin's polyphonic theory springs from his admiration for the freedom of Dostoyevsky's heroes and it is valuable because he plumbs the depths and discovers the foundations of this freedom. We share some of his conclusions and agree with his analysis of dialogue and speech in Dostoyevsky, but the premises are too absolute and his theory is only true as a tool.[1] Bakhtin was like a member of the audience coming to a theatre just as the actors are improvising in a play by Pirandello. He believed in the illusion of the novel, which he transformed into a theory. But he had not seen the rehearsals, he had not read the technical diary of the author – a good part of his notebooks – questioning himself about composition and human architecture, doubting and hesitant: he had not taken part in the brutal experiments with final gestures: he deliberately ignored the dramatist writing the play with his characters, or slipping into the shadow of the chronicler to become a hagiographer. Bakhtin dealt with the fully grown novel and ignored its making. If he had studied the notebooks, which were not available in 1929, he would have seen that in fact Dostoyevsky was using all his skill to transfer his powers to the hero. But he would also have seen how Dostoyevsky's constant study of the act of creation modified the act itself, and that Dostoyevsky, in the notebooks, was an absolute ruler, organising the tortures to seize the suffering in his characters' eyes, forcing them to confess with even more cruelty than in the novel, killing and resurrecting with despotic indifference.

Dostoyevsky constructed his heroes authoritatively, with a will to make his own voice heard and sometimes even to convey a message. As he is like all other novelists in this respect, we shall give only two examples where the writer shows his power over his characters. Versilov, one of the heroes of *A Raw Youth*, is a composite of reality and literature, of flesh and fiction.[2] We know from Dostoyevsky's notes and critical comparisons that he had used features from Herzen, Chaadayev, the Jesuit father Pecherin, J.-J. Rousseau, and probably from Nikolay Aleksandrovich Speshnyov, who was a friend of Dostoyevsky in the Fourierist period and beyond, a strong romantic personality who remained an active socialist and exerted a strong fascination on Dostoyevsky.[3] Versilov was probably influenced by another friend of the difficult years in Semipalatinsk, Chogan Chingisovich Valikhanov, with his 'terrible simplicity' of soul, who later became a famous ethnographer.[4] Great ghosts, such as Hamlet and Faust, presided over Versilov's birth, not to mention Prince Danilo from Salias' novel, and previous heroes of Dostoyevsky's own, such as the Great Sinner from 'The Life' and his relative, Stavrogin, who was also partly inspired by Speshnyov, rather than by Bakunin.[5] Versilov, like most of the great characters in the novels, is a psychological and ideological composite. It is generally true that the more universal a Dostoyevskian character is and the greater his stature, the more difficult it becomes to identify his real and literary prototypes. Inversely, when the characters are less important, the sources become more obvious.[6] Paradoxically research is difficult not because there are no prototypes or because they have become too abstract, but because the borrowings and the different elements which make up the character are so rich, abundant and numerous. Memories, real people, famous or obscure, literary heroes, all these possible sources discovered by critics or noted by Dostoyevsky himself in his notebooks and correspondence, are simply indications, valuable but not at all decisive. Dostoyevsky execrated the genre painter, imprisoned in a false historical reality. He depicted his heroes and nature as they were reflected in his idea after passing, he says, through his senses.[7] 'The ideal must be extracted from reality'; for example, 'Dickens never saw Pickwick with his own eyes, he simply perceived him in the immense variety of observed reality, he created a character and presented him as the result of his observations; so that this character is just as real as if he had really existed, although Dickens had simply taken the ideal from reality.'[8] This is true for all Dostoyevsky's great heroes.

A typical case is Pyotr Verkhovensky, the criminal nihilist of *The Devils*, whose prototype is clearly Sergey Gennadiyevich Nechayev (1847–82). Three times, in the notebooks for the novel, in his letters and later in the *Diary of a Writer* for 1873, Dostoyevsky explained his conception of the character in the novel.

In spring 1870 Dostoyevsky, who sometimes called his hero 'the student', sometimes simply 'Nechayev', noted: 'Nechayev: partly Petrashevsky',[9] and later: 'Follow the type of Petrashevsky more closely.'[10] This is coalescence: experience coheres to the original image, nourishing and fattening it. In autumn, on 20 September 1870, from Dresden, he clarified his position in a letter to the editor, Katkov:

One of the principal events in my story will be Nechayev's murder of Ivanov, well known in Moscow. Let me explain myself. I knew nothing about Nechayev, Ivanov and the circumstances of the murder and have only read about them in the newspapers. And even if I had known them, I should not have copied. I only take the finished act. My intention may be very far from reality as it was and my Pyotr Verkhovensky is possibly not at all like Nechayev, but it seems to me that, spurred by the event, my imagination has been able to create the character, the type corresponding to this crime.[11]

Finally, three years later, Dostoyevsky revealed to his readers in *Diary of a Writer* the reasons for the liberties he took with historical prototypes:

Some of our critics have noted that in my last novel, The Devils, I made use of the data of the famous Nechayev case; but it has been said that there are no portraits in my novel, properly speaking, nor is it a literary reproduction of the Nechayev story; I have only taken the event to try to explain its possibility in the society in which we live, and considering it as a social phenomenon and not just as an interesting story ... I can witness that all this is perfectly true. I leave the well-known Nechayev and his victim Ivanov aside in the novel. The character of my Nechayev, naturally, is not at all like that of the real Nechayev. I wanted to set a problem and, as clearly as the novel form allows, to reply to it: that is, how is it that in our amazing and transitory society of the present day not one but several Nechayevs are possible, and how can it come about that these Nechayevs manage to recruit little Nechayevs to follow them?[12]

The novelist creates his characters in the same way as he seeks the Idea of the novel; he is clearly the boss. From the various prototypes (here Nechayev and the nihilists of *The People's Vengeance*) the Idea, which first aroused Dostoyevsky's interest in them, is extracted. The Idea directs Dostoyevsky's imagination to other related prototypes (here Butashevich-Petrashevsky), mostly linked to the personal experience of the writer or his cultural heritage. Elements of both, chosen for their significance, are added and coalesce, forming an original type, the quintessence of a varied and universal reality.

In the notebooks, at the research stage, there is an undoubted will to speak, and this will selects the human architecture, the Idea of the novel, the composition, and the structure of the heroes. The novelist asserts that he is the master of men.

The truth and limits of polyphony in the novel

However, as soon as the author has noted a character trait or an idea, the hero, his creature, takes possession of it, speaks in his own name and sees with his own eyes; dialogue begins and the idea is examined and judged from different viewpoints. We have seen this in the notebooks for *A Raw Youth* and Dostoyevsky has even said that this was his design, or at least his method. In the finished novel, something which was only a creative rule, tempered by other rules, acquires the force of law: the hero gains a stupefying total freedom. It seems, and Bakhtin has described this well, that the novelist has abdicated, relinquishing his power to the people, his heroes, who are even free to take over the literary comparisons which had been used to create them in the notebooks.

This is not simply the freedom which readers like to see in the successful heroes of great writers: the hero of Dostoyevsky is created so free that he can imitate god and the novelist. Like them, he wants to establish contact with the Other whatever it costs, to penetrate his essence beyond his existence. Vyacheslav Ivanov was the first to note that the moral and religious principle ruling Dostoyevsky's world is that the mind and soul of someone else must not be seen as an object, but as a subject equal to oneself, to escape the ice of reification. The tragic catastrophe which destroys some of his heroes is due to their inability to break free from the prison of their solipsism and to affirm the I of the Other person by a 'thou art' which would establish the Other as an independent mind and soul.[13] Bakhtin did not dispute V. Ivanov's analysis, but he refused to pitch camp on these metaphysical heights. He applied this insight to the formal plane, revealing not a moral and religious principle but a 'principle of an artistic vision of the world and of the artistic structure of a verbal whole, the novel'.[14] Here is his definition at greater length:

Dostoyevsky, like Goethe's Prometheus, does not create mute slaves (as Zeus does), but free men capable of standing beside their creator, of dissenting from his views, even of rebelling against him.

A multitude of distinct and independent voices and minds, a true polyphony of voices which are completely equal is the basic feature of Dostoyevsky's novels. In his works, we do not find a multitude of characters and destinies developing in one objective world in the light of a single author's mind; a multiplicity of minds with equal rights, each with its own world, are combined here, each preserving its own distinct quality, in the unity of an event.[15]

In the polyphonic novel of which Dostoyevsky, according to Bakhtin, is the originator, the mind of the hero is presented 'as another awareness, the mind of the Other, without being reified or closed, without becoming the simple product of the author's mind'.[16] This is obviously too absolute a thesis. One of Bakhtin's predecessors, S. Askoldov, had also shown, from the structure of the novel, that Dostoyevsky's heroes were free and independent, but he ascribed this freedom and independence to the author's plan. He stressed that it was the novelist who predestined his hero to freedom and that this was part of a strictly calculated plan, just as an irrational or transfinite number is part of a precise mathematical formulation.[17] If we substitute 'flexible overall plan whose unity is the dialectic idea of the novel' for 'strictly calculated plan', we see that study of the notebooks confirms this hypothesis. Bakhtin refuted Askoldov's interpretation by saying that it led to the monological traditional novel, contrary to the dialogical and polyphonic system. His passion for theorising led him astray.

In fact, the perfect polyphonic novel could never be finished.[18] Bakhtin agrees:

We do in fact observe in Dostoyevsky's novels a unique conflict between the internal open-endedness of the characters and dialogue, and the *external* (in most cases compositional and thematic) *completedness* of every individual novel. We cannot go deeply into this difficult problem here. We will say only that almost all of Dostoyevsky's novels have a *conventionally literary*, *conventionally monologic* ending (especially characteristic in this respect is *Crime and Punishment*).[19]

This is an important admission: polyphony has its limits and does not explain everything. It seems rather too easy to say that everything, even the subject and the destinies of the heroes, which is controlled by the novelist is mere literary convention. Moreover, patient research on the creative process has shown that while Dostoyevsky predestines his heroes to freedom, he keeps full authority over them by means of the human architecture, the idea of the novel, and its composition in chronicle form with the author's voice included as part of a stereoscopic vision. Bakhtin is right in stressing the importance of the polyphonic structure which signifies the freedom of the heroes and their creation as independent minds, but he is mistaken in thinking that their freedom is absolute. There is an odd parallel between Dostoyevsky's metaphysics and the form of the novel: the more the hero rebels against God or man (Raskolnikov, Stavrogin, Versilov, Ivan Karamazov), the more he fights against the novelist, or in other words, the closer he is to the polyphonic conception of Bakhtin; on the other hand, if a hero is submissive and saintly (Sonya, Tikhon, Makar Ivanych, Zosima), he is close to the classic, monological and more particularly hagiographical tradition. It is at the meeting point of these two freedoms, that of the hero and that of the creator, that we must try to discover the structure of space and time in the finished novel.

Time scheme of the novel

These two freedoms are granted only when the composition has been chosen, and are authorised only in the final spoken improvisation. The novel of Dostoyevsky emerges from this improvisation as a living and fruitful antinomy between the polyphonic structure with its tendency to remain unfinished and the definite statement of the novel's architectonics, with its subject, plot and epilogue. This results in a form of double time; time manipulated by the author and time experienced in the mind of the hero. The reader, however, sees this double time as one time.

Bakhtin explained this perception, this sensation of whirlwind movement by his theory of polyphony, which, characterised by a variety and simultaneity of worlds and independent minds and souls, leads to a space–time structure which Bakhtin, who was later to call it a 'chronotope',[20] defined as follows:

The fundamental category in Dostoyevsky's mode of artistic visualizing was not evolution, but *coexistence* and *interaction*. He saw and conceived his world primarily in terms of space, not time. Hence his deep affinity for the dramatic form. Dostoyevsky strives to organize all available meaningful material, all material of reality, in one time-frame, in the form of a dramatic juxtaposition, and he strives to develop it extensively.[21]

Time, by Bakhtin's rigorous logic, should therefore be devalued in favour of space, and, at the limit, it should be abolished. Whatever the merit of this interpretation, based – as we shall see – on an accurate impression, a question arises: what parts do time and space play in Dostoyevsky's novels and what significance do they have? And first, how far is the novelist a master of hours?

20

Chronology and temporality in *The Idiot*

The splendour of the world is enriched with a new beauty: the beauty of speed.
Marinetti, *Futurist Manifesto (1909)*

The novels of Dostoyevsky are violently at odds with human and biological rhythm. Reader, hero and even author are carried off into a whirlwind of events, dialogues, sensations and ideas, into a world whose natural element is the tempest. In the epilogue, the reader staggers out of the adventure like someone who has jetted through a storm at high speed, exhausted by this extraordinary explosion of vitality. The sensation of speed, however, does not appear fantastic or unreal; it conveys a feeling of superabundant incandescent reality, intense experience, tragic depth. The novels appear realistic partly because Dostoyevsky was passionately interested in the details of contemporary daily life, using the latest news items in his novels (most of his heroes are keen readers of newspapers), drawing migrant images from the collective thought of the time, and invariably setting the action in the changing modern town. But the reader believes in the reality of the novels mainly because the temporality, the time experienced, is accompanied discreetly but continuously by a precise chronology which establishes an objective time, from which the hero is struggling to escape.

Before we analyse the dynamics of the Dostoyevskian novel in the following chapter, we shall consider the time scheme of *The Idiot*, an exemplary work which Claudel admired for its composition, and which we chose because it is a bridge between *Crime and Punishment* and the last three great novels and because it contains nearly all the temporal forms to which we shall make reference.

The Beethovenian crescendo of the first part

The novel begins as follows: 'At the end of November, during a thaw, at about nine o'clock in the morning, a train from Warsaw was approaching Petersburg at full steam.' (5)[1] In chapter 7 we learn that this was on 27 November (70). In a third-class carriage, Prince Lev Nikolayevich Myshkin and Parfyon Rogozhin begin a conversation. An official, Lebedev, joins in to complete the story of Rogozhin's passion for Nastasya Filippovna Barashkova. The past of the two young travellers is revealed in the dialogue and in their mutual confessions.

It is almost eleven o'clock (16) when the prince rings the doorbell of the Yepanchins, to whom he is related. At twelve thirty (33), Myshkin takes a meal in the company of Mme Yepanchin and her three daughters. The author leaves the time of the action several times to introduce the Yepanchin family and to show the desires and calculations which surround Nastasya Filippovna: her seducer Totsky is trying to get rid of her by a gift of 75,000 roubles, so that he can marry a Yepanchin daughter, while Gavrila Ivolgin (Ganya) is planning to marry Nastasya for financial reasons, and seems ready to give her up to General Yepanchin ... On the other hand, Myshkin is presented in scenes and conversations: he talks about the death penalty to a footman, and about his plans for finding work to Yepanchin, does some calligraphy exercises, contemplates and kisses the portrait of Nastasya Filippovna, tells of his life: his childhood, his illness, Switzerland, his feelings about the death penalty (memories of a condemned man). In this naive sketch for his own hagiography, he inserts the parable about the Swiss children and poor Marie. He uses aesthetic parallels to say what he thinks of everyone present and even of the absent Nastasya Filippovna. This is the only example in Dostoyevsky's work where the time of action and the time of elucidation are united in the transparency of the hero.

The action has its first moment of intensity with Ganya's anger when Aglaya Yepanchin answers his note with a scornful 'I don't take part in trading.' This scene takes place two hours later (74) in the street: Myshkin and Ganya are on their way to Ganya's house, where the prince is to stay.[2]

The author interrupts the action to introduce Ganya's family, the Ivolgins. A violent family row breaks out between Varvara, the sister, and Ganya about Nastasya Filippovna ... who suddenly appears and assumes that the prince is a valet. This is the second moment of intensity: everyone is struck motionless. It looks as if a tragedy is about to explode, but a comic intermission slows the effect down when General Ivolgin, a senile teller of lying tales, makes everyone laugh with his story of the cigar and the poodle thrown out of the window.

The respite is short: Rogozhin and his gang appear. The rich heir has come to claim Nastasya Filippovna from Ganya. He offers first 18,000 roubles, then 40,000, then 100,000, if she will marry him. Varvara tries to throw the auctioned lady out, Ganya objects, his sister spits in his face, and, as he is about to strike her, the prince moves between them and receives the blow: third moment of intensity. The tension falls again with Ganya's apology and his sad confession.

An uncertain time of wandering around follows. The prince wants to go to the house of Nastasya Filippovna, who has not invited him, so he is forced to use the services of General Ivolgin, now drunk, who drags him off to see some strangers and then to the house of the widow Terentyeva, mother of Ippolit. It is already evening (107). At half past nine (112), Myshkin and

Kolya, Ganya's young and appealing brother, walk to Nastasya Filippovna's apartment. Eleven people have met in the little apartment: among others, the prince, Totsky, General Yepanchin, Ganya, and Ferdyshchenko, a buffoon who suggests that they should play 'the truth game'. The atmosphere is strained; it is half past ten (119). The game requires everyone to confess the worst action in his life: Ferdyshchenko tells a Rousseau-type story of a theft he blamed on someone else, General Yepanchin the story of the old woman he swore at without noticing that she was dying before his eyes, Totsky tells a story about camellias, ending with the death of a friend in the Caucasus; they are all inverted parables. Suddenly Nastasya Filippovna asks the prince to give a final judgement: should she marry Ganya Ivolgin? Myshkin replies 'No'. She returns the 75,000 roubles to Totsky and the pearl necklace to General Yepanchin. It is the fourth moment of intensity.

A bell rings: it is half past eleven (131). Rogozhin's gang break in, which increases the number of people present to about twenty. It is the fifth moment of intensity: Rogozhin has brought the promised 100,000 roubles and proposes. Nastasya Filippovna bares her heart and her sufferings. Sudden dramatic effect: the prince proposes too: it is the sixth moment of intensity. And, to general stupefaction – seventh moment of intensity – he announces that he has inherited a large fortune. Nastasya Filippovna, weeping and laughing, refuses the prince and his inheritance: she remains 'Rogozhin's property'. In a final gesture of delirium, she throws the parcel of 100,000 roubles on the fire and tells Ganya to pull it out with his bare hands. Ganya cannot bear the test, he faints: eighth and last moment of intensity. The troikas carry Rogozhin and Nastasya Filippovna off into the night. The prince rushes after them.

The first part has finished. As the tension rises, the interventions of the author are less frequent, the moments of intensity rush on and are linked together more closely. The violent surge, as in epilepsy, ends with a descent into darkness. There is a magnificent crescendo where the increase in power is accompanied by mad acceleration and an incredible concentration of events: everything happens in a single day, 27 November. In one day, three loves unfold and rend the soul of Nastasya Filippovna; 'the passionate direct love' of Rogozhin, 'the love through vanity' of Ganya and the 'Christian love' of Myshkin,[3] without counting the lust of General Yepanchin ... Indications of time are rare in this storm of events, less than a dozen at most, slipped in by the author at the beginning, but as the day moves towards night, as the rhythm accelerates and the fever mounts, they become elements of dialogue, significant words for the hero who pronounces them. Nastasya Filippovna keeps on asking the time as she waits to know her fate. Objective time becomes experienced time.

Alternation of accumulations and explosions in the second part

A slow recovery from the night follows. 'Two days after the strange adventure', the prince leaves Petersburg for Moscow to make arrangements about his inheritance. He spends 'exactly six months' (149) there.[4] The strange thing is that this half year is not lived through as a whole. It is retold, reconstituted from rumour and gossip. 'Rumours had certainly reached a few people, though not very often, but they were mostly odd ones and nearly always contradicted each other.'[5] These rumours which were on the point of spreading through the town were gradually 'covered by the darkness of the unknown'.[6] The author adopts the attitude of a chronicler, an outside observer, as he himself says.[7] It is the time of uncertainty and detective work on the truth. The rumours are collected by the Yepanchins, who compare them with solid facts. Nastasya Filippovna is supposed to have fled to Moscow on the day after the scene at her apartment, Rogozhin is supposed to have joined her a week later. Ganya, according to rumour, waited for the prince who returned from his pursuit on the famous night at six o'clock in the morning (151), asked him to give the 100,000 roubles back to their owner and made peace with him. 'This news, which reached all the Yepanchins, was later confirmed to be perfectly correct.'[8]

We even witness the muffled erection of a vast network of signposts concerning the Yepanchins. The mother, Lizaveta Prokyevna, says publicly that she is no longer interested in the prince, but she is corresponding with the old Princess Belokonskaya, who has received Myshkin in Moscow. The three Yepanchin daughters take up with Varvara, who has just married Ptitsyn. This moderately astute businessman hears the gossip in the financial world and is gathering information about the prince's inheritance. General Yepanchin, who has numerous reliable messengers available, is not only spying on the prince, but also on the game of hide and seek which Rogozhin and Nastasya Filippovna are playing. They are supposed to have lost and found each other again three times, but finally Nastasya Filippovna is said to have run away just before the wedding ceremony, at the very time when the prince left Moscow. Even the tender Kolya Ivolgin is not spared: he is wrongly suspected of intrigue when he delivers a letter from Myshkin to Aglaya. The chronicle time is exemplary, in spite of the absence of a chronicler hero. On one hand, the author plays the part of a diligent but rather inefficient reporter, collecting a file of odd rumours and verified information; on the other, he is in charge of coordinating the various inquirers, who are each playing the spy for their own reasons. A succession of flashbacks, punctuated by chronology[9] or indicated by metaphor – frost, thaw, 'frosts of silence' – enable us to follow, in the first months, the passionate interest the Yepanchins take in the prince.

Soon the fever subsides, as two suitors, one for Adelaida, the other for Aglaya, distract the Yepanchins from the enigmatic Myshkin. In the first days of June (156), the prince reappears. The shades of the fatal night of 27 November which swallowed the three heroes and of the mysterious Moscow period have vanished, to be replaced by gaiety, sunshine, 'exceptionally good weather' (158). The Yepanchins and Petersburg society leave for their summer houses in Pavlovsk, not far from Tsarskoye Selo. On the next day or the day after that, the prince gets off the Moscow train and books into an hotel in Petersburg, near the Liteynaya (Foundry Street).

Suddenly, in complete contrast with the original festive atmosphere, the tragic time of crisis begins. Death is all-pervasive, gradually overwhelming the look and word of the hero, though he does not succeed in unmasking its sordid plan. Since his arrival in Petersburg, Myshkin has had the impression that a strange, fiery gaze was following him. He goes to Lebedev's house to hire a summer house and learns that everyone, including Nastasya Filippovna, has gone to Pavlovsk, while Lebedev talks about the end of the world and Mme du Barry on the scaffold. When he goes on to see Rogozhin around midday (169), he finds an immense dark and gloomy house. There, beneath grimy oil paintings on the dark walls, he finds a Rogozhin whose sparkling gaze is only too familiar, a Rogozhin who is not affected by the thought of Nastasya Filippovna with her throat cut, who is nervous when he sees Myshkin fiddling with a new knife with a deer-horn handle. In spite of the exchange of crosses and Rogozhin giving up Nastasya Filippovna to the prince, Myshkin cannot take his eyes from the terrible picture, a copy of Holbein's *Dead Christ*, which leads to a curious conversation about faith and the parable of the peasant who commits a murder as he asks Christ to forgive him.

This is followed by the anxious time of wandering and crisis, where every act is abortive, where the inner and outer shadows grow larger, as the hero longs more and more for light – for sun, clarity of mind and even for the illumination of the epileptic storm. Myshkin has an intense inner experience of time stretching out intolerably and interminably, but this same time is marked for the reader by precise external signals. At half past two (186), Myshkin is at the home of the Yepanchins, who are away, then at the hotel, The Scales, where he waits for Kolya in vain until half past three (186). At four (186) he begins to wander around, only aware of his own increasing torment and tension. At six (186) he finds himself at the Tsarskoye Selo station, buys a ticket, changes his mind and gets off the train. He goes back into Petersburg. The window of a hardware shop fascinates him, he feels that he is about to have a fit and longs to abolish the inexorable length of time, by experiencing the sensation of eternity which epilepsy gives him. In parallel, orchestrated externally by the novelist, but perceived as the beginning of the epileptic crisis, the weather worsens, a storm is threatening, rumbles of thunder approach, the air becomes stifling (189). A whole series of fantastical associations in which recent memories are mingled with present obsessions leads the hero to a 'disgusting' conviction, a 'criminal' supposition: Rogozhin and the object with the deer-horn handle which he saw in the shop-window, the Holbein picture and Nastasya Filippovna threatened by murderous love, the eyes which are continually spying on him, and Rogozhin ... He goes to Nastasya Filippovna's apartment, finds that she too has gone, thinks for a moment of going back to Rogozhin's house and finds himself in front of his hotel. At the very moment when the prince is eagerly seeking illumination, darkness overcomes him. 'The porch of the house, usually dark enough, was very dark at that moment: a threatening storm cloud had swallowed the evening light.' Torrential rain pours down, in the staircase of the old house, there is a shadow, sparkling eyes: Rogozhin! A knife flashes, a terrible wail: the epileptic fit strikes Myshkin down and saves him from certain death. After seven o'clock (196) Kolya appears, discovers what has happened, and arranges for the prince to be cared for at Lebedev's house. Two days later (196), everyone is in Pavlovsk.

This is the first and only moment of intensity of the first five chapters, the explosion, the final chord of a masterly crescendo. It is a pathological climax with the anguished approach of the epileptic fit, a visual and symbolic climax as the light is swallowed by the torn shadows, a dramatic climax as Rogozhin passes from renunciation and brotherhood to jealousy and murder. All this happens in a single day, during the hours of daylight.

Two days later, in Pavlovsk, Yepanchina and her daughters visit the convalescent prince. For the next five chapters there are only three indications of time: 'towards evening' (197), 'after nine in the evening' (227), and 'it struck eleven' (240). They occur so seldom that the time of the action seems to have stopped. In its place there is a block of detached time, the frozen time of dramatic representation, within which the scenes could be arranged in different order. It is not tragedy with its implacable progression, but a modern Beckett-type drama, where the only point of the dialogue is to test the hero. Everything contributes to this impression: the unity of time – the northern twilight that never ends; the unity of place – the terrace of the Lebedev summer house: the number of people present. It is a conclave in which space dominates and the various movements across it are impulses which explore the personality of Myshkin, who is confronted with the aggressive love of Aglaya, confronted with the dilemma of charity and justice (the supposed cheating of the 'son' of Pavlishchev by the prince), confronted with the resentful despair of Ippolit, in his indictment of child-devouring nature.

As soon as the actors leave the stage, the terrace, they enter the time of action once more. At midnight, there is a dramatic event: an eccentric lady, undoubtedly Nastasya Filippovna, familiarly hails Yevgeniy Pavlovich, Aglaya's suitor, from her carriage and reminds him of some promissory notes, casting suspicion on both his honour and his fortune. This is the dramatic event, the moment of intensity of this day which has been compressed into one evening.

Two days later, the Yepanchins make their peace with the prince. The incident of the eccentric lady has assumed 'terrifying and mysterious proportions'. These two intervening days, told in a significant flashback, establish an uncertain anxious suspicious time. Everyone is inquiring, questioning, spying, even the naive Kolya, who admits he has been spying by saying that of course he took care not to spy.[10] On the first of these two days, Adelaida Yepanchina and her fiancé, Prince S., visit the prince, ostensibly to inquire about his health, but really to 'obtain some enlightenment'. Ganya arrives at about seven in the evening (254) and gives the prince some information about Nastasya Filippovna's rowdy and provocative behaviour in Pavlovsk. Varvara arrives and tells Myshkin that her husband, Ptitsyn, is busy sorting out Yevgeny Pavlovich's affairs. Myshkin even conducts an interrogation himself and Lebedev admits that he had told Nastasya Filippovna about the gathering at his summer house. Kolya, after ten (260), arrives with 'a basketful of news' from Petersburg and Pavlovsk, some about Ippolit, some about the Yepanchins. Aglaya is supposed to have quarrelled with her family about Ganya, and Varvara, it is said, was thrown out at about eight o'clock (261) by Yepanchina for intriguing. When Varvara came to see Myshkin at seven (261) – how time flies – she knew nothing about this. Myshkin and Kolya chat for an hour and a half (261). On the second day, Myshkin is in Petersburg, and some time after four (261) he returns to Pavlovsk. At the station, General Yepanchin in a flood of confused words lets some valuable information fall about a mysterious 'conspiracy' by Nastasya Filippovna. It is seven (263) when Lizaveta Prokofyevna comes to interrogate the unfortunate Myshkin with comic despotism. Myshkin is desperately trying to understand what is happening. Does he love Nastasya? Does he love Aglaya? Myshkin's letters to Aglaya and letters from Burdovsky (Pavlishchev's 'son') and Aglaya to Myshkin are added to the interrogation file. The evening ends with a moment of relaxation: Yepanchina drags the unhappy prince off home with her.

To sum up, the second part shows us broken time. Between the crescendos and explosions, gradually diminishing in intensity (the first day of June ending with the murder attempt and the epileptic fit, an evening ending with a scandal directed at Aglaya's suitor, and part of an evening which ends with the prince being kidnapped by the motherly Yepanchina), there are long periods of dead time (six months, two days, then two more days) where in a complex of information – rumour, gossip, facts, confiscated letters – everyone tries to find out the truth, and the elements which form the crisis accumulate.

The two fantastic nights of the third part

The evening which began at the end of the second part goes on in the third as if uninterrupted.[11] The prince is on the terrace of the Yepanchin house. In fact, the time of the novel has frozen. Dostoyevsky, by a laborious detour, a digression on the number of officials in Russia and the absence of 'practical' men, catches up with the Yepanchin family. He rejoins the novel by the back door, using his own personal ideas expressed by the inconsistent Yevgeny Pavlovich.[12] The expression of these opinions, too detached from the actions, lowers the tension, a price Dostoyevsky paid for writing slowly and doing research at the same time.[13]

The action only regains its tempo when the whole company is getting ready to finish the evening at 'Vauxhall', where concerts are held. On the way, the prince delivers an 'unexpected and morbid outburst' about being insulted by nature. Aglaya explodes into a passionate hymn of praise to the prince, followed by an indignant refusal to marry him. As she had not been asked, it is a public admission of love. This is the first moment of intensity, instantly diluted by the laughter of those present. The company mingles with the crowd, and Myshkin in this worldly scene dreams of solitude and sinks into meditation. Suddenly, a drunken group appears with Nastasya Filippovna, whom Myshkin has not seen for three months, at its head. The drama explodes: she again speaks familiarly to Yevgeniy Pavlovich, stunning him by announcing that the uncle from whom he was expecting to inherit a fortune has died with debts of 350,000 roubles; Yevgeniy is forever compromised in the eyes of the Yepanchins. An officer, a friend of Yevgeniy, swears at Nastasya Filippovna, she strikes him with a malacca cane and he rushes to attack her, but is restrained by Myshkin. Rogozhin appears and leads her away. The hour is not indicated, but, as for all moments of intensity, the duration is noted exactly. It has all lasted less than two minutes, and five seconds later the police arrive (291). It is the second moment of intensity.

Very subdued, for a duel is possible, everyone returns to the Yepanchins' summer house. Night has fallen (293) and the prince is alone on the terrace. The prince's 'informers' come to see him one by one, trying to guess the results of the slander. They include Aglaya talking about the art of weapons, Keller the boxer, who suggests at about half past eleven (301) that he should be the prince's second, and others such as General Yepanchin wondering about Nastasya Filippovna's intentions and Rogozhin, who rises from the shadows to confirm Nastasya's generous plan. She has agreed to marry Rogozhin only if Myshkin marries Aglaya, with whom she is conducting a secret correspondence.[14] This is the post-critical time of elucidation, of the police inquest in which Myshkin is a detective in spite of himself. Rogozhin makes fun of him: 'Anyone can see, Lev Nikolayevich, that you're just a beginner. Just wait a while: you'll have your own police force, you'll be on duty day and night, and you'll know every step that's taken.'[15] Suspicion sets the action going again. What does the meeting which Aglaya has arranged with Myshkin mean? Why are the two rivals writing to each other? It is almost midnight (304). Myshkin invites Rogozhin to celebrate his birthday, which he has just remembered. However, when they arrive at the prince's house, a happy company is swigging champagne: the Lebedevs, General Ivolgin, Ippolit, Burdovsky, Ganya, Ptitsyn and even Yevgeniy Pavlovich, who admits that he has come for information. It is so light that one can still read though 'there were at most two hours until dawn' (309).

There is a break in the narrative line. Ippolit forces the company, slightly the worse for drink, to listen to his terrifying 'Explanation'. The form of the text, which is a confession, introduces an ambiguous time. The 'Explanation' has all the features of a confessional diary. It is close to the time it describes since it was written in the hours before its reading, it is by a novice writer who admits his own clumsiness and refuses to correct it because of lack of time, it is not meant for publication, it has a precise chronological structure in which dates and hours are carefully set down, and it contains parables like that of the poor doctor and his family, who are saved by Ippolit and an old friend, Bakhmutov. Like all the chronicles in Dostoyevsky, 'The Explanation' is built on doubt and suspicion: Ippolit, while claiming to express 'the supreme and solemn truth', does not hide the fact that there will be contradictions. He submits to the test of a public reading to find out whether his ideas are true or simply the result of the morbid delirium of a consumptive. However, placed as it is in the frame of the narrative, the 'Explanation' is a true universal parable, set in time like a flash of eternity. Its title could be 'Last days of a man condemned to death by nature'. It is the rebellion of the atheist against the 'periodic zero', which Dostoyevsky was to take up later in his articles, 'Two suicides' and 'The Verdict', in the *Diary of a Writer* for October 1876,[16] and to develop in the ideas of Ivan Karamazov. It is the eternal cry of disgust, the lifelong shrinking of the flesh at the thought of death, 'that infinite force', 'that deaf being, shadowy and mute', 'that enormous and repulsive spider', which swallows life and appears as a scorpion in Ippolit's dream and in the picture of the *Dead Christ* in Rogozhin's house. The strange silent presence of Rogozhin during Ippolit's hallucination clearly has a dramatic role: Rogozhin carries death. The parable has another more profound importance: it continues Myshkin's painful interrogation about the sentence of death. The prince was rebelling against the harshness of society; and now there is a rebellion against the harshness of God. Myshkin's reaction is significant; unlike his companions, who are disgusted by Ippolit's exhibitionism, he is silent, as Christ is silent before the Grand Inquisitor. Ippolit's 'Explanation' reveals the impotence of Myshkin. Set in the brief interval between the two long days, bathed in the nocturnal clarity which Dostoyevsky stresses twice,[17] it is a suspension of time, a frozen cry of horror, like the famous picture of Edvard Munch, a point where action disappears.

At sunrise, Ippolit puts the pistol to his head, but it does not fire because there was no capsule. The moment of intensity which had suddenly invigorated the action ends in derision and pity.

An hour later, it is not yet four in the morning (351), and the prince, with growing anxiety, is wandering through the empty park. He falls asleep on a green bench and dreams of a strange though familiar woman, full of 'repentance and horror'. Light, fresh laughter awakens him: Aglaya has come to the meeting she had arranged for seven o'clock. They are clearly in love with each other, though this is not openly admitted. The prince analyses Nastasya Filippovna's feeling of guilt and Aglaya jealously flings at him the three letters the unhappy woman has written her. At eight o'clock (364) Lizaveta Prokofyevna comes in search of her daughter. There is a frank explanation. At about nine (366) the prince goes home; he is burning to read the letters, but is delayed by Kolya and Lebedev. Four hundred roubles have been stolen from Lebedev during the night and Myshkin is forced to listen to his veiled accusations against General Ivolgin.

Time is broken once more. There follows an inconsistent length of time, made up of agitated sleep, warning dreams, reading the letters. The day passes unnoticed in a painful torpor of body and mind, and so Myshkin goes from one night to another.

By a strange reversal, the rhythm is accelerated in the dream-like light of the 'transparent' June nights. Late in the evening, the prince goes into the park and, in a sort of dream, not noticing the real time – he thinks it is half past nine when it is past midnight (381) – he goes to see the Yepanchins. He is on his way back, confused, when Nastasya Filippovna appears. She falls on her knees before him: 'Are you happy? Happy?' she asks. She tells him she is seeing him for the last time and disappears with Rogozhin. The third part, gathered in two nights, ends on this moment of intensity, in which the reality of the night rises from the dream of the day.

Ritardando and crescendo at the beginning of the fourth part

The last part begins as laboriously as the third, with a digression by the writer about ordinary people and the problem they present to the novelist. This introduces us to the Ptitsyn household, where Varvara and Ganya are talking, roughly a week after the meeting of Aglaya and the prince (383). It is half past ten (383). Varvara has news of the Yepanchins: Aglaya is said to have accepted Myshkin, who is now considered as her fiancé. Ganya listens in disbelief, since Aglaya has promised to meet him on the green bench. But the gossip about his father and the theft of the 400 roubles is interfering with his plans, much to his annoyance; moreover Ippolit, who has been staying with the Ptitsyns for five days, keeps on alluding to the rumour. A violent quarrel breaks out, in which Ganya accuses Ippolit of spying and slander, and Ippolit retorts that Ganya is the incarnation of mediocrity. General Ivolgin, tormented by remorse, enters, flies into a rage and curses Ganya, leaving the house in a fury.

At this point in the narrative, the novelist adopts the tone of chronicler. Forced to go back in time, he declares:

It is sometimes best for the narrator to confine himself to a simple statement of events. This is what we shall do in the further clarification of the present catastrophe concerning the general: for however we may struggle against it, we are faced with the unavoidable necessity of giving this secondary figure in our story somewhat more attention and a somewhat larger place, than we had intended heretofore.[18]

The chronology begins with Lebedev's journey to Petersburg, to inquire about the 400 roubles stolen from him: that is, on the morning following the prince's birthday, and Ippolit's attempt at suicide.

On the first day of this flashback, Lebedev and General Ivolgin are in Petersburg, and in the evening they have come back to Pavlovsk (402). For two whole days the two men do not leave each other.[19] At night, they drink, sing and quarrel. On the next day, about eleven (402), General Ivolgin asks to see Myshkin, who makes an appointment for the following day. In advance, Myshkin summons Lebedev, at about seven in the evening (404), to find out more about it all: Lebedev tells him how he found the 400 roubles, which had been replaced by the unfortunate general, and how he tormented the thief. At midday (409), on the following day as arranged, Myshkin receives the general, who says he has quarrelled with Lebedev and then raves on deliriously about Lebedev's leg buried in the Vagankov cemetery and about being a page with Napoleon in 1812, unable to control his passion for lying, although he is painfully aware that no one believes him. It is two o'clock (417) when the general rushes out, hiding his face. In the evening Myshkin receives a note from General Ivolgin, breaking off relations with him: the prince's kindness has insulted him. The unfortunate general is thrown out of the Yepanchin house after a fresh outburst, passes a bad night and – end of flashback – is struck down in the middle of the street by an attack of apoplexy. The reader has returned to the starting point, and has even passed over it again, since General Ivolgin's fit takes place about two hours after he has cursed his son. Careful calculation proves that it is not in fact a week since Aglaya and Myshkin met on the green bench, but at most four days.[20]

As if the reader were not already unsettled by this flashback, Dostoyevsky introduces a second flashback, which begins a day later. We find ourself at the Yepanchin house, on the morning after the troubled night on which Nastasya Filippovna made her tragic farewell to Myshkin. All the family is wondering what Aglaya really wants. Is the prince a possible fiancé? On the first day, Lizaveta Prokofyevna goes to see the old princess Belokonskaya, her patroness. Back in Pavlovsk (423), she learns what has happened while she was away for the afternoon: the impossible Aglaya has thrown out Myshkin, who had the nerve to beat her at cards, and then sent him a hedgehog as an apology. In the evening (425), while they are drinking tea, Myshkin appears, radiant once more, at the Yepanchins' summer house. Aglaya asks him publicly: is he asking for her hand in marriage or not? He proposes and Aglaya vulgarly questions him about his fortune, his career prospects ... and begins to laugh, immediately apologising with strange seriousness. Myshkin is naively triumphant. On the next day (430) she quarrels with him again. On the evening of the same day (430), she explodes when someone accidentally mentions marriage. Between eleven and midnight, she gives Myshkin a lecture about the way he should behave at the formal party which is to take place on the following day; the engagement will be announced there. She orders him to stay at home and not appear until seven in the evening. The prince goes home, is feverish all night and only wakes at about nine (437). It is not ten o'clock (437) when Levedev appears: he has been thrown out by the worthy Lizaveta Prokofyevna, to whom he was proposing to show the letter from Aglaya to Ganya, which he had intercepted. Myshkin indignantly refuses to unseal it and sends Kolya off to give it to Ganya. Two hours later (441) Kolya returns: General Ivolgin has had an apoplectic fit. Twice during the day, Yepanchina sends for news of the invalid (442). The second flashback is finished: three days only. The two flashbacks match perfectly, given an initial time lag of one day in the second flashback, but this can only be seen on very attentive reading. There is also an acceleration of rhythm; the week originally mentioned at the beginning of part two becomes four days in the first flashback, and three days in the second flashback.

Time is splintered: there is an Ivolgin time and a Yepanchin time. This doubling of duration, planned by the narrator, does not exist for the prince, who assumes temporal unity even inside the split. The Christ-like nature of the Idiot is devoted to others, no matter what they are like: the delightful Kolya, the unfortunate General Ivolgin, the buffoon and master-blackmailer Lebedev, the tragic Ippolit with whom he has a discussion about happiness, on an unspecified date, and the women, Nastasya Filippovna and Aglaya, whom he loves and who are tearing him apart. The shattered time scheme signifies the exhausting struggle of love which

Myshkin is waging on all sides and warns the reader that his soul is breaking. Time is an executioner for Myshkin.

After the two flashbacks, the action begins where the novelist left it. The tension is great: besides the tragedy of General Ivolgin, there is Myshkin's anxiety about the formal party at the Yepanchins'. The author makes a preliminary attack on this smart, empty and hypocritical society, warning the reader of the snare waiting for the naive hero. Using personal comments or stage directions describing the conspiratorial glances of the guests, Dostoyevsky marks the distance between what the prince sees and what the external observer sees. The prince appears at nine (442). encouraged by the apparent goodwill which everyone is showing to him, he takes an emotional part in the conversation, and launches into a long passionate speech containing a violent attack on Caesaropapism, a eulogy on the beauty of the Russian Christ, and a dissertation on the Russians' longing for faith. Everyone is shocked and the prince steps back, whereupon the Chinese vase, which Aglaya had ordered him not to break, falls. The prophecy has come true. Stupefied, Myshkin watches the guests moving about, as if in a dream. They console and forgive him: he begins to speak again, praising the goodness of Russian aristocrats, in which, as he naively admits, he had not believed until then, shudders and ... sinks with a savage cry, struck down by an epileptic fit. Two moments of intensity follow each other in close succession.

On the next day Myshkin emerges from the torpor following an epileptic fit. He has a foreboding that some strange and decisive event is about to happen, a misfortune which all his visitors seem to predict: first, Vera Lebedeva at half past eleven (460), Lebedev at midday (461), then Kolya (461) for a moment, the Yepanchins, after one in the afternoon (461) 'just for a minute'. Aglaya sends a message that he should stay in until seven or nine o'clock. Half an hour later (463) Ippolit comes to see him. Ippolit has been spying on Ganya and Varvara, who were rebuffed by Aglaya when they came to meet her at the green bench. He also tells Myshkin that Nastasya Filippovna and Aglaya are to meet that evening. When Ippolit has gone the prince sinks into dismal thoughts and loses all sense of time: has he had lunch? Has he slept? He does not know (467). At quarter past seven (467), Aglaya takes him to the house of a friend of Nastasya Filippovna. Rogozhin lets them in. In the presence of the two men, the rivals confront each other. Aglaya shows inhuman brutality and coldness. Nastasya Filippovna, at first submissive, rebels and challenges her in return. Myshkin hesitates between them and Aglaya runs away, deeply hurt. Nastasya Filippovna tells Rogozhin to go and then, mad with grief, allows the prince to console her. It is the fourth moment of intensity in less than two days.

After this delayed and thundering crescendo, there is a sharp reaction: a plateau of two weeks (475). The author, who had regained all his omniscience when he described the guests at the Yepanchin party, puts on the mask of chronicler once more: 'We feel that we should confine ourselves to a simple summary of the facts, as far as possible without specific explanations, and for a very simple reason: that we ourselves, in many cases, find it difficult to explain what happened.'[21] He feels that he is in an embarrassing 'false position'. As at the beginning of the second part of the novel, it is a time of uncertainty, of approximate reconstruction of the truth. An immense amount of information about what has happened is collected, especially about the marriage of Nastasya Filippovna and Myshkin, which is the sole topic of conversation in society. First the rumour moves and grows among the crowd. As in Gogol, it ends by filling the whole country:

Two weeks later, that is from the beginning of July, and in the course of these two weeks, the story of our hero, and especially the latest adventure in this story, turned into a strange, quite amusing, seemingly improbable yet at the same time almost incontestable anecdote, which spread gradually through all the streets in the vicinity of the summer houses of Lebedev, Ptitsyn, Darya Alekseyevna, the Yepanchins, in brief, through almost the whole town and even the places around it. Almost the whole of society – local people, owners of summer houses, visitors who had come to listen to the music – all of them began to tell one and the same story, with a thousand different variations.[22]

Then the interpretations begin to spread: 'This funny story was decorated with various dramatic incidents . . . it was given so many various fantastic and mysterious colourings . . . The most subtle, clever and at the same time likely interpretation . . . In their version . . . like this atheist, the prince had, they said . . . a typical feature was added . . . It was said . . . others asserted.'[23] The chronicler admits that he finds 'great difficulty' in drawing any conclusion and is only reporting what he knows about the shocking marriage which is to take place:

besides these, quite accurate, circumstances we know some other facts which are completely bewildering . . . We have a great many of these strange facts before us, but not only do they fail to clarify, but, in our opinion, they positively obscure any interpretation of the affair, however many of them are adduced . . . We know definitely . . . but we know that several times, even often . . . we know that an hour, perhaps even less, after . . . This last news was recognised to be perfectly true . . . It was also said – but this rumour remained vague – that . . .[24]

After leaving the reader lost in doubt, forcing him to feel his way through the thousand possible truths, Dostoyevsky approaches the Truth by arranging a conversation between Yevgeniy Pavlovich and Myshkin. The approach is subtle. As author chronicler overtaken by events, he hastens to agree with Yevgeniy Pavlovich, or almost: 'In general we completely and in the highest degree sympathise with some vigorous, even profoundly psychological words, which Yevgeniy Pavlovich addressed unceremoniously to the prince, in friendly conversation, six or seven days after the scene with Nastasya Filippovna.'[25] But as novelist, he leaves complete freedom to his hero and Myshkin annihilates Yevgeniy's fine analysis by his faith in the power of a loving gesture.[26] Dostoyevsky thus offers a succession of varying points of view about his hero: the anonymous voices of the crowd, avid for scandal, the perplexed voice of the chronicler, the reasonable voice of Yevgeniy Pavlovich, the tormented voice of the hero, firm in his mad conviction. None of them is decisive. Each one has its truth, each independent mind has its own vision of the drama. It is the time of chronicle and stereoscopic vision.

These two weeks, dominated by rumour which is sometimes openly comical, are cut into two equal parts by the visit of Yevgeniy Pavlovich and also by the death of General Ivolgin, eight days after his first attack (485). The funeral, overwhelming the prince with morbid thoughts, marks the beginning of a period of growing anxiety, of muffled menace.

After this break, alarming rumours circulate and a succession of alarmist informers comes to see Myshkin. The dates are no longer in chronological order; the author begins his sentence several times by 'on the eve of the wedding', but then changes his mind and goes back again. The laughter and outbursts of Nastasya Filippovna and the Idiot do not conceal their fear and anguish, as the menacing presence of Rogozhin hovers around: Lebedev says he has seen him at least four times, while Nastasya Filippovna, five days before the wedding (490), thinks she has seen him hiding in the garden, with a knife in his hand. The prince has to convince her that Rogozhin was somewhere else at the time. On his part, the reptile Ippolit, between fits of coughing, enjoys frightening Myshkin: Rogozhin is going to kill Aglaya, 'love for love'. Keller, who is now on the prince's side, tells him that there is going to be a disturbance under his window on the evening of the wedding, and that Lebedev is hatching a plot. Indeed later, 'almost on the day of the wedding' (487), Lebedev, with the narcissistic vileness of the buffoon, confesses to his victim: yes, he has tried to get the Idiot committed, and even to persuade the Yepanchins to help, but, refused by everyone as well as the doctor who has examined Myshkin, he has failed.

On the evening before the wedding, the disordered dance of dates stops, and in the evening chronology takes over once more. At eleven (491), the prince leaves Nastasya Filippovna, who has accepted the challenge of the gossips: she will be dazzling. But at midnight (491), Myshkin is warned that 'it was going very badly'. He rushes to console his fiancée and spends an hour with her. During the night and on the morning of the wedding, he sends to hear news of her: she has recovered and is getting ready for the wedding, which is to take place at eight in the evening (492).

Events rush on but chronicle time is not abandoned. However, it becomes weaker, as instead of admitting uncertainty the chronicler relies on trustworthy witnesses: 'The whole of the following story about this wedding is told by informed people in the following fashion, and, it seems, correctly.'[27] The chronicler has to rely on witnesses because he is trying to describe action as it happens in two places at the same time: the house where Nastasya Filippovna is getting ready, and the church in Pavlovsk where Myshkin is waiting for her. By six o'clock (492) a gaping crowd has gathered around Lebedev's summer house, from which the prince is to set out for the wedding: at about seven (492) the church is filling up, and at half past seven (492) the prince goes to the church and hides for a time in the sanctuary. His witness Keller goes to find Nastasya Filippovna, who has been ready since seven (492). She remarked that she was 'as pale as a corpse', as Keller later reported.[28] She appears on the porch: her tragic beauty makes a great impression on the crowd. Suddenly, on the point of getting into her carriage, she cries out, and rushes through the crowd to find Rogozhin: 'Save me! Take me away!' They escape, race towards the station – 'The news of this adventure reached the church with unusual swiftness'.[29] Myshkin learns of it with grief, but leaves the church 'serene and cheerful: at least this is how many people noted it and then gave an account of it'.[30] Back home, he disarms the people besieging his house by his courtesy. At about half past ten (495), he is left alone. Vera Lebedeva makes a last visit, and he says 'Until tomorrow' with an 'unusual' look, 'at least this was how Vera reported it later'.[31] The chronicler consistently names his sources and quotes from witnesses. Nastasya Filippovna's sudden renunciation and her flight with the dangerous Rogozhin are like the lightning tearing through the heavy clouds which have been massing in the past week, but the use of chronicle, with its shortsighted vision, to describe it suggests that this is only one of the penultimate chords which announce the terrible unleashing of the finale. Myshkin asks to be wakened at seven (495); his short night's sleep is the necessary *ritardando*.

The intense pressure and the power of time in the finale

The time of action begins at daybreak, when the prince sets out to find Rogozhin and Nastasya Filippovna. The chronicler has disappeared. The harsh light of action and the mad whispering of the dialogue dissipate uncertainty and suspicion. It is the moment of truth where the hero finds himself alone, face to face with himself, freed from the observation of others. The chronology then stresses his considerable activity. An hour after being wakened, Myshkin is in Petersburg (495); between nine and ten he rings at the door of Rogozhin's house. Rogozhin is not at home, says the maidservant; but according to the porter he has come back. Puzzled, the prince paces along the pavement: can the figure he sees behind a raised blind be Rogozhin? He goes to Nastasya's last address, the house of a schoolmaster's widow, who gives him another possible address; nothing there. Meanwhile he has been back to Rogozhin's, which is again closed. He wonders whether to rent a room in the hotel where he had the fit 'about five weeks' (497) before. There he wastes half an hour having a meal which he had absentmindedly ordered (498). He goes back to Rogozhin's house a third time; it is useless. It is the same with the widow of the schoolmaster. He asks to see Nastasya's room: she had been reading *Madame Bovary* and playing cards with Rogozhin. Myshkin is in despair, but does not give up: he tries to imagine what Rogozhin would have done. Yes, he would have come to the hotel. The whole passage is given in brief dialogue, in terms of perception and not of sight, in thoughts directed towards action. Space is reduced to topography, movement to an itinerary, surroundings to the feelings experienced. The day is first 'clear and hot' (496), there is 'painfully burning heat' (498) and finally 'The dusty, stuffy Petersburg of summer gripped him like a vice.' (499). It is time in action, which the hero experiences painfully as intense pressure.

Tired of waiting for Rogozhin, at sunset (500), Myshkin goes out into the street. Rogozhin is waiting for him there and asks him to follow. The strange walk, with each of them on opposite pavements, begins again – like a musical theme in reverse, recalling how Rogozhin shadowed Myshkin before trying to murder him. This time they are moving in the opposite direction, from the hotel to the dark house. It is about ten in the evening (501) when they enter the bedroom. A full moon penetrates the lowered blinds; behind a green curtain, in the darkness of the alcove, the corpse of Nastasya is lying, covered with a sheet. The murderer whispers his terrible secrets to the prince. Tears fall from Myshkin's eyes on to Rogozhin's white and silent face. They are found many hours later (507): Rogozhin is unconscious, Myshkin has become the idiot he was before. The whole of this sinister night, except for the final paragraph, is given in dialogue and stage directions. As in a nightmare, length of time is replaced by power.

The fourth part has a more complex movement than the others, but is basically identical. Beginning with a short week, or four days to be exact, where chronicle time is dominant, due to flashbacks, it savagely reaches a summit: this is the fifth day, the double moments of intensity of General Ivolgin's apoplexy and Myshkin's epileptic fit at the Yepanchins' party. Time accelerates. On the next evening, second summit, the rivals tear each other to pieces, and Myshkin makes his choice. Again a long dead time intervenes, a plateau of two weeks. But in the second week the tension rises, death hovers and strikes, the crisis is near. Chronicle time is ripped apart by underground forces. It is the eve of the wedding. On the next day the storm breaks: Nastasya Filippovna runs away with the man who, she knows, will be her murderer. From now on the action has no more pauses: it is the day of Myshkin's search in Petersburg and the tragic culmination of the night spent with the delirious murderer beside Nastasya's corpse.

Remission of time in the epilogue

The epilogue is brief; it is an almost careless 'conclusion', in which a few traces of the chronicler remain. In describing Rogozhin's trial, Dostoyevsky places the adverb 'thoughtfully' (*zadumchivo*) in inverted commas, as if he had taken it from a legal report.[32] Or again, in an account of the correspondence between Yevgeniy Pavlovich and Vera Lebedeva, he feigns surprise and admits he does not know the reasons for this unexpected intimacy.[33] But on the whole he vigorously takes up the rights he had transferred to his heroes during the process of creation and during the actual writing of the novel. His heroes are no longer conducting their own experiments on their own souls: the tormenting fires are out.

While he shows some respect for Rogozhin, who stoically accepts fifteen years in convict prison, while he sheds a few tears over Myshkin, doomed to the eternal shades of idiocy, while he spares Yepanchina, using her as a mouthpiece for his own thoughts about Europe and Russian emigrants, while he gives a pass mark to young Kolya, who has been matured by events, and to the compassionate Yevgeniy Pavlovich and the gentle Vera Lebedeva, he executes the mediocre Keller, Lebedev, Ganya and Ptitsyn in two lines, condemning them to go on as they are, and he punishes Aglaya for her cruelty with particular savagery. Dostoyevsky tenaciously hated Poles, Jews, Catholics and especially Jesuits. No prisoners: Aglaya is condemned to marry a Polish count, a fairly dubious emigrant, whose fortune and nobility are soon revealed as pure inventions, to fall into the clutches of a French Jesuit father and become a fanatical Catholic. Ippolit, who wished to master his death, dies suddenly, sooner than expected. The epilogue is entirely free of the rebellious time of the novel. It is the return to ordinary existence, a remission in life's fitful fever.

21

The ascending spiral

Her soul was mysteriously unable to bear the straight line and had mysterious yearnings for something more complicated.

F. M. Dostoyevsky, 'Two suicides', *Diary of a Writer*, 1876[1]

The sphere, the whirling ellipse, the spiral and all the dynamic forms which the infinite power of artistic genius will be able to discover.

C. D. Carrà, *Futurist Manifesto* (1913)[2]

The spiral curve of The Idiot

On first reading *The Idiot*, the dominant sensation is giddiness, trepidation, stress. The constraining dynamics of the action feels like an attack.

However, when we consider the novel as a whole, we find a strange parallel between the rhythm of the first two parts (first and second) and the last two (third and fourth), although there is noticeable break between them, since the last day of the second part is also the first day of the third. The two wholes thus formed both begin with a crescendo of great purity (one day in the first part, two nights in the third) and continue to alternate doubtful periods, or plateaus where chronicle time is dominant, with dramatic summits when the crisis explodes.

The repetition of figures accentuates this impression of parallelism. Myshkin has two epileptic fits, Nastasya Filippovna directs two libels against Yevgeniy Pavlovich, Ippolit makes two proclamations, one oral, the other read from a script. Nastasya runs off twice with Rogozhin into the night, there are two strange wanderings by Rogozhin and Myshkin through the streets of Petersburg, two meetings fixed by Aglaya on the green bench (first with Myshkin, then with Ganya), two chivalrous interventions by Myshkin to protect women, and both with fairly painful results, Ganya's slap and the officer's blow on the chest. However the movement is not cyclic. The second whole (third and fourth parts) is more rapid and filled with events. The dead times or plateaus are both shorter and less static, the dramatic scenes are more numerous, following closely on each other's heels, and more tragic. The Idiot's first epileptic fit, although spectacular, saves his life; the second condemns him in the eyes of society. The first intervention, when Myshkin prevents Ganya from striking his sister, is less momentous than the second, where the insulted officer is on the point of fighting a duel. The first flight of Nastasya with Rogozhin is only a slap in society's face: the second is suicide.

As if repeating the creative approach, the curve which is drawn moves in a spiral. The second part gives the impression that it is about to return to the figures of the first whole (first and second part), but instead the curve escapes towards drama and catastrophe. This is the ascendant rhythm of *The Idiot*, where the action begins on 27 November and ends in the first days of July. However, in *The Idiot*, where the author is swaying between three attitudes, that of the polyphonic novelist, that of the chronicler and that of the god-like author, the progression has some weaknesses. *The Devils* offers a curve close to perfection.

The Piranesi staircase of The Devils

The chronicle, for such it is with its deliberate ambiguity, begins with a week of exposition, placed at the end of August 1870, in the course of which all the threads are joined together, partly by use of flashbacks:[3] then the rhythm sharply races ahead: three days later, on Friday (it is already September) Varvara Petrovna, the mother of Stavrogin, is trying to understand the Lebyadkin mystery, the chronicler is holding an inquiry about the enigmatic Cripple and on Sunday there is the famous scene-conclave at Varvara Petrovna's house, culminating in the slap which Shatov gives Stavrogin.

Reaching this degree of incandescence, the tension does not sink but stagnates. The next week, with the visits and absences of Pyotr Stepanovich the nihilist as the only indications of time, is full of the maddest rumours. It is a time of uncertainty and suspicion, of insinuation and penetration for Pyotr Stepanovich, and of spying for the chronicler. A sudden burst of fever follows from Monday to Tuesday: the narrator vanishes and Stavrogin appears on the stage. This night is spent in hectic activity; from seven to midnight Stavrogin has talks – and the timing is precise for each meeting – with Pyotr Stepanovich, his mother, Kirillov, Shatov, Fedka the escaped convict, Lebyadkin, Mariya Timofeyevna who throws him out, and Fedka once more. On the next day, at two o'clock in the afternoon, Stavrogin fights a duel and hints that he is preparing to do some monstrous deed.

The story of the duel inaugurates a dead time of about two weeks, during which, to echo a chapter title, 'everyone is waiting'. Rumours become louder, shocking events spring up like mushrooms: the profanation of the icon, prodigies of bad taste, multiple buffooneries by Lyamshin, a case of suicide, one of madness, revolutionary proclamations, the closure of the factory, incitement and commotion among the ruined workers, announcement of false conspiracies to cover up tracks. Stepan Trofimovich cuts off all relationship with his son and Varvara Petrovna. The tension rises unnoticed: disorder and madness settle in everywhere, with the processions as their visual and demonic symbol. Faced with this avalanche of rumour and libel, the chronicler loses his grip; he gives a few indications of time, but cannot regroup the facts in calendar order; he can only deal with limited amounts of time, as in the novella-parable of the young suicide, which he reconstructs from the accounts of witnesses. The rhythm accelerates once more when Pyotr Stepanovich appears on stage and lays his trap: in a day and a night he has converted the governor's wife to his views, changed the governor's mind by gross flattery, incidentally denouncing Shatov, caught Karmazinov 'the great writer' in his nets, reminded Kirillov of his promise to commit suicide, fixed a meeting with Shatov, organised a secret meeting (the chronicler, who had disappeared, reappears for this episode), and finally in a sort of loving delirium has begged Stavrogin to play the part of Ivan the tsarevich, who claimed the Russian throne.

From then on the rhythm takes on a mad cadence. On the next day – the Shpigulin day, in the narrator's words – the inoffensive Stepan Trofimovich's house is officially searched and the governor has the workers of the Shpigulin factory, who have been asking for their due, flogged in public: two flagrant injustices. The next day the boil bursts: there is the shocking literary party organised by the governor's wife, the monstrous literary quadrille at the ball, the governor's fury, the fire which breaks out in the suburbs, the three corpses with their throats cut discovered in the half-burnt house of the Lebyadkins.[4] During this diabolical saturnalia with its tragic climax, Stavrogin and Liza draw a bitter and disgusted conclusion about their night of love. Liza, desperate, runs off in the early morning, pale in the mist and mud, where she meets Stepan Trofimovich who is fleeing this hell. The crowd, turned into a mob by the fire and the wild rumours, murder the girl.

The acceleration is so great that from this tragic instant the action splits off into two directions, the Stepan Trofimovich line and the Pyotr Stepanovich line. There is no pause for breath: on the day of Liza's death, Pyotr Stepanovich prepares Shatov's murder: he stirs up his accomplices, warns Kirillov, and in the course of the night murders Fedya (whose corpse is discovered next day at eleven o'clock). On this same night, Shatov is surprised by a visit from his wife, who had deserted him and who has a baby a few hours later. He forgives her and is himself reborn to life. At six in the evening he is taken off to the meeting. At eight o'clock Pyotr Stepanovich blows Shatov's brains out and throws the corpse into a pond. At two in the morning, Kirillov, as promised, commits suicide. At ten to six, Pyotr Stepanovich gets on the train for Petersburg. A few hours later, Shatov's wife is anxious about her husband's absence, gets up, discovers the corpse of Kirillov and flies in terror with her baby in her arms (they are to die two days later). That evening, the corpse of Shatov is discovered. On the next day,

Lyamshin makes a complete confession. Four days have passed without a pause since the night of the fire and the last meeting of Liza and Stepan Trofimovich.

The last journey of Stepan Trofimovich takes place in this brief period. We follow the old man from stage to stage; on the third day he is delirious and declining hourly; on the fourth, Varvara Petrovna arrives to be present at his long agony. With Varvara Petrovna's return home the two lines meet. The split time becomes whole again for the final effect: Stavrogin is discovered hanged, eight days after the night of blood, and so four after Lyamshin's confession. It is the beginning of October. Everything has happened in five to six weeks, if we include the first week of explanation.

As in *The Idiot*, the rhythm, which is characterised by acceleration and concentration, forms an ascendant curve. But the track of this curve in a spiralling Piranesian staircase with incandescent flights of stairs and precarious landings where people gather to conduct inquisitions is almost ideal in its purity. At the beginning there is a slow ascent of one week, in which the coal of scandal is gradually fanned to flame by the breath of the investigating and spying crowd, ending in three days of increasingly dramatic scenes. There is then a plateau, or landing, of eight days, which rises imperceptibly to end in one dramatic night and day entirely devoted to Stavrogin. We then go up a few steps to reach a final landing of about a fortnight, swarming with dramatic events, processions, and, in the last two days, with incitement and injustice, and leading to five days of tumult, fire, and savage crimes. There follow four days of appalling discoveries, confessions, arrests, and for Stepan Trofimovich, of slow dying agony. The last day, when Varvara Petrovich returns home, is the day when the hanged man is found. Left until the last page of the novel, it reverberates like the final chord of an organ.

This sensation of vortex, as Gide calls it, of whirlwind movement, in Bakhtin's words, or more exactly of an ascending spiral, occurs because the events swell to the point where real time is saturated. We are made aware of this by the discreet chronological scaffolding provided by the novelist, and the repetition of figures which are identical but increasingly tragic.

The effect is increased by the deliberately shown incompetence of the chronicler, his inability to dominate time. The chapter 'After the Party' in *The Devils* is typical. The chronicler, horrified by the events at the literary party, has run away from the scene: he first goes to Stepan Trofimovich's house, where he is refused entrance, then visits the governor's wife, where he bumps into Pyotr Stepanovich and learns too late that Liza has run away, then rushes back to Stepan Trofimovich's house, and then to Liza's for confirmation of what he already knows, then to see Dasha, who does not receive him, then off to see Shatov, who doesn't listen to him, thinks of going to see Liputin, but changes his mind and goes back to Shatov, who answers him with a curse, and finally arrives late at the ball, where the great dramatic scene explodes.[5] From this moment, the chronicler, carried away by the dizzying torrent of dramatic elements, is completely overwhelmed: he disappears, reappears, rushes 'like a madman' – it is his own expression – right and left, always arriving too late, like the detectives who track a criminal by a trail of steaming corpses. If he chances to be at the scene of the action when it is happening, for example, when Liza is murdered by the mob, he is paralysed and impotent, as if in 'a horrible nightmare'.

When there is no chronicler, as in *The Idiot*, the painful sensation of being powerless to dominate time is transferred to the hero: Myshkin runs pointlessly through the whole of Petersburg searching for Rogozhin and Nastasya Filippovna, tracing a spiral route. The acceleration and concentration of the rhythm, deliberately orchestrated by the novelist, are also experienced by the chronicler, the central chronicler-hero (*A Raw Youth*) or the hero himself, entering their mind and speech. A reflection in *The Devils* illustrates this: 'What a pity we have to gallop through the story and have no time for description!'[6] Who is saying this? Is it the chronicler or the novelist, forced to finish his novel for a deadline? Both: their voices are one. The chronicler says it because he is intensely moved by this sequence of events which he is unable to dominate, although he is struggling to set it down: the novelist is using it partly for artistic effect, but mainly because an inner necessity, inherent in his creative logic, forces him to concentrate time to its limit. A last visit to Dostoyevsky's laboratory will prove this.

Contraction of time in the creative process

We have the rough draft of the letter which Dostoyevsky addressed to Katkov, editor of *The Russian Messenger*, at the beginning of September 1865, giving an account of the subject of the novella, which, after radical rewriting in November, was to become *Crime and Punishment*. First he described the beginning of the idea of crime and the murder; he added: 'After this it is less than a month to the final catastrophe.'[7] A page of the notebooks from November to December 1865 seems to indicate that the 'beginning', a 'first section' devoted to the period before the murder of the old moneylender, would cover at least 'ten days'.[8] The action originally took a month and a half. However, when we turn to the novel, we find the following time scheme. On the first day, at the beginning of July, Raskolnikov 'rehearses' his action and meets Marmeladov: on the second he has a letter from his mother and finds out when the moneylender will be alone; on the third, he kills. The following days, Raskolnikov loses all sense of time and stays in bed unconscious. On the eighth day Marmeladov dies; on the ninth, Raskolnikov is visited by Svidrigaylov and confesses his crime to Sonya; on the tenth, the wife of Marmeladov dies. For the next two days,

Raskolnikov wanders through the city, half delirious. On the thirteenth day he has his last conversation with Porfiriy Petrovich and meets Svidrigaylov at the café. At dawn on the fourteenth day, Svidrigaylov blows his brains out: in the evening, the criminal gives himself up. 'So all this mass of events, wanderings, conversations, reflections, rational or pathological states takes place within two weeks', concludes Pierre Pascal.[9] The real time, carefully noted by the author, has been reduced from about five weeks to two.

This contraction of time is also true for historical time in Dostoyevsky's work. We know that *The Devils* was roughly based on the real event of the murder of the student Ivanov, 'executed' on 21 November by the nihilists of 'The People's Vengeance', a terrorist cell directed by Nechayev. The Russian and German press, which Dostoyevsky read with passionate devotion during his exile, had made the most of this horrible political crime, considered a symbol of revolutionary savagery. From the end of November 1869 to the end of February 1870, they collected more and more details about the murder.[10] Dostoyevsky, as he later confirmed to Katkov, had already gathered and stored away a good deal of material about the nihilist organisation and its leader, the prototype of Pyotr Stepanovich Verkhovensky, when in February 1870 he decided, in the notebooks, that the action of the novel should take place in September.[11] Indeed, in the final text, the action begins in the first week of September and ends at the beginning of October 1870.[12] How does this tally with events in real life? On 3 September 1869 Nechayev arrived in Moscow with his accomplices A. K. Kuznetsov, P. G. Uspensky, I. G. Pryzhov and N. N. Nikolayev: on 21 November he murdered Ivanov in the park of the Agricultural Institute, near a grotto, and on 22 November he fled to Switzerland, where his quarrels with Bakunin began. On 25 November, two peasants noticed the corpse of the victim, weighted down with stones, under the ice. The real events took three months, but in *The Devils* the action is compressed into about a month, so that events are much closer to each other: Shatov's body is discovered on the day after the murder.

Moreover, as the example at the beginning of the fourth part of *The Idiot* shows, Dostoyevsky is capable of contracting the duration of time which he has announced in the novel itself. The interval of 'about a week' is reduced to four days by the acceleration of the rhythm.

So, whether we compare it with the historical calendar, or the fictional calendar which the writer proposed for himself in his own novel, or more rarely the calendar announced in the body of the text, the time of action is contracted as much as possible, tightened like a bowstring to speed the flight of the arrow. This is not because Dostoyevsky wishes to make a particular effect; it is an irresistible urge resulting from a structure of thought which culminates in the final great novel, *The Brothers Karamazov*.

The spiral and its golden number

In *The Brothers Karamazov* all the elements which concur in the contraction of time are present, together with the havens of eternity. The movement of the novel is an almost perfect spiral, with three as its golden number.

First, as in *The Idiot* and *The Devils*, the action is so swollen with events that time is saturated and the rhythm becomes stupefying. The novel is Dostoyevsky's final summary, a testament of extraordinary richness, the harvest of a life of thought containing twelve books and an epilogue, where the action takes place in less than a week. Three days and one night – exactly three times twenty-four hours – are enough for the crime, which everyone has foreseen, to be committed and for Dmitriy to be arrested.[13] This is the *fabula*, but it is also the profound subject, so that everyone, either in action or in confession and conversations with Alyosha, reveals his human, spiritual or ideological universe: Father Karamazov with his rows and his buffooneries, Dmitriy in 'The confession of an ardent heart' (in three chapters), Ivan in the chapters 'Rebellion' and 'The legend of the Grand Inquisitor', the elder Zosima in his life, written down by Alyosha, and by his death, of which Alyosha is the witness. After an interval of two months, the action begins again. Two days are enough this time; the day before the trial and the day of the trial itself, which begins at ten o'clock and ends about one in the morning, during which the profound truths by which Smerdyakov and Ivan live and the mental lies leading to judicial error are revealed. Five days pass before the epilogue: the destinies of the women who love Dmitriy are entwined and the hopes represented by Alyosha and the young generation rise. Little Ilyusha is buried. All this happens in one day, icy and limpid, with unity found once more, sealed by sacrifice and suffering. The acceleration of time is exemplary: three days, then two, then one.

The second element described in *The Idiot* with the splitting of time during the two flashbacks, and in *The Devils* with the bifurcation of the narrative into two lines (Pyotr Stepanovich and Stepan Trofimovich) is the dislocation of real time into distinct lengths of time experienced by the heroes and its reassembly by the voice of the chronicler, so that this scission does not seem to be a narrative device, but expresses a superabundance of events which are continually tripping and overtaking each other like runners in a race. In the first part, time is the same for all the Karamazovs: it is the first day in the monastery. In the second, time splits apart: Alyosha is living his second day, which ends with the death of Zosima, while Ivan is living his second and third days (when he departs for Moscow). In the third part, Alyosha spends his third day, which ends in his dream, mainly at the monastery, while Dmitriy, tormented with jealousy, spends his third and fourth days in a desperate search for 3,000 roubles – always the figure three – which would save him. Alyosha-time and Dmitriy-time join at the moment when Dmitriy, after being tempted to kill his father, is flying towards Mokroye to find Grushenka once more: 'The air was sharp and fairly cold, great stars were shining in the pure sky. It was the night, perhaps the moment, when Alyosha, kissing the ground, "was swearing in exaltation to love it for ever and ever".'[14]

The third element which we have seen in *The Idiot*, is the repetitive, mainly ternary, structure, accentuating the impression of a dizzying whirlwind, or rather of a rising Piranesian spiral. Not only are there three Karamazov brothers, as in the folk tales whose link with hagiography has been stressed,[15] but the recurrence of situations, actions, confessions and dreams sketches the loops of time, or more exactly the spirals, whose imperfectly cyclical movement tends to abolish duration, though it never succeeds in doing so. Twice Alyosha, the messenger of the novel, makes a tour, like Myshkin, of all the creatures who are equally embraced by his Christian love: at the beginning of the second day he makes successive visits to Zosima, his father, Liza Khokhlakova who loves him, Ivan and Dmitriy, his brothers, meanwhile meeting the schoolboys: at the beginning of the first day of November he meets Katerina, Grushenka, Liza, Dmitriy and Ivan. Also, twice in the novels, Alyosha, who loves people to the point of imitating them, spontaneously mimics the drama of others. Fyodor Pavlovich, his father, is drunkenly describing a fit of his late wife, Alyosha's mother, when Alyosha falls down, repeating 'exactly' the same gestures.[16] When Ivan Karamazov finishes his legend of the Grand Inquisitor with Christ's silent kiss on the bloodless lips of the terrible old man, Alyosha rises and kisses his brother.[17] Again, Ivan is told twice in a significant negative that he is not guilty of parricide: 'You did not kill him!' says Alyosha: 'It is not you who killed him', repeats Smerdyakov.[18] Three times, five days after the murder, two weeks later, and lastly on the eve of the trial, Ivan interrogates Smerdyakov. And on three occasions, and this is the most conclusive example, dreams (or hallucinations) ratify the destinies of the three brothers.

At the end of the third day, Alyosha falls asleep as he watches over the body of the elder Zosima, while the story of the wedding at Cana in Galilee is being read. Among the wedding guests he suddenly catches sight of Zosima, who signs to him to approach and speaks to him. He awakes, bows down as 'a weak youth' and rises 'a fighter full of strength'. Three days later he leaves the monastery for ever, following the will of Zosima, to begin his journey on 'the crystal road with the sun at its end'.

A few hours later, at dawn, Dmitriy, who has been arrested, falls asleep as the witnesses are being questioned. In his dream he is galloping through a village – burnt skeletons of houses in the barren steppe – and, seeing in the crowd of refugees a 'dried up, black mother' with her crying baby, he asks himself, 'Why are they black with black misery?' When he wakes, Dmitriy accepts the heavy cross which is his destiny. He will go to convict prison to suffer for others.

On the eve of the trial, after a night of suffering, the sick Ivan has a hallucination: the devil. He knows that the devil is an incarnation of himself, but a doubt creeps in; a crack opens in his atheist construction of the world. Henceforward Ivan's faith in humanism is wavering; his certainty about the world has gone.

The last novel of Dostoyevsky is a tragic parabola, a modern philosophic folk tale which could be summed up as follows:

Once upon a time there were three brothers who had a rich and wicked father. The first brother, Ivan, was very clever and rebelled against God: the second brother, Dmitriy, was neither good nor bad, and swayed between the Ideal of Sodom and the Ideal of the Madonna, but the younger brother, pure and innocent, loved all men and worshipped God.[19] Time bore them off into a mad spiral, and they had to face three days of trial. Their father was found dead, and one of the brothers wrongly accused. Three dreams came to them and the three brothers recognised their fates. Then time loosed them from its painful grip.

22

Time of power and power of time

Time, the mark of my impotence, the extent of my power
                                        Jules Lagneau, Fragment 40[1]

The false abolition of time

In all his great novels, with increasing success which culminates in *The Brothers Karamazov*, Dostoyevsky felt the imperious need to compress and accelerate time, to direct it in a spiralling flight of demented rhythm. Why this painful haste? Is time the suffering of the creature? Is the incredible acceleration of rhythm intended to abolish time?

Bakhtin's thesis is that time is abolished in favour of space. He writes:

This characteristic finds its external expression in Dostoyevsky's taste for crowd scenes, in his tendency to concentrate in one single place at one single moment, often in contradiction of practical likelihood, the greatest number of characters and the greatest number of subjects, i.e. to concentrate in one instant the greatest possible qualitative diversity. This is another reason for Dostoyevsky's tendency to observe dramatic unity of time in the novel. It causes the speed of action rushing towards catastrophe, the whirlwind movement, the dynamics of Dostoyevsky. Dynamics and speed here (as everywhere else) are not the triumph of time, but time overtaken, for speed is the only way of overtaking time during time.[2]

This is a just and subtle observation: the famous gatherings, where hoards of characters, arranged with directorial strictness in a drawing room, in a square, or in front of a church, live through those intense and violent moments which would take whole chapters in another novel, or the assemblies, like that in the plan for 'The Life of a Great Sinner', which bring together thinkers and writers from different ages, are perfect illustrations of Bakhtin's idea. He goes on: 'On the plane of Dostoyevsky's abstract intellectual universe, this characteristic is also shown in Dostoyevsky's fondness for eschatology, both political and religious, in his tendency to bring ends closer and to foresee them in the present, to guess the future as if it were already present in the struggle of coexistent forces.'[3]

It is a reasonable impression, but our detailed analysis of chronology in Dostoyevsky's novels does not authorise such an absolute judgement. We agree that Dostoyevsky devalues time in favour of space, and we have shown this process as it develops in the notebooks, but time is not

363

abolished; on the contrary it is used as concrete evidence and accurately noted throughout the novels. Just as fantasy takes the solidity and firmness of the real world for granted, speed and vertigo can be conveyed only by their contrast with the temporal scaffolding deliberately constructed by the novelist. The temporal landmarks are not intended to create 'the illusion of reality' but to confirm that reality, astonishing as it may be, has actually taken place.[4] The stupefying rhythm of the action does not deny time: it indicates the function of time in the novel.

Chronometry of the free act

This function appears at the incandescent moment of the crisis, which, paradoxically, might make the reader believe that time is suspended. In fact, these explosions at crisis point are registered in the real time of the calendar; during the crisis, moreover, time is measured with scientific precision.

The confession of Stavrogin, the chapter 'At Tikhon's' refused by the editor of *The Devils*, is a perfect illustration.[5] This is a text which was originally inserted in the time of the action, as the ninth chapter of the second part. The action splits into two directions: first the Shpigulin day narrated by the chronicler, second Stavrogin's day, in which his conversation with Tikhon in the monastery is described in dialogue and scenes by the novelist. Time has exploded into two points of view. This day follows the night when Stavrogin takes part in the political meeting 'with our lot' and when Pyotr Stepanovich proposes that he should be the new Ivan Tsarevich. Stavrogin does not go to bed, he simply dozes from seven to half past nine. At half past ten he is already at the gates of the monastery (5).

When Stavrogin gives Tikhon the pages of his confession, a new time appears: chronicle time. There is a flashback to Petersburg in the sixties, before Stavrogin's wanderings in the East, in Egypt, in Iceland and in Switzerland. The essential part of the action, the story of the rape and suicide of little Matryosha, is told according to an exact calendar: it begins on a day in June (13). Stavrogin loses a penknife. His landlady accuses her own fourteen-year-old daughter Matryosha of stealing it and whips her. Stavrogin has found his knife again, but says nothing to stop the whipping, as an atrocious idea is forming in his mind. Two days pass (14): Stavrogin questions himself – can he give up his appalling plan? Yes, he can if he wants to, and at once. However, on the third day he goes back to his landlady's: Matryosha is alone in the apartment. An hour passes (16). The same question comes to his mind: can I stop myself? He can. He takes out his watch and looks at the time: it is two o'clock (16). He approaches the frightened child and caresses her: she is first worried and then embraces him with passion and delight. Stavrogin has a reaction of disgust and fear but does not go away. 'When everything was finished, she was confused' (16): nothing else is said about the rape, but the accusation of having 'killed God' which Matryosha takes upon herself is so heavy that there is no doubt of the crime. During the night, Stavrogin has a fight in a tavern; in the morning he cheerfully finds his gang again. He goes back to his landlady's and spends an hour there (17). In the evening, he dreams of convict prison – a proof of his crime – and thinks of killing the child. He wakes at midday, finds a maidservant, with whom he once had an affair, waiting for him in his room and makes use of her services. For two days (17) he does not go to Matryosha's house: he decides to abandon everything. He even announces that he is leaving and then learns that Matryosha is ill and delirious and that her mother has to go out at five o'clock (18). The hallucinating measurement of time, minute by minute, begins.

Stavrogin arrives at a quarter past five (18). 'I remember it all to the last minute', he notes. He waits for a whole hour (18). Suddenly (the adverb is repeated five times in fewer than twenty lines) Matryosha appears, thrusts out her little fist in a threatening gesture and then runs to shut herself in a little room. 'A minute later I looked at my watch and noted the time', writes Stavrogin. The correction given in Anna Grigoryevna's copy is revealing: 'A minute later I looked at my watch and noted the time as accurately as possible. I do not know why I needed this exactness, but in general I wanted to note everything at this instant.'[6] He waits, draws out his watch suddenly: 'It was twenty minutes since she left the flat' (19). Stavrogin gives himself another quarter of an hour (19). Deadly silence; his heart is beating more and more strongly. He looks at his watch: 'There were three minutes to go.' At last he get up, peers through a crack of the door of the little room and sees . . . Three hours later (19) he is playing cards. At eleven (19) someone runs to give him the news: Matryosha has hanged herself.

Watch in hand, Stavrogin has lived through the suicide of the unhappy child. Watch in hand, he has measured the time of his own downfall. Watch in hand, he has tested his own immense freedom.

Dimension of actions and freedom

Like Stavrogin, Dostoyevsky is obsessed by the wish to seize the instant in its essence, the instant swollen with possibilities, the instant when something is about to happen, though no one knows what it will be. At every moment Stavrogin interrogated himself and stated that he could freely choose one way or the other. Sartre writes:

The majority of great authors today, Proust, Joyce, Dos Passos, Faulkner, Gide, Virginia Woolf, each in their own way have tried to mutilate time. Some have deprived it of past and future to reduce it to the pure intuition of the moment: others, like Dos Passos, make it a dead and enclosed memory. Proust and Faulkner have simply decapitated time: they have taken away its future, i.e. the dimension of actions and freedom.[7]

If, following Bakhtin, we were to translate Dostoyevsky's tendency to contract time into a wish to abolish it, we should place Dostoyevsky among the writers whom Sartre is describing, but this would be completely wrong. If Dostoyevsky compresses time, it is not to annihilate it and deprive it of its 'dimension of actions and freedom'. On the contrary, he concentrates and accelerates it to give back to it the fertility of action. He saturates time with what matters in the past and what counts in the immediate future: choice. He is fascinated by the idea of seizing the moment between the present still struggling with the past and the near future where a new impulse, a new free action delivers its challenge: the instant when the freedom and power of the hero are at their height and are acting to their fullest extent.

Many times Dostoyevsky noted, directly or indirectly, the emergence of the free act at the last second. It is a recurrent theme in his stories and novels. In 'The Eternal Husband' Velchaninov questions himself at length about the murderous gesture of Pavel Pavlovich: was it premeditated? He goes over and over the question avidly and feverishly, and sets out a first hypothesis: 'Pavel Pavlovich really wanted to cut my throat, although, perhaps, even a quarter of an hour before, he didn't know himself that he would do it'.[8] A little later he gauges the danger: 'These people, he thought, even a minute before do not know whether they are going to kill or not, but once they have a knife in their hands ...'[9] He comes to a strange conclusion: Pavel Pavlovich wanted to kill him, but the idea of murder had never come into his mind. In short, 'Pavel Pavlovich wanted to kill, but did not know that he wanted to kill.'[10]

Arkadiy, in *A Raw Youth*, analysing the savage action of Versilov, which he explains by a split personality – an intense pathological form of the expansive being – comes to the same conclusion: 'I repeat once more: I believe firmly that he wanted nothing at all and was not even reasoning. He simply had the urge to be there and after that to leap out, to say something to her, and perhaps – perhaps, even to insult her, perhaps, even to kill her ... anything might have happened then.'[11] The Youth shows the same psychological subtlety about himself and often notes this surprising phenomenon of the appearance of the free act. Why, he asks himself, did he hide in the bedroom of Tatyana Pavlovna to spy on the beautiful Akhmakova? 'What was I to do? I am not asking the reader this question, not at all, I am simply imagining that minute at that time, and even now I am totally unable to explain how it happened that I suddenly rushed behind the curtain and found myself in Tatyana Pavlovna's bedroom.'[12] Or again, he asks himself, why did he suddenly threaten to denounce her after being unjustly accused of theft? 'Remembering it now, this is how I sum it up and explain it: but then there was no time for analysis; then I shouted without meaning to, even a second before I didn't know that I was going to shout like that: It shouted itself (*samo kriknulos'*) – for this *trait* was in my soul.'[13]

At each moment, Dostoyevsky is striving to seize the sudden appearance of the free act in the swift flight of time. The frequent repetition of words like 'suddenly', 'all at once', 'sharply', the abundance of perfective verbs denoting the swiftness and unity of the action, of interpolated clauses, reserves, reticences, conditions and flashbacks, which mark the brutal turning point and the infinite number of choices offered, has no other explanation. The hasty rhythm expresses the gap between action and explanation, the vertigo shows that the reign of painful freedom has begun.

Dostoyevsky's dynamics recreate the time of power, in both meanings of the word – in its usual sense of intensity, force and effect, and in the philosophic sense of 'everything is possible' which contrasts power – potentiality (what could happen or be made to happen) with the action itself.

The painful accession of the hero to the time of power

The time of power is, as earlier examples have shown, experienced by the hero as intolerable tension, real suffering. In the world of Dostoyevsky, the exercise of freedom is always painful, even tragic. It emerges in bewilderment, amazement, and constant anxiety. The time of power is the opposite of epic or biographical time, which resolves things painlessly. It is at each instant the reaction, the unexpected rebellion of free will against reason, logical behaviour and conditioned motives. The hero of Dostoyevsky often finds a masochistic pleasure, like the man in *Notes from Underground*, or youthful pride, like the Raw Youth, in 'suddenly' doing the thing he had told himself not to do a few seconds before. The birth of freedom at the heart of the time of power is an eruption of magma which has been too long repressed in the depths of the soul; it is a terrifying pain as well as a violent longing.

There is a large gap between the free act and its rationalisation, and the bewildered hero often has the impression that his choice has been forced on him by time, which Dostoyevsky in his cruel realism refuses to abolish. The hero only becomes aware of what has happened when he is telling the story to himself after the event or when the chronicler (who in this case is also the hero) is writing a diary of events very soon after he has lived through them.

The time of elucidation, the uneasy approach to the truth of the act, then begins. It is a matter of recreating the moment when freedom broke cover. After the dramatic scenes, the moments of intensity, we witness a vast detective operation, whose extent has been shown in analysis of *The Idiot*. The characters in the novel, even the purest of them, such as Kolya Ivolgin, Myshkin and Yepanchina, become a pack of bloodhounds in pursuit of truth. They struggle to explain the past but they also become trapped in disturbing swamps – the plateaus – while the dramatic scene to come is looming over them and the next crisis is about to break. 'Spies' are sent, in all directions, the 'messengers' (Kolya, Myshkin, Alyosha Karamazov) also become reluctant spies. Peaceful gatherings turn into interrogations, cross-examinations or psychodramas, the lie is preached so that the truth may be discovered; one character shouts the opposite of what he thinks to the company at large, another one tells stories, in a less innocent way than General Ivolgin, another hatches plots, another is watching himself closely and does not hesitate to denounce someone else. Some characters are doing all these things at the same time. There is a constant sound of voices, anxiously whispering or chattering or disagreeing with each other, anonymous and inharmonious voices which surround the town with a web of gossip and rumour. Letters proliferate. *The Idiot*, *A Raw Youth* and even *The Brothers Karamazov* are full of missives flying from hand to hand with alarming carelessness, amplifying the rumours or contradicting them, deepening the mystery. A flood of evidence, documents, falsehoods, perjuries comes pouring out, while the chronicler, like an examining magistrate, is trying to get his files in order. But all his information only yields him a quicksilver truth, an incomplete image which is immediately blurred and confused again by the acts of the heroes. It is, in the words of Nathalie Sarraute, 'the era of suspicion', of ambiguity, which, in the self-analysis of the hero, becomes the rationalised face of the time of power.

Arkadiy in *A Raw Youth* is a perfect illustration of this quest for truth and the impossibility of finding it. First, as principal actor he makes the bitter discovery that there is a considerable gap between his praiseworthy intentions and the abject methods to which he resorts in his search for the truth. At the beginning he appears as an impartial inquirer, an incorruptible chronicler, a person, in his own words who 'has become sober long ago and is practically a bystander' with regard to the events which he is describing a year after they happened.[14] He therefore adopts a concise, almost formal style modelled on Pushkin, to make his report, which is based, certainly, on true evidence, on things seen, and on memories, but also, ironically, on eavesdropping, spying, unchecked rumour, and sad bits of gossip which he himself calls hypotheses or 'variants'. The seeker of truth, already wounded in the depths of his heart by recognising his own impulses towards spying, arson, blackmail and rape, sees himself unmasked as a dirty 'little spy' by those who surround him. Unable to hide his need for a father, he ingenuously admits to Versilov: 'The one thing I have been doing is getting details about you, all these nine years.' Versilov retorts: 'A strange admission and a very strange way of passing the time!'[15] But gradually he discovers the extent of the inquiry Arkadiy had been making about his activities, and he counter-attacks: 'Keep at it, my dear, you have definite talents in the secret police department.'[16] Akhmakova, on the other hand, is quite certain that the youth has been placed by Versilov to spy on the old prince. Hidden in Tatyana Pavlovna's bedroom, Arkadiy overhears the two women talking:

– The document exists, and he is capable of anything. I came in yesterday, and the first person I met was *ce petit espion* he has foisted on the prince.

– Oh, *ce petit espion*. In the first place he is not an *espion* at all . . . that coarse vulgar lad is a complete fool, how could he be a spy?[17]

At the very moment when Tatyana Pavlovna is defending him, he leaps out of hiding, completely justifying the accusation. Later, the debauched Lambert, a cynical blackmailer, repeats this double-edged compliment: 'It is lucky you saw everything: I should never have supposed you were such a talented spy and so intelligent.'[18] Throughout the novel, the Youth keeps denying that he is a spy, especially on Akhmakova, with whom he is secretly in love,[19] but each of his actions, premeditated or not, sends him back to this same humiliating image of himself. And, in spite of his accursed gift as a detective, a raw wound which is always being touched, he does not manage to find out the truth, as he is too concerned with his own character: 'Like a blind mole, I understood and saw nothing except myself.'[20]

Next, as chronicler, still stupefied, no matter what he says, by what he has recently experienced, he cannot stop himself, when he calls back this very recent past, from re-living it, and his revived passion ruins the objectivity he is seeking. The amateur chronicler was determined to tell his story in sequence (it is a chronicle with dates) and as objectively as possible, but there is a natural contradiction between this and the fact that the events he is describing involved him very recently as a bewildered witness, a fooled, ridiculed and cheated hero. The youth occasionally spells this out in the novel:

Now I warn you in advance that events from this day until the catastrophe of my illness rushed on with such speed, that, as I now recall it, I am really surprised that I was able to resist them, that fate did not crush me . . . But I will try to describe in strict order, though I warn you that in my thoughts then there was very little order. Events rushed against me like a gale, and my thoughts began to whirl in my mind, like dry autumn leaves.[21]

The contrast between 'now' and 'then' is typical of the subversion of temporality established by the chronicle. Two elements which are absent when the action takes place are introduced: the hero's judgement on himself and his knowledge of certain facts which were then unknown to him. The Youth often stresses the cathartic value of the conclusive memory which the chronicle represents. 'I note all these revolting things to show how shaky I still was at that time in understanding good and evil',[22] he writes. Or again, recalling his intention to go and ask Tatyana Pavlovna for an explanation and his sudden change of mind, he exclaims: 'I shall never forget, and I shall remember with pride, I did *not* go!'[23] At another point, analysing the deep motives, the need for money, the taste for luxury which had impelled him to play roulette, he notes: 'I was aware of it even then, but I didn't struggle against it; now though, writing it down, I blush.'[24] Knowledge alters the narration of facts and the Youth realises that it is impossible to recreate the spontaneity of the time of action. The difficulty of narrative, he says, is not in the 'devices' which every narrator is obliged to use, but in 'the nature of things'. Preparing to set out his idea, the Rothschild idea, he declares: 'even now, when everything that happened has gone by, I feel an insurmountable difficulty in telling this "thought". Besides this, I certainly ought to set it out in the form it had then, that is, how it was formed and thought by me then, and not now, and that is another difficulty.'[25] He is constantly forced to break the narrative line, and to his great disgust, to anticipate events:

I shall now move on to the final catastrophe, which completes my notes. But to go on further, I must first run ahead and explain something, of which I was quite ignorant at the time when I was acting, but of which I learnt and which I explained to myself in full a good deal later, that is, when everything had finished. Otherwise I won't be able to make things clear, since it would all have to be written in riddles. And so I shall make a direct and simple explanation, sacrificing so-called artistry.[26]

So the awareness (*soznaniye*) of what took place after a certain act and the conscience (*sovest'*) with its moral judgement modify the narration of the act. Moreover, the eternal running ahead in advance (*zabeganiye vperyod*) colours the event described with the enigmatic shades of its future, while at the time of the narrative the event is only the past imperfectly explained. Chronicle time rejoins the time of power, or rather struggles to express it. It is trying to recreate, in the light of subsequent knowledge, the action as it was happening – a gamble naturally doomed to failure. The search for 'time past' which the hero of Dostoyevsky conducts is not intended to resurrect the precious intuition of the moment as it is in Proust, but to seize or at least to approach the unseizable moment of choice, the instant when the hero uses his freedom.

The diary–chronicle leads to the impossible exegesis – deliberately willed as impossible by the novelist – of the free act, since an action once committed is seen as determined. Drawn into the spiral of the rhythm, the hero tries to seize the imperceptible shift, the moment when the circle, the time of eternity, changes into a spiral, the elusive moment in his rapidly changing existence when he can exercise his freedom. The hero of Dostoyevsky has no nostalgia about time, he suffers from it and hates it. Time mutilates him by its contingence and while he knows that he cannot abolish it, he tries to escape it to affirm, at every instant, his freedom. As we shall see in the following chapter, his visions of eternity are only dreams and sometimes mirages in which time can be dominated.

The time structure of the novels of Dostoyevsky stresses both the power of time, whose alienating and tragic force is exaggerated by the frantic rhythm imposed by the novelist, and the constantly recurring attempts to defeat time in the hero's painful accession, equivocal as it may be, to the privileged instants of the time of power.

23

The havens of eternity

What is time? Time does not exist: time is numbers, time is the relationship of being to non-being.   F. M. Dostoyevsky, Notebooks for *Crime and Punishment*[1]

Dostoyevsky kneads time like bread, accelerating and contracting it and stuffing it with a thousand events and possibilities, but his sense of reality forbids him to abolish it. However, at the heart of the time of power, the hero catches a glimpse of freedom. In his desire for complete freedom, he breaks through the forbidden doors: the door of real time and the door of suffering, which, as Dostoyevsky repeats throughout his work, is the only way of reaching happiness. The hero plunges into eternity and sees, as in the Book of Revelation, that there should be time no longer. At these instants, Dostoyevsky allows his heroes, exhausted by their painful freedom, a moment of rest to quench their thirst at the spring which he forbids himself to use as a novelist, although he had tasted it as a man.

The experience of eternity

It was a bitter privilege, since Dostoyevsky owed his knowledge of eternity to two terrible experiences which seldom occur together in one human life: the death sentence and epilepsy.

Epilepsy brought him, beyond faith, the sure conviction that eternity exists, that it is indescribable happiness, where the freedom of the creature is serenely at one with the harmony of the universe; epilepsy also gave him the marvellous power of experiencing eternity. Dostoyevsky generously extended this certainty and power to some of his heroes who were epileptic, such as Myshkin, and also to some who were not, such as Kirillov.

The intolerable experience of being condemned to death paradoxically gave to Dostoyevsky not the feeling of eternity, but a perception of time's dimension of eternity. Some hours after the atrocious scene staged on Semenovsky Square and after the reading of the decree of mercy, Dostoyevsky wrote to his brother Mikhail, 22 December 1849: 'Life is a gift, life is happiness, every moment could be a century of happiness.'[2] Later, in *The Idiot*, where Myshkin is discussing the death penalty, he was to recall this scene in intense and precise detail, except for one minor but significant point. It is not after the commutation of the death sentence that the condemned man sings his hymn to life and approaches eternity, but in the seconds preceding the execution: 'He said that these five minutes seemed to him an infinite time, enormous wealth; it seemed to him that in these five minutes he would live so many lives that there was still no point even in thinking of his last moment.'[3] A few lines later, almost literally quoting his letter to Mikhail, Dostoyevsky makes his condemned man say: 'What if I were not to die! What if life were given back, – what an eternity! And all this would be mine! Then I should turn every minute into a whole age, I should lose nothing, I should count out every minute, I should waste nothing!'[4] Strictly speaking, the hero is not granted the sensation of eternity as he is during the epileptic aura; at the heart of the time of power he discovers that time itself is charged with eternity.

The extraordinary thing is that this eternity belongs to living time,[5] not beyond the tomb. The reaction of two others condemned to death, one by nature, Ippolit in *The Idiot*, and the other by himself, Kirillov in *The Devils*, is in strong contrast with that of the two condemned men described by Myshkin, one facing a firing squad – this is Dostoyevsky in 1849 – and the other at the foot of the guillotine. Ippolit and Kirillov reject life, although Ippolit would like to die 'looking straight at the source of energy and life, the sun', and Kirillov is able to love 'the little green sticky leaves' of spring. Both of them abdicate and renounce time. Both atheists, they quote the words of the Angel of Revelation: 'There should be time no longer.'[6] Kirillov stops the clocks, as is the custom when someone has just died. Nothingness laps them round even before the hour of their death. 'As his personal life is finite, he refuses to see life as infinite time'; these words, said of Ippolit,[7] could be applied to both men.

The eternity which Dostoyevsky saw before the firing squad and which the condemned men described by Myshkin also saw is not the immortality in which Dostoyevsky as a Christian wished to believe, but the full and harmonious dimension of time, a kind of ideal reconciliation with the time of power finally accepted and finally without suffering.[8]

The Age of Gold, or eternity found again

The halls of eternity which the hero sees opening before him in life, just before he sinks into the darkness of epilepsy or death, are not the only ones in Dostoyevsky's novels. The dream of the Golden Age, a peaceful vision of primitive Eden, is the most precious among the others. Here again there is an organic link with Dostoyevsky's life, but to rediscover it we must make a long detour, going back to the Fourierist Utopia which Dostoyevsky championed in his youth, at a cost of ten years of convict prison and exile in Siberia.[9]

The dream of the Golden Age is a recurrent theme in Dostoyevsky's work, especially during the last ten years of his life. In chronological order, it was part of Stavrogin's dream in the rejected chapter of *The Devils*; it was then taken up almost word for word to be used by Versilov in *A Raw Youth*; and finally it was the key part of the parable in *Diary of a Writer* for April 1877, 'The Dream of a Ridiculous Man'. We shall take Versilov's dream, which is the version revised and corrected by the author, as our example. It is more universal than the Stavrogin text and less historically ambiguous, as it leaves out the allusion to the 'crosses' on which the prophets died and the evocation of the 'first scenes of mythology'.

I dreamt a dream which was a complete surprise to me, because I had never dreamt anything like that before. In Dresden, in the gallery, there is a picture by Claude Lorrain, which is Acis and Galatea in the catalogue; but I have always called it 'the Golden Age', I don't know why ... I dreamt of this picture, not as a picture, but as something that seemed to have really happened. However, I don't know exactly what I dreamt: it was just as it is in the picture – a remote corner of the Greek archipelago, as if time had gone back three thousand years; blue, caressing waves, islands and rocks, a blossoming shore, an enchanted panorama in the distance, the setting sun calling to me – words can't express it. European humanity was remembering its cradle, and the thought of it seemed to fill my soul with a son's love. Here was the earthly paradise of man: the gods came down and were united with men. Oh, what beautiful people lived then! They rose and lay down to sleep happy and innocent; the fields and groves were filled with their song and their happy cries; a great overflow of unbroken strength spent itself on love and innocent gladness. The sun poured its warmth and light upon them, joying in its beautiful children ... A marvellous dream, a great delusion of humanity! The Golden Age is the most impossible dream that has ever been, but people have given their life for it and all their strength, prophets have died and struggled for it, without it peoples have no desire to live and cannot even die! And all this sensation I seemed to live through in this dream; cliffs, and sea, and the slanting rays of the setting sun – all this I seemed to see still, when I woke up and opened my eyes, which were literally wet with tears. I remember that I was glad. A sensation of happiness, unknown to me before, passed through my heart, even painfully; it was love of all humanity. It was already late in the evening; through the window of my little room, through the greenery of the flowers standing on the windowsill, burst a sheaf of slanting rays, drenching me with light.[10]

This musical lyricism, this emotion is unusual in the caustic Versilov, or the cold and formal Stavrogin, whose style in the rest of the confession is full of 'mistakes and even vagueness'.[11] It is almost as if the writer, rather than the hero, were lulled by the charm of the Attic landscape, the serene freedom in which nature becomes nostalgia, by what used to be called the propriety of Claude's picture. Forms, colours and sounds are all harmony, a perfect balance bathed in sun and sea. Good and evil are suspended: there is no repression of the instincts. The Golden Age is the archetype of a lost freedom, which has been found again with inexpressible joy.

As a return to the springs of innocence and childhood, the Golden Age seen in a dream invites the psychoanalytic interpretation which Alain

Besançon gives it: 'Stretching out like a dream, the scene recalls the happiness of a breast-fed baby: the landscape by the sea is the maternal landscape, narcissistic Arcadia . . . The images of the cradle, of the union of gods and men, recall the happy symbiosis of the dual relation, a happy moment in the hero's life, rediscovered for one instant.'[12] But besides the Freudian explanation of the dream, this vision of the Golden Age contains a double evasion which tarnishes its brilliance.

First there is the desperate evasion of a tortured mind trying to find a state where all individual guilt is wiped out. Dostoyevsky grants this dream only to heroes who are guilty of harming children, which is the sin of sins. Stavrogin has raped a little girl who hanged herself in despair, Versilov has long deserted his son, the youth Arkadiy. The Ridiculous man rejects a destitute child, who was trying to find help for her mother, dying in abject poverty. The dreams of Stavrogin and the Ridiculous man occur when they are painfully remembering the children they have injured.

The Golden Age is an evasion not just of guilt but of the weight of universal historic culture, the mass of knowledge which paralyses the mind, as M. O. Gershenson notes in his *Correspondence from Two Corners* with Vyacheslav Ivanov. 'I do not judge culture, I simply state that I am stifled by it. Like Rousseau, I am haunted by the image of a state of happiness, of complete freedom, where the mind would be released from all its burdens, a state of paradise.'[13] To turn away from the memory of the attainments of humanity and the wanderings of history, to reject real life and one's own history as an individual, to abdicate when faced with the painful time of power and the freedom to create oneself: this is surely a rebellion against time. It links the Golden Age with Utopia, of which it is only a smiling disinfected version, perfectly safe since it is confined, a Hesiod's version of the myth, to the beginning of time. The Faustian Utopians of the nineteenth century, such as Saint-Simon and Fourier, had taken the Golden Age out of its immemorial night to project it into the future as the final goal of Progress; this was the danger. The Golden Age, in Dostoyevsky, is an evasion of historic time and expresses in dream a violent wish, a repressed ideal of universal harmony.[14] Dostoyevsky gives an image of it, possibly a rather insipid one, in a brief fantasy published in his *Diary* for January 1876: 'A Pocket Age of Gold'. The scene takes place at a very formal official ball. Everyone is bored to tears and Dostoyevsky begins to dream:

And if all these honourable and amiable guests really wanted, even for a moment, to be sincere and natural, how this stuffy ballroom would be changed! If each of them were suddenly to discover the secret! If each of them were suddenly to discover how much sincerity, loyalty, open gaiety of heart, purity, magnanimous feelings, desire for good and intelligence he had . . . The things which would happen would surpass anything our sages have dreamt about . . . Do you know that each one of you, if he only wanted to, could at this very moment make everyone present in this hall happy and bring them all to follow him? And this power exists in every one of you, only it is hidden so deep that it has long seemed improbable. Is it possible however, is it possible that the Golden Age only exists on china cups?[15]

Dostoyevsky, suddenly serious, ends with the words: 'What I have just said is not a paradox, but the real truth.'[16] If we compare these two texts, one in a novel and the other in a piece of polemical journalism, we see that the immense happiness which Stavrogin and Versilov find in their dream is not merely an illusion. The Golden Age which they experience in a glow of enthusiasm outside real time, a surrender in both senses of the word, loses its aura of unreality and takes the form of a hope, a prophetic truth. Utopia, once part of pre-historic time, wakes and is filled with energy. Again it looks towards the future. 'The slanting rays of the setting sun', which are always present in the picture of the Golden Age, become the heralds of dawn. Despair is tinged with hope, and the escape into the past becomes a leap into the future. The Golden Age wavers between the beginning and end of time, the end when there will be time no longer, because history will be accomplished.

The myth of the eternal return

However, the true nature of this Golden Age is ambiguous. It could be considered an unacknowledged form of the ideal of Christ which is present in all Dostoyevsky's work,[17] a kind of Church of Atheists,[18] which the author, even before he learnt of its existence in England, had imagined through Versilov in *A Raw Youth*:

These orphaned people would at once begin to press closer to each other and more lovingly; they would seize each other by the hand, understanding that now they alone were everything to each other. The great idea of immortality would disappear, and it would have to be replaced; and all the great excess of people's former love for Him who was eternity would turn towards nature, towards the world, towards people, towards every blade of grass . . . They would wake up and hurry to kiss each other, hastening to love, knowing that the days were short . . . Each child would know and feel that everyone on earth was like father and mother to him. 'Let tomorrow be my last day, – everyone would think, looking at the setting sun, – but it is all the same, I shall die, but they will all remain, and after them their children'; and this thought, that they would remain, still loving and trembling for each other in the same way, would replace the thought of meeting beyond the grave.[19]

It would be enough to re-establish Christ, as Versilov does,[20] when he admits that he is a 'philosophical deist' (another contradiction in terms), for the Golden Age to become an obscure variant of another ideal expressed by Dostoyevsky and his *startsy* (elders): the establishment of a true Church of brothers on earth.

These three dreams of the Golden Age, however, appear in the hearts of men who are profoundly atheist, whatever Versilov may say, in hearts hardened by indifference, by the *taedium vitae* which Tikhon illustrates by reciting the passage 'To the angel of the Church of Laodicea write'. Certainly these atheists are sometimes wavering on the edge of faith, as all believers in Dostoyevsky are sometimes at the point of doubt, but their atheism conquers. There are unambiguous signs; Stavrogin breaks a crucifix, Versilov an icon: the Ridiculous man, at the beginning of his adventure, proclaims himself a perfect agnostic and even an alien in the same sense as Camus. Moreover, the vision of the Golden Age, as Bakhtin and Boris de Schloezer have stressed, remains exclusively pagan, steeped in mythology.[21] The Attic landscape which stretches before our eyes is much closer to Rousseau than to the Garden of Eden.

The Golden Age is not a Christian vision: it is the pagan dream of happiness and love for humanity without God, the door of eternity which the artist opens to his atheist heroes.[22] Alas, the vision is always brief, as it is in the epileptic aura and in the fleeting perception of infinite time before execution, and the dream swiftly topples over into nightmare.

A silent menace hangs over the Golden Age, a menace which is present in Claude's picture. In the foreground the shepherd Acis is embracing Galatea, hiding under a kind of improvised dais, while to the right, in the distance, the jealous Polyphemus is waiting to crush his fortunate rival with a rock. In the same way, in the creation of the novel, a jealous Polyphemus is threatening the unstable and ephemeral universe of the Golden Age. Hardly has Stavrogin seen, through the mist of his own tears of emotion, the indescribable vision fading, when a 'tiny red dot' invades the picture. It happens in a flash: the insect spider on the green leaf, the hanging of the raped child, the derisively threatening ghost of Matryosha, raising her little fist. Hardly has Versilov finished contemplating, in his inexpressible dream, the setting sun of first humanity, than he sees in the same slanting rays the latest agony of humanity, the fires of the Commune reddening before his eyes. The Ridiculous man is triumphant after his journey to the Golden Age, and resolves to show this corner of heaven he has discovered to the world, but there are other things he saw and experienced in this ideal country which he may not be so eager to broadcast: the ruin of the Golden Age, the bloody fratricide which raged over it, the creatures he contaminated by his mere presence. The knowledge of good and evil, of truth and error, in short the terrible freedom of choice which dwells in man, has destroyed this Garden of Eden.[23] What has the Ridiculous man done to prove that the Golden Age is a fragile universe, doomed to vanish as soon as true freedom, the time of power, appears in it? Just as the Utopia of the Grand Inquisitor is incompatible with the freedom and love of Christ, the Golden Age where these marvellous creatures live is incompatible with the freedom to lie which the Ridiculous man brings to them. In the despair which overcomes him on seeing the disaster he has caused, he even carries his unconscious imitation to the point of begging to be crucified.[24]

But the hope which Dostoyevsky placed in the Golden Age is not

destroyed by his eschatological vision, by his premonition of the apocalypse. The Ridiculous man tells us why. His ecstasy after the dream is a
declaration that, although the Golden Age cannot live for ever because it is
doomed to degradation, it can be infinitely reborn. The Golden Age is
dead! Long live the Golden Age! It is repeatable in a cyclic time whose
structure is regenerated with each new 'birth', on whatever plane it takes
place. It is the myth of the eternal return which is found in oriental and
Hellenic civilisations, and later in Nietzsche. The cycle of cosmic time
destined to be repeated is simple: creation – degradation – destruction –
new creation. The first creation always takes place in the perfection of
beginnings, in the Golden Age. In time usury appears and existence is
debased. Destruction is caused by a catastrophe: flood, universal fire, as the
Iranians believed, a sudden reversal of the moment of the planets, as in
Plato. The new creation takes place because a couple of survivors or a
chosen race have escaped the cataclysm, or because a new race of pure and
innocent men has been miraculously born.[25] Dostoyevsky uses this age-old
myth of eternal rebirth in 'The Dream of a Ridiculous Man'. The human
adventure there takes place in three cycles of cosmic time. In the first, the
atheist hero is on the point of committing suicide, it is 'periodic and
perpetual zero': the whole of humanity which exists only in the mind topples
into nothingness; it is destruction. But this is only a dream; the hero survives
his own cataclysm by an interstellar flight to another planet, which is
inhabited by the 'children of the sun'. He has entered the second cycle, the
Golden Age, primitive Eden, the perfection of dawn. Soon this is degraded
by the pestilential germ of the lie, which is a consequence of the freedom
man has to choose bad as well as good, and so to create himself and his own
world; in short, the arrival of continuous time and freedom is followed by
catastrophe, imagined in modern terms of fratricidal war. Shades of horror
invade the picture, the hero is on the point of death. But he escapes, the
eternal elect, from death, and topples back from dream into reality. In the
third cycle, the Golden Age is discovered not in interstellar space, but
within oneself, as Dostoyevsky had suggested in 1876 in 'A Pocket Age of
Gold'. The hero finds innocence again just at the moment when he finds the
child he had formerly thrust aside. The Golden Age has never stopped its
oscillation between past and future.

　　Among the ancients, the myth of eternal rebirth was intended 'to annul
time past, abolishing history by a continuous return: *in illo tempore*'.[26] By
repeating the creation of the world, they were expressing their nostalgia for
the essence of things, their wish to be like the archetypes whose gestures
they are reproducing. In Dostoyevsky's atheist modern heroes, the myth
shows a longing for metaphysical being uncontaminated by continuous time
and a longing to return to the safety of their distant and idealised ancestors.
It is disturbing that Dostoyevsky, just at the time when he was making so

many references to the Golden Age, should have been seduced, as V. S. Solovyov was, by Nikolay Fyodorov's philosophy of the duty of 'bringing ancestors back to life'. In a letter dated 27 March 1878, he even adds that he believes 'in this real, literal, personal resurrection and that it will take place on earth' and that when immortality is thus established there will be no marriages or births.[27] This vision is close to that of Revelation – as Kirillov recalls – but it is also related to the myth of the Golden Age, when men were 'sons of the earth'. Eternity appears as cyclic repetitive time.

The most amazing illustration Dostoyevsky gives of the Golden Age and the myth of eternal rebirth is found early in his novels, although it only becomes clear in retrospect, in the strange dream of Raskolnikov in the epilogue of *Crime and Punishment*, outside the time of power.

If Raskolnikov despised Utopia, he cherished in his heart a dream of the Golden Age, a Golden Age to come. The final version of the novel is silent about this, but a few notes scribbled in the notebooks reveal the hero's thought:

NB. 'Oh, why is everyone not happy?' Picture of the Golden Age. It is already cherished in minds and hearts. How can it not come – and so on.

NB. 'But what right have I, I, a wretched murderer, to wish for happiness for people and dream of the Golden Age!'[28]

How can it not come? Raskolnikov asked himself. It does come in the apparently sybilline dream which precedes the murderer's regeneration, after his stay in the prison hospital, and in this dream the cycle of eternal rebirth is revealed in all its harshness:

In his illness he dreamt that all the world was condemned to be the victim of some terrible deadly plague, never seen or heard of until then, coming from the depths of Asia into Europe. Everyone was doomed to die, except for some, very few, chosen ones. Some new threadworms, microscopic creatures, had appeared, which settled into people's bodies. The people who received them in their bodies immediately became frenzied and mad. But never, never had people thought themselves so intelligent, so unshakable in the truth, as these infected people thought they were . . . Whole villages, whole towns and nations were infected and went mad . . . They gathered in great armies against each other, but even as they marched, the armies suddenly began to prey on each other of their own accord . . . the warriors hurled themselves upon each other . . . Fires began, hunger began. Everyone and every-thing was perishing, dying, . . . In the whole world only a few people could save themselves, they were the pure and elect, destined to begin a new race of people and a new life, to renew and purify the earth, but no one had ever seen these people anywhere, no one had ever heard their words and voices.[29]

'The sad and painful echo' which haunts Raskolnikov after his dream is a nostalgia for first innocence, arising from ancestral depths. And at the same time the annunciation of a new humanity is a presentiment of the Golden Age to come, the hope of regeneration of a new life after the catastrophe.

Raskolnikov has just received the first, healing wound of love for human beings.

And suddenly, on his return to the prison from hospital, this time in a waking state, Raskolnikov sees the mirage of the Golden Age in infinite space, beyond the solid landscape, as the lost and thirsty traveller creates the oasis of his dreams in the desert:

> From the high bank everything around was open to his view. From the other distant bank came the faint sound of a song. There, in the infinite steppe bathed in sunlight, you could only just see the tiny black dots of the nomad tents. There was freedom and there other people were living, not at all like the people here, it seemed as if time itself had stopped, as if the days of Abraham and his flocks were not yet gone.[30]

Freedom of space, time suspended, first innocence, sun, song, eternity reborn...

Eternity repudiated

The cyclic time which makes Stavrogin, Versilov and the Ridiculous man melt with tenderness is ambiguous. It is a source of eternal renewal, the youth of the soul, but it also expresses a refusal to accept living time, 'a fear of History', as Mircea Eliade writes. The Golden Age is a flight from the painful time of power, a dream prison. It recalls the imaginary architecture of the painters and engravers who rivalled Piranesi, where palaces and prisons are strangely alike in their repetitive proliferation of arches and galleries. There is an illusion of seeing space, but in fact it is only a succession of enclosures. Is eternity only time gloomily doubling back on itself? The devil of Ivan Karamazov – a personification of Ivan – imagines the infinite repetition of earthly history:

> Well, take the earth we have now, perhaps it's been repeated a billion times; so, it lived out its time, turned to ice, cracked up, turned to powder, decomposed into its component elements, then came the water, that is above the firmament, then the comet once more, the sun again, and again out of the sun the earth – you know all this development is being repeated from the nth time, and all in the same form, to the tiniest detail. It's obscenely boring.[31]

The cyclic time which the Golden Age inaugurates is an abdication of freedom, a dissolution of the self in universal harmony, a refusal to accept the pain of life. It is the Eastern Nirvana.

Dostoyevsky was aware that the cyclic repetition of time was a synonym for monotony and especially for deprivation of freedom. The prison he experienced and described in *The House of the Dead* is a concentric space where the convicts and time itself turn in circles.[32] This despairing vortex is reflected perfectly in the circular composition of the book.

Eternity seen during the epileptic aura, in the minutes before death, in the dream Utopia of the Golden Age, is a haven in living time, in the cruel time of power which curves in a spiral, not in a circle. The spiral in which the time scheme of the novel is constructed expresses the painful effort of the creature gradually extricating himself from the fascination of the circle, a nirvana where freedom is diluted in universal harmony (for which man is deeply nostalgic), so that he may accede to the true freedom of the time of power.

These flashes of eternity come rarely in the time experienced 'within' the hero. Eternity is revealed only in pathological circumstances, in dreams, or at moments when the soul has a desperate craving for peace. However, these brief moments have a fundamental philosophical content. For the Christian heroes, they are signs which indicate the eternity beyond the grave. For the atheists, they are more than the poetic 'suffering of a soul exiled in the imperfect'. They express the ontological yearning of the human spirit.

24

The dream of space and the space of the real

Full of exaltation, his soul thirsted for freedom, space, vastness.
F. M. Dostoyevsky, *The Brothers Karamazov*

Space in the novel

There is no time without space or space without time. Bakhtin created the instrument of the chronotope, whose name, if not significance, is taken from Einstein's theory of relativity especially to study their interrelationship and thus began a new, though perhaps too systematic, 'historical poetics'.[1] Dostoyevsky has an original place here between Flaubert and Tolstoy, and his novels are used to show the chronotopes of the threshold and of the agora, or market-place, where the time of the mediaeval mystery and the carnival hold sway.[2] In fact, Bakhtin is hardly innovating: he is simply changing the names of aspects already studied by other critics. Moreover he admits that these chronotopes are only specific cases and that there are others, complex and varied, in Dostoyevsky's work.[3] Bakhtin is essentially considering geometrical space and has described only two particular relationships between time and space, but in reality space varies according to the frame of reference: it may be geometrical, topological, philosophical or perceptional. In the novels, space is human without philosophical or scientific pretensions; organised by the novelist, perceived and experienced by the hero, it assumes a variety of solid and living forms, such as isolated places, paths, outlines, colours, landscapes. Moreover, novelists vary in their treatment of space – it is not so much the appearance of space that changes in different novels, but the fact that each author gives space a different significance and relates it differently to time.

The time–space relation in Dostoyevsky's work is best illustrated by a case which seems like an exception: the almost mystic fusion of abolished time and infinite space which his hero yearns for.

The dream of infinite space

In a double negation of finite time and limited space, the hero sometimes – not often, it is true – catches a glimpse of the mirage of supreme freedom. The same yearning for peace leads him to the havens of eternity. At these moments space opens out like a soothing infinity in which mutilating time, experienced as intolerable stress and agony, fades out of sight. Raskolnikov's contemplation of the Kirghizian steppe whilst he is a convict is a call from space, a summons to freedom. The wanderings of Stavrogin and Versilov in Europe, even in Africa, are a painful flight from time and their own selves. The final journey of Stepan Trofimovich in *The Devils* through the vast and bleak Russian landscape is an escape from the accursed spiral of events, while Makar Ivanovich's wanderings in *A Raw Youth* through the immense Russian land are a flight from his own century and a search for freedom by means of space. The glowing ecstasy of Myshkin during the epileptic aura carries him towards infinity and eternity, like the visions of the Golden Age granted to Stavrogin, Versilov and the Ridiculous man.

In another example. Alyosha Karamazov, revived by his daytime dream of the marriage at Cana in Galilee, leaves the cell where he was watching over Zosima's mortal remains. An amazing night scene blazes before him: 'The white towers and golden cupolas of the cathedral sparkled against a sapphire sky.'[4] The link between space and freedom is affirmed stylistically by two sentences, symmetrically arranged to echo each other: 'Full of exaltation his soul thirsted for freedom, for space, for vastness. Above him vast and boundless toppled the cupola of heaven, full of quiet shining stars.'[5]

This desire to be lost in infinite space is a rare sign of grace for the heroes of Dostoyevsky. In fact, the complete triumph of space, so far as it could be attained, would mean that time is dead. Dostoyevsky the poet pursues this impossible ideal through his heroes, but Dostoyevsky the artist, an implacable realist, refuses it. In fact, space originates in the same double freedom which rules in time; it is part of both the creator and the created, and, inside each of them, it is a part of the conflict between the ideal and the way in which the ideal must be tested by experience.

The birth of space

Dostoyevsky's creative interrogation about space is less stormy than his interrogation about time. He never tries to elucidate the nature of human space. Unlike time, space is not an aggression, a painful alienation to overcome but the natural environment where the freedom of man is exercised.

At the planning stage in the notebooks, Dostoyevsky, unlike his rival Turgenev or even Tolstoy, worried very little about the descriptive element, possibly relying on his amazing ability to improvise. He confined himself, whether in portrait or landscape, to defining the composition, the spirit and especially the impression they leave on the hero's mind. Here, for example, are some preparatory notes for *Crime and Punishment*:

Exit [of Raskolnikov] and description of Petersburg. Goodbye to all this world, sadness. Splendid description and suddenly the meeting with the man who has been run over.[6]

And then the last chapter: summer, dust, lime. Lieutenant-Powder and so on, as disgusting, sordid and prosaic as possible.[7]

By the bridge a faint: stopped on the bridge. His head began to go round, fiery wheels, sunset, panorama.[8]

Even the symbolic landscapes are reduced to a mere note, as in this example from the notebooks of *A Raw Youth*:

Finale of the novel. Everyone is dead. The youth remains alone . . . Three days he stayed indoors. Went out in the evening. The idea of profit is tarnished. The sun is setting over the Neva. He wants to live. Each blade of grass is praying.[9]

These dry, laconic notes on scenery are in sharp contrast with the expansive number of notes relating to the time of the chronicle or measuring the time of the action.

The balance is re-established in the novels, where elements relating to space – topography, scenes of action, interiors, exteriors, colours – are as important as the temporal indications. We must conclude that space appears in the novels of Dostoyevsky while he is writing the final version, and so after he has solved the problems about the manner of conducting the narrative. More exactly, space is organised after the temporal choices, such as the time of power, or chronicle time with its perpetual shuttling between the author's point of view and that of the hero.

Space in the Dostoyevsky novel is born with duration. It is not present from the beginning, but appears gradually. The voice of the hero measures it out drop by drop, multiplying its meanders, minute variations and recurrent themes. He slows down so rarely that the appearance of a landscape, swift as it may be, acquires unusual significance and vividness. The nature of space is symphonic. It is organised gradually in an imperceptible but tireless accumulation and the whole which is formed is only perceived over a period of time and by the memory which notes brief, rare, and fleeting indications. Dostoyevsky, although he was hesitant to abandon traditional description in his first works, soon turned away from description and refused to introduce fragments of concrete reality into fiction or to analyse them to exhaustion point like Flaubert or Goncharov, those devourers of the object, or to paint them lovingly, like Turgenev, master of Russian landscape painting. Dostoyevsky's space, which appeared as he was writing the novel, is elaborated only as much as it needs to be, like a country which one discovers as one passes through it. The method is surprisingly effective: space acquires the existential presence of an environment. It does not need to be described in order to exist. It results not from a proposed way of seeing but from a perception which is continuously reorganising it.

All perception is a structuring of space, an organisation of forms. The forms respond to the intentions both of the novelist and of the hero; while the scenery expresses the intention of the writer, the landscape expresses that of the hero. We sense the importance of space in Dostoyevsky: it signifies.

Scenic space

The space structured by Dostoyevsky is essentially theatrical. In his youth, Dostoyevsky had dreamt of being a playwright. In 1858, after his time in prison, he rediscovered the rules of dramatic art while writing *The Village of Stepanchikovo and its Inhabitants*, a comic novel which has often been adapted for the stage and which contains dramatic features typical of later novels, such as the division into scenes, acceleration of rhythm, the action which takes place in scenes of confrontation rather than being narrated. 'When they appear, the characters of Dostoyevsky are already in situation; they do not evolve but act: they do not become, like characters in a novel, but reveal themselves like dramatic personae,' writes Nina Gourfinkel.[10] Finding his gifts renewed, Dostoyevsky carried them into his great novels, *The Idiot, The Devils, A Raw Youth* and *The Brothers Karamazov*, which have often been called novel-tragedies',[11] to take an expression of Merezh-kovsky in 1901, developed by Vyacheslav Ivanov in 1916 in *Furrows and Landmarks*, and since then widely adopted by Russian criticism. Nemi-rovich-Danchenko, one of the directors of the Moscow Arts Theatre, noted: 'If Dostoyevsky wrote as a novelist, he felt as a dramatist. His images, his dialogues are dramatic. How many things in the novels aspire towards the theatre, the stage, and could be easily and naturally placed in a stage setting.'[12]

Following Jacques Copeau, who dramatised *The Brothers Karamazov* in 1911, Albert Camus made the same observation in the programme for the Antoine Théâtre in March 1959, with reference to the characters of *Les Possédés* (*The Devils*) which he had adapted for the stage:

I have been seeing his characters on the stage for almost twenty years. They not only have the stature of dramatic personae, they have the same behaviour, the same explosions, the same rapid and disturbing movement. Dostoyevsky uses theatrical technique in his novels. A man of the theatre, whether he is an actor, a director or an author, can always find in Dostoyevsky all the information he needs.[13]

The parallel which is so often made between dramatic technique and the form of the novel is very instructive, especially with regard to scenic space and scenery. The stage is an environment seen, perceived by the spectator. It exists before the action and has no need of description during the play. Props, stage devices, backdrops have only one function: to serve the action and draw attention to it when necessary. In the novel of Dostoyevsky, the scenery is closer to the concrete and significantly schematic arrangement of the modern stage than to the realistic settings and patiently reconstructed interiors of the nineteenth-century theatre. Everything is stripped bare and the movement is geometrical; there are group scenes carefully prepared, or asides, secrets furtively exchanged, poignant confessions in doubtful places (corridors, closed angles of the stage, in front of the curtain), a complex game moving spotlights with focused lighting and changing colours and everywhere, as if on a screen, the coloured projection of the hero's dreams.

25

The inventory and the expressionist orchestration of scenery and lighting

With delicacy of feeling and mind an artist can make a great deal of effect simply by the way he arranges the parts played by those objects of poverty, the domestic utensils of a poor hovel, and by this amusing arrangement he can impress the heart.

F. M. Dostoyevsky, *Diary of a Writer*, 1877[1]

Inventory of the scenery

Dostoyevsky constructs a scene by enumerating objects, by arranging volumes, and measuring places. Both as props man and as architect and decorator, he limits himself to defining a space in which human beings evolve, choosing only what is strictly necessary for the action and the idea. This is not inevitably sober: occasionally there is a rich abundance of objects, as in a Dutch picture, to convey an idea of profusion. Dostoyevsky does not give descriptions (*opisaniya*) but inventories (*opisi*).

Here, for example, is the surprising 'description' of Ikhmenev's garden in *The Insulted and Injured*:

This little garden belonged to the house: it was about twenty-five paces long and as many paces wide and was all overgrown with greenery. In it were three tall, old, widely branching trees, some young birch-trees, a few bushes of lilac and honey-suckle, there was a little corner for raspberries, two strawberry beds and two narrow winding paths, along and across the garden. The old man was delighted with it and swore that mushrooms would soon be growing there. But the main thing was that Nelli fell in love with this little garden.[2]

The paces define the people who are moving in the garden and the botanical precision is a preparation for the passage where Nelli, the dying child, remembers her love for flowers. Another example can be taken from Dostoyevsky's last work, *The Brothers Karamazov*, where the inventory is fuller, but the spirit is identical. This is the garden next to the house of old Karamazov, the deserted garden where Dmitriy is to make his 'confession of an ardent heart' to Alyosha:

The garden had an area of about a desiatine [an acre approximately] or a little more but it was planted with trees only round the four fences – with apple trees, maple, lime and birch. The middle of the garden was empty, just as a meadow, from which in summer several poods of hay were gathered .. Dmitriy Fyodorovich led his guest to a corner of the garden that was furthest from the house. There suddenly, in the thickly standing limetrees and old bushes of blackcurrant and elderberry, guelder rose and lilac, appeared what seemed to be the ruins of an ancient green summerhouse, which had turned black and twisted, with latticed walls, but with a covered top, in which it was still possible to shelter from the rain .. But the whole had already decomposed, the floor had rotted, all the floorboards were shaky, the wood smelt damp. In the summerhouse there was a green wooden table, dug into the ground, and around it there were benches, also green, on which it was still possible to sit. Alesha immediately noticed the excited state of his brother[3]

It is in this green world that Dmitriy is to sing his hope and his hymn to life. An intentional element, colour, is added to the necessary scenic indications, and this is part of a vast orchestration which is organised not by the hero but by the novelist.

The scenery is part of a knowledge which is rigorously subordinated to the present or future requirements of the action, a knowledge which is meant to be shared with the reader. It is also a part of one of several intentions, which are to be signified to the reader.

The bunch of flowers gathered by the eleven-year-old hero of the novella 'A Little Hero' serves to hide a lost and compromising letter which the child, with charming tact, wishes to return to its owner, the beautiful Madame M., but the bouquet is also, although the boy does not admit it, a declaration of love. Wrapped in 'bright green palmated leaves of maple', it contains sweet-briar and wild jasmine, cornflowers mingled with blades of rye 'the most golden and the fattest', forget-me-nots, blue harebells and wild carnations, yellow water-lilies, pansies, sweet-smelling violets which had been 'hiding in the rich deep grass'.[4] The declaration is modest and discreet – they are wild flowers – but there is a profusion and brilliance of colour unusual in the mature Dostoyevsky, which conveys the child's feeling.

This Flemish profusion, occasionally found in Dostoyevsky's early works, is never purely aesthetic. Here is the amazing inventory of Masloboyev's table in *The Insulted and Injured*, described by Ivan Petrovich:

It was obvious that they expected me. A pretty pinchbeck samovar was boiling on the round table, which was covered with a fine, expensive tablecloth. There was a glistening tea service of crystal, silver and porcelain. On another table, covered with a different kind of tablecloth but no less rich, stood plates of sweets, very good ones, jams and compotes from Kiev, marmalade, pastilles, jellies, French jams, oranges, apples and three or four sorts of nuts, in a word, a whole fruit-shop window. On a third table, covered with a tablecloth white as snow, stood every different kind of hors d'oeuvres: caviare, cheese, pie, sausages, smoked ham, fish and a row of superb crystal jugs with vodka of various sorts and in the most charming colours – green, ruby, brown, gold. Finally, on a little table to the side, also covered with a white tablecloth, stood two vases containing champagne bottles. On the table in front of the divan were three beautiful bottles, Sauternes, Lafite and cognac, very expensive bottles which had been bought at Yeliseyev's.[5]

And all this Gargantuan display is set out for a single guest, Ivan Petrovich. Why this sudden luxuriance, conveyed by adjectives so flat and commonplace that an aesthete would scorn to use them? The festive air of all these objects, as the rest of the page shows, describes Masloboyev psychologically as a pleasure seeker, a lover of good things, but also signifies the feast which the affair of Nelli represents in his shady existence. By organising Nelli's salvation, by conducting an inquiry into Prince Valkovsky's past to help Ivan Petrovich, Masloboyev has regained his lost purity and is celebrating his newly won dignity. As his wife, Aleksandra Semyonovna, says: 'Let good people know that we know how to live, like everyone else.' And further on she adds: 'All year I've been thinking: when a guest comes, a real guest, we will show him all this and give him a feast'.[6]

After *The Insulted and Injured*, Dostoyevsky refined his technique of using scenery. The realism of *Notes from the House of the Dead* played a decisive part in this evolution, whose culmination is the second part of *Notes from Underground*: 'Because of wet snow' of 1864. From then on sobriety dominates. The repetition of recurring elements in the context of the action does not take place on a single page, but is distributed throughout the novel, and it is the significance given to the scenery which is important, whether this is done by an disturbing insistence on 'nothing special', or openly by giving matter its own psychic life.

Still waters

Society drawing-rooms, with their gold and white marble, their long mirrors and suites of rooms into which unexpected silhouettes glide, are not described in detail: only the characters who act in them hold the novelist's attention. It is enough to focus the reader's gaze on one fascinating object: the fireplace of Nastasya Filippovna, where the 100,000 roubles of Rogozhin do not burn, or the Chinese vase in the Yepanchin drawing room, which Myshkin knocks over .. Some middle-class, even modest interiors are treated with the same apparent indifference: nothing special about them, says Dostoyevsky. But this is doubtful; these still waters run deep.

The old money-lender's apartment in *Crime and Punishment* is a significant example:

The small room, into which the young man passed, with yellow wallpaper, geraniums and muslin curtains at the windows, was at that moment brightly lit by the setting sun. '*Then*, of course, the sun will be shining in just the same way! . . ' – the thought flashed apparently by chance through Raskolnikov's mind, and he cast a quick glance round everything in the room, to learn and remember its arrangement as well as he could. But in the room there was nothing special. The furniture, all very old and of yellow wood, consisted of a divan with a huge curved wooden back, an oval table in front of the divan, a dressing table with a mirror between the windows, chairs along the walls and two or three cheap pictures in yellow frames, depicting young German ladies with birds in their hands – this was all the furniture there was. In the corner in front of a small icon a lamp was burning. Everything was very clean:

.. Raskolnikov cast a curious sidelong glance at the cotton curtain in front of the door to the second, very tiny room, where the old woman's bed and chest of drawers were standing and which he had never yet managed to see. The whole apartment consisted of these two rooms.[7]

Nothing special, no doubt, but a strange dominant note of yellow: the evening sun, the wallpaper, the frames, without counting the yellowing furs worn by the old woman, which appear earlier in the text. This dominant note of yellow is to reappear in the dream when the crime is repeated in eerie moonlight. Nothing special, but there is also the deliberate failure to describe the object which is coveted and guessed at, the money chest.

The apartment where Svidrigaylov sets a trap for Dunya, Raskolnikov's sister, is presented in the same way:

Svidrigaylov occupied two furnished, fairly spacious rooms. Dunya looked round mistrustfully, but she noticed nothing special either in the furnishing or the arrangement of the rooms, although something in it might have been noted, for instance, that Svidrigaylov's apartment somehow happened to be between two almost uninhabited apartments. The entrance to it was not directly from the corridor, but through two rooms belonging to the landlady, almost empty.[8]

Absolutely nothing special, except an isolated setting which might have been made for an attempt at rape. In these two examples, the scenery is strictly a function of the action to follow: murder, rape. It is ruled by dramatic ends and its apparent banality is a preparation for dreadful awakenings. These interiors in which there is nothing special are waiting.

Clashing interiors

But there are other, more numerous, interiors, where Dostoyevsky is not intent so much on the action to come but on expression, as in expressionist art. The scenery acquires a significance of its own: it is a concrete expression of the mutilation of human beings. Dostoyevsky, by a dissonance or a flattened chord, extends psychic life to matter. He uses things as signs to convey the soul's anguish without resorting to the hero's vision, as he does in landscape. Three examples, again chosen from *Crime and Punishment*, illustrate this: they are the rooms of the tormented heroes, Raskolnikov, Sonya and Svidrigaylov.

Raskolnikov is lodging under the roof of a high, five-storey house, in an attic room which is like 'a wardrobe', a 'ship's cabin', and even a 'coffin'. He considers it with hatred:

It was a tiny little cage, about six paces long, which had the most pathetic appearance with its yellow, dusty wallpaper, which was coming away from the walls everywhere, and it was so low that anyone who was even moderately tall felt uneasy in it, and it seemed as if you were about to bump your head on the ceiling at any moment. The furniture suited the room: there were three old chairs, which were not completely serviceable, a painted table in the corner with several exercise books and books on it .. covered with dust .. and, finally, a clumsy large sofa, which took up practically the whole of the wall and half the width of the room, and which had once been covered with chintz, but was now in rags and served Raskolnikov as a bed.[9]

Sonya's bedroom is even more depressing:

It was a large room, but extremely low .. Sonya's room looked like a barn, and had the appearance of an extremely incorrect square, and this made it look deformed. A wall with three windows, overlooking the canal, cut across the room somehow sideways, and so one corner, horribly acute, ran away somewhere into the depths, so that, with weak lighting, it was impossible even to see it properly: the other corner was too hideously wide. In all this large room there was practically no furniture. In the corner, to the right, there was a bed; next to it, nearer the door, a chair. Along the same wall as the bed .. was a simple deal table, covered with a dark blue tablecloth; near the table were two wickerwork chairs. Next, by the opposite wall, near the sharp corner, stood a small chest of drawers of plain wood, which seemed lost in the emptiness .. The yellowy, torn and worn-out wallpaper had blackened in all the corners: it must have been damp and smoky here in winter. The poverty was obvious; even the bed had no curtains.[10]

The hotel room where Svidrigaylov spends the night before his suicide is just as bad:

It was a little cage, so tiny that Svidrigaylov only just fitted into it, with one window; the very dirty bed, a plain painted table and chair took up nearly all the space. The walls looked as if they had been roughly knocked together out of planks, with scratched wallpaper, so dusty and torn that the colour (yellow) could only just be guessed at, but it was impossible to make out any pattern. One part of the wall and the ceiling was cut across at an angle, as it usually is in attics, but here over this angle there was a staircase.[11]

As in German films and theatre of the twenties, the scenery is the height of expressionism. Everything is shrieking disharmony, disproportion, deformity, interrupted planes, angles too sharp or too obtuse, poverty, yellowy pus, grey powder, systematic counterpoint: large rooms are empty, small ones are lumbered with some enormous object.[12] These interiors are like 'fissures', as Viktor Shklovsky writes,[13] and their sloping planes, lateral caves of shadow, and cluttered uneven surfaces do not simply evoke poverty, but create unease. They are signs of the convulsion, stifling, mutilation and infirmity of souls. Beyond the social criticism, Dostoyevsky is orchestrating the spiritual dissection and the moral tragedy of his heroes.

Dramatic power of scenery

This expressionism in the scenery, the result of the action and a tragic sign, sometimes casts up fantastic images of almost surrealist power. When the chronicler of *The Devils* ventures into the Lebyadkins' house to find out about the mysterious cripple, he is met by an amazing sight: 'Everything was covered in crumbs, covered in rubbish and soaked in water; large and thick, a completely wet rag was lying in the first room in the middle of the floor, and just there, in the same puddle, was an old worn-out shoe.'[14] By the dim light of a thin candle stuck in an iron candlestick, the chronicler makes out the person he was so eager to see, and the objects which surround her: 'besides the candlestick, in front of her on the table was a small country looking glass, an old pack of cards, a shabby book with a collection of songs and a white German bun, which had had two or three bites taken from it'.[15] The vision is certainly fantastic, but only when detached from the novel. Signs convey an obvious message: the heel-less shoe, in the puddle of water, suggests Mariya Timofeyevna's mental and psychic distress; the candle, the cards and the looking glass reveal her fondness for magical dreams and prophecy. There is nothing really mysterious and this surprising inventory of objects is later explained: 'This is just how she sits, literally for days on end, all by herself, and she doesn't move, she tells fortunes or looks at herself in the glass', Shatov pointed out . . 'you see he doesn't feed her. The old woman from the wing of the house will sometimes bring something out of charity: see how they leave her alone with a candle!'[16] Even the water and the shoe are explained. Mariya Timofeyevna gives the solution: 'Are you talking about Lebyadkin? He's my lackey . . I'll shout to him: "Lebyadkin, bring some water, Lebyadkin, give me my shoes", – and he'll run'.[17]

The scenery precedes the action which explains it. Dostoyevsky uses the duration of reading with consummate art: first comes the effect, and then its significance is explained by action. Expressionism shows its true image: it is the anticipation of dramatic realism. It is subject to the power of time.

Focusing the lighting

The lighting of the scenery is particularly expressionistic. As a master of stage lighting, Dostoyevsky surpasses all his contemporaries, orchestrating shadows and lights as a function of action or dramatic idea. Realistically, he uses only natural phenomena and ordinary sources of light. But he chooses a single dominant tone, ruthlessly eliminating all the ill-timed or chance lighting which reality sometimes offers and preferring the revealing source of light.

His interiors are typical: areas of shadow and lighted planes are distributed from a single source of light, usually a poor candle. We have had some examples: the most famous is in *Crime and Punishment*, where Sonya and Raskolnikov are reading about the resurrection of Lazarus. Dostoyevsky steps back and, giving the picture a title, freezes it into a scene: 'The candle-end had been dying out for a long time in its twisted candlestick, dimly lighting in this beggarly room the murderer and the woman who had sinned, who had strangely come together to read the eternal book.'[18] Less well known, but more revealing is a passage from the *Diary of a Writer* for March 1877, where Dostoyevsky amuses himself by giving a lesson in painting to the genre painters who – the remark is important – don't know how to create a 'normal centre' in their flatly realistic canvases. The subject is a poor Jewess giving birth in a miserable hovel, or 'a night at the Jewish woman's childbed'. Dostoyevsky advises his imaginary pupils to give parts to the objects, so as to 'touch the heart directly', and adds: 'The lighting too could be made interesting: on a warped table a greasy guttering candle is just burning out and through the one tiny window covered with frost the dawn of a new day is already glimmering, a new day of work for the poor'.[19]

In Dostoyevsky's novels the candles of these deformed interiors are never placed on a high surface, but always on a table, even a chair. Lighting is directed from below: it accentuates and hardens the features of the face and deepens the projected shadows. The light given out is not diffused, mysterious, mystical, as in La Tour and Rembrandt, but violently realistic as in Caravaggio. It does not soften, it dramatises. In the wavering blanched light of guttering candle ends the tragedies reach their culmination; the expressions of the heroes, tormented executioners or bearers of monstrous secrets, grow haggard, the faces of the victims are convulsed and the motionless dead, from Prokharchin to the elder Karamazov, chill the onlookers with horror. It is by candlelight that the most terrifying scene in Dostoyevsky's work, the suicide of Kirillov in *The Devils*, takes place. There is the haunting moment when Pyotr Stepanovich gets up and lowers the candlestick to light up 'the different parts of this petrified face' pale as wax, which is observing him from the corner of its eye. The candle is blown out; the sudden darkness of terror is followed by biting, hitting, flight, screams, a pistol shot. Pyotr Stepanovich re-lights the candle; Kirillov is lying dead, splashed with his own blood and brains. As Dostoyevsky suggested in *Diary of a Writer*, he has certainly given a dramatic part to the candle.

This same dramatic part is given to other sources of light, lanterns, lamps in corridors, street lamps, in particularly intense and decisive scenes. Dostoyevsky encloses his characters in a beam of light, as if it were coming from a projector placed high above or to the side, which pierces the darkness and isolates the place and the moment. Lighting focused in this way concentrates the gaze of the reader, giving him a close-up of the hero's face. The instant is crucial, even tragic: a mute confession of crime or the crime itself. In *Crime and Punishment* there is the scene where Raskolnikov silently confesses his double crime to Razumikhin, just after entrusting his mother and sister to his friend:

It was dark in the corridor; they were standing near a lamp. For a minute they looked at each other in silence. All his life Razumikhin remembered that minute.

The burning and concentrated gaze of Raskolnikov seemed to grow stronger with each moment, piercing his soul, his awareness. Suddenly Razumikhin shuddered. Something strange seemed to pass between them .. An idea slid by, as it were a hint; something horrible, ugly and suddenly understood on both sides .. Razumikhin went as white as a corpse.

'You understand now?' Raskolnikov suddenly said, with his face painfully twisted. 'Go back, go to them.'[20]

In *The Brothers Karamazov* the effect is repeated. Ivan and Alyosha, towards the end of the novel, are walking together, and, at each dramatic moment, they stop under a steet lamp. Under the first lamp – from realism as much as scene setting – Ivan unseals the letter where Liza 'the little demon' has offered herself to him like a prostitute. Under a second – 'Both found themselves once more under a lamp'[21] – Alyosha pronounces the terrible words which, by their very negation, underline Ivan's moral guilt: 'it is not you who killed our father.'[22]

We can also quote the violent scene in *The Devils*; in the dark and dismal park of the Stavrogin estate, with its immense aged pines forming black stains in the darkness, a darkness so thick that you can hardly see three steps ahead, 'three lanterns' illuminate the brutal murder of Shatov in their crossed beams.[23]

In these three examples, Dostoyevsky stresses the shadow as well as the light. We are far from the velvety chiaroscuro of Correggio and Rembrandt, with its subtle play of varied gradations of light. In Dostoyevsky the contrast between harshly lighted areas and black masses is stressed and even brutal. It is a world of conflict, of combat.

Cymbals of the storm

Night is the world in which the architect and decorator can organise lighting plans just as he wishes, but Dostoyevsky uses daytime lighting as well. The recurrent themes of the 'slanting rays of the setting sun' is a proof of this, but since this theme is mainly connected with the landscape experienced by the hero, we shall study it in a later example.

Dostoyevsky is not confined by the lighting technique of the playwright, since the novel offers him a stage as vast as the world. With an art closer to music than to painting, he makes a masterly orchestration of natural phenomena such as night, darkness, storm, tempest, or, by contrast, full sun, to serve the action.

The storm with its darkening cloud, its thunder and raging cataracts is a magnificent example of scenery fused with tragedy of the hero. Dostoyevsky first announces the storm by brief notes, apparently remote from the course of events and slipped in at long intervals, and then, suddenly, at the instant of the crisis, he lets it loose, completing and accentuating its progression by a final cadence. So in *The Insulted and Injured*, it is in an atmosphere of storm that Nelli, who is going to die, tells the story of the terrible quarrel between her mother and her maternal grandfather to the Ikhmenevs, who are living through a similar tragedy. At the most touching moment of her story, the point where the old man refuses to see his dying daughter, the storm breaks and the room darkens. At this moment, Natasha, the prodigal and immediately forgiven daughter, arrives unexpectedly, and Nelli is struck down by an epileptic fit. In the same way, in 'The Eternal Husband', the storm which had been threatening all evening breaks on the night when Trusotsky flings himself, razor in hand, upon Velchaninov.

Finally, in *The Idiot*, the orchestration reaches its summit. Dostoyevsky makes three final chords converge: the storm about to break, the crime Rogozhin is about to commit, and the epileptic fit which saves Myshkin at the last moment. The scenery, the dangerous darkness, with the expectation of the epileptic lightning in counterpoint, is conjured up by the novelist. It is a conjugation of darkness: the dark porch of the house, the stormy cloud which has swallowed light from the evening sky, the dark staircase and the darker recess of the alcove where Rogozhin is hiding. The darkness and the storm signify the crucifixion of souls.

The waters of shipwreck

The natural elements unleashed in the night: gusts of wind, deluges of rain with the heavy menace of flood, snowstorms, are all significant orchestrations. This is the setting in which Svidrigaylov, who has just noted the death of all desire in himself, moves towards suicide. He makes his way to death through a Walpurgis night full of tangled nightmares, a night of howling wind, of trees violently overturned, of cold which freezes sweat of thick darkness, above all of dampness: the water of torrential rain, the waters of the Neva which are on the point of flooding, the water which creeps into his dreams in the form of wet flowers, the drenched hair of the drowned girl, the water seeping through the 'thick milky fog' of the morning, the water flooding the whole landscape.

Svidrigaylov set out on the slippery, dirty wooden pavement, in the direction of the Little Neva. He seemed to see the water of the Little Neva which had risen high during the night, Peter's Island, the wet roads, the wet grass, the wet trees and bushes.[24]

The scenery is so powerfully orchestrated by Dostoyevsky that it is real scenery besides being part of the hero's state of mind. Svidrigaylov's 'strange' reflection: 'I have never liked water in my life, even in the landscapes'[25] is a proof of this.

The calm eye of the storm

In *The Brothers Karamazov*, a muffled chronicle, the orchestral volume is consequently more discreet. Dostoyevsky does not use the pedal in his effects, to use a pianist's term which Bakhtin likes, but reaches perfection in sobriety. Each phase of the action, either in the novel or in the novella-parables, is given its own seasonal scenery, the whole of which forms a semantics of scenery. There are numerous examples, so we shall take three strongly contrasted ones.

Ivan Fyodorovich's nightmare, which is both a hallucination of the devil and a schizoid process of dualism – Dostoyevsky leaves this deliberately ambiguous – is the beginning of madness, the unleashing of demonic forces which dwell in man. It happens in a waking state, in Ivan's bedroom with all its peacefully domestic objects: sofa, napkin and jug of water, the inkpot on the desk. There is nothing special, nothing betrays the presence of demons, at least apparently. For outside, and this has been developed copiously at the end of the previous chapter and is to be developed again at the end of this chapter, a snowstorm is raging, hostile and threatening.[26] Ivan's bedroom is the seemingly calm eye of the typhoon, a sign of the furious attack of evil forces. This orchestration seems to require the epigraph which Dostoyevsky chose for his novel *The Devils* – the verses of Pushkin's ballad, also called 'The Devils', describing a snow storm in which travellers are led astray and lost by the devils in the storm.[27]

Season and scenery

In contrast, the weather at Ilyusha's funeral, after which Alyosha and the children swear to keep for all their lives the pure memory of their childhood and their friendship, is serene, with brilliant sun and dry cold. 'The day was clear, calm, it was freezing moderately.'[28] René Girard contrasts this weather in which unity is found once more with the equivocal double weather, mist or snow mingled with rain, which marks the works about underground life: 'The pure light restores clarity and identity to objects; ice compresses and contracts everything. This tragic and cheerful weather is the weather of unity finally conquered and possessed.'[29] It is a fair judgement, although Girard has made a sign into a symbol. The scenery, important as it is, is only one element of the orchestration.

In the novella-parables, the seasonal scenery is usually linked with the moral. In 'A Russian Monk', the sixth book of *The Brothers Karamazov*, which is a narrative of hagiographic character into which Alyosha inserts a few fragments scattered in time, with all the years mixed up, it is striking to note that all the events relating to Zosima, from the moment he enters monastic life, take place in summer, in July and August, the season of harvest, and all those which concern his brother, who, after committing blasphemy, is reborn to spiritual life take place in spring, before and after Easter, the season of birth. Zosima's brother had said, before he vanished, 'Go and live for me'. After his disappearance, years pass and Zosima leaves the army to enter the Order, which he does in summer, with its profusion of trees, birds and sunny hours. He is plucking the fruit born from under the flower. The actual years have been mixed up in his memory, but the scenery establishes a continuity of seasons which has deep, even spiritual significance, as if Zosima and his brother Markel were treading the path of the Great Sinner together, Markel taking on the stage of atheism and conversion, and Zosima the heavier burden of sainthood. Without being a commentary, the seasonal scenery stresses Dostoyevsky's creative intention. A length of time, finally split into two lives, is revealed in a literary space.

Sometimes the orchestration of the lighting covers the whole novel and associates season and night, whether white or shadowy.

The lighting of The Last Day of Pompeii

The title of the novella 'White Nights' is a comment in itself. The Petersburg stories and novels, 'The Eternal Husband', *The Idiot* and *A Raw Youth*, are bathed in the unreal and fantastic glow of the white nights, brilliant, northern and phosphorescent. Apollon Maykov, in his letter to Dostoyevsky of 14 March 1868, defined the lighting of *The Idiot* precisely:

But how much force! How many marvellous passages! How fine the Idiot is! Moreover, all the characters are very strong, very vivid, only they are lit with an *electric light*, in which the most ordinary face and the most ordinary colours have an unnatural glow, so that you want to look at them again .. It is the lighting of *The Last Day of Pompeii*[30]: it is beautiful, it is curious (curious to the highest degree, captivating) and this is foreign to you.[31]

Dostoyevsky was to acknowledge, in his reply, the justice of Maykov's analysis.[32] But in our sense the reproach is unmerited. Maykov had not understood the modernity and the significant nature of the scenery chosen by the novelist, although Bryullov's famous picture should have shown him the way. *The Idiot* is a tragedy of human, almost divine beauty finally defeated by the unleashing of evil forces, very like that represented in *The Last Day of Pompeii* where the beauty of creatures and things, noted and stressed by art critics,[33] is defeated by the eruption of Vesuvius. The lighting orchestrates the tragedy whose victim is beauty.[34]

The shadows of anguish

The most convincing example of seasonal scenery associated with night appears in *The Devils*. The overall dominant tone is the dismal autumn night, sepulchrally cold, with its stagnant water, its fine soaking rain, its dark and muddy streets, its damp parks with their dank smell. The darkness is black as ink, breeding threats like the nightmares of Goya. Outlines of monsters loom in the darkness, evil plots are made, the sombre Stavrogin (the knight of the spider)[35] weaves his web, the blade of a convict's knife gleams, eerie lanterns light a savage killing. The fire glows like a pool of blood in the darkness, a shot rings out and Kirillov is nothing more than splashes of blood and brains in the light of a candle. It is the long night of horror, murder and disintegration. Except for the spurt of light formed by Stepan Trofimovich's flight into the Russian countryside, the novel, from the beginning of the second part on, is almost exclusively nocturnal.

Whether we consider the whole of the work, one of the scenes or a single picture in the novel, the scenery of Dostoyevsky has unique, organised, orchestrated and significant lighting. Is there also a unity of colour?

26

The semantics of colour

I found very interesting, for instance, what Ch. Blanc says about Velasquez' technique in *Les Artistes de mon temps*, his shadows and half-tones consist mostly of *colorless, cool grays*, the chief elements of which are black and a little white. In these neutral, colorless mediums, the least cloud or shade of red has an immediate effect.

Letter from Vincent Van Gogh to his brother Theodore (1884)[1]

Vanity and truth of statistics

Most people think that Dostoyevsky is not a colourist. Except in portraits, where hair must be brown, fair, grey or white, eyes dark, blue, green or hazel, skins pale or waxen or, in contrast, rosy, and lips bloodless or vividly red, there are statistically very few colours in his novels.

The Double, for instance, is strongly influenced by Gogol, an undoubted colourist, but it contains only twelve mentions of green (in a briefcase, carpet, armchair, and uniforms), seven of black, three of which are contrasted with white, five of grey, five of red (excluding references to faces), three of pink, one of crimson, four of sky blue, one of yellow, one of gold.

The Idiot is the most pictorial of all the novels, because of the real pictures it recalls and its creative atmosphere (Dostoyevsky was in Florence and visited art galleries with his young wife), but apart from portraits of characters and the systematic contrast of black and white (fairness of Myshkin and 'blackness' of Rogozhin; the black dress and eyes of Nastasya Filippovna contrasting vividly with her pallor; the clothes and the room of Rogozhin's mother), there is only one mention of dark blue, two of light or bright blue, one of yellow, one of gold, one of purple, two or three of brown, and one of rainbow colours, but at least eight of red and thirteen of green. Colour is rare, but not absent. Moreover, rare as it is, it is striking because of the dominant note it inscribes in the scenery.

Criticism is divided: one school deplores the poverty of colouring and another stresses its dominant note. Both have an element of truth, useful in debate, but insufficient. V. F. Pereverzev states categorically that the world and style of Dostoyevsky are 'poor in colours'.[2] V. Botsyanovsky attempts an explanation:

One of Dostoevsky's characteristic features is his hostility to colour and tone, as if he were deliberately neglecting the pictorial. In the works of Dostoevsky there is an almost complete absence of painting, colours, landscapes ... It is the same thing with his portraits. They are dynamic, but not at all picturesque ... The external appearance of people, as of landscapes, is treated with economy, the portraits are monotonic, black and white predominate ... We might conclude that Dostoevsky had no time to linger over nuances of colouring ... The artist wants to express and transmit the essential as if he were afraid of the secondary, the details which kill the impression.[3]

This is a subtle analysis: Dostoyevsky finds ornament alien. L. P. Grossman agrees: 'In his landscapes, portraits and descriptions, Dostoevsky is as little of a colourist as it is possible to be. He always uses the play of chiaroscuro, a sudden burst of light among the shadows, the light of guttering candles or the slanting rays of the setting sun, which cast long, deep and violent shadows'.[4]

However, another subtle critic, N. M. Chirkov, argues that Dostoyevsky's scenery is not so devoid of colour as it seems. He notes the novelist's preference for 'grey, dark grey, dark brown and black', his 'inclination for brilliant colours and especially for the sunset tones, fiery red and purple'.[5] Another critic, S. M. Solovyov, has studied the use of pink and light blue in Dostoyevsky's work.[6]

The eyes of the writer and the 'farsighted myopia' of Remizov

Writers know how to see. Two of them, tributaries of Dostoyevsky, Andrey Bely, the visionary of the novel *Petersburg*, and Aleksey Remizov, the magician with 'shaven eyes' of *The Fire of Things*, see the author of *The Double*, *Crime and Punishment* and *The Idiot* as an original colourist.

Bely, using both intuition and statistics, has compared the chromatic spectrum of the first Petersburg novellas of Dostoyevsky, *The Double* and 'The Landlady', with that of Gogol's Petersburg stories, *The Greatcoat*, 'The Nevsky Prospect', 'The Portrait' and 'Memoirs of a Madman'. They are identical: first red predominates, then it fades gradually to be replaced by grey and yellow, which, mixed with red, give a blackish brown.[7]

Remizov, with the 'precise inexactness'' of the lyricist, mixes the colours mentioned by the novelist with those suggested by objects and paints a brilliant picture of the scenery in *The Idiot*:

Everything is suffused in green, the bitter green star. In green and red (green inclines to yellow, red to brown). The green trees, the green scarf (Ivolgin), the quilt of green silk (Ippolit), the green bench with a brown back (at Myshkin's), the green house (Rogozhin), the green bed tester, the emeralds of Keller, the green moon of July. And the blood: scarlet with a brilliant beetle in the vivid green of Rogozhin's scarf, the scarlet of Ippolit's bloody handkerchief, the red camellias, the red wall, the caked blood on the stabbed Nastasya Filippovna, the pool of blood on the stone staircase; the brown of the Holbein picture, the scorpion with a brown shell (in Ippolit's dream), the carriage with yellow seats and the red flash of wheels, and the bats in the blackness of misfortune. And piercing this bleeding green, is an endless anguish, the burning flash of eyes (Rogozhin).[8]

We could add the green table, the great plant pots painted green, and the red walls of the staircase of Rogozhin's house, the large divan in red leather, the red seal of the parcel which contains Ippolit's confession. The intuition of Remizov, a colourist and short-sighted calligrapher, is perfect: it reconciles statistics, which he uses to prove his point, and artistic truth. In fact, if green is mixed with red, we obtain brown, as Remizov notes; but if we rotate green and red, complementary and opposed colours, as a pair together, we obtain a grey spectrum which is at its limit a milky white. This pallid spectrum is perfectly in harmony with the 'electric lighting' noted in Maykov's letter, which has been linked with the seasonal scenery of the white nights.

Kandinsky, in *On the Spiritual in Art*, suggests a commentary on grey which forms an astonishing spectral analysis of Dostoyevsky's novel *The Idiot*: 'Gray is therefore the disconsolate lack of motion' (the grey shadows of the room where the murdered Nastasya Filippovna lies illustrate the failure of Prince Myskin). 'The deeper this gray becomes, the more the disconsolate element is emphasized, until it becomes suffocating' (in the tragic instants, the darkness is orchestrated and Myshkin feels a stifling sensation, both material and moral). 'As the color becomes lighter, we feel a breath of air, the possibility of respiring, for it contains a certain element of concealed hope' (the Christ-like figure of Myshkin brings his luminous radiance, hope and love). 'A similar gray is formed by the optical mixture of green and red, arising out of a mixture, in spiritual terms, of self-complacent passivity and a powerful, active, inner glow' (the abandonment of Myshkin to his Christian spontaneity, to the mystical aura and burning passion of the creatures who surround him).[9]

Remizov, revolving the colours of *The Idiot*, reached the spectral synthesis of the novel aesthetically. Art is often more vivid and more exact than exegesis.

Semantic or symbolic?

However, Dostoyevsky's procedure is slower, and more extended in length. He works in Munch's expressionist manner, laying broad firm strokes, but in a discontinuous way. He creates, to return to theatrical technique, the same effect of colour focusing as the stage electrician who uses a projector with a monochrome lens, green, red, or yellow, to enclose a space on the stage in a beam of colour.

Colour is a signal: it announces a theme. Repeated, it becomes a sign. Associated with other colours, it forms a chromatic spectrum which gives the major tone of the novel. Paradoxically, its rarity increases its significance. Colour in Dostoyevsky's scenery is certainly semantic: could we go so far as to call it symbolic?

Symbolism implies three conditions, two objective and one subjective. The symbol must have a permanent and immutable value, as in icon painting: the novelist must be aware of this symbolic value: and he must have a marked inclination for this kind of expression, or in other words, a love of colour. We shall try to answer this question by analysing the use of three colours in Dostoyevsky's work, green, red and yellow; but we shall first deal with the simple question: did Dostoyevsky like colours?

The writer's eye

Dostoyevsky was not a lover of painting. Pictures, as we have seen, interested him only because of the ideas and mythology he could associate with them. Moreover, as Anna Grigoryevna noted:

Fyodor Mikhaylovich was often mistaken about colours and was bad at distinguishing them. He would use the names of colours which had gone completely out of fashion, for instance, the colour 'massak'. He tried to persuade me that this colour would suit me beautifully and begged me to have a dress made of it. I wanted to please him, so I asked for some material of this colour in the shops. The cloth merchants were puzzled by the word, and I learnt only later, from an old woman, that 'massak' was the name of a very distinctive lilac, which they once used in Moscow for the velvet lining of coffins.[10]

Elsewhere, in *The Village of Stepanchikovo*, Dostoyevsky mentions a tie of 'adelaide' colour, a completely forgotten name which used to denote a dark blue very fashionable from 1830–50.[11]

In fact, Dostoyevsky was only completely at ease with black, white, red and green. Yellow is often dirty, dusty, tending to become green or grey, just as all his colours, except for reds and greens, are dulled, degraded, uncertain. Van Gogh might say that he inclines towards the technique of Velasquez, in whose paintings splashes of red and green sing against a background of '*colorless, cool grays*, the chief elements of which are black and a little white'.[12]

The various meanings of green

Dostoyevsky's colour has no conventional and permanent symbolism. The intention expressed by colour varies from one novel to another and within each separate novel. It naturally varies as it is associated and contrasted with other colours. Green is a significant example.

In *The Double* the green is the green of Tsarist officials. The chancellery, men and objects, is green, but not a fresh spontaneous colour as in Gogol's story 'The Nevsky Prospect'; in Dostoyevsky it is the hopeless desperate green of immobility and passivity. 'Pure green is to the realm of color what the so-called bourgeoisie is to human society: it is an immobile, complacent element, limited in every respect.'[13] It is the universe of balance, of self-satisfaction, which opposes its unvarying complacency, its smooth wall, to the unhappy Golyadkin, who is unable to penetrate it, although he knows that his double is moving beyond it with arrogant carelessness. The closed door on which Golyadkin's fragile mind breaks is green.

In *The Idiot*, the green, or shades of green, are different. There is one for Rogozhin, one for Myshkin, one for Ippolit. Rogozhin's green is never absolute and cannot be compared to 'the expansive medium register of the violin', in Kandinsky's phrase.[14] It is sometimes dirty, like the exterior of his house, sometimes too vivid, like his silk scarf, sometimes funereally pale, like the green silk curtains in the study where his murdered mistress is lying. Rogozhin's green is the falsely soothing cover which hides a horrible secret; but each time the colour or associated tones betray him; the dirty green façade of his house masks a blood-red universe (the staircase, the sofa, the mahogany) against a Velasquez background of black and white (the covers of the furniture, the two old women in mourning, the shadow of the labyrinth). The brilliant green of the scarf is significantly contrasted with red; the green silk curtains of Rogozhin's study hide an appalling sight, drawn in black and white ('the sumptuous white silk dress', the heap of white lace, the tip of a naked foot which 'seemed to be carved from marble'). The colour in Rogozhin's world is a chromatic mask.[15]

However, in the world of Myshkin and Aglaya, it is the background for pure and childish love, it is the greenery of Pavlovsk and 'the green bench' where the two young people meet. In Ippolit's mind, the green trees in Pavlovsk which the young consumptive has come to see before his death are a symbol of the feast of life, which he is no longer invited to share. Green is opposed to the red of the brick wall of the Meyer house which faced his window in Petersburg, on which everything is 'written so openly and simply'.[16] The green freshness of life is opposed to the dull glare of red, a sign of death and deadlock: 'When you said goodbye just now, I suddenly thought: here are these people, and they will never be there any more, never! And the trees too, – there'll simply be a brick wall, a red one, on the Meyer house ... opposite my window.'[17] Suffering and rebellion drive Ippolit to renounce the 'ridiculous trees of Pavlovsk' which cannot hide his 'Meyer wall'. He tears off the green mask, 'last ghost of life and love' and discovers the coagulated red of the brick, or, in his nightmare, the reddish brown of the vile crawling scaly beast, like a scorpion or a trident, suddenly appearing near his bed, which was covered with 'a green silk quilt'.[18] The strange relationship between Rogozhin and Ippolit in the novel is echoed by his contrasting use of red and green, similar for both of them.

Reds

Reds also have varied significance in Dostoyevsky, sometimes associated, sometimes opposed. They have a dark and a light side. The red of the slanting rays of the setting sun is a trumpet blast which heralds the great idea of death followed by renewal. The 'red curtains' of the beautiful house cradled in music, which Netochka Nezvanova sees, promise 'an eternal Sunday'. The purple in the Swiss countryside remembered by Myshkin crowns a rainbow universe, a deep luminous blue, with its 'flame'.

But usually red bursts out from a grey, black and white background like an irresistible evil power, like a pool of blood or an infernal flame. In 'The Landlady', red is the sign of demonic presence; Murin, the strange old man who holds the beautiful Katerina in his power, wears an eternal red scarf and offers the young virgin pearls in a red morocco case. Blood covers his hands, his eyes shine like glowing coals and he rises like the Evil One among the flames of the bonfire he has lit, against the background of a night of anguish.

The same nocturnal background of deep black is spattered with demonic red in *The Devils*: it is the little red spider which Stavrogin contemplates while Matryosha hangs herself, the name of the 'great writer' Karmazinov which is only a verbal mask (*karmazin*, crimson), the red tie of Stepan Petrovich described as a 'red idea' by Varvara Petrovna, the reddening fire in the night, the blood of the Lebyadkins, Shatov and Kirillov. This demonic red, in Dostoyevsky's eyes, is also a political red. It is the blood red of the foreign, materialist, atheist revolution: Karmazinov (Turgenev) is the willing ally of the nihilists; Stepan Trofimovich is their irresponsible parent; Shatov and Kirillov are their repentant disciples and their victims; Stavrogin is the idol of their leader; fires and murder are the work of their hands. Russia is trapped in the reptilian folds of the red flag of revolution. The mounting thirst for blood terrifies the novelist, overcome by the spiritual and national crisis passing over Russia, which is symbolised by the town of *The Devils*. These swathes of red are the metaphorical components of Russian fantasy, together with the flaw and the abyss, metaphors first used by Gogol and reaching their apogee in Andrey Bely's *Petersburg*, especially in the theme of the 'red domino'.[19] This essentially conservative fantasy is opposed to the Utopia of the Golden Age, which is also bathed in red, but this time a blazing and radiant red, that of the slanting rays of the setting sun.[20]

Red as a chromatic mask

Allied with 'too white' and 'too black', excessive red expresses an arrogant health which hides evil and spiritual death. These are the masks of the predatory heroes, like the Japanese no masks or the masks of Greek tragedy. There is a rich gallery of these portraits. They begin with the husband of Mme M. in 'A Little Hero', an unsympathetic character who 'has a piece of fat instead of a heart' : 'In appearance he was a dark-haired, tall and particularly solid gentleman, with European sidewhiskers, with a self-satisfied rosy face, with teeth white as sugar.'[21] The theme continues with the portrait of Prince Valkovsky in *The Insulted and Injured* and the painted masks of Svidrigaylov in *Crime and Punishment*, Stavrogin in *The Devils*, and Lambert in *A Raw Youth*. Their relationship is surprisingly close:

Svidrigaylov
It was a strange kind of face, seeming more like a mask: white, rosy, with rosy crimson lips, with a light fair beard and with fair hair which was still quite thick. The eyes were somehow too blue, and their gaze was somehow too heavy and motionless.[22]

Stavrogin
His hair was somehow very black, his light eyes somehow very calm and clear, his complexion somehow extremely soft and white, his colour somehow too bright and pure a red, his teeth like pearls, his lips like coral, – an ideally handsome man, but at the same time he seemed repulsive. People said his face reminded them of a mask.[23]

Lambert
His hair was terribly black, his face white and rosy, as in a mask, his nose long, with a bump, as Frenchmen have, his teeth white, his eyes black.[24]

Elsewhere, red is frankly a sign of lust. Svidrigaylov, for example, dreams that he is wandering through the dark damp corridors of the shady hotel where he is staying. Suddenly he discovers, hidden behind a cupboard, a little girl of five, pale, exhausted, stiff with cold. He takes her in, undresses her and puts her to sleep in his own bed. The child, warm again, is sleeping. The colour has come back into her cheeks. 'But it was strange; this colour somehow appeared brighter and stronger than the usual childish rosiness could be. "It is a feverish redness", thought Svidrigaylov, "it's like a redness from wine, just as if someone had given her a whole glass to drink. Her little crimson lips seem to burn, to flame; but what is this?"'[25] The innocent child flutters her eyelashes, smiles, laughs provocatively, invitingly: she changes into a prostitute offering herself; her burning face issues a monstrous invitation. Here the colour red is a true sign: it precedes the significance, which is transparent if we take into account the transfer phenomenon characteristic of dreams: Svidrigaylov, in spite of his world weariness, has not given up lust, which has grown to be part of his soul. The little red spider which Stavrogin observes on the geranium leaf at the moment when the child he has raped commits suicide, signifies lust, as well as crime and death.

The red blood of the dream

In Dostoyevsky, red is the major sign of blood, blood which the hero dreams of shedding, but fears to shed. The scenery may be real or dreamt.

In the case of dreams, the scenery inclines towards landscape since it is seen 'from inside' by the hero, but it remains scenery because the unconscious mind of the dreamer is deceived, censored by the action of the dream, in which fantasies of condensation, transfer, and determination are indulged, and the dreamer sees himself as actor. In the dream, power is substituted for length of time and an abundance of objects for bareness. With regard to scenery, the dream is the hyperbole of the real, a reality in which the spatio-temporal structure has exploded, but which is, on the other hand, saturated with signs. So colour, as we have just noted in Svidrigaylov's nightmare, plays a determining part, especially red which translates the impulse to murder. For oddly enough Dostoyevsky's heroes dream in brilliant colour.

Three of Raskolnikov's four dreams in *Crime and Punishment* are vividly coloured. One, very short, the dream of the oasis 'somewhere in Africa, in Egypt' is a dream of convenience, as Freud might say: Raskolnikov, before going out to murder, has a fever: he is thirsty and dreams he is drinking from a cool stream.[26] The colours are luminous and pure: 'And it was so cool, and such marvellous blue cold water was running over stones of different colours and over such pure golden glinting sand.'[27]

Two other, more famous dreams, of the poor nag beaten to death and the repetition of the old moneylender's murder, are, on the contrary, predominantly red. More exactly, the original scenery gradually turns red with blood, as if a red disc had been inserted in a projector.

The dream of the beaten horse begins in a grey landscape where, except for the dull green of a church dome, blacks and whites predominate. The weather is grey, there are no trees in the village, though in the distance there is a black wood, and the dust in the road is black. Raskolnikov, who had reverted to his childhood, recalls the *kutya*, the gruel of the dead, made of white rice and raisins, on a 'white dish'. The unbearable scene then begins, the interminable martyrdom of the little horse. With an art which shows an extraordinary knowledge of dreaming, Dostoyevsky slows its progression, freezes its length by repeating actions, words, stereotyped gestures (the old peasant woman who is cracking nuts and laughing occasionally). Time seems to move in a circle, but the murderous violence grows intolerably: gradually the black-and-white picture is overwhelmed with red. First it is the large peasants 'in red and blue shirts', Mikolka with 'his beefy face, red as a carrot', the good wife, fat and rosy, dressed in red cloth and wearing *koty* (fur boots trimmed with scarlet), then again 'red drunken lads', and finally the child sees the eyes of the murderer suffused with blood and the bloodstained mouth of the poor victim.[28]

The dream where Raskolnikov repeats the murder of the old woman is first bathed in a morbid sickly yellow with a background of darkness. 'The shadows thickened, the full moon shone more and more brightly.'[29] Raskolnikov is dragged along by a stranger, who has been treating him as a murderer, to the scene of his crime. As he goes up the stairs, 'the moonlight came through the windows mournfully and mysteriously'.[30] Raskolnikov crosses the 'very dark and empty' ante-room and enters the main room: 'the whole room was brightly bathed in moonlight; everything was just as it had been: chairs, mirror, yellow divan and pictures in their frames. A huge, round, copper-red moon was looking straight through the window. "The moon is making it so quiet, – thought Raskolnikov, – it is probably asking riddles." '[31] The solution of the riddle comes in this abrupt change from yellow to red. In the logic of his dream, Raskolnikov does not know (moral censure) that he has come to commit murder. Red signifies the murder to him and then he discovers the wicked old woman, hidden behind a woman's coat which seems to be hanging on the wall, and strikes her again and again without effect. The red moon is the pool of blood which the dreamer would like to ignore, repress and forget.

Bloodstained reality

This tragic red sometimes escapes from dreams to stain the real scenery with blood. Reality has become a nightmare. The scene where Dmitriy Karamazov, devoured with jealousy – is Grushenka with his father or not? – hidden in the shadow of a tree, observes Fyodor Pavlovich's household and feels a mad parricidal hatred growing inside him is a masterly example of the close interweaving of scenery orchestrated by the novelist and landscape perceived by the hero. Everything is united; shadows and lights, the mass of bushes is lit by the slanting light coming from the window, which later shows the hated profile of his father, and everywhere, over everything, is a thick alarming red. Dmitriy sees only red, or, more exactly, he sees only the red which is abundantly supplied by the novelist. He sees red, as the saying goes. The colour of blood precedes the conscious action; only at the end of his observations does Dmitriy form the clear thought of parricide. Red, to which he gives all the power of his unadmitted impulses, is first outside his conscious mind. ' "The guelder rose, the berries, how red they are", he whispered, not knowing why.'[32] It is the mute call of blood. These red berries are joined explicitly by the red blinds of Fyodor Pavlovich's bedroom and the red sash which he is flirtatiously sporting. ('Red suits him better', as he says) and implicitly by things that the reader knows: the hangings in the dining room are red, the favour knotted around the 3,000 roubles destined for Grushenka is red. There is an amazing convergence of significations here. Red encloses the different motives for the eventual murder: the impulse to kill, the hatred for parental blood, the disgust with sensuality, expressed by the use of the adjective 'Chinese' for the blinds, evoking refined lust. ' "Chinese, – the word flashed through Mitya's mind, – and behind the blinds is Grushenka" '.[33]

Moreover, in *The Brothers Karamazov*, Dmitriy makes a small but

interesting mistake. At the beginning of the novel, when he is telling
Alyosha about his rivalry with his father, he says that the bundle of 3,000
roubles which the old man has prepared for Grushenka is tied up with a 'red
braid'.[34] However, during the trial, a 'thin pink ribbon'[35] is found next to
the torn envelope. The mistake is revealing: Dmitriy is thinking of lust,
while the investigators are only aware of Fyodor Pavlovich's intention to
court Grushenka. This is further proof that there is no permanent symbolic
value of colour in Dostoyevsky but significant values, used only in a precise
context, a complex play of colours which are signs.

The hated sign of yellow

Colour symbolism implies that a novelist must show that he has some
awareness of the symbol, or at least he should make some allusion to it. It is
easy enough to show that this is untrue for green and red, whose various
semantic values have been shown. It is more difficult with yellow, which
apparently had a constant value for Dostoyevsky. His attitude towards it
seems paradoxical at first: he does not like the colour, especially in its sallow
and pale tones, but he spreads it abundantly over things and creatures,
introducing it so generously into interiors and landscapes that he has a
larger percentage of yellow in his works than even Tolstoy, who uses more
yellow in his works than any other nineteenth-century author. If we take
only Russian writers, Gogol has 5 per cent of yellow in his colour spectrum,
Tolstoy 7.9 per cent and Dostoyevsky 10.6 per cent.[36] Certainly Dostoyevsky never expresses his own aversion to yellow, but his heroes,
especially the dreamers of the early works, are closely related to the young
writer. Their unanimous hatred for yellow is too constant not to be shared
by the author, who created the last innocent dreamer, the writer Ivan
Petrovich of *The Insulted and Injured*, in his own image.

On several occasions in *White Nights* the young storyteller denigrates
yellow, or at least sees it as an evil sign. At the beginning of the story he
gives an account of the misfortunes of a pretty little pale pink house:

It was such a dear little stone house, it looked at me in such a welcoming way, and
looked at its clumsy neighbours so proudly, that my heart rejoiced when I happened
to go by. Suddenly, last week, I was going along the street and, as I glanced at my
friend – I heard a piteous cry: 'They're painting me yellow!' The criminals!
scoundrels! barbarians! they had spared nothing: neither columns nor cornices, and
my friend had turned as yellow as a canary. I nearly overflowed with bile on this
occasion, and I have never yet been strong enough to go and see my poor deformed
friend, who had been painted from head to foot in the colour of the Celestial
Empire.[37]

Later on, he paints a sombre picture of the dreamer who has grown old
without ever having lived, with this significant comparison: 'Your fantastic

world will grow pale, your dreams will die and fade and drop like yellow leaves from the trees.'[38] Just before the end, before the appearance of the rival who is to rob him of his dreams and of Nastenka, he praises a landscape without realising the threat it contains: ' "Look at the sky, Nastenka, look! Tomorrow will be a marvellous day; what a blue sky, what a moon! Look: that yellow cloud is spreading over it, look, look! . . . No, it has gone by" '[39] In this poetic novel of the failure of love, yellow is a sign of disaster.

The novella 'A Weak Heart', which ends with the madness of Vasya Shumkov, gives a singular example of yellow seen as a curse. Vasya's friend, Arkadiy Ivanov, is literally paralysed in society by the appalling yellow knitted scarf he is wearing: ' "Look how horrible it is: yellow, abominable, (*poganyy*) disgusting yellow, it's brought me nothing but trouble today!" '[40]

That less innocent dreamer, the anti-hero of *Notes from Underground*, gives a relatively complete commentary on yellow. First it is the signal which arouses painful memories, hours of ignominy;[41] while he watches the snow falling 'almost wet, yellow, hazy', the hero relives his past humiliations and agonies. Yellow represents insult and degradation in the hero's eyes; as he looks through his wardrobe, he feels, like Arkadiy Ivanovich, a complex about yellow: 'But the main thing, on the trousers, right on the knee, there was an enormous yellow stain. I foresaw that this stain alone would take away nine-tenths of my dignity.'[42] Finally, he analyses vivid yellow as a singularly aggressive colour. He first thinks of wearing lemon yellow gloves and then decides on black: 'The colour [yellow] is too sharp, as if somebody wanted to show off.'[43]

In *Crime and Punishment* everything is sulphurous with evil and aggressive yellow. Raskolnikov's Petersburg is gnawed by a sinister leprous yellow, greyish and infectious. The wallpaper in Raskolnikov's room, that 'yellow room which looks like a wardrobe or a chest', where he feels 'stifled and cramped',[44] is dusty yellow. Sonya's licence for prostitution is yellow. So is the wallpaper in the lodging of the old moneylender, together with her furniture and her picture frames and the seedy moth-eaten fur that she wears. The same room is bathed in the mysterious yellow light of the moon in the nightmare when the crime is repeated. The scene of the murder remains yellow in Raskolnikov's memory: when he returns to the room he is irritated to note that it has been re-papered in white with mauve flowers.[45] The official furnishings of the examining magistrate's office are yellow too, and so are the partitions in Svidrigaylov's sordid hotel room. The little wooden houses, dirty and dismal with their closed shutters, which Svidrigaylov sees on his last journey are bright yellow. The copper helmet of the Jewish fireman, a ridiculous and disconcerted witness of Svidrigaylov's suicide, is yellow against a grey background (the military greatcoat). S. M. Solovyov writes that in *Crime and Punishment* Dostoyevsky used 'an exclusively yellow background, creating 'a superb complement, pictorially perfect, for his hero's tragic ordeals'.[46] This needs some modification: the background of Petersburg is rather whitewashed dusty grey, but yellow invades it like alopecia, a disease whose sinister scales stand out with a morbid, oppressive and aggressive force.

However, there is a fundamental difference between the early works of Dostoyevsky and his first great novel, *Crime and Punishment*. In the early novellas, yellow is commented on by the heroes, but in *Crime and Punishment* the characters never refer to it. Yellow explodes in the scenery as a sign arranged by the novelist. In other words, we may answer our previous question by saying that at the beginning of his career Dostoyevsky was tempted by the symbolism of yellow, which is, as Goethe stresses, present in tradition (yellow hats of undischarged debtors, the yellow of cuckoldry, the sulphurous yellow of shirts for heretics), but from *Crime and Punishment* onwards Dostoyevsky chooses a semantics of yellow. The colour is not part of the awareness of the heroes, but is a powerful sign in the orchestration of the novel, just as red and green are. Yellow keeps the qualities which the original symbolism and the traditions of the past had conferred on it: it establishes an atmosphere of infamy,[47] disgust, spiritual oppression, moral illness and even madness,[48] but chiefly of aggression.[49]

Van Gogh and Kandinsky have amazing ideas about yellow which could serve as commentaries on Dostoyevsky's work. Van Gogh always associates this 'diabolic' colour, which he attains at the price of dangerous tension, with ideas of madness and imprisonment and – in his slang expression – of a 'padded cell'. His famous painting *Night Café*, steeped in intense yellow, painted, as he says in 'an infernal atmosphere of pale sulphur' and expressive as the 'power of darkness of a bludgeon', inspires a significant passage: 'In my picture *Night Café*, I have tried to express the idea that the café is a place where one can ruin oneself, go mad or commit a crime.'[50] In the same way, yellow gleams in *Crime and Punishment* like a colour which drives men to crime. Kandinsky also insists on the power of yellow to dissolve the soul: 'Considered directly (in any kind of geometric form)[51] yellow torments man, stimulates and excites him, weighs on him like a constraint, importunes him with a kind of unbearable insolence.'[52] And he adds later:

Yellow is the typically earthly colour. One should not try to give yellow an impression of depth. Chilled by blue, it takes, as we have seen, a sickly tone. If compared with states of mind, it could be the coloured representation of madness, not of melancholy nor of hypochondria, but of an outburst of rage, delirium, furious madness. The man suffering from this illness attacks others, reverses everything, flings everything to earth and disperses his forces, dissipates them without sense and without aim, to final exhaustion.[53]

In the same way, in *Crime and Punishment* yellow creates an intolerable dramatic tension: it is the colour sign of the unbearable convulsion of the soul.

In the great novels which follow, yellow is no longer a dominant note, but it keeps its undoubted power of fascination. In *A Raw Youth*, Dostoyevsky paints a portrait entirely in yellow, where the colour is spread so evenly that its significance becomes obvious. It is the portrait of the mother of Olya, the young girl who committed suicide, which is placed as an introduction to the novella-parable of the story of a soul destroyed by insult and despair:

The mother was still not a very old woman, about fifty at the most, just as fair, but with sunken eyes and cheeks and with yellow, large and uneven teeth. And everything about her was redolent of some sort of yellowness: the skin of her face and hands looked like parchment; her dark dress had gone completely yellow from antiquity, while one nail, on the forefinger of her right hand, for some reason, was carefully and neatly covered with yellow wax.[54]

As with Svidrigaylov, yellow screams of suicide.

To conclude this analysis of the spectrum of essential colours in Dostoyevsky, we note that these, like the scenic lighting, come from a vast orchestration, not at all haphazard, where the sign, placed on the scenery by the novelist, punctuates the action. Colour, rare but insistent, is totally alien to decoration and has no pictorial qualities. It is a code of signs which echo and direct the action, the discreet material transcription of the novelist's intent. Like the scenery, it is one of the score marks and is deciphered not as a system of symbols, but in a simultaneous reading of the other parts of the score.

27

The hero in space: sighting and seeing

It is not surprising that Stendhal never tells us the colour of Fabrice's eyes: they are eyes which see, not eyes which are seen.

G. Blin, *Stendhal et les problèmes du roman*[1]

Movement and look

The setting orchestrated by Dostoyevsky is devoid of ornament but rich in a convergence of signs which anticipate ideas and actions. Lines, volume, lighting and colours are given dramatic, psychological and even philosophical parts, for the scenery reveals the intention of the novelist, master of destinies. Like the sign of fire which appeared to the king of Babylon, it is a tragic sign which cannot be interpreted when it appears, but which stresses the impression of fatality by appearing again and again: the messages of the gods, written in space.

But space is also the natural medium existing *a priori*, in which the characters of the novel move. Considered from this viewpoint, it is closely dependent on the movement and look of the hero, who has two attitudes in space: either he acts in it or he looks at it. In the first case, space is crossed; it is not described or even inventoried, it is simply marked out with references which trace movement. It is a route, a topography of the action. Space is not seen but perceived; it is sighted. In the second case, there is a landscape, space is contemplated by the hero who invests it with his own attributes, and it is then seen. These two attitudes recall the two aspects of time; sighting corresponds to the time of power, when freedom is painfully exercised: seeing is chronicle time, the time of distrustful elucidation.

Having made this first distinction, we must remember that the hero is not the only one to whom the novelist grants independence. While seeing the landscape is obviously individual, sighting is manifold. When the main hero moves through space, he traces the path of his own freedom. But this path crosses the path of others, and these crossroads are privileged places of conflict or elucidation, where movement is annulled and space is scenically frozen. The sighting or seeing of the hero ceases to exist; dramatic representation for the reader-audience takes its place. These are the two chronotopes mentioned by Bakhtin, which are known as the *agora* (market place) and the threshold, which is simply the passage from the hero's path into the market place, his leap into the arena. The novelist then becomes a stage director and shows the audience what is happening.

Memory of the city

For the Dostoyevsky hero, his own action, conscious or unconscious, forms the lens through which he sees the external world. He moves in an urban landscape which he knows and has no need to discover, pacing through the city and observing creatures and things only as they affect his own thoughts and problems. As in all perception, purpose and memory structure the universe, so that the novelist is not bound to recreate reality by traditional description. With Dostoyevsky, reality need not be proved: it is.

But the reader's impression is totally different. Is there a more hauntingly vivid and powerful image of the Petersburg of poor folk than the image of the city in *Crime and Punishment*,[2] although there is no elaborate description or detailed painting of scenery? The one exception is a set piece with the other Petersburg as its subject, the city glittering with palaces, the abnormal, abstract, fantastical and geometric capital of Imperial Russia, icy and inhuman. But even the non-Russian reader has this painful sense of the weird power of the other side of the city, with its brutal July heat, its stifling air, its stink, the bitter stagnant lime dust of its summer building works, its stale smell of alcohol, its swarming crowds, the shouts of prostitutes and drunkards which wake Raskolnikov in the night, its rows of basement gambling dens, its immense sooty tenements crammed with poor lodgers, its grey courtyards hung with washing, its gloomy rubbish-strewn staircases, its rooms misshapen like coffins, cupboards or sheds, its passageways where a fragile girl in a crinoline may be singing or a barrel-organ playing, its fascinating canals far from the flamboyant panorama of the Neva; this city which is like a room without fanlights[3] and which becomes one of the instigators of the crime. It is she who slides the axe into the hand of Raskolnikov, the dreamer caught in the grey net of her alleys and canals. It is she, a pestilential backwater disguised by the scales of her granite pavements, who sucks in the desiccated soul of Svidrigaylov like some gloomy and monstrous spider. Svidrigaylov is perfectly aware of the power of evil which she secretes: 'It is a city where the people are half mad .. There are not many places where one can find so many dark, violent or strange influences acting on a human soul as there are in Petersburg.'[4]

We have made this rough general sketch by collecting together artificially all the indications which are scattered through the novel. How did Dostoyevsky recreate the hypnotic capital with such vivid power? He does not give any panorama of the city, or any artistic or imaginative description. In positive terms, he chooses repetition, topography, surveying, sociological precision; and he respects the exact reality of Petersburg in 1865.

The navel of Raskolnikov's Petersburg is the Haymarket.[5] This is the focal point of a series of interlocking ellipses from which he cannot escape. If he leaves it, he returns, irresistibly drawn by the evil and tempting magnet of its infected air:

But the fact was that, in these latter times, although he was nearly always alone, he could not feel that he was alone. He would leave the town and set off along the highway; once he even reached a small wood, but the more lonely the place was, the more strongly was he aware of a close and troubling presence, not at all frightening, but so irritating that he would go back to town as quickly as he could, lose himself in the crowd, go to cheap cafés or bars, the flea market or the Haymarket. He felt better there, he even felt more alone.[6]

This accursed spiral, to whose depths he always returns, as the prey of the ant-lion slides irrecoverably into the funnel of sand, matches the map of the district; to the north is the Great Neva and to the south the three incomplete spirals of the canals: the Moyka, the Catherine canal[7] and the Fontanka. It is by his inevitable return to this crucial centre, a market place where poor people buy and sell and work, where, in nearby alleys, pubs and tarts tout for customers, that Raskolnikov marks out the city. This incessant return by the same streets, to the same square where his decisive meetings take place, where he finds his inspiration and publicly confesses his guilt, creates an impression of familiarity. The unconscious memory of the hero, the automatic quality of his movements, stressed by Svidrigaylov,[8] finally imprint the image if not the actual plan of this Petersburg of the people on the reader's mind. Raskolnikov has no need to reconstruct his path verbally, as a tourist might do in an unknown town; space is created by his movement and by the repetition of his journeys on foot.

This impression of familiarity, of space verified by movement, is solidly based on topography, on surveying the route and, as in all townscapes, by description of the people in it. The beginning of *Crime and Punishment* gives an example which is valid throughout the novel:

At the beginning of July, in extraordinarily hot weather, towards evening, a young man left the attic which he occupied as sub-tenant in C. Street. He reached the street and slowly, as if undecided, turned towards K. Bridge . . .[9]

Anna Grigoryevna has no difficulty in identifying the side streets, avenues and bridges that Dostoyevsky mentions.[10] C. Street is Carpenter Street (*Stolyarnyy Pereulok*), where Dostoyevsky lived from August 1864 to January 1867.[11] K. Bridge is Kokushkin Bridge, which spans the Catherine canal not far from the Haymarket. This canal is called *Kanava* in the novel, and so is immediately recognisable. The A. Avenue and Bridge are the Ascension Avenue and Bridge, T. Bridge is the Tuchkov Bridge, and so on. Dostoyevsky uses initials for a specific purpose; half naming these places, he stresses the impression of belonging. Why should one notice street names when one is walking through a familiar district?

This kind of sighting also implies approximate pacing out of streets. When the path taken suddenly becomes important, measurement must be precise. So Raskolnikov, going to the old moneylender's house to 'rehearse' his crime, checks the accuracy of his calculations: 'He had not far to walk; he even knew how many paces there were from the door of his house; exactly seven hundred and thirty. One day he had counted them.'[12]

Finally, the people met show the human face of the streets, squares and buildings. But this sociological description is not influenced by the nineteenth-century fashion of describing appearances in the novel; it springs from the perception of the hero. If Raskolnikov, in rags, is trying to go unnoticed, he observes the clothes of the people he passes:

He was so badly dressed that any one else, even if he were used to it, would have been embarrassed to show himself in broad daylight in rags like those. It is true that the district was one of the sort where no kind of clothing would be surprising. The nearness of the Haymarket, the abundance of certain establishments, and the population, formed mainly of working men and tradesmen, which crowded into these streets and alleys was such a motley sight that on the contrary it would have been strange to have been surprised by any picturesque silhouette.[13]

When he examines the place where he is to commit his crime, he notes the sociological variety of the inhabitants and the arrangement of the place to remind himself:

With a tightening of his heart and a nervous shiver he approached a house of colossal dimensions, one side of which overlooked a canal and the other X. Street . . . This house was entirely made up of small lodgings and inhabited by all sorts of poorly paid workers: tailors, locksmiths, cooks, Germans of various kinds, girls making a living with their bodies, petty clerks, etc. People entering and leaving darted beneath the two main gateways and across the two courtyards. There were two or three caretakers in the yard.[14]

All this data, united in the hero's perception, finally create in the reader's mind a specific picture, even a landscape, which has existential force because it appears as observed by the other, the hero, who plays exactly the same role for space as the chronicler plays for time; he is a witness, he guarantees space. Towns in Dostoyevsky's novels are created by the eyes of the characters. G. L. Chulkov has described this landscape as 'anthropological': 'In a landscape of this kind all the elements pass through the soul of the hero; colours, lines, composition, perspective, everything is moving or changing place. We see the landscape through the eyes of the character of the novel, but we still create for ourselves a perfectly definite representation of the landscape.'[15]

To explain this strange quality, we must note that Dostoyevsky is obeying a self-imposed law, simple but very effective. Proceeding by successive brief touches, he never loses sight of the coherence which reality offers him. The topographical description of the hero's route is so accurate and so much based on reality that the paths of Raskolnikov and Svidrigaylov can be precisely traced, and one can even find the houses where the different characters in *Crime and Punishment* lived. The reader can follow the novel with a map of nineteenth-century Petersburg before his eyes.[16]

In Carpenter Street (now Przhevalsky Street) several houses look like Raskolnikov's house, for example, Alonkin House where the writer lived or Yevreynov House. But the house at the corner of Burgher Street (now Citizen Street) and Carpenter Street corresponds precisely with the novel. Under the porch one can see the two steps which led to the caretaker's lodge where Raskolnikov took possession of the axe; the old staircase is still there and, as in the novel, thirteen steps lead to the room–coffin of the student, just under the roof.[17]

Seven hundred and thirty paces separate the house of Raskolnikov from the enormous building where the old moneylender lives. This great tenement building has five storeys. It stands on a bend of the Catherine Canal at the angle it forms with Clerk Street (today No. 104, Griboyedov Canal). The dark staircase and the recess where Raskolnikov hid after his double murder can still be seen there.

When his crime is committed, Raskolnikov, who is afraid of being searched, tries to get rid of the evidence. First he wanders along the Catherine Canal, but he is afraid that the women doing their washing at the bottom of the steps or the men working on the barges might see him throwing the cases away. Then he has the idea of going to the Islands. He turns into Ascension Avenue and suddenly, as he enters Mary Square, he sees a large and isolated courtyard enclosed by blank walls. He goes in, and there, sheltered from witnesses, he hides the stolen cases and purse under a large stone weighing fifty pounds, which he moves. Anna Grigoryevna makes this comment on the passage:

In the first years of our married life, Fyodor Mikhaylovich, while we were out walking, took me to the courtyard of a house and showed me the stone under which Raskolnikov had hidden the objects stolen from the old woman. The courtyard was on Ascension Avenue, the second house after Maximilian Street; an enormous house has been built on this spot, and a German newspaper has its offices there.[18]

This vanished courtyard occupied the sites of the present No. 3 and No. 5, Mayorov Avenue.

Sonya Marmeladova lives near Raskolnikov, in the flat of the tailor Kapernaumov. Sonya's route, as she leaves Raskolnikov's house, tells us her address: she turns twice to her right and comes out by the canal. It is a two-storey house, which until recently was pale green, as in the novel, and which today has an added storey and has been painted yellow. It stands at the corner of the Catherine Canal, at a bend in Treasury Street (today, No. 73, Griboyedov Canal).

In Raskolnikov's shadow, the police station is still to be found at the corner of Clerk Street and the Sadovaya, and the furnished room where the sister and mother of the hero lived is at the point where Ascension Avenue meets Kazan Street, and the restaurant where Svidrigaylov has his interview with Raskolnikov.[19] One can also follow Svidrigaylov's steps as he departs on his great journey. He leaves Vasilevsky Island to reach the Petersburg district (*Peterburgskaya storona*), passes along almost the whole of the Great Avenue, then retraces his steps as far as Sezhinsky Street (still called by this name), and there, at the foot of a large house crowned with a tower, observed by a Jewish fireman, he blows out his brains.[20]

Besides this topographical realism there is a historical and social naturalism which might be thought exaggerated if it were not confirmed by documents of the period. For instance, we can compare the first pages of the novel with an extract from a newspaper, the *Petersburg Paper*, which describes the month of July 1865 in the imperial capital:

PETERSBURG PAPER	CRIME AND PUNISHMENT
The unbearable heat (40 degrees in the sun), the stuffiness, the stink of the Fontanka, the canals and the garbage, the deafening vibration of the carriages, the dust which formed not just a column but an unbroken cloud above Petersburg because the streets were not watered, the lime dust which came from plastering the façades during the day and from unloading the plaster into the canals and the Fontanka during the night, the grey and dusty vegetation of the squares and gardens, etc . . Such has been the picture presented by the Palmyra of the North for more than two weeks.[21]	In the street the heat was terrifying, and then there was the stuffiness, the crowd, lime everywhere, bricks, dust and that characteristic stink, well known by every inhabitant of Petersburg who has no chance of renting a cottage in the country; all this combined had a disagreeable effect on the nerves of the young man, which were already shaken.[22]

The drunkenness and vice which raged among the people at any hour of the day or night in the streets round the Haymarket is in no way exaggerated by Dostoyevsky. If Raskolnikov is awakened at night by the shouts of drunkards being thrown out, it is because Carpenter Street was a paradise for drinkers, as the journalist of the *Petersburg Paper* ironically commented:

There are sixteen houses (eight on each side) in Carpenter Street. In these sixteen houses there are eighteen drinking establishments, so that those who wish to devote themselves to the pleasure of drinking some cordial or some agreable beverage need not bother looking at the signboards; they only have to push a door open to find alcohol.[23]

At another time, Raskolnikov is rebelling against the society which condemns people like Sonya Marmeladova, his sister Dunya, and a child he meets by chance, drunk on a bench, to more or less open prostitution. He comes upon a side street, near the Haymarket, where prostitutes stand herded together in groups, their hair blowing in the wind, without coats, with raucous voices and black eyes; this is Tayrov Street, famous for its two or three gloomy basement brothels.[24]

Each step Raskolnikov takes can be documentally verified. Each of his glances apprehends a part of reality, though only so far as this part corresponds to his own vision. Dostoyevsky does not imagine the city, he throws his hero into Petersburg, in summer 1865, and then borrows the eyes and thought of his character as he walks. Gradually, as if before the eye of a moving camera, as if in a glance prompt to seize whatever suits its inner thought, the city rises. It does not appear in one single moment, as if it were a painting; it is formed by duration and movement, like a piece of music or a sculpture.[25] Its extraordinary power comes from a combination of realism and subjectivity in action. N. P. Antsyferov has written a study of 'Dostoyevsky's Petersburg',[26] but in his second book *The Soul of Petersburg* he recognised that it was difficult to define a purely Dostoyevskian Petersburg,[27] as, strictly speaking, it does not exist. The novels only give us Raskolnikov's Petersburg, Prince Myshkin's Petersburg, the Petersburg of a Raw Youth.

Myshkin's Petersburg in *The Idiot* has none of the crushing presence of the Petersburg of Raskolnikov. Dostoyevsky is just as precise in his topography, but there is not the same sense of lived experience, of repeated pacing over the territory: he was evoking the memory of the capital while living abroad. In *The Idiot*, except for the apparent wanderings of Myshkin spied on by Rogozhin, space is often immobile, enclosed in aristocratic drawing rooms, or made geometrical by terraces overlooking parks. This Petersburg is further to the east than Raskolnikov's. The Yepanchins live on Foundry Avenue, by the Church of the Transfiguration, and a number of scenes take place in Pavlovsk, the town where the prosperous inhabitants of Petersburg spend the summer, twenty-seven kilometres south of the capital, bordered by great parks and steeped in music. But as soon as Myshkin approaches Raskolnikov's Petersburg and enters the district where the merchants live, a few minutes away from the Haymarket, Dostoyevsky recovers his sober and powerful art, bred of exact memory. It is the passage where Myshkin recognises the house of Rogozhin, which he has never seen, simply because it looks like Rogozhin:

As he approached the place where Pea Street crosses the Sadovaya, he was surprised by his own agitation; he had not expected his heart to beat so painfully. A house in the distance had already attracted his attention because of its odd appearance .. He knew that it would be very unpleasant, for some unknown reason, to have guessed right. This house was large, sombre, three storeys high, without any style and dirty green. Some houses of the sort, but very few, built at the end of the last century, survive in those streets of Petersburg ... They are solidly constructed, with thick walls and very few windows; the ground floor windows sometimes have gratings. Usually there is a money-changer's store below. The eunuch who looks after it has his own lodging upstairs. Outside and inside, everything has a dry and unwelcoming air, it seems to be hiding and crouching, but it would be difficult to say why the mere appearance of the house gives this impression. The arrangement of its architectural lines has, of course, its mystery.[28]

This house is now situated, as real and solid as ever, at No. 33, Dzher-zhinsky Street.[29]

Provincial Russia in the last novels

From May 1872, the Dostoyevsky family, whose circumstances were improving thanks to Anna Grigoryevna's financial competence, rented and then bought a holiday house in Staraya Russa, a little watering town near Novgorod, to the south of Lake Ilmen, where the streams of the Polist and the Pererytitsa meet. The family went there every year in summer and even spent the winter of 1874–5 there, when the first chapters of *A Raw Youth* were being written. From then on, the little town entered Dostoyevsky's novels, although first in minor episodes. The main part of the action in *The Devils*, for instance, takes place in a provincial capital, whose place-names recall Tver (now Kalinin), where Dostoyevsky lived from August to December 1859, on his return from Siberia, but the last journey of Stepan Trofimovich takes us to a little fishing village, Ustriki, which recalls Ustevo on Lake Ilmen.[30] While *A Raw Youth* takes place mainly in Petersburg, the parable of the merchant Skotoboynikov and the child with the bird, told by Makar the wanderer, takes us back to Staraya Russa with its large market place and its horse market.[31]

In *The Brothers Karamazov*, however, Staraya Russa becomes the inspiration of the novelist.[32] Its name in the novel is a country landscape in itself: Skotoprigonevsk, or cattle park, furrowed, as such a place could be, by smelly streams like Malashka and Pererytitsa, which isolate the district in which Fyodor Pavlovich's house stands. This is certainly Dostoyevsky's own house; the description in the novel leaves no doubt:

The house of Fyodor Pavlovich Karamazov stood far from the centre of the town, but not quite on the outskirts. It was fairly ancient, but had a pleasant exterior: one storey, with an attic, painted grey and with a red iron roof ... It was spacious and comfortable. There were a lot of different storerooms, hiding places and unexpected steps.[33]

Lyubov, the writer's daughter, describes it in similar terms: the house was full of 'unexpected surprises [sic], secret cupboards, traps leading to dusty spiral staircases'.[34]

All the episodes of *The Brothers Karamazov* can be placed in context, since every time a topographical detail identifies the places. It is so exact that one can easily reconstruct Dmitriy's itinerary on the night of the murder.[35] He leaves Grushenka's house in the Collegial quarter on the other side of the Pererytitsa, crosses the Collegial Bridge, and sets out along the Pererytitsa embankment, which ought to take him to his father's house. A block before he reaches it, however, Dmitriy makes a detour, turning to his left in Dmitriyev Lane, crossing the little bridge over the 'stinking' stream of the Malashka, going right along Dmitriyevskaya Street, and finally taking another right turn along an alley to finish up in Minin Street, which is deserted; before him is the garden with its high wall. This detour is full of premeditation, though unadmitted. Dostoyevsky has rediscovered in his last great novel the same obsessive topographical power he used in *Crime and Punishment*.

Essence of the landscape seen by the hero

Sometimes Dostoyevsky's hero stops, looks and contemplates. Seeing is more important to him than immediate sighting. The world is reified, but only by the will of the character. It exists fully as a collection of objects which are external to the person who contemplates them, external but not indifferent. Love or hate, dream or obsession, sometimes both in disturbing ambivalence, suddenly make the real material world emerge. The subjectivity of the hero is inscribed in a motionless space. This landscape is not however, in Amiel's words, a state of mind, a happy coincidence of being and nature. It is the passionately committed word of the hero about the external world. If we consider, moreover, that Dostoyevsky is the poet of the town, that cityscapes are essentially made by man and that architectural lines have a mysterious language, one can identify the person to whom this word is spoken. Through the stones, the avenues, the panoramas, the interiors, the hero sees man, so that the landscape contemplated in Dostoyevsky appears as the word of the hero about himself and human society, a word of man about men. The landscapes in the novel are like the portrait of Nastasya Filippovna, which Myshkin contemplates even before he knows the heroine: he finds in it the haughty beauty and deep suffering of a soul, but he also inscribes his own love on it with a naive and secret kiss. Each landscape contains a question and a reply. Anthropocentric by nature, the landscape of Dostoyevsky also has an anthropological intention, as Chulkov puts it. The hero of *A Raw Youth* has a confused sense of this relationship between people and places:

I had coffee while I was still on Vasilevsky Island, purposely avoiding the bar I had been in yesterday on the Petersburg district; this bar and the nightingale had become doubly hateful to me. A strange trait: I am capable of hating places and objects, just as if they were people. But I have some happy places in Petersburg, that is, places where I was once happy for some reason – and, in fact, I save these places up and don't go in them for as long as possible, so that when I am quite alone and unhappy, I can go in to be unhappy for a while and remember.[36]

Like Stendhal in *Lucien Leuwen*, Dostoyevsky is always asking: 'How does the hero see this?' In his earliest works, Dostoyevsky had already mastered the essential part of his landscape technique; the hero sees the world with the eyes of his soul and changes its nature. So at the end of 'White Nights', the desperate dreamer sees, as if through the veil of his tears, that the world has suddenly changed:

I looked at Matryona . . She was still a hearty, *young* old woman, but, I don't know why, she suddenly seemed to have a dreary look, wrinkles on her face, bent, decrepit . . I don't know why, it suddenly seemed to me that my room had grown old, just like the old woman. The walls and floors were peeling, everything had gone dark; there were more cobwebs than ever. I don't know why, when I looked out of the window, it seemed to me that the house opposite had gone decrepit and dreary as well, that the plaster on its columns had peeled and fallen off, that the cornices had blackened and cracked, and that the walls from being dark yellow colour had become dappled.[37]

There is already the subtle orchestration between natural causes and subjectivity:

Possibly a ray of sunlight, suddenly glancing out from behind a cloud, was hidden once more under a rain cloud, and everything became dreary again in my eyes: or perhaps it was the whole outlook of my future that flashed before me so unwelcomingly and gloomily.[38]

Later Dostoyevsky was to abandon these commentaries which are impressionistic rather than expressionist, these intermediate links which stress comparison and connections and would have led him to a symbolist technique. Landscape, like setting, was to become a sign, a world which had a direct significance, but this time for the hero. The adjective was to be a realistic description of the material world, besides indicating a subjective vision. Transfer of the mood of the hero to the properties of the object was to become the rule. There were to be 'happy places', as Arkadiy says, and dismal places, landscapes of distress.

The true landscape of Dostoyevsky begins with *Notes from Underground*. A comparison between the works written before and after this story, both in the opposing registers of love and hate, allows us to trace the evolution of Dostoyevsky's technique and to define the singular nature of the Dostoyevsky landscape.

In *Netochka Nezvanova*, written in 1849, Dostoyevsky creates a happy picture inside the nightmare – it is the motif of the rich house with red curtains, steeped in music, which Netochka dreams about before she enters it. The theme traces a melodic line of happiness in the dramatic score, and progresses from dream to reality. Netochka recalls:

However I was somehow particularly happy because everything had ended so well, and all that night I dreamt of the house next door with the red curtains . . Especially I loved to look at it in the evening, when the lights were lighted in the street and when the purple red curtains at the tall windows of the brightly lit house began to glow with a kind of blood-red, special glow . . All this in my childish imagination took on the appearance of something royally luxurious and magical, as if it were in a fairy-tale.[39]

And immediately I formed the idea that we should settle in that particular house and live in it in a kind of eternal holiday and eternal blessedness.[40]

Once after the lesson he began to tell me a fairy tale. It was the first fairy tale I had ever heard. I sat as if enchanted, burning with impatience as I followed the story, I was carried away into a kind of paradise as I listened, and at the end of the story I was in complete ecstasy. It was not that the fairy-tale had such an effect on me, – no, but I took it all for truth, and I immediately let my rich imagination wander and instantly mingled reality with fiction. Instantly the house with red curtains appeared in my imagination . . .[41]

We have mentioned the end of this dream and its passage into reality: the scene blazing with light and music where Netochka, hidden behind a crimson velvet door-curtain, is listening to the concert given by the violinist S. and remembering her dreams. In this treatment of the happy scene of the house with red curtains, everything is explained, prepared at length, carried so far as to become a symbol. Quite different, though still in the happiness register, is the Swiss landscape which Prince Myshkin recalls in *The Idiot*. This is true cosmic ecstasy, a hymn to creation which does not immediately reveal its nature. The splendour which dazzles eyes and heart is not commented on, nor even explained by the hero. It is only signified, as with Stendhal in *La Chartreuse de Parme*, by adjectives which have both material and moral value.

This had been in Switzerland, in the first year of his treatment, even in the first months. Then he was completely like an idiot, sometimes he could not even speak properly . . . Once he went into the mountains, on a clear sunny day, and walked for a long time with a single painful thought which would not take shape. In front of him was the shining sky, below was a lake, all around was the light and infinite horizon, which had no end and no boundary. He looked for a long time and was in anguish. He now remembered how he stretched his hands out towards this light infinite blueness and wept. The thing which was tormenting him was that he was a stranger in all of this. What was this banquet, what was this continuous great festival which never ended and which he had long been drawn to . . . Every morning this same bright sun rises; every morning there is a rainbow on the waterfall; every evening the snowy, highest mountain there, in the distance, on the edge of the sky, burns with a purple flame.[42]

In the contrasting register of hostile, even deadly, landscapes, the distance between works before and after *Notes from Underground* is just as great. In *The Double* the collusion between the gloomy and windswept landscape of Petersburg, directly descended from Gogol, and the imaginary enemies harassing Golyadkin is too explicit, overloaded to the point of being irritating:

The night was horrible, a November night, – wet, misty, rainy, snowy, fraught with fluxes, colds, agues, quinsies, fevers of all possible kinds and sorts, – in short, with all the blessings of November in Petersburg. The wind howled through the deserted streets, whipping up the Fontanka's black water higher than the moorage rings, and provocatively fingering the meagre streetlamps of the embankment, which, in their turn, echoed its wails with a thin piercing creak, which made up an endless, squeaky, rattling concert, well known to every inhabitant of Petersburg. It was raining and snowing at the same time. The streams of rain pierced by the wind were sprinkled almost horizontally, as if from a hose pipe, and were stabbing and flogging the face of the unhappy Mr Golyadkin like thousands of pins and needles . . .
Although all of this together was suddenly attacking the unfortunate Mr Golyadkin, who even without this was nearly dead with misfortunes, not giving him the slightest mercy or the slightest respite, chilling him to the bone, glueing his eyes together, blowing through him from all directions, making him lose his way and the remains of his good sense, although all this toppled on Mr Golyadkin at the same time, as if it were purposely conspiring and making common cause with all his enemies . . . – in spite of all this, Mr Golyadkin remained almost insensible.[43]

The ill-matched comparisons and the journalsitic humour dilute the tragic feeling of growing paranoia. The landscape is impure. It is completely different from the extraordinary landscape of the second part of *Notes from Underground*, 'On the subject of wet snow'.

Here the author does not intervene. Everything appears as the hero sees it, as he projects his deep feeling of inner stagnation and self-disgust on the space around him. The dirty yellowish shades of his soul, 'soaked until it has become mildewed'[44] in the mud of his underground existence, become part of external reality: 'Inexpressibly sad, I went to the window, opened the shutter and peered into the hazy darkness of the thickly falling wet snow.'[45]

The hero only has to think of duel, of death, and the landscape sends him a funereal echo:

The wet snow was pouring down in great flakes: I opened my coat, I was thinking of something else. I had forgotten everything else, because I had finally decided on the slap and I sensed with horror that it would certainly happen now *inevitably, at this very instant* and that *there was no possibility at all of stopping it.* The deserted street lamps gleamed dismally in the snowy darkness, like torches at a funeral.[46]

After his distressing adventure with the trusting Liza, the hero reacts violently. He rushes after her, perhaps to ask for forgiveness for the outrage he has done her. He questions the landscape, he looks at himself in it, and it replies to his unspoken question: give up!

It was quiet, the snow was pouring down and fell almost perpendicularly, spreading a pillow on the sidewalk and the deserted street. No one was passing, there was not a

sound to be heard. The street lamps flickered gloomily and pointlessly. I ran about two hundred paces to the crossing and stopped.
'Where has she gone? and why am I running after her? Why? To fall in front of her, sob with repentance, kiss her feet, beg for forgiveness!... Will I not torture her again?' I stood in the snow, gazing into the hazy darkness, and thought about it.[47]

And in fact he gives up, associating the mud in the road, the melted snow and the brief memory of gravestones with the filth of his soul:

Tomorrow I should certainly have polluted her soul with my filth and wearied heart. But the feeling of insult will never die in her now, and however filthy the mud is that awaits her, – a feeling of insult will raise and purify her ... with hatred ... hm..., perhaps, even with forgiveness.[48]

The hero is literally reasoning in terms of landscape. This last example shows the nature of the landscape seen from inside by the hero. It is essentially musical, not pictorial. Everything in this landscape recalls music: the recurrence of themes, the constant association of colours and sounds, but especially the emotional power.[49] The landscape answers the hero's questions because it is there that he first pursued his obsessions, found his ecstasy, inscribed his hate or read his self-disgust.[50] It is a false mediator of his conscience. In the scenery Dostoyevsky inscribed the message of the gods, the verdict of destiny; in the landscape he leaves the hero alone to argue with his own mind and the minds of others.

The myth of Petersburg

Thoroughly anthropological and anthropocentric, Dostoyevsky's landscapes, particularly those of Petersburg, do not form a continuous whole. Structured as they are by the interrogations of the hero's conscience, they cannot be attributed to the novelist without reference to the heroes. However, when they appear in book after book, they become recurring themes which convey a mythical image belonging to both character and writer, especially when Dostoyevsky, as journalist, for example, takes over the vision of his heroes and when the poets and novelists who follow him adopt the myth which he has created.

For beside the Petersburg of the canals, of populous streets, immense soulless buildings, gloomy courts and apartments like cages, whose centre is the Haymarket, beside the Petersburg of anfractuosities, attics, and basements where the heroes of the early stories before *Crime and Punishment* 'live, drink and fear life',[51] there is another Petersburg, towering, monumental and inhuman, which the hero discovers when he tears himself away from the moist grip of the canals and, leaning on the parapet of a bridge, contemplates the broad panorama of the Neva stretching before his eyes.

The grandiose vision of the Petersburg of palaces, domes, spires, columns, granite and water, with its severe and icy beauty, inspires first Arkadiy, one of the heroes of 'A Weak Heart', then the journalist of 'Petersburg Dreams in verse and prose', then Raskolnikov in *Crime and Punishment*, and finally the Raw Youth[52] with a frank aversion, which is sometimes masked by the violent wish to see the Tsarist capital disappear like a deadly mirage. The landscape is the same for each of these heroes, but sometimes they stress the hostility of the capital and sometimes its deceiving and evanescent side. For all of them it is a snare and a delusion. It is a town of people who are half mad, dreamers, 'the most abstract and premeditated town in the whole of the world'.[53]

In 'A Weak Heart', Arkadiy, the friend of Vasya, who has gone mad because he did not believe in his own happiness, since he was crushed by his feeling of guilt for the oppressed, contemplates this hostile Petersburg:

It was growing dark when Arkadiy returned home. As he approached the Neva, he stopped for a minute and cast a piercing glance along the river into the smoky, icily dim distance, which had suddenly turned to crimson in the last purple of the *blood*red sunset, burning out in the dark heavens. Night was settling over the city, and the whole immense clearing of the Neva, swollen with frozen snow, with the last glow of the sun, was showered with infinite myriads of sparks of needles of frost. It was a frost of minus twenty. A freezing vapour poured from the horses *driven to death*, from the hurrying running people. The condensed air trembled at the least sound, and like giants, from all the roofs of both banks pillars of smoke rose and flared up in the cold sky, twining and untwining as they went, so that it seemed as if new buildings were rising over the old, a new city was being built in the air ... It seemed, at last, that all this world, with all its inhabitants, strong and weak, with all their dwelling-places, beggars' hovels or gilded palaces – *joy of the mighty of this world*, – in this twilight hour was like a fantastical, enchanted vision, like a dream, which in its turn would disappear at once and would float like steam towards the dark blue sky.[54]

Later, in 1861, in an article written in the first person, 'Petersburg Dreams in verse and prose', in which he recalled the period of *Poor Folk*, Dostoyevsky literally repeated the same text, except for a few expressions which stress the hostility of the vision.[55] In 1848, the social accusation was clear:

A strange thought visited the orphaned friend of poor Vasya. He shivered and his heart seemed to be flooded at that moment by a burning fountain of blood, which suddenly boiled up out of a surge of some powerful sensation, which he had never known until then. He seemed only now to understand all this alarm and anxiety and to realise why his poor Vasya, who could not bear his own happiness, had gone mad.[56]

V. Shklovsky asked: whom does Arkadiy resent? He followed Arkadiy's gaze and found that there, where the Neva's waters divide, stands the

Winter Palace, the imperial residence.[57] The frozen empire, a single gigantic machine for crushing men, weak hearts, is to blame for Vasya's destruction. In 1861, Dostoyevsky, who had become more prudent politically and was about to make a complete volte-face, came to a different conclusion; the vision becomes a revelation to the writer of his mission:

It was as if I had just begun to understand, at that precise moment, something which had been moving in me then without my being aware of it. It was as if I had had the sudden vision of something new, a world entirely new, unknown to me and which I had had an idea only by vague rumours and mysterious signs. I think it was precisely at that instant that I began to exist.[58]

In the novella of 1848 there was a hint of the socialist attacking Imperial Russia; in the article of 1861, we are present at the birth of a writer vowed to defend the insulted and injured, morally denouncing the inhumanity of Petersburg, without politically denouncing the underlying cause.

In *Crime and Punishment* Raskolnikov casts an admiring but disturbed look at the same panorama of the Neva:

He took about ten steps and turned to face the Neva, in the direction of the palace. The sky was completely cloudless, and the water almost blue, which so seldom happens at the Neva. The dome of the cathedral, which never appears more clearly from any point of the city than it does from this viewpoint, from the bridge, when you have about twenty paces to go to the chapel, absolutely glittered and through the pure air one could clearly see each one of its distinct decorations ... He stood and looked into the distance long and attentively; this place was an old acquaintance of his. When he went to university, usually – mostly on his way home – he happened, perhaps about a hundred times, to stop just at this very place, to gaze attentively at this truly splendid panorama and each time to be almost surprised at the vague and puzzling impression it made on him. An inexplicable coldness came over him whenever he looked at this splendid panorama; for him this magnificent picture was full of a deaf and dumb spirit ... Every time he was amazed at his own gloomy and puzzling impression and, not trusting himself, he kept putting off any attempt to work it out.[59]

What is this dumb-and-deaf spirit, which Jesus drives out of the epileptic child,[60] if not the breath of the hostile, hated, enchanting city, of this icy Petersburg whose power crushes the insulted and injured, embodying the social injustice against which the poor student rebels, the Petersburg who grips the criminal in her stony hand? The Winter Palace, as Raskolnikov dare not admit to himself, is the obstacle to the golden age which is the dream of his heart. As Prometheus does with Olympus, he fixes his accusing gaze on it, terrified by his own pathetic daring. Andrey Bely, in his fantastic novel *Petersburg*, has pushed Dostoyevsky's timid intuition to its limit. One of his heroes, consumed, like Raskolnikov, by his own solitary and murderous thoughts in the 'yellow space' of his attic, the terrorist of 1905, Aleksandr Ivanovich Dudkin, looks at the Neva with a hatred and fear which is very similar to that of the hero of *Crime and Punishment*.

You are lines!

In you the memory of Peter's Petersburg remains.

Peter once drew these parallel lines; and they were overgrown with granite, or with fences of stone or wood; ...

The stranger remembered ...

He thought that life was getting dearer; that it was hard for the workers to live; from over there, Petersburg drove its way in with the arrows of its avenues and the horde of its stone giants.

Over there, Petersburg was rising; from the wave of clouds, the buildings flamed; over there, it seemed, something malicious and cold was soaring; from over there, from the howling chaos, someone had fixed his stony gaze, and his skull and ears jutted out into the fog.

All this crossed the mind of the stranger; he clenched his fist in his pocket.[61]

For Dudkin, the stone gaze is the gaze of the senator Apollon Apollonovich Ableukhov, rampart of tsarist Russia. In *Crime and Punishment*, the deaf-and-dumb spirit denotes the imperious mind of Peter I, divider of the Russian nation, the inhuman founder of this glacial geometric capital, the iron will which imprisoned the Russian soul in these cubes and parallelepipeds of stone, these rectilinear avenues which have the strange characteristic of 'transforming the passers-by into shadows',[62] as Bely writes, in his inspired continuation of Gogol and Dostoyevsky. The two landscapes are a clash of glances. Dudkin and Raskolnikov, each in his own way, challenge and are challenged by the Enemy City.

From the time of Pushkin's *Bronze Horseman*, the tyranny of Petersburg has been embodied in the equestrian statue of Peter I, the work of Falconet, which stands on Senate Square and looks especially formidable from the Neva embankment. In Pushkin's poem, the statue comes to life and pursues poor Yevgeniy, who has gone mad with grief after the disappearance of his beloved in one of the terrible floods of the Neva and has dared to shake his fist at the statue of the founder of the capital.

This vindictive bronze horseman occupies the centre of Arkadiy's vision in *A Raw Youth* as he passes through Petersburg one cold morning, in 'a moist and milky fog'. But, still obsessed by the Rothschild idea (sighting within seeing), the youth is not remembering the unfortunate Yevgeniy so much as another of Pushkin's heroes, the ambitious and impatient Germann of *The Queen of Spades*, who kills for gain. The two works merge in his mind. In fact, for Dostoyevsky, the characters of Pushkin are old acquaintances knocking at his door: Yevgeniy is the poor Vasya of 'A Weak Heart', and Germann is the Raskolnikov of *Crime and Punishment*. Although Arkadiy's vision is subjective,[63] it is also a synthesis of the Petersburg landscapes of the years 1848, 1861 and 1866, whose two themes are the threat and the mirage:

I consider that the morning in Petersburg, apparently the most prosaic in the whole wide world, is practically the most fantastic in the world. This is my own personal viewpoint or, rather, impression, but I stand by it. On a Petersburg morning like this, decayed, wet and misty, the wild dream of some kind of Pushkinian Germann from *The Queen of Spades* (a colossal figure, unusual, a completely Petersburg type – a type from the Petersburg period!), it seems to me, should become even stronger. A hundred times, amid this fog, I had the strange but insistent vision: 'When this fog is scattered and flies away, perhaps all this decaying slimy town will go away with it, will rise as the fog rises and disappear like smoke, leaving behind only the old Finnish marshes, and in the middle of them, for decoration, there will be the bronze horseman on his driven horse with its burning breath?' In a word, I cannot express my impressions, because all this is fantasy, finally, poetry, and therefore nonsense; however a completely senseless question often occurred to me and still occurs: 'Here they all are, rushing about from place to place tossing and turning, but how can we tell, perhaps all this is someone's dream, and there is not a single real, true person here, and not a single real action? Someone is going to wake up suddenly, who is dreaming all this, – and it will all suddenly disappear.'[64]

The two themes merge: the threat is in the mirage. It is no longer the vengeful animation of the heavy bronze horseman which contains the menace, but the revelation of nothingness, the dispossession of souls. The deaf-and-dumb spirit is that of the myth, in which Petersburg is only an empty cerebral shadow play,[65] a clandestine place, a universe of death where even the self is swallowed up, a fantastic kingdom of the dead, a nineteenth-century Egypt only pretending to be alive.

This powerful and original myth which Dostoyevsky created in his Petersburg stories and novels left its mark on the Russian poets of the end of the nineteenth century.[66] The genius of Andrey Bely seized the myth and used it in all its possibilities, recruiting Gogol and Pushkin as well as Dostoyevsky. He conjugated death by ice (reaction) and death by fire (revolution) to blow up the stones of Petersburg and efface the mirage, the dream of its founder:

And over there were lines: the Neva, the islands. Probably in the distant times when high roofs, masts, spires rose from the mossy marshes, piercing the dank greenish fog with their prongs, –
– on his shadowy sails the Flying Dutchman was flying towards Petersburg from the leaden empty spaces of the Baltic and German seas, to erect his foggy lands here by an illusion, and to give the wave of the gathering clouds the name of islands.[67]

The slanting rays of the setting sun

The dreams of men live in Dostoyevsky's landscapes. But in all his works, from first to last, there is a particular enigmatic lighting of the landscape which plunges the heroes into profound meditation, where the soul questions itself as if astonished. This comes at the time which Dostoyevsky particularly loved, as Anna Grigoryevna repeats,[68] the time when the brilliant purple glow of the setting sun suddenly pierces the greenish or milky fog of Petersburg, lighting its discoloured or dusty interiors, illuminating the dreams of atheist hearts with equivocal happiness. The slanting rays of the setting sun occur so often in Dostoyevsky's novels and stories that they have been seen as a symbol or even a philosophic landscape.[69] However S. N. Durylin has noted that this symbolic landscape is always realistic.[70] The slanting rays of the setting sun are always recalled at the right time of day, and they are always linked with the vision of the hero, so that they sometimes, in their context, have an antinomic sense. Moreover, Dostoyevsky invariably gives several keys to the landscape. The slanting rays of the setting sun are not so much a symbol as a mystagogic sign, whereby the hero is initiated into a mystery. The whole of Dostoyevsky's work illuminates this preparation for the mystery, as if, using this theme again and again, he were developing its meaning and profundity for his own sake.[71]

The sunset hour could be romantic or melancholy, but even in the earliest works of Dostoyevsky, the setting sun does not cause sadness. On the contrary, it brings joy and hope, a kind of glow of the soul. The dreamer of 'White Nights' 'especially' loves this hour, when, free from the constraints of the daytime, he can abandon himself to his dreams. Using the third person, the dreamer describes how he comes back to his house:

He does not look with indifference at the sunset, which is slowly fading in the cold Petersburg sky. When I say that he looks, I am lying: he does not look, he contemplates somehow without taking account of it ... He is rich now *in his own particular life*; somehow he has suddenly become rich, and it is not in vain that the fading sun's ray of farewell glowed so cheerfully before him and summoned up from his comforted heart a whole swarm of impressions.[72]

Netochka Nezvanova gives a more subtle analysis of the immense hope which comes over her soul at the time of the setting sun. She is leafing through *St Ronan's Well* by Sir Walter Scott, opening the book at random to find her fortune. Tears come into her eyes:

The room was brilliantly lit by the last, slanting rays of the setting sun, which poured densely through the high windows on to the gleaming parquet of the floor; ... There are moments when all the mental and spiritual forces, morbidly tense, seem suddenly to flare up with a bright flame of awareness, and at that moment something prophetic appears to the shaken soul, which seems tortured by a feeling of its future, and with anticipation. And every part of you is so eager to live, demands to live, and, catching fire with the most burning, blindest hope, the heart seems to summon the future, with all its mystery, with all its secrecy, even if it brings storms and tempests, if only it brings life.[73]

The same conflagration of the soul, as if lit by the fire of the setting sun, the same mad hope of life, sustains Ivan Petrovich, the writer of *The Insulted and Injured*, at the beginning of the novel:

I love the March sun in Petersburg, especially the sunset, of course, on a clear, frosty evening. All the street suddenly glows, bathed in bright light ... It is as if the weather in the soul had cleared up, as if you had shuddered or someone had nudged you. A new look, new thoughts ... It is amazing what a single ray of sun can do with the soul of man![74]

But this sunny prologue is deceptive, and hope soon falters. The tragedy of *The Insulted and Injured* begins, amid wet snow, rain, storm, and heavy heat. Paradoxically, the setting sun reappears in the epilogue at the moment when little Nelli is dying. From then on the ambivalence of the landscape becomes a theme in Dostoyevsky's work.

The last goodbyes are spoken in the purple rays of the setting sun. This is when children and young people die: Nelli in *The Insulted and Injured*,[75] Liza in 'The Eternal Husband',[76] poor Marie in *The Idiot*,[77] Markel, Zosima's brother in *The Brothers Karamazov*.[78] It is also the hour when the tormented souls decide to end things once and for all. Raskolnikov wants to finish everything before the sunset: will it be a confession or, as Sonya fears, suicide?[79] In *A Raw Youth*, Kraft shoots himself at sunset, to Arkady's amazement: '"Kraft?" I muttered, turning to Akhmakova, – shot himself? Yesterday? At sunset?"'[80] Versilov, in his dream of the Golden Age, sees the death of humanity and the reddening fires of the Commune in the slanting rays of the setting sun.

But people also weep with emotion in the slanting rays of the setting sun. The tormented souls of Stavrogin and Versilov finds the relief of tears in their dreams of the Golden Age. Let us quote the last lines:

cliffs, and sea, and the slanting rays of the setting sun – all this I seemed to see still, when I woke up and opened my eyes, which were literally wet with tears. I remember that I was glad. A sensation of happiness, unknown to me before, passed through my heart, even painfully: it was love of all humanity. It was already late in the evening; through the window of my little room, through the greenery of the flowers standing on the windowsill burst a whole sheaf of bright slanting rays of the setting sun, drenching me with light.[81]

The Ridiculous man, in his triumph and adoration of the 'children of the sun', does not forget the premonition he felt in the slanting rays of the setting sun, when he lived on earth:

I told them often that I had already sensed all this long ago, that all this joy and glory had been seen by me briefly, in our planet, with a painful longing which sometimes led to unbearable sadness; that I had had an intuition of their existence and their glory in the dreams of my heart and the reveries of my spirit, that it had often happened, on our earth, that I could not look at a sunset without weeping ...[82]

All the young people who are spiritually rich remember the happy hours of their childhood spent in the warm purple of the setting sun. Arkadiy, in *A Raw Youth*, declares with youthful arrogance that he does not like sunset,[83] but he cannot help remembering the brilliant light of the evening sun which accompanied an instant of intense happiness, the visit of his mother to the Touchard school.[84] In the same novel, another drifting youth remembers his pure and happy childhood with his sister:

We used to sit together on the terrace, under our old lime-trees, and read this novel, and the sun was setting too, and suddenly we stopped reading and told each other that we too would be just as good, we would be beautiful.[85]

Alyosha Karamazov recalls a decisive instant in his early childhood, which stands out 'like a bright point in the darkness', when he was only four:

He remembered a particular evening, summery, quiet, the open window, the slanting rays of the setting sun (the slanting rays were what he remembered most), in the room in the corner was an icon, in front of it a lighted lamp, and before the icon on her knees sobbing as if in hysterics, with screams and cries, his mother, who had gripped him in both hands, embracing him so firmly that it was painful and praying for him to the Mother of God, stretching out with both her hands and holding him towards the icon, as if putting him under the Mother of God's protection.[86]

It is Mariya Timofeyevna, the Innocent who has the gift of prophecy in *The Devils*, who sums up most simply and strongly the vivid impression of the setting sun on the soul and the ambivalence of the sign:

I climbed this mountain, I turned my face to the east, I fell to the ground, I wept, I wept and I do not remember how long I wept, and I didn't remember then and I don't know anything about it now. I got up then, I turned back, and the sun was setting, and it was so great and splendid and glorious, – do you love looking at the sun, Shatushka? It is good, but it is sad.[87]

The numerous images which accompany the theme of the setting sun – greenery, innocence, birth, universal love – signify that death, which the theme represents, has been transcended. The slanting rays speak of an earthly ending, but also of eternal life, eternal renewal. The perfection of dawn is the great hope which sings in the glorious purple of the sunsets. Eternity endlessly renewed is the mystic message which the slanting rays of the setting sun bring to every soul. 'The sun is the ancient and immemorial symbol of life. The setting sun is the symbol of the indestructibility and infinitude of life: the setting sun, calm and at the end of its career, is also the sun that rises: the unique sun'.[88] With these words, Durylin ends his analysis of the diurnal theme of the setting sun, placing Dostoyevsky's creation in the ancestral tradition of mythologies and solar religions.

But the road of initiation is not yet finished. What is the nature of this longed-for eternity, diffused in the purple of the sunset? Is it Christian immortality? Is it the perpetuity of life which is at the heart of the great pagan mythologies and even of modern Utopias? It is here that the road divides and the univocal symbol is changed by the vision characteristic of

each hero. The artist leaves Christian and atheist to their differing visions of
eternity, never forgetting which stage they have reached in their journey.

Raskolnikov is a good example. At his most difficult moment, before he
officially confesses his crime, the hero of *Crime and Punishment* is still
hesitating between his secret dream of the Golden Age, which he is to find
in his dream in the epilogue, and the Christian path which Sonya indicates
to him. He sees eternity in the setting sun, but he cuts it down to a reduced
space, gloomy and enclosed:

He was wandering without an aim. The sun was setting. A kind of particular grief
had begun to appear in him lately. There was nothing particularly sharp, burning in
it; but it had the sense of something constant, eternal, there was a feeling of endless
years of this cold, killing grief to come, an eternity in a 'yard of space' . . .
'With these stupid, purely physical sicknesses depending on some kind of sunset,
try to stop yourself from doing something stupid! . . .' he muttered with hatred.[89]

For heroes who are committed one way or another, the eternity inscribed
in the slanting rays of the setting sun is more precise. We have seen in our
discussion of the Golden Age that for the atheists, Stavrogin, Versilov and
the Ridiculous man, eternity is an eternal return which is conceived as a
permanent resurrection of the whole of humanity, a kind of fervent
negation of the universal law of entropy, or simply as a continuity of
generations. Versilov, in *A Raw Youth* expresses this idea best:

'Let tomorrow be my last day, – everyone would think, looking at the setting sun, –
but it is all the same, I shall die, but they will all remain, and after them their
children' – and this thought that they would remain, still loving each other and
trembling for each other in the same way, would replace the thought of meeting
beyond the grave.[90]

For Christians, the rays of the setting sun are a divine message and the
promise which exalts their souls is the promise of the Resurrection.
Trishatov, in *A Raw Youth*, describes the sun as the 'thought of God':

And once, the sun is setting, and this child on the porch of the cathedral, bathed in
its last rays, stands and looks at the sunset with quiet thoughtful contemplation in
her childish soul, as if she were facing a mystery, because both of them really are like
a mystery – the sun, as the thought of God, and the cathedral, as the thought of
man.[91]

In the same novel, Arkadiy, who detests sunsets, is almost converted and
begins to love the slanting rays of the setting sun. The scene takes place
during his convalescence, at the moment when he is going to meet his legal
father, Makar the wanderer. He is in his bed:

The day was clear and I knew that after three o'clock, when the sun began to set, one
slanting red ray would strike the corner of my room directly and light that place with
a bright patch of light. I knew it . . . and the fact that I knew this as well as I knew
twice two irritated me intensely. I turned my whole body fitfully, and suddenly, in

the deep silence, clearly heard the words: 'Lord Jesus Christ, our God have mercy on us.'[92]

The youth listens to Makar Ivanovich and they talk of God, of atheism, of the eternal memory of the dead. The word which is sown grows, and brings with it love of the setting sun:

I was lying with my face towards the wall and suddenly in the window I saw the bright patch of light of the setting sun, that same patch which I had cursed as I waited for it just lately, and now I remember that my whole soul seemed to surge up and a new light seemed to pierce my heart. I remember this moment of sweetness and do not wish to forget it. It was only an instant of new hope and new strength.[93]

But the two novels where Christ appears in person complete the explanation of the mystic sign of the slanting rays of the setting sun. In *The Idiot*, where Myshkin appears as an asymptotic image of Christ-like beauty, shining with inner light, the picture described by Nastasya Filippovna gives us the first clue. Christ is openly associated with the setting sun:

Christ has been listening to him, but now has become thoughtful; his hand involuntarily, forgetfully has rested on the bright head of the child. He is looking into the distance, towards the horizon; a thought as large as the whole world is in his gaze; his face is sad .. The sun is setting.[94]

The Brothers Karamazov, where the slanting rays of the setting sun accompany Zosima's departure for heaven and Alyosha's entry into the monastery,[95] gives us the second clue. It has already been said, in the chapter on the Grand Inquisitor, that the crowd of Seville immediately recognise Christ by seeing the rays of light which flow from his eyes. In Alyosha's dream, Christ and the sun are identified with each other. Alyosha is dozing, worn out, while Father Paisy is reading the Gospel, the passage about the Marriage at Cana of Galilee, in the cell where Zosima's corpse is lying. Thoughts pass through the young novice's mind: 'The road is large, straight, light, crystalline, and the sun is at its end.'[96] He falls asleep and in his dream he sees the guests at the Marriage of Cana and among them not only his beloved Zosima, but Christ, the Resurrection incarnate. Zosima points Him out to Alyosha, saying: 'And do you see our sun, do you see it?'[97] For the Christian heroes, the sign of the slanting rays of the setting sun is no longer mystagogic but mystic, denoting faith in the Resurrection.[98] 'The sun which never sets', in the words of the prayer, is Christ.

There are two heroes who refuse to believe in the promise of eternity given by the setting sun. The first is the atheist Ippolit who decides to kill himself at sunrise, in a supreme challenging gesture of despair. The second is the envious ascetic of *The Brothers Karamazov*, Father Ferapont: this uneducated recluse, Zosima's enemy, sees horned and tailed devils everywhere, driving them out of his cell like spiders. In the night, an elm with two branches forms the silhouette of a threatening Christ. As opposed to Zosima, who is full of love and honours life, Ferapont represents a religion based on terror and obscurantism. And when the body of Zosima begins to decay, this spirit gnawed with fears and superstitions cries out: 'My lord has conquered! Christ has conquered the setting sun!'[99] This cry, which contradicts all Zosima's teaching, is a condemnation of the character who utters it and stresses the significance of the landscape of the setting sun, a space of eternity in the earthly existence of Dostoyevsky's heroes.

The crossroads

The sighting and seeing which have been described so far belong to one mind, that of the hero. We have been dealing only with individual space, structured by the intentions of one person. But space is also a crossing and convergence of several individual paths. In this case, looks and sightings meet or clash and the characters become subjects looking at each other or objects looked at by the reader-audience. In this slide from subject to object, public space tends to limit movement which, first suspended in hesitation, is then robbed of its nature in a scenic and frozen geometry. The more people there are in Dostoyevsky's world, the less animation there is, as if a limited space, like that of a stage, restrained the movement of human particles, or as if the mad dynamics of the heroes annihilated each other in their clash and collision.

Time, apparently suspended or detached from the time in the novel, fashions the features of this communal space. Far from being abolished, as Bakhtin thinks, time is exalted and arrested in its power. It is the moment when freedom of choice is exercised, when minds reveal themselves in public. Bakhtin has called these space–time periods 'chronotopes'. The first is the threshold (*porog*),[100] the second is the market square (*ploshchad'*). We should prefer to use the terms 'preliminary space' and 'space of the psychodrama'. In fact, the first is like the introduction to the time of power and the second like the time of crisis, of exposition through dramatic scenes or final gestures.

Preliminary space

The tragic dialectic of desire is at the heart of Dostoyevsky's work. In the early novels and stories, whose symbol might be 'A Weak Heart', the exercise of this dialectic ends tragically in the destruction or ruin of the character. From *Crime and Punishment* onwards, the hero has to commit or, like Dmitriy and Ivan Karamazov, accept an action, in order to test his being. He must therefore, at certain crucial instants, make a decision, a choice of one of the many solutions offered to him. He questions himself:

must he take the step which transforms the free action of the present into
the inescapable past, must he reveal his own nature to the eyes of another
and so expose his guilty desire. This hesitation, which is the true expression
of human breadth, is hesitation between temporal here and beyond. The
preliminary space expresses this hesitation spatially. It takes various forms:
the threshold of a house, a bedroom or a drawing room, an entrance, a
corridor, a staircase, porches or spaces enclosed in the light of a candle or a
shaft of light from a street lamp. In this terrifying dark airlock, the
indecisive mind, tormented by desire, held back by moral, social or political
restraints, wishes and does not wish, advances and retreats, gives itself and
takes itself back.

The Double offers a striking example of preliminary space, where the
hero, alone for three hours in a dark and cold service entry, hesitates to
cross a moral and social threshold. Golyadkin, a petty clerk, knows that
Klara Olsufyevna, the only daughter of the powerful councillor of state,
Berendeyev, the chief director of the ministry where he works, is completely out of his reach and yet he has had the impudence to fall in love with
her. He also knows that he has not been invited to the ball given in her
honour – indeed, on another similar occasion, he had been shown the door –
but he has been bold enough to go to it, in secret. Torn between fear and
desire, he has hidden in the service entry to the apartment:

He, gentlemen, is also here, that is, not at the ball but practically at the ball . . . he is
now standing – it's even odd to say it – he is now standing in the entrance, in the
service entry to Olsufiy Ivanovich's apartment . . . huddling into a place which is now
warmer, but is darker, partly hidden by a huge cupboard and old screens, amid all
sorts of junk, rubbish and throw-outs, hiding himself entirely from time to time and
for the moment just observing how things go in the character of an outside observer.
He, gentlemen, is just observing at the moment; he, gentlemen, can certainly go in
too . . . why not go in? There's only one step to take, and he will go in and go in quite
deftly . . . but he daren't go in any further, obviously he didn't dare to do this . . . not
because there was something he didn't dare to do, but just because he preferred to
be there in secret.[101]

The quotation gives only a slight idea of the interminable quibbles and
hesitations of Golyadkin, but it shows how rapidly his dualism increases.
The terror he refuses to admit is his own, but the daring and deftness he
refers to will be that of his double, Golyadkin the younger. It is immediately
after being thrown out of the ball, where he had finally made an entry which
had unfortunately been noticed, that he sees his persecutor suddenly appear
in the night. The preliminary space, so ironically treated, opens on the
tragic door of madness and shadow: it is the third, pathological, threshold.
This is a typical passage. It contains hesitation before transgression, of
whatever sort, and confession – here subverted by the dual consciousness –
either of which is enough to characterise the threshold. The darkness,

besides being realistic, also signifies the shadow which the mind is struggling to drive away, either by action or by half-confession, another way of committing itself. Finally, there is dialogue: it is true that Golyadkin is alone, but when he repeats 'gentlemen' to his imaginary hearers, he is really turning to the other Golyadkin who is already present.

Many confessions take place on a threshold, at the moment when the path is about to turn in a radically different direction, towards the unknown. So in *Notes from Underground*, the hero has been tormenting Liza the prostitute. Terrified by the effect of his cruel words, he has recovered by saying a few tender words to her. He is about to leave; it is then, 'in the entry, at the door', that the poor girl trustingly holds out to him her only letter of true love, which she has kept devotedly. The repentant executioner feels himself caught in the trap of love. He listens, in the doorway, to Liza's confession.[102] From now on, he must choose and he is furious at being forced into it.

We may recall the preliminary spaces of *Crime and Punishment* and *The Brothers Karamazov*: the badly lit corridor where Raskolnikov, in a silent look, confesses his terrible secret to Razumikhin; the beams of light from the street lamps where Alyosha and Ivan whisper their appalling words of guilt. The half confessions draw the heroes to a decisive choice.

At its extreme, the preliminary space plunged in total darkness becomes a doubtful undistinguished place where emotions can be revealed without constraint. In *A Raw Youth*, for example, Arkadiy, who dare not admit his love for Versilov and is suffering intensely from the need for a father, is walking with him, candle in hand, down the narrow stairs which lead to the youth's bedroom:

> But I did not go away. We were already going down the second flight of stairs.
> 'I have been waiting for you for the past three days,' the remark was suddenly wrenched out of me, as if involuntarily;
> I was choking.
> 'Thank you, my dear.'
> 'I knew that you would certainly come.'
> 'And I knew that you knew I should certainly come. Thank you, my dear.'
> He was silent. We had already come to the outer door, and I was still walking behind him. He opened the door: a swift gust of wind put out my candle. Then I suddenly seized his hand; it was completely dark. He trembled, but said nothing. I pressed my face to his hand and began to kiss it greedily, several times, many times.
> 'My dear boy, why do you love me so much?' he said, but in a completely different voice. His voice trembled and something quite new sounded in it as if it were someone else speaking.[103]

Staircases are in fact Dostoyevsky's favourite preliminary spaces. Besides offering a darkness which is propitious for ambushes, terrors and dangers, as well as admissions and confessions, their steps form a ten-fold, hundred-fold threshold, opening on to numerous apartment or outer doors – for it is always when they are saying goodbye that the heroes suddenly confide in each other – and the steps establish vertical relationships of domination between the protagonists. The staircase theme is treated at length in Bakhtin and P. M. Bitsilli.[104] We shall take one example, very rich, from *The Idiot*, where the preliminary space of the staircase in Rogozhin's house, both labyrinth and graveyard, is used three times.

Myshkin, after his long stay of six months in Moscow, has found Rogozhin again. Rogozhin realises that Nastasya Filippovna has agreed to marry him only out of desperation; he is devoured with jealousy. It is clear from the irritation he shows when Myshkin fiddles with a new knife lying on his table that he is full of murderous hatred. On this note of unease, the two young men get ready to say goodbye. Rogozhin sees Myshkin out. A strange dialogue begins about the copy of Holbein's picture, *The Dead Christ*; each of them asks a question without waiting for an answer. They meet again on the landing, undecided:

Rogozhin laughed caustically; having put his question, he suddenly opened the door and, holding on to the handle, waited for the prince to go out. The prince was surprised, but went out. Rogozhin went out after him on to the landing and closed the door behind him. Both stood facing each other with an expression that seemed to show they had both forgotten where they had come and what they had to do next.
'Goodbye then', said the prince, holding out his hand.
'Goodbye', said Rogozhin, shaking the hand held out to him firmly, but quite mechanically.
The prince went down one step and turned round.
'But with regard to faith', he began:[105]

Still on the point of leaving, Myshkin begins a long speech, full of parables, about true religious feeling. After this he says goodbye and goes down the stairs. He is already on the ground floor landing when Rogozhin calls him from above. The threshold has played its part; the gloomy and jealous man, trying to drive away the call to murder which is torturing him, suddenly decides to exchange crosses.[106] After this ceremony of brotherhood in God, blessed by the mother of Rogozhin, they go down the staircase once more, and there, on the step of the open door (a new preliminary space) Rogozhin grasps Myshkin and (a new sacrifice) cries out that he is giving up Nastasya Filippovna to Myshkin.[107] But passion is too strong for him and Rogozhin is later to try to kill his rival. This attempt also takes place on a staircase, that of the Scales' Hotel, in a darkness where only glances speak intensely and where the two heroes face a terrifying ordeal of death to be given and accepted:

The staircase, to which the prince ran up from beneath the gates, led to the corridors of the second and third floors, along which the hotel rooms were arranged. This staircase, as in all houses built a long time ago, was stone, dark, narrow and wound around a thick stone pillar. On the first landing on this pillar, there was a hollow, a sort of niche, no more than one step wide and about half a step deep . . . Dark as it was, the prince, when he ran up to the landing, immediately made out that for some reason there was a man hiding in this niche. The prince had a sudden urge to go by, without looking to the right. He took another step, but could not bear it and turned round.

The two recent eyes, *the very same*, suddenly met his gaze. The man who had been concealed in the niche had also had time to take a step out of it. For one second they stood face to face with each other, almost touching. Suddenly the prince seized the man by the shoulders and turned him back, towards the staircase, closer to the light; he wanted to see his face more clearly.

Rogozhin's eyes sparkled, and a mad smile distorted his face. His right hand rose, and something gleamed in it; the prince did not even think of stopping it.[108]

In *The Idiot* the staircase is really the favoured image of preliminary space, where Rogozhin hesitates, wavers, commits his contradictory final actions. The staircase is to some extent the spatial translation of his tragic break, his soul's anguish (*nadryv*).

On the demarcation line formed by doubtful and often dark places such as the staircase, the corridor, the doorway, time seems to be suspended, coiled up like a snake. In fact it is compressed and supersaturated. This is the infinite moment when all his life's past with all its contradictory motivations is harrying the hero and when the future which each possible choice would imply is flashing through his mind, although he does not know what his final choice will be. Briefly, it is the free and unavoidable present, 'free in so far as it is creating itself and illuminating its past, inevitable in that it immediately becomes the past and cannot be recaptured.'[109] In *The Devils*, the narrator notes this connection between the preliminary space and the preparations for the time of power. It is the famous scene where Varvara Petrovna orders Stavrogin, who has just come in but has stopped at the door of the drawing room, to say 'without moving' whether Mariya Timofeyevna the cripple is his wife or not: 'The present moment indeed might have been for her one of those moments in which suddenly as if in focus, the whole of life was concentrated, – all she had lived, all her present and perhaps her future.'[110] The numerous expressions such as 'suddenly', 'all at once', 'that very moment', 'instantly', 'immediately', which Dostoyevsky uses in these passages, may be considered as stylistic images of the threshold within the sentence, the space of the line. They punctuate the free and unavoidable present.

The way out of the air lock

In these uncertain preliminary spaces, glances and darkness are of the utmost importance. The hero gives himself up and draws back at the same time. He reveals himself to the gaze of that other person to whom secrets may be confessed, to whom one can show one's inner doubt and suffering, to whom one can make a direct confession. But he draws back too, because he needs darkness as his accomplice, isolating and sheltering him from a more dangerous gaze, that of the crowd, the people whose voice is the voice of God. The preliminary space allows the hero to satisfy, in love or death, 'the terrible desire to establish contact', in Katherine Mansfield's words. The contact between the two heroes is often established for a brief instant at the moment of goodbye, as if the embrace of souls were a touch of fire, from which the hero had to draw back immediately. Half-darkness and the exchange of glances are spatial metaphors for this eternal hesitant movement of man towards the Other person, composed of flux and reflux.[111]

But, when the threshold has been crossed, the act finally chosen commits the hero publicly. The airlock opens – as the example from *The Devils* shows – on to the space of the psychodrama. The hero of Dostoyevsky fears the crowd, but it is there on the market place (the *agora*) that he will make the final gesture committing him to move on towards his destiny. Dostoyevsky has described the judging power of the look of the crowd in two dreams, where the preliminary space is suddenly transformed into the space of psychodrama.

We remember how horrified Raskolnikov is when an unknown man, who seems to 'rise from the ground' shouts at him in a clear voice: 'Murderer!' On coming home, he realises that he is not a true conqueror like Napoleon, but a louse, the trembling creature to whom the Prophet said: 'Do not desire.' He falls asleep and dreams that he is murdering the moneylender again. He hits the old woman with an axe:

But it was a strange thing: she had not even stirred under the blows, as if she were made of wood. He was terrified, bent down closer to her and began to examine her; but she bent her head even lower. Then he bent right down to the floor and glanced at her face from below, glanced and turned to stone: the wicked old woman was sitting and laughing, – she was absolutely overcome with quiet, inaudible laughter, making every effort to keep him from hearing her. Suddenly it seemed to him that the door of the bedroom had opened a tiny crack and there seemed to be laughter and whispering in there as well. Fury overcame him: with all his strength he began to hit the old woman on the head, but with each blow of the axe the laughter and whispering from the bedroom became stronger and louder . . . He rushed to run away, but the whole entrance hall was already full of people, the doors on to the staircase were wide open, and on the landing, on the staircase and down the stairs – it was all people, head to head, all looking, – but all were keeping quiet, hiding and waiting in silence . . . He wanted to shout out and – he awoke.[112]

The dream prolongs the disillusioned reflection of the criminal. Raskolnikov sees himself dethroned in a dream, like Grigoriy, the imposter of Pushkin's *Boris Godunov*:

I had a dream that a steep flight of stairs
Led me up unto a tower, and from its height

> Moscow appeared, an anthill to my view.
> Below the people seethed upon the square
> Pointing at me with laughter; shame and terror
> Came over me – and falling headlong down,
> I woke.[113]

He is the impostor derided.[114] But this dream has an even greater significance: the hero's awareness is projected on to the gaze of the crowd. The people wait in silence (the laugh is Raskolnikov, laughing at himself) while the young man, leaving the preliminary space of the staircase, his private torture-chamber, finally enters public light and goes to bow down and admit his guilt on the market place, in the Haymarket, which he is to do at the end of the novel. The hero of Dostoyevsky needs to reveal himself too in the people's eyes, to leave the shadow of the threshold for the blazing light of communal space. In this way he becomes reconciled with himself.

'The Eternal Husband', written at the same time as *Crime and Punishment*, repeats this episode. Velchaninov, persecuted by a stranger with a black hatband who follows him everywhere, has the same dream:

He slept for about three hours, but with a disturbed sleep; he dreamt some strange dreams, like dreams in a fever. It was a matter of some crime, which he had apparently committed and concealed and he was being accused of this by some people who kept on coming in to see him from somewhere or other. A horrible crowd had gathered, but the people were still coming and coming, so that the door wouldn't shut and stood wide open. But finally all the interest was concentrated on one strange person, who had once been very close and dear to him, who had died, but who now for some reason had suddenly come to see him too.[115]

The two dreams are premonitions; they are followed in reality by the appearance of a character who will soon know the truth (Svidrigaylov) or who already knows it (Trusotsky), who will push the door open and insist on introducing himself. The great door opening on the staircase or the entrance hall is the conscience of the hero offered to the gaze of judgement, the promise of transparence.

The space of the psychodrama

Dostoyevsky's boldness in group scenes has been unanimously admired. He heaps up an improbable number of characters in a space which is too small for such a crowd, whether it is a poor man's room, a rich drawing room, an unexpected meeting place, the terrace of a villa, or even an elder's cell. The arbitrary nature of these assemblies is sometimes irritating, although they are skilfully arranged and the appearance of the crowd of characters is gradual and meticulously timed. But there is no disagreement about their explosive power. They have been called scene-conclaves. Bakhtin, without clearly distinguishing them from the space–time of the threshold, has called them chronotopes of the market place, or *agora*.[116] They are the hot feverish moments of crisis exposed to the common gaze. The most famous are: in *Crime and Punishment* the funeral feast in the Marmeladovs' room, punctuated by a succession of dramatic scenes; in *The Idiot*, the party arranged by Nastasya Filippovna in her drawing-room, where she gambles with her destiny before the three men who love her, Ganya, Myshkin and Rogozhin; in the same novel, the evening parties on the terraces of the summerhouses in Pavlovsk; in *The Devils* the vast general interrogation which Varvara Petrovna conducts in her drawing-room to clear up the mystery of her son's marriage: the secret reunion with 'our lot' in Virginsky's house; and finally at the beginning of *The Brothers Karamazov* the visit of the Karamazovs in a family group to Zosima in the monastery. There are others where the characters are fewer, but which are equally strong, for instance in *The Idiot* the confrontation of Nastasya Filippovna and Aglaya in the presence of Rogozhin and Myshkin.

In all of them, there are conflicts of extreme violence, violent physical or moral reactions, and shocking dramatic scenes, which take place under the gaze of the crowd and are isolated in a space which is usually enclosed or at least geometrical. Their time of action is detached from the time of the novel, like an independent block. In short, they are psychodramas.

In its original sense, the psychodrama is a therapeutic dramatic representation, where the patient, to overcome his psychic problems, plays a role suitable to the situation. In the broader sense, a psychodrama is still a theatrical representation, no longer therapeutic but cathartic, where characters placed in situations of conflict carry their acts to incandescence and, as if rushing headlong into the abyss of their truth, commit themselves to their destiny before everyone's eyes.

In the course of these group scenes where crisis is dominant, the heroes of Dostoyevsky offer up their inner selves as a spectacle for society. They carry their deepest impulses to the point of violence, they reveal their most secret thoughts, and so boldly, so scandalously, so improperly, that the people watching these real psychodramas are stunned and silent until they regain their senses and disperse in disorderly and contradictory hypotheses. There are many varied comments, for instance, about the follies of Nastasya Filippovna at her celebrated birthday party. She refuses a prince, a millionaire besides, throws 100,000 roubles on the fire and runs off with Rogozhin! Is she a queen, a lost woman, a madwoman, a dishonoured victim, who, like the samurai, tears open her stomach in the eyes of the man who has dishonoured her, a woman of extraordinary qualities, a rough diamond?[117] There is a host of commentaries on the slap which Shatov publicly gives Stavrogin in a similar scene in *The Devils*. But the 'what will people say?' aspect, whose only function is to collect all possible motives, is not important to the heroes, who, during the public scenes, are acting out and anticipating, on a lower scale, the tragedies which pursue them. The psychodramas are the first circles of the descent into the realm of tragedy. The destiny of Dmitriy is already blocked out when, at the beginning of *The Brothers Karamazov*, in the presence of Zosima and numerous witnesses, he points at his clown of a father and cries out: 'Why does a man like that live?'[118] This shout of anger is at this point only the expression of a murderous impulse which has not yet been transformed into action, but it is terrible enough for the prescient elder to kneel and bow down before Dmitriy's feet. The numerous spectators do not understand the gesture, but the reader, who is watching through the chronicler's eyes, senses some horrible crime to come.

For the explosive power of these scenes is not so much in the scandalous gesture as in the multitude of pairs of eyes which witness and judge. The psychodrama publicly acted makes the hero transparent to the gaze. The novel, or rather the chronicle, stops, and the theatre begins, with its unity of time, place and action, and its stage directions. The second part of *The Idiot* gives us a striking example, not excessively dramatised, but perfectly characteristic, of theatrical presentation where the heroes exercise neither sighting nor seeing, but in which they are seen, shown, exposed to the universal gaze.

The place is closed, geometrically limited by the sides of the terrace of Lebedev's summer house. It is even elevated like a stage, or like the square in front of a cathedral where the mystery plays were staged,[119] since there are steps leading up to it. Lebedev's apartment, to which the actors sometimes retreat (General Ivolgin, Ganya and Ptitsyn), is used as back stage. Scenery and props are basic: lemon and orange trees in pots on the periphery, chairs which are sometimes arranged in rows and sometimes in a circle, an armchair in which the convalescent Myshkin is sitting, and a small table with a few china cups in centre stage. Time is almost frozen, for it is June and the twilight lingers for ever, but occasional notes of time map out successive entrances, so that time is not abolished. It is, as it were, disqualified in favour of scenic space; power takes refuge in the intensity of the gaze. The movements, in this enclosed, almost motionless space, are limited to the actors' change of position, to moving a few chairs and finally to entrances and numerous false exits. Only Lebedev, the buffoon who totters around being provocative, animates the scene. Sometimes an actor moves and settles near another one, for example, General Ivolgin beside Aglaya. When the curtain rises, Lebedev, his daughter Vera who is carrying her little sister in her arms, and Myshkin are on stage. Then, as in the theatre, the characters enter, appearing from both sides at once: the Yepanchins (Yepanchina and her three daughters, with Prince S., Adelaida's suitor) by the terrace; Ptitsyn, Ganya and General Ivolgin from Lebedev's rooms.[120] As the psychodrama advances to 'new follies', more actors arrive: first General Yepanchin and Yevgeniy Pavlovich Radomsky, the suitor of Aglaya; then Burdovsky, the man who claims to be Pavlishchev's son, with his group, together with Doktorenko (Lebedev's nephew), Ippolit Terentev, and Keller the Boxer. The characters unknown to the reader are described in detail. The stage directions about attitudes are precise: thus General Yepanchin is described for a moment 'on the higher step, with his back to the public'.[121] Individual reactions, pallor, blushes, angry looks, stupefied expressions, as well as group reactions, attentive silence, uproar, stifled laughter, jumping on chairs, are carefully noted. While Prince Myshkin remains the source on which the allusions and attacks are focused, other arrivals are lit up in turn by the spotlight; first Yepanchina, then Aglaya, Burdovsky's group, Ganya and finally Ippolit and Yepanchina again. Sometimes the actors move to the front of the stage to declaim their speeches: Aglaya, firmly planted in the middle of the terrace, recites Pushkin's ballad 'The Poor Knight', a clear allusion to Myshkin, with enthusiastic gravity; Kolya reads aloud the defamatory article accusing the prince of robbing Pavlishchev's son; finally Ganya, playing public prosecutor, sums up Burdovsky's dossier with legal precision and rebuts the false accusations in the article. Time is ignored in favour of effect, of power marked by the accumulation of greater shocks and dramatic effects, more serious allegations, and by the growing embarrassment of Myshkin, who commits more and more mistakes of the heart. The space is the place of the Idiot's painful transparence, as he is attacked by Aglaya's provocative love, the cruel and profoundly unjust accusations of Burdovsky's followers, and the hatred of Ippolit, who is getting his revenge as best he can for the shame of having wept in public. But it is also the place of transparence for the daring Aglaya, who, in her recitation of the 'Poor Knight', transposes the letters AMD (*Ave Mater Dei*) of the poem to AFB (Anastasiya Filippovna Barashkova) and clearly shows her jealousy, and for Yepanchina, who is as open in virtuous indignation as she is in compassion, and for Ippolit, who is full of hatred because he is suffering.

By concentrating the crisis in an enclosed, motionless, theatrical space, the novelist provokes the explosion, which reveals his creatures to the gaze. Psychodramas make psychological analysis theatrical. In fact, movement and gaze no longer belong to the hero, but to a fusion of author and spectator. The chronicler remains backstage: he prepares the crisis and returns when it has taken place, but vanishes when it explodes. In the same way the secondary participants of these psychodramas only retain partial elements of them and do not always understand the significance of a particular gesture. But the reader-spectator, armed with all the previous acquisitions of the chronicler, is dazzled and amazed by the tragedy of the heroes. The space of the psychodrama, by virtue of its collective, public gaze, abolishes the subjectivity of the novel. The tragedy of the hero becomes universal – our own.

Conclusion

After describing the creative environment, after being present at the birth of the novel, after analysing the novel's basic temporal and spatial structures, we are at last in a position to give a reply to our question about the why and how of Dostoyevsky's creation, to attempt a synthesis of his art, or, in other words, to define Dostoyevsky's fascinating and enthralling qualities, and give him his due not only as poet but as artist.

It is in his treatment of time and space that Dostoyevsky reveals his art. Time is the fundamental structure for the tragic experience of the hero, his painful struggle to grasp his freedom when freedom is denied him. Time is an obstacle to the exercise of freedom, since it transforms every free act into a predestined act and thus establishes destiny. But time is also the movement in which freedom, or choice, is accomplished. Instead of recognising this antinomy, as Tolstoy does at the end of *War and Peace* in his long dissertation on necessity and human freedom, Dostoyevsky renounces epic and biographical time. He does violence to nature not by refusing real time but by accentuating its natural contradictions. He subverts it by accelerating and compressing it, saturating it with events; he forces his heroes to experience time more painfully than in everyday life, sometimes allowing them to quench their ontological thirst in the circular time of eternity, in a harmonious and unreal reconciliation with universal being. He saves his hero from the mutilation of time by imprinting on it an ascending spiral movement, a real progression founded on falsely repetitive parallels. It is in the upward curve of this spiral that the hero exercises his power of choice, seizes the moment of the free act and moves towards the higher ring of the helix. The work of Dostoyevsky does not aim to abolish time, but to exaggerate its contradictory power. The writer kneads time, forces it, irritates it to fever point, until it explodes and gives birth, until it yields to man the freedom locked inside it. Destiny is interwoven with freedom. The hero of Dostoyevsky is guilty because he is free and responsible for his destiny, for his own and that of others. Strengthening the terms of this struggle against the cruel power of time, the novelist stresses the power of man, affirming the essential freedom of man faced with the freedom of God. The hot-press chronicle, or the diary, is his favourite form for this unresolved conflict.[1]

This transformation of time, an element both unforeseeable and inevitable, recalls an art which is accomplished over time but which forges its own time: music. Critics from widely differing backgrounds, such as E. M. de Vogüé, Vyacheslav Ivanov, Leonid Grossman, V. L. Komarovich, M. Bakhtin, Paul Claudel and A. A. Gozenpud compare the composition of Dostoyevsky's novels to musical composition. They use the words counterpoint, fugue, symphony, oratorio, polyphony, the mode of Beethoven, the orchestration of Mahler, but their essential point is that, like a musician, the novelist seized time and reconstructed it according to his own laws, which were very close to those of orchestral music. The critics were fascinated by the violence of the rhythms and their imperious variations, the simultaneous development of several melodic lines, the multivocalism, like that of cantata or oratorio, the richness of instrumentation, the masterly progression in large spiral movements towards a grandiose symphonic climax, the play of dissonances and oppositions, but especially the tireless repetition, within the boundaries of one novel or over the work as a whole, of the themes of 'broad nature' freedom, God and atheism, socialism and the city of the future, love and hatred, themes which are ceaselessly debated and explored in their thousand possibilities. To quote Mahler's definition of the symphony, Dostoyevsky used all the technical means at his disposal to create a universe. In his novels everything converges, everything is constructed as a whole, everything echoes. The whole human soul is orchestrated, with all the resources of the universe used in the score. The novelist implacably conjugates all the human data in his possession, such as his experience, newspapers, and literature, without any class distinctions; he interweaves the threads of multiplied intrigues, and, by a thousand paths which are lost and then suddenly found again, leads us towards immense climaxes in which everything is resolved. It is this marvellously constructed complexity which Suarès stresses when he says that in Dostoyevsky 'everything is produced by inner necessity.'[2] The novels of the Russian writer are orchestral works which remodel time in order to stress its power. If a reader sometimes feels irritated, it is because he prefers melodic poverty and sees rich variations simply as repetitions. The power of Dostoyevsky's art constrains and crushes. It is full of stress because it contains a thousand convictions gathered together and driven in. The writer feels ideas and creatures with an extraordinary intensity of images. His frenzied mythologisation of the cultural heritage, his fondness for psychodramas saturated with shocks and final gestures, his hammered redundant sentences, unwinding like labyrinths sown with thresholds full of returns and detours, his disdain for ornament have no other origin than his intense ability to feel more deeply and more strongly than most men and his passionate will to make his readers sympathise with the figures he has created. Dostoyevsky is a powerful writer because he is violent and ardent. It takes a strong soul to endure his works.

If time is the structure of the tragic experience of the hero, space is the structure of its significance, the development of awareness. Dostoyevsky inscribes in the scenery the message of the gods enraged by human freedom, and inserts the dialogue which the hero is conducting with himself and society into the landscape which the hero contemplates. He organises space in a vast geometry, crossed by the intentions of the hero or divided between preliminary spaces where man expresses his burning thirst for the Other and the stages of the psychodrama where the hero comes forward and reveals himself to the public. Above all, in the process of creation he spreads out his human creatures over literary space to express their inner breadth, their vastness, the crucible of their freedom. At the beginning of the novel, an entire world and the great ideas which brought it to life rise in a chaotic wholeness. Dostoyevsky struggles with all his might to make man and world coincide, to focus all humanity and all the multiplicity of human experiences within a single hero, to collect the sum of the universe within one existence, to forge a man-world, as Chirkov expresses it.[3] The expansive beings which are thus created, monsters of universality, form doubles along vertical or horizontal axes, where the break, a sign of their essential dichotomy, is always signified. Around them gravitate a populace of secondary characters committed to one side or another, animated by centripetal or centrifugal forces. Living bridges are constructed between the characters: these are messengers like Fyodor Fyodorovich in the notebooks of *A Raw Youth*, or Alyosha in *The Brothers Karamazov*. Human nature is thus developed geometrically either in real space or in experimental literary space. As opposed to time, which compresses, contracts, squeezes, and paralyses, space develops, explains and clarifies.

This spreading out of the broad nature and the use of signs in space is obviously reminiscent of architecture. Dostoyevsky designs his novels like an architect. He constructs the population of the novels in molecular groups or planetary systems, with their kernels and their satellites. The space of the novel, in which topography is dominant, in which towns appear in the play of movement and look, in which the expressionist scenery multiplies the masses of shade, the amputated corners and the blocks of light, shows the vision of an architect. But the architectural construction is most clearly visible in the composition of the novel, with those almost parallel lines which echo each other and progress towards a culmination. Using the convergence of repeated curves directed towards a keystone or the point of a spiral, and the golden number signified by the gestures, the parallel scenes and dreams, Dostoyevsky builds his novels like cathedrals.

Music composes time, architecture composes space: the composition of Dostoyevsky's novels, the essential principle of his art, goes beyond space and time to relate them to both music and architecture. The Russian novelist is first a bold and despotic composer, subordinating everything to the construction of the whole, as if he wanted to rediscover through form the totality he saw at the beginning of his novels. He is excessively authoritarian. This is not the least of paradoxes in this writer who proves and preserves human freedom so zealously, endowing his heroes with independent sovereign minds. To parody Shigalyov of *The Devils*, it could be said that Dostoyevsky set out from unlimited freedom to end up with unlimited despotism if it were not a matter of two different intentions. The first is philosophical and refers to the hero, the second is aesthetic and relates to the composition of the novel. There is nothing abstract or dry about this artistic despotism.

This powerfully orchestrated music is not obsessed with sound, this daringly constructed architecture is not obsessed with stone. The world of Dostoyevsky's novels is obsessed with men and life. Its material is man, developed, decomposed and recomposed, multiplied, twinned, anatomised, man crucified, torn to pieces by the cruel laws of modern ordeals. The elements of construction or composition are never taken from decorative aesthetics but from the most living and concrete reality, the most everyday fantastic reality: illness, money, press cuttings, contemporary debate, the writer's own experience. The novels of Dostoyevsky are massive architectural and orchestral works, but, powerful though they are in their concentrated beams of convergences, classical though they appear in their lack of ornament, they endlessly respond and vibrate like the flesh and soul of a living creature.

Notes

GENERAL INTRODUCTION

1 *Bakhtin*, p. 5

INTRODUCTION TO PART I

1 Charles Mauron, 'Des Métaphores obsédantes au Mythe personnel', *Introduction à la psychocritique*, Paris, 1962.
2 Anna Grigoryevna made the first catalogue in L. P. Grossman's *Seminariy po Dostoyevskomu*, Moscow–Petrograd, 1922, pp. 54–70.

I FORMS OF CREATIVITY IN EMBRYO

1 *Dostoïevski, Crime et Châtiment*, ed. P. Pascal, Paris, 1958, p. xvi.
2 *A* 22, pp. 27–8. Perhaps the influence of Shakespeare's *Merchant of Venice* is apparent here, or more probably that of George Sand, whom Dostoyevsky mentions later: 'I particularly loved, in her early works, a certain number of figures of young girls, those, for example, of what were then called her Venetian stories (to which *L'Uscoque* and *Aldini* belong)', *A* 23, p. 35. *La Dernière Aldini* had already been published but *L'Uscoque* was not published until 1838 in *La Revue des Deux Mondes*.
3 *Biography*, p. 215.
4 *A* 3, p. 169.
5 *Dostoïevski*, Cahiers de l'Herne 24, Paris, 1973, p. 148.
6 Cf. K. K. Istomin, 'Iz zhizni i tvorchestva Dostoyevskogo v molodosti', in *Tvorcheskiy put' Dostoyevskogo, sbornik statey*, ed. N. L. Brodsky, Leningrad, 1924, pp. 3–49.
7 *Letters* 1, p. 50; *A* 281, p. 54.
8 *LH* 77, p. 64.
9 *Letters* 2, p. 550; *A* 281, p. 63.
10 *Letters* 1, p. 76; *A* 281, p. 108.
11 *LH* 86, p. 328.
12 *LH* 86, p. 329.
13 Open letter of Andrey Dostoyevsky to A. S. Suvorin, 5 February 1881, in *Novoye Vremya*, 8 February 1881, n. 1778 (*A* 281, p. 423, n. 7).
14 *Letters* 1, p. 69; *A* 281, p. 86.
15 The comparison with the Jew Yankel in Gogol's *Taras Bulba* is not convincing: Yankel is practically a generic name. This play, in spite of the fertile imagination of a Soviet novelist (D. D. Bregova, *Doroga Iskaniy. Molodost' Dostoyevskogo*, Moscow, 1962, pp. 259–61) remains a mystery. On this point, cf. David I.

Goldstein, *Dostoyevsky and the Jews*, University of Texas Press, Slavic Studies no. 3, Austin–London, 1981, pp. 3–9.

16 *Letters* 1, p.76, *A* 281, p. 108.

17 He did not know German so well, though he corrected the translation of Schiller's *Don Carlos* made by his brother Mikhail, who was more competent in German.

18 *Letters* 1, pp. 66–71; *A* 281, pp. 83–8, *Letters* 2, p. 555, *A* 281, p. 91.

19 The only edition of the *Complete Works* in which it is to be found is that of L. P. Grossman: *Polnoye sobraniye sochineniy F. M. Dostoyevskogo*, Petersburg, 1911–18, 23, 4.

20 Dominique Arban, *Les Années d'apprentissage de Fiodor Dostoyevski*, Paris, 1968, pp. 228–40. The author, basing her work on the omissions and transpositions of the translator, thinks that Dostoyevsky reveals an obsession with guilt and that Father Grandet is identified with the writer's father and Mme Grandet with his mother. The freedom of the translation makes this hypothesis very weak.

21 L. P. Grossman, *Poetika Dostoyevskogo*, Moscow, 1925, pp. 84–6.

22 *A* 8, p. 172.

23 *Letters* 1, p. 73, *A* 281, p. 100.

24 *Vremya*, January 1861, pp. 1–22; *A* 19, pp. 67–85.

25 *A* 19, p. 69. This impression was so strong that Dostoyevsky used it first in a story of 1848: 'A Weak Heart'. But it was narrowed by the context: through this vision, with which the story ended, Arkadiy Ivanovich suddenly realised why his friend Vasya had gone mad.

26 *A* 1, pp. 279–80.

27 *Biography*, p. 195.

28 *Letters* 1, p. 47; *A* 281, p. 51.

29 *Letters* 1, p. 76; *A* 281, p. 108.

30 Ibid.

31 *Letters* 1, pp. 72–3; *A* 281, pp. 89, 100.

32 *LH* 86, pp. 364–5.

2 THE HERITAGE

1 Yury N. Tynyanov, *Dostoyevsky i Gogol'. K teorii parodii*, Petrograd, 1921.

2 *M* 1, p. 209.

3 Not only the publication of A. G. Dostoyevskaya, *Dnevnik 1867g.*, Moscow, 1923, but also 'Zhenevskiy dnevnik A. G. Dostoyevskoy', recently deciphered by the stenographer Ts. M. Poshemanskaya in *LH* 86, pp. 167–282. It gives an account of the second half of 1867 in Geneva and Anna Grigoryevna frequently refers to 1866.

4 L. P. Grossman, *Seminariy po Dostoyevskomu*, Moscow–Petrograd, 1922, pp. 7–53.

5 In the journal *Sankt-Peterburgskiye Vedomosti*, 1847 (93, 104, 121, 133). Cf. *T* 13, pp. 8–32; *A* 18, pp. 11–34.

6 Cf. our study 'Du Palais de cristal à l'âge d'or ou les avatars de l'utopie', pp. 178–9, in *Dostoïevski*, Cahiers de l'Herne, 24, Paris, 1973.

7 *T* 13, p. 23; *A* 18, pp. 11–34.

8 *A* 8, p. 358.

9 *Letters* 2, p. 139; *A* 28II, p. 319. In *Winter Notes on Summer Impressions* (*A* 5, p. 48) Dostoyevsky remembered drawing Cologne Cathedral 'with awe', when he was studying architecture at the Engineering School, between 1838 and 1843. When he actually saw it, he was disillusioned: 'It was only lace, lace and nothing but lace, an ornament like a paperweight on a desk.' When he saw it for the second time, he wanted to beg its forgiveness because at first he 'had not perceived its beauty'.

10 In an article 'Mr. D[obrolyubov] and Art', published in *Time*, *A* 18, p. 78.

11 *M Anna*, p. 126. Dostoyevsky placed this photograph in Versilov's apartment (*A* 13, p. 82).

12 In Dresden, where he admired Raphael's Sistine *Madonna*, the painting he loved most. His commentary in *Winter Notes on Summer Impressions* (1863) on the attitude of Russian tourists is rather unexpected:

> They walk around with guidebooks and in every town there is a greedy rush to look at rarities ... They gaze at a piece of beef by Rubens and believe that it is the three graces, because the guide tells them so; they rush off to see the Sistine Madonna and stand before her vacantly waiting for something to happen, as if something might crawl out from under the floor and disperse their pointless melancholy and weariness. (*A* 5, p. 63)

13 *M Anna*: for Dresden, p. 102; for Basle, p. 112; for Florence, p. 126; for Bologna, p. 128.

14 Mentioned by Anna Grigoryevna in her diary for 1867, but not in her *Memoirs*. Anna Grigoryevna Dostoyevskaya, *Dnevnik 1867g.*, Moscow, 1923, p. 366.

15 This is the *Madonna with the family of the burgomeister Jacob Meyer* (1525–6), of which the original painting is in the Darmstadt Museum. In 1867, the painting in Dresden was not known to be a copy. In *The Idiot*, Myshkin tells Aleksandra Ivanovna that her face is like that of Holbein's *Madonna* at Dresden (*A* 8, p. 65).

16 *A* 6, p. 369.

17 Mean spirits like Yuliya Mikhaylovna, the governor's wife, and the writer Karmazinov cannot see the beauty of the Sistine *Madonna* (*A* 10, p. 235).

18 *A* 13, p. 82.

19 Presented to him by Countess S. A. Tolstaya (*M Anna*, pp. 257–8).

20 *A* 8, p. 182.

21 *A* 8, p. 339.

22 For a detailed analysis of the symbol, cf. our study 'Du Palais de cristal à l'âge d'or ou les avatars de l'utopie', in *Dostoïevski*, Cahiers de l'Herne 24, pp. 188–94. S. V. Kovalevskaya tells us of a scene in a novel which Dostoyevsky planned in his youth, which is strangely like that of Stavrogin's vision of the golden age in *The Devils*. The hero remembers not *Acis and Galatea*, but 'a ray of light falling on the bare shoulders of St Cecilia, in the Munich Gallery', and at the same time he remembers a book 'about universal beauty and harmony'; then he remembers a child of ten whom he had raped. If Kovalevskaya is correct, it is clear that the actual picture made little difference and only the symbol of the slanting rays of the setting sun was really important (*M* 1, p. 348). The *St Cecilia* which Dostoyevsky admired, by Raphael, is in Bologna, not Munich.

23 *A* 8, pp. 379–80.

24 The painting by Claude Gellée called Le Lorrain: *Seascape with Acis and Galatea* (1657), which Dostoyevsky called 'the Golden Age', is significantly, but wrongly,

mentioned by Anna Grigoryevna by the title *Seascape (Morning and Evening)*. Perhaps she was confusing it with Claude's paintings *Morning* and *Evening*, which are in the Hermitage.

25 Cf. Valentine Marcadé, *Le Renouveau de l'art pictural russe*, Lausanne, 1971, p. 234.

26 *A* 13, p. 319.

27 In *The Idiot*, Myshkin imagines a picture: the head of a man condemned to death a few seconds before he is guillotined. In fact, this still refers to Holbein's *Dead Christ*.

28 *A* 2, p. 48.

29 Holbein used the corpse of a drowned man fished up from the Rhine as his model. The work is sometimes called *The Drowned Man from the Rhine Bridge*. Karamzin, whose works Dostoyevsky knew intimately, says in *Letters of a Russian Traveller* that it was a drowned Jew. N. M. Karamzin, *Izbrannyye sochineniya*, Moscow, 1964, 1, p. 208.

30 *A* 3, p. 212.

31 For the pictures admired by Dostoyevsky and various illustrations of the novels, see the iconography collected in *F. M. Dostoyevsky v portretakh, illyustratsiyakh, dokumentakh*, ed. V. S. Nechayeva, Moscow, 1972.

32 This is the opinion of L. P. Grossman: 'Dostoyevsky-khudozhnik', in *Tvorchestvo F. M. Dostoyevskogo*, Moscow, 1959, p. 411.

33 *A* 5, p. 152.

34 A. L. Rubanovich, 'Peyzazh v romane F. M. Dostoyevskogo *Prestupleniye i nakazaniye*', in *Trudy Irkutskogo gosudarstvennogo universiteta im. A. A. Zhdanova*, 28, 2, 1959, pp. 95–105.

35 Henri Focillon, *Les Maîtres de l'estampe*, Images et Idées, Paris, 1969, p. 77.

36 *LH* 86, p. 329. Riesenkampf tells a picturesque story:

In spite of the exceptional price of tickets (25, then 20 roubles), Fyodor Mikhaylovich and I went to nearly every concert. F.M. often made fun of his friends who wore gloves, hat, hair and cane in the style of Liszt. After one of these concerts, in the crowd a tassel from his sword knot was torn off; and from then until he retired, he kept this sword knot without tassel, which was noticed by many people. If they questioned him about it, he would reply that this swordknot deprived of its tassel was dear to him as a souvenir of Liszt's concerts.

37 *M* 1, p. 357.

38 *M* 2, p. 47. In a letter of 1879 to his wife, Dostoyevsky gives a cutting judgement: 'Although the music is good here [in Ems], Beethoven and Mozart are rarely played, but it is Wagner all the time (a wretched German who is impossibly boring in spite of his fame) and all sorts of rubbish' (*Letters* 4, p. 90).

39 *M* 1, p. 378. The libretto of *Rogneda* is the only musical work found in the catalogue of Dostoyevsky's last library.

40 A. A. Gozenpud, *Dostoyevsky i muzyka*, Leningrad, 1971 (later referred to as Gozenpud).

41 David I. Goldstein, *Dostoyevsky and the Jews*, Austin–London, 1981, pp. 10–13.

42 Gozenpud, p. 53.

43 Gozenpud, pp. 57–63.

44 *M* 1, pp. 377–8.

45 Gozenpud, who is of the opposite opinion, dismisses this awkward witness rather too quickly in a short note (p. 89).

46 *Letters* 3, p. 231.

47 *A* 18, p. 22.

48 Ibid. pp. 22–3.

49 *A* 4, pp. 110–11.

50 Ibid. p. 123.

51 *A* 6, p. 121.

52 *A* 13, p. 222.

53 It was at the literary and musical evening organised at the house of S. F. Durov and A. I. Palm, on 21 April 1849, that Dostoyevsky heard Glinka's romance on the words of the poet Mickiewicz (trans. S. Golitsyn): M. I. Glinka, *Zapiski*, Leningrad, 1954, pp. 207–8. Anna Grigoryevna says that her husband was very moved by this romance played by the composer: L. P. Grossman, *Seminariy po Dostoyevskomu*, Moscow–Petrograd, 1922, p. 61.

54 *M* 1, pp. 377–9.

55 Dostoyevsky is using the fashion for musical parody, in which Mussorgsky and Charles Levi, a musician mentioned by V. Sollogub in his memoirs, excelled. Once Mussorgsky played *Mein lieber Augustin* with the left hand and a waltz from *Faust* with the right (Gozenpud, p. 118). Levi, in 1863, to the disgust of the Polish patriots present, is supposed to have joined the noble strains of the hymn 'To the Fatherland' with the cheerful mocking sounds of a carefree Russian song: M. S. Al'tman, 'Iz arsenala imyon i prototipov literaturnykh geroyev Dostoyevskogo', in V. G. Bazanov and G. M. Fridlender (eds.), *Dostoyevsky i yego vremya*, Leningrad, 1971, pp. 212–13.

56 *A* 2, p. 195.

57 *A* 5, p. 123.

58 S. V. Kovalevskaya says in her memoirs: 'He told us one day that of all musical works he placed Beethoven's 'Pathétique' Sonata highest of all and that this sonata always plunged him into a world of forgotten sensations' (*M* 1, p. 358).

59 Paul Claudel, *Mémoires improvisés*, Idées, Paris, 1969, p. 48.

60 Ibid. p. 48.

61 *A* 13, pp. 352–3.

62 *A* 17, p. 122.

63 V. F. Odoyevsky, *Muzykal'no-literaturnoye naslediye*, Moscow, 1956, pp. 135–6.

64 Gustav Mahler in his *Symphony of a Thousand*, inspired by the second part of Goethe's *Faust*, is nearest the finale imagined by Trishatov.

65 Gozenpud, p. 128.

3 THE HERITAGE: LITERATURE

1 On 17 December 1876, referring to *Netochka Nezvanova*, which he was writing enthusiastically, he confided to his brother Mikhail: 'I keep thinking that I have started a courtcase with our literature, our journals and our critics' (*Letters* 1, p. 104; *A* 281, p. 135).

2 Frederic Schlosser (1776–1861), a German historian, author of a *Universal History* in 18 volumes (1854–6).

3 Sergey Mikhaylovich Solovyov (1820–79), author of *History of Russia* in 29 volumes (unfinished). It ends at the year 1774.

4 Nikolay Mikhaylovich Karamzin (1765–1826) a writer famous, among other works, for his *History of the Russian State*, in 12 volumes, of which the first 8 were published in 1818.

5 Nikolay Ivanovich Kostomarov (1817–85), professor of Russian history at the University of St Petersburg from 1859 to 1861, expelled by the government because of his ideas.

6 William Prescott (1796–1859), American historian, author of *History of the Conquest of Mexico* (1843) and *History of the Conquest of Peru* (1847).

7 *Letters* 4, p. 196.

8 Ibid. p. 222.

9 A. M. Dostoyevsky, *Vospominaniya*, Leningrad, 1930, pp. 44–5. The first of these stories is probably eastern in origin, the second is a descendant of the French *chanson de geste* 'Bueves D'Hanstone' (thirteenth century), which came to Russia through Italian and Serbian versions. Dostoyevsky remembered it in *The Brothers Karamazov*, when he put the words 'your faithful Lichard' in Smerdyakov's mouth (Lichard is a deformation of Richard, the faithful servant of Queen Blonde).

10 A. M. Dostoyevsky *Vospominaniya*, Leningrad, 1930, pp. 68–70.

11 *Letters* 1, p. 302, *A* 28II, p. 19.

12 *Epokha*, May 1864, p. 150.

13 *A* 15, p. 158.

14 *A* 19, p. 70. In 'White Nights', Clara Mowbray is mentioned, as well as Diana Vernon from *Rob Roy*; *Ivanhoe*, *The Pirate*, *The Heart of Midlothian* are also mentioned. In the catalogue of Dostoyevsky's library, *The Monastery*, *Waverley, or Sixty Years ago*, and *Ivanhoe* are listed in French versions; *The Fair Maid of Perth, or St Valentine's Day* in Russian.

15 I. S. Turgenev, *Sobraniye Sochineniy*, Moscow, 1956, 9, p. 122.

16 In *Gambara*, Balzac comments:

> With Beethoven, the effects are as it were distributed in advance. Like the different regiments which contribute to victory by their disciplined move-ments, the orchestral parts of the symphonies of Beethoven follow orders given in the general interest and are subordinate to admirably conceived plans. In this respect, they compare with a genius in another sphere. In the magnificent historical compositions of Walter Scott, the character who is most outside the action comes, at a given moment, by means of threads woven into the canvas of the plot, to attach himself to the conclusion.
>
> (Balzac, 'La Comédie Humaine', in *L'Intégrale*, 6, Paris, 1966, p. 595)

17 *Letters* 1, p. 302; *A* 28II, p. 19.

18 He lent *Lake Ontario* to his friend Grigorovich (*M* 1, p. 128). The complete works of Fenimore Cooper, in French, appear in the catalogue of Dostoyevsky's library.

19 *Letters* 1, p. 58; *A* 28I, p. 69.

20 *Letters* 1, pp. 58–9; *A* 28I, p. 70.

21 Heroes of Schiller's tragedies: *Die Räuber*, *Die Verschwörung des Fiesko zu Genoa*, *Wilhelm Tell*, and *Don Carlos*.

22 *Letters* 1, p. 59; *A* 28I, p. 71.

23 *LH* 86, p. 163, note of 24 August/5 September 1867. In this way the couple read Balzac's *La Cousine Bette* and *Le Cousin Pons* (p. 167); Dickens' *Little Dorrit* (p. 186); George Sand's *L'Uscoque* (p. 270), *L'Homme des neiges* (p. 214) and

Les Dames vertes (p. 246); A. Dumas' *Corricolo*; and Scott's *Heart of Midlothian*.

24 Lyubov Fyodorovna, Dostoyevsky's daughter, says that one day her father wanted to read Schiller's *Die Räuber* to her and her little brother, Fyodor; the children fell asleep and Dostoyevsky laughed and realised he had made a mistake. In the same passage, she says that Dostoyevsky, who was so forgetful that he forgot his wife's maiden name and the names of his own characters, 'remembered all the English names of the heroes of Dickens and Scott . . . and spoke of them as if they were close friends' (L. F. Dostoyevskaya, *Dostoyevsky v izobrazhenii yego docheri L. Dostoyevskoy*, ed. A. G. Gornfel'd, Moscow–Leningrad, 1922, pp. 88–91).

25 *Lebensansichten des Kater Murr nebst fragmentarisher Biographie des Kapellmeisters Johannes Kreisler in zufälligen Makulaturblättern* is the complete title. The musician Kreisler dies mad like Yefimov in *Netochka Nezvanova*.

26 *Letters* 1, p. 47, *A* 28I, p. 51.

27 *Letters* 1, p. 51; *A* 28I, p. 54.

28 *A* 26, pp. 113–14.

29 *Letters* 1, p. 51; *A* 28I, p. 55.

30 *Letters* 1, p. 58; *A* 28I, p. 69.

31 *A* 18, pp. 95–6.

32 In 1840, Dostoyevsky refused to compare Pushkin with Schiller: 'I repudiate this sort of association. I may have accidentally have put Pushkin and Schiller together in general discussion, but I think there is a comma between these two names. They are not at all like each other' (*Letters* 1, p. 57; *A* 28I, p. 69).

33 The first performance took place on 31 January 1829. Although the text was censored, Schiller's tragedy had a resounding success, which was echoed by Belinsky, Lermontov and Herzen.

34 The index of the names of authors and works mentioned in the stories and novels, as well as the notebooks (variants, letters, articles and *Diary of a Writer* excluded) shows the clear predominance of the following writers: Pushkin appears about 120 times, Gogol more than 75 times, Shakespeare more than 70, Schiller about 50. Cf. *A* 17, pp. 463–73.

35 Fyodor thought that his brother's translation of *Die Räuber* was 'incomparable' in the songs, 'excellent' in the prose, but elsewhere too colloquial. He corrected the careless style. Other translations were envisaged: *Die Verschwörung des Fiesko* and *Maria Stuart* (*Letters* 2, p. 553; *A* 28I, p. 90).

36 L. P. Grossman, *Seminariy po Dostoyevskomu*, Moscow–Petrograd, 1922, p. 31.

37 His biography may be found in M. P. Alekseyev, *Ranniy drug F. M. Dostoyevskogo*, Odessa, 1921, pp. 5–8.

38 *Letters* 1, p. 56; *A* 28I, p. 68.

39 Hero of *Maria Stuart*.

40 *Letters* 1, p. 57; *A* 28I, p. 69. A. S. Dolinin thinks that this may also refer to Ivan Ignatyevich Berezhetsky, one of the few students at the Central Engineering School with whom Dostoyevsky had long literary conversations, according to A. I. Savelyev (*M* 1, p. 99).

41 *A* 18, p. 32.

42 *A* 19, p. 71.

43 Ibid.

44 *A* 6, p. 362.
45 *A* 6, p. 371.
46 *LH* 77, p. 59.
47 *LH* 77, p. 87.
48 *A* 23, p. 31.
49 One of the verses from 'An die Freude', celebrated by Dmitriy Karamazov.
50 *LH* 83, p. 628. Attacked by 'Bulgarin and Co.' (Senkovsky, etc.), in a vulgar
   way that Dostoyevsky condemned, George Sand was defended vigorously by
   Belinsky who placed her higher than Balzac, devoted enthusiastic pages to her in
   Annals of the Fatherland from 1841 to 1847, regularly reviewed her new novels,
   and wrote even more laudatory letters to his friends Botkin and Bakunin about
   the Egeria of French socialism. *Paulina Sachs* (1847), perhaps the most successful Russian novel of the time, which deals with the woman question and the
   freedom of the heart, was directly inspired by George Sand's *Jacques*. Its author,
   A. V. Druzhinin, makes the generous husband of Paulina say: 'Ardent youths
   will see a second Jacques in me some day.'
51 *A* 23, p. 30.
52 *A* 23, p. 35.
53 Absent from the catalogue of Dostoyevsky's last library.
54 *LH* 83, p. 420; from the notebooks of 1875–6: 'Excellent in our century:
   Pickwick, Notre-Dame, Misérables. The first novellas of George Sand, Lord
   Byron ... Lermontov, Turgenev, *War and Peace*. Heine, Pushkin.'
55 *LH* 83, pp. 361–2.
   Books to read in Ems library if there is time:
   G. Sand, *Césarine Dietrich. Journal d'un voyageur pendant la guerre*.
   Erckmann-Chatrian, *Histoire d'un Homme du peuple*.
   Belot, *L'article 47*.
   G. Sand, *La Confession d'une jeune fille*.
   Erckmann-Chatrian, *Waterloo*.
   A. Dumas, *Affaire Clemenceau*.
   Proudhon, *La Révolution sociale démontrée par le Coup d'Etat du 2
   Décembre*.
   N.B. Musset Alfred, *La Confession d'un enfant du siècle*.
   Flaubert, *Madame Bovary*.
   Octave Feuillet, *Le Roman d'un jeune homme pauvre*.
56 *Letters* 1, p. 83, *A* 281, p. 114. 8 October 1845 to Mikhail: 'Read *Teverino*
   (George Sand in *Annals of the Fatherland* for October). Nothing like it has
   been written before in our century.'
57 *Letters* 1, p. 108; *A* 281, p. 139. January–February 1847, to Mikhail: 'Have you
   read *Lucrèce Floriani*? Look at *Carol*'.
58 Belinsky reviewed *Bernard Mauprat* in *Annals of the Fatherland*, 6, 1841.
   Dostoyevsky probably read *Spiridion*, which appeared in the *Revue des Deux
   Mondes* for 1838 (where *L'Uscoque* had been published in the same year).
59 Cf. the convincing study of Ivan Pouzyna, 'George Sand et Dostoïevski, la
   parenté littéraire des *Frères Karamazov* et du *Spiridion*', in *Etudes*, 1, 1939,
   pp. 345–60.
60 Cf. our study of the Golden Age in 'Dostoïevski', Cahiers de l'Herne, 24, Paris,
   1973, p. 195.
61 *A* 23, p. 30.

62 *A* 21, p. 11.
63 *LH* 83, p. 542.
64 Ibid.
65 *A* 23, p. 37.
66 Ibid.
67 Ibid.
68 A. A. Gizetti, '"Gordyye yazychnitsy" (k kharakteristike zhenskikh obrazov Dostoyevskogo)', in N. L. Brodsky (ed.), *Tvorcheskiy put' Dostoyevskogo*, Leningrad, 1924, pp. 186–97.
69 Term borrowed from Dostoyevsky: *privit'*.
70 *A* 23, p. 37.
71 Yelena Andreyevna Shtackenschneyder tells the following story – as soon as she arrived at Dostoyevsky's house, he began:
> Yesterday I had an epileptic fit, I have a headache, and that blockhead Averkiyev has just infuriated me. He was abusing Dickens; he said Dickens wrote nothing but trinkets, stories for children. However, how can he possibly understand Dickens! He is not even capable of imagining the beauty of that writer, and he takes to judging him! I was longing to tell him he was an imbecile.   (*M* 2, p. 319)
72 *Letters* 2, p. 71; *A* 28II, p. 251.
73 Although his admiration for Hugo was not unbounded, Dostoyevsky never lost his enthusiasm for Jean Valjean. In 1877 he wrote to S. E. Lurye:
> As for Victor Hugo I have probably said this before, but I see that you are still very young if you are comparing him with Goethe and Shakespeare. I love *Les Misérables* ... The late F. I. Tyutchev, our great poet, and many others then placed my *Crime and Punishment* incomparably higher than *Les Misérables*. But I took them to task and tried to prove to them that *Les Misérables* was superior to my poem, and I did this sincerely, with all my heart ... My love for *Les Misérables* does not prevent me from seeing serious faults in it. The figure of Valjean is admirable.

A merciless criticism of the lovers and republicans in the novel follows (*Letters* 3, p. 284; *A* 29II, p. 178). See also *LH* 83, p. 615.
74 *Letters* 2, p. 71; *A* 28II, p. 251.
75 Dostoyevsky knew Dickens very well, especially this novel. Anna Grigoryevna tells us that in difficult but carefree times 'Fyodor Mikhaylovich would call himself Mister Micawber and called her Mistress Micawber' (*M Anna*, p. 127). *David Copperfield* is mentioned in the notebooks of *A Raw Youth*, where Arkadiy remarks: 'If the Touchard school has to be described, then after Touchard, immediately, a curse on the writers who have described childhood. (Copperfield)' (*LH* 77, p. 256). For a complete study of 'Themes from Dickens in Dostoyevsky's work in the forties and fifties', cf. I. M. Katarsky, *Dikkens v Rossii*, Moscow, 1966, pp. 357–401.
76 *A* 22, p. 28.
77 See Nathalie Babel Brown, *Hugo and Dostoevsky*, Ann Arbor, 1978, pp. 69–142 for a study of the dreams of Raskolnikov and their literary sources.
78 All these phrases are taken from the editorial introduction which he wrote for a translation of *Notre-Dame de Paris*, published in the September issue of *Time*, 1862 (*A* 20, pp. 28–9).
79 *A* 13, p. 353.

80 Ibid.
81 *A* 21, p. 75.
82 While in prison Dostoyevsky, according to P. K. Martyanov, had several opportunities to read books, due to the marine guards, officers who had been demoted for punishment and put in charge of the Omsk fortress. He refused all of them except *David Copperfield* and *Pickwick Papers*, translated by I. I. Vvedensky, of whom he had probably been told before 1849 by A. P. Milyukov a friend of them both (*M* 1, p. 181, and p. 240).
83 This is an additional reason for Dostoyevsky's comparison of Mr Pickwick with Christ.
84 *Biography*, p. 244.
85 *M Anna*, p. 185.
86 He mentions this himself: *A* 21, p. 68.
87 *A* 22, p. 92.
88 *A* 26, p. 25.
89 *A* 26, pp. 25–6.
90 Notes for 1876: *LH* 83, p. 442.
91 *LH* 83, p. 448.
92 *LH* 83, p. 442.
93 *LH* 83, p. 613.
94 *A* 26, p. 131.
95 *A* 11, p. 237.
96 E. M. de Vogüé, *The Russian Novel*, London, 1913, p. 248.
97 Paul Claudel, *Mémoires improvisés*, pp. 48–9.
98 *LH* 83, p. 610.
99 *LH* 83, p. 542: 'George Sand. My youth. The *Faust* of Guber. *L'Uscoque*, College . . .' The first Russian translation of *Faust*, which appeared in 1838, was by the poet E. I. Guber (1814–47). If Bem had known of this note, from the notebooks of 1876, he would not have underrated Goethe's influence on the young Dostoyevsky (A. L. Bem, *Faust v tvorchestve Dostoyevskogo'*, in *Zapiski nauchno-issledovatel'skogo ob'edineniya*, 5, 29, publication of the Free Russian University in Prague, 1937, pp. 109–41).
100 L. P. Grossman, *Poetika Dostoyevskogo*, Moscow, 1925, p. 89.
101 A. Tseytlin, *Povesti o bednom chinovnike Dostoyevskogo. (K istorii odnogo syuzheta)*, Moscow, 1923.
102 L. P. Grossman, *Poetika Dostoyevskogo*, Moscow, 1925, p. 94. The comparison is confirmed by Dostoyevsky, who, in one of the variants of his 'Pushkin speech', recalls the dialogue between Rastignac and Bianchon in *Le Père Goriot* (the million against the distant death of an old Chinese mandarin), which is fairly accurately reflected in the conversation overheard by Raskolnikov before the crime, between an officer and his friend (A. S. Dolinin (ed.), *F. M. Dostoyevsky, Stat'i i materialy*, 2, Leningrad, 1925, pp. 509–36).
103 A. L. Bem, 'U istokov tvorchestva Dostoyevskogo', in A. L. Benn (ed.), *O Dostoyevskom*, 2, Prague, 1933, pp. 37–81.
104 Ibid. pp. 82–126.
105 The three works of Shakespeare which most inspired Dostoyevsky are *Hamlet*, *Othello*, and *Henry IV*. For Shakespeare and Dostoyevsky in general, cf. *Shekspir i russkaya literatura*, ed. M. P. Alekseyev, Moscow–Leningrad, 1965, pp. 590–7.

106 Vyacheslav Ivanov, *Borozdy i mezhi*, Moscow, 1916, pp. 61–72.
107 *A* 19, p. 132.
108 *A* 4, p. 62. The notebooks of *Crime and Punishment* associate Svidrigaylov with Aristov.
109 *A* 19, p. 135.
110 Ibid. p. 136.
111 *A* 7, p. 158.
112 In 1844, Dostoyevsky, rebelling against his guardian Karepin, wrote to his brother Mikhail: 'In his last letter Karepin bluntly told me not to get too keen on Shakespeare. He says that Shakespeare and a soap bubble are about the same thing. I hope you can understand how funny it is, blaming it on Shakespeare!' (*Letters* 1, pp. 73–4; *A* 281, pp. 100–1.)
113 The Menippean satire which Bakhtin finds in Dostoyevsky is only one of the many genres used by the novelist: tragedy, comedy, serial, epic, hagiography, burlesque, etc.
114 'NB. Gogol by the power and depth of his laughter is *first in the world* (not excepting Molière) (direct instinctive laughter, and we Russians ought to note this)' (*LH* 83, p. 608).
115 In his notebooks 1876–7, Dostoyevsky twice compares Gogol with Cuvier (*LH* 83, pp. 606–7).
116 Goethe wrote of the translation of *Le Neveu de Rameau* (which Dostoyevsky read 'with pleasure and profit' in 1868):
     Certainly one finds among the Greeks and often among the Romans also a consummate art in separating and differentiating the different poetic genres; but we cannot be referred to these models exclusively, we who live in the North, for we can boast of other ancestors ... If by the romantic tendency of centuries without culture, a contact with the grandiose and absurd had not been produced, how should we have a Hamlet, a King Lear, an Adoration of the Cross, a Prince Constant! Since we shall never attain the perfection of antiquity, it is our duty as moderns to maintain ourselves courageously on the heights of these barbarian advantages.
     (Goethe, *Sämtliche Werke*, 40 vols., Stuttgart and Berlin, 1902, 34, p. 166)
117 The translator of Eugène Sue and *Le Diable boiteux*, Vasily Andreyevich Gartong, was one of his relatives. Dostoyevsky had intended to translate *Mathilde* with him (*Letters* 1, p. 69; *A* 281, p. 83).
118 *Letters* 1, p. 191; *A* 281, p. 236; *Letters* 3, p. 82; *A* 291, p. 300; and in the novella *The Gentle One*, where he calls *Gil Blas* a 'masterpiece' (*A* 24, p. 31).
119 According to his brother Andrey (*M* 1, p. 80).
120 Respectively of *Viy*, *How Ivan Ivanovich quarrelled with Ivan Nikiforovich*, and *Dead Souls*.
121 Again according to Andrey (*M* 1, p. 80).
122 *Letters* 1, p. 78; *A* 281, p. 110.
123 'Istoriya russkogo romana', Moscow–Leningrad, 1962, 1, p. 275.
124 Ibid.
125 *A* 9, p. 132.
126 *Les Mystères de Bruxelles*, one of the many imitations of *Les Mystères de Paris*, is mentioned in *The Village of Stepanchikovo and its inhabitants* (*A* 3, p. 70).
127 According to D. V. Grigorovich, in the years 1844–5 (*M* 1, p. 131).
128 In 'Petersburg Dreams in verse and prose', 1861, Dostoyevsky remarks: 'If I

were a professional and not an occasional journalist, I think I should like to change myself into Eugène Sue to describe the mysteries of Petersburg. I am very fond of mysteries. I run after phantoms, I am a mystic, and, I confess, Petersburg, for some unknown reason, has always seemed to me a sort of mystery' (*A* 19, p. 68).

129 The complete title shows the relationship between Sue's book and *Netochka Nezvanova*.

130 L. P. Grossman, *Poetika Dostoyevskogo*, Moscow, 1925, pp. 42–3. For *The Insulted and Injured*, which is particularly influenced by E. Sue, see V. Ya. Kirpotin, *Dostoyevsky v shestidesyatyye gody*, Moscow, 1966, pp. 274–8, 308–10.

131 *M* 2, p. 320.

132 *Letters* 1, p. 75; *A* 281, p. 107.

133 *Letters* 1, p. 78; *A* 281, p. 110.

134 Jacques Catteau, 'A propos de la littérature fantastique: André Belyj, héritier de Gogol' et de Dostoïevski', in *Cahiers du monde russe et soviétique*, 3, III, 1962, 327–73.

135 Dominique Barlési, 'La Vision sociale de Pétersbourg chez Dostoïevski des *Pauvres Gens* à *Crime et Châtiment*, *Publications des annales de la Faculté des Lettres d'Aix-en-Provence*, 19, Aix-en-Provence, 1962.

136 In *Winter Notes on Summer Impressions* (1863), an article about his first trip to Europe in 1862, he is particularly hard on London and Paris.

137 *A* 23, pp. 95–9.

138 Albert Camus, 'L'été', in *Essais*, 1965, pp. 854–5.

139 *A* 1, p. 59. The novel of Ducray-Duminil in question is *Le Petit Carillonneur* (1809), about a poor orphan who turns out to be a count.

140 *A* 1, p. 128.

141 The first Russian translation of *Confessions of an English Opium-Eater* appeared in 1834. The second edition, with the name of its real author, appeared in 1856. Turgenev read the book 'twice at a sitting' and warmly recommended it to Herzen, who wrote to him on 25 December 1856: 'Yes, it is a magnificent book. De Quincey is still living ... No Frenchman could write so sincerely, so openly and with so much boldness' (A. I. Herzen, *Sobraniye sochineniy v 30-i tomakh*, Moscow, 1962, 26, p. 60).

142 L. P. Grossman, *Poetika Dostoyevskogo*, Moscow, 1925, p. 34.

143 M. P. Alekseyev, 'F. M. Dostoevsky i kniga De Kvinsi', in *Uchyonnyye zapiski vysshey shkoly g. Odessy*, 1922, 2, p. 102.

144 *A* 1, pp. 279–80.

145 Thomas de Quincey, *Confessions of an English Opium-Eater* (1821), Harmondsworth, 1971, pp. 103–4.

146 Number 91 in the catalogue.

147 *A* 19, p. 70.

148 *A* 19, pp. 88–9.

149 *A* 19, p. 88.

150 *A* 19, p. 89.

151 Albert Béguin, *Création et Destinée (Essais de critique littéraire)*, Paris, 1973, p. 116.

152 For a detailed comparison of the three works, cf. A. L. Bem, *Dostoyevsky. Psikhoanaliticheskiye etyudy*, Berlin, 1938, pp. 119–41.

153 The title, *Die Irrungen*, is significant: Baron Théodore de S. arms himself with a scalpel to kill Schuspelpod. Seized with horror, he flies, giving up his plan. In fact, he ought to be dealing with the tail of the wig, a magic attribute of the old scholar.

154 Schuspelpod is an old Jewish scholar and exegetist of the Koran; Gogol's sorcerer has betrayed his faith and the Ukraine by making an alliance with unbelievers; Murin, which in old Russian means negro, moor and also demon, is the head of a gang of robbers.

155 Jacques Catteau, 'A propos de la littérature fantastique: André Belyj, héritier de Gogol' et de Dostoevskij', *Cahiers du monde russe et soviétique*, 3, III, 1962, 333.

156 *Moskovskiy literaturnyy i uchenyy sbornik na 1847g.*, Moscow, 1847, pp. 33–6.

157 Cf. the excellent linguistic analysis of the 'Petersburg poem', *The Double*, in V. V. Vinogradov, *Evolyutsiya russkogo naturalizma. Gogol' i Dostoyevsky*, Leningrad, 1929, pp. 206–91.

158 Besides the theme of madness, which is a constant in Hoffmann, there are direct links: thus the correspondence between the dogs Madge and Fidèle, in Gogol, recalls the dialogue between the two dogs collecting for the hospital, Scipion and Berganza, of the story *Nachricht von den neuesten Schicksalen des Hundes Berganza*.

159 *Finskiy Vestnik*, 9, v, 1846, p. 30.

160 Here for example is the title of chapter 1 of *The Double, or the Adventures of Mr Golyadkin*, as it was published in 1846, in *Annals of the Fatherland*:
'How the titular counsellor Golyadkin woke up. How he dressed and went off where his way took him. How Mr Golyadkin tried to justify himself in his own eyes and how later he deduced that it was best to act boldly and openly, not without nobility. Where Mr Golyadkin finally called.'
(*A* 1, p. 334)

161 *A* 26, p. 65.

162 *LH* 83, p. 310.

163 *Biography*, p. 373.

164 The difference of opinion between Belinsky and Dostoyevsky about Balzac is striking. Grigorovich says:
But hardly had I begun to say that my neighbour, whose name was still unknown to everyone, had translated *Eugénie Grandet*, than Belinsky burst out in violent imprecations against our idol, saying that he was a bourgeois writer and if he had had this *Eugénie Grandet* in his hands, he would have proved the whole platitude of this work page by page.
(*M* 1, p. 131)

4 THE HERITAGE: HISTORY AND PHILOSOPHY

1 Pushkin says he is 'enchanted' by *Le Rouge et le noir*, in a letter to E. M. Khitrovo, May 1831.

2 Michel Cadot, 'La Double Postulation de Baudelaire et sa version dostoïevskienne', in *Revue canadienne de littérature comparée*, winter 1977, 54–67.

3 A. G. Dostoyevskaya, *Dnevnik 1867g.*, Moscow, 1923, p. 214. Dostoyevsky certainly read *Madame Bovary*. In 1880 he praised the book to L. I. Veselitskaya

(V. Mikulich): cf. V. Mikulich, *Vstrechi s pisatelyami*, Leningrad, 1929, p. 156. The date is uncertain: in 1874–5, the book appears in his list of books to be read in Ems. Perhaps he had simply skimmed through it in 1867.

4 *A* 14, p. 215.

5 *Letters* 3, p. 225; *A* 28ii, p. 100.

6 Letter from Ye. A. Shtackenschneyder to Anna Grigoryevna, 16 January 1879: 'I am sending you the books which Fyodor Mikhaylovich wanted: could you return, if possible, Zola's *Assommoir*, which is on Fyodor Mikhaylovich's desk' (*LH* 86, p. 471).

7 In the notebooks of 1876–7, several notes illustrate this feeling about Zola:
   The realists are not to be believed, for man is a complete whole only in the future, and not everything is exhausted by the present. In realism alone there is no truth. Photography and the artist. Zola overlooked the poetry and *beauty* in George Sand (in the early stories), which is much more real than leaving humanity in the mud of daily life.   (*LH* 83, p. 628)

8 Martin P. Rice, 'Dostoyevsky's *Notes from Underground* and Hegel's *Master and Slave*', in *Revue canadienne–américaine d'études slaves*, 8, 1974, 3, 359–69. Nastasya Filippovna is supposed to be an illustration of the second stage, the 'unhappy awareness' of the dialectic of master and slave.

9 Ya. E. Golosovker, *Dostoyevsky i Kant*, Moscow, 1963.

10 Andrey remarks: 'In general, my brother Fedya read more historical, serious books, and also all the novels he could find' (*M* , p. 80).

11 Ivan Kuzmich Kaydanov (1780–1843), a Russian historian brought up on Bossuet and Herder, author of many textbooks.

12 *A* 25, p. 147.

13 *M* 1, p. 80. There were several editions of this work, from 1818 to 1853, in Dostoyevsky's library, including one signed by Karamzin. This was bought by Anna, who collected autographs.

14 *Letters* 1, p. 126; *A* 281, p. 159.

15 This immense inventory of manners was just as intense in Russia as in France. There were about 700 physiologies from 1838 to 1849, of which the most famous contributors were F. K. Dershau, A. Bashutsky, V. I. Lugansky (Dal'), P. Vistengof, Ye. P. Grebenka, as well as the writers Belinsky, Grigorovich, Zagoskin, Panayev, Nekrasov, Sollogub, Turgenev, Herzen and Dostoyevsky himself. Cf. A. G. Tseytlin, *Stanovleniye realizma v russkoy literature. Russkiy fiziologicheskiy ocherk*, Moscow, 1965.

16 Twice, before the Commission of Inquiry which was interrogating him after his arrest, Dostoyevsky justified his fondness for studying social, political and economic questions (socialism) by his passion for history. In his written deposition, he spoke of the secular order which was cracking in the West: 'Such a spectacle is a lesson! It is History and History is the science of the future.' During another interrogation he repeated that he 'passionately loved historical sciences' (N. F. Bel'chikov, *Dostoyevsky v protsesse Petrashevtsev*, Moscow, 1971, pp. 100, 146).

17 *A* 21, p. 131.

18 N. F. Bel'chikov, *Dostoyevsky v protsesse Petrashevtsev*, Moscow, 1971, p. 214. The wording of the entries about the work of Eugène Sue is worth quoting. First entry: 'Socialist and democratic talks about the Republic and monarchic potentates.' Second entry: 'Socialist and democratic talks about the little books

of the gentlemen of the Academy of Moral and Political Sciences and about the coming elections.'

19 Nearly a quarter of a century later, Dostoyevsky was to recall this 'Petrashevsky' period. He cited some of the names mentioned here, but strangely he placed Strauss, who 'covers Christianity with shame and derision', in the sixties, next to Mill and Darwin (*A* 21, p. 132). Is it an unconscious attempt to avoid the reproach of atheism in 1848?

20 N. F. Bel'chikov, *Dostoyevsky v protsesse Petrashevtsev*, Moscow, 1971, p. 214.

21 Ibid. p. 110.

22 *Life*, p. 52, December 1848.

23 Statement of Dr S. D. Yanovsky in *F. M. Dostoyevsky. Stat'i i materialy*, ed. A. S. Dolinin, Petersburg, 1922, 7, p. 265.

24 Henri Granjard, 'Ivan Tourguénev et les courants politiques et sociaux de son temps', *Bibl. russe de l'Institut d'études slaves*, Paris, 1966, pp. 69–104.

25 The catalogue of Petrashevsky's library is given by V. I. Semyovsky in 'M. V. Butashevich-Petrashevsky', in *Golos minuvshego*, 8, Moscow, 1913, 53–4.

26 *A* 18, p. 26.

27 N. F. Bel'chikov, *Dostoyevsky v protsesse Petrashevtsev*, Moscow, 1971, p. 101.

28 *Letters* 1, p. 124; *A* 281, p. 157.

29 'I came from a pious Russian family ... We knew the Gospel, in our family, practically from earliest infancy ... Every visit to the Kremlin and the cathedrals in Moscow was a solemn event for me' (*A* 21, p. 134).

30 Andrey's account (*M* 1, pp. 74–5).

31 *Biography*, p. 118.

32 A. E. Vrangel, *Vospominaniya o F. M. Dostoyevskom v Sibiri 1854–1856 gg.*, Petersburg, 1912, p. 53.

33 N. F. Bel'chikov, *Dostoyevsky v protsesse Petrashevtsev*, Moscow, 1971, p. 152.

34 *Letters* 1, p. 142; *A* 281, p. 176.

35 Shatov to Stavrogin: 'But was it not you who told me that if it were mathematically proved to you that the truth is outside Christ, you would prefer to remain with Christ, rather than with the truth?' (*A* 10, p. 198).

36 N. F. Bel'chikov. *Dostoyevsky v protsesse Petrashevtsev*, Moscow, 1971, p. 152.

37 The word is *luchinochki*. These are chips of wood cut with an axe. They were used to light the peasant's hut. When several of these chips were joined together in a bundle, for a torch, each one burnt separately, curved and fell away from the others.

38 *LH* 83, pp. 246–50.

39 Pierre Pascal, *Dostoïevski*, Les écrivains devant Dieu, Paris–Bruges, 1969.

40 *Letters* 1, p. 124; *A* 281, p. 157.

41 *Letters* 1, p. 125; *A* 281, p. 158.

42 In prison, by Petrov, a convict who was very fond of him, according to the author of *The House of the Dead*. The episode appears in part 1, chapter 7.

43 Besides this precious Bible, Dostoyevsky's library, on the eve of his death, contained several copies of the Gospel from the sixties and seventies.

44 *Letters* 1, p. 138; *A* 281, p. 171. Later Dostoyevsky lists the modern historians: 'Vico, Guizot, Thierry, Thiers, Ranke'.

45 Jean Drouilly, in his article 'Une erreur dans l'édition russe de A. S. Dolinin des lettres de F. M. Dostoïevski' (in *Etudes slaves et est-européennes*, Montreal, 19, 1974, 118–20) has shown that the word is not *Koran*, but *Karus* (K. G. Carus, the

German philosopher). In the same letter Dostoyevsky asks for a 'German dictionary', which he would not have needed for the Koran. The appearance of the two requests side by side in the letter of 27 March 1854: 'Carus and a German dictionary', is confirmation of this theory. The error is probably due to Dostoyevsky's bad writing. However, the mistake of A. S. Dolinin, one of the leading scholars on Dostoyevsky, is not unreasonable: Dostoyevsky was always extremely interested in the Koran, quoting it several times in his works, and kept a copy of it, a French edition of 1847, in his library. The Academy edition has preserved Dolinin's version, without comment.

46 *Letters* I, p. 139; *A* 28I, p. 173.

47 *Letters* I, p. 145; *A* 28I, p. 179.

48 *Letters* I, p. 150; *A* 28I, p. 184.

49 François Guizot, *Histoire des origines du gouvernement représentatif*; Augustin Thierry, *Histoire de la formation et des progrès du Tiers-Etat*; Louis Adolphe Thiers, *Histoire de la Révolution*.

50 *Histoire de la Conquête de l'Angleterre par les Normands, Récits des Temps mérovingiens*.

51 In his *Scienza Nuova* (1725), Vico considers three ages in the development and decadence of peoples: the age of gods, the age of heroes and the age of men.

52 Dostoyevsky's library, reformed after 1871, was not the same as his library of the fifties. However it contained: Guizot, *Histoire de la République d'Angleterre et de Cromwell* (1854 ed.); Thiers, *Histoire du Consulat et de l'Empire* (1845 ed.) and *Histoire de la Révolution Française de 1789 jusqu'au 18 Brumaire* (1858 ed.).

53 In his library of 1871, Dostoyevsky had the complete works of Tacitus in a French edition of 1865.

54 Pierre Pascal, *Dostoïevski*, Les écrivains devant Dieu, Paris–Bruges, 1969, p. 26.

55 In *The House of the Dead* Dostoyevsky gives an account of a passage from the Koran (III, 43), a legend which is taken from the apocryphal Gospel of Thomas: Isa (Jesus), the prophet of God, made a bird out of clay, breathed on it and it flew (*A* 4, p. 54).

56 *A* 2, p. 313. Kant is mocked for his pomposity as a 'real German professor'.

57 He appears twice in the notebooks of *The Brothers Karamazov*: Ivan says to Satan: 'The meaning of your appearance is to prove that you exist, and are not my nightmare, not a fantasy (Hegel. Iv. Kuzmich)' (*A* 15, p. 335). Satan says to Ivan: 'I love dreams . . . I advise you to stop at this idea (Hegel). Otherwise we shall quarrel' (*A* 15, p. 335).

58 A. E. Vrangel, *Vospominaniya o F. M. Dostoyevskom v Sibiri 1854–1856gg.*, Petersburg, 1912, p. 34.

59 Ibid. p. 33.

60 Cf. the excellent analysis of the works of Karl Gustav Carus, 'the great philosopher of the unconscious' in German romanticism, in Albert Béguin's *Création et destinée, essais de critique littéraire*, Paris, 1973, pp. 57–9.

61 *Biography*, p. 172.

62 *Letters* I, pp. 183–4; *A* 28I, p. 229. The contents of this article are a matter of conjecture. It was to have been an act of repentance, opposing Belinsky's letter to Gogol, and a restatement of the themes set out in the letter to N. D. Fonvizina and the letter in which Dostoyevsky discusses the models which inspired the character of Myshkin.

63 *Biography*, p. 194.
64 *Letters* 1, p. 401; *A* 28II, p. 119.
65 V. S. Nechayeva, *Zhurnal M. M. i F. M. Dostoyevskikh 'Vremya', 1861–1863*, Moscow, 1972, pp. 175–89.
66 From this point references are given in the text, at least for *Time*. The list and references for all articles in *Time* and *Epoch* are to be found in V. S. Nechayeva, *Zhurnal M. M. i F. M. Dostoyevskikh 'Epokha', 1864–1865*, Moscow, 1975, pp. 233–68.
67 Where he attacks Darwin in particular.
68 In Dostoyevsky's library there was an 1874 edition of *The Origin of Species*, and also an 1872 edition of Darwin's *The Expression of Emotions in Man and Animals*.
69 *A* 6, p. 16. Dostoyevsky's library contained an 1876 edition of this book.
70 This did not moderate Dostoyevsky's attacks on the socialism of the ant-heap. His brush with socialist criticism of the conditions of the workers had humanitarian causes but was also fiercely nationalistic: the bourgeois West was hypocritical and cynical, unlike Russia, where, according to Dostoyevsky, this tragedy of the workers did not exist.
71 Marx's reply to Proudhon was in the Butashevich-Petrashevsky library.
72 S. Borshchevsky, *Shchedrin i Dostoyevsky. Istoriya ikh ideynoy bor'by*, Moscow, 1956.
73 Besides two editions (1874 and 1875) of the complete works of Buckle, Dostoyevsky had the first volume of the Tiblen and Panteleyev 1864 edition of Buckle in his library. He knew N. L. Tiblen, who had edited Buckle, Spencer and Macaulay, very well. Cf. *Letters* 1, p. 311; *A* 28II, p. 28.
74 *A* 5, pp. 111–12.
75 *LH* 86, p. 583.
76 For information on this subject, cf. Pierre Pascal, *Avvakum et les débuts du raskol*, Paris–The Hague, 1969 (first edition 1938).
77 *A* 20, pp. 20–1. The last sentence also implies that history is the science of the future.
78 The plan of Pyotr Verkhovensky, who wishes to make Stavrogin a 'Tsarevich Ivan', clearly owes something to this thesis.
79 *A* 7, p. 211.
80 Manuscript Section of Lenin Library, F 93, I, 3, 1. Text quoted by V. S. Nechayeva, *Zhurnal M. M. i F. M. Dostoyevskikh, 'Vremya' 1861–1863*, Moscow, 1972, pp. 201–2.
81 *Letters* 1, p. 349; *A* 28II, p. 66.
82 *Letters* 4, p. 270; *A* 28II, p. 68.
83 *Letters* 2, p. 252; *A291*, p. 107. Turgenev, Goncharov and Kostomarov all contributed to the *Messenger of Europe* in 1870.
84 *Letters* 4, p. 196.
85 Saltykov-Shchedrin's lampoon 'The martinets' on the editors of *Epoch*, in *The Contemporary*, May 1864; Dostoyevsky's mock novel *The Crocodile*, attacking Chernyshevsky, who was then in prison, in *Epoch*, February 1865.
86 In 'Mr Shchedrin or schism among the nihilists' (*Epoch*, May 1864) and 'Puns in life and literature' (*Epoch*, October 1864). For instance, the town of Pupov (*pup* means navel, cf. *glup kak pup*) for the town of Glupov in Shchedrin's novel; Shchedrodarov (from *shchedr–* and *dar*) for Shchedrin; Krolichkov (from *krolik*:

rabbit) for Zaytsev (from *zayats*: hare), the publicist of the nihilist journal, *The Russian Word*.

87 Antonovich in his 'Message to the super-martinet Dostoyevsky' (*The Contemporary*, July 1864) made coarse fun of Dostoyevsky's epilepsy and of his doctor. Dostoyevsky was no less brutal in making fun of Chernyshevsky, who had just been arrested.

88 V. S. Nechayeva, *Zhurnal M. M. i F. M. Dostoyevskikh 'Epokha', 1864–1865'*, Moscow, 1965, pp. 101–5.

89 Ibid. pp. 105–8.

90 The perspicacious Saltykov-Shchedrin noted the religious dimension of *Notes from Underground*, which he calls 'Memoirs of the immortal soul' in his satire 'The martinets' (*The Contemporary*, May 1864). The letter in which Dostoyevsky regrets the censured passages about 'the necessity for belief in Christ' confirms this idea (*Letters* 1, p. 353; *A* 28II, p. 73).

91 *Dostoïevski*, Cahiers de l'Herne 24, Paris, 1973, pp. 59–64.

92 *LH* 83, pp. 173–5.

93 *LH* 83, pp. 246–50.

94 *Letters* 4, pp. 9–10.

95 Anna particularly notes books presented by their authors, historical works, studies of Old Believers, and bibliographical 'rarities' (*M Anna*, pp. 145–6).

96 *Letters* 1, pp. 331 and 335; *A* 28II, pp. 46 and 53.

97 *Letters* 3, p. 177 and notes; *A* 28II, p. 42.

98 Apart from this book, of which Dostoyevsky writes several times in his correspondence (*Letters* 2, p. 149 (*A* 28II, p. 328); p. 181 (*A* 29I, p. 30); p. 293 (*A* 29I, p. 147)), all the books mentioned here are in the catalogue of Dostoyevsky's library (L. P. Grossman, *Seminariy po Dostoyevskomu*, Moscow–Petrograd, 1922, pp. 22–50).

99 *Letters* 3, p. 177; *A* 29II, p. 43.

100 *Letters* 4, p. 136.

101 David Goldstein analyses these two books and their echoes in the work of Dostoyevsky (David I. Goldstein, *Dostoevsky and the Jews*, Austin and London, 1981). See also Jacques Catteau, 'Dostoïevski était-il antisémite?', in *La Quinzaine littéraire*, 241, 1–15 October 1976, 18–19.

102 Even before the article appeared in *Aurora*, Dostoyevsky was impatiently waiting for it at the end of 1868 (*Letters* 2, p. 149; *A* 28II, p. 328).

103 *Letters* 2, p. 181; *A* 29I, p. 30.

104 Ibid.

105 *Letters* 2, p. 271; *A* 29I, p. 125. The Russian word for 'weakish' is *shvakhovat* (from the German *schwach*).

106 *Letters* 2, p. 140; *A* 28II, p. 319.

107 Herbert Spencer's *Intellectual, Moral and Physical Education* was in Dostoyevsky's library.

108 *Letters* 2, p. 271; *A* 29I, p. 125.

109 *Letters* 4, pp. 9–10.

110 Jacques Catteau, 'Du Palais de cristal à l'âge d'or ou les avatars de l'utopie', in *Dostoïevski*, Cahiers de l'Herne 24, Paris, 1973, pp. 188–95.

111 *F. M. Dostoyevsky. Materialy i issledovaniya*, ed. A. S. Dolinin, Leningrad, pp. 89–90.

112 *Letters* 4, p. 7.

113 *LH* 15, p. 135.
114 Pierre Pascal, in his translation of a large part of *The Siberian Notebook* (*A* 4, pp. 235–48), has noted how these expressions were used again in different works (*Dostoïevski*, Cahiers de l'Herne 24, Paris, 1973, pp. 49–58).
115 *A* 21, pp. 88.
116 *Letters* 4, p. 29.
117 In the catalogue of Dostoyevsky's library, nos. 138, 158, 166, 170 (L. P. Grossman, *Seminariy po Dostoyevskomu*, Moscow–Petrograd, 1922, pp. 38–42).
118 *A Anna*, p. 256.
119 V. S. Nechayeva, *Zhurnal M. M. i F. M. Dostoyevskikh 'Epokha', 1864–1865*, Moscow, 1975, pp. 60–4.
120 *Letters* 2, p. 150; *A* 28ɪɪ, p. 329.
121 *Letters* 2, p. 186; *A* 291, p. 35.
122 *A* 23, p. 31. The Russians, Dostoyevsky writes, 'have grafted things borrowed from Europe on to their organism, their flesh and their blood'.

5 ILLNESS

1 *Otechestvennyye zapiski*, 2, 1873, 317.
2 *Sankt-peterburgskiye Vedomosti*, 6, 6 January 1873.
3 *Delo*, 3, 1873, 156.
4 *A* 11, p. 308.
5 *A* 26, p. 107.
6 Dostoyevsky fainted when he was introduced to the beautiful Senyavina in Count Vielgorsky's drawing-room (*Life*, p. 43). He was satirised for this in an epigram attributed to Belinsky, but written by Panayev and Nekrasov, probably aided by Turgenev.
7 *Letters* 4, p. 143, and commentaries by A. S. Dolinin, pp. 413–15.
8 I. S. Turgenev, *Polnoye sobraniye sochineniy*, Moscow–Lenningrad, 1960, 1, pp. 607–8 and *Letters* 4, p. 414.
9 The beautiful Avdotiya Yakovlevna Panayeva, with whom Dostoyevsky fell in love briefly and secretly (*Letters* 1, pp. 85, and 87; *A* 281, pp. 116 and 118) described in a fairly objective manner the reactions and attitude of the young Dostoyevsky in the literary salon over which she presided (*A* 1, pp. 140–3).
10 Pavel Pavlovich Trusotsky, a widower, did not choose the eldest of the eight daughters of State councillor Zakhlebnin as his wife, but the sixth, Nadya, a school-girl of fifteen, undeterred by the repulsion she felt towards him (*A* 9, pp. 66–7).
11 *Perepiska L. N. Tolstogo s N. N. Strakhovym*, St Petersburg, 1914, pp. 307–8.
12 Ibid. Pavel Aleksandrovich Viskovatov (1842–1906): literary historian and biographer of Lermontov, professor at Dorpat University, 1873–95.
13 Pierre Pascal, *Dostoïevski, l'homme et l'œuvre*, Slavica, Lausanne, 1970, pp. 293–4. *The Brothers Karamazov* is the best example of Dostoyevsky's sensitivity to the suffering of children. The Karamazov brothers formulate their questions about the meaning of suffering by using children as examples. Ivan refuses to build universal happiness if it costs the tears of one single child. Dmitriy in his dream of the 'baby' crying with cold and hunger discovers that everyone is responsible for everyone else and accepts his Calvary; Alyosha

discovers his destiny and new strength among children (Kolya Krasotkin, Ilyusha).

14 When Strakhov told Tolstoy of Dostoyevsky's death, Tolstoy replied; 'I have never seen this man and I have never had direct contact with him but now that he is dead I have realised that he was the man who was closest, dearest and most necessary to me.' And he said that he had wept (L. N. Tolstoy, *Polnoye Sobraniye Sochineniy* (Moscow–Leningrad, 1934, p. 43). In another letter of September 1880, he told Strakhov that he knew no 'better book in all modern literature, including Pushkin' than *The House of the Dead* (ibid. p. 24).

15 Ibid. p. 142. 'All composed of struggle' (*ves' bor'ba*) or 'all struggle' (*vsya bor'ba*) according to the text quoted for the first time from the original in the manuscript department of the State Museum of L. N. Tolstoy (*Yasnopolyanskiy sbornik. Stati i materialy god 1960–yy*, Tula, 1960, p. 123).

16 I. Neyfel'd, *Dostoyevsky, Psikhoanaliticheskiy ocherk*, ed. S. Freud, Leningrad–Moscow, 1925, p. 96. The text of Jolanka Neufeld appeared in German in *Imago-Bücher*, 4, 1923.

17 It is the 'Muzhik Marei' episode (*A* 22, pp. 48–9).

18 Neufeld's lack of method is amazing: (1) She has a blind trust in the very doubtful memories of Lyubov Dostoyevskaya, who was only twelve when her father died. (2) Dostoyevsky married Marya Dmitriyevna in 1857, when he was 36. Little is known about his sexual life before 1857. It is known that, unlike his fellow-students, he was apparently not attracted by women. At least apparently, for he fainted before the beautiful Senyavina, fell in love with Mme Panayeva and knew some other ladies who were not so unattainable. In 1845 he wrote to his brother: 'The Minouches, Clairettes and Mariannes etc. have become much more beautiful but they cost enormous sums. And the other day Turgenev and Belinsky scolded me for my irregular life' (*Letters* 1, p. 85; *A* 281, p. 116). Marc Slonim discusses this period in *Three loves of Dostoevsky*, London, 1957, pp. 37–43.

19 He also suffered from haemorrhoids and took castor oil to ease the pain, in the Peter–Paul Fortress (*Letters* 1, p. 126; *A* 281, p. 159).

20 Sigmund Freud, 'Dostoevsky and parricide', in *Dostoevsky. A Collection of Critical Essays*, ed. René Wellek, Englewood Cliffs, N.J., 1962, pp. 98–111. Later referred to as 'Freud'. This is translated from Freud's 'F. M. Dostojewski und die Vatertötung', an introduction to W. Komarowitsch, *F. M. Dostoewski, Die Urgestalt der Brüder Karamazoff, Dostoewskis Quellen, Entwürfe und Fragmente*, Munich 1928.

21 Some of them have been formulated by the psychoanalyst Yvon Belaval in his preface to: Anne Clancier, *Psychanalyse et critique littéraire*, Nouvelle recherche, Toulouse, 1973, pp. 15–16.

22 *Biography*, p. 141.

23 *Life*, p. 33. 8 June 1839. This version has been disputed lately due to the research of G. A. Fyodorov (V. Ya. Kirpotin, 'Oprovergnutaya versiya', in *Literaturnaya gazeta*, 25, 18 June 1975, 7). The facts are as follows: Dr M. A. Dostoyevsky was found dead in the countryside of Darovoye. Two doctors examined the body: both concluded, separately, that it was an attack of apoplexy. Some time later, P. P. Khotyaintsev, a rich neighbour who had his eye on the Darovoye land, accused the serfs of having killed Dr Dostoyevsky: their condemnation and exile would have ruined the heirs, who would then have been

forced to give up their land. Khotyaintsev did not make the public accusation himself, but used an intermediary, Captain A. I. Leibrecht, to make a report of this to the authorities. A fairly long inquest then began: after a year the seven peasants who had been accused were cleared. It was then supposed that the heirs concealed this affair, to prevent their labour force from being deported. This is an unlikely hypothesis: it would have required too many bribes, not only of the two doctors, but of all the people connected with the long inquiry. Moreover, Dostoyevsky, who recalled the death of his father in a letter to his brother, showed no doubt about the truth of the verdict. A century later, V. S. Nechayeva collected from the peasants of Darovoye all the stories which had passed on from generation to generation about the death of Dr Dostoyevsky. An obscure phrase in one of these accounts of rumour inspired a legend which has been cheerfully taken over by Henri Troyat, Dominique Arban and Marthe Robert: Dr Dostoyevsky (who since his wife died had been openly living with a serf woman) is supposed to have been castrated by his murderers in revenge for the rape of two little girls (V. S. Nechayeva, *V sem'e i v usad'be Dostoyevskikh*, Moscow, 1939, p. 54; Henri Troyat, *Dostoïevski*, Paris, 1960, p. 52; Dominique Arban, *Les Années d'apprentissage de Fiodor Dostoïevski*, Paris, 1968, pp. 164–5; Marthe Robert, 'L'Inconscient, Creuset de l'Oeuvre' in *Fiodor Dostoïevski*, Génies et Réalités, Paris, 1971, pp. 148–9).

24 Freud, p. 103.

25 Dominique Arban, *Les Années d'apprentissage*, pp. 31–2.

26 Freud, pp. 101–2. These data, as we shall see, are overwhelming.

27 Freud, p. 101, note 3. An admirable syllogism. Dostoyevsky's epilepsy is neurotic in origin, therefore Dostoyevsky is a neurotic and, since the words of a neurotic are unreliable, all the evidence about his epilepsy must be rejected. 'Biographical data hardly matter, only the interpretation counts!' as J. Schotte remarked at the seventh colloquium of 'L'Association internationale de Recherche en Analyse du Destin' (Szondi), devoted to the theme 'Morbus sacer Homo sacer' and to Dostoyevsky in particular (Paris, 21.9.1975 to 24.9.1975, at the Institut National de Recherche et de Documentation Pédagogiques).

28 Report of 16 December 1857 in *F. M. Dostoyevskii. Sobraniye sochineniy v 10–i tomakh*, 10, Moscow, 1956–8, p. 565. Joseph Frank in the first volume of his monumental biography of Dostoyevsky comes to the same conclusions about Freud's irresponsible way with history as we do. In a valuable appendix, he analyses, by quoting the correspondence between Freud and Stefan Zweig, the way in which this erroneous hypothesis was constructed from an account given by the daughter of Dostoyevsky (Joseph Frank, *Dostoyevsky. The Seeds of Revolt, 1821–1849*, Princeton, 1976, pp. 379–91).

29 Charles Mauron, 'Introduction à la Psychanalyse de Mallarmé', Neuchâtel, 1950, pp. 25–6.

30 This is not the opinion of Janine Chasseguet-Smirgel who, in her introduction to *Pour une psychanalyse de l'art et de la créativité* (Paris, 1971, pp. 13–15), compares those who dispute the use of psychoanalysis in art to Jungians who reject 'the dustbin of infant sexuality'. A person who refuses to psychoanalyse art is thus a victim of that 'unbearable narcissistic wound'. But is not art the illusion without which man would not be human and would sink into Freudian pessimism, which is quite opposed to the fundamental optimism of Dostoyevsky?

31 *A 25*, p. 108.

32 The libido has no ethical value in itself: it aspires to pleasure in total fusion; ethics supposes that one should recognise the other person in that union as a separate being. Ethics is a connection in the distance ... No primary psychic datum is capable of promoting ethics, which is linked with the appearance of a new psychic process: the conscience. This new psychic formation is only possible in a dialectical connection of the libido and the aggressive impulse, as they are connected in two distinct but parallel and complementary processes: the Cain complex and the Oedipus complex ... Szondi affirms that 'from the viewpoint of impulse psychology, the conscience originates not from interiorisation of aggression but from an anxious effort to make reparation for the homicidal tendency of Cain.' 'This will towards reparation – as an impulse tendency – is given the name of "Moses complex" by the Analysis of destiny, and is contrasted with the "Cain complex"' (Antoine Vergote in *Revue de psychologie et des sciences de l'éducation*, 6, 4, Louvain, 1971, 447).

33 Thérèse Neyrant-Sutterman, communication at the colloquium of Cerisy-la-Salle, June 1968, directed by Anne Clancier and André Green: 'L'espace du Tragique'.

34 It is a hystero-epilepsy, according to him.

35 Szondi's *Schicksalanalyse* has an original aspect which is worth summarising. Szondi begins with the question: what could be the secret link, in the character of Dostoyevsky himself, between, for example, the Karamazov brothers: the criminal, the lawyer, the man of God, and finally the epileptic? Szondi used an immense amount of genealogical material to note the statistically revealing frequency of certain professions as well as some illnesses in certain families. 'For example, in the case of Dostoyevsky, the frequency of epileptoid disturbances matching certain professions, which are fundamental in all human societies and often linked with each other, which are the professions or vocations of lawyers and men of God' (J. Schotte in *Revue de psychologie et des sciences de l'éducation*, 6, 4, Louvain, 1971, 423–4).

36   For the person who is aware of the binary or serial law of statistics, according to which no phenomenon occurs which is not the expression of a numerous series of analogous facts, the frequency of epilepsy among great men allows us to suspect that it is more widely diffused than was at first believed, and helps us to realise the epileptoid nature of Genius.
    (Cesare Lombroso, *The Man of Genius*, 1864, quoted by P. G. Loygue in *Etude médico-psychologique sur Dostoïevski. Considérations sur les états morbides liés au génie*, thesis, Lyon, 1903)

37 D. S. Merezhkovsky, *Prorok russkoy revolyutsii*, St Petersburg, 1906, pp. 57–77: 'Besnovatiy ili prorok?'

38 André Gide, *Dostoyevsky*, Harmondsworth, 1967, pp. 31–2.

39 Francois Mauriac, *Le Romancier et ses personnages*, Paris, 1933, pp. 145–6.

40 Thomas Mann, 'Dostojewski mit Maszen', from *Gesammelte Werke* (13 vols.), 9, p. 657.

41 Ibid. p. 661.

42 Ibid.

43 Ibid. p. 666.

44 *M* I, p. 85: evidence of Andrey, his brother.

45 Ibid. pp. 156 and 158.

46 *Letters* I, p. 431; *A* 28II, p. 150.

47 *M Anna*, p. 184.
48 *Letters* 3, p. 247; *A* 29II, p. 125.
49 Ibid. p. 236; *A* 29II, p. 114.
50 *Letters* 4, p. 201.
51 Yakov Bogdanovich Von Bretzel, Professor Dmitriy Ivanovich Koshlyakov and Nikolay Petrovich Cherepnin.
52 *LH* 86, p. 312. Letter of 3 March 1918 to A. V. Zhirkevich. Consumption is a supposition, since, as the prudent Von Bretzel says, Koch's bacillus was not discovered until 1882.
53 *A* 22, p. 48.
54 Now called primary generalised or common epilepsy. In this case, the epileptic discharges depend on a convulsive predisposition and not on a lesion of the brain. For all the technical terms, we are following the *Dictionnaire de l'épilepsie (Partie 1: Définitions)* of the World Health Organisation, under the direction of Professor Henri Gastaut, Geneva, 1973.
55 *M* 1, p. 158.
56 *M* 2, p. 415 (*Novoye Vremya*, no. 1771, 1 February 1881).
57 Viktor Shklovsky, *Za i protiv. Zametki o Dostoyevskom*, Moscow, 1957, pp. 9–10.
58 In particular, the duty officer A. I. Savelyev whose memoirs are very detailed (*M* 1, pp. 96–104).
59 The archimandrite Photius who had just died in 1838 and had acquired a saintly reputation as a humble and gentle soul (*M* 1, p. 97).
60 *LH* 86, p. 331. The memoirs of Aleksandr Yegorovich Riesenkampf (Rizen-kampf), partly known from the extracts quoted by Orest Miller in 1883, were published in a more complete form in 1973.
61 Ibid.
62 Ibid.
63 *Novoye Vremya*, no. 1778, 8 February 1881.
64 *M* 1, p. 100. These 'attacks of death' signify to Freud that Dostoyevsky identified with his dead father, whose death he had wished for, and that he was punishing himself for this (Freud, pp. 102–3).
65 *M* 1, p. 132.
66 Ibid. p. 159.
67 Ibid. p. 155.
68 *Letters* 1, p. 46; *A* 28I, p. 50.
69 *Letters* 1, p. 79; *A* 28I, p. 110.
70 *Letters* 1, p. 78; *A* 28I, p. 110.
71 *Letters* 1, p. 80; *A* 28I, p. 112.
72 *Letters* 1, p. 87; *A* 28I, p. 118.
73 *Letters* 1, p. 89; *A* 28I, p. 120.
74 *Letters* 1, p. 90; *A* 28I, p. 121.
75 *Letters* 1, p. 92; *A* 28I, p. 124.
76 *Letters* 1, p. 115; *A* 28I, p. 147.
77 *Letters* 1, p. 124; *A* 28I, p. 157.
78 *Letters* 1, p. 126; *A* 28I, p. 159.
79 M. Anty, *Psychiatrie à l'usage de l'équipe médico-psychologique*, Paris, 1975, pp. 27–33.
80 *Letters* 1, p. 106; *A* 28II, p. 137.
81 *Letters* 4, pp. 136–7.

82 Letter from A. E. Riesenkampf to A. M. Dostoyevsky, 10 March 1881 (IRLI, f. 56, ed. khr. 100).

83 Letter from A. E. Riesenkampf to A. M. Dostoyevsky, 16 February 1881 (*LH* 86, pp. 548–50).

84 *M* 1, p. 243.

85 *Letters* 1, p. 135; *A* 281, p. 169. The thesis of corporal punishment by flogging is repeated by Sofiya Kovalevskaya (*M* 1, p. 347) and the epilepsy is placed not in the convict period, but during service in the 7th Siberian Battalion of the line, i.e. after 1854. Kovalevskaya's memoirs appear to be less reliable than A. S. Dolinin thinks.

86 In 1857 Dostoyevsky was 36: the error is probably his own, as he often said that he was born in 1822 rather than 1821 (*Life*, p. 23 and *Dostoïevski*, 'Cahiers de l'Herne, 24, Paris, 1973, p. 107).

87 The Russian word *stradaniye* has often been wrongly translated in the medical context.

88 F. M. Dostoyevsky, *Sobraniye sochineniy v 10–i tomakh*, Moscow, 1956–8, 10, p. 565.

89 *Letters* 1, p. 266; *A* 281, p. 386.

90 *Life*, p. 67.

91 Particularly that by Yanovsky, who lingers over the protuberances of Dostoyevsky's forehead and 'Socratic' cranium (*M* 1, pp. 155 and 163–4).

92 Injury to the eye treated with atropine, 4 October 1866 (*M Anna*, p. 28; *LH* 86, p. 221; *Biography*, p. 214); dislocation of a bone in the spine, 6 November 1880, noted by Dostoyevsky himself (*LH* 83, p. 698).

93 Dostoyevsky's own interpretation of his illness is original. On 26 February 1881, the daughter of Andrey Dostoyevsky, Ye. A. Rykachova, describes a talk she had with Dostoyevsky's widow about the date of her uncle's first epileptic fit:

> I asked her if she knew or if my uncle had confided to her the reason for his first fit. She said that my uncle had always asserted that his *epilepsy* began in Siberia ... and that he always supposed his illness came from his passionate (*strastnyy*) temperament which he had not been able to satisfy once in the four years of prison for fear of being flogged. I was extremely surprised by this explanation, but it happens that this was the sort of explanation my uncle gave to Madame Abaza, whom Anna Grigoryevna saw yesterday ... When I let her read the extract from the letter which Riesenkampf sent us, she denied the fact that my uncle had suffered corporal punishment, at least she did not know of it.

(*Dostoyevsky. Materialy i issledovaniya*, 1, Leningrad, 1974, p. 303)

94 Letter from S. D. Yanovsky to A. N. Maykov in *Novoye Vremya*, no. 1793, 24 February 1881, entitled 'The Illness of F. M. Dostoyevsky'.

95 *M* 1, p. 163.

96 N. F. Bel'chikov, *Dostoyevsky v protsesse Petrashevtsev*, Moscow, 1971, p. 99.

97 *Letters* 1, p. 178; *A* 281, p. 224.

98 *Letters* 1, p. 216; *A* 281, p. 270.

99 *Letters* 3, p. 23; *A* 291, pp. 228–9. The style of Dostoyevsky's letters is very casual.

100 A. E. Vrangel', *Vospominaniya o F. M. Dostoyevskom v Sibiri 1854–1856gg.*, Petersburg, 1912, p. 37.

101 *Letters* 1, pp. 137 and 151; *A* 281, pp. 171 and 185.

102 *Letters* 1, p. 146; *A* 281, p. 180.
103 *Letters* 1, p. 198; *A* 281, p. 243.
104 *Letters* 1, p. 215; *A* 281, p. 270.
105 *Letters* 1, p. 222; *A* 281, p. 381. In his chronological canvas, L. P. Grossman places this event in 1856 and 1857. The reference given (Letter 98) proves that this is a mistake (*Life*, pp. 81 and 86).
106 *Letters* 2, pp. 43 and 46; *A* 28II, pp. 223 and 226.
107 *Letters* 2, p. 184; *A* 291, p. 33.
108 *Letters* 2, pp. 239–40; *A* 291, p. 89.
109 *Biography*, p. 213. For the fits of 1869, Dostoyevsky gives the exact calendar in the notebook no. 1/10 (*Zapisnyye tetradi F. M. Dostoyevskogo*, with commentary by N. I. Ignatova and Ye. N. Konshina, Moscow–Leningrad, 1935, pp. 79–80).
110 *Biography*, p. 213.
111 *M Anna*, p. 61.
112 Dostoyevsky worried about his health, but had lost confidence in doctors. On 17 June 1863 he wrote to Turgenev: 'Basically I am going to Paris and Berlin, and if possible for a short time, only to consult specialists (Trousseau in Paris, Romberg in Berlin) about my epilepsy. We have no specialists and the doctors give me such different and contradictory opinions that I have definitely lost all confidence in them' (*Letters* 1, p. 318, *A* 28II, p. 34). The report sent to the Ministry of the Interior on 13 June 1863 by the military Governor-General of St Petersburg when Dostoyevsky asked for a passport says: 'Dostoyevsky has decided to go abroad to consult the most famous European specialists in epilepsy, Professor Trousseau and Drs Herpin and Romberg' (*F. M. Dostoyevsky i I. S. Turgenev. Perepiska. Istoriya odnoy vrazhdy*, ed. I. S. Zil'bershteyn, Leningrad, 1928, p. 58).
113 *Biography*, p. 213.
114 *Letters* 1, p. 430; *A* 28II, p. 150.
115 *Letters* 1, p. 423; *A* 28II, p. 141.
116 *Letters* 2, pp. 59–60; *A* 28II, pp. 239–40.
117 *LH* 86, pp. 167–282. Entitled 'Geneva diary of A. G. Dostoyevskaya'.
118 Ibid. p. 280.
119 *Letters* 2, p. 95; *A* 28II, p. 273.
120 *LH* 83, p. 285.
121 *M Anna*, p. 61.
122 *LH* 83, p. 349.
123 Ibid. p. 350. The mediocrity of the writing, the repetitions and the return to one idea show that Dostoyevsky had difficulty in writing and focusing his thoughts (a phenomenon which specialists in epilepsy call 'glyschroidia').
124 *LH* 83, p. 625.
125 Ibid. p. 698.
126 *A* 15, p. 44.
127 *LH* 86, p. 169.
128 Ibid. pp. 216 and 227.
129 Ibid. p. 181.
130 *M Anna*, pp. 74–5. We have omitted the reactions of other people present.
131 This is not the first time we have had doubts about the 'Memoirs' of the great mathematician.
132 *Biography*, p. 214.

133 *M* 1, p. 347. S. Kovalevskaya is indirectly quoting the words of Myshkin in *The Idiot*.

134 *M Anna*, p. 75 and also *Biography*, p. 214, where Strakhov gives Dostoyevsky's words about his sadness after the fit: 'He had the impression of being a criminal and that an unknown fault, a great crime was weighing on him.'

135 Obviously denotes a sexual relationship.

136 Underlined by us. *Zapisnyye tetradi F. M. Dostoyevskogo*, with commentary by N. I. Ignatova and Ye N. Konshina, Moscow–Leningrad, 1935, pp. 80–3.

137 'It has been established, on neurophysiological, anatomical and clinical grounds, that epileptic fits, even if repeated over a long period, do not cause injury related to the epileptic discharge which accompanies them and so do not cause mental weakening' (Article 'Epileptic dementia', in *Dictionnaire de l'Epilepsie* of the World Health Organisation, p. 46).

138 *Letters* 3, p. 208, *A* 29II, p. 80. For the forgetfulness, delay in correspondence and failure to recognise people which Dostoyevsky blamed on the illness, see also *Letters* 3, p. 283; *A* 28II, pp. 177–8: letter to L. A. Ozhigina, from St Petersburg, 17 December 1877, and *Letters* 4, pp. 14 and 30.

139 *Letters* 1, p. 241; *A* 28I, p. 318.

140 *Letters* I, p. 103; *A* 28I, p. 134.

141 *Letters* 1, p. 107; *A* 28I, p. 160.

142 *Letters* 1, p. 129; *A* 28I, p. 162.

143 *Letters* 1, p. 130; *A* 28I, p. 163.

144 *Letters* 1, p. 131; *A* 28I, p. 164.

145 *Letters* 1, p. 402; *A* 28II, p. 120.

146 See his rough draft, *Letters* 4, p. 338 and p. 472.

147 *Letters* 4, p. 33. Dostoyevsky was 52 in 1873.

148 *Letters* 2, p. 246; *A* 29II, p. 124: 'I know that I have not much longer to live, but not only do I not wish to die, but I still have the feeling that I am just beginning to live. I am not at all tired, but I am already 55, alas!'

149 *M Anna*, p. 227. The 'last novel' is *The Brothers Karamazov*.

150 *Letters* 4, p. 212.

151 *LH* 77, p. 342.

152 Comparison borrowed from Gustave Aucouturier in his preface to *The Double*, in *F. M. Dostoïevski. Récits, chroniques et polémiques*, Paris, 1969.

153 In psychiatric terms, the first would be neurotic, the second psychotic.

154 *A* 2, pp. 151–2.

155 *Letters* 1, p. 126; *A* 28I, p. 159.

156 *A* 3, pp. 425–6.

157 And even concentration, for example, as when driving a car.

158 Henri Baruk, *Traité de Psychiatrie*, Paris, 1959, 1, p. 716.

159 This is Alajouanine's thesis, disputed by H. Gastaut. For the latter, this is a common phenomenon, already described in normal subjects by writers. He quotes Charles Dickens who, in *David Copperfield* (read by Dostoyevsky), wrote:

> We have all had some experience of a sentiment which comes occasionally and during which we have the impression that what we say or do has been said or done before, that we have already been surrounded by the same people, the same objects, the same circumstances, that we know perfectly what is going to be said next as if we had suddenly remembered it.

160 *A* 1, p. 220.

161 Ibid. p. 269.
162 Ibid. p. 274.
163 Ibid. p. 281.
164 *A* 3, pp. 207–8. 'Mystic terror' is the phrase Dostoyevsky uses to describe the sequels of his fits in 1870.
165 Ibid. pp. 260, 370 and 422.
166 *A* 8, pp. 186–96.
167 Ibid. p. 195.
168 Ibid. p. 48.
169 Ibid. p. 188.
170 Ibid. p. 188.
171 Ibid. p. 188.
172 This is the opinion of T. Alajouanine, who compared the literary expression of ecstasy in the novels of Dostoyevsky with the poems of St John of the Cross ('Littérature et Epilepsie' in *Dostoïevski*, Cahiers de l'Herne 24, Paris, 1973, pp. 309–24).
173 This is the opinion of H. Gastaut, who doubts the existence of the ecstatic, or more generally euphoric, aura.

> In 25 years of my medical career devoted exclusively to epilepsy, I have come across very few cases of positively pleasant auras and I have never encountered a single case of ecstatic aura. This is also the experience of Lennox (1960) who, out of 1017 auras, found only 9 cases of pleasant auras (0.9%), out of which only a few expressed positive pleasure. It is also the case with Penfiels who, in six books or articles published from 1947 to 1958 concerning hundreds of cases of epilepsy of the temporal lobe examined neuro-surgically, quotes one single case, with Kristiansen (1951), of a pleasant feeling before the fit accompanied by epigastric discomfort and followed by perceptual illusion, about which he says, before quoting Dostoyevsky: It is rare for a patient to have an aura which he could describe as a pleasant experience. This is also the case with Alajouanine who, in two articles published in 1951 devoted to Dostoyevsky's epilepsy, says that he has only known, among his own patients, a single case of ecstatic aura.
>
> (H. Gastaut, 'L'Involontaire contribution de Dostoïevski à la symptomatologie et au pronostic de l'épilepsie', in *L'Evolution psychiatrique*, 44, 2, April–June 1979, 238)

174 Thomas de Quincey, *Confessions of an English Opium-Eater*, Harmondsworth, p. 33.
175 *A* 6, p. 221.
176 Ibid. This is the argument of the 'Ridiculous' man. Although he had his revelation of the Golden Age in a dream, he proclaims his faith in this Golden Age. Dreams have the same conviction as the phenomenon of illness.
177 Ibid.
178 It is possibly because of this similarity of method, though not of thought, between Dostoyevsky and surrealism, that Max Ernst invited Dostoyevsky to preside among the surrealists in his painting: *A meeting of friends* (1922). (See the commentary of Julien Gracq, interviewed by J. Catteau about the links between Dostoyevsky and surrealism in *Dostoïevski*, Cahiers de l'Herne, 24, Paris, 1973, p. 144.)

179 *A* 10, p. 39.
180 Ibid. p. 41.
181 Ibid. p. 43.
182 *A* 11, p. 260.
183 Ibid. p. 261.
184 *A* 10, p. 182.
185 J. Catteau, 'A propos de littérature fantastique: André Belyj, héritier de Gogol et de Dostoïevski', in *Cahiers du Monde russe et soviétique*, 3, III, 1962, 327–73.
186 Revelation, 10, 6.
187 Koran XVIII, 1.
188 *A* 8, p. 189.
189 'So everything depends on this: is Christ accepted as the final ideal on earth, i.e., on the Christian faith. If you believe in Christ, you believe that you will live for ever' (*LH* 83, p. 174).
190 *A* 1, pp. 277–8.
191 Specialists in epilepsy note an enrichment of the aura (in psychomotive epilepsy) as time goes on.
192 *A* 10, p. 450.
193 Matthew 22:30 and Mark 12:25.
194 *A* 10, p. 451.
195 Dostoyevsky himself stressed the link between reality and epilepsy considered from the viewpoint of extremist expression in art. In a draft of the letter of early December 1879 he replied to Saltykov-Shchedrin's attacks in the journal *Molva* (*Rumour*) of 12 and 18 October on *The Brothers Karamazov*. Among other arguments he challenged the statement: 'The Inquisitor (Ivan is cold.) Ideas like returning his ticket and the Grand Inquisitor seem to hint at epilepsy, at painful nights. – People will ask if you have noted yourself that it may be epileptic in origin.' And he replied: 'But if men like this exist, then how can one fail to describe them? Look around you, gentlemen, are explosions like this so unusual! The thing is finally that you understand nothing of the reality of life today and you do not wish to understand, and this is worst of all' (A. S. Dolinin (ed.), *F. M. Dostoyevsky, Materialy i issledovaniya*, Leningrad, 1935, p. 377).
196 *Complete Letters of Vincent van Gogh*, London, 1958, 3, p. 33.
197 Théophile Alajouanine, 'Dostoïevski épileptique', in *Le Nouveau Commerce*, 2, autumn–winter, 1963, 125.
198 Ibid. p. 126.
199 Epilepsy of the left temporal lobe (or psychomotive epilepsy) was only discovered in the forties in the twentieth century (Jasper and Kershman, 1941, and Gibbs and Fuster in 1948).
200 Théophile Alajouanine, 'Littérature et épilepsie. L'expression littéraire de l'extase dans les romans de Dostoïevski et dans les poèmes de Saint Jean de la Croix, in J. Catteau (ed.), *Dostoïevski*, Cahiers de l'Herne 24, Paris, 1973, p. 314.
201 Ibid.
202 H. Gastaut, 'Fyodor Mikhailovitch Dostoyevsky's involuntary contribution to the symptomatology and prognosis of epilepsy', *Epilepsia*, 19, New York, 1978, 186–201.
203 'Fear in itself' (Jackson), 'fear, vague alarm or profound terror' (Gowers), 'anguish, wish for death' (Voisin).

204 Dostoyevsky and his ecstatic aura have entered medical literature with the inaugural theses of P. G. Loygue, *Etude médico-psychologique de Dostoïevski. Considérations sur les états morbides liés au génie*, Lyon, 1903; of T. Segalov, *Die Krankheit Dostoewskis*, Heidelberg, 1906. Other important theses: J. Figuières, *L'Epilepsie dans l'œuvre de Dostoïevski*, Lyon, 1924 published Valence, 1942; L. Bercovici, *Dostoïevski. Etude de Psychopathologie*, Paris, 1933.

6 MONEY

1 *A* 13, p. 352.
2 In particular, by Sophie Ollivier in her valuable thesis *L'Argent chez Dostoïevski*, Aix-en-Provence, 1970. From now on referred to as S. Ollivier.
3 *Letters* 4, p. 224.
4 *Letters* 1, p. 53; *A* 281, p. 61.
5 *Letters* 1, pp. 242–57; *A* 281, pp. 94–9.
6 *Letters* 4, pp. 222–3.
7 *Letters* 1, pp. 358–60; *A* 28II, pp. 78–80.
8 *Letters* pp. 411–14; *A* 28II, pp. 129–33.
9 *Biography*, p. 221.
10 *Letters* 2, pp. 605–6; *A* 281, pp. 348–9.
11 *Biography*, p. 221.
12 *Letters* 1, pp. 333–4; *A* 28II, p. 51.
13 *Letters* 1, pp. 418–20; *A* 28II, pp. 136–9.
14 *Letters* 2, p. 252; *A* 291, p. 107.
15 *Letters* 2, p. 4; *A* 28II, p. 183.
16 *Letters* 2, p. 47; *A* 28II, pp. 226–7.
17 *Letters* 2, p. 61; *A* 28II, p. 241.
18 As a supporting document, Anna Grigoryevna shows the way in which a bill of change presented to Dostoyevsky worked: X, a mediocre writer, claimed 250 roubles in 1871 for a story which had previously appeared in *Time*, of which Mikhail was financial director. Dostoyevsky trustingly gave X a bill of change, without specifying the date on which the money could be collected. X in difficulties gave the letter to his landlady who hurriedly went to court about it. Dostoyevsky was indignant and X was embarrassed, but it was too late: money had to be borrowed at inflated interest to pay her. Eight years later, Anna discovered in the accounts book of *Time* a receipt signed by X, who had been paid by Mikhail when the story first appeared. Dostoyevsky was indignant, but sympathetic and understanding: 'I would not have believed that X was capable of deceiving me! When a man is in need, he can be brought to anything!' (*M Anna*, pp. 149–50).
19 Dostoyevsky resigned from the committee of this fund to help needy men of letters, since he was about to borrow money from it (*Letters* 1, p. 405; *A* 28II, p. 123).
20 *Letters* 1, p. 401; *A* 28II, p. 119.
21 *Letters* 1, p. 401; *A* 28II, pp. 119–20.
22 V. Shklovsky, opposing Ye. Shtackenschneyder who says that 6,000 roubles always represented a great sum of capital to Dostoyevsky, proves, with several examples, that the decisive sum was 3,000 roubles (Viktor Shklovsky, *Za i protiv (Zametki o Dostoyevskom)*, Moscow, 1957, p. 128).

23 *Life*, p. 150.
24 *Letters* 1, p. 438; *A* 28II, pp. 159–60. Dostoyevsky compares this clause to fire damage clauses in tenancy contracts: in case of misfortune, the charges are crushing. However, 'no use laughing at it', people always sign these contracts.
25 *Letters* 1, p. 436; *A* 28II, p. 157.
26 *Letters* 1, p. 437; *A* 28II, pp. 159–60.
27 *Letters* 1, p. 438; *A* 28II, p. 160.
28 *Letters* 1, p. 333; *A* 28II, p. 50.
29 *M* 1, p. 95.
30 A. E. Vrangel, *Vospominaniya o F. M. Dostoyevskom v Sibiri 1854–1856gg.*, Petersburg, 1912, p. 26.
31 L. P. Grossman says that before reaching Paris, Dostoyevsky won nearly 11,000 francs (*Life*, p. 116). This is a mistake: the 10,400 francs were won at Wiesbaden, in August 1863.
32 *Letters* 1, p. 324; *A* 28II, p. 40.
33 *Letters* 1, p. 330; *A* 28II, p. 45.
34 *Letters* 1, p. 330; *A* 28II, p. 45.
35 The noble motive that Dostoyevsky gives is not supported by facts: Mikhail died in 1864, while Dostoyevsky's passion for gambling began in 1863.
36 *Letters* 2, p. 348; *A* 29I, p. 199.
37 *M Anna*, p. 135.
38 Making Apollinariya the Polina of *The Gambler*, Dostoyevsky expressed the underlying link between the passion of love and the passion for gambling.
39 *Letters* 1, p. 403; *A* 28II, p. 121.
40 His wife and his brother Mikhail.
41 *Letters* 1, p. 398; *A* 28II, pp. 116–17.
42 *Life*, p. 144.
43 *M* 1, p. 370.
44 This does not seem to have been a very serious plan, as the notebooks for *A Raw Youth* show. Dostoyevsky establishes a parallel in the relationships between the young prince [Sokolsky] and the princess [Akhmakova] and those between Yelena Pavlovna and himself:

> He [Sokolsky] asks the advice of the princess (whose relations with him are like mine with Ye.P. while her husband was alive).
> (*LH* 77, pp. 268 and 296)

> The youth explains to Anna Andreyevna the story of Ye.P. It was a joke, I have first hand knowledge of it.　　(*LH* 77, p. 324)

As in the novel, Yelena Pavlovna probably dropped a mischievous 'perhaps' into the conversation, which did not commit her in any way.
45 *Letters* 2, p. 3; *A* 28II, p. 182.
46 The letters which he sent her during his cures abroad show a sexual harmony between them which Anna's modest censorship does not always conceal (*Letters* 4, pp. 83, 84–5, 87, 90). The letter of 28 August 1879, where Dostoyevsky writes of his 'enthusiasm for marriage which grows from year to year' is a good example:

> Show me any other marriage you like, where this feeling is as strong as ours, after twelve years of living together. My own enthusiasm and enchantment are inexhaustible. You will say that this is only one side and the most vulgar. No, it has nothing vulgar about it and, basically, all the rest depends on it.

But you refuse to understand this. To end this lecture, I solemnly swear that
I am burning to cover each tiny toe of your foot with kisses and I will come
and do it, you will see. You write: what if someone is reading our letter?
Well, let them read, let them be envious of us!   (*Letters* 4, p. 103)

47 *M Anna*, p. 135.

48 The image is Dostoyevsky's own:

I live under the influence of sensations which have just passed, under the
influences of fresh memories, under the influence of all that recent
whirlwind, which dragged me at the time into its vortex and tossed me out
again. Sometimes it seems to me that I am still whirling in this blizzard and
that the storm is about to rush by once more, catch me with its wing as it flies
by and again I will leap out of order and feeling of measure and I shall begin
to whirl round and round and round.   *The Gambler* (*A* 5, p. 281)

49 *Letters* 1, pp. 417–20; *A* 28II, pp. 136–9.

50 *Letters* 2, p. 19; *A* 28II, p. 198.

51 *Letters* 2, p. 55; *A* 28II, p. 235.

52 *Letters* 2, p. 105; *A* 28II, p. 286.

53 *Letters* 2, p. 106; *A* 28II, p. 286.

54 *Letters* 2, p. 110; *A* 28II, p. 290.

55 About 320,000 francs in 1971! (Based on calculations given in detail in J.
Catteau, *La Création littéraire chez Dostoïevski*, Paris, 1978, p. 198, note 1.)

56 *M Anna*, p. 150.

57 Ibid. p. 150.

58 Ibid. p. 151.

59 To such a point that in February 1870, he sketches the idea of a novel, never
written, with himself as a character: 'Novelist . . . In old age, but mainly from fits,
his faculties have become blunted and so he has fallen into beggary . . . All his life
he has written to order.' He then compares himself to Turgenev, Goncharov,
Pleshcheyev, Aksakov, Saltykov, the two counts Tolstoy, even Pisemsky and he
notes: 'This is worth 200 roubles a sheet, and I give it them free, and they think
that they are my benefactors' (*A* 12, p. 5).

60 *M Anna*, pp. 150–1.

61 *Letters* 1, p. 97; *A* 28I, p. 128.

62 *Letters* 1, p. 115; *A* 28I, p. 147.

63 *Letters* 4, p. 262–3; *A* 28I, p. 296.

64 *Letters* 2, p. 595; *A* 28II, p. 319.

65 *Letters* 1, pp. 245–6; *A* 28I, p. 325.

66 *Letters* 1, p. 260; *A* 28I, p. 343.

67 *Letters* 1, p. 333; *A* 28II, p. 50.

68 About *The Idiot*, *Letters* 2, p. 141; *A* 28II, p. 321.

69 About *Life of a Great Sinner*, *Letters* 2, p. 255; *A* 29I, pp. 109–10.

70 *Letters* 2, p. 283; *A* 29I, p. 136.

71 About *A Raw Youth*, *Letters* 3, p. 180; *A* 29II, p. 46.

72 *Letters* 2, p. 220; *A* 29I, p. 70.

73 *M Anna*, p. 150.

74 These figures do not mean much without taking the cost of living into account.
From 1840 to 1850 a free weaver received a daily wage of 1 to 1.5 bank roubles
(the bank rouble equalled 28.5 silver kopecks) and a measure of rye of about 210
litres (*chetvert'*) cost 5 bank roubles (or 1.425 silver roubles). In 1855 the wage of

a building worker was 10.7 kopecks and in 1860 114.2 kopecks per day (S. T. Strumilin, *Ocherki ekonomicheskoy istorii Rossii*, Moscow, 1960, p. 107), or if we take, for 1859, the average of 1 rouble per day and 300 days' work: 300 roubles a year.

75 *M Anna*, pp. 174–5. What were the expenses of the Dostoyevsky household and the cost of living? Two series of documents give an approximate idea: the letters and the notebooks which are also used as account books. The letter of 23 December 1868, from Florence, gives an overall picture: 'We have spent for this whole period [March 1867–December 1868] 2,000 roubles a year on average, which we would never have been able to do in Petersburg' (*Letters* 2, p. 149; A 28II, p. 328). Extrapolating, we may estimate that 3,000 roubles a year were needed to live comfortably, if not luxuriously, in Russia.

76 *Letters* 1, p. 76; A 28I, p. 107.

77 *Letters* 1, p. 78; A 28I, p. 109.

78 *Letters* 1, p. 436; A 28II, p. 157.

79 A 4, p. 66.

80 Ibid.

81 *Letters* 4, p. 281–2; A 28II, p. 167. It is true that in this letter Dostoyevsky protests against Katkov censoring the chapter with the famous scene where Sonya and Raskolnikov read the Gospel.

82 The original version has been lost. It is probable that Raskolnikov's revolt was more violent and that Sonya, who had carried 'self-sacrifice to the point of sacrificing her own body', was implicitly compared to Christ, which would have caused great scandal. V. Ya. Kirpotin makes the gratuitous hypothesis that Sonya, at the end of the scene, gave herself to Raskolnikov (V. Ya. Kirpotin, *Razocharovaniye i krusheniye Rodiona Raskol'nikova*, Moscow, 1970, pp. 167–8).

83 The coarse word: *kal* (*Letters* 4, p. 54), the bold phrase 'the hysterical yelping of the cherubim' (ibid. p. 190), the poetic expression of Zosima, inspired by Tikhon of Zadonsk and the travelling monk Parfyony (ibid. pp. 91–2), the popular song noted from life (ibid. p. 54, and p. 119), the concrete details: school uniform (Ibid. p. 135), the exact age of Krasotkin (ibid. pp. 137–8).

84 *Letters* 4, p. 282; A 28II, p. 167.

85 Dostoyevsky did take up the whole ending of *A Weak Heart* thirteen years later (1848–61) in 'Petersburg Dreams in Verse and Prose'. This is one of the few cases where he uses work again, in an article he wrote from necessity, although the symbol studied by V. Shklovsky, the threat of the city, is a recurrent theme, present in both *Crime and Punishment*, and *A Raw Youth* (Viktor Shklovsky, *Za i protiv. Zametki o Dostoyevskom*, Moscow, 1957, pp. 70–3).

86 *Letters* 2, p. 228; A 29I, pp. 77–8.

87 *Letters* 2, p. 255; A 29I, pp. 109–10.

88 *Letters* 2, p. 257; A 29I, p. 12.

89 L. N. Tolstoy, *Polnoye sobraniye sochineniy*, 46, Moscow–Leningrad, 1934, p: 189.

90 A. G. Tseytlin, *Povesti o bednom chinovnike Dostoyevskogo*, Moscow, 1923.

91 Devushkin is formed from *devushka* (a young girl); Golyadkin from *golyadka* (bareness, beggary); Prokharchin from *prokharchit'* (spend money on food *kharchi*); Shumkov from *shumok* (little noise); Marmeladov from *marmelad*, which means both jam and confusion in French.

92 Except for the rare army men, some high officials and Kirillov in *The Devils*, a builder of bridges who dreams of destroying society.

93 The monthly salary of a clerk did not vary much: it could be 10 roubles ('A shocking affair', 'The Eternal Husband'), 17 roubles (*The Idiot*), 23 roubles 40 kopecks (*Crime and Punishment*), 25 roubles ('A Weak Heart'), and 35 roubles (*The Devils*). A teacher's salary was about 80 roubles (1,000 roubles a year, *Crime and Punishment*), a tutor's less than 60 roubles (700 roubles a year, *The Gambler*), a secretary's 50 roubles (*A Raw Youth*). Some prices: renting a room, from 3 to 6 roubles a month; a furlined coat 25 roubles; a uniform 11.50 roubles; a cheap waistcoat and trousers 2.25 roubles; a bottle of champagne, almost 9 roubles; a volume of Pushkin 7.50 roubles.

94 S. Ollivier, p. 137.

95 *A* 14, p. 105.

96 *A* 13, p. 306. 'See what they are capable of, these proud people, in their high society, for money!' Lambert exclaims in the youth's dream (ibid.).

97 *A* 22, p. 30.

98 *A* 23, p. 160.

99 *A* 8, p. 254.

100 *A* 25, p. 62.

101 The wanderer Makar Ivanych is the most completely formed type of this ideal; his surname Dolgoruky, the name of illustrious princes, is like a summons calling the forgetful nobility back to its duties.

102 Nikolay Berdyayev, *Mirosozertsaniye Dostoevskogo*, Paris, 1968, p. 141.

103 N. K. Mikhaylovsky, *Polnoye sobraniye sochineniy*, St Petersburg, 1909, vol. 4, pp. 40–1.

104 *A* 10, p. 64. For the attitude of the socialists towards money, see S. Ollivier, pp. 256–76.

105 *LH* 77, p. 280.

106 Ibid. p. 280. 'Vasin. I need nothing, not a single rouble extra. Vasin dressed in gold and Vasin as he is – is all the same.'

107 In the notebooks for *A Raw Youth*, Dostoyevsky returns to this theme twice. In August–September 1874: 'THE IDEA: "FATHERS AND SONS" – SONS and FATHERS. For the son, who intends to be a Rothschild is in reality an *idealist*, i.e., a new occurrence, as an unexpected consequence of nihilism' (*LH* 77, p. 94). And at a more advanced stage, in October 1874, this fragment of a reply attributed to the future Versilov: 'You, a future Rothschild (He says to the youth). Of course an idealist – and here is a new consequence for you of positivism and that wretched nihilism' (ibid., p. 222).

108 *A* 23, pp. 95–9.

109 Arkadiy, the hero of *A Raw Youth*, quotes these last lines to explain his 'Rothschild' idea.

110 Viktor Shklovsky, *Za i protiv. Zametki o Dostoyevskom*, Moscow, 1957, p. 70.

111 *A* 1, p. 257.

112 *A* 19, p. 72.

113 Ibid. p. 74.

114 *A* 26, p. 122. Nekrasov, whose love of money was noted by contemporaries, had made money at gambling and by editing *The Contemporary* and *Annals of the Fatherland*. Before the passage quoted, Dostoyevsky gives some more verses from the 'attempt at a modern ballad', *The Secret* (1855), which is about the hero's poverty-stricken youth and his present millions.

115 *LH* 86, p. 84.
116 Arkadiy himself says that his thought is 'daring and (consequently) voluptuous'.
117 *A* 5, p. 78.
118 Ibid. p. 229.
119 The theme of Pushkin's miserly knight appears in the notebooks of *Crime and Punishment*: it is the character of Luzhin who was to have been a more developed character than he is in the final novel: 'In his avarice there is something of Pushkin's miserly knight. He has bowed down to money, for everything perishes, but money will not perish; I, says he, am from a low rank, and I want to be at the top of the ladder and dominate' (*A* 7, p. 159).
120 *A* 8, p. 105. Ptitsyn is formed from *ptitsa* (bird).
121 Ibid.
122 *A* 13, p. 74.
123 Ibid.
124 Ibid.
125 Ibid. pp. 74–5.
126 Ibid. pp. 76–7.
127 'SAVING MONEY IS ONLY A POETIC IDEA' (*LH* 77, p. 99).
128 The perspicacious Versilov understands this when he mocks Arkadiy by quoting the first line of a popular song:
'Don't worry, my friend, I know what the point of your idea is; in any case, it's this:
"I am going away to the desert."'
(*A* 13, p. 90)
129 *A* 13, p. 76. 'Like the raven in the desert (*kak vran*)': allusion to 1 Kings 17:4, where the Lord orders Elijah to go east of Jordan and commands the ravens to feed him.
130 *A* 13, p. 68.
131 Ibid. p. 70.
132 Ibid.
133 Here a revealing word is crossed out: 'farming out'.
134 *A* 11, p. 155.
135 The tipsy youth recalls the famous saying of the Girondin Brissot, taken up by Proudhon: 'La propriété, c'est le vol!' (Property is theft!) (*A* 13, p. 361). The saying is noted again in the notebooks for *The Devils* (p. 11, p. 64).
136 Before deciding on the title of *A Raw Youth*, Dostoyevsky had considered other titles, such as 'Taking up a career', 'Disorder', etc. (*LH* 77, p. 114).
137 'Decomposition is the main visible idea of the novel' (*LH* 77, p. 69). 'The whole idea of the novel is to develop the idea that now disorder is general, disorder is everywhere and in everything, in society, in its affairs' (ibid. p. 129).
138 *A* 13, p. 69.
139 Dostoyevsky was inspired by a trial reported by *The Voice* (1874, no. 46 and following): the issuing of false railway shares for the Tambov–Kozlov line. The chief defendant, the gynaecologist Kolosov, had already been in gaol. Among his followers he pretended to be an agent of the Third Section, who had been ordered to get in touch with Marx and seize the nihilists Nechayev and Serebryanikov. Stebel'kov, formed from *stebel'* (stalk) was a clear imitation of Kolosov, formed from *kolos* (ear of corn).
140 *LH* 77, p. 112.

141 S. Ollivier uses the word 'Quicksilver', in comparison with A. N. Ostrovsky's play of the same name (S. Ollivier, pp. 393–5).

142 Ibid. pp. 59–62.

143 *A* 3, p. 84.

144 *A* 14, p. 193.

145 Viktor Shklovsky, *Za i protiv. Zametki o Dostoyevskom*, Moscow, 1957, p. 128.

146 In the notebooks of the end of 1869 to the beginning of 1870, an unwritten plan stresses this theme: 'Extract from a story about a young man. Three thousand roubles found and reported. The other person shouted at him and gave 25 roubles. Through poverty he accepted them. He could not *refuse*. He and his wife, though dreadfully poor, decide to give them back. He tore up the note and threw it in his face' (*A* 9, p. 120).

147 *A* 8, p. 146.

148 *A* 8, p. 146.

149 Ibid. p. 144.

150 Stebelkov's slanders, which present Versilov as a lover of poor young girls, have an influence on the desperate action of Olya. But Versilov is also responsible: he has done too much by offering 60 roubles to Olya as well as trying to find work for her. When Arkadiy asks: 'If it hadn't been for Stebelkov, perhaps it wouldn't have happened?' Vasin replies: 'Who knows? It would certainly have happened. You can't judge in that way, everything was ready for it' (*A* 13, p. 147).

151 An alliance symbolised by the 'copper red' moon lighting the scene of the repeated murder of the old woman in Raskolnikov's dream (*A* 6, p. 213).

152 *A* 9, p. 107.

7 THE WRITER AT WORK

1 *M Anna*, pp. 68–9 and note 1, p. 69.

2 *Biography*, p. 43.

3 *Letters* 2, p. 358 and commentaries of A. S. Dolinin, p. 509 (*A* 291, p. 208).

4 See note 15 to chapter 5 of this book.

5 A study has been made for 'episodes of childhood' by V. S. Pushkaryova in *F. M. Dostoyevsky–N. A. Nekrasov (sbornik nauchnykh trudov)*, Leningrad, 1974, pp. 41–56.

6 *Letters* 4, p. 201. This refers to *The Brothers Karamazov*.

7 Ibid.

8 *M* 1, p. 131.

9 *A* 3, pp. 425–6.

10 A. E. Vrangel', *Vospominaniya o F. M. Dostoyevskom v Sibiri 1854–1856gg.*, Petersburg, 1912, pp. 23–4.

11 This is the reason for V. S. Nechayeva's purely formal distinction between notebooks (*zapisnyye knizhki*) and work books (*rabochiye tetradi*) in her description of the manuscripts. V. S. Nechayeva, *Opisaniye rukopisey F. M. Dostoyevskogo*, Moscow, 1957, p. 24.

12 *Letters* 2, p. 72; *A* 28II, p. 252.

13 Now Dostoyevsky Street. The apartment became the Dostoyevsky Museum of Leningrad in 1971, on the 150th anniversary of the writer's birth.

14 *M Anna*, p. 196.
15 Description taken from Zubchaninov's engraving, made from a photograph in 1881. *Fyodor Mikhaylovich Dostoyevsky v portretakh, illyustratsiyakh, dokumentakh*, ed. V. S. Nechayeva, Moscow, 1972, p. 369.
16 *Dostoyevsky v izobrazhenii yego docheri L. Dostoyevskoy*, ed. A. G. Gornfel'd, Moscow–Leningrad, 1922, 82.
17 L. P. Grossman, *Seminariy po Dostoyevskomu*, Moscow–Petrograd, 1922, p. 58. Anna notes Dostoyevsky's love of fine pens and good paper, which he gives to his hero Myshkin.
18 'Dostoyevsky did not like lamps and preferred to write by the light of two candles' (Lyubov Dostoyevskaya, *Dostoyevsky v izobrazhenii*, p. 84).
19 Sometimes leaving a brief note of instruction to his wife, such as a note of 1 February 1871, written at quarter to five in the morning, where he asks her 'not to recopy what he had dictated to her the previous evening' since he had decided to scrap that passage (*Letters* 2, p. 321; *A* 291, p. 177).
20 Lyubov Dostoyevskaya, *Dostoyevsky v izobrazhenii*, p. 81. This phobia about stains, yellow as it happens, appears in the novels, e.g. in *Notes from Underground* (*A* 5, pp. 140–1).
21 *M Anna*, p. 31.
22 Ibid. pp. 194–5.
23 Lyubov Dostoyevskaya, *Dostoyevsky v izobrazhenii*, p. 83.
24 *M Anna*, p. 73.
25 L. M. Rozenblyum, 'Tvorcheskaya laboratoriya Dostoyevskogo-romanista', in *LH* 77, p. 52.
26 Ibid. p. 50.
27 V. V. Rozanov, *Legenda o velikom inkvizitore F. M. Dostoyevskogo*, St Petersburg, 1906, p. 47.
28 Ibid. p. 48.

8 THE GREAT DIALOGUE: THE NEWS ITEM

1 Anna Grigoryevna is more accurate than Dostoyevsky in this case, as he only mentioned *The Voice* and *The Moscow Bulletin*. She writes: 'He used to go to the café in Mont-Blanc Street and would spend two hours reading *The Voice*, *The Moscow Bulletin*, *The St Petersburg Bulletin*. He also read the foreign press' (*M Anna*, p. 113). In her diary for 1867 she mentions *L'Indépendance Belge* (A. G. Dostoyevskaya, *Dnevnik 1867g.*, Moscow, 1923, p. 36).
2 *Letters* 2, pp. 37, 64, 72; *A* 28II, pp. 216–17, 244, 252.
3 'Geneva Diary' of Anna Grigoryevna in *LH* 86, p. 199.
4 Ibid. p. 215.
5 Communications between Russia and Europe were fairly rapid at the time. A Moscow newspaper could be found in Geneva only two days after it first appeared.
6 *A* 9, p. 140.
7 Ibid. p. 141.
8 Ibid. p. 143.
9 Ibid. p. 145.
10 In 1860, seven years before, Dostoyevsky had thought of writing a story called 'Mignon' (*A* 3, p. 447). It was never written, but Nelli in *The Insulted and*

Injured is possibly Nelly Trent of *The Old Curiosity Shop* fused with Goethe's heroine.

11 *A* 8, p. 94.

12 Ibid. p. 161.

13 *A* 9, p. 269. Dostoyevsky's plan may be compared with Truman Capote's *In Cold Blood* (1967), which is based on similar murders reported in the press.

14 *A* 8, p. 190.

15 Ibid. p. 236 and p. 279.

16 Ibid. p. 237.

17 Ibid. p. 183.

18 This is probably the origin of the Idiot's name.

19 Anna Grigoryevna confirms the origin of this passage of *The Idiot*, in L. P. Grossman, *Seminariy po Dostoyevskomu*, Moscow–Petrograd, 1922, p. 59.

20 V. S. Dorovatovskaya-Lyubimova, '*Idiot* Dostoyevskogo i ugolovnaya khronika yego vremeni', *Pechat' i revolyutsiya*, 3, 1928, 31–53.

21 *A* 8, p. 184.

22 Ibid. p. 380.

23 Ibid. p. 504.

24 Dorovatovskaya-Lyubimova, '*Idiot*', p. 38.

25 *A* 8, pp. 412–13.

26 *Letters* 2, pp. 169–70; *A* 29II, p. 19.

27 Jean-Paul Sartre, 'L'alibi', in *Le Nouvel Observateur*, 19 November 1964.

28 *Letters* 2, p. 43; *A* 28II, p. 223.

29 *A* 22, p. 91.

30 I. I. Lapshin, 'Obrazovaniye tipa Krafta v *Podrostke*', in A. L. Bem (ed.), *O Dostoyevskom*, I, Prague, 1929, pp. 140–4.

31 *LH* 77, pp. 492–5.

32 Ibid. p. 60 and pp. 445–6.

33 *A* 4, p. 195. B. G. Reizov, 'K istorii Brat'yev Karamazovykh'' in *Iz istorii yevropeyskikh literatur*, Leningrad, 1970, pp. 129–38. There may be the objection that this tragic judicial error was not an item published in the Press and that Dostoyevsky only learnt the truth about his fellow-prisoner by a letter sent from Omsk in 1860 and unfortunately lost. But the 'communication' has all the characteristics of the press: correspondence of reader with author, surprise effect, veracity of the document.

34 *Letters* 4, p. 53.

35 *A* 23, p. 144.

36 Dostoyevsky, in spite of his love for the people, never stopped denouncing peasant brutality. In the first drafts of *A Raw Youth*, he notes a case read in *The Moscow Bulletin* for 26 February 1874 entitled 'Correspondence from Bakhmut'. To punish his wife, a peasant had harnessed her to a cart and whipped her almost to death (*LH* 77, p. 59).

37 *A* 21, p. 20.

38 Ibid.

39 Ibid.

40 'At the corner of Sadovaya and Ascension Avenue I came across an hotel; as I knew there were newspapers there, I went in to read what the papers said about the murder of the old woman under the heading of daily news . . . I had just gone in and asked for a glass of tea and *The Voice*, when I noticed . . .' (*A* 7, pp. 74–6).

41 F. M. Dostoyevsky, *Prestupleniye i nakazaniye*, Literaturnyye pamyatniki, Moscow, 1970, p. 779.

42 *The Voice* 1866 (no. 2), 1867 (nos. 24, 49, 52, 66, 303), 1868 (nos. 77, 110, 115, etc.). Dostoyevsky in the third plan for *The Idiot* entitled 'new and last plan' of mid October 1867, returned to the Danilov affair: one of the sons in the general's family is a murderer (*A* 9, p. 154).

43 In fact, at the trial on 22 November 1867, it was learnt that Danilov had forced Glazkov to accuse himself.

44 *Letters* 2, pp. 150–1; *A* 28ii, p. 323.

45 *Letters* 2, pp. 161–2; *A* 291, p. 11.

46 *Letters* 2, p. 44; *A* 28ii, p. 224.

47 There is no contradiction between the two projects. The second, *Diary of a Writer*, in which there are innumerable references to the press, is a personal commentary on the first.

48 It is striking that Anna Grigoryevna, who confirmed that Liza's idea was a project of Dostoyevsky's own, repeated the terms of the letter of 6 February 1869: 'Fyodor Mikhaylovich was thinking of a similar literary enterprise and he was convinced that a book of this sort would sell many copies. He asked me to be his colleague in classifying press-cuttings' (L. P. Grossman, *Seminariy po Dostoyevskomu*, Moscow–Petrograd, 1922, p. 62). She did not relate this to *Diary of a Writer*.

49 *A* 10, p. 103.

50 Ibid. p. 104.

51 Ibid.

52 *A* 14, p. 218.

53 This is an original plan about marital misunderstanding.

> Underground type, could not stand jealousy. NB. Widower, the first wife is dead. He found and chose an orphan girl specially to be more peaceful. He is a real underground man, he has had many blows in his life. He is embittered. Extreme vanity . . . His wife cannot help noticing that he is educated, but she noticed later that he is not highly educated; each sneer (he takes everything as a sneer) irritates him, he is touchy. When he realises that she was not thinking of laughing, he is terribly glad. At the theatre and at the meeting, once only . . . He spied on the lover through the courtyard window. Received a slap on the face in his wife's presence. . . . NB. At one time real love began between himself and his wife. But he wounded her heart.
>
> (*A* 9, p. 119)

In this plan the husband killed his wife: 'After the Bible he knifed her.'

54 *The Voice*, 2 October 1876 (272).

55 *A* 23, p. 146.

56 Ibid. p. 145: 'We only know of obvious daily events, and only by what we see, but ends and beginnings for the time being are still unreal to man.'

9 THE GREAT DIALOGUE: MIGRANT IMAGES

1 Paragraph entitled: 'The natural apple', attacking the aesthetics of Chernyshevsky in the notebook of 1864–5 (*LH* 83, p. 286).

2 Dostoyevsky frequently mentioned *Othello* and *Hamlet* and noted down the date of Shakespeare's birth and death: '23 April (Shakespeare)' (*A* 9, p. 266), in the

notebooks for *The Idiot*. He had read *Much Ado about Nothing*, whose main characters, Beatrice and Benedict, are mentioned in *A Little Hero* (*A* 2, p. 280). All this is in favour of this interpretation, and the idea that 'Hero' is an abbreviation of 'heroine' is less plausible.

3   The prince *simply and clearly* (Othello) tells her why he has fallen in love with her, that it is not simple compassion (as Rogozhin told her and which Ippolit used to torment her), but love and she ought to calm down . . . Here Aglaya enters, calmly, *majestically and simply* mournful, says that she is to blame for everything, that she was not worthy of the Prince's love . . . *that she fell in love with the Prince for such a reason* (Othello here too).

(*A* 9, pp. 284–5)

4   'The woman in black passes. Heroine from the novel by Grech' (*A* 9, p. 265). *The Woman in Black* by N. I. Grech, editor of the conservative journal *Son of the Fatherland*, was written in 1834. The hero of the novel, Prince Kemsky, is, like Myshkin, idealistic, good, gentle and pure. He is haunted all his life by the vision of a woman in black. When he was a child, he saw her fling herself from the balcony into a cart of plague victims, in which was the body of her betrothed. At each crucial moment of his existence, the woman in black appears to him. Dostoyevsky has transposed this theme in the final scenes of his novel, when Myshkin and Rogozhin think they hear someone walking (*A* 8, p. 506) and in Myshkin's dream before his meeting with Nastasya Filippovna (*A* 8, pp. 381–2).

5   L. P. Grossman, *Seminariy po Dostoyevskomu*, Moscow–Petrograd, 1922, p. 10.

6   To support his remark, he quotes Goethe, who gives Lotte's literary opinions in the letters of young Werther (V. Shklovsky, *Za i protiv*, Moscow, 1957, p. 29).

7   *Letters* 1, p. 86; *A* 281, p. 117.

8   Ratazyayev is formed from *rotozey* (literally, some one who has his mouth wide open; gawk, gaper).

9   *A* 1, p. 52.

10 Ibid. pp. 52–3.

11 Ibid. p. 53.

12 Numerous imitators of Gogol multiplied what Tynyanov called Gogol's 'verbal masks', such as Ivan Ivanovich/Ivan Nikiforovich, Uncle Mityay/Uncle Minyay, Kifa Mokevich/Mokiy Kifovich.

13 V. V. Vinogradov, *Evolyutsiya russkogo naturalizma. Gogol' i Dostoyevsky*, Leningrad, 1929, pp. 329–30.

14 Pushkin's *Tales of the late Ivan Petrovich Belkin*, lent by Varenka.

15 *A* 1, p. 59.

16 Ibid.

17 Ibid.

18 Ibid.

19 But not his verbal mask, which is continuously evoked by the theme of shoes. Bashmachkin is formed from *bashmak* (shoe).

20 *A* 1, p. 63.

21 Thérèse and Faldoni, the virtuous (and unfortunate) hero and heroine of a sentimental novel by N. G. Léonard (1744–93): *Lettres de deux amans habitants de Lyon* (1783), translated by M. T. Kachenovsky, published in 1804 and 1816 in Moscow, and imitated by M. Voskresensky in his novel *Thérèse and Faldoni on the banks of the Moskva* (*Literary Gazette*, 7 and 8, 1847), among others.

22 V. V. Vinogradov, *Evolyutsiya russkogo naturalizma*.
23 *A* 23, p. 24.
24 *A* 23, p. 26.
25 Referring to *Poor Folk*, and related by Dostoyevsky in *A* 25, pp. 30–1.
26 *A* 8, p. 207.
27 Ibid. p. 206.
28 *A* 10, p. 36.
29 Ibid. p. 148.
30 *A* 13, pp. 75–6.
31 *A* 15, p. 28.
32 N. N. Strakhov, Dostoyevsky's fellow-worker, was very interested in Claude Bernard and wrote an article 'Claude Bernard and the experimental method' (*Annals of the Fatherland*, 1866), referring to Bernard's *Introduction à l'étude de la médecine expérimentale*.
33 'Yevgeniy Onegin', chapter 2, stanza XIV.
34 *A* 6, p. 211.
35 *A* 5, p. 133.
36 Ibid.
37 Viktor Shklovsky, *Za i protiv*, Moscow, 1957, p. 70.
38 *A* 10, p. 23.
39 Ibid. p. 264.
40 Ibid.
41 Ibid. p. 372.
42 Ibid. pp. 372–3.
43 Ibid. p. 373.
44 N. G. Chernyshevsky, *Sobraniye sochineniy v pyati tomakh*, Moscow, 4, 1974, p. 116.
45 Ibid. p. 48. In the criticism which Chernyshevsky made of his own thesis, there is another ironic comparison between 'a real apple' and the 'adamantine and rubescent fruits of the gardens of Aladdin' (ibid. p. 127).
46 This is the phrase which S. A. Levitsky attributes to Chernyshevsky and which he gives as a quotation from the thesis, where it does not exist: 'A real apple is worth more than a painted apple for it can be crunched, while the other can only be admired, as it rouses your appetite' (S. A. Levitsky, *Ocherki po istorii russkoy filosofskoy i obshchestvennoy mysli*, Frankfurt/Main, 1968, pp. 97).
47 *A* 20, p. 102.
48 *LH* 83, p. 150.
49 Ibid. p. 183.
50 Manuscript of the Lenin Library, 'F. Dostoyevsky', 1.3.5. A fragment intended for the article which was written as 'A necessary explanation' (*Epoch*, July 1864).
51 *A* 18, pp. 93–4.
52 *A* 18, p. 99.
53 '"Pisarev was an intelligent and noble man", Shatov again interrupted brusquely, lowering his eyes' (*A* 11, p. 171).
54 *Russkoye slovo*, no. 5, 1865. The complete text, for it was cut in the first edition of Pisarev's works in 1867, may be read in D. I. Pisarev, *Izbrannyye proizvedeniya*, Leningrad, 1968, pp. 367–85, 562–72.
55 Dostoyevsky, who loved a challenge, chose a 'sybarite and parasite', Stepan Trofimovich, to defend Pushkin in *The Devils*.

56 D. I. Pisarev, *Polnoye sobraniye v 6-ti tomakh*, St Petersburg, 4, 1894, p. 192. *Sapozhnik* (cobbler) has been translated as boot-maker, since the word is formed from *sapog* (boot).

57 V. A. Zaytsev, *Izbrannyye sochineniya*, 1, Moscow, 1934, p. 216.

58 *Russkoye slovo*, no. 3, 1864, p. 64. Zaytsev's anti-aestheticism was total: he rejected Aeschylus, Molière, Shakespeare and Schiller out of hand, whereas Pisarev spared Shakespeare as well as Turgenev, because of Bazarov, hero of *Fathers and Sons*.

59 Discovered in 1820.

60 V. A. Zaytsev, *Izbrannyye sochineniya*, p. 172.

61 The word used by Zaytsev is *zolotar'* which has a dual meaning in Russian: 'jeweller' and 'cesspit cleaner'.

62 *Epokha*, 5, 1864, 274–94.

63 Dostoyevsky combined *shchedryy* (recalling Shchedrin, generous) and *dar* (gift).

64 Puns, *The Opportunist* (*Svoyevremennik*) suggests that *The Contemporary* (*Sovremennik*) only follows fashionable ideas in a demagogic way. *The Foreign Word*, instead of *The Russian Word*, is an accusation: the journal is in the pay of foreigners, and this is causing all the trouble. Skribov (from 'scribe', a Western term) is a pun on Pisarev (formed from *pisar'*: scribe): Krolichkov (from *krolik*: rabbit) is a sneer at Zaytsev (formed from *zayats*: hare).

65 *A* 20, p. 102.

66 *Kraft und Stoff* (*Force and Matter*) (1855), written by the German materialist philosopher Ludwig Büchner and then banned in Russia, was one of the favourite books of the 'new men' and nihilists. In *Fathers and Sons* Arkadiy lends it to his father, on the advice of Bazarov.

67 *A* 20, p. 102.

68 *LH* 83, p. 248.

69 Dostoyevsky uses the word with a French sound, *petroley*, and not the technical terms: *petroleum* or the more widely used *neft'* (petrol).

70 N. I. Solov'yov, 'Teoriya bezobraziya' in *Epokha*, 8, 1864, 1–16. Cf. the commentary of V. S. Nechayeva, *Zhurnal M. M. i F. M. Dostoyevskikh 'Epokha' 1864–1865*, Moscow, 1975, pp. 198–205.

71 *A* 6, p. 285.

72 Jacques Catteau, 'Du Palais de cristal à l'âge d'or ou les avatars de l'utopie', in *Dostoïevski*, Cahiers de l'Herne, 24, Paris, 1973, pp. 176–95.

73 *A* 8, pp. 309–12.

74 *A* 13, p. 173. The dialogue between Versilov and Arkadiy in the novel is as follows:
> 'Well, changing stones into bread – that is a great thought.' – 'Is it the greatest? No, really, you've shown me the way; tell me then: is it the greatest?' – 'It is very great, my friend, very great, but not the greatest; it is great, but secondary, only great at a particular moment; if a man has had his fill of eating, he will forget it: on the contrary, he will immediately say: "Well now I've eaten my fill, what is there to do now?"'

The passage between the image of 'wagons bringing bread to starving humanity' and the Biblical symbol of 'stones changed into bread' may be seen in the notebooks for *A Raw Youth*. The reasoning is the same as in the dialogue just quoted. But instead of the single Biblical image, two images are used: that of the wagons, from the previous novel, and that of the Bible, which occurs in both the novels to come, *A Raw Youth* and *The Brothers Karamazov* (*LH* 77, p. 128).

75 In Dresden, Dostoyevsky had immediately purchased the works of Herzen, which were banned in Russia (*M Anna*, p. 103 and A. G. Dostoyevskaya, *Dnevnik 1867g.*, Moscow, 1923, pp. 17, 29, 46, 177). In Geneva, Dostoyevsky, thanks to N. P. Ogaryov, the revolutionary poet and friend of Herzen, went on reading Herzen with even more enthusiasm and interest. In her *Geneva Diary* Anna Grigoryevna says: 'He brought four books of *My Past and Thoughts* which Ogaryov had given him' (*LH* 86, p. 246).

76 *Polyarnaya Zvezda*, 6, pp. 259–72.

77 This destiny fascinated Dostoyevsky. In *Life of a Great Sinner* the hero becomes a Jesuit at one point.

78 The Raw Youth is to use the same phrase (*A* 13, p. 49).

79 A. I. Herzen, *Byloye i Dumy*, 2, Moscow, 1962, p. 513.

80 Ibid. pp. 514–15.

81 Ibid. p. 517.

82 Matthew 4:3; Luke 4:3. Making the Grand Inquisitor an ally of the Tempter, Dostoyevsky was perhaps remembering Botticelli's painting *The Temptation of Jesus* in the Sistine chapel; the devil is shown as a hermit. Vanquished and thrown down from the top of the mountain, his monk's habit falls off and shows his forked feet.

83 It was in *Diary of a Writer*, 1876 (May), with reference to the suicide of a midwife Pisareva, that Dostoyevsky used the image of 'stones changed to bread' once more. A reader, V. A. Alekseyev, asked him on 3 June 1876 exactly what the phrase meant, and on 7 June Dostoyevsky replied with a detailed letter which forms a valuable commentary on the theme developed in *The Brothers Karamazov* 1879 (*Letters* 3, pp. 211–12; *A* 29II, pp. 84–5).

84 *A* 8, p. 311.

10 THE PLAY OF DIALOGUE

1 Francois Mauriac, *Le Romancier et ses personnages*, Paris, s.d., pp. 95–6.

2 *A* 19, p. 71.

3 Ibid.

4 Ibid.

5 Ibid.

6 Ibid.

7 Ibid. p. 72.

8 Ibid. p. 73.

9 The term 'fantastic' is also used to designate the improbability of the literary procedure, as Dostoyevsky uses it in the introduction to 'A Gentle Soul' (*A* 24, pp. 5–6).

10 *A* 19, p. 73.

11 Ibid.

12 *A* 13, pp. 66 and 76. Arkadiy notes that the episode has been related in the Press.

13 *A* 19, p. 74.

14 François Mauriac, *Le Romancier et ses personnages*, p. 109.

15 *A* 19, p. 74. *La Vie d'un joueur*, or more fully *Trente ans ou la vie d'un joueur*, is a

melodrama by Victor Ducange, 1827. It was very successful when it appeared in St Petersburg in 1828.

16 *A* 19, p. 74.
17 Ibid.

11 THE UNITY OF THOUGHT IN THE NOVEL

1 O. Mandel'stam, *Razgovor o Dante*, Moscow, 1967, p. 19.
2 *A* 26, pp. 129–36.
3 *A* 18, p. 14.
4 *A* 18, p. 15.
5 *A* 2, pp. 95–101.
6 *A* 1, p. 67.
7 *A* 2, pp. 82–94.
8 According to Yanovsky, the original of Astafiy was the retired warrant officer Yevstafiy, Dostoyevsky's servant in 1847.
9 A fragment of this story in folk language has been preserved (*A* 2, pp. 399–402).
10 Later, in 1861, Dobrolyubov noted this absence of an explicit message: 'None of the characters, or particular opinions of Mr Dostoyevsky's give a direct reply to these questions. To find a reply we must group them together and explain each of them by the others' (N. A. Dobrolyubov, *Russkiye klassiki. Izbrannyye literaturno-kriticheskiye stat'i*, Moscow, 1970, p. 321).
11 *A* 2, p. 40.
12 *Sovremennik*, 1861, 11, III, pp. 99–149, and N. A. Dobrolyubov, *Russkiye klassiki*, pp. 301–47.
13 The hero of what is incorrectly called *Raskolnikov's Diary*, the first version of *Crime and Punishment*, is called Vasya.
14 *A* 18, pp. 32–3.
15 Dostoyevsky in his letter to the editor Krayevsky, of 1 February 1849, says 'the first six parts' (*Letters* 2, p. 118; *A* 281, p. 150).
16 As additional evidence of the fascination of previous creations, we may note that the two unfinished works, 'A Little Hero' and *Netochka Nezvanova*, have numerous features in common; in both the surroundings are aristocratic, and tender and beautiful ladies love secretly and stupidly: they lose or forget letters, devious and hypocritical husbands persecute them, the heroes are children, and proud beautiful vicious animals appear as dangerous (Falstaff the bulldog and Tancred the stallion), while red is a dominating theme in dreams (curtains, scarf).
17 18 July 1849, Dostoyevsky wrote to Mikhail: 'I have not been wasting my time: I have imagined three stories and two novels, I am writing one of them at the moment' (*Letters* 1, p. 124; *A* 281, p. 157).
18 Dobrolyubov was the first to note that Dostoyevsky 'likes to return to the same figures several times and try the same characters and situations from different points of view'. He quotes the example of 'the child who is precociously mature, sickly and full of self-love' (N. A. Dobrolyubov, *Sobraniye sochineniy*, 7, Moscow–Leningrad, 1961–4, p. 238).
19 *A* 5, p. 100.
20 Ibid. p. 133.
21 Ibid. p. 100.

22 In the numerous dialogues, Dostoyevsky, who names all the other protagonists, takes care to avoid giving the hero even a Christian name. The first translator of *Notes from Underground*, Halpérine-Kaminsky, made a serious mistake in giving the name Ordynov (hero of *The Landlady*) to the hero of *Notes from Underground* (*L'Esprit souterrain*, Paris, 1886).

23 Letter from Arthur Rimbaud to Paul Demeny, Charleville, 15 May 1871.

24 Nathalie Sarraute, *L'ère du soupçon. Essais sur le roman*, Paris, 1956, p. 51.

25 *A* 6, p. 422.

12 THE SUMMIT OF CREATIVE INTERROGATION: 'THE LIFE OF A
GREAT SINNER'

1 J. P. Sartre, *Situations I*, Paris, 1947, p. 166.

2 In succession and sometimes simultaneously: 'A thought (poem) having as its title: the Emperor', October–November 1867; 'The Innocent', May–September 1868; 'Novel of a land-owner', May–June 1868; 'Atheism', December 1868–May 1869; 'Plan for a story for 'Aurora'', February–March 1869; 'NB. After the Bible, he cut her throat', September–October 1869; 'Death of a poet (idea)', September 1869–January 1870; 'Novel of the prince and the moneylender', end of 1869–February 1870; 'Life of a Great Sinner', June 1869–May 1870. There were also two plans connected with *The Devils*: 'Captain Kartuzov' (end of 1868–beginning of 1869), and 'Envy' (beginning of 1870).

3 *A* 9, pp. 113–14. Capital letters have been added to the possessive adjectives and pronouns referring to Ivan Antonovich to clarify a text which is naturally elliptic.

4 *Otechestvennyye zapiski*, 1866, 4, pp. 530–58.

5 A. V. Alpatov, 'Odin iz neizuchonnykh tvorcheskikh zamyslov F. M. Dostoyevskogo (*Imperator*)', *Vestnik Moskovskogo Universiteta. Filologiya*, 1971, 5, pp. 13–21.

6 'Plan romana iz zhizni Mirovicha i zapiska o nyom G. F. Kvitki (-Osno-viyanen'ka)', *Russkiy Arkhiv*, 1863, 2, 160–70.

7 *A* 7, p. 135.

8 Ibid. p. 147.

9 Ibid. p. 149.

10 Ibid. p. 155.

11 Ibid. p. 167.

12 *A* 9, p. 146.

13 Ibid. p. 180.

14 Ibid. p. 181.

15 *A* 7, p. 90.

16 E. Tur in her 'Memories and Reflections', published in the first journal of the Dostoyevsky brothers, gave the following portrait of F. P. Haas:

> Every feature of his handsome, classical face breathed nobility and an infinite sweetness and goodness ... After distributing all his goods, he did not even take a barouche, but hired the most wretched cab in Moscow for his journeys to the prison-fortress, which was the scene of his truly Christian activity. From the windows of rich dwellings, he was pointed at: 'Look, practical people would say, 'there is that fool Haas going by'.
>
> (*Vremya*, 6, 1862, 64)

Ippolit, in *The Idiot*, has a long speech about Haas visiting the prison: 'In

Moscow there lived an old man, a 'general', that is, an acting state councillor, with a German name; all his life he trailed round prisons and criminals' (*A* 8, 335).

17 *A* 7, p. 80.

18 *A* 9, p. 158.

19 *A* 7, pp. 154–5.

20 M. V. Dzhouns (Jones), 'K ponimaniyu obraza knyazya Myshkina', in G. M. Fridlender (ed.), *Dostoyevsky. Materialy i issledovaniya*, 2, Leningrad, 1976, pp. 106–12.

21 *A* 8, p. 450.

22 *M* 8, pp. 450–1.

23 Ibid. p. 452.

24 Ibid.

25 Ibid. p. 453.

26 *Letters* 2, pp. 148–54; *A* 28ii, pp. 327–33.

27 *Letters* 2, p. 148, *A* 28ii, p. 327.

28 *Letters* 2, p. 150; *A* 28ii, p. 329.

29 *Letters* 2, p. 161, *A* 29i, p. 11. Francisco de Jasser (Francis Xavier) and Ignatius Loyola were the chief founder members of the Jesuit order.

30 *Letters* 2, p. 175; *A* 29i, p. 24.

31 *Letters* 2, p. 195; *A* 29i, p. 44.

32 *Letters* 2, p. 175; *A* 29i, p. 24.

33 *Letters* 2, p. 162; *A* 29i, p. 12.

34 *Letters* 2, pp. 207–8; *A* 29i, p. 58.

35 *A* 9, p. 125.

36 *A* 9, pp. 125–6.

37 *Letters* 2, pp. 244–5; *A* 29i, pp. 93–4.

38 *A* 9, pp. 125–39. The pages must be read in the following order: 8, 7, 6, 9, 22, 11, 9, 11, 12, 13, 23, 13, 16, 15, 18, 17, 70, 71, 20. This order, that of the Academic Edition, is different from that which Ye. N. Konshina adapted in 1935 (*Zapisnyye tetradi F. M. Dostoyevskogo*, with commentary by N. I. Ignatova and E. N. Konshina, Moscow–Leningrad, 1935).

39 Manuscript section of the Lenin Library: F 93.1,1,4.

40 Dostoyevsky fills *The Life of a Great Sinner* with people he knew in childhood; for instance, his brother Mikhail; Ivan Gavrilovich Umnov, his school-fellow, who had recommended that he read *The House of Madmen* by A. F. Voeykov and *The Little Humpbacked Horse* by P. P. Yershov, and, as we learn here, introduced him to the works of Gogol; the serfs at Darovoye (Anna the cook and Vasilisa the laundry maid), the lackey Osip (orderly with the Maslovich family) who were distant relatives of Dostoyevsky; A. A. Alfonsky (1796–1869) who was a colleague of Dostoyevsky's father in 1817 and who became a famous doctor and a great university teacher in Moscow; Souchard and Chermak, heads of the schools where Dostoyevsky studied as a youth; the teachers at the Chermak school: the Frenchman Mango, a former drummer in the Napoleonic army, an excellent teacher of conversation, but very weak in grammar, Karl Teider, an ex-captain who specialised in German literature; Eugène Lambert, a pupil of French nationality, who entered the school in 1833 and whom Dostoyevsky may have known in 1837. For the last three, cf. the contribution of G. A. Fyodorov, 'Pansion L. I. Chermaka v 1834–1837gg.', in *Dostoyevsky. Materialy i issledovaniya*, 1, Leningrad, 1974, pp. 248–9, 252.

41 *A* 9, p. 139. The nouns formed from imperfective verbs show the repetitive nature of the activity.
42 Ibid. p. 130.
43 K. Mochul'sky, *Dostoyevsky. His Life and Work*, trans. M. Minihan. Princeton, 1967, chapter 16, pp. 394–403.
44 *A* 9, p. 126.
45 Ibid. p. 126.
46 Ibid. p. 127.
47 Ibid.
48 Ibid.
49 Ibid. p. 129.
50 Ibid. p. 132.
51 Ibid. p. 126.
52 Ibid. p. 131.
53 Ibid. p. 136.
54 Ibid. p. 127.
55 *Thérèse philosophe, ou Mémoires pour servir à l'histoire du P. Dirrag et de mademoiselle Eradice*, The Hague, 1748. The London edition, 1782–3, has a variation: *Mémoires pour servir à l'histoire de D. Dirag et de mademoiselle Eurydice*. L. Blondeau published an expurgated edition of the text with engravings in 1961. The authorship of this erotic work (kept in the department of 'books not generally available to the public' in the Bibliothèque nationale, 402, 1584, 1592) is uncertain: the author may have been the Marquis d'Argens, Jean-Baptiste Boyer, or Xavier d'Arles de Montigny.
56 *A* 9, p. 133.
57 Ibid. p. 134. Censored in the Academy edition.
58 Ibid. p. 135.
59 Ibid. p. 134.
60 Ibid.
61 Ibid. p. 129.
62 *A* 4, p. 88.
63 This image, which may be a tower, a belltower or a roof, is a recurrent theme throughout the work.
64 Animals, as living beings and creatures of God, play an important part in the evolution of the young hero. Here also the *Life of a Great Sinner* is a synthesis of all Dostoyevsky's work, in which children are often attached to or confronted with animals. Cf. *Netochka Nezvanova*: the bulldog Falstaff; 'A Little Hero': the horse Tancred; *Crime and Punishment*: the mare flogged to death in Raskolnikov's childhood; *The Brothers Karamazov*: the dog Scarab to whom Ilyusha, on the advice of the gloomy Smerdyakov, throws a piece of bread with a pin inside it. *The Brothers Karamazov* also contains the story of the goose whose neck is broken by a cart wheel in a playful device of Kolya's.
65 Kulikov (real name Kulishov) is the prisoner of the Special Section described in *The House of the Dead*, a man 'of great strength and vitality with extraordinary and manifold talents' (*A* 4, pp. 221, 286). In 'The Life of a Great Sinner' he is the valet Osip.
66 *A* 9, p. 130.
67 Ibid. p. 136.
68 Ibid. p. 129.
69 Ibid. p. 125.

70 Ibid. p. 139.
71 Ibid. p. 134.
72 Ibid. p. 136.
73 Ibid. p. 130.
74 Ibid.
75 Ibid. p. 134.
76 Ibid.
77 Ibid. p. 126.
78 Ibid. p. 136.
79 Ibid. p. 130.
80 Orlov is the famous outlaw, a deserter from the army, 'with an iron character', 'with a terrible strength of will', proud of his strength, acknowledging no God nor master, described by Dostoyevsky in *The House of the Dead* (*A* 4, pp. 46–7).
81 *A* 9, p. 135.
82 Ibid. p. 129.
83 Ibid. p. 130.
84 Ibid. p. 139.
85 Ibid. p. 126.
86 Ibid. p. 128.
87 Ibid. p. 135. The Academy edition gives the correct reading for the first time. One would expect *slivayetsya,*
88 Ibid. p. 132.
89 Ibid.
90 Ibid. p. 135. 'Jacob bowed three times.'
91 According to flagellant doctrine, everyone who reaches the supreme degree of perfection called 'the mysterious resurrection' can declare himself Christ (whence the name *khlysty* which is not derived from *khylst*, whip). So Russia had several gods: the 'Sabaoth' Danila Filippovich, the 'Christ' Ivan Timofeyevich Suslov (surrounded by his twelve apostles and the Virgin mother), and their successors, Prokofiy Lupkin, Andrey Selivanov, Vasiliy Radayev. The first, Danila Filippovich, a peasant from the Urevich district, who 'appeared' in 1631 and 'ascended to heaven' in 1700, who preached his twelve commandments in many places, was especially interesting to Dostoyevsky, who mentions him by name in a note of 1 January 1870 (*A* 9, p. 128) in an attempt to define the central character of 'Life of a Great Sinner'.
92 *A* 9, p. 130.
93 Ibid.
94 Ibid. p. 139.
95 Ibid. p. 138.
96 Ibid. pp. 138–9.
97 Ibid. p. 128.
98 E. Behr-Sigel, *Prière et Sainteté dans l'Eglise russe*, Paris, 1950, pp. 121–40.
99 *A* 14, p. 26. In the chapter 'The Elders', Dostoyevsky gives a history of this institution of the Eastern Church, which had developed over thousands of years, and tells several legends about the mysterious and unlimited power with which the Elders are endowed (ibid. pp. 26–7).
100 Pierre Pascal, *La Religion du peuple russe*, Lausanne, 1973, p. 44.
101 Ibid.

102 Ibid. pp. 69–105. Pierre Pascal studies the sources of this monument of Russian religious literature, which he has translated from the two texts of the Slavonic version closest to the oldest Greek text, i.e., the twelfth-century manuscript in the Troitsky–Sergeyevich Monastery and the manuscript of 1602.

103 *A* 14, p. 225.

104 From 1857 to 1863, four editions of *The Pilgrimage of the Mother of God among the Torments* appeared, as further manuscripts were discovered.

105 *A* 9, p. 132.

106 G. B. Ponomaryova, '"*Zhitiye velikogo greshnika*" Dostoyevskogo. Struktura i zhanr', in *Issledovaniya po poetike i stilistike*, Leningrad, 1972, p. 86.

107 *Bakhtin*, p. 7.

108 The last two lines devoted to the end of the *Life of a Great Sinner* envisage a double solution: 'NB. He wanted to shoot himself (a baby abandoned). He ends by making his house into a foundling hospital and becomes a Haas' (*A* 9, p. 139).

109 *Letters* 2, p. 252; *A* 291, p. 107.

110 *Letters* 2, p. 258; *A* 291, p. 112.

111 In the letter to Strakhov, Dostoyevsky says simply 'Tolstoy's novel' (ibid.).

112 In his letter to Strakhov, Dostoyevsky makes it clear that these 'separate novels' could even appear in different journals (*Letters* 2, p. 258; *A* 291, p. 112).

113 *Letters* 2, pp. 263–4; *A* 291, pp. 117–18.

114 A virtuous character who sings the praises of work and economy in the second part of Gogol's *Dead Souls*.

115 Stolz, in Goncharov's novel, is the virtuous friend of Oblomov.

116 Dostoyevsky is thinking of Lavretsky, the hero of Turgenev's *Nest of Gentlefolk*. He has confused the name with that of an acquaintance, Lavrovsky, who appears as a childhood friend of the hero in *A Raw Youth* (*A* 13, p. 62).

117 Rakhmetov and Lopukhov are the positive heroes of *What is to be done?* by Chernyshevsky.

118 *Letters* 2, pp. 264–5; *A* 291, p. 118.

119 Pushkin is mentioned in the plan of *Life of a Great Sinner*, but not as a character in the novel; he appears as a truly Russian writer by comparison with Tolstoy and Turgenev (*A* 9, p. 138).

120 *Biography*, p. 298.

121 *A* 11, p. 131.

122 *A* 11, pp. 121–2.

123 Peter Chaadayev, *Lettres philosophiques adressées à une dame*, Paris, 1970.

124 Ibid. p. 55.

125 *LH* 77, p. 263.

126 Ibid. p. 209.

127 I. S. Turgenev, *Polnoye sobraniye sochineniy i pisem v 28-i tomakh*. Moscow–Leningrad, 1960–8, 14, p. 42.

128 At first Dostoyevsky gave Book VI of *The Brothers Karamazov* ('A Russian monk') the title of 'Pater Seraphicus', which comes directly from the *Second Faust*. Ivan, in the final version of the novel, ironically calls the Elder Zosima 'Pater Seraphicus' (*A* 14, p. 241; *A* 15, p. 202). A. L. Bem and L. P. Grossman, quoted by the former, saw the relationship between *The Brothers Karamazov* – a modified revival of 'Life of a Great Sinner' – and the 'Second

Faust', but they looked mainly for exact thematic resemblances. Bem is approaching our theme when he writes:

For me it is not so much the historiosophic idea of the character of Ivan and his comparison with Faust which are important. The essential point is that Dostoyevsky, when he created *The Brothers Karamazov*, began with a grandiose religious and philosophical conception, for which Goethe's *Faust* – not by its content but by the boldness of its aesthetic plan – could have been the model.

> (*O Dostojevském. Sborník statí a materiálů*, Prague, 1972, p. 197)

129 *Letters* 2, p. 298; *A* 291, p. 151.
130 Ibid.
131 Ibid. p. 301; *A* 291, p. 154.
132 A. L. Bem, *O Dostojevském*, p. 95. 'Evolyutsiya obraza Stavrogina.'
133 Ibid. p. 97.
134 The expression 'L'amour dans la haine' is often repeated in the notebooks for *A Raw Youth*. In *The Brothers Karamazov* Dmitriy speaks of 'love which is only separated from the maddest hatred by the breadth of a hair' (*A* 14, p. 105). This psychological treatment of love and hatred as equivalent is close to that of Racine (Paul Bénichou, *Morales du grand siècle*. Paris, 1967, p. 223).
135 A. L. Bem, *O Dostojevském*, p. 96.
136 *Letters* 2, p. 291; *A* 291, p. 148.
137 *Letters* 2, p. 297; *A* 291, p. 143.
138 'Russkiy sovremennik', 1924, p. 200, note 1. Quoted from Dolinin (*Letters* 2, p. 509).
139 *Letters* 2, p. 358; *A* 291, p. 208.

13 A RAW YOUTH: REASONS FOR CHOICE

1 Virginia Woolf, *The Common Reader*, I, London, 1925, p. 226.
2 A. S. Dolinin, *Posledniye romany Dostoyevskogo*, Moscow–Leningrad, 1963, pp. 196–200.
3 V. S. Nechayeva (ed.), *Opisaniye rukopisey F. M. Dostoyevskogo*, Moscow, 1957, pp. 16–19.
4 These notebooks have been collected in *LH* 77 and *A* 16. The Academy edition follows the version edited by A. S. Dolinin in *LH* 77, to which we refer.
5 Cf. V. S. Nechayeva (ed.), *Opisaniye rukopisey*, pp. 13–19, for a simple presentation of the facts. A vivid description is given by P. N. Sakulin in his introduction to the manuscripts of *The Idiot* (*Iz arkhiva F. M. Dostoyevskogo. Idiot*, ed. P. N. Sakulin and N. F. Bel'chikov, Moscow–Leningrad, 1931, pp. 3–6).
6 For *The Idiot*. Facsimiles of notebook no. 8: *LH* 77, pp. 15, 47, 75, 97, 113, 179; of notebook no. 9: *LH* 77, pp. 237, 267, 271, 283, 287, 402; of notebook no. 10: *LH* 77, p. 197; of the separate sheets: *LH* 77, pp. 127, 359, 365, 383, 421, 426–7, 447, 481, 487.
7 *LH* 77, pp. 105, 215, 491.
8 Ibid. pp. 15, 197, 237, 271, 403, 426–7, 463, 481, 497.
9 Ibid. pp. 47, 75, 113, 179, 365, 429, 463.
10 Ibid. pp. 127, 183, 421, 426–7.

11 Ibid. p. 39.
12 Ibid. 'He' denotes Versilov, he the youth.
13 Louis Martinez, 'Les Carnets de l'Adolescent', in J. Catteau (ed.), *Dostoïevski*, Cahiers de l'Herne 24, Paris, 1973, p. 79.
14 Ibid. p. 80.
15 *LH* 77, p. 286.
16 *LH* 77, p. 291.
17 There were several reasons which led Dostoyevsky to offer *A Raw Youth* to *Annals of the Fatherland*, a radical and even revolutionary democratic publication, and so to renew ties with the poet Nekrasov, with whom he had quarrelled more than nine years ago. A. S. Dolinin exaggerates the ideological reasons: he supposes that Dostoyevsky's action was caused by a feeling of repulsion for the retrograde ideas expressed in *The Devils*. We shall summarise these reasons without comment:
(1) Dostoyevsky was tired of supporting the editorship of *The Citizen*. He wished to return to the writing of novels and he was impatient with the hide-bound conservatism of Prince Meshchersky. He did not change sides, but wanted to go on feeling hope about youth (cf. his quarrel with the dramatist D. Kishensky, where Dostoyevsky was accused of seeing the nihilists as 'bearers of new ideas' (*Letters* 3, pp. 82–4 and commentaries, pp. 311–12; *A* 291, pp. 300–2 and commentary, p. 614), Dostoyevsky said he did not wish to ruin himself and his children and destroy his career as a writer for the sake of Meshchersky (*Letters* 3, p. 88; *A* 291, p. 307).
(2) An article by N. K. Mikhaylovsky, the populist critic of *Annals of the Fatherland*, took up the themes of Belinsky, socialism and atheism in its analysis of *The Devils*. Mikhaylovsky invited the novelist, whose talent he admitted, to turn to another devil:
> What! Russia, this sick man possessed by the devil which you have shown, is girding itself with railways, covering itself with factories and banks, and in your novel there is no trace of this world! You fix your attention on a wretched handful of madmen and rascals! In your novel there is no devil of national wealth, the commonest of devils and the one which has the least knowledge of the frontier between Good and Evil ... Depict sinners who truly do not repent, depict people who are really fanatical about themselves ... and wealth for wealth's sake.
> (*Otechestvennyye zapiski*, 2, 1873, p. 343)
In 'Two notes of the chief editor' of *The Citizen* (2 July 1873, no. 27), Dostoyevsky recalled this article, said he was grateful for this sincere criticism and promised a reply: 'I too find "the face of this world" displeasing' (*A* 21, p. 157 or *T* 13, p. 449). *A Raw Youth* was the reply.
(3) Fees: Katkov's *Russian Messenger*, in which Dostoyevsky used to publish, had grudgingly given him 250 roubles per printed page, while paying L. Tolstoy 500 roubles (*Letters* 3, pp. 95, 145; *A* 291, pp. 318–19, 370). Nekrasov immediately agreed to pay 250 roubles a page. This was probably the decisive reason.
18 *Letters* 3, p. 152; *A* 29II, p. 13.
19 Ibid.
20 *Letters* 3, p. 162; *A* 29II, p. 25.
21 *Letters* 3, pp. 172, 177, 182; *A* 29II, pp. 35–6, 42–3, 48.
22 *Letters* 3, p. 180; *A* 29II, p. 46.

23 *Letters* 3, p. 174; *A* 2911, p. 40.
24 *Letters* 3, p. 175; *A* 2911, p. 41.
25 *Letters* 3, p. 177; *A* 2911, p. 43.

14 A RAW YOUTH: THE APPEARANCE OF THE VISION

1 *LH* 77, p. 59.
2 Ibid.
3 A facsimile of the article, published on page 3 of the *Moscow News* (50), 26 February 1874, is given in *LH* 77, p. 61.
4 *LH* 77, p. 59.
5 Ibid. p. 60. 'Andrieux' in Latin characters.
6 Ibid. p. 62.
7 Ibid. p. 69.
8 Ilyusha prepares to defend his ridiculous father, the retired Captain Snegiryov, while the sons of Karamazov are all guilty of parricide to some degree. This little 'republic' of children, dominated by Krasotkin, is a promise of brightness and happiness.
9 *A* 14, p. 100.
10 *LH* 77, p. 60.
11 Ibid.
12 Ibid. p. 62.
13 Ibid. p. 59.
14 Ibid. p. 62.
15 Ibid.
16 Ibid. p. 63.
17 Ibid. p. 64.
18 Ibid. The whole is entitled 'Embryo of plan'.
19 Ibid. p. 66.
20 Jacques Catteau, 'A propos de la littérature fantastique: André Belyj, héritier de Gogol' et de Dostoïevski', in *Cahiers du monde russe et soviétique*, vol. 3, 1962, 370–3.
21 *LH* 77, p. 66.
22 Ibid. p. 74.
23 Ibid. p. 59.
24 Ibid. p. 62.
25 Ibid. p. 66.
26 Fyodor Fyodorovich, by his Christian name and patronymic, is both the writer himself and the son of his works.
27 *LH* 77, p. 64.
28 Ibid. p. 59.
29 Ibid. pp. 59, 64, 68.
30 Ibid. p. 65.
31 This is what Alyosha Karamazov would have done in the sequel announced for *The Brothers Karamazov*, according to A. S. Suvorin (*M* 2, pp. 329, 423).
32 *LH* 77, p. 68.
33 Ibid. p. 67.
34 In the plan for 'Life of a Great Sinner', the sinner suddenly finds redemption in the same circumstances, another example of the interchangeability of situations.

35 *A* 11, p. 11.
36 *LH* 77, p. 68.
37 This was the opinion of Dostoyevsky in his Fourierist days.
38 *LH* 77, p. 68. In *A Raw Youth* Makar Ivanov was to imagine a paradise on earth
    in a more religious spirit than Fyodor Fyodorovich. When the youth points out
    that he is preaching communism, he asks what that is, but is not embarrassed. He
    takes no notice of the incompatibility between the two philosophies. Prudently,
    Dostoyevsky, instead of giving us a dialogue, sticks to the dry narrative of facts
    (*A* 13, pp. 331–2). The last sentence of the quotation: 'Many people make this
    impossible compromise, it is true, nowadays' foreshadows the attitude of many
    Russian and European Christians in 1917. Cf., for example, Pierre Pascal's
    'What I believe, a declaration to the Central Committee of the Russian
    Communist Party in December 1919' ('*En Communisme. Mon Journal de
    Russie*, Lausanne, 1977, pp. 45–7).
39 The original opposition between predatory (Prince Valkovsky in *The Insulted
    and Injured*, Svidrigaylov) and gentle types (Sonya in *Crime and Punishment*),
    which had a social aspect – the former tortured, the latter suffered – becomes a
    more psychological and spiritual type of opposition, starting with the notebooks
    for *The Idiot*. It is not so much the relationship of masters and slaves as the
    contrast between broad natures struggling with doubt and men of faith commit-
    ted, or about to be committed, to action (Myshkin, Kirillov, Shatov, Tikhon,
    Fyodor Fyodorovich, Arkady, Makar Ivanov, Zosima, Alyosha).
40 *LH* 77, p. 68.

15 A RAW YOUTH: THE HUMAN ARCHITECTURE

1 The broad nature is monstrous only in so far as it is more keenly aware of its
   duality than the ordinary man and has more power of life and so of acting out this
   duality. In *A Raw Youth* and *The Brothers Karamazov* it is often defined by its
   vitality (*zhivuchest'*).
2 This is an aspect of all Dostoyevsky's creative work which could be developed:
   even the atheists are obsessed by this model, the human ideal of Christ. In *The
   Devils*, Shatov praises the Russian Christ; Kirillov wants to die to teach men
   freedom; Pyotr Stepanovich dreams of reviving the life of Christ in Stavrogin,
   when he calls him Ivan-Tsarevich.
3 *LH* 7, p. 66.
4 Ibid.
5 Ibid. p. 62.
6 Ibid. p. 66.
7 Ibid. p. 69.
8 Ibid. p. 74.
9 The unity of fatherhood enlarges the brotherhood to include Smerdyakov but
   the antinomies are stressed: Dmitriy (aged 27) is the half-brother of Ivan (23)
   and of Alyosha (20). Dmitriy is the broad nature which suffers because of its
   immensity, without accepting this until the end of the novel. Ivan and Alyosha
   are the two complementary aspects of the broad nature: the former is the atheist
   who reveals but also refuses the freedom of Christ, the latter is the believer who
   tries to exercise that freedom.
10 *A* 14, p. 74.

11 This expression, from an unsympathetic character, is almost a word-for-word copy of the one which occurs in the notebooks of *A Raw Youth* where Dostoyevsky is characterising the predatory type (*LH* 77, p. 66).

12 *A* 15, p. 129.

13 The insect (*Zhuchok*, lit. little beetle, in allusion to the little red insect on the green leaf which Stavrogin sees while Matryosha is hanging herself) is the 'suffering' which consumes the predator after the child's suicide (*LH* 77, p. 73).

14 Ibid. The hesitation about age is noteworthy: at the beginning a young boy (*molodoy mal'chik*) and at the end, a young man (*molodoy chelovek*). It refers to an adolescent.

15 Ibid. p. 74.

16 Ibid. pp. 74–5.

17 Ibid. p. 77.

18 Ibid. p. 81.

19 Ibid. p. 83.

20 Ibid. pp. 77–80.

21 Ibid. pp. 76–7.

22 Ibid. p. 77.

23 Ibid. p. 78.

24 Ibid. p. 80.

25 Ibid. p. 81.

26 Ibid. p. 80. The rule is immediately applied a few pages later to the predatory type:

> Picture, how he seeks money. (Baseness and breadth). He himself admits it to himself and is amazed at himself. *He himself calls himself a predatory type.* (It should all be explained to the reader). *He seeks a burden, he seeks faith*; but the little beetle has crushed him.
> He talks of the 40 days in the wilderness, but the main thing *he does not believe*. He even asks himself the question. (ibid. p. 86)

27 *LH* 77, p. 84. The fourth estate is the proletariat and the prelude is the Paris Commune and the burning of the Tuileries.

28 Ibid.

29 Ibid.

30 Ibid.

31 Ibid. p. 86.

32 Ibid. p. 82.

33 Ibid. p. 84.

34 Ibid. p. 82. The original word is *klubnichka* (little strawberry). In his notebooks Dostoyevsky uses clear and direct words for sex. The loves he imagines are far from platonic. In the novels, his expressions were restrained by the censorship, but Dostoyevsky needed only allusions, more forceful for being rare, to suggest desire, for instance, the hysterical fits of women in love, the erotic dreams of Svidrigaylov and the youth, the murderous erotic fury of Versilov and those heroes (the Gambler, Svidrigaylov and Rogozhin) whose hearts faint with desire when they hear the swish of the dress of the woman they love.

35 *LH* 77, p. 84.

36 Ibid. p. 77.

37 Ibid. p. 87.

38 Ibid. p. 88.

39 Ibid. p. 91–2.
40 Ibid. p. 92.
41 Ibid. p. 94.
42 Ibid.
43 In 1876, Dostoyevsky admitted to the readers of *Diary of a Writer* that the temptation to rivalry with Turgenev was only brief:

> When, a year and a half ago, Nikolay Alekseyevich Nekrasov invited me to write a novel for Annals of the Fatherland, I was about to begin a Fathers and Sons in my turn, but I restrained myself, and thank goodness, I wasn't ready. While I was waiting, I wrote only A Raw Youth: it is a first test of my idea. (*A* 22, p. 7)

44 *LH* 77, p. 173.
45 The action is noted without comment several times (*LH* 77, pp. 77, 111, 156, 170, 175, 203).
46 Ibid. p. 80: 'The boy with the little bird.' It is the theme of Skotoboynikov's picture.
47 *A Raw Youth*, 3, III, iv.
48 *LH* 77, p. 75.
49 *A* 11, p. 197.
50 *LH* 77, p. 85.
51 Ibid. p. 105.
52 Ibid. pp. 106–7.
53 Ibid. p. 109.
54 Ibid. p. 139.
55 Ibid. p. 170.
56 Ibid. p. 236.
57 Ibid. p. 74.
58 *A* 13, p. 169.
59 *LH* 77, p. 238.
60 Ibid. pp. 163–9, 214–17.
61 Like Tikhon in 'The Life of a Great Sinner' he is a teacher: there is much use of 'thou shalt'.
62 *LH* 77, pp. 164, 166–8. Liza Smerdyashchaya (stinking Liza) disappears in the finished novel. She was reborn in *The Brothers Karamazov*, where Smerdyakov is her son. But, probably to keep the secret of Smerdyakov's paternity, Dostoyevsky made her a simpleton incapable of speech. It is only in this passage of the notebooks, where she proposes that God should pardon all sinners and take her into hell in their place, that her nature as a *strastoterpets* (martyr) is defined by the dialogue.
63 19 February 1861: emancipation of the serfs.
64 *LH* 77, pp. 169–70.
65 Ibid. p. 240.
66 Alyosha Karamazov, another youth, has two fathers even more clearly: Fyodor Pavlovich and Zosima.
67 *LH* 77, pp. 172–3.
68 Ibid. p. 178.

16 A RAW YOUTH: THE IDEA OF THE NOVEL

1 Cf. Vladimir Seduro, *Dostoyevsky in Russian Literary Criticism, 1846–1956*, New York, 1957; Vladimir Seduro, *Dostoyevski's Image in Russia Today*, Belmont, Mass., 1975 (the book has an appendix: 'Dostoyevsky in Russian émigré criticism'); Jean-Louis Backès, *Dostoïevski en France, 1884–1930*, doctoral thesis, Paris-Sorbonne, 1971.

2 This is the attitude, for example, of Albert Camus, who is interested in Kirillov and the philosophical suicide in *Le Mythe de Sisyphe*, and in the heroes of *The Devils* and individual terrorism in *L'Homme révolté*; also that of R. Guardini, who in *L'Univers religieux de Dostoïevski* (Paris, 1947, trans. from German) analyses the different characters of the novels on the religious plane.

3 B. Engel'gardt, 'Ideologicheskiy roman Dostoyevskogo', in *F. M. Dostoyevsky. Stat'i i materialy*, ed. A. S. Dolinin, 2, Leningrad, 1924, p. 105.

4 V. Ya. Kirpotin, *Dostoyevsky v shestidesyatyye gody*, Moscow, 1966, pp. 553–4.

5 *Bakhtin*, p. 43 (p. 31).

6 Apart from the Russian and Christian idea of strength in submission, none of the universal ideas which obsess the masculine heroes is attributed to the heroines. Dostoyevsky has deprived women of ideological passion.

7 *Crime and Punishment* is a perfect illustration of the distinction between the emotional Idea of the heroes and the idea or thought of the novel. The former is the antinomic dream of universal happiness and of Napoleonic power (Raskolnikov). The latter is given in the title: the punishment is contained in the crime, and this is the subject of the novel.

8 *LH* 77, p. 64.

9 Cf. pp. 277–8 of this book.

10 *LH* 77, p. 69.

11 Ibid. pp. 124, 170–1.

12 Dostoyevsky stresses that the predatory nature is inevitably linked with 'the urge towards disorder and adventures' (*LH* 77, p. 102).

13 Ibid. p. 92.

14 Ibid. p. 84. Later (p. 105) Liza realises the character of the predator: 'i.e. decomposition and nothing whole'.

15 Ibid. p. 102.

16 Ibid. p. 79.

17 Ibid. p. 106.

18 Ibid. p. 131.

19 The expression is reiterated on pp. 158, 159, 160.

20 Ibid. p. 274.

21 Ibid. p. 276.

22 Ibid. p. 118. Dostoyevsky stresses the organic link between the emotional idea of Kraft (the logical deduction that the Russian people is a second-class people degenerates into a 'violent feeling which takes over his whole being, which is difficult to expel or modify') and the Idea of the novel, which is that of ever-present and all-powerful disorder.

23 Ibid. p. 362.

24 Ibid. pp. 129–30: A. V. Dolgushin (and his wife A. D. Dolgushina). Dolgushin, who is to be called Dergachev, the one who 'pulls strings', is the leader of a

revolutionary group. The Dolgushintsy, his followers, are the historical originals of the revolutionaries in the novel.

25 Ibid. p. 146.
26 Ibid. p. 148.
27 Ibid. p. 268.
28 Ibid. p. 95.
29 Ibid. p. 98.
30 Ibid. p. 114.
31 Ibid. p. 101. Here Dostoyevsky makes a semantic distinction between the idea felt by the hero (*ideya*) and the idea of the novel (*mysl'*).
32 Ibid. p. 104.
33 Ibid. p. 112.
34 Ibid. p. 74.
35 Ibid. p. 92.
36 Ibid. p. 93.
37 Ibid. p. 94.
38 Ibid. p. 96.
39 'There is the story' (ibid. pp. 98, 101, 102).
40 Ibid. pp. 136–7.
41 V. Ya. Kirpotin, *Dostoyevsky v shestidesyatyye gody*, Moscow, 1966, p. 554.
42 Ibid.
43 The novel is less violent and erotic than the notebooks. One example will show what we mean: the comparison between the last lines of the penultimate chapter of the novel (*A* 13, p. 445) and the notes in the notebook (*LH* 77, p. 207). This is the dramatic scene where Versilov, after knocking Lambert senseless, holds the fainting Akhmatova in his arms, embraces her and wants to kill her. This is the text of the notebooks, with our comments in square brackets:

When He bestially [theme of sex, the adverb 'bestially' is suppressed in the novel] rushes with the half-dead princess [theme of death, the word in the novel is 'senseless'] in his arms, He suddenly with all his strength, and when he has already placed her on the bed [theme of sex, *postel'* in the notebooks for bed, the more colourless word *krovat'* in the novel], hits her (after kisses) on the face with his fist [theme of death, in the novel, he waves the revolver over her and then aims it at her face] (he has bared her leg) [theme of sex absent in the novel]. Here the youth tries to kill him [theme of death, in the novel the youth and Trishatov simply try to disarm him].

44 Action attributed to a secondary character, the youth's landlord (*LH* 77, pp. 179–93).
45 Ibid. p. 70. 'Story of the slap; endurance (*pereneseniye*) the slap.'
46 Ibid. p. 241. 'But in the plot there must continually be the main idea: the youth's will towards arson, leading him astray from his own idea and an unsuccessful first step.'
47 The epilogue of *A Raw Youth* is particularly significant; when Bioring appears on the scene, the victims, except for the wounded Versilov, have already disappeared (*A* 13, 448). There is no trace of violence, the stage is empty: the youth is meditating.
48 N. S. Leskov, in a text published only in 1977, *Happiness on two floors (a Kievan variant of real people addressed to cardboard people on the Neva)*, attacks *A Raw Youth*, accusing Dostoyevsky of lacking truth and simplicity. The 'Achilles heel

of all his creation', according to Leskov, is that Dostoyevsky makes life more complicated and colourful than it really is. 'Where the waves are crashing against the rocks under the pen of Mr Dostoyevsky, in real life there is a peaceful current of concession and reconciliations' (*LH* 87, pp. 97–8, 111–12).

49 In spite of some brilliant psychological guesses by the youth: the analysis of the 'duality' of Versilov and the 'malicious allegory' represented by the breaking of Makar's icon (*A* 13, p. 446). But is it really the youth who is speaking? See the problems of composition in the following chapter.

50 The word means both outrage and deformity.

51 *LH* 77, pp. 390–1.

52 Versilov says to the youth: 'I am the same as you, I am your image' (ibid. p. 233).

17 THE COMPOSITION OF THE NOVEL IN DOSTOYEVSKY'S WORK: CHOICE OF CHRONICLE FORM

1 E. M. de Vogüé notes of *The Insulted and Injured*:
The slow development, the double dramatic action, shocks all our ordinary conceptions of good composition. As soon as we are interested in an intrigue, a second appears unexpectedly, quite distinct, but seemingly a copy of the first. I am quite willing to believe that the writer has in this separation of the two parts made rather a subtle artistic attempt borrowed from a process well known to the musical world. The principal drama awakes a far-away echo. It is the melody arrangement for the orchestra, transposing the chorus heard on the stage. Or, if preferred, it is as if the two novels together imitate the play of two mirrors when on opposite walls, both reflecting the same object to each other simultaneously.
(E. M. de Vogüé, *The Russian Novel*, London, 1913, p. 237)

2 V. Ivanov writes of the novel-tragedies of Dostoyevsky: 'To construct his tragedies, he has used the procedures of the symphony: he applies a method corresponding to musical themes and counterpoint in his novels. He makes an appeal to their amplifications, meanders and variations, such as the composer uses, to make us psychologically perceive and feel his constructions as a whole' (Vyach. Ivanov, *Borozdy i mezhi*, Moscow, 1916, p. 20).

3 *Bakhtin*, pp. 58–9 (pp. 41–2).

4 A mistake in L. P. Grossman. It refers to the journal *Epoch* (1864).

5 *Letters* 1, p. 365; *A* 28ii, p. 85.

6 L. P. Grossman, 'Dostoyevsky-khudozhnik' in *Tvorchestvo F. M. Dostoyevs-kogo*, Moscow, 1959, pp. 341–2.

7 V. L. Komarovich, 'Roman *Podrostok* kak khudozhestvennoye yedinstvo', in *F. M. Dostoyevsky. Stat'i i materialy*, ed. A. S. Dolinin, vol. 2, Leningrad, 1924, pp. 67–8.

8 Jean Fleury, 'Deux Romanciers russes contemporains Dostoïevski et Pissemski', in *Revue politique et littéraire*, called 'Revue bleue', 26 February 1881, 278.

9 However, it may be thought that Dostoyevsky was trying to do, in a completely different composition, what Turgenev did for the Russian serfs in *A Sportsman's Sketches*: that is, to plead the cause of the outcast. The two books had a decisive effect on consequent reforms: *A Sportsman's Sketches* on the freeing of the serfs in 1861, *The House of the Dead* on the abolition of the most barbaric corporal punishments in 1863.

10 For the history of the stormy relationship between the two writers, cf. Yu. Nikol'sky, *Turgenev i Dostoyevsky*, *Istoriya odnoy vrazhdy*, Sofia, 1921; A. S. Dolinin, 'Turgenev v *Besakh*' in *F. M. Dostoyevsky. Stat'i i materialy*, ed. A. S. Dolinin, 2, Leningrad, 1924; *F. M. Dostoyevsky i I. S. Turgenev, Perepiska. Istoriya odnoy vrazhdy*, ed. I. S. Zil'bershteyn, Leningrad, 1928.

11 In *The Brothers Karamazov* the unsympathetic and unscrupulous seminarist Rakitin and the feather-brained Khokhlakova, Liza's mother, both read Saltykov-Shchedrin.

12 L. P. Grossman supports Tver (now Kalinin), which has a partial topographical resemblance to the town of *The Devils*.

13 M. S. Altman, basing his argument on the initial which is repeatedly given to the province where the action of *The Devils* takes place and on the real events which are recalled in the novel, proposes Kharkov (*Dostoyevsky. Materialy i issledovaniya*, 2, Leningrad, 1976, p. 53).

14 *A* 25, p. 51.

15 In his notebooks, Dostoyevsky mentions 'Childhood' and 'Boyhood' only once. Liza is talking to the youth: 'No, it is you who are the poet of petty self-love, and not Count Tolstoy (but the bird-cherry)' (*LH* 77, p. 116). The allusion to the bird-cherry is significant: at the end of the second chapter of 'Boyhood', entitled 'The Storm', the young hero breaks off some flowering branches of bird-cherry, strikes his face with them and is intoxicated with their marvellous scent. In Tolstoy, everything is poetry, calm and beauty, for Arkadiy everything is anxious passion, disorder and 'precocious hatred for the pettiness and chance of his condition', according to the analysis of Dostoyevsky himself in *Diary of a Writer*, January 1876 (*A* 22, p. 8).

16 *A* 17, pp. 142–3.

17 *A* 13, p. 455.

18 *A* 25, p. 173. In February 1877, in *Diary of a Writer*, Dostoyevsky had reproached Tolstoy for repeating himself in *Anna Karenina* which was then being published: 'I constantly had the impression that I had already read that somewhere, and namely in Childhood and Boyhood of the same Count Tolstoy, and in War and Peace, and of finding rather more freshness there. Still the same historical chronicle of the noble Russian family, although certainly that is not the subject.'

19 *A* 13, p. 455.

20 *A* 17, p. 142. Variant of chapters 7 and 8 of the third part. The sketch of this variant in the notebooks is much less acid (*LH* 77, pp. 408–9).

21 It might be objected that these assertions belong to the heroes (Versilov in the variant, Nikolay Semyonovich, the teacher and protector of the youth during his school years in Moscow, in the novel) and not to the author. The quotations made from *Diary of a Writer* in 1876 and 1877 enable us to attribute them also to Dostoyevsky. We may note only that the transfer of the idea of the writer to the word of the hero forms a screen behind which Dostoyevsky is hiding two of his own features: his jealousy as a writer, shown by Versilov's caustic irony, and his modesty as an innovator in form: the invention of a new aesthetics of chaos is postponed until the distant future by the prudent Nikolay Semyonovich.

22 Note at the bottom of page 435, L. P. Grossman, *Dostoyevsky*, 'Zhizn' zamechatelnykh lyudey', Moscow, 1962.

23 Chronology of the story: first meeting with Maksim Maksimych ('Bela'); next

day, the second meeting ('Maksim Maksimych'); shortly afterwards, the author, having learnt of the death of Pechorin, publishes Pechorin's diary (1. 'Taman'; 2. 'Princess Mary'; 3. 'The Fatalist'). Chronology of the events: 'Taman', 'Princess Mary', 'Bela', 'The Fatalist', 'Maksim Maksimych'.

24 B. M. Eykhenbaum, 'Geroy nashego vremeni', in *Istoriya russkogo romana v dvukh tomakh*, 1, Moscow–Leningrad, 1962, p. 297.

25 *Vremya*, 1862, 10, 11, p. 26.

26 The reference to Dickens is instructive. Dostoyevsky read *The Posthumous Papers of the Pickwick Club* in prison. Published from March 1836 to December 1837 in illustrated monthly instalments, it was probably read by Lermontov, who knew English perfectly, on its first appearance.

27 *Letters* 1, p. 221; *A* 281, p. 281.

28 Ibid.

29 Ibid. p. 166; *A* 281, p. 209.

30 *Letters* 4, p. 262; *A* 281, p. 295.

31 *Letters* 2, p. 585; *A* 281, pp. 288–9.

32 *Letters* 4, p. 262; *A* 281, p. 295.

33 *Letters* 2, pp. 585–6; *A* 281, pp. 288–9.

34 *Letters* 2, p. 589; *A* 281, p. 299.

35 F. M. Dostoyevsky. *Materialy i issledovaniya*, Leningrad, 1935, p. 515. *Wilhelm Meisters Lehrjahre* appeared in 1797, *Wilhelm Meisters Wanderungen* in 1821–9. Mikhail Dostoyevsky, who was mad about German literature, is here referring to the novel of education or apprenticeship (in German, *Bildungsroman*), whose originals are the novels of Goethe. He is reasoning by analogy, which is deceptive. Only *A Raw Youth* and the part dealing with Alyosha in *The Brothers Karamazov* can be related to this type of novel. There is a clear distinction between the *Bildungsroman* and Dostoyevsky's novel of a life: the *Bildungs-roman* is only a pre-novel, a sort of anti-drama where conflicts which are always temporary are always resolved in a happy ending. It ends with the beginning of adult life. The novel of a life is a drama in successive phases where the conflicts are permanent and end only in the final tragedy. It ends in death, redemptive or not. The first is a climb, the second a balancing act.

36 F. M. Dostoyevsky. *Materialy i issledovaniya*, Leningrad, 1935, p. 527.

37 *Letters* 2, p. 605; *A* 281, p. 348.

38 *Letters* 2, p. 608; *A* 281, p. 351.

39 If we remember that every time, as we see from the years 1857–9 and later years, the subterranean line fails, either because the poet expects too much from the power of the artist, or because the 'desire for the topical' exerts too great a fascination, it is probable that *The Brothers Karamazov* would never have had the sequel which Dostoyevsky was still intending to write on the eve of his death.

40 Or even the 'student' (Pyotr Verkhovensky) who was originally designated as the main hero: 'THE STUDENT IN THE FORM OF A "HERO OF OUR TIME"' (encircled by a line in the notebook) (*A* 11, p. 115).

41 D. D. Blagoy, 'Dostoyevsky i Pushkin', in *Dostoyevsky khudozhnik i myslitel'*, Moscow, 1972, pp. 344–426.

42 Ibid. p. 404.

43 In *Uncle's Dream*, subtitled *Fragment from the Mordasov chronicle*, Dos-toyevsky notes: 'The instinct of provincial gossips sometimes attains the miracu-lous, and of course there is a reason for this. It is based on the closest, most

interested, and long-lasting study of each other. Every provincial lives, as it were, under a glass dome' (*A* 2, p. 236).

44 *Letters* 1, p. 86; *A* 281, p. 117.

45 N. M. Chirkov, *O stile Dostoyevskogo*, Moscow, 1963, p. 55.

46 D. S. Likhachov, *Poetika drevnerusskoy literatury*, Leningrad, 1971, p. 358.

47 In the sense that Dostoyevsky gives some of his heroes, without interfering with their freedom in the novel, some of his own experiences (death-sentence, gambling, love, epilepsy, etc.) or some of his own ideas, which are easily traced by comparing, for example, *The Diary of a Writer* or his correspondence with some committed statements by his heroes.

48 *A* 10, p. 95.

49 *Bakhtin*, p. 336 (p. 250).

50 *A* 11, p. 261: 'Nechayev [Pyotr Stepanovich] and the Prince without explanations, but in action, while about Stepan Trofimovich *always with explanations.*' And 'The tone is that Nechayev and the Prince [Stavrogin] are not explained. Nechayev begins with malicious gossip and ordinariness and the Prince reveals himself gradually in action and without any explanations.'

51 He said it openly in 1876: 'I love him deeply, my Stepan Trofimovich, and I respect him deeply' (*A* 23, p. 64).

52 Cf. the chapter about *The Devils* and Lyamshin in David I. Goldstein, *Dostoyevsky and the Jews*, Austin–London, 1981, pp. 68–87.

53 *A* 10, pp. 69–70.

54 V. A. Tunimanov, 'Rasskazchik v *Besakh* Dostoyevskogo', in *Issledovaniya po poetike i stilistike*, Leningrad, 1972, p. 134. The article is a detailed analysis of the narrator in *The Devils*.

55 *LH* 77, p. 90.

56 They even make efforts to improve their style. Devushkin in *Poor Folk* makes the naive admission: 'To make a confession, my dear, I began to describe all this to you partly to unburden my heart to you, but more to show you a sample of the good style of my works. Since you probably will admit, my dear, that recently I have been forming my style' (*A* 1, p. 88).

57 Chapters 5 and 6 of the first part of *The Insulted and Injured* are a living postscript to *Poor Folk*. The novelist's voice replaces that of the chronicler.

58 *A* 3, p. 178.

59 *A* 13, p. 5.

60 A sub-title later abandoned but given in *Annals of the Fatherland*.

61 The chronicler of 'Uncle's Dream' is a good example of the amateur writer. He suffers from 'innate literary timidity'. Without worrying about literature, he first simply notes events (the arrival of Prince K. and the revolution he causes); then, after many hesitations, he finally decides to 'clothe in literary form' one of the most striking pages of the Mordasov chronicle (*A* 2, p. 299).

62 This procedure is like that of Lermontov in *A Hero of Our Time*: the narrator meets Maksim Maksimych, who tells him about Pechorin, and like that of Pushkin in *Tales of Belkin*: the author obtains the writings of Belkin through a friend.

63 *A* 4, p. 8.

64 An illustration of this thought is given in the rejected chapter of *The Devils*, 'At Tikhon's. Stavrogin tells the Elder that he is going to publish and distribute the pages of his confession where he describes the rape of Matryosha. Tikhon sees in

this choice a desire to suffer and bear the cross, but also an immeasurable pride, a wish to challenge and scandalise society (*A* 11, p. 24 and *A* 12, p. 108, where in another variant the chronicler expresses this idea).

65 In the same way, the chronicler of *The Brothers Karamazov* says that the detective part of the story, the crime and the judicial error, is only the 'external form' (*vneshnyaya storona*) of the work (*A* 14, p. 12).

66 *A* 5, p. 122.

67 Ibid. p. 179.

68 Literary confession, sometimes in public, is not rare in Dostoyevsky's novels. Raskolnikov, Ippolit ('My necessary explanation' in *The Idiot*), Stavrogin (the pages he makes Tikhon read, the letter to Dasha), Versilov, Dmitriy Karamazov confess with more or less sincerity, often from pride or exaltation. But these are quite different from the chronicle which follows shortly after the events, implying a difficult attempt at elucidation; they are actions in public.

69 I. I. Glivenko, who was the first to publish the three notebooks of *Crime and Punishment in extenso*, had already stated the hypothesis that notebook 2 preceded 1. Komarovich had confirmed this. Recent editions, those of the 'Literary Memorials' and the Academy (*A* 7, p. 400), due to dates established by textual scholars, give the notebooks in their right order: 2, 1, 3.

70 This story, 'the psychological account of a crime' committed by a student, should have contained only five or six signatures (*Letters* 1, pp. 417–18, *A* 28II, p. 136). The novel *Crime and Punishment* was born of the meeting between this 'story' and the 'novel' of at least twenty signatures, *The Drunkards*.

71 Instead of 'It will be a document' there was 'Let it be a report . . . What sort? For whom?'

72 *A* 7, p. 6.

73 Ibid. p. 5.

74 Ibid. p. 81: 'Here the story finishes and the diary begins.' 'Here' is probably after the meeting of Zamyotov and Vasiliy at the café.

75 Ibid. p. 83.

76 Ibid. p. 92: 'Notes for the Confession'.

77 Ibid. Dostoyevsky used many passages in the confession in the final novel, simply replacing the first person by the third.

78 *A* 7, p. 96. Instead of 'This is a confession. I shall hide nothing', Dostoyevsky had written: 'It is a complete confession. I am writing for myself, for my personal need, and this is why I shall hide nothing.'

79 Ibid. p. 138.

80 Ibid. p. 141.

81 Ibid. p. 144.

82 Ibid. p. 146.

83 Ibid. pp. 148–9.

84 There are fourteen days of action in *Crime and Punishment*, nine if the days when Raskolnikov is ill and unconscious are subtracted (A. G. Tseytlin, 'Vremya v romanakh Dostoyevskogo', in *Rodnoy yazyk v shkole*, 5, 1927, 3–17).

85 *A* 9, p. 235.

86 Ibid. p. 276.

87 Ibid.

88 Cf. the study 'Vymyshlennyy rasskazchik' in V. E. Vetlovskaya, *Poetika romana 'Brat'ya Karamazovy'*, Leningrad, 1977, pp. 13–51. The Soviet critic forms the

same connections between Pushkin's chronicler Belkin and Dostoyevsky's chronicler as we do. She also compares the chronicler of *The Brothers Kara-mazov* to the chronicler in *History of a town* by Saltykov-Shchedrin.

89 *A* 15, p. 89.
90 Ibid. p. 118.

18 COMPOSITION OF THE NOVEL IN *A RAW YOUTH*: CHRONICLE AND STORIES

1 *Letters* 2, p. 294; *A* 291, p. 148.
2 The journalist works in the same way. He brings voices to life. The article about the environment in *Diary of a Writer 1873* is a good example:

But let us suppose – a voice whispers to me – that your solid assumptions . . .

– Certainly, there is truth in your remark, – I must reply to the voice . . .

– The Russian people? Allow me, – another voice whispers to me – this is what people say . . .

– Well, yourself after all, – whispers some caustic voice to me . . .

(*A* 21, pp. 14–15)

3 *LH* 77, p. 85.
4 Ibid. p. 92.
5 In the finished novel, Raskolnikov is present in thirty-seven scenes out of forty. Some important episodes take place without him: for instance, the meeting between Svidrigaylov and Dunya, and Svidrigaylov's suicide.
6 *LH* 77, p. 92.
7 Ibid. p. 95.
8 Ibid. p. 96. Towards 20 August Dostoyevsky confirmed his choice: 'Principal note: The youth tells the story: i, i' (Ibid. p. 106).
9 Ibid. p. 135.
10 Ibid. p. 145.
11 Ibid. p. 177.
12 Ibid.
13 Ibid. p. 162. On 12 August Dostoyevsky had envisaged another solution: 'One QUESTION only: about His sufferings on the death of his wife, the flight of the child, etc. And, especially, about the little beetle. Narrative in the third person, will it be natural there. *The father* might, however, tell this to the youth himself, just before the suicide' (ibid. p. 96).
14 *LH* 77, p. 96.
15 Ibid. p. 111.
16 Ibid. p. 174.
17 Ibid. p. 180.
18 Ibid. p. 198.
19 Ibid. p. 214.
20 Ibid. p. 284.
21 Ibid. p. 96. In capitals in the text.
22 Ibid.
23 Ibid. p. 108.
24 Ibid. p. 135.
25 Ibid.
26 Ibid. p. 139.

27 Ibid. p. 140.
28 Ibid.
29 Ibid. p. 141.
30 Ibid. pp. 144-5.
31 Ibid. p. 146.
32 Ibid. p. 148.
33 Ibid. p. 152.
34 Ibid. pp. 161-2.
35 Ibid. p. 177.
36 As we have seen, Dostoyevsky believed that this was impossible.
37 *LH* 77, p. 144.
38 Ibid. p. 145.
39 Ibid. p. 318.
40 Ibid. p. 232.
41 Ibid. p. 263. The context does not allow us to say whether this refers to the youth or to Versilov (He).
42 Ibid. p. 268. All these expressions within the system of the chronicle are identical with those which characterise the narrative of the author, as found in *Crime and Punishment*.
43 Ibid. pp. 211-12.
44 Ibid. p. 114.
45 *A* 13, pp. 142-7. This story is artificially linked with the action: the youth sees Olya several times and Versilov helps the girl as he would have helped any other teacher in difficulties. Vasin denies the fatal part played by Versilov, seeing the drama as a universal image of tragic destiny.
46 Ibid. pp. 165-7.
47 Ibid. pp. 288-9.
48 Ibid. pp. 309-10.
49 Ibid. pp. 313-22.
50 *A* 13, p. 309.
51 L. P. Grossman has tried to set this passage in free verse (L. P. Grossman, *Poetika Dostoyevskogo*, Moscow, 1925, p. 155).
52 *A* 13, p. 313.

INTRODUCTION TO PART 3

1 There is an identical structure in *The Brothers Karamazov*. Two brothers, Ivan, the rebel against God, and Alyosha, the seeker after holiness, represent the two extremes: in the centre Dmitriy is fighting between heaven and hell. V. E. Vetlovskaya has observed that in the novel Dostoyevsky reverses the real order of ages. Chronologically Dmitriy is twenty-seven and his two half-brothers, Ivan and Alyosha, are twenty-three and twenty respectively. But Ivan is promoted to elder brother (*starshiy brat*, *A* 15, p. 135) and even elder son (*starshiy syn*, *A* 15, p. 97 and pp. 136-7) with reference to Dmitriy who is thus placed in the middle in spite of the truth (V. E. Vetlovskaya, *Poetika romana 'Brat'ya Karamazovy'*, Leningrad, 1977, pp. 194-5).
2 As M. Bakhtin says:
  Whatever these meanings turn out to be, in order to enter our experience (which is social experience) they must take on the *form of a sign* that is

audible and visible for us (a hieroglyph, a mathematical formula, a verbal or linguistic expression, a sketch, etc.). Without such temporal–spatial expression, even abstract thought is impossible. Consequently, every entry into the sphere of meanings is accomplished only through the gates of the chronotope. (M. Bakhtin, 'Forms of time and of the chronotope in the novel', in Michael Holquist (ed.), *The Dialogic Imagination*, Austin, Texas, 1981, p. 258, translated from 'Formy vremeni i khronotopa v romane', in *Voprosy literatury i estetiki*, Moscow, 1975, p. 406.)

19 THE MASTER OF MEN AND HOURS

1 In art, theories are not worth much ... But this is a libel. The truth is that they have no universal value. They are theories for one person. Useful for one person. Made for him, to match him, and by him. Criticism, which can easily destroy them, lacks the knowledge of the needs and inclinations of the individual; and even theory cannot declare that the theory is not true in general but true for X, whose instrument it is.

                (P. Valéry, 'Rhumbs. Tel quel', in *Oeuvres*, 2, Paris, 1960, 638)

2 Versilov, 'He' at the beginning of the notebooks for *A Raw Youth*, was first called Brusilov. The name Versilov was probably suggested by Dostoyevsky's stay in Staraya-Russa in winter 1874, where a landowner called Andrey Petrovich Versilov lived a few years earlier (L. M. Reynus, *Dostoyevsky v Staroy-Russe*, Leningrad, 1969, p. 28).

3 *LH* 77, p. 115 and commentaries p. 479.

4 Ibid. p. 92.

5 Cf. the argument between L. Grossman, who supports Bakunin, and V. Polonsky, who supports Speshnyov: L. P. Grossman and V. P. Polonsky, *Spor o Bakunine i Dostoyevskom*, Leningrad, 1926. In the light of recent documents, we have investigated this debate and have unhesitatingly come down on the side of Polonsky, while stressing that there is a relationship between Stavrogin and the Great Sinner (J. Catteau, 'Bakounine et Dostoïevski', communication to the 'Colloque international Bakounine', 28 and 29 January 1977 at the Institut national d'études slaves, Paris, partly published in *Magazine littéraire*, 134, March 1978, 32–6).

6 This is true, for example, of the members of the group of five (*pyatyorka*) of the Vengeance of the People (the Nechayev affair – Pyotr Verkhovensky in *The Devils*) and of the Dolgushin group (Dergachëv in *A Raw Youth*). But even at this level of transparency, there is always supercomposition in the novel and the judgement of the novelist intervenes.

7 *A* 21, p. 75.

8 Ibid. p. 76.

9 *A* 11, p. 106.

10 Ibid. p. 107.

11 *Letters* 2, p. 288; *A* 291, p. 141.

12 *A* 21, p. 125.

13 V. Ivanov, *Borozdy i Mezhi. Opyty esteticheskiye i kriticheskiye*, Leningrad, 1916, pp. 33–4.

14 *Bakhtin*, p. 13 (p. 11).

15 Ibid. p. 7.

16 Ibid.
17 S. Askol'dov (S. A. Alekseyev), 'Religiozno-eticheskoye znacheniye Dostoyevskogo', in A. S. Dolinin (ed.), *F. M. Dostoyevsky. Stat'i i materialy*, 1,
   Petersburg, 1922, pp. 1–32.
18 Viktor Shklovsky has stressed this aspect of Dostoyevsky's creation:
   > I presume that if he was short of time, it was not because he signed too many
   > contracts and was putting off the end of the work. While his work kept its
   > variety and number of plans and voices, while the creatures continued their
   > struggle, he did not despair about the absence of a solution. The end of a
   > novel meant the collapse of a new tower of Babel for Dostoyevsky.
   >   (V. Shklovsky, *Za i protiv*, Leningrad, 1957, p. 172)
19 *Bakhtin*, pp. 55–6.
20 M. Bakhtin, 'Forms of time and of the chronotope in the novel', in Michael
   Holquist (ed.), *The Dialogic Imagination*, Austin, Texas, 1981, pp. 84–258,
   translated from 'formy vremeni i khronotopa v romane' in *Voprosy literatury i
   estetiki*, Leningrad, 1975, pp. 234–407.
21 *Bakhtin*, p. 38 (p. 28).

20 CHRONOLOGY AND TEMPORALITY IN *THE IDIOT*

1 *A* 8, p. 5. References to chronological data, which are widely scattered, will be
  inserted in brackets in the text for this analysis, so that the reader may see how
  sparingly the information is doled out.
2 These are the first seven chapters of the first part. At this stage of the writing of
  the novel nothing has been resolved; the chapters had been sent off to the editor
  while several versions of the novel were still possible. Without going into detail
  over the notebooks, Dostoyevsky's letter from Geneva to A. N. Maykov of 12
  January 1868 is enough to show his extraordinary power of improvisation:
  > On the whole the plan is made. I see in the following part details which
  > attract me and sustain my interest. But the whole? But my hero? Because
  > the whole for me depends on the hero. This is the position where I have
  > stopped. I must draw him. Will he develop as I write? And imagine the
  > catastrophe which is naturally happening to me: besides the hero, there is a
  > heroine, which makes two heroes! And besides these two heroes, there are
  > two more characters of the first importance, almost heroes . . . Of these four
  > heroes, two have their outlines firmly traced in my mind, one not at all and
  > the fourth, the principal, the first of all, is still very wavery.
  >   (*Letters* 2, p. 61; *A* 28ɪɪ, p. 241)
3 Return to the notes in the notebooks of 12 March 1868 (*A* 9, p. 200).
4 Dostoyevsky hesitated for a long time about the length of Myshkin's stay in
  Moscow. It was first three weeks (7 March 1868), then three months (12 March),
  then five days (10 April), then a month and a half (14 April), and finally six
  months (15 April). Contrary to his usual inclination, he slows time down. This is
  because it is a time of ripening and not of crisis (*A* 9, pp. 216, 224, 247, 255).
5 *A* 8, p. 149.
6 Ibid. p. 150.
7 Ibid.
8 Ibid. p. 151.
9 'At the beginning' (149); 'About two days later' (150); 'About ten days later'

(150); 'A month after the departure of the prince' (152); 'The day when the letter from princess Belokonskaya arrived' (152); the next day (152); the evening of this next day (152); the following week (152), etc.

10 'I obviously wasn't spying and didn't want to question anybody' (*A* 8, p. 260).

11 In fact it refers to the day before, since General Yepanchin has not yet returned from Petersburg (275).

12 These ideas were to become themes in *The Devils* and *A Raw Youth*: the Russian liberals despise and hate Russia; indifference towards crime comes from the disorder and moral and intellectual depravity which are present everywhere.

13 Dostoyevsky had finished the second part with an impression of uneasiness. He wrote to Maykov on 21/22 August 1868: 'I am dissatisfied with my novel to the point of being disgusted with it. I have made dreadful efforts, but have not been able to work: my heart isn't in it. Now I am bringing all my efforts to bear on the third part' (*Letters* 2, p. 130; *A* 28II, p. 310). Moreover he had not yet fixed the plot. Contrary to what he tells S. A. Ivanova 26 October/7 November 1868 – that he had written and imagined the whole novel in terms of the final scene: Rogozhin and Myshkin by the corpse of Nastasya Filippovna (*Letters* 2, p. 138; *A* 28II, p. 318) – Dostoyevsky only thought of this 'poetic' idea on 4 October. 'Rogozhin and the prince near the corpse. Final. Not bad' (*A* 9, p. 283).

14 The meeting with Rogozhin takes place between eleven and midnight, as Myshkin later tells Aglaya (*A* 8, p. 362).

15 *A* 8, p. 304.

16 *A* 23, pp. 144–8.

17 *A* 8, pp. 309–52.

18 Ibid. p. 402.

19 In these two days, it is probably necessary to include the morning of the following day.

20 Dostoyevsky had written 'about a week' (*proshlo s nedelyu*).

21 *A* 8, p. 475.

22 Ibid. p. 476. Every statement is accompanied by a reticence, which signifies both the probing power and the fragility of what is said and which preserves the uncertainty of reality.

23 Ibid. pp. 476–7.

24 Ibid. pp. 477–8.

25 Ibid. p. 479.

26 Yevgeniy Pavlovich's analysis is convincing, at least at the beginning, in the negative part where he enumerates the reasons which would explain the strange conduct of Myshkin: 'congenital inexperience', 'abnormal naivety', 'phenomenal absence of a sense of measure', 'enormous flood of cerebral ideas', 'nostalgia for Russia'. But when he makes these the motives for the actions of the prince, he is mistaken. He confuses environment and freedom. Myshkin tells him so by the statement that he (Myshkin) 'did not let anything go on' (*nichego ne dopuskal*) (*A* 8, p. 483).

27 *A* 8, p. 492.

28 Ibid.

29 Ibid. p. 493.

30 Ibid. p. 494.

31 Ibid. p. 495.

32 Ibid. p. 508.
33 Ibid. pp. 508–9.

21 THE ASCENDING SPIRAL

1 *A* 23, p. 146.
2 In Giovanni Lista, *Futurisme. Manifestes, documents, proclamations*, Lausanne, 1973, p. 184.
3 Contrary to what Bakhtin too categorically says: 'Thus there is no causality in Dostoyevsky's novels, no genesis, no explanations based on the past, on the influences of the environment or of upbringing' (*Bakhtin*, p. 40 (p. 29)). The first two chapters of *The Devils* are an attempt, imperfect, it is true, since it is made by the chronicler, to collect all the important biographical data about Stepan Trofimovich and Stavrogin, according to a discreet but dated chronology.
4 This crescendo, introduced by the mad processions, is so powerful that Fyodor Sologub, in his novel *The Petty Demon*, constructed his dénouement, prepared by the numerous mad escapades of Peredonov and the little grey creature which is harassing him, on the same contrasted elements: formal ball, fire, murder.
5 The chronicler, by returning to the same places (he twice visits Stepan Trofimovich, Liza and Shatov) traces the coils of a spiral. Michel Cadot has discovered similar structures in the metaphors of *Crime and Punishment* and *The Idiot*. (Communication to the 'Third International Dostoyevsky Symposium', 14–20 August 1977, Copenhagen: 'Can some constructions in the novels of Dostoyevsky be described as engendered by a helicoidal movement?')
6 *A* 10, p. 223.
7 *Letters* 1, p. 419; *A* 28II, p. 137. 'The final catastrophe': the confession of the criminal.
8 *A* 7, p. 138.
9 Pierre Pascal (ed.), in *Crime et Châtiment*, Paris, 1958, p. xxviii.
10 In Dresden Dostoyevsky read the Russian newspapers every day: *The Moscow Bulletin*, *The Voice*, *The St Petersburg Bulletin* and the journals *Russian Messenger* and *Aurora*. His attention was attracted by the character of Nechayev long before the crime took place. In fact, in *The Moscow Bulletin*, 112, 24 May 1869. M. N. Katkov had mentioned Nechayev as a person 'who led a band of rebellious students'. An argument followed in which *Aurora* took part (6, 1869, 170–5) with many quotations from Katkov. L. P. Grossman has made use of the legend, supported by Anna Grigoryevna, according to which Dostoyevsky is supposed to have heard of events at the Moscow Agronomical Institute, where Ivanov was a student, from I. G. Snitkin, Anna's brother, who came to spend his holidays in Dresden in 1869 (*Life*, pp. 184–5). I. G. Snitkin, according to Anna, mentioned the sudden change in Ivanov, whom he knew, to Dostoyevsky (*M Anna*, pp. 130–1). Now the trial showed that Ivanov had not changed his views at all and that his conflict with Nechayev originated in personal rivalry (a recent confirmation of this is given by publication of the letter of 1 August 1870 from G. Lopatin to Natalya Herzen, in Michael Confino, *Violence dans la violence (le débat Bakounine-Nechaev)*, Paris, 1973, pp. 206–9). However it is probable that Dostoyevsky, alerted by the press, interrogated his young brother-in-law about student unrest. Since Snitkin stayed in Dresden until October 1870, he and Dostoyevsky possibly had long talks about Ivanov's murder, which was first

revealed by the *The Moscow Bulletin* of 27 November 1869, in its account of the discovery of Ivanov's body. The affair was widely reported, but Nechayev was not mentioned until 20 December. On 25 December, in the same newspaper, Nechayev was named as the murderer of Ivanov. From then on, using the German and even the French press (in *La Marseillaise*, Rochefort wrote an article about Nechayev, entitled 'the great Russian patriot' and even published a letter from him), *The Moscow Bulletin* and *The Voice* were full of details about the life, activities and proclamations of Nechayev. As is shown by a number of notes in the notebooks, all prior to 1 July 1871, when the trial of the Vengeance of the People took place in Petersburg, Dostoyevsky constructed his Nechayev essentially from accounts in *The Moscow Bulletin* and *The Voice*. When he returned from exile and was in the capital from 8 July 1871 onwards, he evidently used the minutes of the trial, and in particular *The Catechism of a Revolutionary* and N. Ogaryov's poem 'A Luminous Soul', written in honour of a teacher who died in Siberia but re-dedicated at this time to Nechayev. This however affected only part of the novel, since the first part and two chapters of the second had already been published before this date.

11 *A* 11, p. 94.

12 In the tradition of Russian novelists which Nabokov mocks in the first lines of his novel *The Gift*, Dostoyevsky only mentions the first three figures '187' (*A* 10, p. 311, in Shigalyov's speech). As the first chapters of *The Devils* were published at the beginning of 1871 and as it is a chronicle of events which took place in September, the year is logically taken by the reader as 1870. In fact the writer was thinking of the year 1869. Though he introduces allusions to later years (the incomplete data given by Shigalyov, Lyamshin's musical parody on the Franco-Prussian war mentioning Jules Favre 'weeping on Bismarck's lap' and abandoning everything, which refers to the year 1871), it is because he is using events which are as recent as possible. The chronological contradiction is invisible to present-day readers.

13 The visit to the monastery begins on the first day, towards the end of August, at half past eleven, and Dmitriy is taken away three days later, at eight o'clock in the morning.

14 *A* 14, p. 369.

15 V. E. Vetlovskaya, *Poetika romana 'Brat'ya Karamazovy'*, Leningrad, 1977, pp. 193–6.

> The number three, repeated in different variants, is an organic part of *The Brothers Karamazov*. It indicates to the reader the relationship between the novel and the fairytale and perhaps stresses the conventional slightly fabulous character of the heroes, events and relationships, realistic as they are, giving them a hint of universal significance.' (Ibid. p. 196)

16 This mimicry is stressed by Dostoyevsky and noted by Fyodor Pavlovich:

> The old man leapt up in fright. The moment Alyosha began to speak about his mother, his face gradually began to change. He grew red, his eyes burned, his lips trembled . . . The drunk old man was spluttering and noticed nothing until something very strange suddenly happened to Alyosha; the same thing, which the old man had just been saying about the 'hysterical female', was repeated in him. Alyosha, who had been sitting at the table, suddenly leapt up, exactly as his mother had done in the story, clasped his hands, then covered his face with them, fell back on the chair as if struck

down, and suddenly began to shake all over with a hysterical attack of sudden, convulsive and inaudible tears. The unusual resemblance to his mother particularly amazed the old man. (*A* 14, pp. 126–7)

17 Here again the mimicry is noted by Ivan: 'Alyosha rose, went up to him and silently kissed him on the lips. – Literary theft! – exclaimed Ivan, suddenly changing his mood to a kind of ecstasy, – you stole it from my poem!' (ibid. p. 240).

18 At this moment Ivan remembers Alyosha's words.

19 A parody of the formula of Russian fairy-tales: 'The eldest was a clever lad, the second neither good nor bad, the third would give you all he had.' In many passages of the novel, the innocence and simplicity of Alyosha are stressed (*A* 14, pp. 5, 20, 25, 175, 183, 319). The third son, traditionally the simpleton in Russian fairy-tales (*Ivan-durachok*), is always triumphant.

22 TIME OF POWER AND POWER OF TIME

1 Jules Lagneau, *Célèbres leçons et fragments*, Paris, 1950, p. 62.

2 *Bakhtin*, p. 39.

3 Ibid. p. 41.

4 This is the thesis defended by Likhachov in his article: 'In quest of the expression of reality', in *F. M. Dostoyevsky. Materialy i issledovaniya*, 1, Leningrad, 1974, pp. 5–13.

5 This chapter exists in three versions, all incomplete:
   (*a*) The first version (TsGALI, F.212.1.10) is known to us by the fifteen pages of proofs of the issue of *The Russian Messenger* of December 1871.
   (*b*) The corrections Dostoyevsky made on these proofs. These corrections are of different dates and are later than *c*.
   (*c*) The copy which Anna Grigoryevna made of a second version, the manuscript of which has been destroyed or lost. This is the version most often published.

   Variant *a* is most adapted to the novel and the least prolix, as well as being the most brutal: the rape is implied, but indubitable. There is no page missing in the confession, as there is in version *c* and the chronicler is logically absent. Variant *b* is an attempt to make the Stavrogin–Tikhon meeting later, in the third part, in chapter 1 (*A* 12, p. 119). Variant *c* shows the desperate effort Dostoyevsky made to make his chapter acceptable: Stavrogin does not give Tikhon the page where the rape is implied and even affirms that possibly nothing happened, which transforms his confession into a fiction meant to provoke and challenge; moreover the chronicler gives commentaries which are absolutely incompatible with the time of the action, since at the same time he is a spectator of the 'Shpigulin day' (*A* 12, pp. 108–18). This is why the first version has been preferred (*A* 11, pp. 5–30). The references are given in the body of the text.

6 *A* 12, p. 113.

7 Jean-Paul Sartre, *Situations*, 1, Paris, 1947, p. 71.

8 *A* 9, p. 100.

9 Ibid. pp. 100–1.

10 Ibid. p. 102.

11 *A* 13, p. 446.
12 Ibid. pp. 126–7.
13 Ibid. p. 268.
14 Ibid. p. 22.
15 Ibid. p. 96.
16 Ibid. p. 110.
17 *A* 13, p. 127.
18 Ibid. p. 419.
19 Ibid. p. 204.
20 Ibid. p. 200.
21 Ibid. pp. 240–1.
22 Ibid. p. 240.
23 Ibid. p. 225.
24 Ibid. p. 230.
25 Ibid. p. 65.
26 Ibid. p. 322.

23 THE HAVENS OF ETERNITY

1 *A* 7, p. 161.
2 *Letters* 1, p. 131; *A* 281, p. 164.
3 *A* 8, p. 52.
4 Ibid.
5 In Myshkin's description of a condemned man on his way to the scaffold, time is experienced both as pain and as ultimate freedom. The more it accelerates, the richer it becomes (the brain works intensely, thoughts multiply to infinity). The progression is minuted cruelly and in masterly fashion by counting in reverse and by the space which remains to be crossed (the term 'chronotope' is perfectly appropriate here). At the beginning, the unhappy man has a week to live; it is curtailed: at five o'clock he is awakened, with four hours left to live; three hours later, he is being taken through the town ('I think, that here too it seemed that there was an infinity of time left to live, while he was being driven to the scaffold. I think he probably thought on the way: "It's a long way yet, there are three streets left to live..."'); then it is the steps of the scaffold which he climbs 'with tiny steps', 'some seconds', 'the very last seconds', 'the last quarter of a second', 'the tenth of a instant' in which he hears the sound of the slithering steel (*A* 8, pp. 55–6).
6 Ippolit twice (*A* 8, pp. 318–19). Kirillov takes up this formula, quoted to him by Stavrogin, and approves of it (*A* 10, p. 188). For him 'time is not an object, but an idea which will be extinguished'.
7 T. S. Karlova, *Dostoyevsky i russkiy sud*, Kazan', 1975, p. 77.
8 An ideal and therefore impossible reconciliation as the rest of the dialogue between Myshkin and his questioner, Aleksandra Yepanchina, makes clear:

This friend, who told you about these sufferings ... the punishment was changed surely, so that he was given this 'endless life' as a gift? Well, what did he do with these riches then? Did he keep a score of every minute he lived?

– Oh no, he told me himself, – I asked him about this – he didn't live like that at all and he wasted no end of minutes.

– So there is an experiment for you, then, and it is impossible to live really 'keeping a score'. For some reason it is impossible.

– Yes, for some reason it is impossible, – repeated the prince, – I thought that too. But all the same I don't believe it somehow.   (*A* 8, p. 53)

9 This is what we have done in our study: 'Du palais de cristal à l'âge d'or ou les avatars de l'utopie' (in J. Catteau (ed.), *Dostoïevski*, Cahiers de l'Herne 24, Paris, 1973, pp. 176–95). In our view, the vision of the Golden Age in Dostoyevsky's works is one facet of the syncretism of the writer, which gathers in an act of faith in man, deeply optimistic, the Christian inspiration of Revelation and the pagan inspiration of the myth of eternal rebirth and reunites Christian and atheist heroes in the same struggle. The philosophic meaning and religious ambiguity of the theme do not concern us here. We are only interested in the temporal structure of the dream Utopia of the Golden Age.

10 *A* 13, p. 375.

11 *A* 11, p. 12.

12 Alain Besançon, *Le Tsarévich immolé (La symbolique de la loi dans la culture russe)*, Paris, 1967, p. 214.

13 Vyacheslav Ivanov and M. O. Gershenson, *Perepiska iz dvukh uglov*, Petersburg, 1921, p. 16.

14 Numerous Soviet scholars have studied this theme of the Age of Gold and universal harmony: V. L. Komarovich, 'Mirovaya garmoniya Dostoyevskogo', in *Ateney*, 1–2, 1924, 112–42; N. F. Bel'chikov, 'Zolotoy vek v predstavlenii Dostoyevskogo', in *Problemy teorii i istorii literatury*, Moscow, 1971; A. S. Dolinin, 'Zolotoy vek u Dostoyevskogo', in *Neva*, 11, 1971; N. I. Prutskov, 'Sotsial'no-eticheskaya utopiya Dostoyevskogo', in *Idei sotsializma v russkoy klassicheskoy literature*, Leningrad, 1969; N. I. Prutskov, 'Dostoyevsky i khristianskiy sotsializm', in G. M. Fridlender (ed.), *Dostoyevsky. Materialy i issledovaniya*, 1, Leningrad, 1974, pp. 58–82.

15 *A* 22, pp. 12–13.

16 Ibid. p. 13.

17 In an article sketched in 1864–5, 'Socialism and Christianity', Dostoyevsky noted: 'Not a single atheist who disputed the divine origin of Christ has denied that He is the ideal of humanity' (*LH* 83, p. 248).

18 In his *Diary of a Writer* of March 1876, Dostoyevsky says that he has only recently learned of this 'Church of Atheists' into which only non-believers who worship humanity are admitted, long after finishing and publishing *A Raw Youth*: 'There is something moving there in many respects and much enthusiasm. It is a true deification of humanity and a passionate need to show love for it.' And to show the full value of this thought, he quotes at length the passage from which we have only given extracts here (*A* 22, pp. 97–8).

19 *A* 13, pp. 378–9. Ivan Karamazov develops the same theme in what he calls 'The geological revolution' (*A* 14, p. 83).

20 But it is remarkable that I have always ended my picture with a vision like the one in Heine, of Christ on the Baltic Sea. I could not manage without him, I could not fail to imagine him finally, among orphaned people. He would approach them, stretch out his hands to them and would say: 'How could you forget him?' And here a kind of veil would fall from their eyes and the great triumphant hymn of the new and last resurrection would ring out.

(*A* 13, p. 379)

In the same way Blok ends his revolutionary poem, 'The Twelve' with the appearance of Christ.

21 'And in general what dominates in "The Dream of a Ridiculous Man" is not the Christian but the ancient spirit' (*Bakhtin*, p. 200 (p. 149)). 'The golden age of the Christian Dostoyevsky undeniably bears the trace of its mythological origin: God is absent from this Eden. His name is not even pronounced in it, and no prohibition weighs on these fortunate people' (Boris de Schloezer, 'Sur trois nouvelles de Dostoïevski', in *La Nouvelle Revue française*, 157, 1966, 106).

22 Soviet criticism is more interested in the sources of this dream of the Golden Age than in its significance in Dostoyevsky's work. Komarovich sees mainly the influence of the French utopians and particularly that of *Social Destiny* by Considérant (Komarovich, 'Mirovaya garmoniya Dostoyevskogo', p. 139): Pogozheva sees a form of the 'reactionary' vision of the kingdom of God (L. P. Pogozheva, 'Mechta Dostoyevskogo o zolotom veke', in *Krasnaya Nov*, 2, 1941, 177); finally, Lebedeva believes that the literary sources of the 'paradise of the children of the sun' are to be found in the old Russian apocrypha of the sixteenth century, *The Tribulations of Zosima among the Rahmans* (probably the Brahmins) (T. B. Lebedeva, 'Sotsial'naya utopiya Dostoyevskogo i 'zemnoy ray' drevnerusskoy literatury', in *Puti russkoy prozy XIX veka*, Leningrad, 1976, pp. 75–85).

23 Shestov sees the dream of the Golden Age as a version of the Fall, of original sin (L. Shestov, *Kirkegard i ekzistensial'naya filosofiya*, Paris, 1939, pp. 18–21). The Russian philosopher places more stress on the fact that the knowledge of Good and Evil brings Evil to birth, than on the painful freedom that it brings.

24 *A* 25, p. 117.

25 Mircea Eliade, *Le Mythe de l'éternel retour*, Paris, 1949.

26 Ibid. p. 125.

27 *Letters* 4, pp. 9–10.

28 *A* 7, p. 91.

29 *A* 6, pp. 419–20.

30 Ibid. p. 421.

31 *A* 15, p. 79.

32 T. S. Karlova, *Dostoyevsky i russkiy sud*, Kazan', 1975, pp. 42–6.

24 THE DREAM OF SPACE AND THE SPACE OF THE REAL

1 M. Bakhtin, *Voprosy literatury i estetiki*, Moscow, 1975, pp. 234–5; *The Dialogic Imagination*, ed. Michael Holquist, Austin, Texas, 1981, pp. 84–5.

2 Ibid. pp. 397–8.

3 Ibid. p. 398.

4 *A* 14, p. 328.

5 Ibid.

6 *A* 7, p. 90.

7 Ibid. p. 149.

8 Ibid. p. 205.

9 *LH* 77, p. 124. *Final* in French.

10 Nina Gourfinkel, 'Les Eléments d'une tragédie moderne dans les romans de Dostoïevski', in *Le Théâtre tragique*, Paris, 1962 and reprinted in *Dostoïevski*, Cahiers de l'Herne 24, Paris, 1973, p. 242.

11 Clearly this is only a tendency. Dostoyevsky's novels cannot be called theatrical works. The obvious reasons, a complication which wishes to express the whole, a powerful complexity, are supplemented by structural reasons. The theatre forbids the stereoscopic vision which is characteristic of chronicle time. Scenic time, distributed among acts of the same length, is totally incapable of expressing the ascending spiral with its false repetitions. Finally, as Bakhtin stresses, drama is foreign to authentic polyphony, since it can include only a multiplicity of levels, not a multiplicity of worlds (*Bakhtin*, p. 47). Moreover, Dostoyevsky himself explained the problem. When Princess Obolensky wanted to dramatise *Crime and Punishment*, he wrote to her on 20 January 1872:

> I consent willingly, and besides I make it a rule never to oppose attempts of this kind; however I must note that they are never entirely successful. It is one of the mysteries of art that an epic form can never find its equivalent in dramatic form. I even think that different artistic forms imply series of specific poetic thoughts, so that no thought could ever be expressed in a form which was not suited to it. It would be another thing if you were to redo and change the novel from beginning to end, only keeping a few episodes to transform it into a drama; or if, taking your inspiration from the original idea, you were to modify the subject entirely.
>
> (*Letters* 3, p. 20; *A* 291, p. 225)

12 Quoted by A. Dikiy, *Povesti o teatral'noi yunosti*, Moscow, 1957, p. 62, from *Sovremennoye slovo*, St Petersburg, 21.9.1910.

13 Albert Camus, *Théâtre, récits, nouvelles*, Paris, 1967, p. 1886.

25 THE INVENTORY AND THE EXPRESSIONIST ORCHESTRATION OF SCENERY AND LIGHTING

1 *A* 25, p. 91. The epithet 'amusing' (*zabavnaya*) does not imply any idea of frivolous or pointless pleasure. Dostoyevsky's conception of humour is completely different from the usual definitions. For him humour does not hide pain, nor does it save us from feeling pain (Freud). The secret of humour, as he once wrote in reference to Pickwick, is in 'arousing compassion' (*Letters* 2, p. 71; *A* 28II, p. 251).

2 *A* 3, p. 425.

3 *A* 14, p. 96.

4 *A* 2, p. 293.

5 *A* 3, p. 330.

6 Ibid. p. 331.

7 *A* 6, p. 8.

8 Ibid. p. 376.

9 Ibid. p. 25.

10 Ibid. pp. 241–2.

11 Ibid. p. 388.

12 The chapter: 'Impression and expression', in N. M. Chirkov, *O stile Dostoyevskogo*, Moscow, 1963, pp. 83–107.

13 V. Shklovsky, *Za i protiv. Zametki o Dostoyevskom*, Moscow, 1957, p. 41.

14 *A* 10, p. 113.

15 Ibid. p. 114.

16 Ibid.

17 Ibid. p. 115.
18 *A* 6, pp. 251–2.
19 *A* 25, p. 91.
20 *A* 6, p. 240.
21 *A* 15, p. 40.
22 Ibid.
23 *A* 10, p. 460.
24 *A* 6, p. 394.
25 Ibid. p. 389.
26 *A* 15, pp. 57, 68–9, 84.
27 The significance of this scenery (the unleashing of the elements and of demonic forces) like that of the death of Svidrigaylov (shipwreck of the being and the watery universe with its threat of flooding) is strengthened by their common literary descent from Pushkin. The first is linked with the ballad *The Devils*; the second to 'The Bronze Horseman'.
28 *A* 15, p. 191.
29 René Girard, *Du double à l'unité*, La recherche de l'absolu, Paris, 1963; pp. 164–5.
30 Picture by Karl Pavlovich Bryullov (1799–1852). Exhibited in Milan, Rome and Paris, where it won a gold medal in 1834, it is now in the National Russian Museum, Leningrad, which contains both the original (1830–3) and a preliminary sketch (1828–30). In Petersburg, Gogol hailed this vast dramatic composition in which Hellenistic beauty of body is contrasted with theatrical and romantic scenery as a masterpiece and declared it 'the first day of the Russian palette'.
31 Quoted by A. S. Dolinin in *Letters* 2, p. 419.
32 *Letters* 2, p. 103; *A* 28II, p. 283: 'But your judgement is probably quite correct.'
33 *Istoriya russkogo iskusstva*, 8, Moscow, 1964, 2, p. 72. The commentator quotes Herzen who used the picture for political purposes: 'They [the characters in Bryullov's painting] fall beneath the blows of a savage, blind, unjust force, against which all resistance would be useless. This is the sort of inspiration drawn in from the atmosphere of Petersburg.'
34 *Dostoïevski, L'Idiot*, ed. Pierre Pascal, Paris, 1977, p. xxxiii.
35 See Pierre Boutang's study 'Stavrogin', in J. Catteau (ed.), *Dostoïevski*, Cahiers de l'Herne 24, Paris, 1973, pp. 259–65.

26 THE SEMANTICS OF COLOUR

1 *The Complete Letters of Vincent van Gogh* (3 vols.), London, 1958, p. 297.
2 B. F. Pereverzev, *Tvorchestvo Dostoyevskogo*, Moscow, 1912, pp. 73–4.
3 V. Botsyanovsky, 'Kraski u Dostoyevskogo', in *Zhizn' iskusstva*, 15 November 1921, no. 817.
4 L. P. Grossman, *Poetika Dostoyevskogo*, Moscow, 1925, p. 119.
5 N. M. Chirkov, *O stile Dostoyevskogo*, Moscow, 1963, pp. 108–11.
6 S. M. Solov'yov, 'Kolorit proizvedeniy Dostoyevskogo', in *Dostoyevsky i russkiye pisateli*, Moscow, 1971, pp. 414–46.
7 A. Belyy, *Masterstvo Gogolya. Issledovaniye*, Moscow–Leningrad, 1934, p. 286. Andrey Bely excludes green which appears mainly in official uniforms, which partly explains why this contradicts the statistics we gave at the beginning of the chapter.

8 A. Remizov, 'Ogon' veshchey', *Opleshnik*, Paris, 1954, p. 204.
9 W. Kandinsky, *Complete Writings on Art*, ed. K. C. Lindsay and Peter Vergo, 1, London (2 vols), 1982; p. 186.
10 Ibid. *M Anna*, p. 216. Bagautov's coffin in 'The Eternal Husband' is lined in 'massak' velvet and Anna Grigoryevna repeats her testimony when this detail is mentioned. L. P. Grossman, *Seminariy po Dostoyevskomu*, Moscow–Petrograd, 1922, p. 60.
11 *A* 3, p. 41.
12 Cf. the quotation at the beginning of the chapter.
13 Kandinsky, *Complete Writings on Art*, p. 183.
14 Ibid. p. 183.
15 In *Netochka Nezvanova* an unsympathetic hero, the husband of Aleksandra Mikhaylovna, the gloomy Pyotr Aleksandrovich, seems to hide his look 'behind large green glasses' (*A* 2, p. 226).
16 *A* 8, p. 343.
17 Ibid. p. 247.
18 Ibid. p. 323.
19 J. Catteau, 'A propos de la littérature fantastique: André Belyj héritier de Gogol' et Dostoïevski', in *Cahiers du monde russe et soviétique*, 3, III, 1962, 327–73.
20 The dream of the Golden Age reveals the perversion of red. For Stavrogin the scarlet of the setting sun, swollen with hope, changes into a bleeding wound, the little red insect on the geranium leaf at the moment when Matryosha hangs herself. Similarly, for Versilov, the setting sun, recalling the dawn of humanity, suddenly changes to the deep red of the fires of the Commune.
21 *A* 2, p. 275.
22 *A* 6, p. 357.
23 *A* 10, pp. 37 and 145, where the word 'mask' is repeated.
24 *A* 13, pp. 27 and 274, where the word 'mask' is repeated.
25 *A* 6, p. 393.
26 'Like as a thirstie man dreameth, and loe, he is drinking, and when he awaketh, behold he is faint, and his soule longeth' (Isaiah 29:8).
27 *A* 6, p. 56. The dream hides a symbol revealed by the economy of the novel. In the epilogue, Raskolnikov is dreaming of the Golden Age, which he evokes in the image of the happy time of Abraham. The dream of the oasis is a desperate attempt to escape tragic determinism, representing a haven clothed in the perfection of dawn, sheltered from the storm which Raskolnikov's will to power has called up. It illuminates the idealistic side of the hero at the very moment when he is preparing for the crime.
28 *A* 6, pp. 46–9.
29 Ibid. p. 212.
30 Ibid. p. 213.
31 Ibid. p. 214.
32 *A* 14, p. 353.
33 Ibid.
34 'Krasnaya tesemochka.' *A* 14, p. 111, line 32.
35 'Tonen'kaya rosovaya lenta.' Ibid. p. 410, line 44.
36 S. M. Solov'yov, 'Kolorit proizvedeniy Dostoyevskogo', in *Dostoyevsky i russkiye pisateli*, Moscow, 1971, p. 433.

37 *A* 2, p. 103.
38 Ibid. p. 119.
39 Ibid. p. 139.
40 Ibid. p. 29.
41 *A* 5, p. 123.
42 Ibid. pp. 140–1.
43 Ibid. p. 131.
44 *A* 6, p. 35.
45 Ibid. p. 133.
46 S. M. Solov'yov 'Kolorit proizvedeniy Dostoyevskogo', pp. 433–42.
47 Cf. the yellow star which the Jews were forced to wear by the Nazis.
48 In *The Master and Margarita* Bulgakov uses these implications of yellow; when the Master meets Margarita for the first time, she is carrying some repulsive, alarming yellow flowers (*otvratitel'nyye, trevozhnyye, zholtyye tsvety*) against her black coat and responding to this yellow sign (*zholtyy znak*) he follows her. The first word she pronounces resounds like an echo sent back by the 'dirty yellow wall': (M. Bulgakov, *Master i Margarita*, Frankfurt/Main, 1971, pp. 176–7). In Russian, madhouses were called 'the yellow house'. Although this originated in the fact that the Obukhov hospital where madmen were locked up in Petersburg was painted yellow, the expression has some aesthetic truth.
49 V. Mayakovsky and the futurists used the aggressive quality of yellow. S. Yesenin ends his *Confession of a Hooligan*, with these words of aggression and suicidal despair:
    I want to be a yellow sail
    Sailing towards the land where we are going.
50 *Letters of Vincent Van Gogh*, London, 1958, vol. 3, p. 31.
51 The remark is interesting: yellow must be enclosed within a form and not spread out in the background.
52 Kandinsky, *Complete Writings on Art*, London, 1982, pp. 180–1.
53 Ibid. p. 181.
54 *A* 13, p. 142.

27 THE HERO IN SPACE: SIGHTING AND SEEING

1 Georges Blin, *Stendhal et les problèmes du roman*, Paris, 1953, p. 150.
2 For a detailed study of the landscape of *Crime and Punishment*, see A. L. Rubanovich, 'Peyzazh v romane F. M. Dostoyevskogo *Prestupleniye i nakazaniye*', in *Trudy Irkutskogo universiteta*, 28, 2, 1959, 91–105.
3 As Raskolnikov's mother says (*A* 6, p. 185).
4 *A* 6, p. 357.
5 Now Ploshchad' Mira (Peace Square).
6 *A* 6, p. 337.
7 Now the Griboyedov Canal.
8 When Raskolnikov, after turning into the –sky Avenue (Obukhovsky, later Zabalkansky Avenue, which goes south from the Haymarket and crosses the Fontanka) sees Svidrigaylov, whom he was going to visit in his apartment, in a bar, he is amazed. Here is the dialogue between them:
    – I was going to your apartment and I was looking for you, – began Raskolnikov, – but somehow I suddenly turned into —sky Avenue from the

Haymarket! I never turn down here and never come here. I turn right from the Haymarket. And this isn't the way to your apartment . . . This is strange!
– Why don't you say right out: this is a miracle!
– Because it may be just chance. . . .
– And as for miracles, I can tell you that you seem to have been sleeping through these last two or three days. I mentioned this inn to you myself and there was no miracle about your coming straight here; I explained all the way here myself . . .
– I forgot, – Raskolnikov answered in amazement.
– I believe you. I told you twice. The address was imprinted mechanically in your memory. You turned this way mechanically, but strictly according to the address, without realising it.   (*A* 6, pp. 356–7)

Here the unconscious sighting is clarified by someone else. In the same way, in *The Idiot*, Rogozhin knows where Myshkin is going (to see Nastasya Filippovna) before Myshkin is clearly aware of it himself.

9 *A* 6, p. 5.
10 Marginal notes of Anna Grigoryevna for the 1906 edition of Dostoyevsky's *Complete Works*, collected in L. P. Grossman, *Seminariy po Dostoyevskomu*, Moscow–Petrograd, 1922, pp. 56–8.
11 Dostoyevsky lived in the house of the merchant Alonkin, at the corner of the Little Citizens Street (now no. 7 in Treasury Street) and Carpenter Street, a house of two storeys mainly occupied by clerks and artisans. The apartment of the writer (11) is on the first floor above the porch.
12 *A* 6, p. 7.
13 Ibid. p. 6.
14 Ibid. p. 7.
15 G. Chulkov, *Kak rabotal Dostoyevsky*, Moscow, 1939, pp. 329–30.
16 Or have the privilege – due to the excursions organised by the Institute of Russian Literature in Leningrad – of following the itineraries of Dostoyevsky's heroes district by district.
17 In fact, nothing is certain. The house identified has only three floors and not four as it says in the novel (*pyatietazhnyy dom*). Sylvie Luneau, who made a pilgrimage to these places in the company of Dostoyevsky's grandson, Andrey Fyodorovich, raises other possibilities and stresses that 'the whole district bears the same stamp' (J. Catteau (ed.), *Dostoïevski*, Cahiers de l'Herne, 24, Paris, 1973, pp. 130–5).
18 L. P. Grossman, *Seminariy po Dostoyevskomu*, Moscow–Petrograd, 1922, p. 56.
19 All the details for *Crime and Punishment* are given in Yevgeniya Sarukhanyan, *Dostoyevsky v Peterburge*, Leningrad, 1970, pp. 160–83.
20 The Petersburg district, situated to the north of the little Neva and the Peter-Paul Fortress, was familiar to the writer as Anna Grigoryevna again shows in one of her marginal notes about Svidrigaylov's last walk:
Svidrigaylov went towards X Avenue. He walked along this interminable avenue for a long time, almost half an hour, sometimes going down into the darkness on the wooden pavement'. This refers to the Grand Avenue of the Petersburg Quarter. This district was well known to Fyodor Mikhaylovich, in fact his sister Aleksandra Mikhaylovna Golenovskaya had a house on Grand Avenue . . . and when Fyodor Mikhaylovich went to see her, he

always found it wearisome to have to go along this interminable avenue, which was then fairly deserted and bordered with wooden houses.

(L. P. Grossman, *Seminariy po Dostoyevskomu*,
Moscow–Petrograd, 1922, pp. 57–8)

21 Quoted by Yevgeniya Sarukhanyan, *Dostoyevsky v Petersburge*, pp. 168–9.
22 *A* 6, p. 6.
23 Quoted by Yevgeniya Sarukhanyan, *Dostoyevsky v Peterburge*, p. 164.
24 *Peterburgskiy Kalendar' na 1870g.*, St Petersburg, 1870, 2, p. 103.
25 For this reason, as N. S. Durylin notes, it is impossible to make an anthology of landscapes in Dostoyevsky (N. S. Durylin, 'Ob odnom simvole u Dosto-yevskogo', in *Dostoyevsky, sbornik statey, Trudy gosardarstvennoy Akademii khudozhestvennykh nauk. Literaturnaya sektsiya*, 3, Moscow, 1928, p. 165).
26 N. P. Antsiferov, 'Peterburg Dostoyevskogo. Opyt literaturnoy ekskursii', *Ekskursionnoye delo*, Petrograd, 1921, 2–3, 49–68.
27 N. P. Antsiferov, *Dusha Peterburga*, Petersburg, 1921, pp. 138, 147.
28 *A* 8, p. 170.
29 Yevgeniya Sarukhanyan, *Dostoyevsky v Peterburge*, p. 187. G. A. Fyodorov has established that 'Rogozhin's house' did not really begin to look like the house in the novel until after some restoration work done after the publication of *The Idiot* and that Dostoyevsky was inspired by similar merchants' houses belonging to relatives of his, the Kumanins (G. Fyodorov, 'Moskva Dostoyevskogo', in *Literaturnaya Gazeta*, 43 (4329), 20 October 1971, 7).
30 L. M. Reynus, *Dostoyevsky v Staroy Russe*, Leningrad, 1969, p. 21.
31 Ibid. p. 30.
32 L. M. Reynus finds amazing coincidences in the toponymy of Staraya-Russa: Ilinskaya street is supposed to remind Dostoyevsky of Lieutenant Ilinsky of Tobolsk, wrongly accused of parricide (ibid. pp. 43–4), the house of a Russian general K. K. Von Sohn recalls the sad Von Sohn affair which is mentioned in the novel (ibid. p. 46). The love affair of an inhabitant of Staraya Russa, Grushenka Menshova, which aroused the sympathy of Anna Grigoryevna, is supposed to have influenced the portrait of Grushenka in the novel (ibid. pp. 47–53), etc.
33 *A* 14, p. 85.
34 L. F. Dostoyevskaya, *Dostoyevsky v izobrazhenii yego docheri L. Dostoy-evskoy*, Moscow–Leningrad, 1922.
35 L. M. Reynus, *Dostoyevsky v Staroy Russe*, pp. 60–7, and the plan of Dmitriy's route to his father's house, p. 71.
36 *A* 13, p. 115.
37 *A* 2, pp. 140–1.
38 Ibid. p. 141.
39 Ibid. pp. 161–2.
40 Ibid. p. 163.
41 Ibid. p. 165.
42 *A* 8, p. 351.
43 *A* 1, p. 138.
44 V. Shklovsky, *Za i protiv. Zametki o Dostoyevskom*, Moscow, 1957, p. 153.
45 *A* 5, p. 141.
46 Ibid. p. 151.
47 Ibid. p. 177.

48 Ibid. pp. 177–8.
49 The themes mainly associate music with scenery: in *Netochka Nezvanova*, the enchanting theme of the music at the concert and the house with red curtains opposite; in *Notes from Underground*, the painful theme of moral decomposition and the wet, yellowish misty snow, described as a haunting musical theme by the hero himself; in *Crime and Punishment*, the melancholy theme of the refrains of the barrel organ and the autumn evenings, damp and cold, when a damp snow falls in the light of the streetlamps. On the other hand, in *A Raw Youth*, Versilov associates music with an interior scene:

> He [Versilov] took me to a little tavern on the Catherine canal, downstairs, in a basement. It had few visitors. A tuneless barrel organ was playing, there was a smell of greasy napkins; we settled down in a corner. – Perhaps you don't know? I love sometimes, from boredom ... from terrible spiritual boredom ... to call in at sewers like this. This setting, this hiccuping aria from *Lucia*, the waiters in their indecently Russian costume, this stink of tobacco, these shouts from the billiard room – all this is so vile and prosaic that it almost becomes fantastic.   (*A* 13, p. 222)

50 E. Sturm in his parallel between *Notes from Underground* and *The Fall* by A. Camus, compares the moral and material landscape of the wet yellowish and dirty snow, a vision of decay and spiritual death, with Camus' sentence: 'I love the breath of stagnant mossy waters, the smell of dead leaves soaking in the canal, and the funeral scent which rises from barges full of flowers' (Ernest Sturm, *Conscience et impuissance chez Dostoïevski et Camus, parallèle entre 'Le Sous-sol' et 'La Chute'*, Paris, 1967, p. 58).
51 V. Shklovsky, *Za i protiv. Zametki o Dostoyevskom*, Moscow, 1957, p. 41.
52 Successively in 1848, 1861, 1866, and 1875.
53 *A* 5, p. 101. The expression is that of the Underground man.
54 *A* 2, pp. 47–8. The passages, which reveal an intention to accuse, are those which Dostoyevsky did not use again in 'Petersburg Dreams'.
55 *A* 19, p. 69.
56 *A* 2, p. 48.
57 V. Shklovsky, *Za i protiv*, pp. 72–3.
58 *A* 19, p. 69.
59 *A* 6, pp. 89–90.
60 Mark 9:25.
61 Andrey Belyy, *Peterburg*, Moscow, 1928, I, pp. 33–34.
62 Andrey Belyy, *Peterburg*, p. 49.
63 These three works, where Petersburg is the object of a vision by the heroes, are also linked by the names of the characters: the chronicler-murderer of the first version of *Crime and Punishment* (*The Diary*) is called Vasya, as in 'A Weak Heart'; and the hero of *A Raw Youth* is called Arkadiy, like the friend of Vasya in 'A Weak Heart'.
64 *A* 13, p. 113.
65 This is the theme of the novel of A. Belyy, *Peterburg*. Cf. G. Nivat, *Le Jeu cérébral, étude sur 'Pétersbourg'*, in Andréi Biély, *Pétersbourg*, Lausanne, 1967, pp. 321–67. And J. Catteau, 'A propos de la littérature fantastique: André Belyj, héritier de Gogol' et de Dostoïevski', in *Cahiers du Monde russe et soviétique*, 3, III, 1962, 327–73.
66 N. P. Antsiferov, *Dusha Peterburga*, Petersburg, 1921, p. 153.

67 *Peterburg*, ch. 1, p. 30.
68 The first time in a marginal note in *The Brothers Karamazov* (L. P. Grossman, *Seminariy po Dostoyevskomu*, Moscow–Petrograd, 1922, p. 68) and the second during a conversation reported by Grossman in his preface to the *Memoirs* of Anna Grigoryevna (*M Anna*, p. 16).
69 A. A. Belkin, 'O realizme Dostoyevskogo', in *Tvorchestvo F. M. Dostoyevskogo*, Moscow, 1959, p. 49.
70 S. N. Durylin, 'Ob odnom simvole u Dostoyevskogo', in *'Dostoyevsky' (sb. statey). Trudy gosudarstvennoy Akademiy khudozhestvennykh nauk. Literaturanya sektsiya*, Moscow, 1928, pp. 163–99.
71 The setting sun is one of the rare landscapes noted in the notebooks even before the novel is written.
72 *A* 2, p. 114.
73 *A* 2, p. 239.
74 *A* 3, p. 169.
75 Ibid. p. 441.
76 *A* 59, p. 59.
77 *A* 8, p. 63.
78 *A* 14, p. 263.
79 *A* 6, pp. 398 and 402.
80 *A* 13, p. 128.
81 *A* 11, pp. 21–2.
82 *A* 25, p. 114.
83 *A* 13, p. 61. It is a rebellion, like that which makes him say he does not want to become a Schiller.
84 Ibid. p. 267.
85 Ibid. p. 353.
86 *A* 14, p. 18. The author-chronicler of *The Brothers Karamazov* several pages later stresses the important part played by this image of the sun in Alyosha's monastic vocation: 'Probably the slanting rays of the setting sun, in front of the icon towards which his mother "the possessed" was stretching her hands, had played their part' (ibid. p. 25).
87 *A* 10, p. 117.
88 Durylin, 'Ob odnom simvole u Dostoyevskogo', p. 194.
89 *A* 6, p. 327.
90 *A* 13, p. 379.
91 Ibid. p. 353.
92 Ibid. p. 283.
93 Ibid. p. 291.
94 *A* 8, p. 380.
95 *A* 14, p. 265: 'I bless the daily rising of the sun . . . but I love its setting still more, its long slanting rays.'
96 Ibid. p. 326.
97 Ibid. p. 327.
98 For J. Drouilly, the theme is symbolic of light, of beauty and faith (Jean Drouilly, 'L'Image du soleil couchant dans l'œuvre de Dostoïevski. Essai de critique thématique', in *Etudes slaves et est-européennes*, 19, Montreal, 1974, 3–22).
99 *A* 14, p. 304.

100 Cf. the analysis of Dominique Arban, 'Le *Seuil*, thème, motif et concept', in *Dostoïevski*, Cahiers de l'Herne 24, Paris, 1973, pp. 205–14, and in Russian in *Dostoyevsky. Materialy i issledovaniya*, 2, Leningrad, 1976, pp. 19–29.

101 *A* 1, pp. 131–2.

102 *A* 5, pp. 162–3.

103 *A* 13, p. 169.

104 *Bakhtin*, pp. 227–30; P. M. Bitsilli, 'K voprosu o vnutrenney forme romana Dostoyevskogo', in *O Dostoyevskom. Stat'i*, Providence, Rhode Island, 1966, pp. 53–6.

105 *A* 8, p. 182.

106 Ibid. p. 184.

107 Ibid. p. 186.

108 *A* 8, pp. 194–5.

109 Jean Pouillon, *Temps et roman*, La jeune Philosophie, Paris, 1946, p. 168.

110 *A* 10, p. 145.

111 Without being a preliminary space, since it is a motionless place carried along in movement, the third-class compartment where Myshkin and Rogozhin meet at the beginning of the novel, where Arkadiy was supposed to meet his sister Liza in the notebooks of *A Raw Youth*, is one of those uncertain places, like bars, which are favourable to confidences and confessions. In 'Little Pictures on a Journey' (March 1874), Dostoyevsky notes that in Russia travellers on a train often tell their life stories (*A* 21, p. 162). Tolstoy was to remember it in *The Kreuzer Sonata*, 1887–89.

112 *A* 6, p. 213.

113 *Boris Godunov* (night, a cell in the Chudov monastery).

114 Bakhtin analyses this passage from the point of view of the carnival (*Bakhtin*, pp. 226–8 (pp. 167–9)).

115 *A* 9, p. 15.

116 *Bakhtin*, p. 39 (pp. 28–9) and pp. 226–8 (pp. 167–9).

117 *A* 8, pp. 146–9.

118 *A* 14, p. 69.

119 This is the scene of a conclave in *The Devils*.

120 *A* 8, p. 199.

121 Ibid. p. 222.

CONCLUSION

1 Tolstoy noted this in the epilogue of *War and Peace*:
The degree of freedom or necessity attributed to an act depends on the greater or lesser length of time that has gone by between the accomplishment of the act and the judgement upon it.
If I consider an act that I have just accomplished a moment ago in conditions almost the same as those in which I now find myself, my act appears indubitably free.'
(L. N. Tolstoy, *Polnoye sobraniye sochineniy*, 12, Moscow–Leningrad, 1933, p. 330)

2 A. Suarès, *Dostoïevski*, Cahiers de la Quinzaine, 18, 3, Paris, 1911, p. 37.

3 About Myshkin (N. M. Chirkov, *O stile Dostoyevskogo*, Moscow, 1967, p. 143).

Select bibliography

A complete bibliography of the critical literature on Dostoyevsky would require many volumes. This section is confined to works used in the preparation of this study and relevant material which has appeared since the publication of the original French edition, and is arranged under the following headings: bibliography; Dostoyevsky's works; correspondence; memoir material; essential monographs; critical works.

BIBLIOGRAPHIES

For the period 1846–1903

Dostoyevskaya, A. G., *Bibliograficheskiy ukazatel' sochineniy i proizvedeniy iskusstva, otnosyashchikhsya k zhizni i deyatel'nosti F. M. Dostoyevskogo, sobrannykh v Muzeye pamyati F. M. Dostoyevskogo v Moskovskom Istoricheskom muzeye, 1846–1903*, St Petersburg, 1906

For the period 1903–23

Sokolov, A. N., 'Materialy dlya bibliografii F. M. Dostoyevskogo', in A. S. Dolinin (ed.), *F. M. Dostoyevsky. Materialy i issledovaniya*, 2, Leningrad, 1924, pp. 3–122

For the period 1923–30

'Bibliografiya Dostoyevskogo', in F. M. Dostoyevsky, *Polnoye sobraniye khudozhestvennykh proizvedeniy*, Moscow–Leningrad, 1926–30, 13, pp. 617–25

For the period 1917–71

Belkin A. A., Dolinin, A. S., Kozhinov, V. V. (eds.), *Bibliografiya proizvedeniy F. M. Dostoyevskogo i literatury o nyom 1917–1965*, Moscow, 1968. [Supplement in V. G. Bazanov and G. M. Fridlender (eds.), *Dostoyevsky i yego vremya*, Leningrad, 1971, pp. 353–6.]
Belov, S. V., 'Bibliografiya proizvedeniy F. M. Dostoyevskogo i literatury o nyom 1966–1969', in V. G. Bazanov and G. M. Fridlender, *Dostoyevsky i yego vremya*, Leningrad, 1971, pp. 322–53
'Proizvedeniya F. M. Dostoyevskogo i literatura o nyom 1970–1971', in G. M. Fridlender (ed.), *Dostoyevsky. Materialy i issledovaniya*, 1, Leningrad, 1974, pp. 305–38
F. M. Dostoyevsky (1821–1881). Izdaniye proizvedeniy i literatura o nyom (1956–

1971), compiled by G. A. Petrova, ed. L. N. Podgut, Moscow, 1971 (duplicated publication of the Lenin Library, Moscow)

Other sources

Belov, S. V., 'Bibliograficheskiye materialy po F. M. Dostoyevskomu', in *Dostoyevsky–Nekrasov*, Leningrad, 1973, pp. 217–33
Dostoyevsky i teatr 1846–1977. Bibliograficheskiy ukazatel', Leningrad, 1980
Nechayeva, V. S. (ed.), *Opisaniye rukopisey F. M. Dostoyevskogo*, Leningrad, 1957
Opisaniye materialov Pushkinskogo Doma, 5, Moscow–Leningrad, 1959, pp. 81–208
Rice, M. P., *F. M. Dostoyevsky: A Bibliography of Non-Slavic Critical Literature about Him, 1900–1980*, Knoxville, Tenn., 1984
Terry, G. M., 'Dostoyevsky studies in Great Britain: a bibliographical survey', in M. V. Jones and G. M. Terry, *New Essays on Dostoyevsky*, Cambridge, 1983, pp. 215–44
Current bibliographies of work on Dostoyevsky appear in publications of the *International Dostoevsky Society*, compiled by R. Neuhäuser, M. P. Rice, *et al.*: *Bulletin of the International Dostoevsky Society*, 1–9 (1972–9) and *Dostoevsky Studies*, 1–6 (1980–5)

F. M. DOSTOYEVSKY: WORKS

Complete works

Polnoye sobraniye sochineniy F. M. Dostoyevskogo v 14-i tomakh, St Petersburg, 1882–3, 1: Biography, letters and extracts from notebooks
Polnoye sobraniye sochineniy F. M. Dostoyevskogo v 12-i tomakh (free supplement to the journal *Niva*, 1894–5), 1: *Povesti i rasskazy*, with a critical–biographical sketch by V. V. Rozanov
Polnoye sobraniye sochineniy F. M. Dostoyevskogo v 14-i tomakh (6th Jubilee edition, ed. A. G. Dostoyevskaya), St Petersburg, 1904–6:
    Vol. 10: *Dnevnik pisatelya za 1873 god. Politicheskiye stat'i. Kriticheskiye stat'i.* Reprinted as F. M. Dostoyevsky, *Dnevnik pisatelya za 1873 god*, Paris, no date [D 1873]
    Vol. 11: *Dnevnik pisatelya za 1876 god.* Reprinted as F. M. Dostoyevsky, *Dnevnik pisatelya za 1876 god*, Paris, no date [D 1876]
    Vol. 12: *Dnevnik pisatelya za 1877, 1880 i 1881 gody.* Reprinted as F. M. Dostoyevsky, *Dnevnik pisatelya za 1877 god*, Paris, no date [D 1877]
Polnoye sobraniye sochineniy F. M. Dostoyevskogo, Petersburg, 1911–18. Vol. 18 contains Dostoyevsky's translation of Balzac's *Eugénie Grandet*
Polnoye sobraniye khudozhestvennykh proizvedeniy v 13-i tomakh, ed. B. Tomashevsky and K. Khalabayev, Moscow–Leningrad, 1926–30, Vol. 13 contains Dostoyevsky's articles 1845–78
Sobraniye sochineniy v 10-i tomakh, Moscow, 1956–8
Polnoye sobraniye sochineniy v 30-i tomakh, Leningrad, 1972– . As publication of this Academy edition nears completion (vol. 29 has appeared at the time of writing) it is clear that this will stand as the definitive edition of Dostoyevsky's works. [Referred to in notes as *A* plus volume number.]

Published manuscripts

Dokumenty po istorii literatury i obshchestvennosti, 1, F. M. Dostoyevsky, Moscow, 1922

Prestupleniye i nakazaniye. Iz 'Zapisnykh knizhek' F. M. Dostoyevskogo, in *Krasnyy arkhiv*, 7, Moscow, 1925

Iz arkhiva F. M. Dostoyevskogo. Idiot, in P. N. Sakulin and N. F. Bel'chikov, *Neizdannyye materialy*, Moscow–Leningrad, 1931

Zapisnyye tetradi F. M. Dostoyevskogo, with commentary by N. I. Ignatova and Ye. N. Konshina, Moscow–Leningrad, 1935

Dolinin, A. S. (ed.), *F. M. Dostoyevsky. Materialy i issledovaniya*, Leningrad, 1935

'F. M. Dostoyevsky: Pervaya zapisnaya knizhka. Sibirskaya tetrad', in *Zven'ya*, 6, Moscow–Leningrad, 1936, pp. 413–38

Dolinin, A. S. (ed.), *F. M. Dostoyevsky v rabote nad romanom 'Podrostok'. Tvorcheskiye rukopisi*, Literaturnoye nasledstvo, 77, Moscow, 1965, pp. 59–518. [Referred to in text as *LH* 77.]

Dostoyevsky, F. M., *Prestupleniye i nakazaniye* (Literaturnyye pamyatniki), ed. L. D. Opul'skaya and G. F. Kogan, Moscow, 1970. Notebooks: pp. 427–596. Manuscript fragments: pp. 597–678

Neizdannyy Dostoyevsky. Zapisnyye knizhki i tetradi 1860–1881, Literaturnoye nasledstvo, 83, Moscow, 1971. [Referred to in text as *LH* 83.]

F. M. Dostoyevsky. Novyye materialy i issledovaniya, Literaturnoye nasledstvo, 86, Moscow, 1973. [Referred to in text as *LH* 86.]

Dostoyevsky, F. M., *Polnoye sobraniye sochineniy v 30-i tomakh*, Leningrad, 1972– , contains what are now the most authoritative versions of Dostoyevsky's notebooks and drafts

Wasiolek, E. (ed.), *Fyodor Dostoyevsky: The Notebooks for Crime and Punishment*, Chicago and London, 1967

Fyodor Dostoevsky: The Notebooks for The Idiot, Chicago and London, 1967

Fyodor Dostoevsky: The Notebooks for The Possessed, Chicago and London, 1968

Fyodor Dostoevsky: The Notebooks for A Raw Youth, Chicago and London, 1969

Fyodor Dostoevsky: The Notebooks for The Brothers Karamazov, Chicago and London, 1971

Proffer, Carl R. (ed.), *The Unpublished Dostoyevsky. Diaries and Notebooks 1860–1881*, 3 vols., Ann Arbor, Michigan, 1972–6

CORRESPONDENCE

Dostoyevsky's letters

Dostoyevsky, F. M., *Pis'ma v 4-kh tomakh*, ed. A. S. Dolinin, Moscow–Leningrad, 1928–59. [Referred to in text as *Letters* 1–4.]

Letters not included in the above
1. Botkina, A. P., *Pavel Mikhaylovich Tret'yakov v zhizni i iskusstve*, Moscow, 1951, pp. 216–7. [Letter to V. N. Tret'yakova, 13 June 1880.]
2. Simmons, J. S. G., 'F. M. Dostoevsky and A. K. Tolstoy: Two letters', *Oxford Slavonic Papers*, 9, 1960, pp. 64–71. [Letter to an unknown correspondent.]

3. Kautman, F., *Sborník Narodního Musea v Praze*, 7, 1960, 4, pp. 220–3. [Letters to N. P. Vagner, 24 October, 4 and 21 December 1875, January 1876, 24 October 1876, 17 January 1877.]
4. Bityugova, I., 'Neopublikovannoye pis'mo F. M. Dostoyevskogo', *Russkaya literatura*, 1961, 4, pp. 143–7. [Letter to L. G. Golovina, 4 August 1876.]
5. Zhavoronkova, A. and Belov, S., 'Delo o podporuchike Dostoyevskom', *Russkaya literatura*, 1963, 4, pp. 200–1. [Contains requests to the authorities of 1872 and 1875.]
6. Bessonov, B., 'Novyye avtografy russkikh pisateley', *Russkaya literatura*, 3, 1965, p. 206. [Letter to A. A. Krayevsky, 11 January 1874.]
7. Krasovsky, Yu. A., 'Kazanskiy korrespondent F. M. Dostoyevskogo', *Vstrechi s proshlym*, Moscow, 1971, pp. 47–50. [Letter to N. F. Yushkov, 5 February 1876.]
8. Bazanov, V. G. and Fridlender, G. M. (eds.), *Dostoyevsky i yego vremya*, Leningrad, 1971, pp. 248–9. [Letter to V. M. Kachenovsky, 25 November 1880.]
9. Legras, J., 'Lettres inédites de F. M. Dostoïevski', *Le Monde Slave*, 3, 1930, 321–36

Other sources
Lansky, L., 'Utrachennyye pis'ma Dostoyevskogo', *Voprosy literatury*, 1971, 1, 196–222
Lowe, D. and Meyer, R. (eds.), *F. M. Dostoevsky: Complete Letters*, 5 vols., Ann Arbor, Michigan, 1987– (forthcoming)
Zil'bershteyn, I. S., 'Novonaydyonnye i zabytyye pis'ma Dostoyevskogo', *F. M. Dostoyevsky. Novyye materialy i issledovaniya*, Moscow, 1973, p. 114–52

Letters to Dostoyevsky

Piksanov, N. P. (ed.), *Iz arkhiva Dostoyevskogo. Pis'ma russkikh pisateley*, Moscow–Petrograd, 1923
Suslova, A. P., *Gody blizosti s Dostoyevskim*, Moscow, 1928
Zil'bershteyn, I. S. (ed.), *F. M. Dostoyevsky i I. S. Turgenev. Perepiska. Istoriya odnoy vrazhdy*, Leningrad, 1928
Dostoyevsky, A. M., *Vospominaniya*, Leningrad, 1930, pp. 365–406 [Contains Dostoyevsky's correspondence with his brother.]
Dolinin, A. S. (ed.), 'Pis'ma A. N. Pleshcheyeva k F. M. Dostoyevskomu', *F. M. Dostoyevsky. Materialy i issledovaniya*, Leningrad, 1935, pp. 429–502
'Pis'ma M. M. Dostoyevskogo k F. M. Dostoyevskomu', in *F. M. Dostoyevsky. Materialy i issledovaniya*, Leningrad, 1935, pp. 503–79
Barsukova, A. (ed.), 'Perepiska F. M. Dostoyevskogo s M. P. Pogodinym', *Zven'ya*, 6, Moscow–Leningrad, 1936, pp. 439–54
Prokhorov, G., 'Nerazvernuvishiysya roman F. M. Dostoyevskogo', *Zven'ya*, 6, Moscow–Leningrad, 1936, 582–600. [Contains letters from Marfa Braun to Dostoyevsky.]
Ulanovskaya, B. Yu. *et al.*, 'Neizdannyye pis'ma k F. M. Dostoyevskomu', in V. G. Bazanov and G. M. Fridlender (eds.), *Dostoyevsky i yego vremya*, Leningrad, 1971, pp. 250–79
Volgin, I., 'Pis'ma chitateley k F. M. Dostoyevskomu', *Voprosy literatury*, 1971, 9, 173–96

Belov, S. V. and Tunimanov, V. A. (eds.), *F. M. Dostoyevsky i A. G. Dostoyevskaya: Perepiska*, Leningrad, 1976
Udina, I. M., 'Neizdannyye pis'ma k Dostoyevskomu', in G. M. Fridlender (ed.), *Dostoyevsky. Materialy i issledovaniya*, 2, Leningrad, 1976, pp. 297–322

Letters concerning Dostoyevsky

Dostoyevsky, A. M., 'Otkrytoye pis'mo k A. S. Suvorinu, 5-ogo fevralya 1881', *Novoye vremya*, 1778, 8 February 1881
Yanovsky, S. D., 'Bolezn' F. M. Dostoyevskogo' [letter to A. N. Maykov], *Novoye vremya*, 1793, 24 February 1881
Perepiska L. N. Tolstogo s N. N. Strakhovym, St Petersburg, 1914
Nechayeva, V. S., *V sem'ye i v usad'be Dostoyevskikh* [letters of M. A. and M. F. Dostoyevsky], Leningrad, 1939
Yanovsky, S. D., 'Pis'mo k O. F. Milleru, 8-ogo noyabrya 1882', *Literaturnaya gazeta*, 39, 23 September 1970
'Dostoyevsky v neizdannoy perepiske sovremennikov (1837–1881)', in *F. M. Dostoyevsky. Novyye materialy i issledovaniya*, Literaturnoye nasledstvo, 86, Leningrad, 1973, pp. 349–564
Rykachyova, Ye. A., 'Pis'mo k A. M. i D. I. Dostoyevskim, 26 fevralya 1881', in G. M. Fridlender (ed.), *Dostoyevsky. Materialy i issledovaniya*, 1, Leningrad, 1974, pp. 302–4.
Kumpan, K. A. and Konechnyy, A. M., 'Pis'ma Mikhaila Dostoyevskogo k ottsu', in *Pamyatniki kultury. Novyye otkrytiya*, Leningrad, 1981, pp. 69–86

MEMOIR MATERIAL

Dolinin, A. S. (ed.), *F. M. Dostoyevsky v vospominaniyakh sovremennikov*, 2 vols., Leningrad, 1964. [Referred to in text as *M* 1 and *M* 2.]
Dostoyevskaya, A. G., *Vospominaniya A. G. Dostoyevskoy*, ed. L. P. Grossman, Moscow–Leningrad, 1925. [Referred to in text as *M Anna.*]
Dnevnik 1867g., Leningrad, 1923
'Zhenevskiy dnevnik A. G. Dostoyevskoy (2-aya ch. dnevnika 1867g.)', in *F. M. Dostoyevsky. Novyye materialy i issledovaniya*, Literaturnoye nasledstvo, 86, Leningrad, 1973, pp. 167–290
'Primechaniya A. G. Dostoyevskoy k sochineniyam F. M. Dostoyevskogo', in L. P. Grossman, *Seminariy po Dostoyevskomu*, Moscow–Petrograd, 1922, pp. 54–70
Dostoyevskaya, L. F., *Dostoyevsky v izobrazhenii yego docheri L. Dostoyevskoy*, ed. A. G. Gornfel'd, Moscow–Leningrad, 1922
Dostoyevsky, A. M., *Vospominaniya*, Leningrad, 1930
Dostoyevsky, Fyodor, *The Gambler with Polina Suslova's Diary*, ed. E. Wasiolek, Chicago–London, 1972
fon Brettsel', Ya. B., 'O Dostoyevskom', in *F. M. Dostoyevsky. Novyye materialy i issledovaniya*, Literaturnoye nasledstvo, 86, Moscow, 1973, pp. 309–14
Mikulich. V. [Veselitskaya, L. I], *Vstrechi s pisatelyami*, Leningrad, 1929
Miller, O. F., 'Materialy dlya zhizneopisaniya F. M. Dostoyevskogo', in *Polnoye sobraniye sochineniy F. M. Dostoyevskogo*, St Petersburg, 1883, pp. 1–176
Perlina, N. M. 'Dostoyevsky v vospominaniyakh A. I. Suvorinoy', in V. G.

Bazanov and G. M. Fridlender, *Dostoyevsky i yego vremya*, Leningrad, 1971, pp. 295–305
Rizenkampf (Riesenkampf), A. Ye., 'Vospominaniya o Fyodore Mikhayloviche Dostoyevskom', in *F. M. Dostoyevsky. Novyye materialy i issledovaniya*, Literaturnoye nasledstvo, 86, Moscow, 1973, pp. 322–31
Strakhov, N. N., 'Vospominaniya o Fyodore Mikhayloviche Dostoyevskom', in *Polnoye sobraniye sochineniy F. M. Dostoyevskogo*, St Petersburg, 1883, 1, pp. 177–322
Suslova, A. P., *Gody blizosti s Dostoyevskim. Dnevnik-povest'-pis'ma*, ed. A. S. Dolinin, Moscow, 1929

ESSENTIAL MONOGRAPHS

Arban, D., *Dostoïevski par lui-même*, Paris, 1962
Les Années d'Apprentissage de Fiodor Dostoïevski, Paris, 1968
Bel'chikov, N. F., *Dostoyevsky v protsesse Petrashevtsev*, Moscow, 1971
'Biografiya F. M. Dostoyevskogo', in *Materialy po istorii literatury i obshchestvennogo dvizheniya*, Literaturnyy arkhiv, 6, Moscow–Leningrad, 1961
Carr, E. H., *Dostoyevsky (1821–1881)*, London, 1931
Catteau, J., 'Chronologie Dostoïevski', in *Magazine Littéraire*, March 1978, 134, 9–23
Dolinin, A. S., 'Dostoyevsky i Suslova, K biografii Dostoyevskogo', in A. S. Dolinin (ed.), *F. M. Dostoyevsky. Materialy i issledovaniya*, 2, Leningrad, 1924, pp. 153–284
Frank, J., *Dostoevsky. The Seeds of Revolt, 1821–1849*, Princeton, 1976
Dostoevsky. The Stir of Liberation, 1860–1865, Princeton, 1986
Dostoevsky. The Years of Ordeal, 1850–1859, Princeton, 1983
Fyodorov, G. A., 'Pansion L. I. Chermaka v 1834–1837gg.', in G. M. Fridlender, *Dostoyevsky. Materialy i issledovaniya*, 1, Leningrad, 1974, pp. 241–53
Grossman, L. P., *Dostoyevsky*, Moscow, 1962. [*Dostoevsky*, tr. M. Mackler, London, 1974.]
Zhizn' i trudy Dostoyevskogo. Biografiya v datakh i v dokumentakh, Moscow–Leningrad, 1935. [Supplement in A. M. Konechnyy, 'Dostoyevsky v 1840-e gody', in V. G. Bazanov and G. M. Fridlender (eds.), *Dostoyevsky i yego vremya*, Leningrad, 1971, pp. 280–3.]
Knapp, L. (ed.), *Dostoevsky as Reformer: the Petrashevsky Case*, Ann Arbor, 1986
Mochul'sky, K., *Dostoyevsky. Zhizn' i tvorchestvo*, Paris, 1947. [*Dostoevsky. His Life and Work*, trans. M. Minihan, Princeton, 1967.]
Natova, N. A., *F. M. Dostoyevsky v Bad Emse*, Frankfurt, 1971
Nechayeva, V. S. (ed.), *F. M. Dostoyevsky v portretakh, illyustratsiyakh, dokumentakh*, Moscow, 1972
Pascal, P., *Dostoïevski, l'homme et l'œuvre*, Lausanne, 1970
Reynus, L. M., *Dostoyevsky v Staroy Russe*, Leningrad, 1969
Sarukhanyan, Ye., *Dostoyevsky v Peterburge*, Leningrad, 1970
Seleznev, Yu., *Dostoyevsky*, Moscow, 1981
Slonim, M., *Three Loves of Dostoevsky*, London, 1957
Volgin, I., *Posledniy god Dostoyevskogo: istoricheskiye zapisi*, Moscow, 1986
Volotskoy, M. V., *Khronika roda Dostoyevskogo 1506–1933. Zapiski proshlogo. Vospominaniya i pis'ma*, ed. M. Tsyavlovsky, Moscow, 1933
Yermilov, V. V., *F. M. Dostoyevsky*, Moscow, 1956

CRITICAL WORKS

Alajouanine, T., 'Dostoïevski épileptique', *Le Nouveau commerce*, 2, 1963, 114–33
'Dostoievski's epilepsy', *Brain*, 86, 1963, 209–18
'Littérature et épilepsie. L'expression littéraire de l'extase dans les romans de Dostoïevski et dans les poèmes de Saint Jean de la Croix', in J. Catteau (ed.), *Dostoïevski*, Cahiers de l'Herne, 24, Paris, 1973, pp. 309–24
Alekseyev, M. P., 'F. M. Dostoyevsky i kniga De Kvinsi', *Uchonnyye zapiski vysshey shkoly Odessy*, 2, 1922, 97–102
Ranniy drug F. M. Dostoyevskogo, Odessa, 1921
Allain, L., *Dostoïevski et l'Autre*, Paris, 1984
Alpatov, A. V., 'Odin iz neizuchonnykh tvorcheskikh zamyslov F. M. Dostoyevskogo: "Imperator"', *Vestnik Moskovskogo Universiteta: Filologiya*, 1971, 5, 13–21
Al'tman, M. S., 'Gogolevskiye traditsii v tvorchestve Dostoyevskogo', *Slavia*, 30, 3, 1961, 443–61
'Iz arsenala imyon i prototipov literaturnykh geroyev Dostoyevskogo', in V. G. Bazanov and G. M. Fridlender (eds.), *Dostoyevsky i yego vremya*, Leningrad, 1971, pp. 196–216
'Toponomika Dostoyevskogo', in G. M. Fridlender (ed.), *Dostoyevsky. Materialy i issledovaniya*, 2, Leningrad, 1976, pp. 51–6
Antsiferov, N. P., 'Peterburg Dostoyevskogo. Opyt literaturnoy ekskursii', *Ekskursionnoye delo*, 2–3, Petrograd, 1921, 49–68
Arban, D., *Dostoïevski le 'coupable'*, Paris, 1953
'Les lieux dostoïevskiens et leur signification', in *Fiodor Dostoïevski*, Paris, 1971, pp. 174–91
Ardens, N. N. (Apostolov, N. N.), *Dostoyevsky i Tolstoy*, Moscow, 1970
Askol'dov, S. (Alekseyev, S. A.), 'Religiozno-eticheskoye znacheniye Dostoyevskogo', in A. S. Dolinin (ed.), *F. M. Dostoyevsky. Stat'i i materialy*, 1, Petersburg, 1922, pp. 1–32
Aucouturier, G., Introduction to *F. M. Dostoïevski, Récits, chroniques et polémiques*, ed. G. Aucouturier, Paris, 1969
Bakhtin, M., *Problemy poetiki Dostoyevskogo*, Moscow, 1963. [M. Bakhtin, *Problems of Dostoyevsky's Poetics*, tr. Caryl Emerson, Manchester, 1984.] [Referred to in text as *Bakhtin*.]
Bel'chikov, N. F., 'Zolotoy vek v predstavlenii Dostoyevskogo', in *Problemy teorii i istorii literatury*, Moscow, 1971, pp. 357–66
Belik. A. P., *Khudozhestvennyye obrazy F. M. Dostoyevskogo*, Moscow, 1974
Belkin, A. A. (ed.), *F. M. Dostoyevsky v russkoy kritike*, Moscow, 1956
'O realizme Dostoyevskogo', in *Tvorchestvo F. M. Dostoyevskogo*, Moscow, 1959, pp. 45–54
'*Vdrug i slishkom* v khudozhestvennoy sisteme Dostoyevskogo', in *Chitaya Dostoyevskogo i Chekhova. Stat'i i razbory*, Moscow, 1973, pp. 129–34
Belknap, R., 'Memory in The Brothers Karamazov', in R. L. Jackson (ed.), *Dostoyevsky. New Perspectives*, Englewood Cliffs, N.J., 1984, pp. 227–42
The Structure of The Brothers Karamazov, Paris, 1967
Belov, V. S., 'Nesluchaynyye slova i detali v *Prestuplenii i nakazanii*, *Russkaya rech'*, 1, 1975, 37–40
Belyy, A., *Tragediya tvorchestva. Dostoyevsky i Tolstoy*, Moscow, 1911
Bem, A. L., *Dostoyevsky. Psikhoanaliticheskiye etyudy*, Berlin, 1938

'*Faust* v tvorchestve Dostoyevskogo', *Zapiski nauchno-issledovatel'skogo ob'edi-neniya* (publication of the Free Russian University in Prague), 5, 1937, 109–41

O Dostojevském. Sborník statí a materíalů, Prague, 1972

'U istokov tvorchestva Dostoyevskogo', in A. L. Bem (ed.), *O Dostoyevskom*, 2, Prague, 1933, pp. 37–81

Bem, A. L. *et al.*, 'Slovar' lichnykh imyon v proizvedeniyakh Dostoyevskogo', in A. L. Bem (ed.), *O Dostoyevskom*, 2, Prague, 1933, and 4, Prague, 1936

Berdyayev, N., *Mirosozertsaniye Dostoevskogo*, Paris, 1968

Bitsilli, P. M., 'K voprosu o vnutrenney forme romana Dostoyevskogo', Sofia, 1946, in *Godishnik na Sofiyskiya universitet. Istoriko-filologicheski fakultet*, 42, 1945–6. Reprinted in *O Dostoyevskom. Stat'i*, Providence, Rhode Island, 1966, pp. 1–71

Blagoy, D. D., 'Dostoyevsky i Pushkin', in *Dostoyevsky: khudozhnik i myslitel'*, Moscow, 1972, pp. 344–426

Borshchevsky, S., *Shchedrin i Dostoyevsky. Istoriya ikh ideynoy bor'by*, Moscow, 1956

Botsyanovsky, V., 'Kraski u Dostoyevskogo', *Zhizn, iskusstva*, 817, 15 November 1921, 3

Brown, N. B., *Hugo and Dostoyevsky*, Ann Arbor, 1978

Bursov, B. I., *Lichnost' Dostoyevskogo. Roman-issledovaniye*, Leningrad, 1964

Cadot, M., '*La Double Postulation* de Baudelaire et sa version dostoïevskienne', *Revue canadienne de littérature comparée*, winter 1977, pp. 54–67

'Peut-on décrire certaines constructions romanesques de Dostoïevski comme engendrées par un mouvement hélicoïdal?', *Bulletin of the International Dostoevsky Society*, 7, 1977, 35–7

Catteau, J., 'A propos de la littérature fantastique: André Belyj, héritier de Gogol' et de Dostoïevski', *Cahiers du monde russe et soviétique*, 3, III, 1962, 327–73

'Bakounine et Dostoïevski', *Magazine littéraire*, March 1978, 134, 32–6

'De la structure de *La Maison des Morts* de F. M. Dostoevskij', *Revue des études slaves*, 54, 1982, 63–72

(ed.), *Dostoïevski*, Cahiers de l'Herne 24, Paris, 1973

'Dostoïevski était-il antisémite?', *La Quinzaine littéraire*, 241, October 1976, 18–19

'Du palais de cristal à l'âge d'or ou les avatars de l'utopie', in *Dostoïevski*, Cahiers de l'Herne 24, Paris, 1973, pp. 176–95

'Du visionnaire de l'humanité au romancier de l'homme', *Dostoevsky Studies*, 3, 1982, 53–60

'Le Christ dans le Miroir des Grotesques (*Les Démons*)', *Dostoevsky Studies*, 4, 1983, 29–36

'The paradox of the Legend of the Grand Inquisitor in *The Brothers Karamazov*', in R. L. Jackson (ed.), *Dostoyevsky. New Perspectives*, Englewood Cliffs, N.J., 1984, pp. 243–54

'Prostranstvo i vremya v romanakh Dostoyevskogo', in G. M. Fridlender (ed.), *Dostoyevsky. Materialy i issledovaniya*, 3, Leningrad, 1978, pp. 41–53

'Structures Récurrentes et Répétitives dans la Composition du Roman Dostoevskien', *Dostoyevsky Studies*, 1, 1980, 41–6

Catteau, J. and Rolland, J. (eds.), *Dostoïevski*, Les Cahiers de la nuit surveillée, Lagrasse, 1983

Chicherin, A. V., 'Poeticheskiy stroy yazyka v romanakh Dostoyevskogo', in *Idei i stil'. O prirode poeticheskogo slova*, Moscow, 1968, pp. 175–227

Chirkov, N. M., *O stile Dostoyevskogo*, Moscow, 1963
O stile Dostoyevskogo. Problematika, idei, obrazy, Moscow, 1967

Chulkov, G. I., *Kak rabotal Dostoyevsky*, Moscow, 1939
'Posledneye slovo Dostoyevskogo o Belinskom', in *Dostoyevsky. Trudy gos. Akad. khudozhestvennykh nauk. Literaturnaya sektsiya*, 3, Moscow, 1928, pp. 61–82

Dalton, E., *Unconscious Structure in 'The Idiot'. A Study in Literature and Psychoanalysis*, Princeton, 1979

Delcour, J., 'Dostoïevski et le parricide', in *Dostoïevski*, Cahiers de l'herne 24, Paris, 1973, pp. 270–5

Dneprov, V., *Idei, strasti, postupki. Iz khudozhestvennogo opyta Dostoyevskogo*, Leningrad, 1978

Dobrolyubov, N. A., 'Zabityye lyudi', in N. A. Dobrolyubov, *Russkiye klassiki. Izbrannyye literaturno-kriticheskiye stat'i*, Moscow, 1970, pp. 301–46

Dolinin, A. S., *Posledniye romany Dostoyevskogo. Kak sozdavalis' 'Podrostok' i 'Brat'ya Karamazovy'*, Moscow–Leningrad, 1963
'Turgenev v Besakh', in *F. M. Dostoyevsky. Stat'i i materialy*, Leningrad, 1925, pp. 119–38
V tvorcheskoy laboratorii Dostoyevskogo. Istoriya sozdaniya romana 'Podrostok', Leningrad, 1947
'Zolotoy vek u Dostoyevskogo', *Neva*, 11, 1971, 179–86
ed., *F. M. Dostoyevsky. stat'i i materialy*, 1, Petersburg, 1922
ed., *F. M. Dostoyevsky. stat'i' i materialy*, 2, Leningrad, 1925

Dorovatovskaya-Lyubimova, V. S., '*Idiot* Dostoyevskogo i ugolovnaya khronika yego vremeni', *Pechat' i revolyutsiya*, 3, 1928, 31–53

Dowler, W., *Dostoevsky, Grigor'ev, and Native Soil Conservatism*, Toronto, 1982

Drouilly, J., 'L'image du soleil couchant dans l'œuvre de Dostoïevski. Essai de critique thématique', *Etudes slaves et est-européennes*, Montreal, 19, 1974, 3–22.
'Une erreur dans l'édition russe de A. S. Dolinin des lettres de F. M. Dostoïevski', *Etudes slaves et est-européennes*, Montreal, 19, 1974, 118–20

Dryzhakova, Ye., 'Dostoyevsky, Chernyshevsky and the rejection of nihilism', *Oxford Slavonic Papers*, 13, 1980, 58–79
'Dostoyevsky i Gertsen. Londonskiye svidaniya 1862g', *Canadian–American Slavic Studies*, 17, 1983, 325–48
'Segmentatsiya vremeni v romane *Prestupleniye i nakazaniye*', *Dostoevsky Studies*, 6, 1985, 67–90
'The fifties in transition: A. S. Dolinin and Yu. G. Oksman, our remarkable teachers', *Oxford Slavonic Papers*, 18, 1985, 120–49

Durylin, S. N., 'Ob odnom simvole u Dostoyevskogo', in '*Dostoyevsky' (sb. statey). Trudy gosudarstvennoy Akademiy khudozhestvennykh nauk. Literaturnaya sektsiya*, 3, Moscow, 1928, pp. 163–99.

Engel'gardt, B. M., 'Ideologicheskiy roman Dostoyevskogo', in A. S. Dolinin (ed.), *F. M. Dostoyevsky. Stat'i i materialy*, 2, Leningrad, 1925, pp. 71–109

Etov, V. I., *Dostoyevsky. Ocherk tvorchestva*, Moscow, 1968

Fanger, D., *Dostoyevsky and Romantic Realism: a Study of Dostoevsky in Relation to Balzac, Dickens, and Gogol*, Cambridge, Mass., 1965

Figuières, J., *L'Epilepsie dans l'œuvre de Dostoïevski*, Lyon, 1924, published Valence, 1942

Fortunatov, N. M., 'Cherty arkhitektoniki Dostoyevskogo', in *Puti iskaniy. O masterstve pisatelya*, Moscow, 1974, pp. 84–104

Freud, S., 'Dostoevsky and parricide', in R. Wellek (ed.), *Dostoevsky. A Collection of Critical Essays*, Englewood Cliffs, N.J., 1962, pp. 98–111

Fridlender, G. M., *Dostoyevsky i mirovaya literatura*, Moscow, 1979
   (ed.). *Dostoyevsky. Materialy i issledovaniya*, 6 vols. to date, Leningrad, 1974–85
   'Estetika Dostoyevskogo', in *Dostoyevsky: khudozhnik i myslitel'*, Moscow, 1972, pp. 97–164
   Realizm Dostoyevskogo, Moscow–Leningrad, 1964
   'Roman *Idiot*', in *Tvorchestvo F. M. Dostoyevskogo*, Moscow, 1959, pp. 173–214
   'Romany Dostoyevskogo', in *Istoriya russkogo romana v dvukh tomakh*, 2, Moscow–Leningrad, 1964, pp. 193–269

Fyodorov, G. A., 'Moskva Dostoyevskogo', *Literaturnaya gazeta*, 43 (4329), 20 October 1971, 7

Gastaut, H., 'Fyodor Mikhailovitch Dostoevsky's involuntary contribution to the symptomatology and prognosis of epilepsy', *Epilepsia*, 19, New York, 1978, 186–201

Gessen, S. I., 'Tragediya dobra v *Brat'yakh Karamazovykh* Dostoyevskogo', *Sovremennyye zapiski*, 25, Paris, 1928, 308–38

Gide, A., *Dostoevsky*, tr. A. Bennett, London, 1925

Gizetti, A. A., 'Gordyye yazychnitsy' (k kharakteristike zhenskikh obrazov Dostoyevskogo), in N. L. Brodsky (ed.), *Tvorcheskiy put' Dostoyevskogo*, Leningrad, 1924, pp. 186–97

Goldstein, D. I., *Dostoevsky and the Jews*, Austin–London, 1981

Golosovker, Ya. E., *Dostoyevsky i Kant. Razmyshleniye chitatelya nad romanom 'Brat'ya Karamazovy' i traktatom Kanta 'Kritika chistogo razuma'*, Moscow, 1963

Gozenpud, A. A., *Dostoyevsky i muzyka*, Leningrad, 1971

Grishin, D. V., *Dnevnik pisatelya F. M. Dostoyevskogo*, Melbourne, 1966

Grossman, L. P., 'Dostoyevsky-khudozhnik', in *Tvorchestvo F. M. Dostoyevskogo*, Moscow, 1959, pp. 330–416
   'Gorod i lyudi', in F. M. Dostoyevsky, *Prestupleniye i nakazaniye*, Moscow, 1935, pp. 5–52
   Poetika Dostoyevskogo, Moscow, 1925
   Seminariy po Dostoyevskomu, Moscow–Petrograd, 1922
   (ed.), *Tvorchestvo Dostoyevskogo*, Odessa, 1921

Grossman, L. P. and Polonsky, V. P., *Spor o Bakunine i Dostoyevskom*, Leningrad, 1926

Guardini, R., *L'Univers religieux de Dostoïevski*, Paris, 1947

Gus, M., *Idei i obrazy F. M. Dostoyevskogo*, Moscow, 1962

Hackel, S., 'F. M. Dostoevsky (1821–1881): Prophet manqué', *Dostoevsky Studies*, 3, 1982, pp. 5–26

Holquist, M., *Dostoevsky and the Novel*, Princeton, 1977

Ivanchikova, Ye. A., *Sintaksis khudozhestvennoy prozy Dostoyevskogo*, Moscow, 1979

Ivanov, V., *Borozdy i mezhi*, Moscow, 1916
   Freedom and the Tragic Life. A Study in Dostoevsky, New York, 1966

Istomin, K. K., 'Iz zhizni i tvorchestva Dostoyevskogo v molodosti', in N. L. Brodsky (ed.), *Tvorcheskiy put' Dostoyevskogo, sbornik statey*, Leningrad, 1924, pp. 3–49

Jackson, R. L. (ed.), *Dostoevsky. New Perspectives*, Englewood Cliffs, N.J., 1984
Dostoevsky's Quest for Form. A Study of his Philosophy of Art, New Haven and London, 1966
The Art of Dostoevsky. Deliriums and Nocturnes, Princeton, 1981

Johnson, L. A., *The Experience of Time in 'Crime and Punishment'*, Columbus, Ohio, 1985

Jones, J., *Dostoevsky*, Oxford, 1983

Jones, M. V., 'An aspect of Romanticism in Dostoyevsky's *Netochka Nezvanova* and Eugène Sue's *Mathilde*, *Renaissance and Modern Studies*, 17, 1973, 38–61
'Dostoyevsky and an aspect of Schiller's psychology', *The Slavonic and East European Review*, 52, 1974, 337–54
'Dostoevsky, Rousseau and others (a study of the "Alien Voice" in Dostoevsky's novels)', *Dostoevsky Studies*, 4, 1983, 81–94
Dostoyevsky. The Novel of Discord, London, 1976
'K ponimaniyu obraza knyazya Myshkina' in G. M. Fridlender (ed.), *Dostoyevsky. Materialy i issledovaniya*, 2, Leningrad, 1976, pp. 106–12

Jones, M. V. and Terry, G. M. (eds.), *New Essays on Dostoyevsky*, Cambridge, 1983

Jonge, A. de, *Dostoevsky and the Age of Intensity*, London, 1975

Kabat, G. C., *Ideology and Imagination. The Image of Society in Dostoevsky*, New York, 1978

Karlova, T. S., *Dostoyevsky i russkiy sud*, Kazan, 1975

Karyakin, Yu. F., *Samoobman Raskol'nikova. Roman F. M. Dostoyevskogo 'Prestupleniye i nakazaniye'*, Moscow, 1976

Kashina, N., *Chelovek v tvorchestve F. M. Dostoyevskogo*, Moscow, 1986

Kashina, N. V., *Estetika F. M. Dostoyevskogo*, Moscow, 1975

Katarsky, I. M., 'Dostoyevsky i Dikkens', in G. M. Fridlender (ed.), *Dostoyevsky. Materialy i issledovaniya*, 2, Leningrad, 1976, pp. 277–84
'Dostoyevsky i nekotoryye voprosy estetiki romana', in G. M. Fridlender (ed.), *Dostoyevsky. Materialy i issledovaniya*, 1, Leningrad, 1974, pp. 83–99
Khudozhestvennaya struktura rannikh romanov Dostoyevskogo, Moscow (MGU dissertation), 1969

Kirpotin, V. Ya., *Dostoyevsky i Belinsky*, Moscow, 1976
Dostoyevsky-khudozhnik. Etyudy i issledovaniya, Moscow, 1972
Dostoyevsky v shestidesyatyye gody, Moscow, 1966
Mir Dostoyevskogo. Etyudy i issledovaniya, Moscow, 1980
'Oprovergnutaya versiya', *Literaturnaya gazeta*, 25, 18 June 1975, 7
Razocharovaniye i krusheniye Rodiona Raskol'nikova. Kniga o romane F. M. Dostoyevskogo 'Prestupleniye i nakazaniye', Moscow, 1970

Kjetsaa, G., *Dostoevsky and his New Testament*, Atlantic Highlands, N.J., 1984

Kobylinsky, M., 'Bolezn' Dostoyevskogo', *Vrachebnoye delo*, Kharkov, 1927, pp. 1–9

Kogan, G. F., 'Zhurnal *Vremya* i revolyutsionnoye studenchestvo 1860-kh godov. Razyskaniya o Dostoyevskom', in *F. M. Dostoyevsky. Novyye materialy i issledovaniya*, Literaturnoye nasledstvo, 86. Moscow, 1973, pp. 581–93. [*LH* 86]

Komarovich, V. L., 'Mirovaya garmoniya Dostoyevskogo', *Ateney*, 1–2, 1924, 112–42. Reprinted in *O Dostoevskom. Stat'i*, Providence, Rhode Island, 1966, pp. 119–49
'Roman *Podrostok* kak khudozhestvennoye yedinstvo', in A. S. Dolinin (ed.), *F. M. Dostoyevsky. Stat'i i materialy*, 2, Leningrad, 1925, pp. 31–71
Kovacs, A., 'O khudozhestvennoy strukture povesti F. M. Dostoyevskogo *Dvoynik*', *Revue canadienne-américaine d'études slaves*, 8, 1974, 408–26.
Roman Dostoyevskogo, opyt poetiki zhanra, Budapest, 1985
Kovsan, M. L., 'Khudozhestvennoye vremya v romane F. M. Dostoyevskogo *Besy*, *Filologicheskiye nauki*, 5, 1982, 24–9
Kravchenko, M., *Dostoevskij and the Psychologists*, Amsterdam, 1978
Kudryavtsev, Yu. G., *Tri kruga Dostoyevskogo. (Sobytiynoye. Sotsial'noye. Filosofskoye)*, Moscow, 1979
Kuznetsov, B. G., *Einstein and Dostoyevsky*, tr. V. Talmy, London, 1972
'Obrazy Dostoyevskogo i idei Eynshteyna', *Voprosy literatury*, 3, 1968, 138–65
Lapshin, I. I., 'Obrazovaniye tipa Krafta v *Podrostke*', in A. L. Bem (ed.), *O Dostoyevskom*, 1, Prague, 1929, pp. 140–4
Lary, N. M., *Dostoyevsky and Dickens. A Study of Literary Influence*, London and Boston, 1973
Leatherbarrow, W. J., 'Apocalyptic imagery in *The Idiot* and *The Devils*', *Dostoevsky Studies*, 3, 1982, 43–52
Fedor Dostoevsky, Boston, Mass., 1981
Lebedeva, T. B., 'Sotsial'naya utopiya Dostoyevskogo i 'zemnoy ray' drevnerusskoy literatury', in *Puti russkoy prozy XIX veka*, Leningrad, 1976, pp. 75–85
Levin, Yu. D., 'Dostoyevsky i Shekspir', in G. M. Fridlender (ed.), *Dostoyevsky. Materialy i issledovaniya*, 1, Leningrad, 1974, pp. 108–34
Likhachov, D. S., 'Letopisnoye vremya (u Dostoyevskogo)', in *Poetika drevnerusskoy literatury*, Leningrad, 1971, pp. 347–63
'V poiskakh vrazheniya real'nogo', in G. M. Fridlender (ed.), *Dostoyevsky. Materialy i issledovaniya*, 1, Leningrad, 1974, pp. 5–13
Linner, S., *Dostoevsky on Realism*, Stockholm, 1967
Loygue, P. G., *Etude médico-psychologique sur Dostoïevski. Considérations sur les états morbides liés au génie*, thesis, Lyon, 1903
Matlaw, R. E., *The Brothers Karamazov: Novelistic Technique*, The Hague, 1957
Meier-Gräfe, J., *Dostojewski der Dichter*, Berlin, 1926
Meijer, J. M., 'A note on time in *Brat'ja Karamazovy*', in J. van der Eng and J. M. Meijer, *The Brothers Karamazov by F. M. Dostoevskij*, Paris–Hague, 1971, pp. 47–62
Merezhkovsky, D. S., *Prorok russkoy revolyutsii*, St Petersburg, 1906
Meserich (Meszerics), I., 'Problema muzykal'nogo postroyeniya v povesti *Zapiski iz podpol'ya*', in V. G. Bazanov and G. M. Fridlender (eds.), *Dostoyevsky i yego vremya*, Leningrad, 1971, pp. 154–65
Meyer, G., *Svet v nochi, o 'Prestuplenii i nakazanii'. Opyt medlennogo chteniya*, Frankfurt, 1967
Meylakh, B., *Na rubezhe nauki i iskusstva. Spor o dvukh sferakh poznaniya i tvorchestva*, Leningrad, 1971
Miller, R. F., *Dostoevsky and 'The Idiot'. Author, Narrator, and Reader*, Cambridge, Mass., and London, 1981

Morson, G. S., 'Dostoevskij's anti-Semitism and the critics: a review article', *Slavic and East European Journal*, 27, 1983, 302–17

Morson, G. S., *The Boundaries of Genre. Dostoyevsky's 'Diary of a Writer' and the Traditions of Literary Utopia*, Austin, Texas, 1981

Moser, C. A., 'Dostoyevsky and the aesthetics of journalism', *Dostoevsky Studies*, 3, 1982, 27–42

Myslyakov, V. A., 'Kak rasskazana "Istoriya" Rodiona Raskol'nikova (k voprosu o sub'ektivno-avtorskom nachale u Dostoyevskogo', in G. M. Fridlender (ed.), *Dostoyevsky. Materialy i issledovaniya*, 1, Leningrad, 1974, pp. 147–63

Nazirov, R. G., 'Geroi romana *Idiot* i ikh prototipy', *Russkaya literatura*, 2, 1970, 114–22

Nechayeva, V. S., *Ranniy Dostoyevsky 1821–1849*, Moscow, 1979

Zhurnal M. M. i F. M. Dostoyevskikh 'Epokha' 1864–1865, Moscow, 1975

Zhurnal M. M. i F. M. Dostoyevskikh 'Vremya' 1861–1863, Moscow, 1972

Neyfel'd, I., *Dostoyevsky. Psikhoanaliticheskiy ocherk*, ed. S. Freud, Leningrad–Moscow, 1925

Nikol'sky, Yu., *Turgenev i Dostoyevsky. Istoriya odnoy vrazhdy*, Sofia, 1921

Ollivier, S., *L'Argent chez Dostoïevski*, Aix-en-Provence, 1970

Pascal, P., *Dostoïevski*, Paris–Bruges, 1969

'Le prophète du Christ russe', in *Fiodor Dostoïevski*, Paris, 1971, pp. 113–29

Peace, R., *Dostoyevsky. An Examination of the Major Novels*, Cambridge, 1971

'Dostoyevsky and the "Golden Age"', *Dostoevsky Studies*, 3, 1982, 61–78

Pereverzev, V. F., *Tvorchestvo Dostoyevskogo*, Moscow, 1912

Perlina, N., *Varieties of Poetic Utterance. Quotation in 'The Brothers Karamazov'*, New York, 1985

Petrovsky, M. A., 'Kompozitsiya *Vechnogo muzha*', in *Dostoyevsky. Trudy gos. Akad. khudozhestvennykh nauk. Literaturnaya sektsiya*, 3, Moscow, 1928, pp. 115–62

Pogozheva, L. P., 'Mechta Dostoyevskogo o zolotom veke', *Krasnaya nov'*, 2, 1941, 173–81

Pokrovskaya, Ye., 'Dostoyevsky i Petrashevtsy', in A. S. Dolinin (ed.), *F. M. Dostoyevsky. Stat'i i materialy*, 1, Petersburg, 1922, pp. 257–74

Ponomaryova, G. B., '*Zhitiye velikogo greshnika* Dostoyevskogo. Struktura i zhanr', in *Issledovaniya po poetike i stilistike*, Leningrad, 1972, pp. 66–86

Pouzyna, I., 'George Sand et Dostoïevski, la parenté littéraire des *Frères Karamazov* et du *Spiridion*', *Etudes*, 1, 1939, 345–60

Prutskov, N. I., 'Dostoyevsky i khristianskiy sotsializm', in G. M. Fridlender (ed.), *Dostoyevsky. Materialy i issledovaniya*, vol. 1, Leningrad, 1974, pp. 58–82

'Sotsialno-eticheskaya utopiya Dostoyevskogo', in *Idei sotsializma v russkoy klassicheskoy literature*, Leningrad, 1969, pp. 334–73

'Utopiya ili antiutopiya?', in V. G. Bazanov and G. M. Fridlender (eds.), *Dostoyevsky i yego vremya*, Leningrad, 1971, pp. 88–107

Pushkaryova, V. S., 'Detskiye epizody v khudozhestvennykh proizvedeniyakh i v publitsistike Dostoyevskogo', in *F. M. Dostoyevsky–N. A. Nekrasov (sbornik nauchnykh trudov)*, Leningrad, 1974, pp. 41–56

Raether, M., '"La grande action future" de Raskolnikov. Dostoïevski et la littérature de l'*acte gratuit*', *Revue de Littérature Comparée*, 45, 1981, 342–57

Reizov, B. G., 'K istorii Brat'yev Karamazovykh', in *Istorii yevropeyskikh literatur*, Leningrad, 1970, pp. 129–38

Rice, J. L., *Dostoevsky and the Healing Art. An Essay in Literary and Medical History*, Ann Arbor, 1985

Rice, M. P., 'Dostoyevsky's *Notes from Underground* and Hegel's *Master and Slave*', *Revue canadienne-américaine d'études slaves*, 8, 3, 1974, 359–69

Robert, M., 'L'Inconscient, creuset de l'œuvre', in *Fiodor Dostoïevski*, Paris, 1971, pp. 130–50

Rozanov, V. V., *Legenda o velikom inkvizitore F. M. Dostoyevskogo*, St Petersburg, 1906. [*Dostoevsky and the Legend of the Grand Inquisitor*, tr. S. E. Roberts, Cornell, 1972.]

Rozenblyum, L. M., 'Tvorcheskaya laboratoriya Dostoyevskogo-romanista', in *Literaturnoye nasledstvo*, 77, Moscow, 1965, pp. 7–56. [Referred to in text as *LH 77*.]
Tvorcheskiye dnevniki Dostoyevskogo, Moscow, 1981

Rubanovich, A. L., 'Peyzazh v romane F. M. Dostoyevskogo *Prestupleniye i nakazaniye*', in *Trudy Irkutskogo universiteta im. A. A. Zhdanova*, 28, 2, 1959, pp. 91–105. [Cover says 1958, 18, 1.]

Rzhevsky, L., *Tri temy po Dostoyevskomu*, Frankfurt, 1972.

Sarraute, N., *L'ère du soupçon. Essais sur le roman*, Paris, 1956

Seduro, V., *Dostoyevsky in Russian Literary Criticism 1846–1956*, New York, 1957
Dostoevski's Image in Russia Today, Belmont, Mass., 1975

Segalov, T., *Die Krankheit Dostoewskis*, dissertation, Heidelberg, 1903

Seleznev, Yu., *V mire Dostoyevskogo*, Moscow, 1980

Semyovsky, V. I., *Butashevich-Petrashevsky i petrashevtsy*, Moscow, 1922
'M. V. Butashevich-Petrashevsky', *Golos minuvshego*, 8, 1913, 53–4

Serman, I. Z., 'Dostoyevsky i Ap. Grigor'ev', in V. G. Bazanov and G. M. Fridlender (eds.), *Dostoyevsky i yego vremya*, Leningrad, 1971, pp. 130–42

Shestov, L., *Dostoyevsky i Nitshe. Filosofiya tragedii*, St Petersburg, 1903
'F. M. Dostoyevsky', in *Povesti o proze. Razmyshleniya i razbory*, 2, Moscow, 1966, pp. 153–261

Shklovsky, V., *Za i protiv. Zametki o Dostoyevskom*, Moscow, 1957

Simenon, G., 'Ya romanist, a ne pisatel' voobshche . . .', *Inostrannaya literatura*, 10, 1971, 259–66

Skaftymov, A. P., *Nravstvennye iskaniya russkikh pisateley*, Moscow, 1972

Solov'yov, S. M., *Izobrazitel'nyye sredstva v tvorchestve Dostoyevskogo*, Moscow, 1979
'Kolorit proizvedeniy Dostoyevskogo', in *Dostoyevsky i russkiye pisateli. Traditsii, novatorstvo, masterstvo*, Moscow, 1971, pp. 414–46

Solov'yov, V., *Tri rechi v pamyat' Dostoyevskogo*, Moscow, 1884

Steiner, G., *Tolstoy or Dostoevsky*, New York, 1959

Stepun, F., *Vstrechi: Dostoyevsky, L. Tolstoy, Bunin, Zaytsev, V. Ivanov, Belyy, Leonov*, New York, 1968

Terras, V., 'The art of fiction as a theme in *The Brothers Karamazov*', in R. L. Jackson (ed.), *Dostoevsky. New Perspectives*, Englewood Cliffs, N.J., 1984, pp. 193–205
The Young Dostoyevsky 1846–1849, The Hague, 1969

Toporov, V. N., 'Poetika Dostoyevskogo i arkhaichnyye skhemy mifologicheskogo myshleniya', in *Problemy poetiki i istorii literatury*, Saransk, 1973, pp. 91–109

Tseytlin, A. G., *Povesti o bednom chinovnike Dostoyevskogo. (K istorii odnogo syuzheta)*, Moscow, 1923

'Vremya v romanakh Dostoyevskogo', *Rodnoy yazyk v shkole*, 5, 1927, 3–17

Tsiv'yan, T. V., 'O strukture vremeni i prostranstva v romane Dostoyevskogo *Podrostok*', *Russian Literature*, 4, 1976, 203–55

Tunimanov, V. A., 'Rasskazchik v *Besakh* Dostoyevskogo', in *Issledovaniya po poetike i stilistike*, Leningrad, 1972, pp. 87–162

'Satira i utopiya (*Bobok*, *Son smeshnogo cheloveka* F. M. Dostoyevskogo)', *Russkaya literatura*, 4, 1966, 70–87

Tvorchestvo Dostoyevskogo 1854–1862, Leningrad, 1980

Tynyanov, Yu. N., *Dostoyevsky i Gogol'. K teorii parodii*, Petrograd, 1921

Van der Eng, J., *Dostoevskij romancier. Rapports entre sa vision du monde et ses procédés littéraires*, The Hague, 1957

Verret, G., 'Temps et conscience chez Dostoïevski (De *Crime et Châtiment* à *l'Adolescent)'*, in J. Catteau (ed). *Dostoïevski*, Cahiers de l'Herne 24, Paris, 1973, pp. 196–204

Vetlovskaya, V. E., *Poetika romana 'Brat'ya Karamazovy'*, Leningrad, 1977

'Simvolika chisel v *Brat'yakh Karamazovykh*', in *Drevnerusskaya literatura i yeyo traditsii russkoy literature XVIII–XIXvv*, Leningrad, 1971, pp. 143–61

Vinogradov, V. V., *Evolyutsiya russkogo naturalizma. Gogol' i Dostoyevsky*, Leningrad, 1929

'Stil' peterburgskoy poemy *Dvoynik*', in A. S. Dolinin (ed.), *F. M. Dostoyevsky. Stat'i i materialy*, Petersburg, 1922, pp. 211–56

Vladiv, S. B., *Narrative Principles in Dostoyevsky's 'Besy': A Structural Analysis*, Berne–Frankfurt–Las Vegas, 1979

Voloshin, G., 'Prostranstvo i vremya u Dostoyevskogo', *Slavia*, 12, Prague, 1–2, 1933, 162–72

Wasiolek, E., *Dostoevsky. The Major Fiction*, Cambridge, Mass., 1964

Yevnin, F. I., 'Roman *Prestupleniye i nakazaniye*', and 'Roman *Besy*', in *Tvorchestvo F. M. Dostoyevskogo*, Moscow, 1959, pp. 128–72 and 215–64

Zundelovich, Ya. O., 'O romane Dostoyevskogo *Besy*. O pamfletnom stroe romana', *Trudy Samarkandskogo gos. universiteta. Problemy khudozhestvennogo masterstva*, new series, 112, Samarkand, 1961, 3–36

Romany Dostoyevskogo. Stat'i, Tashkent, 1963

Index of names